Keep this book. You will
need it and use it throughout
your career.

HOSPITALITY
SALES
and
ADVERTISING

Educational Institute Books

HOSPITALITY SALES and ADVERTISING

Second Edition

James R. Abbey, Ph.D., CHA

EDUCATIONAL INSTITUTE
of the American Hotel & Motel Association

Disclaimer

This publication is designed to provide accurate and authoritative information in regard to the subject matter covered. It is sold with the understanding that the publisher is not engaged in rendering legal, accounting, or other professional service. If legal advice or other expert assistance is required, the services of a competent professional person should be sought.

   —From the Declaration of Principles jointly adopted by the American Bar Association and a Committee of Publishers and Associations

The author, James R. Abbey, is solely responsible for the contents of this publication. All views expressed herein are solely those of the author and do not necessarily reflect the views of the Educational Institute of the American Hotel & Motel Association (the Institute) or the American Hotel & Motel Association (AH&MA).

Nothing contained in this publication shall constitute a standard, an endorsement, or a recommendation of the Institute or AH&MA. The Institute and AH&MA disclaim any liability with respect to the use of any information, procedure, or product, or reliance thereon by any member of the hospitality industry.

Printed in the United States of America
   2 3 4 5 6 7 8 9 10 00 99 98 97 96

Library of Congress Cataloging-in-Publication Data
Abbey, James R.
   Hospitality sales and advertising/James R. Abbey.—2nd ed.
      p. cm.
   Includes bibliographical references and index.
   ISBN 0-86612-070-X
   ISBN 0-86612-108-0 (pbk.)
   1. Hospitality industry—Marketing. 2. Advertising—Hospitality
industry. 3. Market segmentation. I. American Hotel & Motel
Association. Educational Institute. II. Title.
TX911.3.M3A23 1993
647.94'0688—dc20   93–1515
                                                             CIP

Editor: Jim Purvis

Contents

About the Author

James R. Abbey, Ph.D., CHA, is a professor of hotel marketing and management at the University of Nevada, Las Vegas. He also has executive experience with clubs, restaurants, and hotels. As a consultant and researcher, he has worked with many prominent companies in the areas of sales management and marketing research and strategy. He is active in the Society of Company Meeting Professionals and the Hospitality Sales & Marketing Association International. The author has won awards from the Travel Research Association of America, the National Institute of Foodservice Instructors, and the Statler Foundation. He is a graduate of Michigan State University's School of Hotel, Restaurant & Institutional Management, and holds a master's degree in finance and a Ph.D. in tourism from Utah State University.

James R. Abbey

Dr. Abbey is a contributor to leading hospitality publications and is co-author of *The Art and Science of Hospitality Management* and *Convention Sales and Services.*

Preface

THE BASIC FUNCTION OF MARKETING, sales, advertising, and promotion is to find and retain enough guests to maintain a profitable level of business. In this age of new construction and investment, modernization, consolidation and mergers, automation, and growing competition, the name of the game in the hospitality industry is to "wear out the carpet"—that is, bring in the business.

In large hotels, there is usually a full-time marketing and sales division or department; midsize properties may have a marketing and sales department or a sales office; in small properties, marketing and sales may be among the many duties of the general manager. Regardless of the property's size, a continuous sales effort is required to fill guestrooms, dining rooms, lounges, and meeting space. Sales must never be considered the sole responsibility of a single individual; sales is an important part of every employee's job. Knowledge and application of the sales and advertising fundamentals presented in this text can benefit the reader professionally as well as help boost a hotel's profits.

The second edition of *Hospitality Sales and Advertising* includes new material on a number of topics: employee empowerment, yield management, marketing teams, relationship selling, positioning, internal marketing, and travel distribution systems, to name a few. Each chapter contains insights from hospitality leaders from around the world. New photographs, forms, and advertising pieces have greatly increased the educational value of the text. Additional industry examples make the text more effective and appealing. All tables, charts, and references have been thoroughly updated.

The text's coverage of negotiating with meeting planners, tour wholesalers, and other travel intermediaries has been increased substantially. Because of the tremendous growth of hospitality marketing computer applications, the discussion of sales office automation has been expanded. New information on soliciting such special market segments as reunion groups, truckers, government employees, and sports teams are included in this edition.

Hospitality Sales and Advertising, second edition, contains many features to help students. Exhibits and other boxed material illustrate key concepts. Each chapter begins with an outline and ends with review questions and a list of key terms. An extensive glossary at the end of the book defines the key terms, providing a handy student resource.

The text is divided into four parts. Part I begins with an introduction to hospitality sales and marketing, then discusses marketing plans and examines the organization of a sales office in small, midsize, and large properties. Part II, Sales Techniques, explores personal, telephone, and internal sales, and promotion of on-site revenue centers such as restaurants, lounges, banquet facilities, and meeting rooms. In Part III—Advertising, Public Relations, and Publicity—we look at advertising media and review guidelines for writing and producing advertising that sells. Part IV, Marketing, discusses some of the major market segments (both individual and group) and how to reach them.

In writing a textbook, an author usually starts out with a strong idea of what the book should be like. However, before the manuscript is published, there are a number of suggestions made by students, colleagues, friends, editors, and industry professionals that contribute to the author's original idea and improve the book. I particularly want to acknowledge the helpful comments and contributions of my editor and friend, Jim Purvis. I also wish to thank Paul Wise, Jim Peckrul, Michael Holt, and Ed Sansovini for their work on the first edition.

Finally, I owe a special thank-you to Tom McCarthy. Tom is a veteran of hospitality marketing whose outstanding career and commitment to helping others are shining examples for those aspiring to be hotel sales professionals. His seminars and magazine articles are valuable sources of education for hospitality sales and marketing executives. For his suggestions and contributions to this second edition, and his great contributions to the industry, I dedicate this book to Tom McCarthy.

James R. Abbey
Las Vegas, Nevada

Part I

Introduction

Chapter Outline

1

Introduction to Hospitality Sales and Marketing

IN 1948, THE TYPICAL HOTEL* (84.4% of all properties) was located in a population or trade center, had fewer than 50 rooms, and was independently owned. Only 4.7% of all properties belonged to a chain, and there were only two prominent chains—Sheraton and Hilton. Rooms were small, most had no telephone, and a few lacked a private bath. There was no standardization of product, amenities, or services. Rates averaged $3.75 per night.

Only large properties could afford to support restaurants and bars, and hotels with swimming pools were uncommon. There were a few resorts (most were located in the mountains or near a lake or an ocean), but these properties were primarily seasonal and catered to wealthy individuals.[1]

Beginning in the 1950s, however, hotels began to change, driven by changes in the society around them:

1. *Population growth.* The population began growing significantly, especially in the South, Mountain, and Pacific regions. In addition to this growth, the population began shifting; the Sunbelt (especially Florida and Texas) and the western states (Colorado, Arizona, and California in particular) experienced a tremendous influx of people.

2. *Longer life span.* Not only did the population grow, it became older, and a significant number of new households were formed. Many of these new families relocated, moving across the country as never before.

3. *Improved incomes.* Family incomes improved in the post-war economy, and two-income families became more prevalent. After the belt-tightening war years, families suddenly had more money to spend on travel and leisure. It wouldn't be until the 1970s, when inflation began running rampant, that this trend would be curtailed to any great extent.

4. *Increased leisure time.* Leisure time increased when the 40-hour workweek became commonplace and additional legal holidays were given to workers. Other job market factors such as part-time work and job sharing also contributed to the increased amount of leisure time available to workers.

---

*Except where otherwise noted, the term "hotel" will be used generically to represent all types of commercial lodging properties, including motels, motor hotels, and resorts.

5. *Expanded highway system.* Construction of the interstate highway system began in earnest in 1956, and the 42,500-mile system soon became an important factor in the number of Americans traveling, both for business and leisure. Vehicle registrations grew phenomenally and Americans took to the roads in great numbers.

6. *Development of suburbs.* Not only did the interstate highway system facilitate long distance travel, it also made local travel simpler. As a result, new residential neighborhoods were established in the suburbs. These were followed by retail shopping centers, office buildings, and recreational and entertainment facilities, all of which attracted increased traffic and the need for accommodations and meeting space.

7. *Increased air travel.* Air travel also became a commonplace part of the American business and leisure scene. By the early 1980s, there were over 700 airports certified for passenger service, including 23 large hub airports (in Chicago, New York City, Los Angeles, Dallas, and so on). Hub airports not only served their own cities (which were destinations in their own right), but also served as connection points for an increasing number of domestic and international flights. In addition, 35 medium hubs served regional areas such as the Southwest or Northeast, and 62 small hubs provided statewide connections for a growing number of business and leisure travelers.

8. *Convention center expansion.* The 1950s and 1960s ushered in a booming U.S. economy. As businesses (and business and fraternal organizations) grew, businesspeople needed facilities for conventions and meetings. Some cities already had civic centers or auditoriums that could accommodate groups, generally served by a small number of downtown hotels. But as businesses expanded into the suburbs or outgrew the limited civic center facilities, there was a boom in the construction of convention hotels, both in the cities and in regional and resort destinations.

But what do these factors have to do with hospitality sales and promotion? The answer is simple: everything! Changing times have had a great impact on the hospitality industry, and the industry has had to evolve tremendously to meet the new challenges posed by a changing society.

To meet the demands of road travelers in the 1950s, the industry responded with the development of a number of chain properties: Holiday Inns, Ramada Inns, Howard Johnson's, and Travelodge were among the lodging pioneers along interstate highways. Each of these chains introduced its own standardized designs, amenities, services, and referral networks; each became easily recognizable (both in terms of service and market image) in the eyes of the traveling public.

The growth of these and other chains—coupled with developing technology—ushered in the first toll-free reservations systems in the 1960s, a decade that also introduced the first budget hotels. These "back to basics" budget properties did not come into great prominence until the 1970s, when runaway inflation, fuel shortages, and budget cutbacks on the part of many companies resulted in an unprecedented belt-tightening among travelers.

The 1970s also introduced the traveling public to the first all-suite properties. These properties were largely ignored by travelers in the '70s, but today—two decades after their introduction—they have become an important part of the hospitality industry. An increasing number of "extended-stay" travelers—businesspeople or vacationers who spend a week or more in the same location—prefer a suite to a conventional hotel room.

Large convention hotels such as the Las Vegas Hilton, the New York Marriott Marquis, and the Hyatt Regency Maui were built in the 1980s. Hotels catered to the business traveler with executive floors, business services, and fitness amenities that were virtually non-existent in the 1970s.

The 1980s also ushered in another major building boom in the hospitality industry, largely due to the 1981 Economic Recovery Act, an attempt to stimulate capital investment in the United States. The lure of investment tax credit resulted in a glut of hotel construction—largely by builders and developers who had no knowledge of hotel markets or management. Most properties were built without regard for market demands or the amount of time necessary to establish a guest base; still other, "luxury" properties were constructed at costs that would prove almost impossible to recover. The Tax Reform Act of 1986 put an end to this irresponsible building, but the American hospitality market would feel the effects of overbuilding for years to come.

Today's Hospitality Trends

Successful hospitality management depends on keeping abreast of current trends and acting on them before the competition does. Pro-acting rather than reacting is the key to success. The study of trends is often referred to as "environmental scanning" in marketing circles, and is an integral part of hospitality sales. Current trends affecting the hospitality industry include:

- Globalization
- Consolidation
- Product segmentation
- Expansion of legalized gambling
- Distribution methods
- Computers
- Media planning
- Environmental awareness
- Guest preferences
- Relationship marketing

Globalization

The early 1990s saw changes that would have been unthinkable a few short years ago: the dissolution of the Soviet Union; the opening of eastern European bloc

Hotels with No Guestrooms:
All-Suite Hotels

All-suite hotels have taken the lodging industry by storm. While they comprise only 8% of today's market, that figure is expected to more than double in the 1990s. Why the increased interest in all-suite properties? The answer is simple: profitability.

All-suite properties are currently averaging substantially higher occupancy rates than conventional hotels, and can command higher room rates for a number of reasons. First, suites are typically larger than most conventional guestrooms. While conventional guestrooms average 300 to 400 square feet, all-suite hotels generally offer combination living/working areas, separate bedrooms, and (often) kitchenettes, with a total size of 500 to 800 square feet.

Second, suites often do not provide on-premises restaurants, but rather provide a complimentary breakfast or cocktail hour. While these amenities generally cost between $3.50 to $4.50 per guest, the perceived value by the guest enables operators to increase room rates by $5 to $15! Limiting the scope of a food and beverage operation results in increased profits for the operator as well.

All-suite operators also benefit from the wide appeal of their properties. While many convention hotels are typically occupied at greater levels either during the week or on the weekend, all-suite properties appeal to both business travelers (who generally travel on weekdays) and leisure travelers (who are taking more frequent mini-vacations on weekends). Therefore, occupancy at all-suite properties tends to remain high, rather than rising and falling as it does at many conventional hotels.

But why are all-suite properties so popular? The spacious accommodations, the home-like atmosphere, and the functional work areas (which are ideal for working and entertaining) appeal to business travelers (the largest growing segment of the hospitality market) and to those on extended stays, including leisure travelers with families. But, there is a proliferation of these properties, and confusion is rampant as to which property serves what segment—and with what product.

All-suite properties vary widely in concept and amenities offered. As mentioned, many limit their food and beverage service, while other properties, such as the Washington, D.C.-based Guest Quarters, offer restaurants and lounges similar to those found in first-class hotels. Some properties concentrate on a traditional atrium-style mid-rise construction, while other all-suite hotels position themselves as residential-type complexes complete with landscaped areas and recreational facilities. Some of these last, such as Residence Inns, offer amenities designed to make guests feel right at home—grocery shopping services, baby-sitting services, and so on.

With the varying concepts and services offered, it is becoming increasingly necessary for an all-suite hotel to position itself for particular target markets, and to promote its positioning so that the public will know exactly what the property has to offer. The increased proliferation of all-suite properties is expected to continue into the next decade, and competition for all-suite guests will grow more heated as more and more travelers discover the properties that have come to be called "the standard of tomorrow."

countries to free trade; and the creation of a single European market, the European Economic Community. In addition, despite dramatic fluctuations in the economy, the early part of the decade ushered in a worldwide boom in tourism. People had the freedom, time, and money to travel—and were taking full advantage of the tourism bargains resulting from a sluggish economy. Travelers were crossing international boundaries in huge numbers and spending trillions of dollars on travel at home and abroad.

This trend led to a new industry buzz word, "globalization." Globalization has had—and will continue to have—a significant impact on the hospitality industry. First, the American hospitality industry no longer perceives its market as 240 million Americans; the new hospitality market is 5 billion people worldwide. Most of the major domestic chains are not only stepping up efforts to more effectively promote their American properties to the international traveler, but are also developing global networks of properties to take advantage of the international tourist boom. Choice Hotels International (formerly Quality Inns), for example, has set a goal of 10,000 properties and one million guestrooms worldwide by the year 2000, while the southeast Asian tourist boom has resulted in international expansion in the Pacific Rim by Hilton International Resorts, Hyatt International, and Sheraton.

Globalization has not been a one-way street. Foreign hotel chains, taking advantage of a slow American economy, have expanded their own international bases by acquiring domestic properties as never before (see Exhibit 1). Accor, the French hotel chain which is Europe's largest, purchased Motel 6 in 1990, and New World Hotels, based in Hong Kong, added the Ramada group to its worldwide holdings. The involvement of overseas investors will no doubt lead to changes in how their American properties are managed—and, hopefully, will increase their appeal to international visitors.

Consolidation

Globalization can be extremely costly. It requires advanced technology to process international reservations and develop marketing strategies for specific countries and regions, and there is the expense of additional promotional costs. High costs

Exhibit 1   Foreign Hotel Affiliations in the United States

HOTEL	COUNTRY
ANA (All Nippon Airways)	Japan
Delta Hotels and Resorts	Canada
Doubletree (Canadian Pacific)	Canada
Dusit Hotels and Resorts	Thailand
Four Seasons	Canada
Hilton International-Vista Hotels (Ladbroke)	England
Holiday Inn Worldwide (Bass PLC)	England
Inter-Continental (Saison Holdings)	Japan
Mandarin	Hong Kong
Meridien (Air France)	France
Miyako Hotels	Japan
Motel 6 (Accor)	France
New Otani	Japan
Nikko (Japan Air Lines)	Japan
Omni (Wharf Ltd.)	Hong Kong
Pan Pacific (Tokyu Hotel Group)	Japan
Park Land Hotels International	Hong Kong
Park Suites (Sara Hotel Group)	Sweden
Penta (Lufthansa Airlines)	Germany
Prince Hotels	Japan
Ramada International/New World	Hong Kong
Stouffer	Hong Kong
Swissotel (Swissair)	Switzerland
Travelodge (Forte Hotels)	England
Westin (Aoki Corp.)	Japan

Many foreign interests now have hotels in major U.S. cities. There are several reasons for this move to the "internationalization" of U.S. hotel chains: first, the United States is a strong market, enjoying a recent surge in visitors; second, the U.S. economy is more stable than that of most countries; and third, foreign hotel chains see a variety of bargains in the United States, including lower construction and operating costs and relatively inexpensive land.

have led to another hospitality trend that is expected to play a key role in the industry into the next century: product consolidation.

The high price of globalization has made it nearly impossible for small chains to operate on a worldwide level, and there has been a frenzy of mergers and acquisitions within the hospitality industry. In 1990, Choice Hotels International started the trend when it purchased the Rodeway, Econo Lodge, and Friendship chains. Another large, industry-changing merger occurred in 1992, when Days Inns was sold to Ramada's domestic parent company, Hospitality Franchise Systems, which also owns Howard Johnson. On the international level, in addition to the purchase of Motel 6 by Accor, London-based Bass PLC bought Holiday Inns (although former Holiday brands Embassy Suites, Hampton Inns, Homewood Suites, and Harrah's fell under the umbrella of Promus).

In the March 1992 issue of *Lodging Magazine,* Henry Silverman, the chairman of Hospitality Franchise Systems, stated that consolidation was inevitable—just as it had been in the auto industry (there were 53 American auto companies in the

1950s; now there are a handful), and with the airlines (in 1992, 8 major airlines dominated the industry; in 1979, there were 24 carriers). Silverman predicts that it will only be a matter of time before five or six major chains will dominate the hospitality industry.[2]

Is this trend good or bad? Benefits of consolidation include the availability of the capital required to purchase new technology and marketing and the resources to assist properties individually as needed. Streamlining at the corporate level also eliminates duplication of efforts and the resulting overhead expenses, helping to keep rates down.

Consolidation has drawbacks, however. There are justifiable fears that employee layoffs will result as operations are streamlined, and hospitality products will suffer. Will the individual franchisees get lost at the corporate level? Will individual brands lose their integrity? How will the corporation determine which property needs the most attention, and will this attention come at the expense of another struggling property? Dealing with these drawbacks will be a major concern in the hospitality industry as the trend toward consolidation continues to have an impact on today's market.

Product Segmentation

Product segmentation—that is, designing, building, and marketing hospitality properties for a specific market segment—is not entirely new. The hospitality industry has traditionally positioned itself into three broad product categories or segments: luxury, mid-price, and budget. But now there are segments within these segments, and hotels are creating "brand" images and names to distinguish their properties from competitors (see Exhibit 2). Today, product segmentation has taken three basic forms:

1. Tier marketing
2. Hotels within hotels
3. All-suite hotels

Tier Marketing. Tier marketing (also called niche or product portfolio marketing) was established as properties became aware that there were an increasing number of market segments with varying preferences and budgets. Choice Hotels International was the first chain to adopt a multi-tiered marketing strategy, and introduced Comfort Inns (budget properties) and Quality Royale (upscale properties) to complement its mid-priced Quality Inns product. Other chains quickly followed suit, some by developing different "brand" names to attract new market segments, others by buying existing chains (as in the case of Holiday Inns, which purchased Granada Royale Hometels).

There were several reasons for this sudden diversification of hospitality properties:

- The recognition on the part of some chains that they had to target additional markets to meet the goals of aggressive growth plans

Exhibit 2   Product Segmentation in the Hotel Industry

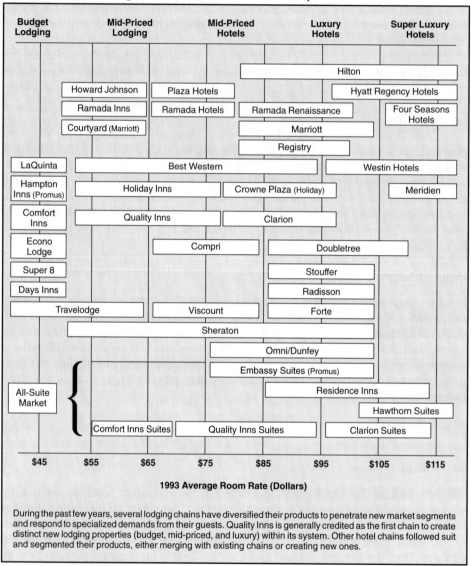

During the past few years, several lodging chains have diversified their products to penetrate new market segments and respond to specialized demands from their guests. Quality Inns is generally credited as the first chain to create distinct new lodging properties (budget, mid-priced, and luxury) within its system. Other hotel chains followed suit and segmented their products, either merging with existing chains or creating new ones.

Source: Updated and adapted from "An Investor's Scorecard," *Hotel and Motel Management*, April 1985, p. 1.

- The need to identify the variations in facilities, price, and service between properties within a chain
- The chains' attempt to instill "brand loyalty" in their guests, a strategy that has long been used in the sale of consumer goods
- The trends toward upscale and economy properties

- The fact that many mid-priced properties were finding it difficult to compete because of their age and condition

With so many hotel chains diversifying to reach as many market segments as possible, it is important that a chain make clear the distinctions among its different types of properties. The Radisson hotel chain, for example, uses different names to distinguish its properties:

- Radisson "Plazas" are deluxe facilities featuring a minimum of 250 guest-rooms and 40 to 50 square feet (3.7 to 4.7 square meters) of meeting and function space per guestroom.

- Radisson "Hotels" feature a minimum of 200 guestrooms and 50 to 70 square feet (4.7 to 6.5 square meters) of meeting and function space per guestroom.

- Radisson "Inns" cater to the roadside traveler, and have a minimum of 150 guestrooms and 30 to 40 square feet (2.8 to 3.7 square meters) of meeting and function space per guestroom.

- Radisson "Resorts" are designed to serve incentive groups and high-class meetings with a minimum of 200 guestrooms and 45 to 50 square feet (4.2 to 4.7 square meters) of meeting and function space per guestroom.

These properties are promoted differently, but are promoted (as are the properties of other chains) to generate a "brand loyalty"—in this case, a brand loyalty to Radisson properties. Brand loyalty has been used in other industries, such as the automobile industry, for years, and involves "capturing" the consumer and moving him or her up to the next product tier as wants and desires change. In the case of the automobile industry, for example, a young man might purchase a Ford Escort for his first new car, then later "graduate" to a Ford Taurus as his family grows. As his career and salary rise, he will, if he remains loyal to the Ford "brand," choose another Ford product—a Lincoln or Thunderbird—over other luxury cars.

Marriott has also created several different types of properties in an effort to develop brand loyalty among travelers (see Exhibit 3). Marriott currently offers the following product line:

- Fairfield Inns—an economy product

- Courtyard by Marriott—moderately priced accommodations

- Residence Inns—all-suite properties designed for extended-stay corporate travelers

- Marriott Hotels and Resorts—full-service luxury properties marketed to upscale leisure travelers and to the convention market

- Marriott Suites—accommodations that target the business traveler who requires "more than a guestroom"

The Fairfield Inn product is relatively new, and was designed to introduce new guests to the Marriott organization. According to Michael R. Ruffer, vice president and general manager, the Fairfield Inn's prime objective is to widen the

Exhibit 3   The Marriott Product Line: Developing Brand Loyalty

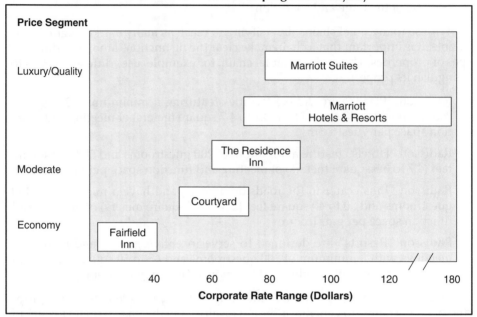

Many chains now offer a number of hospitality products in a variety of price ranges to attract guests and build brand loyalty. Just as someone starting a career may begin with an economy model automobile, a business traveler on a limited budget can choose Marriott's Fairfield Inn. Familiarity—and satisfaction—with the product often leads to guest brand loyalty. As the guest becomes more successful, he or she will "graduate" to middle of the line products (in both cars and hotel accommodations), and later choose the "luxury" product offered by the familiar automobile maker or hotel chain. (Courtesy of the Marriott Corporation)

chain's guest base and build brand loyalty: "Hopefully, if we have a chance to service them [economy travelers] well at a Fairfield Inn, to let them touch and feel the things that make Marriott the excellent lodging company that we are, then they will stay with us in the Marriott family."[3]

Hotels within Hotels. Product segmentation is not limited to chains acquiring or building different types of properties, however. The "hotel within a hotel" concept has proven popular, especially with upscale guests who appreciate having a club or floor reserved exclusively for their use. Sheraton and Hilton hotels offer Tower sections, Hyatt promotes a Regency Club, and Marriott offers a Concierge level. Other properties also promote business clubs, floors, and services.

All-Suite Hotels. The all-suite hotel, as mentioned, has become an integral part of the hospitality industry, and appeals to value-conscious travelers who do not want to pay for extra amenities they would not use at a traditional hotel (a lounge, swimming pool, health club, and so on), as well as to travelers who enjoy the extra comfort a suite can provide during extended business or pleasure stays. To meet a variety of needs—from budget to executive tastes—all-suite hotels vary from complete resort-like properties that offer meeting facilities, restaurants, and recreational amenities for the upscale traveler to those that have trimmed the extras while still providing the comforts of home to value-oriented travelers. Many all-suite hotels offer a continental or cooked-to-order breakfast as part of the room rate, and a full-service restaurant is usually located nearby for the convenience of guests.

Expansion of Legalized Gambling

A relatively new hospitality trend has resulted from efforts to raise needed state revenues in a sluggish economy. Once forbidden except in the gaming meccas of Las Vegas and Reno, Nevada (and later gaining a foothold in Atlantic City, New Jersey), legalized gambling in various forms has spread across the United States. According to the National Association of Attorneys General, in the second quarter of 1992, 33 states had lotteries, 11 had video gaming, 13 had sanctioned Indian casinos, and 9 (Colorado, Illinois, Iowa, Louisiana, Mississippi, Montana, Nevada, New Jersey, and South Dakota) offered casino gambling, either on land or on riverboats. Only 9 states (Alabama, Alaska, Arkansas, Georgia, Hawaii, Oklahoma, Tennessee, Texas, and Utah) and Washington, D.C., had no form of legalized gaming, but gaming legislation was pending in Arkansas and Hawaii.[4]

How will this trend affect the hospitality industry over the next decade? Benefits include the development of additional gaming complexes (proposals in Chicago and in Connecticut were under consideration in 1992), an increased need for qualified management employees, and increased tourism. The greatest argument against gambling as a fund-raiser, however, cites studies that have shown that government gambling revenues are a regressive tax that adversely affects the poor. Opponents of the spread of legalized gambling also point out that most jobs created by gambling businesses are low-paying. Perhaps the objection that most affects the hospitality industry, however, regards possible over-saturation of the market. As more states "get into the act," there may be no need to travel to gamble. Two questions remain to be answered: Will the increase of local gambling options adversely affect established gaming areas such as Las Vegas and Atlantic City, which have already experienced their share of financial woes? Will new gaming complexes enhance tourism in cities such as Chicago, or merely draw revenues away from non-gaming properties in the area?

Distribution Methods

Since Holiday Inns ushered in the "computer revolution" with the first automated central reservations system (CRS) in the mid-1960s, computers have played an increasingly important part in the distribution of hotel rooms. Today, not only do most properties offer CRS, but many are linking up with other properties—and services, such as airlines and rental car firms—to provide increased accessibility to hospitality products.

One of the industry's most innovative systems is UltraSwitch, operated by The Hotel Industry Switch Company (THISCO). UltraSwitch links the central reservations systems of major North American hotel chains with those of major airlines. This type of system is essential in today's global market, and has resulted in a

Insider Insights

J. Raymond Lewis, Jr.
Executive Vice President
  Worldwide Sales & Marketing
Holiday Inn Worldwide
Atlanta, Georgia

Ray Lewis majored in marketing at the University of Tennessee. He has also attended executive development programs at the University of Chicago and the Wharton School of Business at the University of Pennsylvania. Lewis began his sales and marketing career in 1966 with the Monsanto Company. Immediately prior to his association with Holiday Inn, Lewis was senior vice president and director of marketing for an Atlanta-based advertising agency.

In February 1985 Lewis joined Holiday Inn, where he was assigned the responsibility for directing the corporation's national consumer marketing programs. In April 1990, after Holiday Inn was acquired by Bass PLC, he was named senior vice president in charge of all U.S. marketing for Holiday Inn Worldwide.

Holiday Inn has a new parent. Bass PLC acquired the company in 1990 in order to realize one of its major goals: to become a global company. To acquire Holiday Inn, Bass sold a very successful hotel chain in the United Kingdom, Crest Hotels. The divestiture enabled Bass to focus on Holiday Inn, now called Holiday Inn Worldwide.

Holiday Inn Worldwide continues to see growth opportunities in North America. We are also looking at Europe, and as the infrastructure improves in Eastern Europe it will become a major area of opportunity. There are many growth opportunities in Asia as well.

Our brand strategy has always been to be the best in the middle market. Some see that market as shrinking, but we think it has tremendous growth potential because we are a world of middle-market consumers. There is a well-defined high and low end of the market, and everything else is in the middle. It's the middle market that's growing, whether it's in cars, fast-food, TV sets, or housing. Our goal is to continue to be the dominant hotel company in the middle market.

Today's guest has more options than ever, but by the same token, there are a wide variety of guests. Not everyone wants the same thing. We identify the guest groups we want to serve, determine their economic value, and define what they want. Then, to meet their needs we create "brand extensions" under the Holiday Inn umbrella. A well-known brand extension we established ten years ago for the upper end of the middle market is the Holiday Inn Crowne Plaza. More recent additions include Holiday Inn Express, a streamlined facility geared to travelers who don't need the amenities of a full-service hotel; Holiday Inn SunSpree Resorts, full-activity hotels in preferred leisure destinations; and Holiday Inn Crowne Plaza Resorts, affordably priced for the upper range of the middle market.

The world is changing and globalization is not an empty word anymore. The 1990s will see an enormous rise in travel and tourism among the peoples of the world. Fortunately, technology enables us to operate on a global basis and on a consistent basis. We intend to be the leaders of change, not the victims of it.

number of additional innovations, including a Hotel Clearing Corporation that provides centralized payment of travel agent commissions (thus encouraging additional bookings).

Computer technology is not limited to use by the hospitality industry itself. Potential guests already have direct access to property information through the use of data banks at airports, and new computer data bases, such as The Eaasy Sabre, enable consumers with home computer systems to directly make hotel reservations and book flights.

Computers

As just mentioned, state-of-the-art computer technology has revolutionized central reservations systems, and has provided hotels with a direct link to travel agents and airline reservations systems for virtually instantaneous verification of room arrangements. Computers also play an important role in areas as diverse as generating marketing data bases, following up on sales efforts, and sending personalized sales letters. Computer technology is an indispensable tool for managing research information, generating monthly reports, and planning sales efforts.

The computer has also enabled hotels to increase room revenues through the management of rates and occupancy, using yield management systems. Yield management systems take into account potential room supply and demand to determine whether a lodging facility should raise or lower its room rates on a particular date. The idea of yield management is not new, but advances in computer technology now make it possible to update prices according to demand with much greater frequency.

Media Planning

Media planning also plays an important role in hospitality sales. In past decades, a general manager had few media options. He or she could advertise in the local newspaper, perhaps place an ad in one of the nation's general readership magazines, or purchase radio spots. Today, however, there is a wide variety of both print and broadcast media available. In addition to general magazines, thousands of special interest magazines, trade journals, and consumer publications are now available. In the broadcast area, television is playing a more significant role. The hotelier has a choice of commercial television (both local and national), public television sponsorship, and a myriad of cable television options. With this wide range of media choices, audiences have become smaller, and it has become necessary to "narrowcast" advertising. Marketers must develop advertising and promotions that appeal to specific markets rather than employ national "broadcast" strategies that were once the norm.

With the increased focus on international markets, an awareness of foreign media sources and a knowledge of the target country's culture is essential. An unintentional cultural *faux pas* can destroy the image a property is trying to project and undermine future marketing efforts in that country. Sensitivity to a country's culture is a crucial part of international sales and marketing, and many chains that have expanded into foreign markets have established international branch offices with a knowledgeable staff, or rely on international experts to assist them in correctly promoting their hospitality products.

Environmental Awareness

Concern about the environment is no longer the province of a few fringe groups; many of today's consumers are genuinely concerned about environmental issues. Consumers are opting for more environmentally sound vacations in greater numbers, giving rise to another new industry buzz word: "ecotourism."

Ecotourism can be easily confused with adventure travel, but it is much more. Not only does ecotourism promote an enjoyment of nature (without harming the environment), it also entails a responsibility for helping to protect the visited region.

This responsibility is shared by visitors and developers alike. At one time, developers often built in the middle of a resource because of its view. Cancun, Mexico, and parts of Hawaii are examples of areas where overbuilding has destroyed precious natural resources and dimmed the beauty that originally attracted visitors.

Fortunately, many developers are now taking an active interest in preserving our fragile environment. One of the pioneers of environmental responsibility was the Ramada chain (see Exhibit 4), which was purchased by New World Hotels (Holdings) Limited of Hong Kong in 1989. Ramada's international division adopted the slogan "Hotels of the New Wave[SM]," and began a campaign "to position Ramada International Hotels & Resorts as a visionary international hotel company for the new age, where technology, business values, and hospitality reflect our concern for the world environment...."[5]

Many other hospitality properties have followed Ramada's lead, and subscribe to more environmentally sound programs, including water conservation (in some cases, guests are charged for excessive usage), the use of recycled paper and biodegradable products, recycling programs (including the use of recyclable packaging materials), and involvement in local conservation efforts.

Guest Preferences

Just as changing guest preferences altered the face of the hospitality industry in the 1980s, two major trends of the 1990s will greatly affect the hospitality industry into the next century: the "graying" of America and a shift in the demographics of the American family. In 1960, only 9.2% of the population was over the age of 65; this percentage is escalating rapidly as the baby boom generation matures. This age group is especially important to the hospitality industry because it has both the time and the discretionary income to travel.

The demographics of American households are also changing dramatically; more women are opting for careers and marrying later. Because of this trend (and a high divorce rate), there is also an increase in the single adult market segment, which has the freedom—and the discretionary income—to travel.

Two-income families are also on the increase. In 1960, only 28.5% of American families were headed by two-income couples. By the year 2000, that percentage is expected to almost triple to 75%![6] This trend, which has resulted in more disposable income but less time for extended vacations, has led to shorter, multiple vacations spread throughout the year or, if time permits, "adventure" or "fantasy" vacations (which is good news for resorts).

Exhibit 4   Environmental Awareness Advertising

This ad, from Ramada International Hotels & Resorts, was designed to promote the chain's commitment to preserving the natural sites chosen for its properties. Other corporate ads also express the chain's concern for the health of its guests, and the advertising campaign as a whole reflects each property's commitment to "environmental integrity through preservation, conservation and recycling programs initiated by the property's staff and by the group." (Source: Ramada International Hotels & Resorts Communications Manual, January 1991.)

Changing modern lifestyles have also given rise to two very different types of travelers: a sophisticated, discriminating traveler and a new breed, the "do-it-yourselfer." As Americans travel more for both business and leisure, they become more discriminating and expect personalized service and quality amenities. Gone are the days when in-room amenities were an option; today's traveler expects fine soaps, shampoos, lotions, and quality stationery. The sophisticated traveler *expects* to be pampered.

At the opposite end of the spectrum are those who are comfortable with helping themselves. Like the discriminating travelers, the do-it-yourselfers expect a trouble-free vacation, including an emphasis on service, but for them efficient service doesn't necessarily mean pampering. These travelers are used to self-services—from using automated teller machines to pumping their own gas to bagging their own groceries—and are willing to do more for themselves. To meet this demand, some properties are offering buffets in their restaurants; various degrees of self-service during check-in and check-out; and such amenities as in-room self-service beverages, microwavable foods, and video entertainment.

While the type of hotel a guest prefers will vary depending on the guest's reason for travel, budget, and other factors, it is interesting to note that both all-suite properties (typically upscale) and economy or limited-service properties are experiencing acceptance and growth.

Today's traveler, no matter what category he or she falls into, is more likely to be health conscious than the traveler of ten years ago. In addition to the nationwide trend toward no-smoking, the consumption of "hard" liquor has declined. Today's guest is likely to demand "healthy" foods (lower cholesterol, sodium, and fats, as well as fewer calories and preservatives) and cross-cultural "ethnic" fare (especially Asian and Hispanic). Many guests expect exercise facilities at hotels, so they can continue working out while away from home.

Relationship Marketing

With the wide range of hospitality choices available to travelers today, properties are finding it essential to build a repeat customer base. This trend has resulted in "relationship marketing," which is defined as businesses seeing their customers as assets and protecting their customer bases by maintaining and enhancing relationships with guests.

Although the word "hospitality" suggests a relationship, the industry as a whole has been lax when it comes to fostering a bond between properties and guests. Good service has come to be *expected* by guests, and properties of the past stopped there; good service was provided, but there was no concentrated effort to develop guest-property relationships. This is changing, and many properties are taking the time to foster friendships by making guests feel more special. For example, it is no longer unusual for a repeat guest to be treated to a basket of his or her favorite fruit or receive another favorite amenity.

Making guests feel welcome and pampered still begins with the property's staff, however, and "internal marketing" has become an integral part of today's industry. Internal marketing seeks to employ and retain the best people possible doing the best possible work by focusing on the human aspect of the industry. Each employee is "sold" on the property and on his or her value in terms of providing guest satisfaction and building relationships. This type of education promotes greater awareness of the importance of conscientious service and its role in building a satisfied, loyal guest base.

Marketing and Sales

In the 1980s, competition among hotels became fierce, and it was no longer adequate to place a few advertisements, send a few salespeople out on personal calls, and rely on word-of-mouth advertising to fill guestrooms and property revenue centers. As the hospitality industry faces the changes of the 1990s and looks ahead to the next century, the need for concentrated marketing and sales strategies has never been greater. The success of today's—and tomorrow's—hospitality products will be the direct result of the combined efforts of highly trained, competent, and innovative sales and marketing professionals who are dedicated to making an impact on the ever-changing, challenging hospitality industry.

Marketing vs. Sales

For years, the hospitality industry focused on *selling* guestrooms and other services and facilities. In today's sophisticated marketplace, however, *marketing* has become the buzzword; properties have shifted from a strictly sales orientation to marketing in order to understand and manage the relationship they have with the client or guest.

What is the difference between marketing and sales? Marketing is the study and management of the exchange process. It involves those things that the property will do to select a target market and stimulate or alter that market's demand for the property's services. While marketing includes sales, it also includes a number of other elements: research, action strategies, advertising, publicity, and sales promotions, as well as a means to monitor the effectiveness of the marketing program.

Sales consists of direct efforts to sell the property by personal contact, telephone, and mailings. Although we will discuss the importance of sales later in the chapter, it is important to note that the sales process has been changed considerably by new marketing concepts that focus on what consumers want rather than on what the property has to sell. An example of this shift is the establishment of no-smoking rooms in response to requests from health-conscious guests. Because of marketing research, more properties are developing features for salespeople to sell, rather than just trying to sell existing features.

Marketing differs from sales in these key ways:

Marketing focuses on:	Sales focuses on:
Market analysis, planning, and control	Field work and desk work to sell to consumers
Long-term trends, and how to translate problems and opportunities into new products, markets, and strategies for long-term growth	Short-term considerations, such as today's products, markets, consumers, and strategies

Insider Insights

Thomas T. McCarthy, CHA, CHSE
Owner
Tom McCarthy Associates
Falls Church, Virginia

After graduating from Villanova University, Tom McCarthy began his hotel career in 1953 as a room clerk at the Warwick Hotel in Philadelphia. Eventually he joined Hilton Hotels, where he held a variety of sales positions, including director of sales at the Capitol Hilton in Washington, D.C., before joining Marriott. McCarthy served as national sales manager, director of advertising, and vice president of advertising and public relations in his 11 years with Marriott before leaving to establish his own hotel marketing consulting firm, Tom McCarthy Associates. He co-founded the Hotel Professional Educational Series, which specializes in hotel sales and marketing training, and has served as international president of the Hospitality Sales & Marketing Association International. He has been the sales/marketing columnist for Hotel & Resort Industry *magazine since 1981.*

Those who are successful in hotel sales know what it means to "pay your dues." They have experienced long hours, rejection, frustration, enormous work loads, difficult guests, and uphill battles with supervisors, but have found that the personal satisfaction they experience far outweighs all the negatives.

The thrill of closing the sale after competing with four or five other hotels is one of the greatest compensations for hard work I can think of. I'll never forget how excited I was when I booked my first convention at the Waldorf-Astoria—and the excitement that came with every close since.

Another compensation is the satisfaction of being a member of a winning team that takes that extra step to satisfy guests' needs. There's nothing more satisfying than having a meeting planner tell you that your efforts—and the efforts of your staff— contributed to the most successful convention in the history of their organization. And let's not forget that a hotel is an exciting place for a salesperson to work. It's a place where important events are happening; a place where interesting, and often famous, people congregate; and a place where new challenges await you every single day.

Over and above these compensations, there's the opportunity to build friendships with people from all over the world. Very few people in other businesses have the opportunity to meet so many people from so many places. Building friendships with others within the worldwide hotel community is another compensation that keeps the successful salesperson's enthusiasm high. There's no question that camaraderie with the many wonderful people in our industry, often built through active participation in organizations such as Hospitality Sales & Marketing Association International and the American Hotel & Motel Association, is an enriching experience.

I've been asked by many people entering hotel sales to comment on what makes a hotel salesperson successful. To name a few of the many ingredients, successful salespeople are:

Insider Insights *(continued)*

- True believers in their products
- Honest, sincere, and ethical beyond reproach
- Enthusiastic even when feeling low
- Optimistic and able to spring back quickly from defeat
- Concerned about delivering more than what was promised, not just concerned about closing the sale
- Able to put themselves in the prospect's shoes and sell only what they would buy themselves
- Creative in finding ways to make the guest's experience better
- Motivated to do their most persuasive selling when the prospect says no
- Not content with the ways of the past if better ways can be found
- Aware that continuing education to improve sales skills is a career-long activity
- Willing to make an investment in time and effort to be successful

Because of intense competition, owners and operators have been forced to recognize that hotels can no longer be successful without strong selling efforts. This has created a demand for better educated, highly motivated sales executives. There's no question that opportunities for hotel sales professionals are greater now than at any time in the history of our industry.

Profit planning, such as determining the appropriate mix of business from individual market segments	Volumes and quotas, current sales, bonuses, and commissions

Marketing, then, focuses on the researching of trends and the development of successful sales techniques and efforts. Successful sales of the property depend on effective marketing strategies, which can only be developed by focusing on market variables—the environment in general (uncontrollable or external variables), and controllable variables inherent in the property (the marketing mix).

The Marketing Mix

The term *marketing mix* is used to indicate the integrating of several variables to satisfy specific consumer needs. The task of the marketing manager is to form these variables into a marketing mix that meets the needs of each consumer group or market segment targeted by the property.

What makes up the marketing mix? The most widely used model of the marketing mix is the familiar "four Ps" set forth by E. J. McCarthy in his classic *Basic Marketing.* This model can be represented by three concentric circles:

1. The innermost circle contains the focal point of the marketing effort—the *consumer.*

2. The middle circle illustrates the marketing mix of product, price, promotion, and place (the four Ps). These are termed *controllable variables*.

3. The outer circle identifies *uncontrollable variables* such as the economic environment, political and legal influences, and the cultural and social environment.

The problem with this model is that it is too restrictive for the hospitality industry, which has unique characteristics that prohibit an unadulterated application of the four Ps. This doesn't mean, however, that the hospitality industry needs a new marketing mix. The wheel has been invented; all the industry need do is add a few spokes to make it work for hospitality properties.

The four Ps developed for the consumer goods industry have been broadened in this chapter to account for the unique way in which the hospitality industry operates. *Product* has been expanded to *product-service* because of the service orientation of hospitality properties. *Place,* the second element in the marketing mix, has been broadened to *place-distribution* to include the channels of distribution or the intermediaries who aid in the flow of the hospitality offerings to the guest. The *promotion* "P" is now *promotion-communication,* since marketing communication is different from promotion. Promotion is a one-way flow of information from the seller to the consumer; marketing communication is a two-way exchange. Effective marketers listen to the consumer before developing a product-service based on what they have learned the consumer wants. The last "P," *price,* has been expanded to *price-rate* since the word "price" is seldom used when discussing lodging accommodations.

Conceptually, the marketing mix might be seen as:

*   Developing a product-service mix based on the wants and needs of the target market(s)

*   Determining the most appropriate channels (place-distribution) or ways to reach the market(s)

*   Determining promotion and communication strategies and informing markets of the property's product-service

*   Establishing a price-rate mix that is competitive and will assure a fair return for fulfilling the needs of consumers

In other words, the hospitality marketing manager must have the right facilities and services (product), make them easily accessible to guests (place), with the proper amount of promotion—at the right price. This can be accomplished if the marketing manager can develop a marketing mix that will be effective in reaching his or her property's target markets.

Product-Service. The product-service mix is considered first because without a product the industry has nothing to distribute, promote, or price. Hospitality properties offer products such as guestrooms, banquet space, and food and beverages; and services such as parking, housekeeping, and express check-in/check-out.

This product-service mix must be tailored to the needs and wants of the guests sought. A hospitality firm's offerings are based on research of who its guests are and what benefits they seek. It is important to remember that most hospitality properties serve more than one market segment, each with somewhat different needs and wants. A Four Seasons hotel might define its market segments as families, business travelers, and small business meeting groups, for example. Each of these groups will seek different benefits from the property: the family might desire recreational amenities, the business traveler may require a secretarial service or on-site copying facilities, and the meeting group might be most interested in sound-proof meeting rooms.

While the marketing and sales department cannot actually produce the physical product or render the intangible service, it is responsible for researching the guests' product-service needs and wants and then working with management to develop the property so that it meets those needs and wants. Marketing also evaluates the existing product-service mix and the property's brand name identity for possible improvements. For example, Western International Hotels changed its name and logo to Westin Hotels; the old name was believed to be too long, and many guests were unaware of the chain affiliation of many of the hotel's properties.

The market-oriented hospitality firm attempts to match its product and service offering to the needs and wants of its target markets, but it can face difficulty due to the fixed nature of the product. Hotel rooms and facilities are just not that versatile: a guestroom cannot become a suite, a convention center cannot be converted into a golf course, and a coffee shop cannot be transformed into a lounge without considerable effort and expense.

Service, the other element of the product-service mix, is considerably more flexible, but also poses problems for marketers desiring to meet the needs and wants of guests. It is nearly impossible to standardize hotel services. The front desk agent at night cannot duplicate exactly the service provided by the front desk agent who works the morning shift. A complicated service such as a lavish once-a-year banquet featuring 12-foot-high ice sculptures and exotic menu items is impossible to create the same way each time, and some guests may be disappointed when the banquet is "not as good as last year's." This is in sharp contrast to the consistency of consumer goods. The Nautilus sit-up machine used in a gym in New York, for example, will not differ from the Nautilus sit-up machine found in a health club in California.

In addition to this challenge, providing some services may negatively affect a property's profitability. Two cases in point are telephone and room service; both generally lose money on an annual basis, but failure to provide these services could result in lost business.

Place-Distribution. Place-distribution refers to the accessibility of the product to consumers. With consumer goods, producers use distribution channels to ship their product to consumers. In the hospitality industry, however, distribution is far different: instead of the product traveling to the consumer, the consumer travels to the product.

In the marketing of consumer goods, the role of intermediaries is to ensure that the product is available to the consumer when and where it is needed, and in sufficient variety and quantity. In contrast, hospitality products—clean guestrooms, a pleasant dining experience, and so on—are neither shipped nor stored.

The problems of warehousing and inventory control do not arise, making distribution much simpler for hospitality firms.

The distribution channels available to lodging establishments can be viewed as either direct or indirect. If a hospitality firm seeks to reach potential guests with its own sales force through direct mail, telephone solicitation, personal sales calls, or media advertising, the effort is said to be direct marketing. Indirect distribution channels include intermediaries such as travel agents, tour operators, and independent hotel representatives.

Promotion-Communication. It is the task of the director of marketing to blend the most effective promotion-communication mix. Promotion is the way a hotel or restaurant communicates to target markets, and can involve advertising and direct sales techniques. Communication is different from promotion; promotion implies persuasion (something the marketer does *to* the consumer) while communication is a two-way exchange (something the marketer does *with* the consumer). Determining what the consumer wants and needs through communication is much more effective than trying to sell a product or service that is not needed.

Price-Rate. If a potential guest rejects the property and its services because of price, all of the previous efforts were wasted. Therefore, price-rate determination is one of marketing's most crucial concerns. Consumers are strongly influenced by prices, and the guests a property is seeking to attract must be taken into consideration when establishing room rates and menu prices. Guests who stay at a budget motel, for example, have different wants, needs, and expectations from those who choose an expensive resort property.

Hotels, particularly large properties, may employ a variable rate policy to meet the needs of different market groups. A variable rate policy is characterized by charging different prices to different buyers of the same product, depending on the competitive situation and the bargaining position of the buyer.

The bargaining position of buyers (individual guests, meeting planners, and so on) will vary depending on the hotel's level of business, which can be broken down into three categories:

1. *Peak.* Also known as "in-season," this is the period when demand for a property and its services is highest and the highest prices can be charged. Peak periods vary for different types of properties. A resort, for example, may experience a peak period during the middle of the summer if it is a popular seaside destination, or in the winter if it is a popular ski resort.

2. *Valley.* This period, also known as "off-season," characterizes times when demand is lowest. Reduced rates are often offered during valley periods to attract business.

3. *Shoulder.* This period falls between a peak and a valley, and can be an excellent opportunity to build business—rooms are available and a mid to high rate can be charged. Many properties target sales and marketing efforts toward these shoulder times.

Meeting planners know they can generally negotiate better rates during valley or shoulder periods than during peak convention months, and vacationers often wait to take advantage of special reduced rates during the off-season. Commercial downtown hotels, recognizing that their peak periods occur during the week, often promote special weekend package rates to encourage business during that shoulder period.

A property's pricing policy can also affect its image. Upscale properties, for example, are generally cautious about offering deep discounts. In fact, if famous five-star hotels such as The Ritz-Carlton in Boston or the Regent in Hong Kong were to reduce their prices significantly, guests might become suspicious that product quality was being reduced or services curtailed. Guests at luxury properties expect to pay top rates, and marketers at such hotels feel it hurts their hotel's upscale image to discount.

Pricing strategies may vary, depending on the goals of the property. A new property, for example, may introduce itself at low rates in order to build guest awareness and sales volume, sacrificing some immediate profits.

Reputation can play a significant role in the pricing of hospitality products. A lodging facility may charge a higher rate for similar rooms and service because it enjoys a better reputation than its competitors. A Holiday Inn, for example, can demand a higher rate than a comparable independent property simply because of the market value travelers have placed on the chain's good reputation.

Marketing Mix Decisions. It is important to stress that a decision concerning any one of these controllable variables within the marketing mix often affects the others. One element may be emphasized over another when appealing to a specific target market, but the elements of the marketing mix are interrelated (see Exhibit 5), and a decision with respect to one variable usually affects other variables of the mix.

While the four Ps of the marketing mix are called controllable variables, it is important to realize that control is not absolute. For example, the lodging marketer has product limits. He or she is not free to convert conventional guestrooms to suites without substantial expense. Similarly, a property cannot raise its prices from one day to the next without feeling some repercussions from its guests. In addition, place and promotional commitments are frequently handled on a long-term basis. An agreement with a travel agent or a contract with a tour operator must be honored to protect the property's credibility, and media contracts for print or broadcast advertising must be honored even if the market changes.

Uncontrollable variables—external environmental factors—will also affect a marketing effort. A recession cannot be controlled by a marketing staff, nor can an energy crisis, natural disasters such as earthquakes and floods, or weather conditions such as heavy snowfalls that adversely affect travel.

Successful marketing efforts don't just happen. They must take both controllable and uncontrollable variables into consideration, and a carefully researched, planned, and managed sales effort must be developed to ensure that the property attracts guests and keeps them.

Management's Role in Marketing and Sales

On the property level, three key management positions in the marketing and sales area are the property's general manager, the director of marketing, and the director of sales.

Exhibit 5   The Interaction of the Marketing Mix

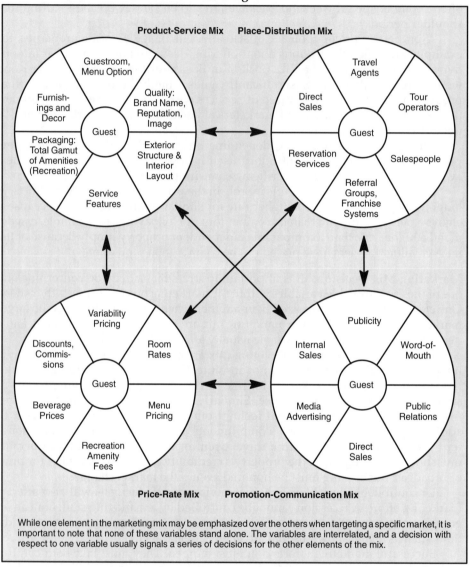

Product-Service Mix   Place-Distribution Mix

- Guestroom, Menu Option
- Quality: Brand Name, Reputation, Image
- Furnishings and Decor
- Guest
- Packaging: Total Gamut of Amenities (Recreation)
- Exterior Structure & Interior Layout
- Service Features

- Travel Agents
- Tour Operators
- Direct Sales
- Guest
- Salespeople
- Reservation Services
- Referral Groups, Franchise Systems

- Variability Pricing
- Room Rates
- Discounts, Commissions
- Guest
- Beverage Prices
- Menu Pricing
- Recreation Amenity Fees

- Publicity
- Word-of-Mouth
- Internal Sales
- Guest
- Media Advertising
- Public Relations
- Direct Sales

Price-Rate Mix   Promotion-Communication Mix

While one element in the marketing mix may be emphasized over the others when targeting a specific market, it is important to note that none of these variables stand alone. The variables are interrelated, and a decision with respect to one variable usually signals a series of decisions for the other elements of the mix.

The General Manager

The success or failure of a hotel's marketing and sales program starts with top management, and a marketing-oriented general manager is the key to a property's sales efforts.[7] In small to medium-size properties, the general manager may take on the responsibilities of advertising and public relations to enable the sales

Insider Insights

Dario dell' Antonia
General Manager
Hotel de Paris
Monaco

Dario dell' Antonia's first job after his 1956 graduation from the Ecole Hoteliere in Lausanne, Switzerland, was in the auditor's office of the Savoy in London. He later transferred to the London Berkeley to install the auditing system he had learned at the Savoy. In 1970 he became reservations manager of The Grand Hotel in Paris, and was promoted to general manager in 1973. In 1975, dell' Antonia was hired by the Societe des Bains de Mer (SBM), which manages most of the Principality of Monaco's hotel and leisure interests. He initially oversaw all of SBM's seventeen restaurants, spread over a dozen properties, and later became general manager of Monaco's Hotel de Paris. He has been president of the European Hotel Managers Association since 1983, and has been instrumental in making the organization an important force in the industry.

As general manager of Monaco's Hotel de Paris, I have the pleasure of receiving the members of the world's elite in one of its truly privileged corners. But our hotel is facing a changing market. The hotel formerly catered to long-term guests—many of whom would stay a month or more—who would return season after season and receive truly personalized service from a staff attuned to their individual needs.

Now, however, the hotel must change to meet the needs of today's guests. Our biggest challenge is to maintain our appeal to traditional clients while also attracting the modern clientele, which includes conference and seminar attendees. Our competition comes not from other hotels, but from the discovery by the world's elite of new places. So we can take nothing for granted. Once the wave moves elsewhere, nothing you can do will bring it back. People are not obliged to come to Monaco. We have to attract them.

To do this, an establishment needs character. Part of our character here at the Hotel de Paris is our natural and authentic style of service. This cannot be taught—it results in part from the fact that our staff has truly local roots and we have an exceptionally low turnover. This is more like a club than a hotel; the guests are really "at home." We must be constantly on the alert to maintain that ambience.

I greet the most important clients personally—not for show but because it makes everything else easier. The client feels important, and thus is happier with things; the staff sees the boss single out that particular guest and assumes he or she must require special attention.

The most important responsibility of a manager is to be, at every instant, an example—to inspire others to excel. Since service is paramount when it comes to attracting and keeping guests, I involve the staff in decision-making and empower them to make those decisions that will result in immediate customer satisfaction. This is especially important in the affluent market; it is vital not to alienate guests because there are proportionally fewer of these truly up-scale clients.

(continued)

Insider Insights *(continued)*

Hotelkeeping is a long-term commitment. A general manager can achieve nothing in a hotel in less than five years. The first year is spent getting acquainted with the product and its environment, the second year convincing those who must be convinced that there is a need to do something, and the following three years to motivate everybody, start to implement the changes, evaluate the consequences, and redefine the concept. Exposure to new methods and ideas is the way forward. Hospitality management must keep abreast of world events, social customs, styles of living, and even currency exchange rates to have an edge over the competition.

And, last but not least, a successful manager must have vision. You must always be able to see the horizon. The day you cannot see further than what is just in front of you, you cannot make any more strategy, and so you cannot build or develop anything. It is creation, not power, which is interesting.

---

manager to devote his or her time to selling. The general manager may also make personal sales calls outside the office on high priority business, and spend a half hour a day at the front desk during check-out thanking guests for their business.

The degree to which the general manager becomes involved depends on the size of the property and the sales staff, but many general managers assist the sales staff (especially with difficult or key accounts). While a general manager's involvement and duties will vary, there are five basic areas that all general managers should be concerned with:

1. Directing the sales effort
2. Developing the sales staff
3. Participating in the sales effort
4. Supporting the sales staff
5. Evaluating the sales effort

Directing the Sales Effort. The general manager is usually directly involved in the development of the marketing plan, and is often responsible for the delegation of duties to ensure that sales goals are met. It is the general manager's job to monitor the marketing plan and spot-check the function book and other sales office records to ensure that all is proceeding according to plan.

Developing the Sales Staff. The general manager should encourage the sales staff to be as productive as possible, and show an active interest in the development of salespeople and programs. The general manager may become actively involved in the actual training of the sales staff, or may closely monitor the training efforts of the sales manager or other training personnel.

Participating in the Sales Effort. A good general manager knows that sales is everybody's business, and he or she will make every effort to meet with sales managers or hotel salespeople to help close sales. The general manager may also keep up-to-date with community developments, participate in community groups and functions, and extend invitations to new business executives to develop business for the property. The general manager should be available to welcome guests to the property and thank them for visiting. This is particularly important in the case of key accounts—the general manager should be introduced to all key clients (especially those who have the potential for bringing in extensive group business) and make a special effort to extend a warm welcome.

Supporting the Sales Staff. Adequate information plays a large part in sales, and the general manager should see that salespeople are kept informed of the activities of the competition as well as new developments at the property. The general manager should be sure that the sales office is conveniently located and staffed with enough secretarial help to free the salespeople for making sales calls. Occasional meetings with the sales staff, and personal review of sales call reports and correspondence from time to time, demonstrate personal concern and help motivate salespeople.

Evaluating the Sales Effort. A good general manager becomes familiar with the results generated by the sales effort, and is actively involved in analyzing the revenue produced by the sales office, the areas in which business needs to be developed, and the effectiveness of the sales staff. The general manager will also compare results with marketing plan strategies and recommend changes or revisions as necessary to meet sales goals.

The Director of Marketing

Since marketing is largely a management function, it is important that the director of marketing be capable of performing a variety of management tasks: setting objectives and policies; making decisions; organizing, selecting, and supervising staff; and planning, delegating, directing, and controlling the work of the sales and marketing staffs (see Exhibit 6).

A marketing director's job can be divided into five functions: planning, organizing, staffing, directing, and controlling. Of these, planning is probably the most important. Planning is determining what needs to be done and deciding how to meet the goals and objectives set. Without proper planning, the other functions are meaningless.

Organization is also important, as a structured approach is necessary when developing strategies or employing the marketing and sales staff to fullest advantage. Staffing—getting the right people into the right place at the right time—plays a key role in organization. Staffing also involves training employees so they can reach their highest potential, and helping them develop the ability to take on additional responsibilities.

Directing involves overseeing both programs and employees. Directing incorporates motivating and guiding the staff to do its best, and requires well-developed

Exhibit 6   The Director of Marketing's Job in Marketing and Sales

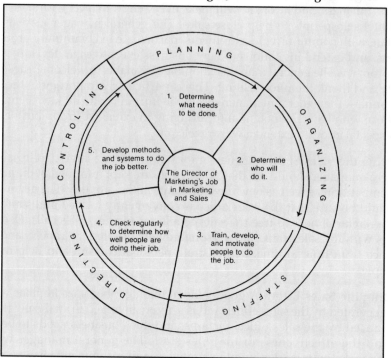

interpersonal skills. Controlling involves setting standards, measuring performance on a regular basis, and taking corrective action if needed.

Looking for new opportunities—and redirecting or modifying strategies that are not working well—is an ongoing process, and requires the skills of a full-time marketing director, so many medium-size and large properties also use the services of a director of sales to motivate the sales staff and to oversee the direct sales effort.

The Director of Sales

A director of sales differs from a director of marketing, although many properties use the terms interchangeably. The two positions have entirely different focuses: a director of marketing deals more with research and strategy and is concerned with identifying the needs and wants of consumers; a director of sales carries out marketing strategies and directs the sales staff in motivating clients to make purchases that will benefit them (fulfilling needs and wants).

While marketing affects everything a hotel does (from operations to advertising), sales is a more narrow focus. The most important responsibility of a salesperson is to sell the product—the property and its facilities and services—that management and the marketing and sales department have created. An effective director of sales will see that the sales staff is doing just that—contacting prospective or current clients (either in person, by phone, or by letter) and selling the benefits of the property, rather than wasting precious sales time on areas that belong to marketing.

The Importance of Sales

While many people have become "hung up" on the marketing function, it is important to note that both marketing and sales are vital parts of a process that will fill guestrooms and sell function and meeting room space. Both are necessary; neither works well without the other.

Putting business on the books is critical to every property's economic health and growth, and it is essential to realize that direct sales are as important today as they were before marketing efforts came to the forefront of hospitality promotion. Marketing activities such as publicity and advertising are one-way communications; in an industry that is consumer-oriented, the value of personal contact (especially in today's computer age) cannot be overstated. A prospect can pick up a newspaper, read a property's ad, and remain uninvolved and uncommitted; but consider the impact of a salesperson's fifth visit to a prospect. Most prospects will be impressed by the salesperson's persistence and the fact that the salesperson really cares about landing the business.

Sales as a Career

In today's marketing-oriented industry, is it possible to find job satisfaction and career mobility as a salesperson? There's no doubt about it. Consider these statistics:

- Hotel salespeople are young—70% are under 40 years of age; 31% are 30 or younger.

- There are an equal number of men and women in hotel sales, but a significantly higher number of entry-level salespeople are women.

- Very few hotel salespeople are involved in marketing functions; most are sufficiently challenged by the sales profession and intend to stay in sales.

- Hotel salespeople are well-educated. A vast majority (90%) have at least some college background; 57% are college graduates.

- Over 89% of hotel salespeople believe they are moving forward in their professions.

- Most hotel salespeople have been in the business from three to ten years, and most have been with their current property for two years or less.

- Of those who have worked at more than one property, over 40% have remained with the same company (changing properties rather than chains).[8]

These statistics show that sales is indeed a profession to take seriously (see Exhibit 7). In fact, the sales profession today is vastly different than it was just a decade ago, both in attitude and method. Sales has become a scientifically designed function, from the way leads are generated, to the study of the psychology of buying, to the professional identification and handling of clients. Rather than

Exhibit 7   The Sales Career Path

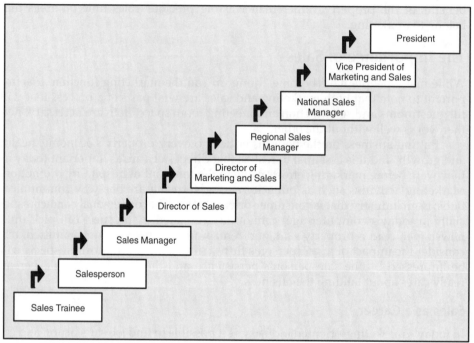

relying on hit-or-miss efforts, sales leads are typically generated by computers relying on detailed consumer profiles or through lists scientifically developed for each property's target markets. In addition to being trained in practical sales techniques, professional salespeople are now trained in the psychology of selling, and in both verbal and non-verbal communication. They are becoming experts in people-handling skills, such as the recognition of common personality types, and methods of dealing with each type of client.

Why all this emphasis on new techniques and sales methods? First of all, the value of a concentrated sales effort—whether a personal one-on-one sales call or an organized sales blitz—has finally been recognized. Secondly, hospitality sales has become more than just a job, more than a springboard to higher or more prestigious positions. Hotel salespeople are recognized as professionals—highly trained and service-oriented members of the marketing team. And last, but certainly not least, there is the uniqueness of hospitality sales itself—the personal and professional challenge of selling an intangible rather than a tangible product.

The Challenge of Hospitality Sales

Hospitality sales differs greatly from consumer goods sales in that the hospitality salesperson is selling something—a hospitality experience—that has both tangible and intangible elements. The product offered (guestrooms, dining facilities, etc.) is tangible, but the services provided are intangible. Guests can't take the hotel's products or services home to use or admire; when the hotel experience is over, all they have is a memory (pleasant or otherwise).

Hospitality salespeople have to take the following characteristics of hospitality products and services into consideration when selling potential clients on a hotel:

1. *Intangibility.* Salespeople do not sell guestrooms or banquet rooms; they sell the *use* of these rooms. Since hospitality salespeople are not selling something clients can take home with them, they must sell the *benefits* or experience the property's products and services will provide to prospective clients. And since clients cannot see, touch, or use the hospitality experience before they buy, they must rely on the hospitality salesperson's description of the property. Therefore, the salesperson's credibility plays an important role in the sale.

2. *Perishability.* The perishability of the hospitality product presents challenges for hotel salespeople that are different from those faced by their counterparts in consumer goods. An unused guestroom, an empty restaurant seat, or an unfilled tee-off time represents business lost forever. In contrast to consumer goods, the hospitality product has no shelf life; it cannot be stockpiled or inventoried to sell later. This perishability places heavy pressure on hospitality marketing and sales executives to develop innovative pricing, promotion, and planning schedules.

3. *Inconsistency.* The service rendered by a housekeeper or a food server can vary widely from hotel to hotel—or even at the same property. This much variability is not found in consumer goods, and maintaining a consistent level of service is a challenge to all hospitality properties. Inconsistency is a special challenge to chain properties. As mentioned, clients tend to expect the same type of experience from each property in a chain, but, even with standardized training programs, employee skills and the level of service provided change from property to property. Even the same employee may provide varied levels of service from day to day.

4. *Inseparability.* Production and consumption are largely simultaneous with services. The hospitality consumer comes to the property, and services are consumed at the place and time they are created. This is totally different from the sale of such consumer goods as automobiles or appliances. In many cases, the purchase or consumption of a consumer good takes place several months after production has been completed.

While general marketing methods advanced for consumer goods industries may be borrowed by the hospitality industry, a number of modifications must be made in order to sell the intangible hospitality product. Hospitality products are obviously not the same as tangible goods, and the marketing and selling of rooms and services requires a different selling approach. As you will see and discover, the hospitality industry has met its sales challenge in a number of exciting ways.

Endnotes

1. Some of the information in this and the previous paragraph was adapted from Laventhol & Horwath, *Hotel/Motel Development* (Washington, D.C.: The Urban Land Institute, 1984), p. 7.

2. Phillip Swann, "The Selling of Days Inns: What Does it Mean to You?" *Lodging Magazine*, March 1992, p. 12.

3. Alan L. Dessoff, "Marketing the Economy Product," *Lodging*, June 1988, p. 24.

4. National Association of Attorneys General Report, reprinted in *Las Vegas Review-Journal*, May 24, 1992.

5. Ramada International Hotels & Resorts Communications Manual, January 1991.

6. Marvin Cetron and Owen Davies, *American Renaissance: Our Life at the Turn of the 21st Century* (New York: St. Martin's Press, 1989).

7. General managers seeking more information on how to give salespeople the leadership and direction they need to be more effective should see *Feiertag on Sales: Tips for General Managers* (East Lansing, Mich.: Educational Institute of the American Hotel & Motel Association, 1992). Audiotape.

8. Hotel Sales Management Association International, 1983.

Key Terms

all-suite hotel

ecotourism

environmental scanning

globalization

marketing

marketing mix

peak period

product segmentation

relationship marketing

sales

shoulder period

tier marketing

valley period

Review Questions

1. What changes in U.S. society beginning in the 1950s had an impact on the hospitality industry?

2. What factors influenced the growth of budget hotel chains in the 1970s?

3. What were the reasons for the overbuilding of lodging properties in many market areas during the 1980s?

4. What are some of today's hospitality trends?

5. What are several reasons for the lodging industry's move to product segmentation?

6. What impact has computer technology had on marketing lodging properties?

7. What is the concept of a "hotel within a hotel"?

8. What is the difference between marketing and sales?

9. Why must each of the four controllable variables that make up the marketing mix be carefully researched and planned to ensure a successful marketing effort?

10. What are the five management functions typically inherent to the position of director of marketing?

11. Who is the "typical" hotel salesperson?

12. How does the challenge of hospitality sales compare with that of selling consumer goods?

Chapter Outline

The Marketing Plan
    The Marketing Team
    Steps of a Marketing Plan
        Conducting a Marketing Audit
        Selecting Target Markets
        Positioning the Property
        Determining Marketing Objectives
        Developing and Implementing Action Plans
        Monitoring and Evaluating the Marketing Plan
Appendix: Sample Marketing Plan

The Marketing Plan: The Cornerstone of Sales

IN TODAY'S COMPETITIVE HOSPITALITY MARKET it is especially important for properties to increase their market share and profits. No business can afford to rest on its laurels, yet far too many hotel and restaurant owners fail to recognize the benefits of a structured marketing plan.

The Marketing Plan

Both marketing and sales are necessary if a property hopes to effectively compete in today's marketplace. Marketing is the foundation upon which sales are built. Marketing seeks out demand, identifies the products and services that will satisfy demand, and then employs strategic sales and advertising techniques to reach customers. If we try to sell without first utilizing marketing, we could easily sell to the wrong markets. Without a well-defined marketing plan, based on thorough research, sales efforts may be wasted. Since the marketing plan is a guide for the two primary means of selling hospitality properties—direct sales and advertising—it is necessary to understand the marketing plan's role in sales before delving into sales and advertising methods.

The ever-changing nature of the hospitality industry seems to lend itself to short-term sales efforts rather than long-term marketing efforts. This is probably why some properties do not take the time to develop a marketing plan. In other cases, usually at small properties, the general manager has his or her ideas in focus and doesn't feel a need to commit strategies to writing. Still other properties may enjoy high occupancy and management may feel that advance planning is not needed. Whatever the reason for the lack of a marketing plan, you should not overlook the obvious benefits of long-range marketing planning. A marketing plan:

- Forces managers to think ahead and make better use of the property's resources

- Sets responsibilities and coordinates and unifies efforts to reach the property's sales goals

- Helps evaluate the results of marketing and sales efforts

- Creates an awareness of problems and obstacles faced by the property

- Identifies opportunities to increase market share in some market segments and open new opportunities in previously ignored areas

- Provides a source of information for present and future reference

Insider Insights

Lynn O'Rourke Hayes
Consultant
Choice Hotels International
Paradise Valley, Arizona

After graduation from Arizona State University, Lynn O'Rourke Hayes began a career as a business reporter. But an interview and subsequently published profile of Robert C. Hazard, Jr., who was then president of Best Western International, led to a job as manager of corporate communications for "the world's largest lodging chain."

A few years later, when Hazard and several members of his top management team were reinvigorating the Quality Inns International chain (now Choice Hotels International), Hayes was again hired by Hazard—this time as director of marketing programs. Following a year of service to the United States Travel and Tourism Office, Hayes returned to Choice Hotels as vice president for international marketing, and presently serves as a consultant to Choice. Hayes is also co-author of Crisis Management for American Hotels *and has contributed to two other travel-related books.*

A well-researched, well-developed marketing plan is particularly important in an international environment because the management team can't be physically on the property every day to monitor market developments. In some cases, the marketing team isn't even in the same country! It's for this reason that a definite plan of action is of utmost importance to me.

A good marketing plan should take all of the factors affecting the success of your product into account. In putting the plan together, it's important to determine the goals and objectives of the entire organization. Objectives should always be in line with the philosophy of the property's leadership. But when putting the marketing plan together, it's also important to "put on your detective hat" and find out what the successful competition is doing right—and what the unsuccessful competitor is doing wrong, so your property can avoid the same mistakes.

It's important for the property to find a vacant niche and fill it. How the property is positioned in the marketplace is critical. This area should not be taken lightly—positioning mistakes are costly to reverse!

The marketing plan, and the creative plans and activities developed to make the marketing plan work, must be cost-effective as well. While budget guidelines are often unwelcome visitors to the marketing and sales professional, it's essential that all marketing and sales activities fit in with the economic framework of the property and its organization.

Once a cost-effective, action-oriented marketing plan is developed, it's important to *use* it. Often, many weeks are spent brainstorming, crunching the numbers, and seeking out just the right combination of thoughts, dollars, and plans—only to have the completed plan sit on the shelf collecting dust. Refer to your marketing plan! Update it. Make it a working document that helps bring you well-thought-out, long-haul success.

- Ensures that sales promotions and advertising are not wasted because of misdirected efforts

A property's marketing plan should include programs to attract business to each of the property's revenue centers, with individual programs complementing, not fighting, one another.

The marketing plan should be developed for at least a three-year period, although the marketing strategies of many properties are planned only a year at a time. In most cases, one year is not long enough, because when sales objectives are limited to 12 months, salespeople tend to stay with the existing guest base rather than target new—and often more profitable—market segments that might take two or three years to develop. (Tour operators, associations, incentive groups, and many corporations are often committed well beyond one year.) Therefore, strict adherence to a one-year planning cycle can restrict growth and long-term profits. If management is uncomfortable with a three-year plan, a compromise can be reached by setting broad goals over the three-year period and well-defined objectives and strategies for the first year of the three-year cycle. See the chapter appendix for a sample one-year marketing plan.

The marketing plan is the property's road map. It should be regularly reviewed and updated, not left sitting on a shelf to collect dust or stashed in a drawer until year's end. While the plan is a guide, it is not etched in stone; from time to time, certain activities will not be completed as scheduled or some action plans may be delayed or deleted due to changes in the economy, marketplace, or personnel. Advertising and direct sales efforts may need to be increased or decreased due to these changes.

The Marketing Team

While the head of the marketing and sales department is ultimately responsible for the marketing plan, he or she may seek assistance and advice from other property staff members to ensure that all areas of the property are represented in the final marketing plan. A property-wide marketing team, sometimes called a "sales committee," can be established to work together to create and implement marketing strategies for the entire property.

The marketing team should include at least one representative from each revenue center who is assigned planning responsibilities for that area. The team member or "team leader" from the restaurant, for example, may be the food and beverage director. Non-revenue areas of the property can be represented on the marketing team as well. The director of sales may be responsible for providing input and plans relating to group business; the general manager may be assigned to gather information about specific market segments; and the public relations director may be responsible for documenting successful advertising strategies used by competitors. The marketing team can also include employees who are directly involved in day-to-day operations—front desk agents, housekeeping staff, kitchen personnel, and so on.

Once the marketing team is established, team members can develop strategies for their revenue centers. These strategies are presented to the marketing team for review and revision. The revised strategies are then incorporated into the property's overall marketing plan. Planning by the marketing team ensures that areas that might be overlooked by marketing and sales personnel are included in the marketing plan. For example, a salesperson may know basic facts about the property's restaurant, but input from the food and beverage director—perhaps the information that the head chef has served important officials or celebrities—can result in new promotional directions that otherwise would not have been considered.

Marketing teams can be excellent vehicles for unified efforts to sell the entire property. The team member responsible for a marketing strategy for his or her revenue center can often devote more time to that area than could one person from the marketing and sales department developing marketing plans for a number of areas. The resulting strategies, developed by team members who understand all that is involved in their areas of expertise, are often more effective than a marketing plan developed by a director of sales who has only general knowledge of the property's revenue centers.

Steps of a Marketing Plan

A good marketing plan can take a number of forms and may be developed by using any one of several techniques, but there are six key steps that must be included (see Exhibit 1):

1. Conducting a marketing audit
2. Selecting target markets
3. Positioning the property
4. Determining marketing objectives
5. Developing and implementing action plans
6. Monitoring and evaluating the marketing plan

This six-step process or cycle can minimize wasteful efforts. It is a systematic approach to increasing sales and developing long-term growth in the property's targeted markets.

The development of a marketing plan is a never-ending process. After one marketing plan cycle has been completed, results must be evaluated, and the process returns to the research or marketing audit portion of the marketing cycle.

Conducting a Marketing Audit. The foundation of any marketing plan is the marketing audit. The marketing audit is the research step in the planning process, and is sometimes referred to as "gathering marketing intelligence." Marketing audits are a careful evaluation of the factors relating to sales potential. Systematically gathering, recording, and analyzing information about your property, your competition, and the marketplace is of great benefit in decision-making and in selecting appropriate target markets. Marketing audits consist of three parts: property analysis, competition analysis, and situation or marketplace analysis.

Property analysis. A property analysis is a written, unbiased self-appraisal used to assess the strengths and weaknesses of your property (see Exhibit 2). More than a simple checklist, a property analysis takes into account both revenue- and

Exhibit 1   The Marketing Plan Cycle

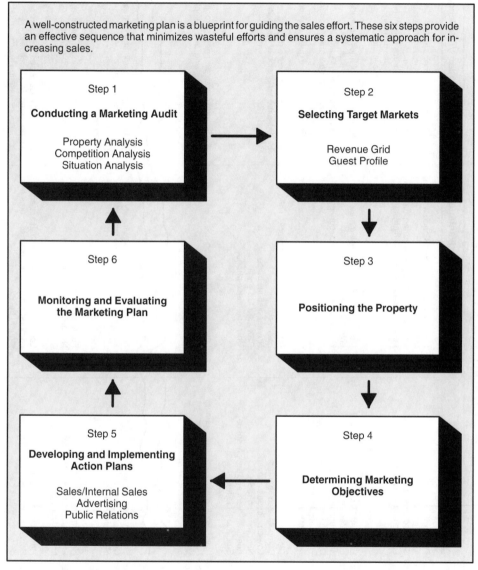

A well-constructed marketing plan is a blueprint for guiding the sales effort. These six steps provide an effective sequence that minimizes wasteful efforts and ensures a systematic approach for increasing sales.

Step 1

Conducting a Marketing Audit

Property Analysis
Competition Analysis
Situation Analysis

Step 2

Selecting Target Markets

Revenue Grid
Guest Profile

Step 6

Monitoring and Evaluating the Marketing Plan

Step 3

Positioning the Property

Step 5

Developing and Implementing Action Plans

Sales/Internal Sales
Advertising
Public Relations

Step 4

Determining Marketing Objectives

non-revenue-producing areas, as well as intangibles such as reputation and location.

First, a detailed room-by-room and facility-by-facility inspection should be made. Building exteriors, landscaping, and the property's sign should also be examined. The entire property should be carefully evaluated in terms of traffic flow, accessibility, eye appeal, and compatibility with local surroundings. Areas for change can be noted, but changes must be feasible. It would not be practical, for

Exhibit 2   Sample Property Analysis

PROPERTY ANALYSIS—CENTER CITY HOTEL

Area/Facility	Strengths/Advantages	Weaknesses/Disadvantages	Recommendations/Challenges
Exterior	a. Pool centrally located b. Ample parking space c. Covered breezeways d. Luxurious landscaping	a. Handicap parking not positioned well in all lots b. Inadequate lighting for security purposes c. Lobby located too close to highway	a. Add more handicap spaces b. Increase lighting in parking areas c. Roving security guard d. Add trees and shrubs in front of lobby area to reduce noise from highway e. Invite local police for coffee
Food and Beverage	a. Excellent food b. Live entertainment c. Ample seating space d. Coffee shop open 24 hours e. Food cost 33% f. Low employee turnover	a. No outside entrance to dining areas b. Low % of local patrons c. No room service or poolside service	a. Look into costs of adding outside entrance to dining room b. Advertising (see marketing) c. Portable bar in pool area for summer months d. Room service (see guest services)
Front Desk	a. Close to lobby and entrance b. Computerized operation c. Low employee turnover d. Near meeting rooms e. Adequate work and supply space f. Safe available for guests	a. No designated areas for check-in and check-out b. No reservations office c. PBX area too small d. Only one house phone	a. Add additional house phones b. Possible expansion of reservations and PBX
Housekeeping	a. Loyal employees, there since opening b. Guest praise of room cleanliness c. Modern equipment	a. Laundry is in bad location b. Excessive lag time	a. Schedule housekeepers to rooms in one area so walking time is kept to a minimum
Reputation	a. Friendly, clean hotel b. Courteous staff c. Moderately priced rooms	a. Positioning is as an average facility b. More individual than group business	a. Use slogan or marketing strategies to enhance image b. Involve hotel in more community support
Location	a. Near airport b. Easy access to industrial park c. Located on highway	a. Far from downtown b. No rapport with cab drivers	a. Billboard advertising on highway b. Free coffee for cab drivers
Recreational Areas	a. Heated swimming pool b. Pool area has potential for food and beverage functions c. Game room is good for family market	a. Lack of recreational areas that appeal to corporate market; no exercise rooms or jogging track	a. Promote use of pool area for receptions and F&B functions b. Explore installing exercise room and jogging track

example, for a 20-room property to spend $50,000 remodeling the outside of its building if changes in occupancy would be minimal. Only changes with a reasonable return on the investment should be considered for the final marketing plan.

It is also important to analyze the property from a guest's perspective. In other words, management should try to see the property as guests see it. Sales staff members and the property's management should stay overnight at the property to form an impression of the property as a product. An uninvolved outsider should also be invited to spend a night or weekend at the property to provide additional input.

Competition analysis. The objectives of a competition analysis are to discover (1) profitable guest groups being served by competitors that are not being served at your property, (2) some competitive benefit or advantage your property enjoys that cannot be matched by major competitors, and (3) weaknesses in the marketing strategies of the competition that your property can capitalize on. This analysis should be done at least four times a year.

Before the competition can be evaluated, it is necessary to know who the property's competitors are. Simply stated, competitors are properties in the immediate area that sell to similar market segments and offer similar products and services at similar prices. To make this comparison, a competitive rate analysis should also be done at least four times a year. This analysis should not only compare competitors' rack and corporate rates, but also group rates, local corporate rates, government rates, senior citizens' rates, tour and wholesale rates, and special package rates. Once this information is obtained, the property's marketing and sales force can be mobilized against the competition in each market segment, and market share and fair share can be calculated.[1]

The first step in calculating market share and fair share is to set up a table of descriptive data, including each competitive property's number of rooms, available nights for sale (the total rooms multiplied by 365), occupancy percentage, and actual room nights sold over the course of the year:

	Number of Rooms	Available Rooms*	Percentage Occupancy	Room Nights Sold
Your Property	300	109,500	76.5	83,768
Downtown Hotel	454	165,710	70.0	115,997
Airport Hotel	400	146,000	75.0	109,500
TOTAL	1,154	421,210	73.8#	309,265

*Number of rooms multiplied by 365 for yearly total.
#Average occupancy.

The market share is determined by dividing the number of property room nights sold by the total market room nights sold (in this case, total room nights is 309,265). Using this formula, your property would have a market share of 27% based on 83,768 room nights sold, the downtown hotel would have a market share of 38% based on 115,997 room nights sold, and the airport hotel would have a market share of 35% based on sales of 109,500.

But market share alone does not provide enough information to accurately assess how well your property is doing in the marketplace. To get a more accurate analysis, you must also determine your property's "fair share"—the number of room nights your property would sell if demand were distributed based on the number of rooms in each property.

Fair share is determined by dividing the number of rooms available at each property by the number of rooms available in the market as a whole. Using the figures above, for example, your property would have a fair share of 26% (109,500 rooms divided by 421,210), the downtown property would have a fair share of 39% (165,710 rooms divided by 421,210), and the airport property would have a fair share of 35% (146,000 divided by 421,210):

Market Share vs. Fair Share

Your Property	27%	26%
Downtown Hotel	38%	39%
Airport Hotel	35%	35%

In this example, your property's market share is 1% more than its fair share, the downtown property's market share is 1% less than its fair share, and the airport property's fair share and market share are the same. These figures show that your property is enjoying a small measure of success, while the downtown property is losing ground in the market and the airport property is just holding its own. This market analysis is helpful both in terms of tracking area market trends and in measuring the impact of various marketing strategies.

A comparison of your property with the competition can reveal strengths, weaknesses, and important characteristics that will assist in positioning and selling your property. A comparison helps to delineate differences between properties and explains why similar hotels may be performing at different occupancy and room rate levels. Statistics to be considered for comparison include number of available guestrooms, total meeting space, largest ballroom, restaurants, overall condition of the property, annual market segmentation, published room rates, estimated annual average occupancy, management company/franchise affiliation, and other pertinent data that can assist you to evaluate your property's strengths and weaknesses against those of the competition. But simply taking inventory—comparing the number of rooms, restaurants, and other facilities with those of the competition—will not get the job done. Like a property analysis, a competition analysis needs to be much more than a checklist.

A competition analysis involves walking the properties of competitors, talking with competitors' employees, and studying the advertising of competitors. For an even clearer picture, actually staying at the properties of competitors is essential. Driving through their parking lots at night on a regular basis, paying special attention to the types of cars, the states represented by their license plates, and the number of commercial vehicles; eating in their restaurants; reading rack brochures and internal literature; and conversing with their guests are excellent ways of determining differences between your property and other properties. Once these differences are determined, it is possible to set goals to "sell the differences" to each targeted market segment.

Other information needed for a competition analysis is available from a number of sources:

- Local convention and visitors' bureaus
- Chambers of commerce
- Local, county, and state room tax reports[2]
- Telephone yellow pages
- Hotel chain directories
- Travel guides

Making personal contact with other area hotel managers is also an effective information-gathering tool, although one must be careful not to violate the Sherman Antitrust Act.

Situation analysis. In order to plan marketing strategies, it is essential to know as much as possible about the marketplace or environment in which the property operates. A situation analysis researches the property's current position in the marketplace and reveals potential opportunities to promote the property.

A situation analysis consists of two parts: the *marketplace analysis* and the *occupancy and activity analysis*. The marketplace analysis identifies environmental opportunities and problems that can affect business. Just a few of the marketplace factors that influence occupancy and the average daily rate are changes in demographics; positive and negative events in the community, region, state, and nation; the cost and availability of energy; government regulation; and the cost of travel. The statistics for projecting environmental effects on business can be found in census data, information from industrial commissions such as the state or city division of economic development, and industry reports such as Sales and Marketing Management's *Survey of Buying Power*. Other sources of information are listed in Exhibit 3. The marketplace analysis checklist in Exhibit 4 can assist in revealing new opportunities or problems that may require attention to keep the property competitive and profitable.

The second part of a situation analysis, the occupancy and activity analysis (also called business status and trends summaries), is an analysis of the property's past, present, and potential operating statistics, and is used to track sales history patterns over a three- to five-year period. This analysis helps determine "soft spots"—low business periods—that most hotels have in their sales pattern. This analysis aims to disclose sales areas that can be improved, and should be prepared for all the property's revenue centers. Most hotels keep guestroom statistics, but fewer track restaurant, lounge, and function space statistics such as total covers (meals served), seat turnover, average guest check, function room bookings, and average size of functions. Room statistics (see Exhibit 5) focus on occupancy and average rate, occupancy by day of the week, geographic origin of bookings, group and individual room nights by segment and source, and the status of future group business already on the books.

One of the key summaries in the situation analysis is the *geographic origin study.* Not only is it important to know who guests are, what they need and want in a hospitality product, and when and how they buy; where they come from can play a crucial part in selecting target markets and marketing effectively to market segments.

Exhibit 3   Sources of Information for Preparing a Marketplace Analysis

POPULATION AND DEMOGRAPHICS

Sales and Marketing Management
New York, NY
212/986-4800
   Ask for *Survey of Buying Power* ($65)

American Demographics Institute
Ithaca, New York
800/828-1133
   Statistical highlights are published in *American Demographics* ($62/year).
   Contact Michael Edmondson.

Donnelly Marketing Information Services
Stamford, CT
   Current year estimates with five-year projections for population, income, and employment available by zip code and geographic areas. Report fees begin at $50.

Woods & Poole Economics Inc.
Washington, D.C.
202/332-7111
   Population statistics for 1970 to 2010 by age, race, and sex; income and employment by county, state, and metropolitan areas. Contact Sally Poole.

U.S. Bureau of Census
Population Information Division
301/763-5002

State Office of Demographics and Economic Analysis (sometimes called the Division of Research and Statistics)
   Found in the governmental pages under the state name

INCOME

Sales and Marketing Management

American Demographics Institute

Donnelly Marketing Information Services

State Office of Demographics and Economic Analysis

U.S. Bureau of Census
Ed Welniak
301/763-5060

State Commerce and Economic Development Department
   Division of Economic Development found (in telephone directory) in governmental pages under state name.

EMPLOYMENT

Donnelly Marketing Information Services

Woods & Poole Economics Inc. (Sally Poole)

State Office of Demographics and Economic Analysis

U.S. Bureau of Census
Thomas Polumbo
301/763-2825

State Commerce Department
Division of Economic Development

U.S. Bureau of Labor Statistics
Labor Force Statistics Division
202/523-1944

RETAIL STATISTICS

Sales & Marketing Management

State Office of Demographics and Economic Analysis

State Commerce Department
Division of Economic Development

Donnelly Marketing Information Services

U.S. Bureau of Census
Ronald Piencykoski
301/763-5294

COMMERCIAL & INDUSTRIAL ACTIVITY

State Banking Department
   See governmental pages of telephone directory under state name.

U.S. Treasury
   Controller of the Currency, listed in governmental pages under "United States"

Chamber of Commerce (Local)

State Department of Commerce

TOURISM

State Highway Department
   State Department of Transportation; Traffic and Safety Division; found in government pages under state name

Local Airport Authorities
   State Department of Transportation; Public Transportation Division; found in governmental pages under state name

Area Attractions

Area Hotels

TRANSPORTATION

State Highway Dept. (above)

Local Airport Authority (above)

Community Planning Agencies
   Regional Office of Housing and Urban Development; Community Planning and Development Division; found in governmental pages under United States

Exhibit 3 *(continued)*

AREA ATTRACTIONS	POTENTIAL COMPETITION
Chamber of Commerce (local)	**Building permits**
Convention and Visitors Bureau	Local Department of Buildings found in governmental pages under County or State.
SITE ADAPTABILITY	**Project Status**
Community Planning Agencies See above.	Local Department of Buildings in conjunction with local banks.
MARKET SUPPLY/DEMAND	**DEMAND**
Local Hotel and Motel Association	**U.S. Department of Commerce directories**
Convention and Visitors Bureau	**Local Chamber of Commerce statistics**
Interviewing Hotels	**Hotel sales tax figures** (if available)
	Monthly and yearly lodging reports
DIRECT COMPETITION	**Visitor and Convention Bureaus**
On-site inspections	**Local hotel managers**
Directories (chain, AAA, Mobil)	
Interviews with hotel managers	

Source: Updated from information originally found in Kirby Payne, "How to Assess the Market for a Hotel," *Lodging,* November 1987, pp. 22–32.

Identifying major "feeder cities" or "catchment areas" is extremely valuable information; identifying which cities and zip codes most guests come from results in a more effective use of time and money. Knowing that 30% of a property's business traveler market comes from southern California, for example, provides more pertinent information than the general fact that 40% of total business comes from that state. Geographic origin information is relatively easy to obtain if the property uses computers to register guests.

Selecting Target Markets. Although many hoteliers erroneously promote a property as though it were a single business serving one market, a hotel is actually a series of businesses that cater to a number of different markets. The hotel's guestrooms, for example, may appeal primarily to leisure travelers on the weekends and to business travelers during the week; the property's restaurant may serve a local business clientele at lunch and hotel guests at dinner; and meeting rooms may be used primarily by convention groups from out of town during the week and by local groups on weekends.

Most consumer industries are keenly aware of the importance of selling to specific market segments, and steer clear of the broad market categories generally used in the hospitality industry. But as demographics change and guests are placed in ever-narrower market segments, the hospitality industry is targeting more segments than ever before. This *market segmentation* consists of viewing a market as a number of smaller market segments, each segment a group of consumers with similar product and service preferences. Markets can be segmented in a number of ways: demographically (senior citizens, young marrieds); by purpose of trip (busi-

Exhibit 4   Sample Marketplace Analysis Checklist

A. Local Community
  1. Track trends in population and growth projections.
  2. Determine demographic profiles of locals secured through census data.
  3. Research local sports groups; social clubs; and trade, educational, professional, and political associations.
  4. List local events and attractions—historical, scenic, cultural.

B. Local Industry
  1. Assess economic and employment trends secured from Economic Industrial Commission.
  2. Research proposed, new, and recently closed office and industrial complexes.
  3. Document details of main employers by industry type. Information to document includes:
    a. Name and address
    b. Number of employees
    c. Independent or chain business
    d. Names of managing director and key contacts
    e. Assessment of their lodging and function needs
    f. Expansion plans

C. Traffic Assessment
  1. Assess the location of property with respect to highways, train stations, airports, and bus stations.
  2. Determine traffic counts for highways, railroads, airports, and buses.
  3. Obtain names and addresses of decision-makers for airline and travel companies.

D. Recreational
  1. List the amusement, recreational, and sports facilities that attract visitors from outside the community.
  2. Obtain information on source, volume, and seasonality of use.
  3. Obtain information on expansion plans, if any.

E. Unusual Area Activities
  1. List all special events of a recurring nature that attract visitors.
  2. Obtain data on volume.

ness, leisure); geographically (international, local); by life-style (sports-minded, culture seekers); by usage (frequent business travelers, occasional business travelers); and by intermediary (travel agent, incentive travel planner, meeting planner).

It is impossible, however, to be all things to all people. Properties must realistically define their product in terms of the major market segments they can best satisfy. A property should determine the market segments for which it is best suited, the areas of least competition, and modifications (if any) necessary to reach its targeted market segments.

Before a property decides which market segments to go after, the present guest base should first be determined. Determining the guest base and the decline or growth of a market segment can be facilitated by the use of two basic forms: a

Exhibit 5   Sample Occupancy and Activity Chart

Room Occupancy and Average Room Rate

Four-Year Trends

MONTH	19XX/19XX		19XX/19XX		19XX/19XX		19XX/19XX	
	% OCC.	AVERAGE RM. RATE	% OCC.	AVERAGE RM. RATE	% OCC.	AVERAGE RM. RATE	% OCC.	AVERAGE RM. RATE
OCT.	77.9%	$73	72.7%	$74	71.5%	$75	71.2%	$75
NOV.	76.7	72	74.1	73	72.9	74	70.9	74
DEC.	73.1	71	70.9	72	69.7	72	70.6	73
JAN.	83.9	74	80.3	74	78.9	74	77.4	75.50
FEB.	84.3	74	81.2	73	79.9	74	79.2	75
MAR.	85.7	74	83.9	74.50	82.1	75	80.1	76
APR.	77.4	72	75.3	73	73.5	74	72.4	74
MAY	71.8	71	69.7	72	67.8	73	64.3	72
JUNE	69.8	70	66.3	71	65.5	70	61.3	61
JULY	60.3	69	58.1	70	55.5	69	54.8	69
AUG.	65.2	66	56.3	66.50	54.1	67	53.9	68
SEPT.	68.5	70	65.7	70.50	62.4	71	63.1	72
Average Total for Year	74.6%	$71.33	71.2%	$71.96	69.5%	$72.33	68.3%	$72.04

This is one of many occupancy and activity charts that may be used in a situation analysis. This analysis is basically a historical trends study. Occupancy and activity charts should be prepared and tracked for each revenue center.

revenue grid, which details statistics and revenue for each source of business (see Exhibit 6); and an occupancy chart, which provides insight into the growth patterns of each market segment (see Exhibit 7).

Guest profiles also help identify the market segments the property is currently appealing to. For best results, guest profiles should be prepared for each revenue center—guestrooms, restaurants, lounges, banquet facilities, and any other revenue-producing service (valet, laundry, health club, and so on). You can then use this information to create a clearer picture of the types of guests that patronize each revenue-producing area.

Information that should be considered in a guest profile includes: name of guest, address, and zip code; sex and age of guest; place or type of employment; place of residence; mode of transportation to property (car, airplane, bus, train); guest status (new, repeat, corporate); date and method of reservation; arrival and departure dates; length of stay; number in party; room rate paid; type of room chosen; type of guest (convention delegate, businessperson, leisure traveler, and so

Exhibit 6   Sample Revenue Grid

MARKET SEGMENTS	Room Nights	Average Guest per Room	% of Occupancy	Average Room Rate	Room Revenue	% of Room Revenue	F&B Revenue	% of F&B Revenue	Other Revenue	% of Other Revenue	% of Repeat Business	Time of Year to Promote
Individual Traveler Business Leisure												
Group Traveler Tour Convention												
Other Airline Crews Sports Teams Government												

This chart helps to determine which market segments are most profitable. It not only shows occupancy and average rate, but also details all revenue from each market segment to help determine which guest mix is most profitable. Knowing the most profitable guest mix helps ensure that sales and advertising dollars are spent in the proper proportion to achieve or maintain the desired mix.

on); total folio charges and method of payment (cash, credit card, company billing); and salesperson making the booking if the guest is part of a group. This information will reveal:

- The makeup of the present guest base

- The demographics of each guest (age, sex, marital status, family size, income, occupation, and so on)

- The point of origin, or the "feeder city" or area from which each guest arrives

- The average length of stay and the pattern of occupancy (revealing peak, shoulder, and valley periods)

- How guests get to the property (modes of transportation)

- Sources of reservations

- Which segments of the market are most lucrative and which should be sought in future promotions

Exhibit 7   Sample Occupancy Chart

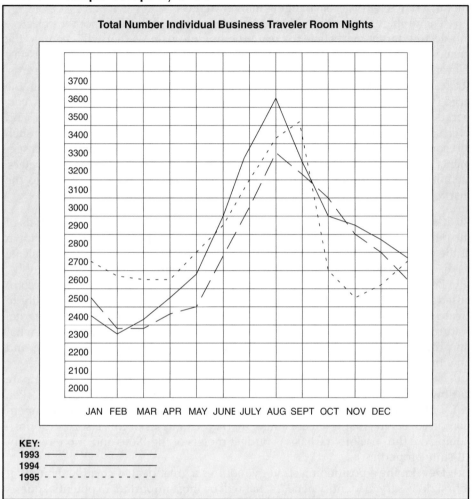

Occupancy charting details the monthly room nights for a particular market segment (in this case, the business traveler). All market segments should be charted in this way. Similar activity charting should be done for restaurants, lounges, and other revenue centers to facilitate assessment of market trends.

Compiling guest statistics by state, city, or zip code permits the ranking of geographic areas in terms of potential. Sales and advertising efforts can be concentrated on those zip codes with high potential.

When selecting markets, you should keep in mind that a balanced guest mix is ideal. A full-service hotel, for example, will want to target several markets: business travelers during the week, leisure vacationers on the weekends, local food functions, convention business, and perhaps group tours during shoulder or valley periods. This mix will ensure that the property maintains a fairly steady occupancy rate regardless of changing market trends.

The property's guest mix should be reviewed periodically. Since the objective in selecting target markets is to create the mix of business that will generate the greatest revenue and produce the most profit, changes in strategy may be necessary during the course of the year. Unforeseen events, such as economic downturns, strikes, highway reroutings, and weather may alter the guest mix and result in the need for a change in the mix of business. For example, in economic recessions, corporations cut back on travel, laid-off workers drop out of the leisure market, and even senior citizens with discretionary income travel less. To fill guestrooms in such an economic climate, hotel marketers might decide to go after specialty market segments such as sports teams, family reunion business, and government travelers. Defining and redefining markets is a continual process, and adjustments to the marketing plan are frequently required as conditions change.

Positioning the Property. Every property projects a certain image in the minds of the public; this perception of a property by its guests or potential guests is known as the property's *position*. It is of utmost importance for a property to communicate its distinctive position to each targeted market segment.

Positioning is much more than just advertising. A property's position is composed of the hospitality it offers and the management's and marketer's ability to create unique selling points based on the property's location, internal or external features, and personnel. Without positioning, it is impossible to determine what the property has to offer, where the property is going and how it will get there, and how the property will stand out in a highly competitive arena.

There are two basic positioning choices. A property can (1) directly compare itself with the competition and compete head-on for a share of a particular market, or (2) identify a need in the marketplace and fulfill that need before the competition discovers it—that is, create a new market. Examples of this last type of positioning are the "back to the basics" budget motels of the 1960s and, more recently, all-suite properties.

Developing a positioning strategy requires a great deal of creative thought. It is first necessary to identify benefits that will be most important to potential guests by knowing exactly what the property has to offer:

1. Who are we? What do we stand for?

2. How is our property different from the competition? Are there ways in which we can set ourselves apart?

3. What areas are not producing the desired revenue or response? Are there other areas that show a high potential for increased business?

4. Does our property have a liability that can be turned into an asset?

5. Which target market segment can be most beneficial to us?

6. Is there a way to change the use of a specific area in order to make it more profitable? Would it be more cost-effective to turn a restaurant into a cafeteria, for

example? Or, would it be beneficial to remove a lounge to expand an existing restaurant?

7. Does our property have tangible or intangible advantages over competitors?

8. Does the property offer any features or services that are unique? Atrium areas, complimentary limousine service or an on-property attraction (museum, park, etc.) are examples of unique features that appeal to travelers.

The answers to these questions will greatly assist in the development of a position that will affect everything the property does and stands for. The property's uniqueness can then be expressed in what is known as a "positioning statement." The positioning statement must communicate the property's advantages to its selected target markets. Of course, this statement must reflect what the property actually offers. A positioning statement such as "Friendliest service west of the Mississippi," for example, may be too general; if a guest is greeted by a discourteous employee, the guest will certainly question the property's positioning statement. On the other hand, if a property positions itself as offering "Leisure for less," and offers economy rates, recreational amenities, and a relaxing atmosphere, it has lived up to its positioning statement.

To analyze the effectiveness of a positioning statement, the following questions must be answered:

- Do we really know who our guests are and what they are looking for?

- How do our guests perceive our property versus our competition? How do we rate in terms of price, service, facilities, and amenities?

- What do the competition's guests think of our property? Do they know what we have to offer?

The positioning statement should be targeted to a market segment of sufficient size to warrant the expenditures required to attract additional business from that segment, and the property must have the ability to meet that market segment's demands. Strong positioning creates an image, outlines guest benefits, and distinguishes a property from its competition.

Determining Marketing Objectives. Once the marketing audit is completed, the target market segments identified, and the positioning established, the next step in the marketing plan is to establish specific marketing objectives. This is one of the most difficult steps in the planning process because it involves establishing goals for each market segment.

At the beginning of the year, goals such as number of room nights, average room rate, and revenue targets should be established for each month. Sales objectives and quotas can be developed as a result of these marketing objectives. Since marketing objectives cannot be reached without sales, it is important to answer the following questions before setting specific marketing objectives:

- Which revenue centers would benefit from additional sales activity? Would offering two-for-one coupons increase restaurant business, for example? Would offering a discounted rate for families attract more business to the property? Or do such areas as the lounge, banquet facilities, room service, or recreational facilities need additional promotion to increase profits?

- When are the peak periods? the shoulders? the valleys?

- Which marketing segments can be reached, and what priority should be given to each segment?

- What can be done to ensure increased sales in each market segment?

Marketing objectives should be simple and should be set for each market segment, revenue center, and revenue-producing service—valet, laundry, and so on. To be effective, marketing objectives must be:

1. *In writing.* Putting objectives in writing provides concise information that can be referred to as necessary by both managers and employees. Written objectives ensure that everyone has the same information.

2. *Understandable.* Performance will suffer if objectives cannot be understood by both management and staff. Objectives should be written clearly, and adequately explained.

3. *Realistic and challenging.* Objectives must be attainable, but they must also present some challenge to the staff. For example, an objective to maintain 100% occupancy year-round is unrealistic for most properties, but an objective to increase rooms business by 20% over the summer months is probably realistic.

   One way to ensure realistic goals is by *forecasting.* Occupancy and other forecasts, however, should not be based simply on prior years' performance. Factors noted in the marketing audit (changes in the economy, competitive room supply, market share, etc.) should be taken into consideration when forecasting future potential and setting goals.

4. *Specific and measurable.* Objectives must clearly define the expected results, and should be as specific and measurable as possible. For example, rather than having a general objective to "raise room occupancy," you might restate your objective as follows: "To achieve an average occupancy rate of 75% (900 room nights) during June and July and maintain an average room rate of $65."

Marketing objectives should be:

- *Time-specific.* While the average marketing plan is developed for a minimum of three years, objectives should be broken down into annual, quarterly, monthly, weekly, or even daily objectives to make it easier to evaluate the success of marketing efforts.

- *Quantity-specific.* Detail expected sales in terms of number of room nights, number of covers, number of banquets, and so on. Expected dollar value (such as average daily rate and average guest check) might also be specified, although inflationary trends may force re-evaluation of these figures.

- *Bottom line-specific.* Since properties often experience a loss while trying to obtain business from new market segments, acceptable loss amounts (as well as desired gains) should be specified.

- *Market share-specific.* Objectives should be set for target markets that offer the highest potential to the property. In many cases, this may mean going after a larger share of an existing market rather than trying to generate business from totally new (and possibly less profitable) market segments.

As mentioned earlier in the chapter, a marketing team is perhaps the most effective way to ensure that all revenue centers are included when setting marketing objectives. Individual revenue center objectives can be reviewed by the team to determine their feasibility, and revisions can be made as necessary before the objectives are incorporated into the property's marketing plan.

Developing and Implementing Action Plans. The core of the marketing plan is step 5, developing and implementing action plans. The statistical report generated by the marketing audit may encompass more pages, but a marketing audit alone is useless. Success comes to those hotel marketers who make decisions and take action based on what they've learned about their property, the competition, the marketplace, and their guests. Their analysis of this data helps identify:

- What areas need sales activity (the three to six most important priorities for the coming year)

- When business is needed

- The appropriate market segments to be targeted to fulfill objectives

Once these facts are known, action plans can be created.

While the marketing plan may be designed to market the entire hotel, it is actually, in effect, many small marketing plans—one for each market segment in each of the profit centers (rooms, banquets, restaurant, lounge, etc.)—combined into one document. There should be detailed action plans for *each* market segment and revenue center, and responsibility for implementing action plans should be assigned to specific individuals in each of the property's revenue centers (this accountability allows for monitoring the progress of marketing efforts).

Action plans can be as simple or as complicated as necessary (see Exhibit 8). They should be very specific, incorporating the following five areas:

1. *A description of the types of business and the market segments to be solicited.* A property might wish to increase meeting room business, for example, and target local associations to help to meet its goal.

2. *Target customers—a specific definition of who will be solicited.* In the case above, for example, "local associations" is not very specific. Listing the names, addresses, and contact persons for local associations will facilitate implementation of action plans.

3. *Rates/special plans/packages/promotions—a listing of the rates that will be charged for business within each segment.* To attract association business, an incentive package may be developed that includes reduced room rates or complimentary meals for association attendees.

4. *Objectives.* It is not enough to say "increase meeting rooms business." A specific goal—"increase meeting rooms business by 20% over weekend periods in

Exhibit 8   Sample Action Plans

I. Market Segment—Association Meetings

Objective: Increase room nights from 10,000 to 20,000 per year while maintaining an average rate of $74 for this segment.

Advertising Action Plans:
1. Review the files at the Convention and Visitors' Bureau and develop a list of association prospects that could meet in our area and have sleeping requirements that we can accommodate. Develop three direct mail campaigns a year for this list.

2. Place three insertions per year in *Meeting News* and *Association Management* magazines.

Direct Sales Action Plans:
1. Develop a good working relationship with the local Convention and Visitors' Bureau. Make sure it is stocked with collateral material. Invite the bureau's personnel to the hotel for cocktails and reacquaint them with the hotel.

2. Follow up all Bureau leads. Whenever possible, the site selection chairperson for an association will be invited to dinner and given a complimentary overnight stay.

3. Continue membership in local American Society of Association Executives (ASAE). Purchase a booth at the local ASAE annual meeting and trade show.

II. Market Segment—Individual Business Traveler

Objective: Increase total annual room sales revenue from this market segment from $1,600,000 to $1,850,000 by the end of the fourth quarter of this year.

Advertising Action Plans:
1. Contract for an attractive billboard placed permanently on the interstate which gives the name of the hotel and directions to the property. In addition, contract for billboards in prime commercial business districts of the city.

2. Send direct mail to a list of corporate travel decision-makers in the local market, developed through analysis of past reservation cards and through outside calls.

Direct Sales Action Plans:
1. A Secretary's Club will be made up of secretaries who have the potential to make reservations for their bosses and businesspersons coming into our city. As a member of our club, the secretary will receive the following:

   - Discounted guaranteed rate on guestrooms (subject to availability)

   - VIP treatment for their guests (quick check-in, check cashing privileges, turn-down service)

   - Free morning newspaper for their guests

   - Free local telephone calls for their guests

   - A free drink ticket when used with dinner

   Two club parties will be given throughout the year, one in April to celebrate National Secretaries Day, and one at Christmas. Birthday and anniversary cards will be sent to each club member. To qualify for membership, a secretary must make reservations totaling 12 room nights per month.

2. A "Seventh Stay Is Free" program will be geared to the traveling businessperson. The first time the guest stays at the hotel he or she will be given a card listing the rules and regulations of the program. Each stay thereafter, this card can be presented to the front desk agent for validation. At the completion of the seventh stay, regardless of

Exhibit 8   *(continued)*

room nights used, the guest will be entitled to one free room night. Every member of the program will be given VIP service, quick check-in, free newspapers, free local phone calls, and a free drink coupon to be used with the purchase of a dinner at the hotel restaurant.

III. Revenue Center—Catering

Objective: Increase annual food and beverage banquet sales revenue from $200,000 to $225,000 during this fiscal year.

Advertising Action Plans:
1. Develop special event banquets for New Year's Eve, July 4th, and Mother's Day. Promote each banquet with in-house posters prior to the event, and in local newspapers using 3 column × 5 column ads placed three times prior to the banquet.

Direct Sales Action Plans:
1. Work with the chef and food and beverage director to develop new catering menus. Prices should be competitive with major competition.

2. Develop a personal sales and telephone sales campaign for catering clients who have the potential to rebook with the property.

3. Use the community business directory to research and compile a list of new banquet prospects, concentrating on corporate, civic, and fraternal groups.

4. Develop a wedding package that includes the reception, two hours of open bar, the cake, entertainment, and free overnight accommodations for the bridal couple. Price at $45 per person with a 100 person minimum.

July"—will help in establishing action steps and monitoring progress toward meeting the objective.

5. *Action steps—the specific steps that will be taken to achieve objectives.* For association business, these may include a direct mailing to all association meeting planners in the area, an "open house" to introduce meeting planners to the property, and so on.

Each action plan should include the "who," "what," "why," "when," and "where" of each step if it is to meet its objectives. If an objective is to increase covers in the restaurant next month by an average of ten per evening, for example, one action plan might be stated as follows: "Restaurant manager will contact 20 local businesses and invite owners to drop by for a complimentary dessert with dinner." This places the responsibility for implementing this part of the plan—targeting local businesses—on the restaurant manager. Another action plan to meet the same objective can be created to involve a number of employees: front desk agents can suggest to registering guests that they reserve a table in the dining room, or switchboard operators may call guests in the early evening to offer information about the restaurant's dinner special.

This scenario is an excellent example of involving a number of property employees to meet a marketing objective. The property's entire staff should always be aware of both individual revenue centers and overall marketing efforts. Cooperation can make it much easier to attain marketing objectives, and employee involvement may result in excellent suggestions for more effective action plans.

Budgeting. Action plan expenses must be figured into the marketing budget. Most marketing budgets include sales, advertising, and promotional expenses; direct mail postage and handling charges; promotional premiums; and salaries of the marketing and sales staff. Individual budgets should also be established for each market segment and each action plan designed to reach that market segment. As a rule of thumb, budgeting should be broken down into quarterly segments to make effective monitoring possible. The exception is media advertising, which is often budgeted on an annual basis. There are four common types of marketing budgets:

1. *Percentage-of-sales.* These budgets are based on the previous year's sales, and usually work best for properties that enjoy a significant base of repeat business. The budget is three to six percent of last year's sales in most cases, although this may vary depending on the size and needs of the property.

2. *Competitive-parity.* This type of budget is based on what the competition is doing. A property spends according to what the competition spends, a practice which may or may not result in effective budgeting.

3. *Affordable-funds.* This type of budget uses a portion of the property's profits as the basis for marketing expenditures. Sometimes referred to as the "whatever's left over" technique, this is the least desirable method of determining a marketing budget.

4. *Zero-base.* This type of budget is based on the task method; monies are budgeted at levels to get the job done, and all expenses must be justified. This is considered the best way to budget for marketing, although a number of variables—room occupancy, the business mix, gross revenues, and so on—must be taken into account when establishing a sound budget.

   The principal advantage of zero-based budgeting is that it questions every expenditure. The budget is established after each detailed marketing plan is prepared and the amount required to complete each task estimated, rather than assuming expenditures at a fixed percentage of gross income and then deciding how to spend it. The premise underlying zero-based budgeting is that the marketing effort is budgeted at the level required to accomplish the action steps needed to capture business. While using this approach takes much more time and effort than required for percentage of sales, competitive parity, or affordable funds budgeting, this type of "bottom up" budgeting ensures that the necessary funds are available to reach the marketing objectives for each target market.

A great deal of attention must be given to establishing a budgeting system that works. The overall result should be a budget that provides funds for producing new business as well as allocations for maintaining the property's established business.

In most cases, it is advantageous to develop a budget form that provides instant access to information. The budget form shown in Exhibit 9 breaks the marketing plan down into specific segments such as "Advertising," then divides these segments into expenditure categories. This type of detail is helpful for a number of reasons:

Exhibit 9   Sample Budget Form

SALES — MARKETING BUDGET — NEXT YEAR

Expenditure Item	JAN $	JAN Budget %	FEB $	FEB Budget %	MAR $	MAR Budget %	Quarter 1 $	Quarter 1 Budget %	APR $	APR Budget %	MAY $	MAY Budget %	JUN $	JUN Budget %	Quarter 2 $	Quarter 2 Budget %
Advertising																
Consumer Magazine																
Trade Magazine																
Radio AM																
Radio FM																
Television																
— Network																
— Cable																
Newspaper																
Direct Mail																
Outdoor Specialty																
Other																
1.																
2.																
Public Relations & Sales Promotion																
Trade Shows																
Sales Force																
Promotion																
Events																
FAM Trips																
Writers																
Tour Operators																
Travel Agents																
Others																
Receptions																
Travel Missions																
Chef Luncheon																

This is one page from a sales and marketing budget form that, when filled out, will show the budgeted funds for each expenditure item listed, broken down by month and subtotaled for each quarter. A detailed marketing budget is much better than one that simply allocates lump sums to general categories such as "Advertising," "Public Relations," "Corporate Travelers," and so on. (Source: James C. Makens, The Hotel Sales and Marketing Plan Book [Winston-Salem, North Carolina: Marion-Clarence Publishing House, 1990], p. 227.)

1. *It ensures that all expenses are planned for and documented.* Using a less detailed form can mean that expenses may be overlooked. In the case of "Public Relations & Sales Promotion," for example (see exhibit), it is far better to list the individual items that will require funds—"Trade Shows, Sales Force Promotion, Events, FAM Trips," and so on—than to allocate one sum for a general public relations and sales promotion category. Otherwise, it is too easy to forget to include funds for expenses that do not occur often, or forget specific products or services that are involved in the advertising process.

2. *It helps prevent arbitrary budget cuts.* When the budget is not broken down into specific expenditures, it is much more likely that money will be moved from one category to another without regard for the consequences. For example, if a sales manager needs more money for a sales blitz, it may appear that funds are available from another category. This, however, may not be the case, and only a specific budget shows exactly what is needed in each area.

3. *It is a step toward increased accountability for marketing plans.* Having a detailed budget provides a means of monitoring anticipated and actual expenses for each area of the marketing plan. Actual expenditures can be measured against the results obtained from various marketing programs, and the budget can more easily be adjusted to meet changing trends. If a sales manager finds that direct mail campaigns are more effective than billboard campaigns, for example, the next budget might see more money allocated to direct mail and less to billboards.

4. *It provides a financial road map that guides expenditures by market segment.* The budget should represent allocations of dollars on a segment-by-segment basis. The allocation of marketing expenditures by target markets enables the marketing director to assess the return from specific marketing investments, such as the hiring of a salesperson to develop individual corporate business, for example. This person's salary, benefits, and expenses can be directly allocated to this market segment and compared with the revenue the position generates to determine cost-effectiveness.

Monitoring and Evaluating the Marketing Plan. The more carefully the marketing effort is measured, the easier it will be to plan future activities and programs for building business and profitability. While the cost-effectiveness of some public relations and sales promotions may be difficult to measure because of their inherent long-term effects, it is important to establish a monitoring system at the same time that action plans and specific promotions are developed.

Monitoring the marketing plan can be fun as well as enlightening, especially if the plan is reviewed periodically so that corrective action can be taken throughout the planning cycle (see Exhibit 10). Methods of monitoring the marketing plan include:

1. Recording the number of room nights for each market segment. While it may seem tedious to count and code room nights by market segment, this method results in a report that facilitates the comparison of actual results with marketing plan goals.

Exhibit 10   Monitoring the Marketing Plan

The specific methods listed here were used by one property to evaluate marketing and sales efforts.

1. Make daily comparison analyses for room sales, restaurant charges, and occupancy percentages in relation to last year's, the year-to-date, and forecasted figures.

2. Use registration card data to survey zip codes to determine which media are working well for the property's shoulder and valley periods.

3. Tabulate senior citizen discount coupons, children's fun packs, and employee paycheck coupons at the end of each week during shoulder periods to determine which segments are responding.

4. Maintain a clippings file of the property's public relations material (and that of competitors).

5. Monitor restaurant and bar sales and the comment cards received from each of these revenue centers. Offer a weekly drawing for a free meal to individuals who have filled out cards during shoulder and valley periods. Use the addresses obtained from these cards to determine where guests are coming from.

6. Keep a daily record of comment card responses. Follow up on consistent problems with employees, maintenance, and so on. Break the cards down by geographic location, income, and how respondents heard about the property.

7. Keep a weekly record of phone sales and bookings made by each salesperson. Check back with potential guests, and check the "dead files."

8. Set goals for each market segment; color code and count room nights by each market segment, and develop a monthly report that compares actual results with goals.

9. Have weekly meetings with the sales staff. Discuss the week's activities and pinpoint areas needing attention. Inform staff of upcoming events in the hotel and the surrounding area.

10. Monitor restaurant covers before and after promotions to evaluate the cost-effectiveness of the promotions.

11. Record direct mail responses. Break them down by geographic location, level of income, group or individual traveler.

12. Keep track of specials and regular items that sell well in the coffee shop. Project sales for each food server, and monitor actual sales generated against projected sales.

13. Monitor motorcoach tour packages based on information obtained from the reservations department. Each reservation taken should include the following information:

    a. Package code
    b. Guest zip code
    c. Code for media reference

    This information should be compiled weekly and turned in to the marketing and sales department for analysis.

14. Monitor all discounts given by the rooms department in the following manner:

    a. Place a code for each discount on each folio.
    b. Compile a room count of discounts nightly. This can be done by the night auditor and can be turned in to the marketing and sales department at the end of each week.
    c. Keep records of all discounted rates requested. This information should be forwarded to the marketing and sales department on a monthly basis.

15. Evaluate internal promotions by measuring the average expenditure per guest prior to and throughout each promotion.

2. Charting and comparing the number of restaurant covers sold before and after advertising. Evaluation should take a number of factors into consideration, including the cost of the promotion compared to the increase in profits. If profits increased by 20% but promotional costs exceeded the profits realized, the promotion should be re-evaluated.

3. Surveying zip codes to determine which media are most effective in local advertising. This type of analysis is especially effective for restaurant promotions and weekend packages.

4. Tracking prospecting results and sales production versus goals by salespeople. If, for example, a salesperson started the year with a prospect list of 750 companies, the director of marketing might expect that one quarter of these companies had been contacted by the end of the first quarter.

5. Keeping track of each salesperson's: (1) production of room nights by market segment; (2) business booked by peak, shoulder, and valley periods; and (3) repeat business versus new business booked.

6. Evaluating internal merchandising campaigns by monitoring the average expenditure by each guest prior to and throughout the promotion.

7. Recording direct mail responses and telephone inquiries in a log book that indicates the specific salesperson to which each lead was assigned. Six months later, conversions (the actual bookings realized as a result of the inquiries) can be measured. This type of monitoring not only gives an indication of the effectiveness of the advertising piece, but may also provide insight into the strengths and weaknesses of the sales staff. If a mail campaign generated inquiries that did not convert to definite bookings, for example, the problem may lie more with the product or the sales staff than with the media.

8. Using return mail coupons and tabulating responses to coupons distributed to guests and employees can assist in determining who is using the services and products offered by the property.

9. Using specific response techniques, such as using special telephone numbers or instructing respondents to ask for a specific individual. These techniques can help track the effectiveness of both print and broadcast advertising.

Remember, control is an essential part of the marketing plan cycle, and periodic evaluation should be designed into the plan from the beginning. Waiting until the end of the marketing cycle can be risky. A record should be kept each time an advertising campaign is run; any strategies that do not contribute to the bottom line can be immediately re-examined.

If action plans are effective and objectives are realized within established budget limits, corrective action need not be a part of the process. But it is a painful fact that some strategies just do not work. If hotel sales goals are not being met, the problem can often be traced to one or more of the following:

1. *Lack of responsibility.* The marketing team member or team leader for a revenue center has not assumed responsibility for seeing that schedules are met and evaluations of results have been made.

2. *Lack of communication.* Salespeople or other employees are not aware of their part in the marketing plan.

3. *Lack of time.* Insufficient time has been allocated for making outside sales calls or directing advertising efforts in the required markets.

4. *Lack of authority.* Salespeople have not been given the authority to commit the budget to specific marketing efforts.

5. *Lack of appeal.* Guest benefits are overrated or pricing is not competitive.

6. *Lack of control.* Outside factors (the economy, an energy crisis, inclement weather) have made it necessary to lower marketing plan goals.

7. *Lack of realistic goals.* Guests have been targeted at a time when they are not planning to buy, or sales goals are simply too high.

Whatever the reason for lagging sales, you must determine that enough time has been given for the plan to work and that corrective measures have been taken to build sales in each market segment. Objective evaluations and corrective actions may prevent costly mistakes and can lead to more effective marketing strategies in subsequent years.

Endnotes

1. Information on the calculation of market share and fair share is updated and adapted from Robert C. Mackey, "The Savvy Marketing Executive's Guide to Budgeting," *HSMAI Marketing Review,* Winter 1987/88.

2. In some areas, it is possible to get breakdowns of occupancy tax by individual property. By knowing how much tax was collected each month, the monthly room revenue can be computed, and, by dividing this figure by the estimated average rate, the occupancy percentage can be fairly accurately determined.

Key Terms

affordable-funds budget
competition analysis
competitive-parity budget
fair share
feeder city
marketing audit
marketing plan
marketplace analysis
market segmentation

market share
occupancy and activity analysis
percentage-of-sales budget
positioning
property analysis
situation analysis
target markets
zero-base budget

Review Questions

1. The marketing plan should be developed for what time frame?

2. What are six steps in developing a marketing plan?

3. The marketing audit consists of what three analyses?

4. What are the objectives of a competition analysis?

5. What two forms are suggested for helping to determine the guest base?

6. What types of information are found in a guest profile?

7. What are two basic positioning choices?

8. What are four guidelines for marketing objectives?

9. Which type of budget is considered best for marketing?

10. What are seven reasons sales goals are not met?

Appendix

Sample Marketing Plan

This is an excerpt from a hotel marketing plan. It shows one-year strategies for increasing business from one market segment—corporate or business travelers.

Market Segment Plans

Corporate

1. Description

    a. Individual business travelers

    b. Relocation/Extended Stay projects—people staying seven days or more

    c. Meetings—corporate sales, training and development, distributor and dealer, executive conferences, product presentations, stockholder, board and management meetings

    d. Catering—Christmas parties, other employee and client receptions, luncheons, dinners

2. Target Customers

    a. Present local files   141
           (300 by end of year)

    b. Priority Accounts—largest local accounts that aren't using us at present (list to be established)   15

    c. Anytown Prospects

       — Companies of over 10 employees within selected SIC number in following zip codes: 07314, 07315, 07318   275

       — Companies of over 50 employees within selected SIC numbers in following zip codes: 07329, 07330, 07331, 07332   150

       — Companies of over 100 employees within selected SIC numbers in all other zip codes within metropolitan area   100

    d. All realtors within metro area   75

    e. ASTD (American Society for Training and Development) members in six-state region   1,400

    f. Travel agents who used us in past two years   210

                Total Target Customers   2,366

3. Rates, Special Plans, Packages and Promotions

    a. Regular Corporate $75 sgl. $80 dbl.

    b. VIP Frequent Traveler Club $72 sgl. $72 dbl.

       Membership benefits include newspaper, complimentary coffee, check cashing, points for gifts/travel, upgrade/availability

       Membership for special rate based on volume of at least one reservation per month.

    c. Relocation/Extended Stay $65 sgl. $65 dbl.

       Minimum of 7-night stay. Assign king room, refrigerator, coffee maker and supplies, no charge for spouse or children, check cashing, and newspaper

    d. Meetings   Rates depend on dates/size of meeting. Will average:

                                                 $72 sgl. $77 dbl.

    e. Seminar/Training/Corporate Group Package

       Available on an excellent selection of specific dates

       Minimum of 15 sleeping rooms includes:

	Single	Per Person Double
Room	$ 60.21	$ 30.16
Tax (6.5%)	3.91	1.96
Meeting Room	–	–
Continental Breakfast	3.50	3.50
Lunch	10.00	10.00
AM and PM Breaks	3.00	3.00
All Food Tax (4.5%)	.74	.74
All Food Service (16%)	2.64	2.64
	$ 84.00	$ 52.00

Above package including dinner:

	Single	Per Person Double
Dinner	$ 14.12	$ 14.12
Tax	.64	.64
Food Service	2.24	2.24
	$ 101.00	$ 69.00

The hotel may, at its discretion, serve group lunch and/or dinner with a preset menu in the dining room or a private room.

4. Goals/Objectives

Based on the marketing audits and a thorough review of the property, the competition, and the marketplace, we have identified midweek business as our most important priority for the coming year. We will target the corporate (individual and group) market as the primary segment to solve this need. Our objective is to increase total annual room sales revenue from $1,267,322 to $1,372,400 (an 8.3% increase) and to maintain an average room rate of $72 for this segment. Monthly targets are identified in the following chart:

Individual Room-Night and Revenue Goals

	J	F	M	A	M	J	J	A	S	O	N	D	Total	ADR	Room Revenue
VIP Club	100	150	200	200	200	200	150	150	175	200	150	150	2025	$72.00	$145,800
Relocation/Other Extended Stay	60	180	250	350	500	500	500	500	400	600	400	300	4540	$65.00	$295,100
Other Corporate	100	200	300	500	500	500	400	400	600	800	400	400	5100	$76.00	$387,600
Total	260	530	750	1050	1200	1200	1050	1050	1175	1600	950	850	11665	$71.02	$828,500

Group Room-Night and Revenue Goals

	J	F	M	A	M	J	J	A	S	O	N	D	Total	ADR	Room Revenue
Group Total	400	600	700	800	800	750	400	400	500	900	700	400	7350	$74.00	$543,900

Corporate Individual and Group Room-Night and Revenue Totals

	J	F	M	A	M	J	J	A	S	O	N	D	Total	ADR	Room Revenue
Combined Total	660	1130	1450	1850	2000	1950	1450	1450	1675	2500	1650	1250	19015	$72.17	$1,372,400

5. Action Steps

Sales/Direct Mail

Step No.	Method	Target Customers	No.	Details	Qtr.	Sales Days	Resp.
1	Direct Mail	a. Present local files	141–300	Send personal letters week of Jan. 5 thanking them for past business and asking them to rate satisfaction with our services by returning postage-paid return card.	1	–	M.S.
2	Telephone	a. Present local files that don't return card	100 est.	Survey their satisfaction over the telephone. Give comp one-night stays to any who were dissatisfied.	1	4	M.S. T.M. M.C.

Step No.	Method	Target Customers	No.	Details	Qtr.	Sales Days	Resp.
3	Personal Blitzes	a. Present local files	141–300	Deliver small gifts for Valentine's Day, Easter, 4th of July, Halloween, and Christmas	1 2 3 4	15	M.S. T.M. M.C.
4	Party	a. Present local files	141–300 (est. 300 pp)	Thanksgiving party to show appreciation for past business. Invite customer and guest.	4	1.5	M.S. T.M. M.C.
5	Personal calls / Telephone calls	b. Priority Accts	15	Have contact with these accounts a minimum of once a month. Include entertainment at hotel, sporting events, or other local activities to build relationship.	1 2 3 4		M.S. T.M. M.C.
6	Telephone	c. Other Anytown prospects of over 10 employees in selected ZIPs	275	Call for initial qualification to determine if file should be set up (at least 50 room-nights per year). For those with potential, set up appointment with prospect at his or her office or hotel.	1	10	M.S. T.M. M.C.
7	Telephone	c. Other Anytown prospects of over 25 employees in selected ZIPs	150	Call for initial qualification (see Step 6 details)	2	6	T.M.
8	Telephone	c. Other Anytown prospects of over 100 employees All other ZIPs in metro area	100	Call for initial qualification (see Step 6 details)	2	4	M.C.
9	Personal Blitzes	d. All realtors in metro area	75	Drop off relocation brochures and do survey of needs. Set up files for those that have two or more relocations per month.	3	3	M.S. T.M. M.C.
10	Direct Mail	e. ASTD members in six-state region	200 (of 1400 total)	Do two-part mailing test of 200 throughout six-state region to determine potential for long-term training.	2	–	M.S.
				The first part of the mailing will include personal letter; meetings brochure, and postage-paid return card.		–	M.S.
				The thrust of letter will be economy, privacy, and the fact that a training meeting of 20 is a major meeting at our hotel.			
				The second part of the mailing will consist of a copy of first letter, reminder note, and another return card.		–	M.S.
11	Telephone call-backs	e. ASTD members in six states	30 est.	Respondents to mailing (Step 10) showing potential to be called within 1 day of response.	2	–	T.M.
12	Direct Mail / call-backs	e. ASTD members in six states	1200	If response from 1st mailing is positive, additional names to be contacted as in Steps 10 and 11.	3	7	T.M. M.C.
13	Phone Blitzes	f. Travel agents who used us in the past two years	210	Call all agents to thank for business, qualify for future. In each case talk to manager and determine whether agent should be on our mailing list.	4	5	M.S. T.M. M.C.

Step No.	Method	Target Customers	No.	Details	Qtr.	Sales Days	Resp.
14	Direct Mail	f. Travel agents who used us in the past year	175 est.	Send rate letter updating them on all programs and offering complimentary rooms for their personal travel on a space available basis.	4	–	M.S.

5. Action Steps (*continued*)

   ### Advertising

   #### Media

   Journal/South Metro (2 col. × 5") 8 times
   Journal/Center Metro (2 col. × 5") 4 times
   Connection Newspapers/Springfield (2 col. × 5") 4 times
   Springfield Chamber Brochure—Annual (1×)
   Chamber Directory—Annual (1×)

   #### Merchandising

   ##### Development of the Following Brochures and Flyers

   Local corporate VIP Club   4p, 2c 1,500
   Relocation/Extended Stay   2p, 1c 1,500
   Hotel fact sheet (group)   8" × 10", 2c   3,500
   Meeting Packages   4p, 2c 2,500

   #### Public Relations and Publicity

   Column items dealing with prominent corporate guests or meetings will be given to major dailies as well as community media.

6. Budget

   ### Sales

   #### Dues/Subscriptions

   Springfield and Metro Chambers, MPI $ 2,100

   #### Entertainment (over and above normal entertainment)

   Meet the Manager-Prospect
   Get Togethers   12 × $75 $ 900
   Thanksgiving party   300 @ $20 (cost) $6,000   6,900

Advertising

Media

Journal/South Metro		
2 col. × 5″ × $550 × 8	$4,400	
Journal/Central Metro		
2 col. × 5″ × $450 × 9	$4,050	
Connection Newspapers/Springfield		
2 col. × 5″ × $1005 × 4	$4,040	
Springfield Chamber brochure—annual ¹/₂ pg.	450	
Chamber Directory—annual ¹/₂ pg.	500	$13,440

Media Production

Corporate headquarters ad	425	
Meetings ad	350	
Meetings package	450	
Chamber, individual and group × 2	800	2,025

Direct Mail

Present local files 1,400 × $1.00	1,400	
ASTD		
#1 2-part—200 × $1.50	300	
#2 2-part—1200 × $1.50	1,800	
Travel Agent—175 × $1.00	175	3,675

Brochures/Flyers

Local corporate VIP club 1,500	$1,150	
Relocation/Long Term Stay 1,500	450	
Hotel fact sheet 3,500	600	
Meeting Packages 4p, 2c 2,500	900	3,100

Other Selling Aids

Holiday Gifts for blitzes $5 × 200		1,000
Total Corporate		$32,240

Summary

Midweek corporate business is our top priority for the coming year. The estimated 19,015 room-nights is 41% of total rooms business. And the $32,240 is 16.6% of the total marketing budget.

Courtesy of Tom McCarthy, Tom McCarthy Associates, Falls Church, Virginia

Chapter Outline

The Marketing and Sales Division
Organizing a Sales Office
    The Sales Area
    Hiring Effective Salespeople
    Training Salespeople
        Property Knowledge
        Office Procedures
        Performance Standards
        Salesmanship
        Training Techniques
    Managing Salespeople
    Evaluating Salespeople
    Compensating Salespeople
        Sales Incentive Programs
    Supplemental Sales Staff
        The Regional Sales Office
        Hotel Representatives
Developing the Sales Office Communication System
    Sales Meetings
    Sales Records
        The Function Book
        The Guestroom Control Book
    Filing Systems
        The Master Card File
        The Account File
        The Tickler File
Evaluating the Sales Office
The Automated Sales Office
    Computerized Client Information
    Lists, Reports, and Analysis Applications
    Yield Management

3

The Sales Office

THE MOST IMPORTANT PART OF any property's sales team is the sales office. Whether it stands alone at a small property or is part of a larger marketing and sales department or division at a mid-size or large property, a well-organized sales office staffed with enthusiastic, knowledgeable salespeople is the key to a property's success.

The Marketing and Sales Division

Marketing and sales divisions or departments vary with the size, type, and budget of the property. Exhibit 1 shows typical organization charts for the sales personnel of a small and a mid-size property.

Exhibit 2 presents a sample organization chart for the marketing and sales division of a large hotel. Although the responsibilities of the division staff may vary among properties, a brief description of typical duties and responsibilities of division members follows:

Vice President or Director of Marketing and Sales—Considered the head of the sales effort at large properties, the vice president or director of marketing and sales usually serves on the executive committee of the property. Some directors of marketing and sales are actively involved in sales; others confine themselves to administering the division.

Director of Convention Service or Convention Service Manager—Hotels that have substantial convention and group meeting business will generally employ a director of convention service or convention service manager who is responsible for overseeing the servicing of group business once it has been sold. The director of convention service is available to meet with clients and sales personnel to discuss the feasibility of bookings and the specifics of meetings. This person must work closely with all departments, coordinating the efforts of the food and beverage department, the front office, and the banquet setup crew.

Director of Advertising and Public Relations—The job of the director of advertising and public relations is to coordinate all promotional materials, establish a good public image for the property, and help select advertising media for the property.

Telemarketing Director—This member of the marketing and sales division manages the telemarketing center and works closely with the sales staff. It is the telemarketing director's job to supervise and manage the telephone sales staff, which is responsible for developing leads, making prospecting calls, and following up on leads and previous clients.

Market Research Coordinator—Many large properties employ a marketing professional who oversees the development of information regarding the history

Exhibit 1   Sample Organization Charts for the Sales Personnel at Small and Mid-Size Properties

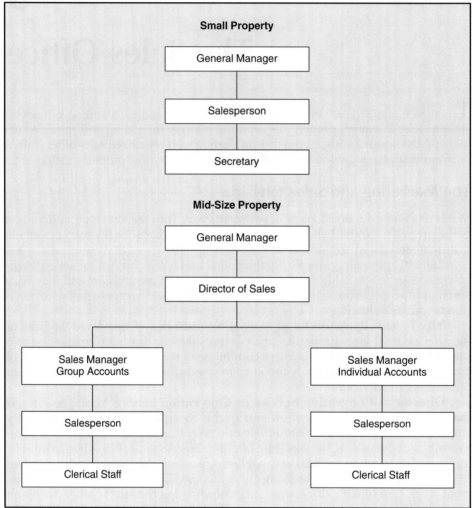

and past performance of each account being solicited. The market research coordinator may also research current market trends, the strategies used by competing properties, and general consumer trends. The property uses this research to develop sales strategies.

The following positions form the heart of the marketing and sales division—the sales office:

Director of Sales—The director of sales is usually in charge of the sales office and supervises the sales office staff. In addition to administrative duties, the director of sales may also handle key accounts, assist salespeople when necessary, and prepare sales reports for top management (see Exhibit 3).

Exhibit 2   Sample Organization Chart for a Marketing and Sales Division

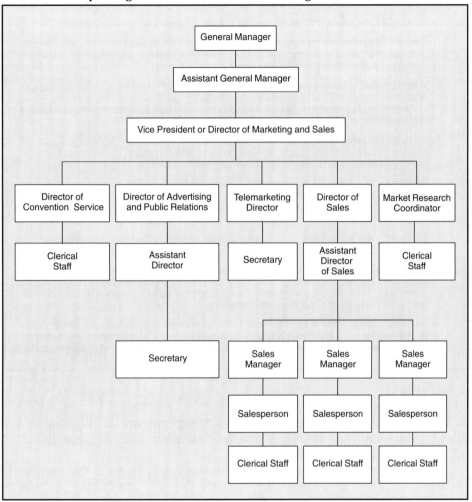

Sales Manager—In small properties, this position might be synonymous with the director of sales while, in larger properties, the sales manager would report to the director of sales. Sales managers usually assign territory or accounts to salespeople, monitor the progress of salespeople, and handle their own accounts, although specific duties will vary depending on the structure of the sales office.

Assistant Director of Sales—When this position is used, the assistant director of sales serves as the chief aide to the director of sales. The assistant director of sales may manage the sales office, supervise sales staff, and handle his or her own accounts. If the sales office is headed by a sales manager, this position would be called the assistant sales manager.

Exhibit 3   The Role of a Director of Sales

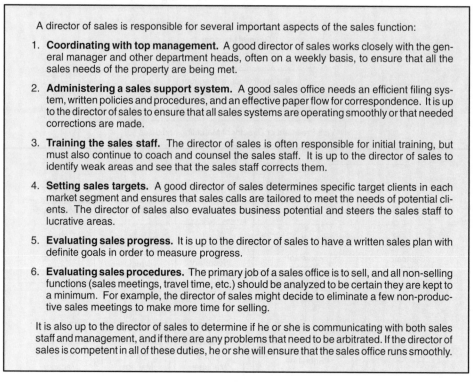

A director of sales is responsible for several important aspects of the sales function:

1. **Coordinating with top management.** A good director of sales works closely with the general manager and other department heads, often on a weekly basis, to ensure that all the sales needs of the property are being met.

2. **Administering a sales support system.** A good sales office needs an efficient filing system, written policies and procedures, and an effective paper flow for correspondence. It is up to the director of sales to ensure that all sales systems are operating smoothly or that needed corrections are made.

3. **Training the sales staff.** The director of sales is often responsible for initial training, but must also continue to coach and counsel the sales staff. It is up to the director of sales to identify weak areas and see that the sales staff corrects them.

4. **Setting sales targets.** A good director of sales determines specific target clients in each market segment and ensures that sales calls are tailored to meet the needs of potential clients. The director of sales also evaluates business potential and steers the sales staff to lucrative areas.

5. **Evaluating sales progress.** It is up to the director of sales to have a written sales plan with definite goals in order to measure progress.

6. **Evaluating sales procedures.** The primary job of a sales office is to sell, and all non-selling functions (sales meetings, travel time, etc.) should be analyzed to be certain they are kept to a minimum. For example, the director of sales might decide to eliminate a few non-productive sales meetings to make more time for selling.

It is also up to the director of sales to determine if he or she is communicating with both sales staff and management, and if there are any problems that need to be arbitrated. If the director of sales is competent in all of these duties, he or she will ensure that the sales office runs smoothly.

Salespeople or Sales Representatives—Salespeople are the backbone of any sales organization. They are responsible for contacting, soliciting, and providing follow-up service to clients (see Exhibit 4).

Although for the sake of clarity we will refer to employees in this position as "salespeople," in today's hospitality industry the title "salesperson" is seldom used. Salespeople are usually given titles such as "account manager" to give them increased credibility. In some operations, even members of the sales office clerical staff are called "account managers." Senior salespeople are sometimes given the title of "sales executive" or "account executive."

At small properties, a salesperson usually handles all types of business. He or she may call on meeting planners, travel agents, tour operators, and other sources of potential business. At medium, large, and convention properties, each salesperson may be given a specific assignment: individual sales (sales to leisure or business travelers who are not traveling with a group); group sales (sales to associations or corporations in which a number of rooms and/or meeting rooms and other facilities are sold); international sales (sales to guests from foreign countries); group or individual sales to tour brokers, tour operators, and travel agents; or food and beverage sales (banquets, functions, and so on).

Exhibit 4   Sample Job Description—Group Salesperson

Job Title:	Group Salesperson
Department:	Marketing and Sales
Reports To:	Director of Sales
Basic Functions:	Review the marketing strategy that will obtain maximum occupancy levels and average rate with the director of sales. Responsible for all group business within the western territory.
	Consult daily with the director of sales concerning the western territory and how it relates to the sales success of the hotel. Effective merchandising, prospecting, solicitation, and booking of business are among the areas that will be discussed.
Scope:	The group salesperson will be the primary person responsible for booking long-term group business (long-term being more than six months out).
Work Performed:	Initiate prospecting and solicitation of new accounts in the western territory; manage current accounts to maximize guestroom nights; responsible for administrative efforts necessary to perform these tasks.

Quotas for this position are:

Room nights per month:	1,200
Soft spot percentage:	20%
Phone calls per week:	
Trace/Follow-up	20
Prospecting	25
Personal calls per week:	10
New accounts per month:	10
Referrals per month:	5

The group salesperson must supply weekly, monthly, and annual reports supporting productivity standards.

Probe for client needs: rooms, suites, desired dates, day-of-week pattern, program agenda, food and beverage requirements, and degree of flexibility in each of these areas.

When available, obtain information on a group's past history; i.e., previous rooms picked up, arrival/departure pattern, and double occupancy percentage.

Review availability of clients' required dates and research any alternative dates which should be offered. The dates presented to clients should satisfy their needs while allowing the hotel to maximize occupancy and average rate.

Negotiate with clients the day or days of the week that rooms will be needed (and held), the number of rooms that will be blocked for each day of the function, and group rates (within guidelines as set by the director of sales regarding comps and function space).

Tentatively block rooms and function space in accordance with office policy.

Confirm in writing, according to office standards (via short-term contract or long-term contract and function room outline), all aspects of the meetings. Track to ensure groups receive signed contracts.

Alert all necessary departments (i.e., front office and credit) of pending tentative bookings.

Upon receiving a signed contract, process definite booking ticket, definite function room outline, and credit application.

Oversee, manage, and track the way in which reservations are made, the pick-up of group blocks, adherence to cut-off dates, and any subsequent adjustment to room blocks (positive or negative).

(continued)

Exhibit 4 *(continued)*

Periodically contact clients while in-house to be certain all is in order and going well; handle any last-minute needs as they arise.

Conduct an exit interview with clients to determine level of satisfaction and ask for additional business.

Send letter of appreciation to clients. Letter should include actual room night consumption and should be tailored to previous exit-interview discussions.

Attend extra-curricular activities and meetings, and accept any responsibilities or projects as directed by the director of sales.

Supervision Exercised: Supervise one secretary.

Supervision Received: Primary supervision from the director of sales. Initial training, and retraining as needed, also received from the director of sales. Receive direction from the director of sales in regard to room merchandising.

Responsibility Upon satisfactory completion of rooms merchandising and operational training, the group salesperson will have the authority to confirm dates, room blocks, and rates directly with clients.

Minimum Requirements: Bachelor's degree, preferably in business, hotel, or restaurant administration. Individual must also be professional in appearance and approach.

Experience: Minimum of two years' experience in hotel sales.

Sales Competencies:
1. Ability to negotiate.
2. Ability to prioritize and manage accounts.
3. Ability to prospect.
4. Ability to judge the profitability of new business.
5. Knowledge of product.
6. Knowledge of competition.
7. Ability to make sales presentations.
8. Ability to organize and plan.
9. Ability to utilize selling skills.
10. Ability to overcome objections.
11. Ability to solve problems and make decisions.
12. Ability to write effectively.

A job description is a detailed statement about a job, including work to be performed and organizational relationships. Job descriptions aid in the hiring process by defining the specific criteria needed to fill a position effectively; note that this sample job description lists activity goals (phone calls and personal sales calls required per week), but also lists productivity goals—performance measured by the number of room nights booked per month. Job descriptions also serve as a general guideline for training personnel. It is the responsibility of the general manager or the head of the marketing and sales department or sales office to develop job descriptions for each sales position.

Clerical Staff—The clerical staff is responsible for maintaining sales paperwork, freeing salespeople to solicit clients. A good clerical staff is essential for the maintenance of sales reports, and may do research for salespeople. As mentioned above, the clerical staff is often included in the "sales manager" category. In many cases, the clerical staff knows as much about the property as the salespeople, and they can often generate leads or actually "sell" a client.

No matter what structure is ultimately chosen—or what positions are created within the sales structure—every effort should be made to motivate the entire staff and create a sense of teamwork. This involves instilling a sense of community, and ensuring that everyone involved—from the general manager or director of sales to the relief receptionist—shares a common direction and a willingness to play whatever part is necessary to achieve the goals set for the property.

Organizing a Sales Office

Whether it stands alone at a small property or is included within a marketing and sales division or department at a large property, a sales office can be organized in a variety of ways, based on a number of factors:

- The property's goals and objectives

- The budget available for sales

- Available outside assistance (travel agents, chain referrals, reservation systems, and so on)

- The total market potential and the number of people needed to take advantage of that potential

When organizing a sales office, it is important to note the objectives of the sales team and select supervisory personnel to oversee the typical operations of a sales office, which include:

- Increasing property revenue through personal sales calls, telephone calls, and correspondence

- Establishing guidelines for the number of personal sales calls, telephone calls, and sales letters required from each salesperson

- Assisting the general manager with obtaining the maximum sales effort from all employees

- Holding weekly and monthly sales meetings

- Maintaining sales reports and establishing a sales filing system to ensure that all files are processed and kept up-to-date

The property's sales office must be organized so that every employee's responsibilities, authority, and accountability are clear. Three classic organizational principles should be a part of every sales office:

1. *Unity of command.* The effectiveness of the sales office can be seriously hampered if employees have two or three bosses giving conflicting orders. By ensuring that each employee has only one boss, accountability is established.

2. *Authority commensurate with responsibility.* A sales manager who is given the responsibility to increase sales must also have the authority to secure those sales. For best results, authority should be commensurate with responsibility.

3. *Span of control.* There is a limit to the number of employees that supervisors can effectively manage. While there is no universally accepted figure, it is important that supervisors be given a reasonable number of people to deal with.

Exhibit 5   Sample Interview Questions for Hiring Salespeople

1. What do you like most about selling?
2. What is the greatest lesson you have learned from your sales experience?
3. How do you organize your time to maximize your sales effectiveness?
4. What would your plan be if you were asked to sell to a market segment that was new to you?
5. How do you schedule appointments?
6. How would you rate your ability to schedule appointments? Your ability in one-to-one selling?
7. How do you service and follow up an account?
8. What information is most important to collect on competitors?
9. What do salespeople need to know about their product? What is the most important thing?
10. How did you handle a difficult client objection that you have faced?
11. Can you describe a time when you didn't quit when making a difficult sale?
12. What techniques do you use for getting by intermediaries when making telephone sales calls?
13. What has been the most difficult thing for you to learn in selling?
14. What resources do you use for prospecting new leads?
15. What is your approach to closing a sale?

Each of these open-ended questions is an opportunity for the applicant to talk about him- or herself—and for the interviewer to determine sales strengths and weaknesses.

The sales office must be structured in such a way that business is handled profitably. This necessitates the delegation of the proper authority for the sales office to carry out its work. To function well, the head of the sales office must have full authority over all aspects of the sales office and sales promotional tools.

The Sales Area

Whether the property is large or small, the sales offices may be the first property area a potential client sees, and the importance of first impressions cannot be overstated.

Potential clients should be properly greeted by the sales secretary or receptionist. The sales area should be accessible but private—no "goldfish bowl" off the main lobby, but not stuck away in a basement or unused guestroom. (If the hotel has meeting and banquet rooms, the ideal location is adjacent to these facilities.) The furniture should be tasteful, the offices well lit and properly ventilated, and the design uncluttered and professional. The decor should include photographs of events, guestrooms, meeting rooms, and the property's staff, as well as awards received by the property. Above all, every member of the sales office—from the sales manager to the file clerks—should be knowledgeable about the property and ready to share information about the property's benefits.

Hiring Effective Salespeople

Since effective salespeople are so important to the property's sales efforts, it is essential that a good sales staff be hired (see Exhibit 5). Hiring—and retaining—good salespeople also makes good business sense, since replacement costs can be extremely high—both in terms of training a replacement and in business lost over the hiring and training period.

Consider the case of salesperson Jim Dandy, for example. Jim, an experienced sales rep, sells an average of 1,250 room nights per month at $100 each (including food and beverages)—a total revenue of $125,000 per month. Should Jim leave, the director of sales estimates it will take approximately three months to find and hire a qualified replacement—a loss of $375,000 to the property!

After the replacement is found, it may take three to six months for the new hire to work at Jim's full capacity. If the new salesperson works at one-half of Jim's capacity for the first three months and increases productivity to three-fourths of Jim's capacity in the fourth through sixth month on the job, the property has still sustained a loss of $656,250 in revenue![1] No wonder, then, hiring the right people for the job—and keeping them—is so important.

To build an effective sales team, the sales manager should be aware of a number of characteristics common to successful salespeople:

1. *Professionalism.* Successful salespeople present a professional image. They dress well, but conservatively, and are well groomed. A successful salesperson projects honesty, reliability, and enthusiasm, and potential clients sense he or she is sincerely interested in meeting their needs.

2. *Ability to communicate.* Successful salespeople are excellent communicators, both in speaking and in writing. Their sales presentations are clear and interesting, they are able to build rapport with clients through small talk, and they can handle questions and objections calmly.

3. *Intelligence.* Successful salespeople are knowledgeable and learn very quickly. They have the ability to share their knowledge with a client, thus boosting their credibility.

4. *Ability to analyze.* Successful salespeople can objectively analyze their property's strengths and weaknesses and use their findings to benefit potential clients. They are also adept at analyzing clients, and are able to suggest additional products or services to meet clients' needs.

5. *Motivation.* Successful salespeople have a positive mental attitude and are goal-oriented. They understand that sales is often a "numbers game," see each rejection as a step closer to closing a sale, and refuse to let failures keep them from going after additional business. They are extremely self-disciplined, and have the ability to sell in a variety of situations.

6. *Efficiency.* Successful salespeople are experts at managing their time and sales territory. They turn waiting time into sales time, and waste little effort on unproductive activities and accounts.

7. *Persistence.* Successful salespeople use a steady and systematic selling approach, and follow up consistently on their prospects and customers. Rather than communicating through a quarterly newsletter, for example, they will make repeated contacts—a sales letter followed by a telephone or personal call, another follow-up letter or visit, and so on.

Insider Insights

Danielle Imming
Director of Sales and Marketing
Bally's Resort
Las Vegas, Nevada

Danielle Imming began working in the hospitality industry while attending the University of Nevada, Las Vegas. Initially she worked for a company bringing charters to Las Vegas from the East Coast, then for the Riviera Hotel as a front desk agent. She has worked as a tour and travel coordinator, director of catering/convention services, director of sales, and is now director of sales and marketing for Bally's Resort, Las Vegas.

After graduating from college I assumed—as we all do—that all the major companies would beat a path to my door. Wrong! Without the needed sales experience and contacts, I was not a hotly pursued candidate. Reality soon set in and I realized that the "real world" is nothing like college.

I continued to network through the Hospitality Sales & Marketing Association International, the American Marketing Association, and any other organization that could give me the contacts I needed. Finally it all fell in place, and I began my sales career at the Hacienda Hotel working in Tour and Travel Sales. Then I was hired as National Sales Manager for Bally's Resort. After three years with Bally's, I was promoted to Director of Sales and Marketing.

The role of the sales department at Bally's is vitally important. And in order to reach occupancy and revenue goals, our sales office must be organized.

Each salesperson is assigned accounts to work on and maintain. In addition, salespeople are responsible for researching and developing new accounts. This can be done through directories published by organizations or the government, attendance at trade shows, and personal sales calls. Once a sale is made, salespeople continue to interact with their clients until the function is over. This keeps the lines of communication open and, when the function concludes, the salesperson can begin the process of rebooking immediately.

Our marketing plan is our road map for sales efforts. Once a year, a plan for the next selling year is determined. We look at guest mixes and the percentage of tour/travel versus convention business we need to book on a monthly basis in order to achieve our contribution to the occupancy level. We also establish our upcoming travel schedule—from trade show and conference attendance, to personal sales trips, to our participation in special events such as the Detroit Auto Show and the AFL-CIO Executive Council Meeting.

Standard operating procedures provide a reference for our sales and catering personnel and are a great tool for training new salespeople. When procedures and policies are clearly defined in writing, communication is improved. Having the lines of communication open is very important because we all must know what others are doing in order to sell productively. Business should never be lost because someone didn't go that last step.

Another quality that successful salespeople share is curiosity. They are alert to new developments that might result in business for the property, and are interested in the property's guests.

It is important to note that salespeople are not "born salespeople." Almost any enthusiastic, intelligent applicant, properly trained, can become a real asset to a property's sales staff.

Good salespeople can be found through word of mouth, advertising in newspapers or trade publications, employment agencies, and contacts through associations or organizations that deal with the sales profession, such as the Hospitality Sales & Marketing Association International (HSMAI). They can even be found among the property's existing staff!

Training Salespeople

Once selected, salespeople (even experienced new hires) must be trained.[2] Effective initial training can mean the difference between bookings and lost business, but far too often sales training consists of a tour of the property, a slap on the back, and then the new hire is urged to hit the bricks and get some business. Far more extensive sales training, however, is crucial for salespeople to sell productively. Each salesperson should have a firm foundation in the following key areas:

- Property knowledge
- Office procedures
- Performance standards
- Salesmanship

Property Knowledge. Each new salesperson should have a complete tour of the property to become familiar with the property's staff; the facilities, services, and products offered; and the strengths and weaknesses of the property. Salespeople should also be presented with an overview of the entire operation and shown the role they play in reaching the hotel's financial objectives.

It is important that new salespeople learn about the financial status of the property. Salespeople need to understand the economics of the hotel, and should be coached regarding:

1. The property's rate structure.

2. The profit contribution of each of the hotel's revenue centers. While margins may vary from one property to another, departmental profit margins run about 75% for guestroom sales, 15% for restaurant food sales, 40% for beverage sales, and 35% for banquet revenue. Because of its high profit margin, the major source of profits lies in guestroom sales rather than the food and beverage area.

3. The present percentage of business from each market segment, and the targeted optimum business mix.

4. The property's slow business periods, so that sales efforts can be directed to times when business is most needed. The negative effects of booking low-rated business during peak periods, or reserving banquet or function space for local groups when that space could have been reserved for groups needing guestrooms, should be explained.

5. The targeted average rates for each market segment, and authoritative guidelines for quoting rates.

Office Procedures. Each salesperson should know the sales office routine. A supervisor should explain sales office hours; booking policies; the function and guestroom control books; sales forms and reports; paper flow; and past, present, and future promotional material.

To avoid confusion and poor communication, each salesperson should have just one boss (the unity of command principle). Each salesperson should know the chain of command in the sales office, and how he or she fits into the general sales picture. Salespeople should also know how much of their work can be delegated to the sales clerical staff.

Equally important is knowledge of the office's **standard operating procedures** (SOPs). SOPs are written instructions explaining how recurring business activities should *always* be handled. Each property has different policies regarding expense reports, VIP and complimentary room policies, sales office room allotments, and booking procedures, so it is essential that salespeople know the guidelines and limits set by the property. SOPs should be in writing, and salespeople must study and learn them.

Written SOPs can serve as a training manual for new salespeople and a ready reference for the experienced. Salespeople who have been given written policies on room rates and meeting room charges do not have to waste time questioning a director of sales about how much to charge. Clear operating procedures enable salespeople to answer such questions themselves, greatly enhancing productivity.

Performance Standards. Every salesperson should know exactly what is expected of him or her in terms of deadlines, sales quotas, numbers and types of sales calls (personal, telephone, and so on), correspondence, and inter-property communications. New salespeople should be given a detailed, written job description, specific long-term and short-term goals, and a territory or number of accounts. A good sales manager will give a new salesperson at least one or two high-potential accounts. It is discouraging to new salespeople to get accounts that no one else wants. Success builds enthusiasm, so some "live" accounts should be given to new hires.

It is important that salespeople understand the market segments they are expected to target. A salesperson working with corporate group accounts, for example, will have to learn the common procedures used by corporations for booking guestrooms and meeting facilities. He or she will need to determine which corporations use a travel department for making accommodations, and which corporations have a secretary or clerical employee handle travel arrangements.

It is vital that new salespeople learn how to recognize profitable and non-profitable accounts. Some accounts produce more business than others, and it is usually up to the individual salesperson to determine which accounts are producing—and, consequently, which accounts should receive more of the salesperson's time.

Salesmanship. It is important to note that instruction in the psychology of selling is part of successful sales training. More and more properties are realizing the value of training salespeople to recognize motivations for buying decisions and the types of buyers salespeople will typically encounter. The information presented in the following two sections is just a sample of the many different theories, systems, principles, and hypotheses available to salespeople seeking to learn more about selling psychology.

Buying motivations. Most people purchase products and services to meet one or more of four basic needs: biological needs, social needs, self-fulfillment needs, and psychological needs.[3]

Biological needs are basic needs for food, shelter, and clothing. A hotel salesperson can appeal to a traveler's need for shelter while traveling, and to basic food needs to sell the property's food and beverage facilities.

Social needs include people's desire to belong, and their need to feel at home even in a strange city. Hotel salespeople can sell the property to individuals with strong social needs by stressing the property's friendly service, its appeal to travelers with similar interests (business travelers, families, tourist groups, and so on), and special social amenities such as complimentary "get acquainted" cocktail parties.

Self-fulfillment needs are represented by an individual's desire to live graciously or to reward one's self for fulfilling personal or business goals. People who are primarily motivated by this need may be more responsive to hotel salespeople who represent a property that offers luxury and status.

Exhibit 6   Four Personality Types

Source: Adapted from information developed by Jim Cathcart of Cathcart, Alessandra & Associates, Inc.

Psychological needs are largely undefinable, even by those who are motivated to buy as a result of them. Most people traveling, for example, need shelter for the night, but what makes them choose one property over another? Perhaps they stayed in a Holiday Inn as a child, and staying in Holiday Inns as an adult provides a satisfying re-creation of that childhood experience. Whatever the deep-seated psychological reason, it is often difficult for a salesperson to know exactly what will appeal to a person who makes a decision based on psychological needs.

The personality types of buyers. Not only do buying motivations vary, the personalities of clients also vary. Learning to recognize a client's basic personality type can greatly increase a salesperson's chances of selling to him or her.

Like buying motivations, personalities can be divided into four basic types: the director, the socializer, the relater, and the thinker (see Exhibit 6).[4] Remember that these types are generalizations, and an individual may have traits of more than one of these personality types. What follows are guidelines, not hard-and-fast rules.

The *director* is interested in getting results quickly, and is assertive and often blunt. He or she is interested in facts and the bottom line. To successfully sell to a director, salespeople must be prepared, organized, fast-paced, and to the point. A director must be made to feel that the decision to buy is his or her own; it is best for the salesperson to present two or three options and let the director select the one most suitable.

The *socializer,* on the other hand, is playful and talkative. Socializers enjoy the opportunity to talk about personal ideas and opinions, and are usually in no hurry to end a discussion. To successfully sell to socializers, salespeople must be stimulating and interesting but give socializers the chance to speak. Socializers usually respond to stories or illustrations that relate to them and their goals.

Like the socializer, the *relater* is a people person. Relaters tend to view things in terms of how they affect people and relationships. Relaters also need a lot of reassurance once the sale has been completed. To successfully sell to a relater, salespeople must be supportive and somewhat personal. They must never seem to be in a hurry to get the sale and terminate the contact. It is important that salespeople study the relater's feelings and emotional needs as well as his or her business needs.

The *thinker* is an idea person who is precise, efficient, and well-organized. Thinkers are not interested in words; they must be won through actions, and it is important that they be given solid, factual evidence to digest. To successfully sell to a thinker, salespeople must be well-prepared and have all the answers to any questions the thinker may ask. Since thinkers are task-oriented, they will get right to the point and will want the facts presented in a logical manner. In fact, logic is the key word when dealing with thinkers; they want logical solutions to problems. Documentation is essential when dealing with this personality type.

Training Techniques. Although methods of training vary from property to property, there are several common techniques that many properties use:

1. *Simulated sales calls.* These are sales calls acted out by the sales staff. A new salesperson can make a sales presentation and be critiqued by other staff members. When videotaping is used, the new salesperson can view his or her performance and make corrections as necessary.

2. *Double calling.* With double calling, a sales presentation is made by a new salesperson accompanied by the director of sales or a senior salesperson. There are drawbacks to this method, however. The new salesperson may feel nervous, resulting in a poor presentation. And it takes two people to make a call.

3. *Market segmentation drills.* Since all selling is based on customer needs satisfaction, it is important that salespeople understand the needs, characteristics, and requirements of each market segment. New and experienced salespeople can meet to discuss market segment characteristics and the sales tactics that work best with each segment.

4. *Case study exercises.* In this training exercise, a hotel's sales staff is challenged to formulate a sales action plan for a property other than its own. It may be a competitor's property or an imaginary property. This exercise hones sales strategies that may then be applied to the staff's own property.

5. *In-basket drills.* The trainee is given a stack of written communications (letters, messages, memos, and directives) to order and act on within a limited period of time. This exercise provides insights into how well the salesperson judges priorities and uses time.

The success of sales training can be measured by the performance of the sales staff. At the end of training, each salesperson should be able to:

- Explain the property's marketing plan.

- Prepare a property fact book.

- Conduct sales tours of the property.

- Understand how accounts are established and approved, the property's policy on advance deposits for groups, and credit policies of the hotel as they apply to functions.

- Research information on current and potential accounts.

- Prepare sales correspondence.

- Prepare for and complete sales calls.

- Prepare sales call and booking reports and interpret monthly sales progress reports.

- Use the sales office's filing system.

- Analyze the financial performance of the sales office by interpreting the income and expense items on the hotel's profit and loss statement that are directly affected by the sales office.

Time spent giving the sales staff a firm training foundation is time well invested. The value of continuing education for the sales staff is also important. In-house seminars and industry courses such as those offered by the Educational Institute of the American Hotel & Motel Association will help ensure that a sales staff develops to its full potential.

Managing Salespeople

Managing hospitality salespeople is a specialized type of personnel management for several reasons.[5] First, in today's highly competitive market, it is often necessary for salespeople to be away from home and family for extended periods of time. Salespeople are also away from the sales office, making it difficult for them to form close ties with the rest of the property's sales team. Additionally, the business of selling can have certain psychological effects. For example, it is normal for a salesperson to get depressed or feel discouraged if he or she has put on a dynamic presentation and the client doesn't buy.

A sales manager must become involved in a number of areas to ensure that sales volume goals are met or exceeded and costly personnel turnover is kept to a minimum. Sales management involves training and motivating salespeople, scheduling them and assigning accounts, and supervising them.

As just mentioned, training involves both the beginning and continuing instruction of salespeople in many areas. Salespeople often learn at different rates, but the sales manager should check with the sales trainer to see that salespeople meet expectations and minor problems are corrected before they become major ones.

Scheduling salespeople involves analyzing both the needs of the property and the strengths and weaknesses of individual salespeople. If a property targets the business traveler, for example, it is important to select a salesperson who can relate well to and is well-received by this market segment. In addition, other factors must be considered when assigning salespeople to accounts. Does the account require extensive travel? If so, is the salesperson free to travel, or does his or her family situation prohibit extensive travel? Is the salesperson people-oriented or detail-oriented? Would he or she work better with decision-makers who are "directors," for example, or "relater" types? Does the salesperson have good time management skills, or instead require close supervision?

Even if the sales manager places salespeople in accounts suitable for their talents and strengths, salespeople still need motivation on a periodic basis. In most cases, money is a less effective motivator than personal recognition. It is important that salespeople be given incentives, of course, but it is often more effective to provide personal encouragement, especially if the salesperson is having an "off" period.

Supervising the efforts of the sales staff is an ongoing process, but it is often difficult to gauge efforts in selling situations. Many sales managers feel that monitoring sales quotas is enough, and a periodic review of a salesperson's weekly activity report (see Exhibit 7) is all the supervision given. Other sales managers more closely supervise their personnel by periodically testing them on their knowledge, including asking them to give sample presentations to ensure that their performances are up to property standards. Their personal quotas are also reviewed on a regular basis to ensure that they are performing to the best of their ability.[6]

One of the key elements of sales management is the assigning of accounts. Unfortunately, this is often done in a haphazard manner. A director of sales may have three salespeople, for example, and decide to assign one to each targeted market segment: one to corporate business, one to the leisure market, and one to tour and wholesale business. While this may seem adequate on the surface, how equitable—and effective—are these assignments if 65% of the property's business comes from the corporate market, 30% is from leisure travelers, and only 5% comes from tours?

The director of sales may realize this, and decide instead to put two of the salespeople on corporate accounts; one will handle corporate group business while the other will handle individual transient business. But this arrangement leaves other business, such as catering, relegated to yet other contacts at the property—a situation that can pose problems, since most businesses prefer to work with one

Exhibit 7   Sample Weekly Activity Report

Weekly Booking Activity Report

Comfort Inn · Quality Royale

Page____ of ____

Hotel _____

Reporting Period_____ Year _____

Name of Group	*DCT	Dates	Room Nts	Room Rates	Room Revenue	Food Covers	Bev. Covers	F&B Revenue	MTG RM Revenue	**DES.

*D–Define
C–Cancellation
T–Tentative
**–Designation
N–New Business
R–Repeat Business
U–Unsolicited Business
CW–City Wide
SO–Regional Sales Office

	Room Nights	Covers	$
Group Rm Sales			
Group Rm Cxl.			
Net Sales			
Total Food			
Total Beverage			
Total Mtg. Rm.			
F&B Cxl.			
Mtg. Rm. Cxl.			
Net Sales			
TOTAL NET SALES			

GM
DDS
DOS
SR
SR
SS
TOT

	Per Calls			Telephone Calls			Correspondence		
	WK	MTH	YTD	WK	MTH	YTD	WK	MTH	YTD

Manager _____   Sales Director _____   Date _____

A weekly activity report is used to monitor the performance of the sales staff. This form not only tracks the number of sales calls made and other activity goals, but also details room nights booked and the dollar value of group business. (Courtesy of Quality Inns)

individual, and the property is wasting valuable time and labor by having two or more people servicing the same account.

One answer to this dilemma is to assign salespeople to particular accounts rather than to market segments. That is, give one salesperson responsibility for all business generated by an organization. Rather than having three or four salespeople calling about different segments of a company's business—corporate, individual, relocation, catering, etc.—the salesperson assigned to an account is the property's contact for all types of business. This type of account assignment is helpful both to the client, who can now contact one person for all company needs, and to the salesperson, who can learn the client's preferences and build the rapport necessary to solicit additional business.

When assigning account responsibility, several factors must be considered. These include the number of accounts, the geographic area (territory), and the market segments that will be covered by each salesperson. In terms of the number of accounts, the general manager or director of sales must determine how many can be adequately handled. If, for example, the property expects to target 1,200 accounts over the coming year, it is usually best to assign the same number of accounts to each salesperson rather than having one responsible for 500, another for 250, etc.

The location of accounts must also be considered when determining the number of accounts a salesperson can adequately handle. A salesperson assigned to a local area, for example, would have far easier access to his or her accounts than a salesperson who must spend a great deal of time traveling to service accounts. The market segment(s) assigned to salespeople can also be a determining factor in the number of accounts to be assigned. A salesperson handling the account of a large corporation, for example, may have to spend more time on this account, which could involve monthly meetings, quarterly sales rallies, and a large yearly convention, than a salesperson who is handling the account of a non-profit organization that stages one benefit a year.

Since there are so many variables in assigning account responsibility, and changes such as shifts in market segments or increases or decreases in the sales staff may lower effectiveness, account assignments should be evaluated periodically. This would allow the sales manager to make adjustments when necessary, such as assigning additional salespeople to a particularly productive market segment or repositioning a salesperson who shows particular strengths in a marketing area.

Evaluating Salespeople

Evaluating the hotel's salespeople plays an important part in evaluating the success of the property's sales efforts. Evaluation usually covers personal quotas (expected number of phone calls, personal sales calls, new accounts, etc.) and the actual performance of the salesperson (a salesperson can make more than the number of calls assigned, but still bring in less business than expected). Evaluation can also cover a number of other areas. Good salesmanship is more than successful selling. It is a continual growth process that includes the salesperson's appearance and demeanor, time management and organizational skills, ability to prospect for and develop leads, ability to follow up on accounts, and attitude toward the property and selling.

To improve sales performance, evaluations should be made on at least a quarterly basis. Waiting for a yearly review leaves too much time for minor areas of difficulty to develop into major problems. Frequent evaluations allow for timely feedback that can enhance the salesperson's performance. Frequent feedback also allows management to determine if suggested changes are actually being put into action.

With new salespeople, frequent evaluations are especially crucial. Managers must take the time to work with these salespeople on at least a weekly, or, better still, a daily basis to ensure that they understand what is expected of them.

To assist with evaluations, each salesperson should be required to maintain a "reader file." A reader file is a file folder that contains copies of all internal and external memos and correspondence. This file can be reviewed on a weekly basis by the director of sales or general manager to make certain that each salesperson's appraisal is not only based on the volume of correspondence, but on its quality as well.

Compensating Salespeople

Most properties pay a new salesperson a straight salary for the first six to twelve months on the job. This policy enables new salespeople to establish a client base, since most commissions are paid only after business is realized. After the prescribed salary-only period, salespeople are usually compensated on a salary plus commission basis.

There are many variables for determining the salary structure for salespeople: the geographic area, the level of experience, salaries offered by competitors, and sales quotas are a few examples.

Sales Incentive Programs. Sales incentive programs offer rewards separate from a salesperson's regular pay and commissions, and are provided to build a team spirit, give extra recognition to good performers, and reduce sales staff turnover. Incentive programs can also be used to spark competition between departments. Incentives may include cash bonuses (on top of commissions), merchandise (cars, furs, and so on), vacation trips (in the case of chain properties, sometimes to another property in the chain), or a combination of rewards. No matter what type of incentive program is developed, it must be designed to give individuals or departments a specific reward for meeting a specific objective.

One example of an incentive program is the multi-faceted program developed by The Ritz-Carlton Hotel Company. Annual sales quotas (gross room revenues booked) are established jointly by each salesperson and his or her immediate supervisor. Ritz-Carlton salespeople are eligible for a bonus of up to 15% of their annual salary for achieving 100% of their annual sales quota. Additional cash awards are given to recognize outstanding accomplishments such as reactivating lost accounts, salvaging cancellations, creating new business, or greatly exceeding set quotas. The size of these cash awards is determined by the hotel's corporate management.

Whatever a property's choice of incentives, the main goal is to produce a motivated, productive sales staff. Properties as well as salespeople can profit from incentive programs, since such programs often result in more business.

Supplemental Sales Staff

It is often impractical or uneconomical for individual hotels to be represented nationwide by their in-house sales staff. Therefore, many properties have looked for ways to supplement their staff's sales efforts. Many chain properties are turning to regional sales offices to help them with regional, national, and even worldwide sales efforts. Sheraton, for example, operates regional offices around the globe in such cities as Brussels, London, Melbourne, Paris, Tokyo, and Toronto. Many hotels with no chain affiliation have hired hotel representatives to assist their sales teams.

The Regional Sales Office. A regional sales office usually consists of a regional director of sales, area directors of sales, senior account executives, account executives, a research director, an office manager, and a clerical staff.[7] Regional sales personnel often work in individual hotels within the region before advancing to the regional level.

A hotel chain's regional sales office may present workshops, seminars, and receptions to attract local executives desiring to learn more about the chain, and may provide news releases and feature columns for use in local newspapers. While the responsibilities of regional sales offices are typically directed toward promotions and public relations, the offices can also scout potential business and develop sales leads in a particular geographic area. For example, a regional sales office for Hilton in Chicago not only sells Hilton's Chicago hotels to people in other cities; it also sells Hilton hotels from all over the country to people within a prescribed radius of Chicago.

Regional sales offices maintain extensive records regarding business prospects in the region. The regional office's computer data banks can offer concise listings of group business; provide information on a client's needs, past meeting history, and the suitability of a property for a particular group; and serve as a central clearinghouse for public space, guestrooms, date availability, and rate information for all the properties in the region.

Today, most U.S. hotel chains have regional offices in major cities such as New York, Los Angeles, and Washington, D.C., particularly if the chain serves groups. Washington, D.C., for example, has over twenty-five regional offices to serve the potential business of that city. A number of hotel chains also maintain a regional sales office at their corporate headquarters. This allows the close monitoring of the chain's operations, and is especially effective if corporate headquarters happens to be located in an industrial or population center or in a popular travel destination.

Hotel Representatives. Many independent properties are turning to outside hotel representatives for sales assistance. These representatives or "reps" serve as out-of-town or market-source business representatives for non-competing properties. Because hiring hotel representatives is often more economical than setting up an individual property sales outlet, hotel reps can be extremely effective for hotels that are not a part of a chain or franchise system (although hotel reps may also be used for supplemental promotion by chain properties).

Since hotels have different needs, the services provided by hotel reps can vary widely. In some cases, the rep may be hired as a field salesperson, soliciting clients who are impractical for the hotel's in-house staff to reach. A property in Florida, for example, may find it more economical to hire a hotel rep in Boston than to send its own salespeople to that city. Other hotels use large representation companies, such as Robert Warner and Loews Representation International. Services provided by these firms include consulting, market analysis, advertising, and public relations in addition to field sales.

For the most part, hotel reps usually serve as:

- *Agents for clients who want to book individual room reservations.* The hotel rep may list his or her phone number in advertising targeted in a specific area by a distant property. A hotel in the Virgin Islands, for example, may target a New York City market; the property's hotel rep in New York would answer local phone calls and confirm specific reservations or answer inquiries.

- *Agents who book individual room business through business contacts.* The hotel rep's contacts with travel agents, airline companies, and other sources in the area can mean business for the property.

- *Agents who provide detailed data on properties.* Most hotel reps are located in major population areas where many corporate and association groups are headquartered. Hotel reps in these cities serve as a clearinghouse for information on the products and services offered by a number of hotels. Corporate and association executives make extensive use of this convenient service, which can lead to a vast amount of business at a minimal expense for a number of properties.

Since a property's hotel rep is an extension of the property's own sales and reservations offices, it is important that the property choose a rep who understands the property's marketing needs. There are several questions that should be answered before selecting a rep:

1. Does this rep represent any major competitors?
2. Does this rep specialize in our property's target markets?
3. Can this rep provide individual attention to our property or does his or her workload preclude working closely with our sales staff?
4. Can this rep's marketing contacts and sales techniques benefit our property?
5. What is this rep's record of client satisfaction?
6. Does this rep operate adequate facilities—telephone services, field sales staff, reservation capabilities, and so on?
7. Can this rep deliver the supporting services (advertising, computerized booking, and so on) our property needs?
8. How does this rep compare in cost with other reps who represent properties similar to ours?
9. Does the rep have offices or contacts in the cities that are likely to be our major market areas?
10. Is this rep truly interested in representing our property?

It is also important to determine how the hotel rep will fit into the property's sales organization and how the rep will be paid. Will the rep be a salaried agent of the property, or will he or she become an extra salesperson who works on a commission basis only? A hotel rep is often hired on a contract basis—paid a set fee plus a predetermined commission percentage on the volume of business that he or she directly books for the hotel. It is important with commission arrangements to set clear booking and pricing guidelines; reps should be given acceptable rate structures to ensure that they don't "give away the house" just to receive their commissions!

Once a hotel rep has been selected, the property's sales staff should establish a defined line of communication between the property and the rep. The rep's productivity and level of service will largely depend on input from the property.

Developing the Sales Office Communication System

For a sales office to operate at maximum efficiency, clear lines of communication must be established both within the sales office and with other areas of the property. Good communication ensures that all members of the property's sales team have the same information and that potential problems are kept to a minimum. A sales office relies on various methods to communicate ideas and information, including holding meetings, keeping sales records, and establishing filing systems.

Sales Meetings

Regularly scheduled sales meetings are an essential part of a successful sales effort. To ensure maximum production and communication, the head of the sales office may want to hold brief daily meetings with salespeople to discuss daily sales calls and the next day's schedule. He or she may also schedule various other meetings, including:

- Weekly staff meetings
- Weekly function meetings
- Monthly sales meetings
- Marketing team meetings
- Annual or semi-annual sales meetings for all employees

Weekly Staff Meetings. Weekly meetings of the sales staff should be conducted by the head of the sales effort—the director of marketing and sales, the director of sales, or the sales manager (the person heading up the meeting will vary depending on the size of the property and the structure of the marketing and sales department or sales office). These meetings should include the general manager and any department heads whose departments will be discussed. Topics that may be covered in a typical weekly staff meeting are new business prospects, tentative and new bookings, conventions, client service procedures, promotions, publicity, and lost business. An open discussion and brainstorming period should be a part of weekly sales meetings to encourage a mutual exchange of ideas and information.

Weekly Function Meetings. These meetings are held with department heads to review upcoming group events. At these meetings, departments involved in serving groups review each group's meeting agenda (commonly called the specification sheet or meeting resume) item by item to ensure that everyone understands what is going to take place and to nail down any last-minute details.

Monthly Sales Meetings. These meetings are held to discuss tentative and definite bookings for the next month or quarter, review progress made in achieving sales goals, and discuss new property promotions. Monthly sales meetings are usually attended by all sales personnel.

Marketing Team Meetings. These meetings involve department heads and knowledgeable representatives from each area of the hotel. They are essentially "meetings of the minds" to ensure that every area of the property is adequately covered in the property's marketing plan. The frequency and types of meetings held by marketing teams are usually determined by the head of the marketing and sales department or the general manager.

Annual or Semi-Annual Sales Meetings for All Employees. These meetings are held to discuss the marketing plan with the property's entire staff. Such meetings provide an opportunity to obtain ideas and suggestions from all employees.

The marketing plan presented to the staff can be fairly simple and abbreviated, but it should give all employees an overview of the function of the marketing and sales department and outline each employee's role in the plan. Sales and advertising programs should also be discussed.

Sales Records

Sales records are a vital part of a sales office's communication system. They are important in servicing accounts and generating repeat business. It is essential that salespeople familiarize themselves with sales forms, learn to complete them properly, and file them in accordance with sales office procedures. In sales offices with computers, the data from the forms is input by the clerical staff, and the information is used to produce a variety of computer-generated reports and analyses.

In most cases, the salesperson's involvement with sales records will begin with a call report, a form generated during a cold call on a prospective client (see Exhibit 8). The call report is then placed in the organization or individual's account file, and a notation for follow-up is placed in the tickler file. (Account and tickler files will be discussed later in the chapter.)

When a sales presentation is made, a tentative booking is usually offered if no definite booking is sold (see Exhibit 9). Once a definite booking has been made, the salesperson may be required to write and/or sign a contract with the client. If the original booking information changes, a change sheet is required. If the meeting or convention is canceled, a lost business report must be filled out and filed with the sales manager (see Exhibit 10).

The Function Book. The key to successful function and banquet space control is the hotel's function book. This record shows the occupancies and vacancies of function and banquet rooms and aids in the effective planning of functions.

Function books are normally divided into pages for each day of the year, with sections set aside for each meeting or function room. Information recorded in the function book includes the organization or group scheduling the space; the name,

Exhibit 8   Sample Sales Call Report

054492

EMBASSY
SUITES ℠

Sales Call Report

Type of Call: _____ Personal

_____ Telephone

_____ Walk-in/Call-in

Trace Date _____

(Month)   (Year)

GENERAL INFORMATION

Account Name _____

Division/Department _____

Address _____

City _____ State _____ Zip _____

Telephone (   ) _____

Individual Called _____

Title _____

Other Contact(s) _____

_____

_____

REMARKS

SAMPLE

ACTION STEP

Potential for other Cities _____

Sales Representative _____ Hotel _____

Date of Call _____

File Copy

Welcome to the Suite Life℠

This form is used by salespeople to document information gathered from personal, telephone, or walk-in sales calls. The form provides for general information about the account, remarks on the needs of the group, and action steps that can be taken to sell business to the account. A notation to call the account on the date indicated on this form will be placed in the tickler file for the salesperson's future reference.
(Courtesy of Embassy Suites, Inc.)

address, and telephone number of the group's contact person; the type of function; the time required for the function; the total time required for preparation, break-down, and cleanup; the number of people expected; the type of setup(s) required; the rates quoted; the nature of the contract; and any other pertinent remarks to assist property personnel in staging a successful function. Function book entries are

Exhibit 9   Sample Booking Form

METROPOLITAN BUSINESS FORMS – DALLAS, TX

LOEWS ANATOLE DALLAS CONVENTION BOOKING FORM

DATE:_____

_____Definite   _____Tentative   _____Option

Booked By:_____

Decision Date:_____

Assisted By:_____

Group

Contact

Phone

Address

City	State	Zip

Assigned To:
Convention Services:_____ Catering_____

Reservations:
_____Direct
_____Res. Card
_____Rooming List
_____Housing Bureau
_____Cut Off Date

Comp Policy
_____1 per 50
_____Spec. Staff Rate
No._____Rate_____
Extra Comps_____

Scope
_____Nat'l
_____State
_____Corp.
_____Tour/Travel
_____Market

Attendance:

Overflow:

Billing:
_____I.P.O.
_____Rm/Tx To Master
_____All to Master
_____Catering to Master
_____Advance Deposit

Rates: Singles	Doubles	Suites	Concierge	Guest Room Block:	
				Day/Date	Room/Suites

Special Instructions:

Credit References:

Meeting Space	_____Yes	_____No	TOTAL ROOM NIGHTS

Meeting & Catering Requirements: EXHIBITS_____Yes_____Number_____ Set Up_____ Tear Down_____

DAY	DATE	TIME	FUNCTION	SETUP	ATTENDANCE	ROOM	RENTAL

Book Administrator_____ Date Posted_____

FILE

This sample booking form, for booking firm convention dates, is one form that may be used to process sold business. In some sales offices, there may be separate forms for tentative and firm bookings as well as change forms that reflect changes to an initial booking. (Courtesy of Loews Anatole Hotel, Dallas, Texas)

Exhibit 10 Sample Lost Business Report

OPRYLAND HOTEL

Group Booking Status Change or Lost Business Report

Today's Date _____ Salesperson _____ FILE# _____   ☐ Group Name Change
                          Month   Day   Year   ☐ Contact Name Change

Current Meeting Dates _____   ☐ Change in # of Rooms

New Meeting Dates _____   ☐ Change in dates

Organization _____   ☐ Tentative Cancellation

Contact _____   ☐ Def. Cancellation

Address _____

_____ / Phone# _____

Status Change

YEAR	DAY												
	DATE												
	RMS												

Reason for Cancelling (Tentative or Definite) _____

_____

Where is Business going? _____

_____

Comments _____

_____

_____

_____

_____

_____

_____

_____

_____

This form is used to document any business either canceled or changed. In some sales offices, change forms are separate from a lost business report, and serve to note changes in the name of the group, the name of the contact person, the number of rooms reserved, and/or booking dates. A lost business report, which can also be a separate form, documents bookings which have been either tentatively or definitely canceled. This form is used to follow up on the reason(s) for the cancellation, and is forwarded to the head of the sales office for review. (Courtesy of Opryland Hotel, Nashville, Tennessee)

always made in pencil because changes can occur even when a commitment seems firm.

Control of the function book. To prevent mismatching of entries or double bookings, a property should have just one function book maintained by only one person. In many cases, the person having control of the function book is the senior sales executive, but because sales personnel often travel frequently, the senior sales executive may designate one clerk to coordinate all entries.

When a property has a catering department, it is wise to locate it close to the sales office so that the function book can be easily shared. (Like the sales office, the catering department does its own selling, usually soliciting local banquets and functions.

Having a single person control the function book is essential. It is not uncommon for the sales office and the catering department to compete for the same function space. At many properties, sales office and catering department managers who want to reserve function space must submit a function book reservation sheet (see Exhibit 11) to the person in charge of the function book. This ensures that difficulties do not arise from a decentralized, undefined procedure of recording function arrangements.

The Guestroom Control Book. Every hotel soliciting group business should have a guestroom control book. A guestroom control book is used to monitor the number of guestrooms committed to groups. The guestroom control book should list the number of guestrooms allotted to each group and indicate whether the allotment is firm or tentative. To make changes easier, entries are penciled in.

Most properties want a mix of group, individual, and tour business, so they establish a maximum allotment of guestrooms available to groups. This quota is usually set by the general manager and the head of the marketing and sales department, and special care must be taken to ensure that the sales staff does not exceed the prescribed allotment.

Because front desk, reservations, and sales office employees all book guestroom business, it is important that they all be aware of group allotments. The guestroom control book provides the sales office with the maximum number of guestrooms it may sell to groups on a given day. The remaining guestrooms (and any rooms allotted to groups that are not sold) are available for individual guests—these are the rooms that can be sold by front desk and reservations staff. Therefore, there should be constant communication between these personnel to avoid any overlapping room sales.

The guestroom control book is kept in the sales office and is usually administered and controlled by the director of sales. In large hotels with a sizable volume of group sales, however, entries are often coordinated by a diary control clerk, so-called because the guestroom control book is called the hotel diary at some properties.

Confirmations, options, and holds. The guestroom control book is used to record all pertinent details regarding group room sales, including confirmations, options, and holds on rooms. A *confirmation* is definite group business that has been confirmed in writing and gives the specific dates on which the group will be using the facilities of the hotel. An *option* is given when a group is unable to make a firm confirmation of room dates—perhaps a board meeting or approval by a superior is required. A *hold* is then placed on the rooms requested and an *option date* is set. The group must then confirm the requested rooms by the option date or release the rooms to enable the property to sell them to other clients. Reputable hoteliers will not confirm other orders for the requested rooms during the hold period. If a

Exhibit 11 Sample Function Book Reservation Sheet

FUNCTION BOOK RESERVATION SHEET

Group Name _____   Comments _____

Contact _____   _____

Address _____   _____

Phone _____   _____

Dates in House _____   _____

AGENDA

DAY/DATE	TIME	FUNCTION	SET-UP	# OF PEOPLE	ROOM NAME

Meeting Space Charges: _____

Sales Rep _____

Date _____

Option Date _____

Date Entered _____

Entered By _____

At many properties, sales office and catering department managers fill out reservation request forms and submit them to the one person responsible for monitoring the hotel's function space. Use of forms such as this one helps prevent double bookings. (Courtesy of US Grant Hotel, San Diego, California)

second group is interested in the same dates, this group may be given an option after being told about the first group's option. This puts the second group in a position to book if the first group releases the rooms on its option date.

Filing Systems

For maximum efficiency in the sales office, an effective filing system is required. Up-to-date information is essential for a successful sales effort, and information must be available quickly.

There are several types of filing methods that may be used for storing client data and other sales information. These methods fall into three general categories:

1. *Alphabetical filing.* Records are filed in alphabetical order by the title of the organization, firm, or association with whom the property is doing business. Many properties also file the names of contact people in alphabetical order. This system seems to be the easiest to implement and use.

2. *Key word alphabetical filing.* Client information is filed alphabetically by a general category key word that appears in the name of the client's organization; the Association of Petroleum and Oil Products would be filed under "Petroleum," for example. While this system has its advantages when a firm or organization's exact name is not known, the system may also result in accounts requiring filing under several key words. For example, perhaps the hotel serves a police fraternal organization. The account could be filed under "Police," "Fraternal," and "Law Enforcement."

3. *Numerical.* Sales files are assigned a number and a corresponding set of file cards is kept by account number, with the name of the account listed after the number. This system is often used with computers—the salesperson or sales clerk can either key in the account number or, if the account number is not known, type in the name of the account.

Once the filing method has been established, the next step is to determine the elements of the filing system. Most hotels use three separate files to record client information: the master card file, the account file, and the tickler file. Before each of these is explained in the following sections, it is important to note that these files may vary slightly from property to property.

The Master Card File. Master cards are instrumental in establishing data banks of information on the needs of clients. Each master card (usually a standard index card) contains a summary of everything needed for an effective sales effort: the organization's name, the names and titles of key executives, addresses, phone numbers, month or months in which the group meets, the size of the group, where the group has met in the past, the group's decision-maker, and other pertinent data that can help to obtain and keep that account's business (see Exhibit 12). In many cases, a trailer card—an additional card that lists divisions or departments within the account's organization—may be filed behind the master card to serve as a source of additional business.

The master card file is also a cross-reference. It can be used to see if an account file exists for a particular group without having to go to the file cabinet to look. Master card files are also used to create mailing lists and quickly obtain addresses or phone numbers for additional sales efforts or follow-ups.

Exhibit 12   Sample Master Card

Jan.	Feb.	Mar.	April	May	June	July	Aug.	Sept.	Oct.	Nov.	Dec.	1 to 100	100 to 250	250 to 350	350 to 500	Over 500

Convention Group   *National Livestock Dealers Asso.*   *N-02197*

Main Contact   *David Pritchard*   Title   *Asso. Manager*

Address   Phone

City

Other Contacts

How is Decision Made   When

Date	City	Hotel	Attend	No. of Hotel Rms.
				Exhibits
				Functions

Master cards are often color-coded to draw attention to specific areas of consideration: geographic location, months of meetings, follow-ups required, and size of group. Some properties also arrange master cards alphabetically by market segment. For example, IBM and Xerox would be sorted alphabetically under "Corporate Business." Other properties may not separate master cards by market segment, but may use a color code system to easily identify specific market segments within the file—an association account may be flagged in blue, a government account in yellow, and so on.

Some properties keep a geographic file of master cards. These cards are organized according to the geographic location of the decision-maker. This type of file enables sales personnel to quickly identify accounts in cities to which they are traveling. Salespeople can simply pull the names of the decision-makers located in the area they are visiting and call on them during the sales trip.

The Account File. An account file is a standard-size file folder holding information needed for serving a client's basic business needs. An account file is started at the time of initial contact with a prospective client and may include programs from previous conventions or meetings the organization has held, convention bureau bulletins, and information relating to the organization that has appeared in newspapers or trade journals. Sales reports and all correspondence relating to previous efforts to secure business should also be in the file. All information in the account file should be in reverse chronological order—that is, the newest paperwork first. Account files are usually filed alphabetically.

Exhibit 13 Sample Tickler File

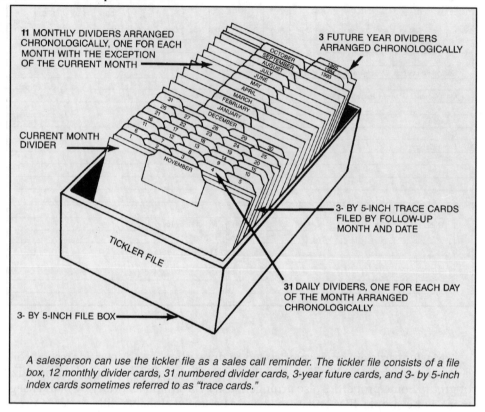

A salesperson can use the tickler file as a sales call reminder. The tickler file consists of a file box, 12 monthly divider cards, 31 numbered divider cards, 3-year future cards, and 3- by 5-inch index cards sometimes referred to as "trace cards."

The account file includes files on potential business as well as files on groups currently booked at the property and groups that have booked with the property in the past. Like master cards, account files are often color-coded by geographic location or, more commonly, by market segment. When a color-coding system is used, the colors used for the account files should correspond to the colors used for the master cards.

When an account file is removed, a guide card noting the name of the group, its file number, the date of removal, and the initials of the person removing the file should be left in the file drawer in place of the file. This ensures that the sales staff will always know the whereabouts of the file.

The Tickler File. This file, also known as a tracer file, bring-up file, or follow-up file, is an effective aid for following up an account. A reminder note or card is filed in the tickler file by month and date; as seen in Exhibit 13, daily dividers are arranged chronologically for the current month. The system is used as a reminder of correspondence, telephone calls, or contacts that must be handled on a particular date.

How the tickler file works. Suppose a client has reserved space for a training meeting at the property in April. The salesperson will want to contact the client no later than February 15 to finalize meeting plans, so the salesperson would slip a note or an index card (often called a "trace card") dated February 15th into the February tickler divider. On February 1, the notes and trace cards for February would be arranged according to date, and the reminder to contact the meeting planner would be placed into the 15th slot. This system, as long as it is updated and checked daily, works well, costs very little, and takes very little time to implement. An added bonus is that if a salesperson is transferred or leaves the property, there is a record of future contacts to be made that can be followed up by other members of the sales team.

Evaluating the Sales Office

Even established sales offices should not be regarded as permanent or unchangeable. If sales responsibilities are not being handled in the most efficient way possible, the head of the sales office should seek ways to improve procedures. Periodic reviews can help ensure that sales duties are handled properly. The following questions should be considered when evaluating the sales office:

1. Does the organizational structure of the sales office make the most of the property's sales strengths?

2. Does the present structure encourage improvement, innovation, and creativity?

3. Is the sales structure compatible with the overall organizational structure of the property?

4. Is authority properly delegated and understood at all levels?

5. Do all members of the sales office understand and properly carry out their duties and responsibilities?

6. Is the clerical staff performing duties that help sales personnel spend as much of their time as possible selling?

7. Have effective lines of communication been established within the sales office and with other departments in the hotel?

8. Is correspondence being handled in a timely, orderly fashion?

9. Are all necessary elements for operating a successful sales office in place; i.e., a written marketing plan, employee job descriptions, standard operating procedures, an efficient filing system, a system for monitoring sales performance, a training program for new employees, and a continuing education program for veteran salespeople?

The Automated Sales Office

A typical sales office generates an incredible amount of paperwork, and a great part of each day is spent in managing the information collected through prospecting, selling, booking, and reporting. At many properties today, much of

Exhibit 14   Manual vs. Automated Systems

Manual	Automated
1. Account and booking information is entered on a scratch sheet.	All information is entered directly into the computer. If the account is an established one, entering the first few letters brings the name, address, contact person, and all other relevant information onto the screen. If the new booking is similar to a previous booking, the old entry can be duplicated and modified if necessary.
2. The same account and booking information is entered into the group room control log—the log is summarized manually.	The log is updated automatically; summary and forecast are calculated automatically.
3. The secretary types up group room block and function information.	The recap is automatically printed and includes all details on the group room block and the function events.
4. The same account and booking information is retyped in a condirmation letter.	Confirmation is produced automatically.
5. The same information is retyped in a contract.	Contract is produced automatically.
6. The banquet event order is typed and retyped with corrections using the same information as well as detailed menus, resource items, and comments.	Banquet event order is automatically generated by selecting menus and resources from the screen. Costs, consumption, and use at the time of the event are displayed.
7. Related follow-up correspondence is typed, referring to the same account and booking information.	Follow-up correspondence is traced and generated automatically.
8. In order to execute market research and/or telemarketing activity, a database is built by re-entering the same booking and account information.	Integrated account booking information is available for database search for marketing, telemarketing, service history, and lost business tracking.
9. Reports are created by a review of the forecast books, diaries, and booking recaps. Summary of data is entered.	Diary is automatically updated each time a booking is entered; summary and forecast are automatically calculated.
10. Salesperson booking pace and productivity reports are created through manual tabulation.	Reports are generated automatically using data in the system.
11. Tracing is done by manual entry on 3- by 5-inch cards. Traced files are delivered by secretaries to salespeople where they pile up on desks.	All activities are traced to the salesperson in accordance with a pre-developed plan. Daily trace reports remind the sales staff of such critical account and booking details as contracts due, credit checks to be done, block pick-ups, menus, and follow-up sales calls. Tentative and definite bookings are displayed and traced for follow-up. Numerous user-defined account traces and booking traces are generated for action steps.

Source: Adapted from *HSMAI Marketing Review,* Spring 1987, p. 27.

this time-consuming and costly effort is handled with one of sales' most effective tools: computer systems (see Exhibit 14).[8]

While many hotels have used computer systems to book reservations for some time, only in the last decade have sales offices been automated. Computer systems provide up-to-date information to salespeople, greatly enhancing the sales effort.

The benefits of an automated sales office are many. Computers:

• Allow tedious tasks to be accomplished quickly and efficiently.

• Allow immediate access to sales information.

Automating the Sales Office at a Small Hotel: The Daytona Inns

Al Szemborski, a Daytona Beach hotelier with 15 years' experience in innkeeping, operates two properties: the Daytona Inn at Seabreeze with 98 rooms, and the Daytona Inn Broadway with 150 rooms.

Szemborski purchased a table model IBM computer and several software packages for both accounting and marketing purposes. His computer is used extensively for mailings to past guests (the computer selects and prints labels at a rate of 5,000 names and addresses in 10 to 12 hours) after a market analysis of (1) where the guests come from, and (2) in what month of the year they visit a Daytona Inn. Over 30,000 guest history records are used.

By using the computer, Szemborski found that ten states and Canada accounted for 85% of his business in the last three years. But lucrative states are not just lucrative states, period. Lucrative states are big producers during particular months of the year. Each state (or more precisely, zip code) has a visitation profile of its own. More guests come from Michigan, for example, than any other state. But virtually all Michigan guests arrive in the winter season. Therefore, advertising in Michigan is done two or three months before the winter season. (Georgia ranks second in number of guests, but all Georgia guests arrive in the summer!)

Taking advantage of his computer's capability, Szemborski can now find out how much money guests spend per day, where they come from, whether they are repeat guests, or whether they come once to see Disney World and don't constitute a good prospect for repeat business.

- Facilitate personalized mailings based on the data in their memory banks.

- Reduce the risk of human error. When specific procedures are implemented, there is less chance of information being lost or misplaced.

- Result in decreased training costs for clerical personnel. Set procedures result in faster training time and less deviation from standard practices.

- Store information that can help the sales office direct specific sales promotions or programs to prospective clients or individual guests based on zip code, desired time periods, areas of interest, and so on.

- Enhance communication among properties, greatly facilitating the sales effort in large hotel chains.

The proliferation of personal computers and the variety of software available from a multitude of vendors have made data processing an increasingly effective and accessible tool in hotel sales offices. A typical example of hospitality industry software programs is the Delphi system. Used by over 100 properties, the Delphi system includes programs designed specifically for the hotel industry. Among its many applications, the Delphi system has the capability to provide an "Available Dates Search" that attempts to match the needs of a prospective group with those of the hotel by providing a list of best available dates to accommodate the group (based on projected occupancy). This allows a hotel salesperson to quickly tell if a specific date is available. If an association executive calls to arrange a meeting on April 7–10, for example, a salesperson or any authorized person in the sales office can use a computer to immediately check the status of these dates, and suggest other days that the computer indicates are open if the requested days are already booked.

Computerized Client Information

Automated systems can be used in many day-to-day sales office operations. In Exhibit 15, for example, the computer provides an alternative to a master card file. The salesperson can simply call up information needed for an account, whether it be the names of contacts, specifics on follow-up calls, or remarks that can assist other members of the sales team in the absence of the salesperson who made the call(s). This application is also an excellent management tool: the sales manager can tell at a glance exactly how many calls were made, and their results.

In a computerized sales office, the tickler or tracer file is also automated. A trace report is printed for each salesperson every morning, and the salesperson can decide whether to trace each entry to another day or act on the trace. If the salesperson acts on a trace, he or she records notes on the report; these notes are entered into the computer by a staff person and updated for the next day's report. Traces that have been completed will no longer appear on the trace report; traces awaiting action will continue to appear on future trace reports until action is taken.

Another computer application can be used by both the sales office and the catering department. We have already seen that the key to successful function and banquet space control is the function book, with the sales staff eventually transcribing information from the function book and other files onto a function sheet (also called a banquet event order or BEO). Automated sales systems can build a function sheet as information is gathered and input by the salesperson into the client's account file (see Exhibit 16). Sample function book reports can be displayed on a salesperson's terminal or printed as a report to banquet and convention service departments (see Exhibit 17). These reports list each function room, and give an overall picture of the property's monthly activities to prevent double booking or unsold business.

Sales and catering software packages that supplement information on the function sheet are also available. An automated sales system can produce kitchen reports (menu items needed, listed by preparation area), room setup reports (resources requested for events on function sheets), and revenue forecast reports (anticipated revenue based on function sheets).

This type of application can also be used for the guestroom control book. A major challenge for non-automated sales offices is maintaining an up-to-date and accurate guestroom control book that indicates the status of guestroom sales to groups. For example: a meeting planner calls and requests the best rate the hotel can offer for 50 rooms for three nights in April. The planner also requires a general session meeting room and three break-out rooms. To respond to this request, a salesperson would first have to match availability dates in April in the guestroom control book with open dates for four meeting rooms in the function book. The salesperson would also want to double-check the accuracy of the information in

Exhibit 15   Sample Computerized Master Account File

Window (or Screen) A

Account Master Acct #003	Contacts Sales Calls Remarks Traces Bookings

AcctName	Water Wonders	Cr Stat GOOD
Abbr	WW	Payment DB /Approved Credit
SlsID	SSH	Comm?
Cntc/Ttl	McFadden, Bill /Mr.	TA#
Position	Senior Vice President	
Address	101 River Blvd.	Lst Call JUL24,90
		Lst Book DEC12,90
City,St	Waterloo, IA	
Zp/Ct/Nt	87655 /USA /USA	
Phone	(515) 678-4564	
Telex		
AcctType	SC State Corporate	
Region	MW Midwest	Status A
SIC	79 Recreation Services	Created JUL01,90 LD
Assn	17 Recreation	Changed JUL01,90 LD
Origin	SL Solicited	
Quality	G Good	

Window (or Screen) B

Account Master Acct #003	Contacts Sales Calls Remarks Traces Bookings

AcctName	Water Wonders
Abbr	WW
SlsID	SSH
Cntc/Ttl	McFadden, Bill /Mr.
Position	Senior Vice President
Address	101 River Blvd.

---- Contact ----

Cntc/Ttl	Keinig, Cheryl /Ms.
Position	Administrative Assistant
Address	101 River Blvd.
City, St	Waterloo, IA
Zp/Ct/Nt	87655 /USA /USA
Phone	(515) 678-4564
Comments	Cheryl accumulates info and makes site recommendations to Mr. McFadden.

---- Contact Name ----

L#	Contact	Position
1	Keinig, Cheryl	Administ
2	Hill, Mary	Meeting

This computer program allows a salesperson to get detailed information on an account instantly. Window A is similar to the information recorded manually on master cards like the one in Exhibit 12. But by simply pushing additional keys, the salesperson can obtain detailed information on key contacts for the account (Window B). Other "windows" provide a summary of sales calls made on the account, specifics about each sales call, salesperson remarks, and specifics on tracing and following up the account. (Source: Lodgistix, Inc., Wichita, Kansas.)

each book with several members of the sales staff—and check with the department manager—before quoting a rate.

Exhibit 16   Sample Computerized Function Sheet

THE RIVERVIEW HOTEL
FUNCTION SHEET
44 Newmarket Road   Durham, NH 03824   603/868–1592

Group: Kollmorgen Corporation
Contact: David Kornfeld
Title: Director of Conference Services   Agreement #: 17892
Address: 3131 Campus Drive   Acct. ID: Corp–4758

Plymouth   MN

Day: Thursday August 13, 1995
Function Name: Awards Banquet
Post As: Sales Meeting
Conf. Coordinator: David Kornfeld

SPECIAL INSTRUCTIONS

Valet service for all attendees who arrive between 6:45PM and 7:00PM.

VIP Basket #2 in all rooms by 5:00PM.

Date	Time	Function	Room	Setup	Spec	People
8/13/95	3:00PM – 3:15PM	Coffee Break	MEZZLNGE	BREAK	No	75
	6:00PM – 7:00PM	Coffee Break	VIKING	BAR	No	200
	7:00PM – 11:00PM	Banquet Dinner	OSLO	RD10	HEAD	200
8/14/95	8:00AM – 5:00PM	Meeting	STOCKHOLM	USHP	No	35

BILLING INSTRUCTIONS
All charges expect incidentals to Master

MENU

Banquet Dinner 1   From 7:00PM to 9:00PM
Room: Oslo Room   Attendance 200

Fillet of fresh Trout marinated with Saffron	200 Serving
Chilled light Chicken Veloute with Herbs	200 Serving
Roast Leg of Lamb in Crust, Madeira Sauce	200 Serving
Milk Chocolate Mousse	200 Serving
Coffee, Tea	200 Serving

Price: $38.00 per person

SETUP REQUIREMENTS

Room: OSLO   From 7:00PM to 9:00PM

60" Rounds	10
Pink tablecloths	10
White napkins	200
All wood lectern	1
Head table for 12	1
Rear screen projection	1
12" screen	1
Hand-written name tags	200
Flowers by Valentine Florists	

Room: STOCKHOLM   From: 8:00AM to 5:00PM

VIP pen and pads	12
Flipcharts with markers	2
Lamp Screen Pointer	1

BEVERAGE SERVICE

Raymond Chardonnay	
Served with Chicken Veloute	7.00 pp
Clos de la Roche	7.50 pp
Served with Lamb	

ADDITIONAL INFORMATION

1. Allen Doyle, Executive Vice President will sign check.

2. Have photographer available through reception and dinner.

CUSTOMER AUTHORIZATION AND APPROVAL

I have read both sides of this document and agree to abide by the terms and conditions set forth by the Riverview Hotel. All arrangements and specifications contained herein are:

_____ Approved   _____ Approved with changes as indicated.

Date: _____   Signature: _____

GUESTROOMS
Arrival Date: August 12, 1995

Booked By: David Sullivan
Date Booked: February 1, 1995

This function sheet draws together relevant booking information and important information about the account, and merges the data on one display screen. (Source: Newmarket Software Systems, Inc., Durham, New Hampshire.)

In an automated sales office, however, the salesperson would be able to respond much more quickly. Both the guestroom control book and the function book could be displayed simultaneously on the salesperson's computer terminal, and the salesperson could use a search function to match the meeting planner's needs with the property's guestroom and meeting room availability. This would enable the salesperson to check the status of the meeting planner's preferred dates and suggest alternate dates if the requested dates are booked. In many cases, rates are also programmed into the system, eliminating the need for the salesperson to check with the department manager for room rates.

Exhibit 17   Sample Function Book Report

THE RIVERVIEW HOTEL

Date Printed: October 1, 1995   Time Printed: 11:59 AM

—DELPHI – Function Space Profile   Page: 1

Report for Oct 1 1995 to Oct 31 1995

Room Name	Time Period	Sa 1	Su 2	Mo 3	Tu 4	We 5	Th 6	Fr 7	Sa 8	Su 9	Mo 10	Tu 11	We 12	Th 13	Fr 14	Sa 15	Su 16	Mo 17	Tu 18	We 19	Th 20	Fr 21	Sa 22	Su 23	Mo. 24	Tu 25	We 26	Th 27	Fr 28	Sa 29	Su 30	Mo 31
WASHINTN	M	D	D	D	D				D	D						T	T	T														
	L	D	D													T	T	T														
	A	D														T	T	T														
	E															T	T	T														
ADAMS	M																															
	L															DD	DD															
	A																		DD	DD												
	E	T	T	T		T	T																									
JEFFERSN	M	D	D	D		VD	VD	VD	VD	VD	VD																					
	L					VD	VD	VD	VD	VD	VD																					
	A																															
	E																															
MADISON	M											T	T	T												T	T	T				
	L				VD	VD										DD	DD	DD							T	T	T					
	A				VD	VD						T	T	T		DD	DD	DD							T	T	T					
	E											T	T	T																		
MONROE	M															T	T	T														
	L															T	T	T														
	A															T	T	T														
	E															T	T	T														
JACKSON	M								D	D	D																					
	L			VD	VD	VD			D	D	D																					
	A			VD	VD	VD																										
	E																															
VAN BURN	M		T	T	T							D	D	D												T						
	L		T	T	T							D	D	D												T						
	A											D	D	D												T						
	E																									T						
HARRISON	M																															
	L																															
	A																															
	E																															

This report displays the status of all of a property's function rooms for a month. Each day is broken down into four periods: Morning (M); Lunchtime (L); Afternoon (A); and Evening (E); and there are four different levels of room status: Definite (D); Deposit Due (DD); Verbal Definite (VD); and Tentative (T). (Source: Newmarket Software Systems, Inc., Durham, New Hampshire.)

In addition to being displayed on a computer terminal, information in the guestroom control book can easily be printed in concise, accurate computer reports (see Exhibit 18). These reports, too, offer instant access to the same information to authorized staff members. "Definites" and "tentatives" are clearly defined to prevent booking errors.

Exhibit 18   Sample Group Room Control Report

THE RIVERVIEW HOTEL

Date Printed: August 27, 1995   Time Printed: 11:41AM

—DELPHI – Group Rooms Control Report for 1995 August   Page: 1

	1 Sun	2 Mon	3 Tue	4 Wed	5 Thu	6. Fri	28 Sat	29 Sun	30 Mon	31. Tue	Total. Rooms	Total Guests	Ave Rate	Room Revenue	Decision Date	RT SRC	Stat	Date Entered
DEFINITES for Corp.																		
D.E.C.											500	500	124.00	62,000.00	8/25/95	TRB	D	8/25/95
MASS. BAY CO											200	200	118.00	23,600.00	8/25/95	TRB	D	8/25/95
I.B.M.											90	90	125.00	11,250.00	8/25/95	TRB	D	8/25/95
COASTAL INC.											15	30	128.00	1,920.00		TRB	D	2/ 3/94
Corp.	0	0	0	0	0	0	0	0	0	0	805	820	122.69	98,770.00			D	
TENTATIVES for Corp.																		
LOTUS DEV CO		5	5	5	5						20	40	145.00	2,900.00	8/25/95	SB	T	8/25/95
CRIMSON TRVL						6					24	48	118.00	2,832.00	8/25/95	RWH	T	8/25/95
EASTERN INC.											35	70	130.00	4,550.00	8/25/95	RWH	T	8/25/95
LOTUS DEV CO											15	30	121.00	1,815.00	8/25/95	SB	T	8/25/95
INTEL CORP.											9	27	121.00	1,089.00	8/25/95	SB	T	8/25/95
EASTERN INC.											4	8	145.00	580.00	8/25/95	RWH	T	8/25/95
Corp	0	0	5	5	5	11	0	0	0	0	107	223	128.65	13,766.00			T	
DEFINITES for Assoc.																		
TRAVEL ASSOC	25	25	25								75	75	108.00	8,100.00	9/30/95	KL	D	3/10/95
N.A.F.E.											30	60	127.00	3,810.00	8/12/95	CRW	DD	8/12/95
U.S. ASSOC.											120	240	120.00	14,400.00		TS	D	8/ 1/95
U.S. ASSOC.							7	7	7	7	63	126	112.00	7,056.00		TS	D	8/10/95
U.S. ASSOC.							5				20	20	120.00	2,400.00		TS	D	8/22/95
Assoc.	25	25	25	0	0	0	12	7	7	7	308	521	116.12	35,766.00			D	
TENTATIVES for Assoc.																		
VETS ASSOC.	2	2	2								6	12	121.00	726.00	8/25/95	TRB	T	8/25/95
N.A.R.R.P.	10	10									20	40	110.00	2,200.00	8/25/95	TRB	T	8/25/95
DATA SYSTEMS			6	6	6	6					48	96	131.00	6,288.00	8/25/95	TRB	T	8/25/95
D.P.A.			10	10	10						30	60	145.00	4,350.00	8/25/95	TRB	T	8/25/95
MUTUAL ASSOC.					3	3					24	48	131.00	3,144.00	8/25/95	TRB	T	8/25/95
MONT WARD CO											40	80	100.00	4,000.00	6/24/95	EP	T	6/24/95
NEWSWEEK											16	32	131.00	2,096.00	8/25/95	RWH	T	8/25/95
N.A.F.E.											36	72	127.00	4,572.00	8/12/95	CRW	T	8/12/95
INTRNTL ASSC											8	16	118.00	944.00	8/25/95	TRB	T	8/25/95
WOMENS ASSOC											4	8	110.00	440.00	8/25/95	TRB	T	8/25/95
MANUFACT ASC											48	96	127.00	6,096.00	8/25/95	RWH	T	8/25/95
N.A.T.C.O.							45				270	540	234.00	63,180.00	8/25/95	TRB	T	8/25/95
DENTAL ASSOC								2	2		4	8	110.00	440.00	8/25/95	TRB	T	8/25/95
CENTRAL ASSC									30	30	60	120	120.00	7,200.00	8/25/95	TRB	T	8/25/95
US YACHT CLB									4	4	8	16	131.00	1,048.00	8/25/95	TRB	T	8/25/95
Assoc.	12	12	18	16	19	9	45	2	36	34	622	1244	171.58	106,724.00			T	

The report illustrated here is from an automated system which can replace the guestroom control book. This report provides a concise summary of bookings for the month. The bookings are broken down into Definites (including deposit due and verbal definites) and Tentatives. Each block is listed by day, with totals for rooms, guests, average rate, and revenues. The decision date, sales source, and date entered are also given. (Source: Newmarket Software Systems, Inc., Durham, New Hampshire.)

Lists, Reports, and Analysis Applications

An automated sales office can quickly generate lists and reports that would take hours to produce manually. Computers can store mailing lists of prospective clients, previous guests, and organizations and associations. These lists can be printed out in a variety of applications—by zip code, by type of guest or prospect, etc.—and can be "merged" into word processing functions to provide "personalized" sales letters. Computerized systems make short work of large mailings, providing cost-effective, targeted advertising and promotion for the property.

Exhibit 19   Sample Sales Performance by Market Segment Report

Sales Source Activity Report by Market Segment
Sales Performance Market Segment
Sales Activity between 12/6 and 12/21
Arrivals beginning 1/1

Booking Source: Ralph Johnson

Market Segment	Room Nights Current	(+/–)	Average Rate Current	(+/–)	Room Revenue Current	(+/–)	Food Revenue Current	(+/–)	Beverage Revenue Current	(+/–)
Corporate										
TENTATIVE:	0	0	0.00	0.00	0	0	0	0	0	0
DEFINITE:	130	130	125.00	125.00	16,250	16,250	1,150	1,150	0	0
National Association										
TENTATIVE:	435	–262	170.00	35.00	73,950	–20,145	250,000	221,851	6,100	1,420
DEFINITE:	1,267	1,267	128.80	128.80	163,195	163,195	73,149	73,149	12,680	12,680
Regional Association										
TENTATIVE:	0	0	0.00	0.00	0	0	0	0	0	0
DEFINITE::	2,225	85	134.24	2.58	298,704	16,949	41,190	0	13,845	0
SHERF										
TENTATIVE:	0	–360	0.00	–135.00	0	–48,600	0	–10,657	0	0
DEFINITE:	360	360	135.00	135.00	48,600	48,600	10,657	10,657	0	0
Social										
TENTATIVE:	0	0	0.00	0.00	0	0	0	0	0	0
DEFINITE:	0	–25	0.00	–94.00	0	–2,350	0	0	0	0
State Association										
TENTATIVE:	0	0	0.00	0.00	0	0	0	0	0	0
DEFINITE:	550	450	115.45	20.45	63,500	54,000	153,991	150,000	5,000	5,000
Tour & Travel										
TENTATIVE:	0	0	0.00	0.00	0	0	0	0	0	0
DEFINITE:	50	50	120.00	120.00	6,000	6,000	4,320	0	1,170	0
TOTAL										
TENTATIVE:	435	–622	170.00	35.00	73,950	–68,745	250,000	211,194	6,100	1,420
DEFINITE:	4,582	2,317	130.12	0.50	596,249	302,644	284,457	234,956	32,695	17,680

Source: Delphi/Newmarket Software Systems, Inc., Durham, New Hampshire.

Data entered into computer systems is often used to generate reports, such as a sales performance by market segment report (see Exhibit 19) that analyzes a salesperson's booking activity by market segment during a specified time period. This report is valuable to both the salesperson and the director of sales for evaluating performance, and is just one example of the various types of reports that sales offices can generate to provide up-to-date information for a wide variety of applications.

One of these applications is market analysis. Market analysis begins with master cards or other basic information on present and potential business. The computer sorts the information into several categories, generating reports that will allow the sales staff to determine a number of statistics at a glance. Reports may include arrivals and booking dates, length of stay, rates, room type chosen, or other information, such as the zip code areas that produce the highest business or the types of rooms that are most popular during a particular season of the year.

These statistics are a vital tool to help management plan sales strategies, especially at a time when advertising costs are escalating. A computer-generated market analysis provides the information necessary to know just where to target promotional efforts.

Yield Management

The increasing use of computers in market analysis has led to yet another new application: yield management. Yield management is a technique used to maximize room revenues. "Yield" is based on a simple percentage that involves revenue potential and revenue realized:

$$\frac{\text{Revenue Realized}}{\text{Revenue Potential}} \ = \ \text{Yield}$$

Revenue potential is the revenue that would be realized if all of the property's rooms were sold at full rack rates; revenue realized is actual sales receipts.

Yield management has been used by airlines and cruise ships to fill empty seats and cabins for some time, but the hospitality industry has been relatively slow in using this technique to fill empty rooms (usually limiting application to seasonally adjusted rates). One reason for the hospitality industry's late entry into full-fledged yield management has been the way it looks at pricing: most room prices have been based on the product—location, square footage, amenities, etc. Yield management, however, requires that room prices be based on demand; room rates are raised when demand is high and discounted when the supply exceeds the demand. During a slow period, for example, rooms may be offered for discounted rates rather than letting them go unsold; conversely, when demand is high, it is not good business to offer discounts on rooms that can be sold for higher rates. But, until computer technology was available, the most crucial part of yield management—predicting or forecasting demand—was tedious and haphazard at best.

Forecasting demand involves looking at a number of factors, including data on previous bookings and projections of guest trends. In addition, forecasting must also include current data, such as weather, the activities of competitors (special packages, contract discounts, etc.), and events in the local area (a highly publicized festival, concert, or other event that will likely increase bookings). While these statistics and trends can be analyzed without using computers, the computer has made it far easier to predict demand by generating a number of reports that help in forecasting. A price-value report, for example, compares how your property's rates relate to those charged by competitors in your market area. Market segmentation reports, which should be done for all market segments targeted, enable property managers to discover patterns in lead times, arrivals and departures, and price considerations, which help in forecasting. A demand analysis can chart how demand builds over time, and can assist management in evaluating the property's market and adjusting strategies to meet market demand.

But computerized reports are only as good as the data entered. In some cases, for example, reservations data may show that room revenue was lost, but doesn't tell why. Was the business lost to a competitor? Was a trip canceled? Could something have been done to save the reservation? Whenever rooms revenue is lost, reservations can assist marketing by gathering and recording information helpful to

Insider Insights

Robert W. Horgan
Chief Executive Officer
Newmarket Software Systems, Inc.
Durham, New Hampshire

Robert Horgan was formerly a general manager with Marriott Hotels. He is a 1969 graduate of Cornell University, with over 16 years of experience in hotel operations. Newmarket Software Systems, Inc., is a privately held corporation founded in 1985 by Horgan. Its staff designs, develops, and markets Delphi, the world's leading sales and catering computer system (licensed in more than 400 hotels worldwide). Delphi's acceptance is reflected in its sales, which averaged an annual growth rate of over 85 percent for the past three years.

The hotel sales manager who doesn't have a personal computer on his or her desk is at a distinct disadvantage compared to the competitor who does. A well-trained sales manager with a PC can cover the ground of two people without computers and do it better.

A new generation of sales and catering software for hotels has grown up around the power of today's PCs. Features that weren't possible just a few years ago are now available in a number of systems.

These features can help sales personnel in a number of ways. The first is decision support, or the "what-if" capabilities that can give salespeople the ability to maximize the hotel's yield on every booking.

Office automation is another feature of sales software systems. A recent study showed that more than 70 percent of a typical salesperson's time is spent on such paperwork as contracts, proposals, internal records, and reports. An effective software package can free up a salesperson from the mountain of paperwork that even a single proposal or booking can generate.

In a manual system, the bible for the rooms side is the guestrooms control book; for the function side, it's the function book. An automated sales office no longer needs these big books. Both guestroom and function room details are now produced automatically as a result of the booking process. With personal computers, several salespeople can now simultaneously check and book space. In addition, computerized systems can offer a combined view of both books for up to two weeks at a time.

In an electronic function book, events can be shuffled, stored as prospects, or held to be assigned (TBA) when space loosens up. Salespeople can store events in a diary "window" while they flip through other events to achieve a better "fit."

Automated sales systems offer other advantages. Capacity checks are easy to perform, and a capacity warning in the system indicates when numbers exceed the limits of a function room. Pop-up windows show details from both the account file and the booking file that would be impossible to record in a manual function book.

(continued)

Insider Insights *(continued)*

No one suggests that a PC will replace a sales department's day-timer, but automated systems have built-in tracing systems and perpetual calendars with holidays, special events, and red-flag days.

Another major feature of a PC-based system is the report and analysis capability. Interactive sales and catering systems offer both system-generated reports and reports produced through a report generator. Daily, weekly, monthly, and annual information is available without further input.

A well-conceived computer program relates accounts in a hierarchy and summarizes total account productivity. For instance, a corporate account might have several sources of business—its headquarters, a few regional offices, and any number of branch offices. The PC can quickly summarize all of a firm's data—room nights, average rates, revenue, customer counts, average check, and so forth—and put it on the screen or into a report.

Today's fast, inexpensive, and easy-to-use personal computers have changed the sales and catering office forever. Without a doubt, the sales department produces the largest return for the smallest investment in dollars and time when it's equipped with a PC and a comprehensive sales and catering system.

the marketing effort (reason for revenue loss, market segment represented, and so on).

To better use yield management, many properties have formed forecast committees or yield management teams that meet regularly to evaluate demand trends. These teams usually consist of executives from reservations, sales, and the rooms division, and may also include marketing and front office personnel. These executives meet regularly to forecast demand and establish systems and strategies for dealing with changing demand patterns.

But properties also need feedback to assess the application of yield management strategies and offer suggestions for improving performance. For example, marketing's goal may be to fill 80 additional rooms over a typically low demand weekend period, so a discounted room rate of $65 is quoted to potential guests. This rate may meet the immediate objective of filling guestrooms, but suppose the guest wants to stay five days, three of which involve days on which room rates are typically $110 per day? The reservations and marketing departments need feedback in this case to develop a different yield management strategy which would ensure that the property realizes maximum revenue.

Managers who wish to make good yield management decisions can also take advantage of sophisticated yield management software. This software can provide a vast amount of information on a number of market factors, such as the property's booking history, market conditions, and bookings by market segment, and can help the manager project the highest revenue-generating guest mix. This software can also be used to monitor and evaluate yield management decisions, and, over time, can be used to create "models" that show the probable results of marketing decisions.[9]

Even the most efficiently organized office and the best computer system that money can buy cannot guarantee that the property's sales efforts will be successful, however. The key to sales success is always the property's *people*, and how effectively the property's sales staff can sell the property.

Endnotes

1. One half of Jim's monthly capacity of $125,000 is $62,500; three-fourths of Jim's capacity is $93,750. Three months at half capacity ($62,500) equals $187,500; three months at three-fourths capacity ($93,750) equals $281,250. Therefore, the new salesperson brings in $468,750 in revenue in the first six months ($187,500 + $281,250 = $468,750). However, Jim Dandy would have brought in $750,000 during those six months ($125,000 × 6 = $750,000). Subtracting the new salesperson's revenue ($468,750) from the revenue Jim Dandy would have brought in had he remained at the property ($750,000) shows that the new salesperson's revenues are $281,250 less than Jim Dandy's would have been ($750,000 − $468,750 = $281,250). Adding this revenue shortfall to the revenue lost during the three months it took to find and hire the new salesperson ($125,000 × 3 = $375,000) reveals that the property lost $656,250 during this nine month period ($375,000 + $281,250 = $656,250).

2. For more information on training, see Lewis C. Forrest, Jr., *Training for the Hospitality Industry*, 2d ed. (East Lansing, Mich.: Educational Institute of the American Hotel & Motel Association, 1990).

3. Jay Diamond and Gerald Pintel, *Principles of Selling* (Englewood Cliffs, N.J.: Prentice-Hall, 1985), pp. 54–55.

4. The information in the following section was developed by Jim Cathcart of Cathcart, Alessandra & Associates, Inc., and is used with permission.

5. Some of the material in this section was adapted from Richard R. Still, Edward W. Cundiff, and Norman A. P. Govoni, *Sales Management: Decisions, Strategies, and Cases* (Englewood Cliffs, N.J.: Prentice-Hall, 1988).

6. For more information on hospitality management, see Jerome J. Vallen and James R. Abbey, *The Art and Science of Hospitality Management* (East Lansing, Mich.: Educational Institute of the American Hotel & Motel Association, 1987); Raphael R. Kavanaugh and Jack D. Ninemeier, *Supervision in the Hospitality Industry*, 2d ed. (East Lansing, Mich.: Educational Institute of the American Hotel & Motel Association, 1991); and Robert H. Woods, *Managing Hospitality Human Resources* (East Lansing, Mich.: Educational Institute of the American Hotel & Motel Association, 1992).

7. Some of the material in this section was adapted from Edward E. Eicher, "The Role of the Regional Sales Office in Hotel Sales and Marketing," *HSMAI Marketing Review*, Spring 1984, pp. 9–15.

8. For more information on computers in the hospitality industry, see Michael L. Kasavana and John J. Cahill, *Managing Computers in the Hospitality Industry*, 2d ed. (East Lansing, Mich.: Educational Institute of the American Hotel & Motel Association, 1992).

9. Forecasting, systems and procedures, and strategies and tactics of yield management are explained in *Yield Management*, a two-videotape program (including companion materials) available through the Educational Institute of the American Hotel & Motel Association, East Lansing, Michigan. *Yield Management 2.0*, a software program also available through the Educational Institute, provides several scenarios (at increasing

levels of difficulty) for users to practice achieving the best yield through the optimum combination of rate and occupancy.

Key Terms

account file

call report

director

double calling

function book

guestroom control book

hotel representative

master card

reader file

relater

socializer

standard operating procedures (SOPs)

thinker

trace card

yield management

Review Questions

1. What positions are typically found in a large property's marketing and sales division?

2. What factors influence the organization of a sales office?

3. What are three classic principles of organization?

4. What are seven characteristics common to successful salespeople?

5. Personalities can be divided into which four basic types?

6. What are several training techniques for developing new sales personnel?

7. What is the role of a regional sales office?

8. What are the functions of independent hotel sales representatives?

9. What are some of the facts recorded about an upcoming function in the function book?

10. What is an option?

11. What is contained in an account file?

12. The tickler file serves what purpose?

13. What are some of the things that should be considered when evaluating a sales office?

14. What are some of the benefits of an automated sales office?

15. What is yield management?

Part II

Sales Techniques

Chapter Outline

Prospecting
    Qualifying Prospects
Preparing for the Presentation Sales Call
    Pre-Presentation Planning
        Property Research
        Competition Research
        Client Research
    The Sales Kit
    Projecting a Professional Image
        Non-Verbal Communication
        Voice Quality
        Listening Skills
        Negotiating Skills
The Presentation Sales Call
    Opening the Sales Call
        Introduction
        Purpose Statement
        Benefit Statement
        Bridge Statement
    Getting Client Involvement
        Questioning
    The Presentation
        Organization
        Effective Speaking
        Visual Aids
        Closing the Presentation
    Overcoming Objections
        Types of Objections
    Closing and Following Up
        Following Up
Improving Sales Productivity
    Time Management
    Key Account Management
Appendix

4

Personal Sales

THIS CHAPTER DISCUSSES ONE OF the most effective tools for selling a property and its services: the personal sales call. A personal sales call is used to build rapport with clients or potential clients and sell them the property's products and services.

There are several types of personal sales calls:

1. *Cold or prospect calls* are usually made within a small geographic area with a minimum amount of time spent on each call. Generally, little is known about the person or organization being called on; this is strictly a fact-finding or exploratory call. The objective is not to make a sale, but to gather information so that a selling strategy can be developed and a follow-up visit made. Of course, if you run into someone really interested in doing business, you can present the property's benefits and try to make a sale.

2. *Public relations or service calls* are made on companies and individuals who are already clients. These calls serve to promote goodwill and indicate your willingness to meet the future needs of the client.

3. *Appointment calls* are used to introduce a prospective client to the features and services offered by the property. You may book business or develop information so a follow-up call can be made at a future date. The person being called on is usually busy (that's the reason for requiring an appointment); therefore, you should obtain as much information as possible about the prospect's needs before making the call.

4. *Presentation calls* are usually the result of several previous calls. The objective is to have the individual, committee, or group make a decision in favor of the property. It is very important that you use visual aids and other support materials during the presentation. If you are making the presentation to a committee or group, you should know who the decision-makers are. You must have the confidence to make a strong sales pitch, overcome objections, and ask for the sale.

5. *Inside sales calls* are made to walk-ins inquiring about the property.[1]

This chapter looks at the components of successful face-to-face salesmanship, beginning with a discussion of the importance of prospecting and the need for thorough preparation before making a sales call. Next, it focuses on the presentation sales call, and describes how pre-presentation planning and the five basic steps of a presentation sales call can lead to bookings for the property. The final sections of the chapter discuss time and key account management.

Prospecting

In today's competitive environment, few hotels can be certain that their current client base will be adequate for the future. Prospecting for new business is essential and should be a continual part of hotel sales. Individuals and groups must constantly be cultivated to ensure that the hotel keeps pace with market trends and the competition.[2]

But properties should not just send salespeople out to find new business by going up and down the street and knocking on doors. According to Tom McCarthy, who has over 35 years in hotel marketing, properties need a planned approach to prospecting:

> For example, a salesperson might have a territory that includes 35,000 companies. If a salesperson can qualify 20 new prospects a week, it doesn't take much figuring to determine that the salesperson can qualify about 1,000 accounts a year.
>
> Wouldn't it make more sense to work with a list broker and pick the 1,000 companies in advance that will be assigned the salesperson (based on proximity, size, and type of business), rather than just telling the person to "hit the bricks"? Do we think the person will call on the best 1,000 out of the 35,000 by chance?
>
> Here we are working with computers and sophisticated software and still living in the 19th century when it comes to the most basic principles of prospecting.[3]

McCarthy has also found that sales managers in other industries find it unbelievable that many hospitality salespeople are sent into the field without any training. How can a salesperson adequately sell the property without training in sales procedures and an understanding of the property and its objectives?

Many salespeople see prospecting as a difficult, frustrating, and thankless job. Prospecting, however, serves two essential purposes: first, it increases sales by bringing in additional individual and group business; second, it brings in new clients to replace former clients who have been lost over a period of time. Prospecting is the lifeblood of sales because prospecting identifies the individuals or groups that may become the property's client base of the future.

Prospect research information is as close as the sales office files. The function books and other records from previous years are excellent sources of prospects. These records provide information on groups that have booked and not returned, the names of key contact persons, and the names of satisfied past clients.

Other sources for prospect research include:

1. *Referrals from past and present clients.* In addition to being excellent prospects for future bookings, satisfied clients can also be excellent sources for leads. Not only might your clients personally recommend the property to friends or business acquaintances, they may also have an extensive sphere of influence within other areas of their own organizations—or with peers from other firms. Asking current clients to identify others who might be interested in your property's facilities and services is an excellent business practice called "referral prospecting."

2. *Other departments within large corporations or groups that the property is currently serving.* If the property is dealing with one department within a large

Insider Insights

Greg Hendel
Co-Owner
Best Western Host Hotel
Palm Springs, California

Greg Hendel graduated from Sacramento State in 1974 with a degree in Criminology, and worked as a supervising probation officer in Palm Springs, California, for the next four years. In 1979, Hendel purchased 6% of a 160-unit property, and began a career in the hospitality industry as manager and director of sales. He now owns 50% of the Best Western Host Hotel in Palm Springs, and is currently working on the development of a 125-unit full-service property (to include meeting rooms) in northern California.

Some people refer to sales and marketing as prospecting, but I like to think of it as detective work. The good sales and marketing person is constantly asking questions: "Who's coming into town?" "Who utilizes rooms of this type?" "How can we determine additional sources for business?"

The "leisure-overnight" type of property is perhaps the most difficult to sell. Commercial/convention and "tour" properties can be contracted; after a meeting between the prospect and the salesperson, a signature indicating future business can be obtained. But all a leisure property can do is educate the prospect in the hopes that he or she will stay at the property when in the area. In other words, the leisure property is more likely to take any type of business it can get.

As a starting point, we use a daily manager's report that puts each room rented into a category: AAA, Travel Agent, Special Package, et cetera. From this information, we can focus a plan of attack. For example, if we see that we're generating a good deal of travel agent business we'll focus on travel agents. We want travel agents to single out the Host over 100 other properties in the area, so we want travel agents to know they are important. This month, we are sending the "Official Desert Bookmark" to tell them we care; next month, we will send out a photograph of the entire staff, so the agent can associate a face with a call.

And we don't neglect potential business from unexpected sources. Last week, for example, a brochure crossed my desk asking for a donation to a local, non-profit educational institute called "Guide Dogs of the Desert." I asked myself, "Who from that organization could use hotel rooms?" I met the director of the institute and gave him my five-minute slide presentation. He advised me that the blind students attending the institute must live in dorms, but after asking some pertinent questions I found that rooms would be needed for graduation ceremonies and a yearly golf tournament held to raise funds.

When I heard that as many as 100 golfers came from out of town, I advised the director that our property would pay the postage if the organization would mention us and allow us to include a brochure with their mailing to the golfers. His eyes lit up, as postage is one of the organization's biggest expenses. We both won!

(continued)

Insider Insights *(continued)*

Sales and marketing are limited only by a salesperson's imagination. One of my sayings is, "There are no bad programs, just bad implementation and execution." In the example above, selling was accomplished "an inch wide and a mile deep," and through meticulous detective work during the interview a greater amount of business was realized than a few rooms for a small graduation exercise. May all of *your* prospecting produce nuggets of new business. Good luck!

---

corporation or association, there may be a number of other departments within the organization that need hotel accommodations or services.

3. *Local organizations and companies.* You should not neglect local firms when prospecting. Business directories, chamber of commerce publications, and industry reports will often yield important information. A local firm, for example, may be a branch of a national organization and the potential source of a large amount of business.

4. *Community contacts.* Don't discount the potential of casual contacts. Delivery and repair personnel; department store managers, who entertain sales suppliers and often come in contact with residents new to the area; real estate salespeople, who also deal with new residents and help to relocate corporate executives; and even service station attendants, who are often asked for directions and information on places to eat or stay, are all excellent sources for a number of types of business.

5. *Front desk personnel.* Many individual guests have the potential to bring group business to the property. The front desk staff can provide referrals that may result in additional individual or group business.

6. *Other property employees.* Many property employees belong to groups or organizations such as bowling leagues and church groups that can become potential clients. You should ask staff members for leads.

7. *The property's competitors.* You can even get prospect leads from the competition, so knowing what competitors are doing and whom they are serving is important. Consider these questions when researching competitors:

   • Who are our top three direct competitors?

   • What are the five major accounts for each competitor?

   • How many room nights is each account booking and at what rates?

   • What will it take (lower rates, better product-service, more promotion, etc.) to get our competitors' major accounts to use our facilities?

8. *Other sources.* You can find both individual and group business through a number of other sources (see Exhibit 1). The local newspaper is an excellent starting point; a careful review of the business, local news, and sports sections—as well as local advertisements—can prove productive (a single newspaper could result in 15 to 25 promising leads). Leads may include names of people and businesses that have recently located to the area; presidents, officers, and committee persons of local civic and social clubs; sponsors of sporting or entertainment events; newly engaged couples; couples celebrating anniversaries; sponsors of class or family reunions; or businesses sponsoring special events.

   The local library, chamber of commerce, convention and visitors' bureau, and state industrial commission are also excellent sources for local leads. Most offer publications that list businesses according to the Standard Industrial Classification (SIC), developed by the federal government. In many cases, your property may already have a breakdown of business booked by SIC code; this makes it particularly easy to target other businesses from the same category.

   In addition to the SIC code, which categorizes virtually every type of business, many publications also list businesses in terms of geographic area, volume of business, number of employees, and names of officers. This information is particularly useful in determining the prospects that would most likely be interested in your property's facilities.

9. *The national level.* Although it is always best to begin with "backyard" prospecting, it is also important to target travel intermediaries such as meeting planners, corporate travel managers, incentive travel buyers, travel agents, tour operators, and tour wholesalers. Lists of these travel intermediaries can be found in directories issued by national organizations. These directories can be found in large libraries.

   Many travel intermediaries belong to professional associations that offer allied memberships to hotel salespeople (see chapter appendix). By joining these associations and attending their meetings or conventions, you can network with travel intermediaries and develop relationships that may lead to increased sales.

Once prospect research has been done, goals can be set. If, for example, the sales department's goal for each salesperson is to develop three new accounts a week, it may be necessary to set a prospecting goal of 15 contacts per week to realize three new prospects. Many hotel sales offices assign such specific goals, while others allow individual salespeople to set their own goals within property guidelines. In either case, you should keep accurate records of prospecting efforts for evaluating your progress in meeting goals (see Exhibit 2).

Qualifying Prospects

Qualify and *quantify* are two of the most important steps in the solicitation of any account. Unfortunately, not every prospect qualifies as a potential client; in many

Exhibit 1   Sources for Individual and Group Business

Companies

Potential business: Guestrooms, meeting rooms, office and holiday parties, retirement and award banquets, training schools and employee indoctrination sessions, recruiting programs, sales incentives (vacations for top-producing salespeople, and so on).

Sources: Chamber of commerce listings, Polk's city directory (available in libraries), telephone directory yellow pages, business sections of newspapers, National Passenger Traffic Association directory, leads from clients and acquaintances, competitors' function boards (the listing of daily functions that is usually posted in the lobby or meeting area).

Contact persons: Sales managers, personnel and training directors, department or division officers or heads, traffic managers, key secretaries.

Local Clubs and Professional and Fraternal Organizations

Potential business: Guestrooms for guest speakers, regularly scheduled chapter meetings, installation of new officers (banquets), holiday parties, special project events, state and regional conventions.

Sources: Chamber of commerce listings, telephone directory yellow pages, newspaper stories, leads from clients and acquaintances, competitors' function boards.

Contact persons: Local community professionals, fraternal organization administrators, club officers and members, key secretaries.

Hospitals, Schools, and Government Agencies

Potential business: Guestrooms, meetings and seminars, recruiting programs, parties, award banquets, training schools, conventions.

Sources: Chamber of commerce listings; telephone directory yellow pages; government, school, and hospital directories; leads from clients and acquaintances; competitors' function boards.

Contact persons: Directors and administrators, athletic directors or team managers, department heads, military recruiting officers, key secretaries (court bailiffs and judicial secretaries, secretaries to principals, and so on), personnel and public relations managers.

Family Social Functions

Potential business: Guestrooms for out-of-town family members (for family reunions or funerals), guestrooms for out-of-town wedding guests, a honeymoon guestroom or suite, receptions, rehearsal dinners, showers.

Sources: Retail store managers, church officials, newspaper stories, leads from clients and acquaintances.

Contact persons: Family reunion organizers, retail store managers, church officials, the bride or her parents, the groom or his parents, friends or relatives of the wedding party or family.

Travel Industry Accounts

Potential business: Guestrooms (individual and corporate), guestrooms for bus tours, tour bus meal stops, familiarization seminars.

Sources: American Society of Travel Agents membership directory, National Tour Association membership directory, telephone directory yellow pages, mailing houses, newspaper stories, leads from clients and acquaintances, competitors' function boards.

Contact persons: Company presidents; national sales managers; local airline, bus, and train station managers.

Professional and Trade Associations

Potential business: Guestrooms for guest speakers or members, regularly scheduled chapter meetings, installation of new officers (banquets), holiday parties, state and regional conventions, meetings and seminars, special project events, auxiliary activities.

Sources: Chamber of commerce listings, telephone directory yellow pages, newspaper stories, leads from clients and acquaintances, competitors' function boards.

Contact persons: Executive directors, association officers, local association members, committee chairpersons.

Exhibit 2   Sample Prospect Card

Prospect's Name _____

Company Name _____

Address of Prospect _____

Type of Business _____

Pertinent background information on the company and/or contact person:

_____

_____

_____

Prospect's estimated sales potential in:

    Room Nights _____

    Dollars _____

Facilities and/or services needed by prospect:

_____

_____

Has the prospect been qualified? ☐ Yes ☐ No

Action required to:

    a. Qualify the prospect _____

    b. Follow-up _____

Salesperson's Name_____

Date of Contact _____ Follow-up Date _____

hotels, 80% of business is generated by 20% of their accounts. Merely collecting the names of prospects, then, does not warrant calling on each one personally.

Full qualification involves gathering all the information necessary to place a dollar value on the potential business from the account. For example, a company executive may indicate that she has 40 executives visiting from out of town two days each month of the year, a three-day sales training seminar for 25 persons twice a year, and the need for 10 room nights per month for visiting clients. This makes it possible to estimate the potential yearly dollar volume from this account for your property—$98,100:

40 persons	×	2 days	×	12 months	=	960 room nights	×	$80	=	$76,800
25 persons	×	3 days	×	2 months	=	150 room nights	×	$70	=	$10,500
10 persons	×	1 day	×	12 months	=	120 room nights	×	$90	=	$10,800
										$98,100

By estimating potential value, you can focus on "big dollar" accounts, the key prospects that could really make a difference in occupancy and revenue should they become steady clients. Simply estimating potential revenue is not enough, however. The potential may indeed be there, but are there other factors that may affect the account's profitability? To fully determine if the prospect is indeed qualified involves three basic criteria: financial status, the need for the product or service, and the ability to purchase.

Financial status information may be obtained from national or local credit rating organizations as well as from annual reports. This information will provide an overview of the prospect's financial standing and enables a salesperson to weed out certain prospects. An organization that does a low volume of business, for example, probably cannot afford an upscale property for a business meeting or convention. Spending time on such an account would likely be a waste of time for a salesperson from an upscale property. Conversely, a large, multimillion dollar corporation might be interested only in upscale accommodations for its executives and meeting attendees; a salesperson for a budget property would probably be unable to solicit business from a corporation of that size.

Need for the product or services offered by the property can be determined by researching the prospect's previous buying record. This information can be obtained through telephone surveys, by contacting the prospect directly, or through information supplied by clients or other business contacts. Has the prospect used other facilities similar to those offered by the property? Is the prospect's company part of a chain or conglomerate that may be affiliated with other hospitality properties? Does the prospect have a need for the special services offered by the property?

The prospect's ability to purchase is based on a number of factors. Even if a prospect's company is financially secure, there may be budget limitations for travel and business expenses, or restrictions on which hospitality properties may be chosen (the company may have a preferred list of acceptable accommodations). Other companies, although prosperous, may still be risky from a salesperson's point of view: payment may have to be routed through corporate offices, the company may be in the midst of a reorganization or takeover by another company, or the prospect's authority for buying may be limited. When qualifying a prospect, therefore, it is important to do your homework in these areas.

Preparing for the Presentation Sales Call

Once a qualified prospect has been called on and has expressed an interest in the property, a presentation sales call can be made.

Although you should approach each presentation sales call with confidence, you should realize that not all presentations lead to a sale. There are three reasons within a salesperson's control why a presentation sales call fails:

1. Planning for the call was inadequate.

2. The salesperson was anxious or nervous.

3. The salesperson failed to reach the decision-maker.

All of these problems can be overcome if you thoroughly prepare for your presentation.[4] Thorough preparation results in:

1. *Increased credibility.* A prepared salesperson knows what the property has to offer, has translated property products or services into benefits, and has determined the needs of the client before attempting to make a presentation. A client will have much more confidence in you if you know the property and how it can benefit the client.

2. *Increased confidence.* Salespeople must sell themselves as well as the property; a nervous or anxious salesperson can lose an important sale. Knowing the product, the competition, and the client increases your self-confidence and ability to influence clients.

3. *Increased probability of reaching the decision-maker.* Research gives you a better chance of talking to the right person, which means a better chance of making a sale.

Pre-Presentation Planning

To be effective, pre-presentation planning should include property research, competition research, and client research.

Property Research. You must have a thorough knowledge of your property. There are two basic methods of improving property knowledge: studying a property fact book, and developing a working knowledge of all the property's departments. The facts obtained through either method should be studied, memorized, and updated when necessary.

    The property fact book. Your property fact book should include pertinent information on the following:

- General property description—location, age, layout, and so on

- Guestrooms—number, types, rates, special rooms, amenities, security

- Restaurants and lounges—number, hours, menus (including room service menus), seating capacities, types of seating, entertainment, special promotions

- Meeting and banquet facilities—number of rooms, seating capacities, services offered, banquet menus, rates

- Audiovisual equipment—types of equipment offered, availability, and prices

- VIP packages—amenities and prices

- Transportation—availability and rates, with special attention to airport transportation

- Recreational facilities—types, rates, hours, lessons available, rental equipment, supervision

- Outside services—secretarial services, shopping services, and so on

- Vendors—florists, photographers, musicians, and their rates

- The community and surrounding areas—area attractions (locations, fees, hours, group rates, etc.) and community atmosphere (rustic, metropolitan, suburban, and so on)

- Guests and finances—guest profiles; present guest mix; optimum guest mix; peak, valley, and shoulder periods; average daily rate from each market segment

During a presentation sales call, products and services listed in the property fact book should be presented as benefits to the client. A property's total number of guestrooms, for example, may not be important to a client, but he or she may be influenced by amenities, room dimensions, the number of no-smoking rooms, check-in/check-out times, deposit policies, or other property fact book information presented as benefits to meet specific needs.

A good exercise for new salespeople touring their property is to list every feature of the property they think a guest might desire—remote color television, a private floor for corporate executives, full-length mirrors, a desk with a telephone, well-lit bathrooms, and so on—and write down how these features will benefit guests.

Competition Research. You must know as much about competitors' properties as the home property in order to sell successfully against the competition. It is almost impossible to sell a property if you are unable to show clients how the property can serve their needs better than the competition can.

By taking a hard, objective look at competitors' properties, you can note strengths and weaknesses and emphasize your property's strengths in areas that relate to client needs. One salesperson was able to book a weekend convention after visiting a competitor's property and noting that his own property's ballroom—although approximately the same size as his competitor's—seated 40 additional guests. Research allows you to downplay those features and services in which a competitor has an advantage, and play up those areas in which your property can best serve the client (see Exhibit 3).

Information required for competition research may be obtained through visits to the competition, inquiries to competitors' properties, and studies of the competition's marketing plans and annual reports. In researching the competition, don't overlook the competition's sales methods, pricing strategies, promotional methods, and sales staff size and ability. In addition to comparing features and services, you must consider such intangibles as the reputation, friendliness, and service standards of other properties.

Exhibit 3   Sample Competition Analysis

NEEDS AND WANTS OF TARGET MARKET	CENTER CITY	OUTLAW INN	LAST RESORT	EMPTY ARMS	BEST HOTEL	COMMENT
Family Leisure Traveler						
Swimming Pool	Yes	—	Yes	—	Yes	
Children's Activities	Yes	Yes	Yes	Yes	Yes	
Recreational Facilities	Yes	Yes	—	Yes	Yes	
Game Room	Yes	—	—	—	Yes	
Double-Doubles	Yes	—	—	—	Yes	
Attractions/Tours	Yes	—	Yes	—	Yes	
Extra Towels	Yes	Yes	Yes	—	Yes	
Family-Oriented Menus	Yes	—	—	—	Yes	
Information Center	Yes	—	Yes	—	Yes	
Corporate Meetings						
Audiovisual Equipment	Yes	Yes	Yes	Yes	Yes	
Security	—	—	—	Yes	Yes	
Training Atmosphere	Yes	Yes	Yes	Yes	Yes	
Well-Lighted, Quiet Meeting Rooms	Yes	Yes	Yes	—	—	
Space on Short Lead Time	Yes	—	Yes	Yes	—	
Soundproof Meeting Rooms	Yes	—	Yes	—	Yes	
Comfortable Chairs	Yes	Yes	Yes	Yes	Yes	
Master Account Billing	Yes	—	—	—	—	
Copy Equipment	Yes	—	—	—	Yes	
Efficient Check-In and Check-Out	Yes	Yes	—	Yes	—	
Association Meetings Market						
Complimentary Room Policy	Yes	—	Yes	—	Yes	
Exhibit Space	Yes	Yes	Yes	Yes	Yes	
Accessible Location	Yes	Yes	—	Yes	Yes	
Overflow Arrangements	Yes	—	—	—	Yes	
Assistance with Housing	Yes	—	—	—	Yes	
Media Coverage of Event	Yes	—	Yes	—	Yes	
Spouse Programs	Yes	Yes	Yes	—	Yes	
Overflow Activities	Yes	—	Yes	—	Yes	
Breakout Meeting Rooms	Yes	—	Yes	—	Yes	
Copy Services/Rates	Yes	Yes	Yes	Yes	Yes	
Recreation Amenities	—	—	—	Yes	Yes	
Convention Coordinator	Yes	Yes	Yes	Yes	Yes	
Sight-Seeing and Recreational Activities	Yes	Yes	Yes	—	—	
Motorcoach Tour Market						
Double-Doubles	Yes	Yes	Yes	—	—	
One Large Meeting Room	Yes	—	Yes	Yes	—	
Highway Accessibility	Yes	Yes	Yes	Yes	Yes	
Confidential Rates	—	Yes	—	Yes	—	
Group Check-In and Baggage Service	Yes	—	Yes	—	Yes	
Bus Parking	Yes	—	Yes	—	Yes	
Welcome Reception	Yes	Yes	—	Yes	—	
Comp Rooms for Drivers	Yes	—	Yes	—	Yes	

A competition analysis form such as this one can reveal property strengths, in relation to competitors, that may be used in a sales presentation.

Exhibit 4   Sources for Client Research

National, State, and Regional Association Meetings Market

Who's Who in Association Management, published by the American Society of Association Executives, 1575 I St., N.W., Washington, DC 20005, sells for $80 and lists approximately 7,000 associations. A valuable reference; the names and addresses of those listed in this directory are also available for direct mail rental for properties that wish to use the names on a one-time basis rather than purchasing the book.

The Nationwide Directory of Association Meeting Planners, available from The Salesman's Guide, Inc., 1140 Broadway, New York, NY 10001, sells for $160 and lists the names and titles of over 10,000 meeting planners from 6,500 major associations. The directory also details the number of meetings held annually, the months in which the meetings are held, the approximate number of attendees, and the geographic location of the meetings. Of special interest to hotel salespeople: the type of facilities used by each group.

Corporate and Incentive Meetings Market

The Directory of Corporate Meeting Planners, available from The Salesman's Guide, Inc., 1140 Broadway, New York, NY 10001, lists the names, addresses, and phone numbers of 12,000 meeting planners. Also listed: the number of meetings held annually, months held, and locations.

Meeting Planners International Membership Directory is available to members and allied members of Meeting Planners International, 1950 Stemmons Freeway, Dallas, TX 75207. Hotel salespeople wishing to obtain a copy of this guide—the best-known source of corporate meeting planners—must join the organization with a meeting planner.

Group Tour and Travel Market

The National Tour Association Membership Directory, available from the association's headquarters, 120 Kentucky Ave., Lexington, KY 40502, lists approximately 3,000 air and motorcoach tour companies and affiliate suppliers.

The American Society of Travel Agents Membership Roster is available to allied members, and lists travel agents and suppliers. For additional information, write: 4400 MacArthur Blvd., N.W., Washington, DC 20007.

These sources are invaluable guides for the names, addresses, and phone numbers of potential group-business clients.

Client Research. Before calling on clients, learn as much as possible about them and their organization. Information is available from a number of sources: other clients who know the client, annual reports, business directories, articles, trade journals, and membership directories and lists (see Exhibit 4).

The information obtained during pre-presentation research allows you to custom-tailor a presentation for each client. Needs, characteristics, and requirements vary from one market segment to another, and you must gain an understanding of these differences before making sales calls.

Good salespeople are empathetic; they can put themselves in the other person's shoes. They understand their clients' viewpoints and concerns, and they consciously question, "If I were this prospect, why would I choose my hotel?" It is sometimes difficult to develop empathy, especially if you have never been a frequent business traveler, a honeymooner, or a meeting planner.

To become knowledgeable about market segments, their needs, and requirements, you should:

- *Study research done on market segments.* Periodicals such as *Lodging Magazine, Hospitality,* and *Nation's Restaurant News* regularly report on the needs of

Exhibit 5   Examples of Market Segment Needs

Relocation/Extended-Stay Executive

- Large guestroom, work area, closet
- Refrigerator
- Health/fitness center
- Variety of food
- Safety deposit boxes

Retail Travel Agent

- Competitive commission rates
- Commissions paid promptly
- 800 number reservation service
- Assurance the hotel will service their clients
- Good stock of current hotel brochures

Sports Teams

- Assignment to one area of the hotel
- Split folios when team members pay their own expenses
- Free meeting space for pre- and post-game meetings
- Extra security
- Excellent meals
- One contact in the hotel

Different market segments have different requirements. To more effectively sell to each segment, hotel salespeople must take the needs of each segment into consideration, and prepare presentations that address these needs.

market segments. (See the chapter appendix for a list of hospitality-oriented publications, many of which can be found in local libraries.)

- *Brainstorm with hotel staff to complete a customer needs analysis for each market segment (see Exhibit 5).*

Thorough knowledge of the property, the competition, and the client can lead to booked business.

The Sales Kit

Before making a sales call, you should prepare a well-organized and professional sales kit. Only the information pertinent to the client's particular needs should be included; too much information results in clutter and appears unprofessional.

Information basic to nearly every sales call includes a general property information sheet—a summary of what the property has to offer. A property information sheet should include the location of the property, the number and types of guestrooms, a description of the atmosphere of the hotel, parking information, number and types of restaurants, meeting room capabilities, and special amenities and features.

A meeting and banquet room information sheet may also be part of the sales kit. It should cover each meeting room's seating capacity (figured for various set-ups) and breakfast, lunch, dinner, and break menus. Testimonials or endorsement letters are often included in the sales kit. When using endorsement letters, however, the market segment targeted is a prime consideration; a training director is more likely to identify with an endorsement letter from another training director, for example, than with a letter written by a motorcoach tour organizer.

And, while they are not usually considered part of the sales kit, business cards also play an important role in a sales appointment. You should have at least three business cards readily available for each sales call—one for the receptionist, one for the secretary, and one for the prospect. Business cards should not be carried in the sales kit, but in a convenient pocket.

Information in the sales kit is more meaningful if it is accompanied by visual aids such as color photographs of rooms, restaurants, banquet facilities, and the exterior of the property. A map of the hotel's general vicinity indicating transportation terminals and nearby attractions can also prove beneficial. For best results, list major attractions below the map, along with the mileage from the property to the attractions.

Projecting a Professional Image

Once the pre-call research is complete, it is time to attend to personal factors that can affect the success of the sales call. You are an official representative of the property, and your appearance, attitude, and approach to clients can mean the difference between new business and a negative response to the property. Remember, you never get a second chance to make a first impression.

First and foremost, never smoke, chew gum, or drink during a sales call. These activities detract from the presentation and may create a communications barrier. Other distractions or unnecessary materials (coats, umbrellas, newspapers, literature for other sales calls, and so on) should be kept to a minimum. Leave any unnecessary items outside the office and avoid distracting motions such as shuffling papers and fumbling with visual aids.

Never neglect the importance of punctuality; salespeople who are habitually late for appointments are wasting their time and their clients' time. They also send the message that the client is not important to the property.

Other factors in projecting a professional image include non-verbal communication, voice quality, listening skills, and negotiating skills.

Non-Verbal Communication. According to one prominent researcher, 65% of face-to-face communication is non-verbal.[5] A presentation, no matter how well-researched, will not generate a sale if your non-verbal communication is not accepted by the client. Non-verbal communication can be divided into four general categories: appearance, the handshake, territorial space, and body language.

Insider Insights

David O'Connor, CHSE
Director of Northeast and Insurance Sales
Saddlebrook Resort
Wesley Chapel, Florida

After his graduation from Old Dominion University in Norfolk, Virginia, David O'Connor began his hotel career as a conference services manager at the Williamsburg Inn, a Five-Star hotel and conference facility in Williamsburg, Virginia. Over the years, O'Connor has advanced through various management and sales positions at Innisbrook Resort, the Key Biscayne Hotel and Villas, and the Colony Beach and Tennis Resort. He is currently employed at Saddlebrook, a Florida resort, where he is responsible for over $2.5 million in rooms sales annually. As director of northeast and insurance sales, he concentrates his nationwide sales efforts on the lucrative insurance company market, but also solicits short-term corporate business from the Northeast.

Having the opportunity to start my hotel career at a complex like Colonial Williamsburg was truly a break for me. The Williamsburg Inn was really unique; I was able to handle the details of every conceivable type of conference—from a weekend for Amway distributors and their families to the coordination of the Emperor of Japan's first stopover on his historic visit to the United States in 1976.

As conference services manager, I began with the assumption that the client was basically sold, or I would not be sitting in front of him or her. I would immediately ask questions about the group and start to form clear ideas in my mind—and sometimes in the mind of the client, I suspect—regarding just what was the purpose of the meeting. Once I had determined this, I came up with ideas on how the hotel could help the client accomplish those objectives. When I shifted from this service role to sales, however, I had to change the way I worked. I had to convince my prospects of the various wonders of the properties that I represented!

Every sales book in the world says the same thing: "satisfy the customer's needs," but I had to learn it the hard way. And it seemed so obvious once I realized it. I try to say practically nothing about the property until I gain the same information from the prospect that I asked for as a service manager. Essentially, the client tells me exactly what will sell him or her and what will turn him or her off.

The resort I represent, Saddlebrook, fulfills so many different corporate and incentive needs that it isn't often that I can't meet the needs of the client. If my property can't meet a prospect's needs, however, I say so, and try to direct him or her elsewhere. Then the client thinks of me as a friend who has been of help.

Appearance. Your appearance (especially your hairstyle) is the first thing a client notices. For this reason, you should have a well-groomed and inoffensive hairstyle.

Your wardrobe is another important success factor. You should wear conservative clothing that suggests success and authority. Dark suits for men and conservative, tailored suits for women project an image of stability and credibility, setting the stage for a businesslike presentation. Clothes should be clean, well-pressed, and appropriate for the region's business community.

Even the most expensive wardrobe won't erase negative impressions caused by bad grooming. Hair should be clean; makeup moderate and well-applied; fingernails neatly manicured; and perfume, colognes, or aftershaves kept to an acceptable level for business.

The handshake. The handshake, when done correctly, helps establish an atmosphere of mutual respect and leads into a positive presentation. As a general rule, you should extend your hand first and maintain eye contact with the client while gripping the client's hand firmly. The handshake should be fairly brief. A long handshake may cause discomfort for a new client because it implies intimacy, but a limp "cold-fish" handshake should also be avoided—it implies unfriendliness.

Territorial space. There are four socially acceptable distances that most people try to keep between themselves and others: public space, social space, personal space, and intimate space.[6] Since any unwelcome invasion of these spaces can make the client defensive, an understanding of territorial space is essential to successful selling.

Public space is a non-threatening area over twelve feet (3.7 meters) away from potential clients. This type of space can be used when selling to a group because a group usually feels more at ease and more willing to communicate at this distance. This much distance is not particularly helpful when making a presentation to an individual, however, as it limits his or her involvement.

Social space is an area four to twelve feet (1.2 to 3.7 meters) from the client, and may be an ideal beginning area for a presentation to an individual, especially if you are not acquainted with him or her. Clients often use a desk to maintain this distance.

Personal space is an area two to four feet (.6 to 1.2 meters) from the client, and is often the closest you may get to a client. Depending on a person's background, even this distance may be too close, and barriers (desks, tables, and so on) may be used by some clients to protect their personal space.

When clients are comfortable with you, they may invite you into their personal space zone; this gesture shows friendliness and greatly enhances your chances of giving a successful presentation. If you are given a choice of a seat in the social space (in front of the desk) or in the personal space (beside the client on the side of the desk), you should indicate friendliness and interest by accepting the chair in the personal space. However, chairs should not be moved closer unless the client is a friend. To do so might be an unwelcome intrusion into the client's personal space, which could lessen the chance for a sale.

Intimate space is an area within two feet (arm's length) of the client and is usually reserved for close friends and loved ones. A salesperson's invasion of this space may be offensive or cause the client to feel dominated or overpowered.

Body language. One of the most interesting parts of non-verbal communication is body language—signals sent from a person's face, arms, hands, legs, and posture. Your body language is very important to your presentation. Your body should be erect to project confidence, you should smile to show warmth and interest in the client, and your gestures should complement, not detract from, the sales presentation.

Understanding body language can increase your chances of making a sale. Since non-verbal communication tends to be spontaneous and unconscious, people tend to believe the non-verbal message even if it contradicts what is being said. Therefore, it is important to make a conscious effort to display positive body language:

- Face—Maintain a pleasant expression, make direct eye contact with the client, and smile frequently.

- Arms—Keep them relaxed and uncrossed.

- Hands—Offer a firm handshake; make arm gestures with extended hands, palms open.

- Legs—Cross them in the direction of the client or leave them uncrossed.

- Posture—Lean forward to express interest or sit upright to project confidence and credibility.

You should also be alert to any negative body language sent by the client. *Caution signals* include the client leaning away from you, very little eye contact, puzzled facial expressions, a neutral or questioning tone of voice, crossed or tense arms, clasped hands, fidgeting, or legs crossed and turned away from you. *Disagreement signals* include the client leaning away from you, retracted shoulders, a tense face, a wrinkled brow, very little or no eye contact, arms crossed over the chest, hand motions expressing rejection or disapproval, tense or clenched hands, or legs crossed and turned away from you.

It is important to deal with negative body language as soon as you note it. In the case of caution signals, you can depart from the planned presentation and ask questions to encourage the client to express attitudes and opinions. By listening carefully, you can address the client's particular concerns, modify your presentation, and possibly re-establish rapport.

When disagreement signals are evident, it is important to *immediately* stop and adjust to the situation. Again, you may use questions to determine what is wrong, and it is acceptable to let the client know you are aware that something upsetting has occurred. Direct questions, such as "Have I said something that you do not agree with?" can be used to re-establish communication and lead the client back into the areas in the presentation that caused concern.

Since non-verbal communication plays such an important role in sales, you should know:

- How to recognize non-verbal signals.

- How to interpret non-verbal signals correctly. Some signals, such as facial expressions, may not always be genuine; a client may feign interest or enthusiasm.

- How to alter a selling strategy as needed for a particular situation. You should be able to slow, change, or even stop a presentation in order to remove communication barriers.

- How to respond verbally as well as non-verbally to a client's body language.

Voice Quality. Every sales presentation must be clear and understandable to be effective. The human voice is a persuasive instrument when used properly, and it is vitally important that you learn to use your voice as a selling tool.

You should be aware of the importance of voice tone, inflection, and enunciation during a sales call. Avoid slang and technical jargon, and speak slowly. If you speak too quickly and do not allow the client to speak, the client may feel overwhelmed by a verbal barrage.

A salesperson's accent may also be a factor in giving a presentation. A New Englander may need to adapt to the slow drawl of westerners, for example. If you are uncertain of how you sound to others, you may wish to tape-record your voice to analyze strengths and weaknesses.

Listening Skills. At the other end of the spectrum, you must know when to stop talking. You need to show a genuine interest in your clients' needs, and listening is an important part of building rapport. Although the average American adult has a listening efficiency of only 25%,[7] there are ways you can increase your listening efficiency—and the likelihood of making a sale.

First, when the client is speaking, face him or her and eliminate as many distractions as possible. Show the client that you are really listening by maintaining eye contact (without staring) and nodding in agreement. Appropriate facial expressions are another non-verbal way to assure the client that you are listening.

Pay careful attention to what is being said; this is not the time to be thinking about what to say when the client stops talking. It is often effective to repeat, in your own words, what has just been said as you understand it. Avoid adding content when rephrasing and refrain from agreeing or disagreeing with the client; the important thing is to communicate to the client your understanding of what was said.

Being attentive to the client, taking notes, and not interrupting while the client is speaking can build listening skills and sales success.

Negotiating Skills. Listening plays a key role in yet another important sales skill: negotiating. Negotiating involves two or more parties coming together to reach an agreement for their mutual benefit. This process should be viewed as a friendly, problem-solving partnership, but many salespeople are fearful and uncomfortable in a negotiating situation. This shouldn't be the case; negotiating can result in a win-win situation for both the property and the prospect if handled properly.

The first step involves preparation by gathering information. Knowledge is power, and a successful salesperson will thoroughly research four key areas: his or her product, the competition, the prospect's position, and the property's position. We have already discussed the importance of property and competition research, but there are still many cases in which a prospect (a meeting planner, corporate travel manager, travel agent, tour operator, etc.) knows more about the property than the property's negotiator. This situation puts the property's representative at a distinct disadvantage, and makes it nearly impossible to effectively sell features and benefits or to demonstrate how the property is better equipped to meet the prospect's needs than the competition.

There are several key factors to consider when evaluating the prospect's position:

1. *Deadline.* How soon will the function be held?

2. *Competitors.* Is the prospect negotiating with other properties as well? If so, how well can your property compete in terms of product, services, and prices?

3. *Past problems.* Has the prospect experienced problems with another property? Knowing what went wrong enables you to point out features and benefits that will ensure that disasters will not be repeated.

4. *Budget.* Knowledge of the prospect's past and present event budgets is essential. How much has the prospect been willing to spend on similar events in the past? Is price a major concern?

5. *Other key issues.* What are the prospect's other concerns? The availability of special services, such as transportation, VIP check-in/check-out, or special meals? Payment arrangements? By knowing what is important to the prospect in advance, you can be ready with a solution that is equitable to both parties.

6. *Decision-maker.* Is the prospect the decision-maker or will he or she have to "sell" the property to another party? If another decision-maker is involved, you must provide the prospect with enough information and supporting material for an effective presentation.

The property's position is usually based on profitability requirements—how badly the property needs the prospect's business. Will this business fill a particular need—generate revenue during a "soft" period, for example? Will it be necessary to forgo this piece of business because more lucrative accounts take precedence during a particular time period? Or does this prospect have unreasonable demands that are not cost-effective?

When evaluating these points, it is essential to consider opportunities for future business. Would servicing a minor function for the client today result in additional, possibly more lucrative business tomorrow? Are there other departments within the company that might use the property's facilities in the future? Would company executives generate profitable word-of-mouth business?

Trade-offs or concessions are often part of negotiating, and the property must set its limits. Many salespeople think they must give something away to close a sale, but successful salespeople do not enter into discussions with that attitude. They sell value, and offer concessions only when absolutely necessary. Concessions should not cut too deeply into the property's profitability. Free meeting space may be offered if the prospect agrees to pay standard room rates, for example, or rooms may be upgraded if the prospect agrees to pay standard banquet costs.

Successful negotiating is a give and take process, but the end result is that both parties are satisfied. The prospect can look forward to a properly handled function that falls within his or her budget guidelines, while the property benefits not only from the revenue generated from the function, but also from the rapport that may result in additional business in the future.

The Presentation Sales Call

Regardless of the type of sales call, you must have a planned objective for the call, whether it is to establish a personal relationship with the client, invite the client to visit the property, qualify the client for potential business, or obtain a provisional or definite booking. In general, some type of commitment from the client is the main objective of any sales call. Having an objective in mind helps keep you on track.[8]

The objective of a presentation sales call is to book business for the property. Once you have prepared yourself for a presentation sales call, it is time to meet with the client and follow the five steps that will help ensure success:

1. Opening the sales call

2. Getting client involvement

3. The presentation

4. Overcoming objections

5. Closing and following up

These five steps follow the same order in every presentation sales call, and most can be prepared in advance.

Opening the Sales Call

All sales calls begin with an opening. The opening should put the customer at ease, establish rapport, and build the prospect's confidence and trust in you. The opening includes an introduction and a purpose statement, benefit statement, and bridge statement.

Introduction. The first step is to introduce yourself and your property: "Good morning, Mr. Smith. I'm Terry Jones from the Red Rock Resort in Boulder, Colorado." If you have already spoken with the client, either in person or over the telephone, it is appropriate to say something like "Good afternoon, Mr. Baker. It's nice to see you again" or "Hi, Jean. It's a pleasure to finally meet you after talking with you on the telephone."

During the introduction, offer a brief but firm handshake, maintain eye contact, and present a business card. Then, you should immediately begin to build rapport through a brief conversation (mutually interesting "small talk") or, better yet, by expressing interest in the prospect.

Communicating your knowledge of your prospect's organization or needs is particularly effective (this information can usually be obtained through client research). A comment such as "I've heard so much about what your firm has been doing in the field of laser technology, and I've been looking forward to meeting you and finding out more about laser surgery" can go a long way in building rapport.

If the client still seems nervous after the introduction, more small talk, such as commenting on the office decor or mentioning how much you enjoy going out in the particularly good weather the community has been enjoying, usually helps break the ice.

Exhibit 6   Sample Features-Benefits Worksheet

Features	Benefits
1. Firm, king-size beds	A good night's sleep
2. Health club and spa	An opportunity to relax and unwind at the end of a busy day
3. Corporate rate program	Savings, value, investment
4. Electronic door locks	Safety, feeling of security
5. Quality gourmet restaurant	Impress clients
6. Express check-in/out	Save time and hassle
7. Honored guest program	Recognition
8. Frequent airport limo service	Convenience, savings
9. No-smoking rooms	Health and comfort
10. Turn-down service	Feeling of contentment, personal pleasure

This features-benefits worksheet for individual corporate travelers clearly spells out the intangible benefits of each hotel feature.

Purpose Statement. Soon after the introduction, state the purpose of the visit. Are you calling to present a new idea, service, or product? To renew a business relationship?

Benefit Statement. The next step in the opening is to present a benefit (or benefits). The benefit statement is the most important part of the opening because it gives the client a reason to listen to you.

Most clients become interested in a hotel's facilities and services only if the facilities and services can benefit them directly. Therefore, it is important to not sell the product; you must sell what the product can do for the client. In other words, you must be a problem-solver, rather than a product-seller.

Translating features and services into client benefits takes practice, but one good way to organize features-benefits information is to prepare a features-benefits worksheet for each targeted market segment (see Exhibit 6). In the hospitality industry, the benefits of a product or service are often intangible. What the client really buys is a feeling, a pleasure, an image. Therefore, that is what you should be selling (see Exhibit 7).

Bridge Statement. Once you have stated property benefits, you are ready to lead into the body of the sales presentation. Bridge statements are a way of asking for permission to continue the sales call, and are usually made in the form of a question: "Would you be interested in learning how other companies such as yours have benefited from our frequent guest programs?" or "Ms. Townes, is it all right if I take a few moments to ask some questions and jot down some notes about your business to give me a better idea of how we can serve you?"

Exhibit 7   Turning Features into Benefits

Feature	Benefit
"I'm glad you asked about our guestrooms! We have the latest in keyless lock technology;	cards for guestroom locks are simple to use and more secure than keys."
"As for the furnishings, the mattresses are firm but not rock-hard;	you're sure to enjoy a comfortable night's sleep."
"The television and lights may be operated from a remote control panel on the nightstand between the beds,	so you don't have to get out of bed to change the channel after you're comfortable."
"And each room has a desk and a love seat:	the desk gives you plenty of room to work, and the love seat is great for relaxing after a hard day."

If salespeople present only features, they leave it to the client to interpret how those features can benefit him or her. Salespeople should try to influence this interpretation by explaining the benefits that the client will receive from each feature.

These questions ask for a response from the client. If the client is not interested in answering these questions, permission to continue has not been granted, and you can thank the client for his or her time and ask for an appointment in the future. If these questions elicit positive responses, however, you have received permission to continue, and can proceed to the next phase of the sales call: getting client involvement.

Getting Client Involvement

Step two in the sales call focuses on determining the client's specific needs and involving the client by asking questions. Questioning precedes any sales presentation; this is a fundamental rule. Questioning and presenting are separate steps. *Always* complete the questioning before presenting—don't question and present, question and present, etc. This type of approach results in a "stop-start" sales call that tends to confuse prospects and can cause them to lose interest.

Sales presentations are much more understandable and interesting when they flow in a logical progression rather than jumping from topic to topic. If you do not complete the questioning before your presentation, you may have difficulty remembering the points that have been covered and may not adequately cover the client's concerns later.

Getting client involvement serves several purposes. Involvement helps build the client's interest and helps you determine the client's needs and the areas of greatest importance to the client. You should take notes during this step; these notes should later become a part of the client's account file. Questioning helps you custom-tailor the sales call. With the knowledge gained during this questioning step, you can anticipate objections and adjust your presentation accordingly.

Questioning. The use of questions such as "Don't you agree?" "Does that sound fair?" "Isn't it?" "Wouldn't it?" and "Aren't you?" help you identify areas of concern to the client. Such questions can also be used throughout the presentation itself, either at the beginning or end of a sentence. For example, if a meeting planner is visiting the property, you could show him or her the ballroom and ask, "Wouldn't this room be suitable for your closing banquet?" Or, in showing the property's executive suite, you might say, "Your president would like this suite, wouldn't he?"

You need to ask two types of questions: close-ended questions and open-ended questions. Close-ended questions generally require a specific reply and can often be answered in one or two words. "How many training meetings did you stage last year?" is a close-ended question. Open-ended questions give clients the opportunity to express their feelings and knowledge. For example, you might say "In researching your company, I noticed that last year's attendance at your annual convention was at an all-time high. Why do you think last year's meeting was so successful?" The client's answer may give clues about what is important to the client.

Questions can also be divided into three broad categories: *fact-finding* questions determine specifics and facts; *feeling-finding* questions reveal the feelings, attitudes, and opinions of the client; *problem-solving* questions uncover the problems faced by the client and pave the way for the presentation.

Fact-finding questions are generally close-ended questions such as "How long have you been with the Builder's Association?" or "How often do you hold these meetings?" Open-ended fact-finding questions can prove more effective; by asking open-ended questions ("Could you tell me about your needs for hotels in our area?"), you can determine some of the client concerns you need to address during your presentation.

To effectively sell to a client, you must accurately determine a client's feelings. This is done by asking such feeling-finding questions as "What factors are most important to you personally in deciding on a lodging site?" Other examples of feeling-finding questions are: "What did you like about last year's convention?" "What do you feel made your last meeting such a success?" and "What do you think would make this year's meeting an even greater success?"

Problem-solving questions focus on the considerations that weigh most heavily on the client's mind. By beginning problem-solving questions with a statement that demonstrates the concerns of others in a specific area, you may get a more honest response: "Ms. Jones, many of our clients tell us they're concerned about delays during check-in and check-out. Do you have any concerns in that area?" The client is encouraged to reply since he or she knows others have the same concern, and you can then respond.

The most important skill in gaining client involvement is *listening* to the client's responses. The successful salesperson is an active listener who can identify and relate to the prospect's needs and desires. Careful listening can help you anticipate and overcome objections in order to close the sale.

Successful salespeople not only listen closely, but, whenever possible, they reinforce and confirm by agreeing with the prospect. "Rewarding remarks" such as "Right," "I understand," "That's great," and "I agree" encourage the prospect to continue—especially when they are reinforced by positive body language like smiling, leaning forward, maintaining good eye contact, and nodding in agreement.

After you have established rapport during this questioning phase, you may use a transition statement ("Now that I understand your needs, I can show you how our property can—") to lead into step three of the presentation sales call—the presentation.

The Presentation

You should have a prepared, rehearsed sales presentation that addresses the needs of each of the major market segments the property has targeted; for example, a general sales presentation for meeting planners that relates specifically to the needs of that segment. But successful salespeople do not stop there; they custom-tailor this basic presentation to the needs of the particular meeting planner they are calling on, based on their research or questioning of the client.

There are three skills required for a successful presentation: organization, effective speaking, and intelligent use of visual aids.

Organization. Writing a presentation in advance is a good way to ensure that all important points are covered in logical order. You can then give the client an overview of the presentation ("I want to explain how our hotel will eliminate the concerns we've discussed") and present each point individually. At the end of the presentation, you can summarize the points covered. A presentation checklist containing the key elements of the opening and presentation can be a useful planning aid (see Exhibit 8).

Effective Speaking. The most important ingredient in effective speaking is enthusiasm. No salesperson wants to sound "canned." If you have memorized your presentation, make a special effort to put feeling and energy into your voice. Every salesperson's voice and manner should express a sincere desire to assist the client. Avoid using hospitality jargon.

Since it is important to continue the client's involvement throughout the sales call, you should ask questions periodically during the presentation. This not only involves the client, but assures you that the client understands the presentation.

Besides monitoring yourself for proper voice tone, inflection, and enunciation, make sure you are not using gestures or facial expressions that could distract the client.

Visual Aids. While people recall only 25% of what they hear, they retain 50% of what they both see *and* hear,[9] making visual aids an important part of your sales presentation. Visual aids such as pictures, charts, and graphs also build credibility. It is seldom enough to simply state the benefits of property products or services;

Exhibit 8   Sample Presentation Planning Checklist

Presentation Planning Checklist

1. Who is the client? _____
   Company Name _____
   Type of Business _____
   Contact Person _____
   Address _____
   Phone _____
   Receptionist's Name _____
2. Date and time of appointment _____
3. Statements of client problem and/or opportunity as related to my offering:
   _____
   _____

4. Major buying motives of the client (if known):
5. Objectives of the presentation:

Major	Minor
_____	_____
_____	_____
_____	_____

6. Important guest benefits to be stressed:
   _____
   _____

7. Evidence needed to support my claims (competitive comparisons, public relations pieces, testimonials, etc.):
   _____
   _____

8. Other information needed (color photographs of the property, list of guest references by market segment w/phone numbers, etc.):
   _____
   _____

9. Sales tools required (brochures, audiovisual equipment, samples, etc.):
   _____
   _____

10. To start the presentation, I will:
    a. Build rapport in this way: _____
    _____

    b. Capture attention, interest, and move on to the presentation in this way: _____
    _____

(continued)

Exhibit 8 *(continued)*

---

11. I anticipate these objections during my sales presentation:

Objection	Response
_____	_____
_____	_____
_____	_____

12. To close the sale, I will ask for the business in this way:

_____

_____

The use of this type of form enables a salesperson to plan each phase of a sales presentation. The form provides space to list objectives, benefits to be stressed, sales aids needed, ways to overcome objections, and techniques to close the sale. (Source: Adapted from Danny N. Bellenger and Thomas N. Ingram, *Professional Selling Test and Cases* [New York: Macmillan, 1984], pp. 167–168.)

visual aids provide proof and increase believability. Ideally, you should carry visual aids that have been specifically selected for each target market.

In addition to brochures, color photographs of the property, reports of favorable publicity, testimonial letters, and third party endorsements, there are a number of more sophisticated visual aids available. Some recent innovations include portable videotape and film equipment, multimedia presentations, and portable computer terminals. You should not make indiscriminate use of these high-tech visual aids, however. When using visual aids, the guideline should be: use the simplest and most effective method to increase believability. A well-planned presentation supplemented with endorsement letters and a presentation book that pictures past successful functions may be just as effective as a multimedia show. The important thing is that the visual aid relates to the needs of the client.

If a presentation book or brochure is used to increase believability, however, don't give up control of the item during the presentation itself. Rather than handing the item to the prospect, continue to hold on to it and explain features and benefits relevant to particular photos. If you give the brochure or presentation book to the prospect before or during the presentation, the prospect may become distracted by thumbing ahead while you are still focusing on an earlier point.

Closing the Presentation. When you have concluded the presentation, a transition phrase, which may be as simple as "Do you have any questions?" can lead to the next step of the sales call—overcoming any objections expressed by the client.

Overcoming Objections

Step four of the sales call deals with those times when the client has objections to your sales presentation.[10] Objections can occur at any time (one salesperson had his business card torn up by a client before he even got started), and there is no reason to panic when an objection is raised. Some objections are a client's way of asking for more information—and some may offer an opportunity to close the sale!

Objections can be verbal or non-verbal. If a client asks a number of pointed questions about food and beverage service, for example, it is possible that he or she has heard negative reports about the property's food and beverage operation. On a non-verbal level, clients may move back, clench their fists, become restless, glance sideways, or cross their arms when there is an objection to a suggested benefit.

Most objections should be handled immediately. The exception is an objection concerning price: if you talk about price too early, the client may think about rates throughout the presentation instead of paying attention. Deal with all other objections as soon as they come up. If you don't, the client may think you are trying to avoid them and you lose credibility.

Address objections with empathy and without arguing. You may need to ask questions to clarify the objection. If you feel that questions are necessary, do not interrupt the client. Wait until the client has finished voicing the objection, give a sympathetic response, and restate the objection in your own words before asking questions.

The majority of sales objections are predictable. You can minimize objections in a number of ways (see Exhibit 9) or prepare answers to common objections well in advance of the presentation. This is one area in which pre-presentation planning really pays off: you have a better chance of dealing successfully with objections you anticipate. Brainstorming with other salespeople about the client is an extremely effective technique for preparing answers to objections. When a number of people are involved in the creative process, more ways to handle an objection can be developed. These answers can be written down and memorized by the entire sales force.

Types of Objections. Objections fall into three basic categories:

1. Price or rate

2. Product or service

3. Lack of interest or urgency

Price or rate objections ("Your competition offers a better rate" or "My wife and I can't afford to spend that much for a wedding reception") can often be deferred to the end of the presentation, after you have had the opportunity to further detail the benefits offered for the price quoted. Price objections can also be avoided by questioning the client on other areas of concern, rather than directly answering the price question. You can say something like: "Putting price aside for a moment, what else, if anything, is of concern to you?"

Product or service objections ("Our previous experience at your property was not very good" or "Your guestrooms just don't compare with those offered at newer properties") and lack of interest or urgency objections can be handled in a number of ways. One way is to restate the objection and offer a positive response to the objection:

Salesperson:	"Mr. Stubbs, from your comments I gather that you don't feel our location is suitable for your training meetings."
Client:	"That's right."

Exhibit 9   Handling Objections During a Sales Call

Objections will be raised in most sales calls. But the salesperson can take several steps to avoid objections, and has several options for taking positive action when an objection is raised.

WAYS TO MINIMIZE OBJECTIONS

* *Listen* to your prospect. Don't interrupt; let the prospect finish talking about concerns before responding. Be alert for body language that may signal unspoken objections.

* *Empathize* with your prospect. Try to see the prospect's needs and concerns from his or her point of view. Show respect for prospects, and show them that you understand their needs.

* *Convince* your prospect. If a dialogue seems to be headed for trouble, restate benefits or offer additional benefits. Show proof of these benefits, such as a testimonial letter from another client.

WAYS TO HANDLE OBJECTIONS THAT ARE RAISED

* *Direct response.* Clarify the objection (by asking a question or restating it in your own words) and respond directly with a solution.

* *Compensating benefit.* When the objection is valid—a meeting room will not be available until 8:00 A.M., and a group of members will be arriving at 7:00 A.M., for example—offer a compensating benefit, such as complimentary coffee and donuts while the members wait.

* *Indirect denial.* When an objection is raised, acknowledge it (don't directly agree with the prospect, but simply say, "I see," or "I understand"), but then show how your property is still able to meet the prospect's needs.

RESPONSES THAT SHOULD ALWAYS BE AVOIDED

* *Never* assume that you understand the objection from the prospect's point of view. Always clarify the objection by asking questions or restating the objection in your own words.

* *Never* argue with or respond negatively to the prospect. This includes trying to intimidate or make your prospect look foolish or criticizing the competition.

* *Never* take the objection personally—or give up. In many cases, an objection is just the prospect's way of getting assurance that the property is indeed interested and can meet his or her needs. Don't make the mistake of getting up to leave too early—always try a close ("Mrs. Jones, if our property can provide the equipment you need, shall we confirm for June 13th?").

Salesperson: "What is it about our location that concerns you?" (Because of thorough pre-presentation research, the salesperson has a good idea of what the client's objection will be.)

Client: "I guess the biggest problem is arranging transportation for our delegates."

In this scenario, the salesperson has identified the client's concern and can then present a benefit offered by the property that will answer that concern: complimentary bus transportation to and from the airport, bus station, and train terminal.

A salesperson can also agree with an objection but point out a compensating benefit:

Client:	"Your room rates are $10 to $15 higher than your competitor's."
Salesperson:	"Yes, our room rates are higher, but our hotel offers 24-hour transportation to the airport, a complimentary breakfast in our deluxe coffee shop, and the finest room service in the area. We also offer no-smoking rooms, and all of our rooms have special electronic locks for extra security."

Lack of interest objections can be handled by questioning the client about his or her feelings about present arrangements:

Client:	"We're happy with our present hotel."
Salesperson:	"Is it the facilities or the service you are most pleased with?" (The salesperson is already aware that the client has complained about the poor service she received at a recent award banquet.)
Client:	"Their meeting rooms and audiovisual equipment are excellent. But sometimes we have had problems with the food service."
Salesperson:	"So you need a hotel that can equal your existing hotel in meeting rooms and audiovisual assistance, but provide better food service. Ms. Stern, our property has an excellent reputation for food service, and we can meet or exceed the meeting room and audiovisual services offered by your present hotel."

When answering objections, never knock the competition or downgrade their product or services. This tactic insults the client's judgment if he or she uses the services of the competitor, and may provoke the client's natural reaction to speak up and defend his or her previous decision. It can also destroy your credibility as an advisor.

There may be times when you are unable to overcome an objection (a meeting planner or training director may say "no" to a sale and mean it), but, in many cases, objections can be answered to the satisfaction of the client.

Closing and Following Up

Many salespeople enjoy presenting their product, but hesitate when it comes to closing. Closing is not difficult, however, when you understand some fundamental principles involved.[11]

There are two basic types of closes: test closes and major closes. Test closes try to draw a reaction from the client. For example, when a salesperson shows a client a meeting room and asks, "How do you like our meeting facilities?" the salesperson is hoping to get a favorable response from the client.

Test closes can be used throughout a presentation to build an "agreement staircase" that will make the major close easier. Asking questions that invite a positive response helps to get the client to say "yes" and be more receptive to the presentation. Using test closes also helps solidify key points and lets you know where you stand with the client before attempting a major close.

A major close is a question or statement that asks for the sale. The major close should elicit a commitment on the part of the client and should be attempted as soon as the client has reached a peak of excitement.

Before attempting a major close, you should keep in mind that some closing situations are better than others. For example, trying to get an affirmative answer from a client who has been sitting in a cramped sales office for twenty minutes is more difficult than getting a positive response from a client who is basking in the luxury of a suite or lush atrium lobby.[12]

There are a number of major closing techniques that can be used (see Exhibit 10). You can determine if a client is ready for a major close by observing these clues:

- Continual agreement throughout the presentation.

- The client's agreement to your response to an objection.

- Repetition of a benefit by the client.

- Positive non-verbal signs—the client smiles frequently or re-examines property brochures, for example.

- The client requests further details or asks questions throughout the presentation.

After using a major close, stop talking and give the client the chance to think things over and respond. Far too many salespeople get nervous after a major close and blurt out information or otherwise distract the client from making a decision.

It is also important to refrain from talking too much after the sale has been made. Too much talking can actually result in the loss of the sale if you say something that brings up doubts or objections that the client had not previously considered! After the sale has been made, thank the client and leave as soon as politely possible. The one exception to this rule is when you are attempting to get the names of other potential clients.

Closing is a skill that can be learned and improved like any other. Salespeople who are uncomfortable with closing should remember that clients *expect* salespeople to ask for the sale (see Exhibit 11).

Following Up. You should follow up all presentation sales calls. If a sale was not made, following up can consist of a brief thank-you letter. The letter should be accompanied by additional collateral material not given to the client at the time of the presentation and any materials specifically requested by the client, such as a copy of the property's contract, rate sheets, maps of the area, and so on.

If a sale was made, following up is even more important. Following up after a sale consists of providing excellent post-sale service. Certainly, follow-up service takes time, but it is usually easier and more cost-effective to keep a client satisfied than to replace a dissatisfied client.

Follow-up confirmation of a sale is extremely important, especially with group business. While a firm handshake may have closed the sale with the client, most meeting or other group business also requires a signed proposal, contract, or

Exhibit 10 Examples of Major Closing Techniques

Technique	Characteristic	Example
Direct Close	The salesperson asks for the business directly.	"May I reserve the space on a definite basis?"
Summing-up Close	The salesperson summarizes the benefits and then asks for the business.	"Our meeting rooms are more than adequate to accommodate your group, the rates I've quoted are within your budget, and the dates you desire are available. May I reserve the space for you?"
BIQ Close	The salesperson uses the following format: "**B**ased on _____, **I**'d like to suggest _____." **Q**uestion: "_____?"	"Based on the success that other companies in your field have had in using our meeting facilities, I'd like to suggest that we book your training seminar in our Gold Room." Question: "Does that sound good to you?"
Assumptive Close	The salesperson assumes that the sale is a sure thing.	"Shall I block 45 rooms for you?"
Alternative Choices	The salesperson suggests a choice between two positive alternatives.	"Would you prefer that your trainees be housed in our standard rooms or in the Tower section?"
Contingency or Closing on an Objection	The salesperson makes an agreement based on a concession from the property (overcoming a final objection).	"If we can revise the awards banquet prices to fit within your budget, then could I have your definite commitment?"
Trial Order	The salesperson suggests that the client try the facilities for an evaluation period.	"Why don't you book just one of your training seminars with us?"
Special Offer	The salesperson provides an added inducement.	"If you confirm next year's convention before the end of this month, we can offer this year's rates."

Source: Adapted from Tom Hopkins, *How to Master the Art of Selling* (New York: Warner Books, 1982).

confirmation agreement. Prompt attention to paperwork and other post-sale details reinforces the client's belief that he or she chose the right property.

Keeping the client informed between the time of the sale and the time of the meeting, convention, or other function is one of a salesperson's post-sale responsibilities. Meeting planners in particular want to be kept posted on the number (and often the types) of guestrooms actually reserved by members of their group(s), changes in hotel personnel, potential hotel labor problems, and any other changes that might affect their function.

During the function, you should check with the client to see that all is well. This might be done during a coffee break or meal function when the client is free. If

Exhibit 11   Steps in the Selling Process

The sales process is a logical series of actions that directs the client toward taking a desired action—buying the property's products and services.

Step 1: Opening the Sales Call

The opening consists of an introduction, a purpose statement, a benefit statement, and a bridge statement asking for permission to continue. The opening must interest the client enough so that he or she will want to hear more.

Step 2: Getting Client Involvement

The object of this step is to build rapport and get the client to talk about problems and needs. Most sales are made or lost during this step.

Step 3: The Presentation

This is the heart of the selling process. During this step, the salesperson explains the hotel's products and services to the client. It is impossible to over-emphasize that the salesperson must sell *benefits*, not features, and that the salesperson must serve as a problem-solver.

Step 4: Overcoming Objections

Resistance is a normal and expected part of the sales process. When clients raise objections, they are not necessarily reacting negatively to the salesperson's proposal, but may only be seeking clarification of it. A solid objection gives direction to the sales effort—it tells the salesperson what he or she needs to do to make the sale!

Step 5: Closing and Following Up

A successful close is the ultimate objective of the sales call. Closing is asking for the sale, and a good close is a logical finish to a good sales presentation. Following up is the crucial work to ensure client satisfaction after the sale.

the client says the audiovisual equipment for a meeting is not working well, for example, you can immediately see that the problem is corrected. This personalized attention shows the client and the meeting attendees that the property is genuinely interested in the needs of the group.

After the function, a phone call or letter to determine client satisfaction is advised. Never assume that a lack of complaints means the client was satisfied; you must make sure that the client was pleased with the hotel and its service. If the response is positive, you can seek rebookings at a later date and ask the client for the names of others who would benefit from the services provided by the property.

Improving Sales Productivity

Sales is a highly competitive field, and you should constantly monitor your performance in a number of areas. In sales, good presentations are not enough. Results are what counts, and good salespeople must look at their actual productivity and search for ways to improve it.

In order to measure your productivity, you must first have a written list of goals; goals keep you on track and allow you to gauge your success. The basis for

The Transition

At some small hotels, all follow-up duties fall to the salesperson who makes the sale—that is, the salesperson helps the meeting planner plan the function and coordinates the meeting or conference when it takes place. At large hotels, salespeople typically turn their clients over to a convention service manager or meeting coordinator after the sale, which frees up the salespeople to pursue other sales.

A frequently debated subject in meetings and convention management is, "How and when should a salesperson turn the meeting planner over to the individual within the hotel who will be in charge of coordinating the client's conference?" Timing depends greatly on the meeting planner, the size and type of the meeting, and how far in advance the meeting has been booked. In all cases, the transition must be handled smoothly and with sensitivity. Usually, the client has dealt exclusively with the salesperson for some time and has complete trust in the sales staff. The salesperson's exit can be traumatic if the planner has not been reassured of the convention service manager's competence.

Although there are no hard and fast rules, the convention service manager is usually introduced to the client at one of four preferred times:

1. *During the site inspection.* Even though the hotel salesperson is the key contact when booking the event, some meeting planners try to meet the convention service manager during the site inspection visit. Planners say there is a "reassurance factor" in making early contact with the person who will be handling the details of their meetings.

2. *Right before signing the contract.* Some meeting planners ask for an interview with the convention service manager before signing the contract. This helps reassure them that promises the salesperson made regarding space, setups, and meeting services will be met. As one meeting planner put it, "Before signing a contract, I want to meet the convention service manager and let him or her know who I'm bringing in and what my meeting is all about. The salesperson may wine and dine me, but the convention service manager makes it happen. That's the person I'm married to for three days."

3. *Immediately after the sale.* If the convention is large and complex and will take place relatively soon after the sale (within a year), some planners like to start working with the convention service manager as soon as the contract is signed to resolve details as far in advance as possible.

4. *One year before the meeting or convention.* In cases when the meeting or convention has been booked several years in advance, the client can be introduced to the convention service manager approximately one year before the event is scheduled, and the detailed planning process can begin. Many meeting planners feel no need to involve the convention service manager any sooner.

It is difficult to divorce the salesperson entirely from the service function, nor is it desirable. The salesperson who simply dismisses a client after the sale, assuming that the convention service manager will shoulder the burden, will probably not get a rebooking. When the convention or meeting actually takes place, the salesperson should greet the client and check with him or her throughout the event to make sure everything is going well.

Source: Milton T. Astroff and James R. Abbey, *Convention Sales and Services,* 3d ed. (New Jersey: Waterbury Press, 1991), pp. 282–284.

goals should always be the hotel's marketing plan, and success should be evaluated in terms of achieving the optimum marketing mix set by the property. An evaluation may show, for example, that although you are seemingly productive, you are not generating the type of business desired by the property.

Once corporate and personal goals are clearly defined, you can use two invaluable tools to attain these goals: time management and key account management.

Time Management

Good time management is crucial to a successful sales career. Time management starts by knowing where time goes. You should keep a daily log for a minimum of two weeks to determine how much time you spend on sales activities; paperwork; meetings; telephone calls; non-productive activities such as travel time, interruptions, waiting on the telephone, and waiting at appointments; and other activities (see Exhibit 12). Once you see where your time is going, you can establish priorities—urgent, important but not urgent, and tasks to be delegated—to ensure greater production.

Your work day should be planned. Non-selling tasks should be eliminated during prime selling times, and emphasis given to work items with deadlines. Hotel salespeople should be using 60 to 75 percent of their time selling aggressively. A full-time person working 50 hours a week, for example, should spend 30 to 35 hours per week making sales calls, and only 15 to 20 hours servicing accounts, filling out reports, attending meetings, and taking orders. Time must also be available to handle unexpected but important tasks when required.

Time management begins with planning on a yearly basis at the property management level (establishment or evaluation of the marketing plan, action plans, and planning for major events). Individual salespeople deal primarily with monthly, weekly, and daily planning to achieve these corporate goals.

Daily planning involves reviewing information to ensure that available time is used for maximum effectiveness. Getting an overview of daily responsibilities and activities as early as possible promotes more efficient handling of appointments and prioritizing of "to do" lists.

Weekly planning does not focus on the minute details inherent in daily planning, but is used to define objectives and set goals for the coming week. In many cases, for example, Mondays may be used for scheduling appointments and supplemental sales activities, Tuesdays through Thursdays set aside for extensive selling efforts, and Fridays spent finishing uncompleted tasks and planning next week's activities.

Monthly planning focuses on major events, such as conventions, community events, etc., and sets general sales goals and strategies based on those activities. A large convention, for example, can provide the opportunity to secure future business—and may prove to be more profitable to the sales effort than prospecting during that week.

In order to use time most effectively, time spent on routine work should be minimized. Delegate routine tasks if possible. A sales secretary can handle a simple inquiry letter, for example. If delegation is not possible, group similar tasks to save time. Salespeople who have to attend to the bulk of their own paperwork can

Exhibit 12 Sample Sales Time Record Analysis

	PROSPECTING			FACE TO FACE			FOLLOW-UP			Travel	Waiting	Paperwork	Meeting	Interruptions	Misc.
	High	Med	Low	High	Med	Low	High	Med	Low						
7:00 – 7:15															
7:15 – 7:30															
7:30 – 7:45															
7:45 – 8:00															
8:00 – 8:15															
8:15 – 8:30															
8:30 – 8:45															
8:45 – 9:00															
9:00 – 9:15															
9:15 – 9:30															
9:30 – 9:45															
9:45 – 10:00															
10:00 – 10:15															
10:15 – 10:30															
4:15 – 4:30															
4:30 – 4:45															
4:45 – 5:00															
5:00 – 5:15															
5:15 – 5:30															
5:30 – 5:45															
5:45 – 6:00															
Total Time in Hours															
Percent of Total Day															

Sales Time Record Analysis. Salesperson _____ Day of the Week _____ Date _____

Source: William T. Brooks, *How To Do It All … On Time: A Time Management Workbook for Hotel Sales Executives* (Washington, D.C.: The Foundation of the Hotel Sales & Marketing Association International, 1986), p. 10.

save time by avoiding as many interruptions as possible. It may be cost-effective to provide each salesperson with a private office or have a sales secretary screen routine calls.

The saying "Time is money" is especially true for salespeople. There are a number of ways for you to save time and money during everyday activities.

When on the road making personal calls, you can prospect for new business by making short cold calls between scheduled presentations.

When making telephone calls, it is important that you know exactly what you want to talk about and that you have all the information needed to answer any

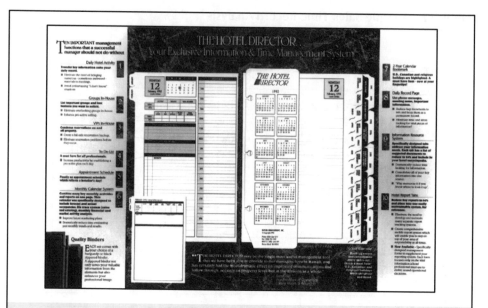

THE HOTEL DIRECTOR

Two of the characteristics of a successful salesperson are organization and follow-up, two activities made easier through the use of a good time management system. The time management system shown here, "The Hotel Director," was designed by hotel professionals to meet the unique needs of hotel salespeople.

In addition to the appointment schedule and weekly and monthly calendar systems found in other planners, The Hotel Director also contains such special features as:

- Areas for listing daily hotel activity, such as occupancy, room rate, and revenue from rooms and food and beverage

- Area to list visiting groups and VIPS

- "To do" list to prioritize sales activities

- Appointment schedule with entries from 7:00 A.M. to 8:00 P.M. to reflect a typical sales day

- Monthly calendar system including file trace system, monthly financial and market activity analysis, market

trends, city-wide activities, and a monthly "to do" list to help with forecasting and evaluating monthly trends and results

- A two-year calendar bookmark highlighting United States, Canadian, and religious holidays for easy reference

- Daily Record page for phone messages, meeting notes, and other information

- Information Resource System to consolidate key information into one source

- Hotel Report Tabs to enable a salesperson to easily find key reports such as group bookings and revenue, and the property's budget

- A 20-year calendar to enable the salesperson to book events and conventions in future years

This type of system provides all the information salespeople need in one convenient place, and helps them better manage valuable selling time.

questions that might arise. If the office is automated, a personal computer greatly facilitates obtaining information. In non-automated offices, you should have immediate access to clients' files, property information, function book information, and so on. When you are prepared, the business portion of the call should go quickly, allowing time for rapport-building small talk with the client.

You should have a specific time set aside for accepting routine calls, and should advise clients of the best time to call; most clients are aware that salespeople are often on the road and will try to schedule their calls for a time when you are available. Emergency calls or client service calls, of course, should always be put through.

Personal telephone calls may be handled by a secretary or through an answering machine. You may set aside a small block of time each day for personal calls, but family and friends should be asked not to call at the office except in an emergency.

Drop-in visitors can mean potential business, and time should be allocated for them in daily scheduling. You can discourage lengthy stays by a visitor who is "just looking" by offering property brochures or pamphlets and encouraging the visitor to look them over and call back with any comments or questions, or suggesting a convenient time for an appointment. In many cases, the clerical staff can answer questions for drop-in visitors, freeing the sales staff for more productive work.

Paperwork can take up much valuable sales time, so you should delegate routine paperwork to the clerical staff. Since clutter breeds confusion, you should be encouraged to generate as little paperwork as possible. This is easier in automated offices, of course. In non-automated offices, you should refrain from writing down suggestions or ideas that you can just as easily tell someone. It is also important for you to learn to file, not pile. Each piece of paper should be handled just once—by personal action, delegation, filing, or discarding.

Travel time can be turned into productive time by using it to catch up on reading (if driving, you can listen to motivational tapes or mentally plan the work day) or correspondence (every salesperson should have access to a hand-held cassette recorder). On the road, you can save time by planning ahead, keeping a realistic schedule, and combining meetings with meals. Luncheon appointments or dinner meetings should be scheduled with high-priority clients; this is prime selling time that shouldn't be spent alone or with low-potential prospects.

Efficient time management can mean increased sales for the property. Each salesperson should be able to account for productive sales time and efforts. Time management plays a major part in the second aspect of personal planning, key account management.

Key Account Management

A typical salesperson at properties of all sizes handles 300 to 400 accounts. Landing new accounts does not mean that you must service an ever-increasing number of clients. New accounts with high potential will replace those with the lowest potential for business, so that the total number of accounts you service will remain relatively stable.

With so many accounts to service, how much time should you spend on an account? One way to determine this is to rank accounts according to their profitability. This is important because in most cases 20% of a salesperson's accounts

---

SALES TIME QUIZ

	Yes	No			Yes	No
1. Do you always complete and forward paperwork when due?	☐	☐	14. Do you always know where your first sales call will be when you make plans the previous day?		☐	☐
2. Do you have a list of your key accounts?	☐	☐				
3. Do you have a list of your highest priority prospects?	☐	☐	15. Do you set objectives for occupancy rates, dollar/volume group meeting bookings, and for each client, prospect, or account?		☐	☐
4. Do you get enough face-to-face selling time?	☐	☐				
5. Do you use your waiting time effectively?	☐	☐	16. Do you spend much time on non-selling activities?		☐	☐
6. Do you have a clearly defined list of objectives in writing?	☐	☐	17. Do you know how many calls per account it is economical to make?		☐	☐
7. Do you always complete what needs to be accomplished daily?	☐	☐				
8. Do you squeeze every available minute from your trade show experience?	☐	☐	18. Do you feel that you spend enough time on formal professional sales training?		☐	☐
9. Do you have a set of weekly objectives in writing?	☐	☐	19. Do you feel you are earning your full potential?		☐	☐
10. Do you procrastinate when you must tackle difficult, demanding, or unpleasant tasks?	☐	☐	20. Do you spend adequate time prospecting?		☐	☐
11. Do you spend leisure time handling clerical duties or paperwork?	☐	☐				
12. Do you know what your time is worth by the minute?	☐	☐				
13. Do you have a five-year plan for your sales career?	☐	☐				

Scoring Key

Add all **Yes** and **No** answers. Determine your score below:

17-20 **Yes** You're an all-pro salesperson.

14-16 **Yes** You aren't starving (yet).

11-13 **Yes** You are heading for problems.

10 or more **No** You need help—NOW!

Source: William T. Brooks, *How To Do It All … On Time: A Time Management Workbook for Hotel Sales Executives* (Washington, D.C.: The Foundation of the Hotel Sales & Marketing Association International, 1986), p. 2.

generates 80% of the business. This prioritizing provides an overview of the potential profitability and importance of each account, and helps you allocate time to the most promising accounts.

A salesperson's accounts fall into three general priority categories—high, medium, and low—whether they are established accounts or potential business sources. Accounts can also be assigned levels that reflect the account's impact, present or potential, on the property's sales:

- *Level 1.* These are new accounts with high potential, or present accounts with high potential but lower than expected profitability. These accounts should be your top priority. (As a general rule, you will make a minimum of five personal calls and five telephone calls to each of these accounts annually.)

- *Level 2.* High potential accounts that are already providing an acceptable share of business. While these accounts deserve a high investment of time, they don't require the amount of personal attention needed for Level 1 accounts. (These accounts will typically be serviced with four personal calls and four telephone calls annually.)

- *Level 3.* New accounts with medium potential, or present accounts that have medium potential but aren't providing an acceptable level of business. (These accounts are generally serviced with three personal calls and three telephone calls each year.)

- *Level 4.* Accounts that have medium potential and are providing an acceptable level of business. (These accounts may require two personal calls and two telephone calls annually.)

- *Level 5.* New or present accounts that have low potential and do not warrant a great deal of your time. These accounts may be given token attention over the course of the year. (You may visit once annually while on a sales trip or prospecting, or may make a telephone call to the account after all other business has been taken care of.)

How do you determine an account's level of potential? Most information on present accounts comes from internal invoices (past performance records, advance registrations, survey sheets indicating potential booking dates, and so on), while other information on present and new accounts such as credit information and references can come from outside sources.

To help rate accounts, you should list every account on a time management spread sheet (see Exhibit 13). A spread sheet includes such important information as the name of the account, the name of the contact person, how often each account was called in a certain time period, how often each account is expected to be called in the future, an estimate of the account's guestroom revenue, revisions of this estimate after review, and the account's priority level.

It is fairly easy to determine the amount of time that should be spent on each account in light of the spread sheet information. The number of calls must be proportionate and manageable, and will vary with the number of clients each salesperson serves, the property's geographic location, and other commitments the salesperson may have. A typical salesperson is usually responsible for 40 to 50 sales calls per week. These calls are normally broken down into three categories: 15 presentation calls, 15 to 20 telephone follow-ups, and 10 to 15 cold or prospecting calls.

After the accounts have been rated, you can discuss the ratings with your supervisor, develop a strategy for each established and potential account, and begin the exciting job of selling the property.

Endnotes

1. Some of the information in this list was adapted from Howard Feiertag, "Making Effective Sales Calls," *The Complete Travel Marketing Handbook* (Chicago: NTC Business Books, 1988), pp. 153–155.

Exhibit 13 Sample Key Account Management Spread Sheet

		KEY ACCOUNT MANAGEMENT SPREAD SHEET						
Name of account	Account contact(s)	How often these accounts were called on in 1995	How often we expect to call on them in 1996	Estimate of the account's room nights	Current rates	Estimate of food and beverage revenue	Estimate of meeting rooms revenue	Account priority (1 through 5)

It is vital to concentrate on those accounts that are likely to produce the most significant profits. Salespeople should evaluate their accounts by completing a key account management spread sheet similar to the one shown. (Source: Adapted from Christopher W. L. Hart and David A. Troy, *Strategic Hotel/Motel Marketing*, Rev. ed. [East Lansing, Mich.: Educational Institute of the American Hotel & Motel Association, 1986], p. 154.)

2. Ideas on how to prospect and develop leads, as well as information on how to make a sales call, negotiate, close a sale, and manage time, can be found in *The Best of Howard Feiertag: Successful Sales Ideas* (East Lansing, Mich.: Educational Institute of the American Hotel & Motel Association, 1992). Audiotape series and workbook.

3. Tom McCarthy, "Get Your Sales Management Ready for the 21st Century," *Hotel and Resort Industry*, December 1990, pp. 30–31.

4. See also *Hospitality Sales: Preparing for the Sale* (East Lansing, Mich.: Educational Institute of the American Hotel & Motel Association). Videotape.

5. Julia Crystler, "The Importance of Selling Silently," *HSMAI Marketing Review*, Winter 1985, p. 8.

6. Charles M. Futrell, *ABC's of Selling* (Homewood, Ill.: Irwin, 1985), p. 77.

7. Terry C. Smith, *Making Successful Presentations: A Self-Teaching Guide* (New York: Wiley, 1984), p. 51.

8. See also *Hospitality Sales: Making the Sales Call* (East Lansing, Mich.: Educational Institute of the American Hotel & Motel Association). Videotape.

9. Smith, p. 51.

10. See also *Hospitality Sales: Overcoming Objections* (East Lansing, Mich.: Educational Institute of the American Hotel & Motel Association). Videotape.

11. The art of closing is also explored in Tom Hopkins, *How to Master the Art of Selling* (New York: Warner Books, 1982) and the videotape *Hospitality Sales: Closing the Sale*

and Following Up (East Lansing, Mich.: Educational Institute of the American Hotel & Motel Association).

12. Adapted from Tom McCarthy, "Sales Success Starts with Closing," *Hotel and Resort Industry*, December 1986, pp. 29–30.

Key Terms

appointment call
body language
close-ended question
cold call
inside sales call
intimate space
major close
open-ended question
personal space

presentation call
property information sheet
public relations call
public space
referral prospecting
rewarding remark
social space
test close

Review Questions

1. What are five types of sales calls?

2. What are some sources for prospect research?

3. What are three basic criteria for qualifying prospects?

4. What are three reasons within a salesperson's control why a presentation sales call fails?

5. To be effective, pre-presentation planning should include research into which three areas?

6. What are four general categories of non-verbal communication?

7. What should a salesperson do if he or she is given a choice of a seat in the client's social space or personal space?

8. What are the five basic steps of a presentation sales call?

9. Why should product features be converted to benefits?

10. What are the elements of a sales call opening?

11. What are three skills needed for a successful presentation?

12. What are three basic types of objections?

13. What are some of the techniques used to overcome objections?

14. When should a sale be closed?

15. What is key account management?

Appendix

The following is a list of some of the professional associations and hospitality periodicals that might be of interest to hospitality salespeople. Phone numbers are not included because they change somewhat frequently.

Professional Associations of Travel Intermediaries

Association of Corporate Travel Executives (ACTE)
P.O. Box 5394
Parsippany, NJ 07054

American Society of Association Executives (ASAE)
1575 I Street, NW
Washington, DC 10005-1168

American Society for Training and Development (ASTD)
Box 1443, 1640 King Street
Alexandria, VA 22313

American Society of Travel Agents (ASTA)
1101 King Street
Alexandria, VA 22314

Insurance Conference Planners
Minnesota Mutual Life Insurance
  Company
400 N. Robert Street
St. Paul, MN 55101

Meeting Planners International (MPI)
1950 Stemmons Freeway
Information Building, Ste. 5018
Dallas, TX 75207-3109

National Association of Business Travel Agents
3255 Wilshire Blvd., Suite 1514
Los Angeles, CA 90010

National Association of Exposition Managers (NAEM)
719 Indiana Avenue, Suite 300
Indianapolis, IN 46202-3135

National Business Travel Association (NBTA)
1650 King Street, #301
Alexandria, VA 22314-2747

National Coalition of Black Meeting Planners (NCBMP)
50 F. Street, NW, Suite 1040
Washington, DC 20001

Professional Convention Management Association (PCMA)
100 Vestavia Office Park, Suite 220
Birmingham, AL 35216

Religious Conference Management Association (RCMA)
Hoosier Dome, Suite 120
Indianapolis, IN 46225

Society of Corporate Meeting Professionals (SCMP)
2600 Garden Road, #208
Monterey, CA 93940

Society of Government Meeting Planners (SGMP)
219 E. Main Street
Mechanicsburg, PA 17055

Society of Incentive Travel Executives (SITE)
21 W. 38th Street, 10th Floor
New York, NY 10018

National Tour Association (NTA)
546 E. Main Street, P.O. Box 3071
Lexington, KY 40596

American Bus Association
1015 15th Street, NW, Suite 250
Washington, DC 20005

Hospitality-Oriented Publications Meetings Magazines

Association and Society Manager
1640 Fifth Street
Santa Monica, CA 90401

Association Meetings
Laux Company
63 Great Road
Maynard, MA 01754-2097

Convene
PCMA
100 Vestavia Office Park, Suite 220
Birmingham, AL 35216

Corporate Incentive Traveler
Coastal Communications Corp.
488 Madison Avenue
New York, NY 10022-5772

Insurance Conference Planner
Laux Company
63 Great Road
Maynard, MA 01754-2097

Medical Meetings
Laux Company
63 Great Road
Maynard, MA 01754-2097

Meeting News
P.O. Box 8391
Boulder, CO 80329-8391

Meeting Manager Magazine
Meeting Planners International
1950 Stemmons Freeway
Information Building, Ste. 5018
Dallas, TX 75207-3109

Meetings and Conventions
Cahners Publishing Co.
44 Cook Street
Denver, CO 80206
Attn: Customer Service

Resorts and Incentives
Gralla Publications, Inc.
Two World Trade Center, 18th Floor
New York, NY 10036-5753

Successful Meetings
633 3rd Avenue
New York, NY 10017

U.S. Association Executive
Custom News, Inc.
4341 Montgomery Avenue
Bethesda, MD 20814

Tour and Travel Publications

ASTA Notes
American Society of Travel Agents
Box 23992
Washington, DC 20026-3992

ASTA Travel News
Yankee Publications
Main Street
Dublin, NH 03444

Business Travel Management
Coast Communications Corp.
488 Madison Avenue
New York, NY 10022-5772

Business Travel News
CMP Publications
600 Community Drive
Manhasset, NY 11030-3847

Canadian Travel Press Weekly
Baxter Publications Co.
310 Dupont Street
Toronto, Ontario
Canada M5F 1V9

Corporate Travel
Gralla Publications
Two World Trade Center, 18th Floor
New York, NY 10036-5753

Recommend Magazine
P.O. Box 69-3780
Miami, FL 33169

Travel Agent
7 East Twelfth Street
New York, NY 10003-4404

Travelweek Bulletin
P.O. Box 575, Station F
Toronto, Ontario
Canada M4Y 2L8

Travel Weekly
Reed Travel Group
44 Cook Street
Denver, CO 80206

Motorcoach Publications

Agent Ontario
Bizletters Publishers
1534 W. Second Avenue, Suite 300
Vancouver, BC
Canada V6J 1H2

Bus Tours Magazine
9698 West Judson Road
Polo, IL 61064-9015

Courier
National Tour Association
546 East Main
Lexington, KY 40508-2342

Destinations
American Bus Association
1015 Fifteenth Street, NW 250
Washington, DC 20005-2681

Tour and Travel News
600 Community Drive
Manhasset, NY 11030-3847

Travelage East
OAG Travel Magazines
1775 Broadway
New York, NY 10019-1992

Travel People
CMP Publications
600 Community Drive
Manhasset, NY 11030-3847

Travel Today
Fairchild Publications
7 East Twelfth Street
New York, NY 10003-4404

Hospitality Management Publications

AH&MA Reports
American Hotel & Motel Association
Communications Department
1201 New York Avenue, NW
Washington, DC 20005-3931

Canadian Hotel & Restaurant
Maclean Hunter Ltd.
Maclean Hunter Building
777 Bay Street
Toronto, ON M5W 1A7
Canada

Casino World
Gramercy Information Services, Inc.
Madison Square Station, Box 2003
New York, NY 10010-9998

Cornell Quarterly
Elsevier Science Publishing Co.
Subscription Customer Service
655 Avenue of the Americas
New York, NY 10010

F&B News
Hospitality Communications
1251 West Webster Street, Suite 2
Chicago, IL 60614

Foodservice & Hospitality Magazine
Kostuch Communications Ltd.
980 Yonge Street, Suite 400
Toronto, ON M4W 2J8
Canada

Healthcare Foodservice Magazine
International Publishing Company of
     America, Inc.
665 La Villa Drive
Miami Springs, FL 33166-6095

Hospitality Law
Magna Publications
2718 Dryden Drive
Madison, WI 53704-3005

Hotel & Motel Management
Advanstar Communications
7500 Old Oak Boulevard
Cleveland, OH 44130

Hotel & Resort Industry
Coastal Communications Corporation
488 Madison Avenue
New York, NY 10022-5772

Hotel Business
ICD Publications
1393 Veterans Highway, #214N
Hauppauge, NY 11788

Hotels
Cahners Publishing
1350 East Touhy Avenue
Des Plaines, IL 60018-3358

HSMAI Marketing Review
1300 L Street NW, Suite 800
Washington, DC 20005

International Hotel Trends
Pannell Kerr Forster
420 Lexington Avenue, Suite 2400
New York, NY 10170

Lodging
American Hotel & Motel Association
1201 New York Avenue, NW
Washington, DC 20005-3931

Lodging Hospitality
Penton Publishing
1100 Superior Avenue
P.O. Box 95759
Cleveland, OH 44114-2518

Nation's Restaurant News
Lebhar-Friedman, Inc.
425 Park Avenue
New York, NY 10022-3506

Resort Management
Western Specialty Publications, Inc.
2431 Morena Boulevard
San Diego, CA 92110

Restaurant Business
Bill Communications, Inc.
355 Park Avenue South, 3rd Floor
New York, NY 10010-1706

Restaurants USA
National Restaurant Association
1200 Seventeenth Street, NW
Washington, DC 20036-3097

Chapter Outline

Basics of Telephone Communication
    Telephone Etiquette
    Telephone Communication Skills
    Listening Skills
Outgoing Calls
    Prospect and Qualifying Calls
    Appointment Calls
        Reaching the Decision-Maker
        Opening the Call
        The Presentation
        Overcoming Objections
        Setting the Appointment
    Sales Calls
        Closing Techniques
    Promotional Calls
    Service Calls
    Public Relations Calls
Incoming Calls
    Reservations
        Central Reservations Systems
    Responses to Advertising
    Inquiries
Telephone Sales Operations
    Telephone Sales Blitzes
    Telemarketing Operations
        Telemarketing Scripts
        Telemarketing Programs

5

Telephone Sales

WHILE FACE-TO-FACE SELLING is the most effective way to sell, the telephone, if used properly, can be one of the most economical ways to find—and sell to—prospective guests and clients. Salespeople and other employees can use this sales instrument to:

- Search for sales leads
- Identify most-likely-to-buy prospects (qualify accounts)
- Make sales appointments
- Blitz a market to reach prospects and clients (this technique will be discussed later in the chapter)
- Service local accounts in an economical and timely manner
- Service geographically isolated accounts
- Assist guests in making reservations and arranging for return visits to the property
- Inform callers about higher-priced rooms and suites that would be better suited to their needs
- Sell additional services, such as room service and the hotel's restaurants, to registered guests
- Receive direct mail response inquiries
- Convert inquiries generated by ads (especially ads with toll-free numbers) into sales
- Secure market research data quickly
- Penetrate new markets
- Reactivate former accounts
- Increase the profitability of marginal accounts
- Announce promotional news to clients and generate business for special promotions
- Follow up bids, proposals, direct mail campaigns, and leads developed at trade shows

Since the telephone is used in so many different ways, telephone sales may be delegated to several groups of employees within a property. Incoming calls for individual guest reservations may go through a front desk or reservations staff; calls promoting room service or the property's restaurant may be made by switchboard operators; sales calls may be handled by salespeople or top management. No matter how calls are delegated, both incoming and outgoing calls play an important role in a property's overall sales effort.

Large independent hotels and hotel chains may employ a telemarketing staff to research data, sell, and/or set appointments for the sales staff. Telemarketing—used solely or in combination with media advertising, direct mail, and face-to-face selling—is being increasingly used to build business, offer better service, and generate market data. In this chapter, we will discuss this trend in marketing as well as detail the telephone's value as both a sales and public relations tool.

Basics of Telephone Communication

Many telephone calls are potential sales calls, so it is important that property employees have good communication skills. Telephone selling is more difficult than face-to-face sales because you can't read the prospect's body language during a telephone call or see the prospect's office decor, which often provides insights into the prospect through family photographs, trophies, and recognition plaques.

Since a friendly smile and a firm handshake can't be conveyed over the telephone, the words you use and your pronunciation, tone of voice, and delivery take on greater importance. Methods most commonly used to make a good impression and sell the property over the telephone include telephone etiquette, telephone communication skills, and listening skills.

Telephone Etiquette

The lodging industry offers more than just rooms and guest services. It offers hospitality, and friendliness and courtesy are an important part of any interaction between a property employee and a potential guest. When using the telephone, property employees must communicate warmth and a willingness to be of service.

Unfortunately, sensitivity, empathy, and politeness are often lacking in telephone calls selling hospitality products. The salesperson who employs these courtesies, then, can stand out from the crowd and make a positive impression. You can get this "edge" from the very beginning, by simply asking the prospect if it is a convenient time to talk!

If it is a bad time for the prospect, sales efforts are hampered before they even begin. By respecting the prospect's time, you greatly increase the chances of a successful future contact. If the prospect suggests calling at another time, it is important to follow through. Many salespeople fail to follow up, and those who do have a much greater chance of success.

Telephone etiquette begins by letting the potential guest know that he or she is important to the property. One way to do this is to use phrases that will put the potential guest at ease and show the property's concern for him or her (see Exhibit 1). It is important that the property's representative be polite and understanding, and that the unseen guest feels that someone is concerned about what he or she has to say.

There are a number of other ways salespeople can make a good impression:

Exhibit 1   Sample Telephone Etiquette Guidelines

THIS IS BETTER	THAN THIS
Answering the Call	
"Days Inn Reservations, Mr. Eaton speaking. How may I help you?"	"Days Inn Reservations."
"Days Inn Reservations, Ms. Wood speaking. How may I help you?"	"Days Inn, can I help you?"
Making Sure	
"Would you repeat your name for me please?"	"What name did you say? I can't hear you."
"Would you spell that for me, please?"	"What did you say? Talk a little louder."
"I'm sorry. I didn't get the name of the person."	"I can't understand what you're trying to say."
Acknowledging	
"Yes, Mr. Martinez. I'll be happy to request that for you."	"O.K. I'll do what I can."
"Yes, Ms. Jones, I'd be glad to check that for you."	"All right. Let me see."
Leaving the Line	
"Would you mind waiting while I check, please?"	"Just a minute."
	"I'll try to find out."
Returning to the Line	
"Mr. Glazer, thank you for waiting. I have that information."	"The date on that reservation was June 18."
"Ms. Muzzall, I'm sorry to have kept you waiting."	"Are you still waiting?"
Completing the Call	
"Thank you for calling Days Inn, Ms. Yang."	"Bye-bye." "OK." "So long." "That's OK." "All right, bye."

Courtesy of Days Inns of America, Inc.

1. *Adequate preparation.* Always have pertinent information at hand before calling a client. By being prepared, you can organize your thoughts, be ready to answer questions, and avoid wasting the client's time.

2. *Adequate time.* Take steps to make sure you will not be interrupted while calling a client. An interruption can irritate a client and may result in the loss of a sale. Clients deserve your undivided attention. Some properties even have a policy of allocating specific blocks of time during which salespeople can make calls without interruption.

3. *Direct contact.* Always dial the call personally. It can irritate a client if a secretary or receptionist places the call and the client is put on hold or asked to wait for you to come to the phone.

4. *Courtesy and respect.* Intermediaries (secretaries, receptionists, clerks, assistants, etc.) should be treated courteously. Being arrogant or disrespectful greatly decreases chances of getting through to a prospect.

5. *Brevity.* Calls should be kept short and to the point unless the client wants to chat. When the call has been completed, let the client hang up first. Avoid giving the impression of being in a hurry, and never slam the receiver down while the client is still on the line.

6. *Timing.* It is important to respect the hours kept by clients. As a general rule, avoid calling during the late afternoon or early morning hours. Of course, the client's time zone should also be considered.

These simple guidelines will go a long way toward building courteous telephone habits among the sales staff. But sales and goodwill can be increased even more by understanding how to speak effectively over the telephone.

Telephone Communication Skills

You should check yourself often on these important communication skills:

1. *Tone of voice.* Your voice should reflect sincerity, pleasantness, confidence, and interest. It is especially important to have a "verbal smile"—something you can achieve by smiling as you speak. Also, too many salespeople make the mistake of shouting into the receiver, especially on long distance calls. Speak into the receiver as if the client were sitting across the desk.

2. *Pitch.* A low-pitched voice is desirable. Low voices carry better and are more pleasant to the listener.[1]

3. *Inflection.* Avoid talking in a monotone. Enunciate clearly and emphasize key words; you can generate interest by the way you raise or lower your voice.

4. *Understandability.* Avoid talking with anything (gum, a cigarette, pen or pencil, etc.) in your mouth. Be careful not to talk too fast. If you talk too rapidly, your words may be misunderstood, or the listener may be so fascinated by your talking speed that the message is lost.

It is a good practice for employees who use the telephone a lot, whether they be salespeople, switchboard operators, front desk agents, or top management, to check their voices on a tape recorder. Every employee should work to develop a pleasant telephone voice free of slang, jargon, and irritating habits. An enthusiastic, well-modulated voice is half of a successful telephone call.

Listening Skills

The other half of a successful telephone call is listening to what the prospective client or guest has to say. A salesperson in particular should be aware of several keys to good listening:

1. *Limit talking.* No one can talk and listen at the same time. The prospect should get a chance to air his or her views, and these views should be given careful attention—no interrupting or jumping to conclusions before the prospect has

finished speaking. As a general rule, if the prospect does most of the talking during a telephone sales call, it is much easier to make a sale because you will know the prospect's needs and concerns.

2. *Get involved.* It is usually much easier to be enthusiastic and alert when sitting erect; leaning back and relaxing often interferes with listening. You should also try to put yourself in the prospect's place, listening for clues to what is important to the prospect. You can learn a great deal about the prospect's needs by the way things are said.

   Successful salespeople also get involved by empathizing with the caller. Phrases such as "I know how you feel" are excellent ways to show the prospect that what he or she is saying is important to you.

3. *Ask questions.* Asking questions generates prospect involvement and shows that you are interested. Questions are an effective way to keep the prospect talking and gather additional information. Ask "Why is that important to you?" or "What else can you tell me about that?" and take notes as the prospect shares views and needs. These responses can be used later in a presentation to build support for the sales message.

Outgoing Calls

Outgoing telephone calls can be divided into a number of categories: prospect calls, qualifying calls, appointment calls, sales calls, promotional calls, service calls, and public relations calls. Since most salespeople use the telephone to set appointments rather than make a sale, this section will focus mainly on appointment telephone calls.

Prospect and Qualifying Calls

The objective of prospect calls is to gather information and learn the names of decision-makers. Many calls that start out as prospect calls end up as qualifying calls. Qualifying calls determine if prospects need or can afford the products and services offered by the property (see Exhibit 2). Qualifying calls are not sales calls, but are used to find out if an individual or company warrants an in-person sales call. This can be determined by asking several questions:

- Does your company have a need for hotel accommodations, meeting rooms, or banquet facilities?

- How many people travel for your company? What is the destination of most company travel?

- Who decides where your traveling staff stays? What hotels are you currently using?

- Who usually makes the reservations for your traveling staff?

If a prospect seems a likely candidate for an in-person sales call, further information may be gathered by asking these questions:

Exhibit 2   Sample Prospect Qualification Form

Prospect Qualification Form

COMPANY NAME: _____

ADDRESS: _____

CITY/STATE/ZIP: _____

PHONE: _____   CONTACT: _____

1. *Introduction*: "My name is _____, and I'm calling you on behalf of L'Ermitage Hotels located in West Hollywood/Beverly Hills. Can you tell me who handles the travel and meeting arrangements for your company?"

   _____

   _____

2. After locating the right contact, state the purpose of your call and ask if any of the company's business travelers stay overnight in the Los Angeles area. If so, ask "Are you familiar with our hotels?"

   _____

   _____

3. "Do you use an outside travel agency?"

   _____

4. If so, "What is the name of the agency involved?"

   _____

   OR

   "Do you use an outside travel agency? If so, may I ask which one you work with?"

   _____

5. "Can you estimate how many room nights annually you reserve in the Los Angeles area?"

   _____

6. "Aside from individual travel, do you hold meetings in the Los Angeles area?"

   _____

   "How often?"_____

7. "Would you be interested in speaking with one of our sales managers regarding our corporate rate program for your upcoming meetings?"_____

8. Thank the individual for his or her time, and state that you will follow up in an appropriate manner (via telephone or by sending brochures and a general information letter).

Forms such as this one are used to determine if corporations or firms have a need for the products or services offered by a property. Qualifying saves the property time and money by ensuring that salespeople call on promising accounts. (Courtesy of L'Ermitage Hotels, Beverly Hills, California)

- How many meetings does your company hold throughout the year? What time(s) of the year are meetings normally held and how long do they last?

- What types of meetings do you typically hold? What types of facilities do you need?

- How do you decide where to hold a meeting? What criteria do you use to decide on a location?

- When are location decisions made, and who makes them?

When researching information on national corporations, it is necessary to probe deeper and get the answers to these questions:

- Does the corporation have a travel department or a corporate travel directory that advises the corporation's business travelers of properties in which they are authorized to stay? Who heads the department for corporate travel?

- Who decides which properties are used? Who makes guestroom and meeting room reservations? Why are certain locations chosen?

- Is there a written contract or any kind of obligation to the property currently being used? If so, when does this obligation expire?

- How many people travel for the corporation? How many guestroom nights are reserved? What department has the most travelers? Do business travelers carry corporate identification?

- Do business travelers pay their own bills or are accommodations billed to the corporation? Do travelers pay on a per diem (by the day) basis?

- From which company properties do most business travelers originate? What is the destination of the majority of the corporation's business travelers?

A good approach to take when making telephone prospect calls is to follow a simple who, what, when, and where format:

Fact-Finding Question	Follow-Up Information Generated
Who?	Future account data—name, address, etc.—as well as description of prospect's business.
What?	Prospect's needs for guestrooms, meeting space, catered events, and other facilities/services.
When?	Months, weeks, or specific dates for which hotel facilities or services are needed.
Where?	Properties with whom the prospect is currently dealing.

The answers to these questions will give the information necessary to prepare a sales presentation. You are now in a position to answer exactly how your

Exhibit 3   Sample Appointment Telephone Call Dialogue

Reaching the Decision-Maker

"Hello, my name is Dan Stern. Could you help me by giving me the name of the person who makes the convention planning decisions for your firm?"

Opening the Call

"Good morning, Ms. Merrill. My name is Dan Stern. I'm with Complete Resorts International. I'm calling to explain one of the most innovative programs in convention planning available today!"

The Presentation

"Our unique services will help you save time and money on all of your convention meeting room and banquet needs. We have recently developed a program that includes three exciting features to help you stage successful meetings: your own private operations-headquarters room adjacent to the meeting area; the use of our hotel's limousine to pick up your VIPs; and your own personal meeting aide—a fully qualified staff assistant, supplied by our hotel—to handle any last-minute problems for you!"

Setting the Appointment

"I know you will be as excited as we are about our new services that will help you stage successful meetings. When can we meet for just 30 minutes to discuss your upcoming convention for your independent distributors?

"Which day of the week would be best for you, Tuesday or Wednesday?

"What time is most convenient for you on that day, 10:00 A.M. or 2:00 P.M.?

"Great! I'll see you on Tuesday at 2:00 P.M. in your office at 1234 Goodsale Road just west of the Interstate. Thank you for your time, Ms. Merrill. I'm looking forward to meeting you in person. Have a good day!"

Note that in setting the appointment, the salesperson did not set up the possibility of a "no" answer, but asked a forced-choice question that gave the prospect a choice of two alternatives: Tuesday or Wednesday. Other typical forced-choice questions include: "Would you prefer to meet in the morning or afternoon?" and "Is the beginning or the latter part of the week best for you?"

---

property can meet the prospect's needs, and, when appropriate, you can end the prospecting call with a request for an appointment.

Appointment Calls

Telephone appointment calls are used to briefly introduce a prospective client to the features and services offered by the property and ask for an appointment to meet face-to-face (see Exhibit 3). The object of an appointment call is to get the prospect to agree to an appointment, not to make a sale. Appointment calls save time for the salesperson and the prospect because they allow time for both to prepare for a future face-to-face sales presentation. Having an appointment also reduces the likelihood that the sales presentation will be interrupted.

Before making an appointment call, you should have all necessary information available—prospect sheets, account records (if any), prices, firm and tentative booking dates (if applicable), and general property information. You should also develop an outlined presentation to help you remember key questions and sales points.

Exhibit 4   Reaching the Decision-Maker

Intermediary:	"Why do you want to know [the name of the decision-maker]?"
Salesperson:	"I'm putting together a list of people who would like to be kept abreast of some of the ways other local businesses are reducing their costs through the use of training meetings. I'm sure your manager would be interested in receiving this information."
Intermediary:	"What is the purpose of this call?"
Salesperson:	"I'm sorry, but I can only discuss that with your manager. Can you put me through to her, please?"
Intermediary:	"Is this a sales call?"
Salesperson:	"No, I'm not trying to sell anything on the phone. I'm just doing research on how area businesses are meeting their training needs. I was hoping that your manager could give me some ideas."

Handling the objections of a secretary, receptionist, or other intermediary is often necessary to determine the name of or reach the decision-maker. These questions are typical of those used to screen calls; the responses given are guides to handling these objections.

Like face-to-face selling, the telephone appointment call is made up of several steps:

1. Reaching the decision-maker

2. Opening the call

3. The presentation

4. Overcoming objections

5. Setting the appointment

Reaching the Decision-Maker. If a prospect call has not been made, you can learn the name of the decision-maker through an intermediary at the firm or corporation. While intermediaries can be helpful in providing the name of the decision-maker, they can also prove to be obstacles when it comes to reaching him or her (see Exhibit 4). Appealing to the intermediary's sense of responsibility—presenting ideas that might help the decision-maker, for example—often helps you avoid the objections and barriers that intermediaries can present.

Prepare an opening statement. You must initiate the conversation when the telephone is picked up, so you should prepare an opening statement. Since the intermediary is paid to protect the time of the decision-maker, an introductory statement such as "This is Donna Scott from the Concorde Hotel. May I speak with Bob Cross?" is not likely to get you through the ring of protection surrounding most decision-makers.

Instead, you should appeal to a need—of either the decision-maker or the company—and to the intermediary's sense of responsibility: "The reason I'm calling today is because our hotel has recently developed an incentive tour package that other top incentive companies have said is the best hotel value in years. I'd like to ask Mr. Cross a few questions to determine if this would be of any value to him." This type of opening, spoken in a confident, expectant tone of voice, will appeal to the intermediary's need to keep the decision-maker abreast of ways to save time and money for the firm.

Develop respect and rapport. Since many decision-makers rely on their secretaries or associates to screen calls and advise them of calls worthy of reply, it is important to show respect to intermediaries. Learn the names of secretaries and receptionists and list these names in your diary of clients' telephone numbers. Calling the intermediary by name is highly effective, as is timing the call so it will not interrupt a busy schedule. (You should especially avoid making calls on Monday mornings and Friday afternoons.) Timing the call shows that you respect the time of both the intermediary and the decision-maker.

Don't leave a message. There may be times when a decision-maker cannot be reached. In most cases, when you are told that the decision-maker is out of town, out on a business call, or on the telephone, the intermediary is telling the truth, but you should be concerned if you are repeatedly told "He isn't available," "She's in a meeting," or "He's in conference." In these cases, *never* leave a message asking the decision-maker to call back; instead, ask the intermediary to suggest a time when it is more convenient to call. This technique is both polite and effective because it puts the intermediary's credibility on the line. You can call back and begin with this type of statement: "Good afternoon, Ms. Smith, this is Ms. Jones calling from Best Resort. When I called before, you suggested that this would be a good time to reach Mr. Sullivan. Is he in?"

Opening the Call. Once you have reached the prospect, a good opening is essential to hold the prospect's interest. As with a face-to-face sales call, you should introduce yourself, give the name of the property you represent, and immediately state the purpose of the call. A statement such as "The reason for my call is that most companies want to house their relocating executives in hotels convenient to company headquarters. Our hotel is located just three blocks from your offices, and we are now offering a special corporate program" is far more effective than opening with "I just called to say hello," or "I'm calling because my general manager suggested you might be a good account, and you're on my list of prospects to call today."

Presenting a benefit—and showing sincere interest in meeting a prospect's needs—is a vital step in opening a call. Developing rapport is important at this early stage, and there are several techniques that can be used to make the prospect more receptive to the presentation to follow.

First, use the prospect's name often. The prospect's name is important to him or her and, in most cases, the more you use it (without becoming overly familiar or offensive), the better the prospect will feel toward you.

Another good way to build rapport is to use a third-party endorsement. You might say: "Mr. Pritchard, a friend of yours—Jane Steward of Woodcraft, Incorporated—suggested that I call because she felt you would be interested in our banquet facilities." The use of third-party endorsements gives credibility to the sales message and provides a common meeting ground between you and the prospect.

An appointment call should be kept short, unless the prospect wants to chat or ask questions. If it is obvious that the prospect is busy or in a totally unreceptive mood, try to get a brief message across and offer to call back at a more convenient time. If the prospect seems interested or at least willing to listen, you can move on to the presentation.

The Presentation. For an appointment call, the purpose of the presentation is to get the prospect interested enough in your property to agree to a face-to-face meeting. During the presentation, refer to your notes, if necessary, to make sure you stay on track. Remember to sell the benefits of the property rather than the features. In telephone selling, you must paint "word pictures." Benefit statements must be specific. When talking to a meeting planner, for example, it is far better to give a descriptive benefit ("When you book your meeting with us, your group is assigned to one person who has the authority to ensure that everything is handled to your satisfaction; this person will have all the answers for you at every stage to make sure your meeting is successful") than a vague benefit ("We have a great convention service department").

The use of power words such as "excellent," "guaranteed," "quality," and "successful" greatly enhances a presentation and can generate prospect interest. Power words are words that have more "sales power" than others. Power words are dynamic, expressive, and highly descriptive, helping clients to "see" the hotel's services over the phone. Power words are an important part of a sales vocabulary, along with personal words like "you," "me," "we," "us," and "our."[2]

The importance of power words is well-known in the industry. Jeff Erickson, a hospitality sales and marketing trainer, says that when his salespeople call a prospect or client, "they use the pronoun 'we' instead of 'I.' Using 'we' communicates they have the power of the company behind them. We have three words we stress, 'please,' 'thank you,' and 'you.'"[3]

Overcoming Objections. Be prepared to overcome objections to specific points of the presentation. It is much easier to handle objections if you have planned some answers to common objections and have backup material available that will support your claims (see Exhibit 5). Positive public relations pieces and complimentary letters from satisfied customers are important sales aids. Such material also can be read before a sales call to give you the enthusiasm you need to sell the benefits of the property.

As with in-person selling, it is very important during an appointment telephone call to listen carefully to objections and avoid arguing with the prospect. The prospect's objections will often provide clues that will enable you to revise the presentation to meet the prospect's needs or concerns.

Setting the Appointment. Since most appointments are made or lost during the first few minutes of the telephone call, you will want to ask for the appointment early. By offering choices of a day—"Would Wednesday or Thursday be more convenient?"—you can lead the prospect into a commitment to a face-to-face sales call.

Sometimes the prospect may be unwilling to set an appointment or may request that you send additional information or a brochure for review. If you are

Exhibit 5   Overcoming Common Prospect Objections

Common objections should be anticipated, and responses readied, before a salesperson makes a sales call. These are typical objections that might be voiced by a prospect.

Prospect:	"I'm not interested."
Salesperson:	"I can understand that you might not realize the values offered by our resort from just a brief explanation over the phone, Ms. Kingsbury. But didn't you tell me that you were considering an incentive package for your top salespeople? I'd like to show you in person how our resort can give you just the package you need—at a good value."
Prospect:	"I don't have time to see you now."
Salesperson:	"Mr. Portigo, I realize you have a busy schedule. That's why I want to invite you to visit our hotel for a complimentary lunch or dinner. We can discuss your convention needs over a delicious meal, without taking a lot of time from your business day."
Prospect:	"Just send me a brochure."
Salesperson:	"I'd be happy to send our brochure, but I'd prefer to deliver it personally so I can answer any concerns you might have and explain how groups similar to yours have benefited from our facilities and services. Would 1:30 on Wednesday or Thursday be a good time to visit with you?"
Prospect:	"We can't afford to hold outside training seminars."
Salesperson:	"I know you are aware that sales is a highly competitive area, and that training has proven to be an effective sales tool. Our low rates make it possible for firms like yours to hold sales training seminars at a price you can afford."

unable to get an appointment during the conversation, make arrangements to call back on another day:

Salesperson:	"I'd be happy to send a brochure on our sports program. If you receive it by Tuesday, would you have a chance to review it before the end of the week?"
Prospect:	"Oh, certainly."
Salesperson:	"Good! I'll give you a call next Friday morning to see if you have any questions."

This type of approach opens the door for the salesperson's next call:

Intermediary:	"What is this regarding?"
Salesperson:	"Mr. Prospect is expecting my call to discuss the literature I sent regarding saving money on your school's team travel expenses."

Exhibit 6   Turning Features into Benefits

It is important that salespeople sell benefits, not features. To assist salespeople in thinking "benefits," the words "so that" can be used.

Feature		Benefit
"We have electronic door locks	SO THAT	you will enjoy a feeling of security."
"We offer 24-hour room service	SO THAT	you may enjoy a meal in the comfort of your own room."
"Every room has a desk with a telephone	SO THAT	you can take care of personal business efficiently."
"Every room features a complete package of name-brand amenities	SO THAT	you can travel light."
"We have express check-out	SO THAT	you can enjoy the convenience of a timely departure."

The selling sentence could also be reversed—starting with the benefit and backing it up with the feature. The word "because" would link the benefit to the feature:

Benefit		Feature
"You will enjoy a feeling of security	BECAUSE	we have electronic door locks."
"You can enjoy a meal in the comfort of your room	BECAUSE	we offer 24-hour room service."

If an appointment is made, end the call by confirming the date, time, and location of the appointment, express thanks, and promise to follow up the conversation with additional details (property brochures, menus, etc.) and a letter confirming the date of the face-to-face meeting. Ideally, this meeting should be held at your property so you can show the prospect the property's features and facilities.

Sales Calls

Telephone sales calls may be made by a salesperson or by a telemarketer working with a sales script. Hotel chains and many large independent hotels work with specially trained telephone sales teams that call on prospects and concentrate on getting bookings or commitments by phone. Unlike an appointment call, the objective of a telephone sales call is to make an immediate sale, and the caller must either close during the conversation or make arrangements to call back on another day.

Just as in a face-to-face sales presentation, it is important that you sell benefits rather than features when you sell over the phone. If you tell a prospect "We have electronic door locks," you've only done half the job; you can't assume that the prospect will understand the benefits of this feature (added security, for example.) People buy benefits, not features, and benefits must be clearly spelled out to avoid misinterpretation by the potential guest or client (see Exhibit 6).

Closing Techniques. There are several techniques that can be used to close a telephone sale.

Asking for a sale can be as simple as saying, "Shall I reserve a meeting room for your district managers on Monday, July 12th?" However, this technique limits the prospect to a yes or no response, and limits you to one specific area.

A more effective technique is to *assume a sale*. Assuming a sale assumes a "yes" answer on the part of the prospect: "All right, Mrs. Grauberger, I'll confirm your group at our Lakeview Downtown Inn on the 30th of November. As I said, the rates are $42. Now let me read back the booking requirements."

Forced-choice questions limit the prospect to choosing from the alternatives presented by the salesperson, and provide the salesperson with more control than the previous two methods. Examples of forced-choice questions include: "Shall I book your tour group for Friday night or Saturday morning?" and "Would your distributors like to try our buffet when they arrive or will they be dining in our Red Lion restaurant?" Forced-choice questions make an effective close because they create a choice between positive alternatives; the salesperson is asking not *whether*, but *which*.

The *pause close* is uniquely effective in telephone selling because silence in a strictly audio medium is difficult for most people to tolerate. A typical pause close may be set up as follows: "Okay, Mr. Fritz. Can I go ahead and book you at the Bayside Inn in Bayport at $65?" (Pause.)

The first person to speak following the pause loses. If the salesperson speaks, the prospect is taken off the decision "hook"; if the prospect speaks, he or she must make a decision.

Closing on an objection acknowledges the prospect's objection, but counters the objection with a benefit (or benefits) and asks for the sale: "That may be true, Mr. Butler. However, the guestrooms will have tables, making your employees' stay more conducive to after-meeting work sessions. Shall I reserve the large meeting room or the two small ones?" or "I agree, Mr. Morton, that our property is away from the big city and its entertainment, but imagine how distraction-free this sales meeting will be! How many rooms will you be needing?"

A *series-of-minor-agreements close* summarizes the positive statements made by the prospect: "You said that our rooms are comfortable, correct? And you agreed that our location was suitable. And didn't you say that our 'Budget Meeting Plan' is just what you're looking for? Then may I set up your annual sales meeting for the 20th to the 25th?"

As you can see, there are a number of effective telephone techniques that may be used in obtaining a commitment from a prospect. Even though many telemarketing operations use a standardized telephone sales script, telemarketers as well as salespeople should become familiar with these closes.

Promotional Calls

Promotional calls can be made by salespeople, the telemarketing staff, or top management to introduce special promotions. For example, one hotel advertised in community newspapers to promote its wedding reception package. The ad requested that recently engaged couples contact the catering sales manager by dialing the "hot line" telephone number listed in the ad. The catering sales manager supplemented these incoming calls by calling couples who had recently announced their engagements in the local newspaper and explaining the wedding reception package. The property was able to secure 15 new accounts in one week!

Service Calls

Client satisfaction and loyalty can be developed through service calls, whether the calls are made just to keep in touch or are follow-up calls to clients after a sale has been made. Clients need to know they are important, and service calls are essential to maintaining and building business for the property. If changes are anticipated before a function, or if problems occurred during a function, a service call does far more to show concern and smooth over the situation than a letter.

Public Relations Calls

Public relations calls are made to generate goodwill. In one case, a restaurant manager made low-key telephone calls to past regulars who had not been to the restaurant for some time. The impact was immediate—the restaurant had 25 additional covers per day! Such person-to-person contact can generate additional rooms business as well. If a general manager picks up the telephone to respond to a guest's complimentary letter, it can have a great impact on the guest—he or she is more likely to feel that the property values his or her business and will want to return.

Incoming Calls

No matter what type of call is received by a hotel, it is essential that the caller receive a positive first impression. When a call is answered at the hotel, the spotlight is on the person representing the property, and any unprofessional behavior, such as carrying on a conversation with a co-worker while the caller is on the line, may result in thousands of dollars in lost business.

It is both a courtesy and good business to answer the telephone *promptly*. When a call is not answered right away, the caller may become impatient and hang up; waiting time always seems longer than it is, and time is especially valuable to busy executives. Nancy Austin, co-author of *A Passion for Excellence*, explained in a speech how many callers may feel:

> During the first ring, we can hardly wait to speak to someone on the other end! But by the third ring your patient customer has already decided, 'This is it, if they don't answer the phone I'm calling the next hotel.' And by six rings, forget it! They are so thoroughly disgusted that if they are asked for a recommendation, the research shows they will *go out of their way* to disrecommend that place that didn't bother to pick up the phone. And you know why? They say, 'They didn't care.'[4]

Once the telephone receiver is picked up, the hotel's representative must be ready to talk. Whether the call is to the switchboard, the reservations department, or a sales office extension, the property's representative should begin the call with a greeting, the name of the property, his or her name, and a courteous phrase:

Insider Insights

Thomas A. Elbe
Vice President, Sales
Meridien Hotels
New York City

Thomas Elbe originally had his mind set on restaurant management, but soon after enrolling in the Hotel and Restaurant Department of New York City Technical College he focused on hotel management and continued in that direction at the University of Nevada, Las Vegas. Immediately after graduation, he joined Americana Hotels in an operations position, and never considered sales as an option. But after 2 1/2 years, an opportunity arose and he joined the sales force of the 1,850-room Americana Hotel in New York City. Elbe is now celebrating his 18th anniversary in hotel marketing and sales—including positions as director of sales for the Loews Hotels, director of convention sales for the New York City Convention and Visitors Bureau, regional director of marketing for Inter-Continental Hotels, vice president/sales for Nikko Hotels International, and his present position as vice president, sales for Meridien Hotels.

The telephone is valuable not only as a selling tool, but also for prospecting and qualifying potential business. While there are many sources for client lists, the information on those lists is limited, and it would be impossible to qualify each person face-to-face, especially since it's estimated that personal sales call costs run as high as $250.

By using the telephone, you can inexpensively and efficiently determine if a client has the potential for your product. You can virtually initiate contact with a client, qualify the business, and "seal the deal" over the telephone. Although this type of selling isn't as personal as direct contact, it's certainly an important and cost-effective way of doing business.

Some companies have the luxury of a telemarketing staff, while others use existing staff to prospect. Another idea that is becoming more prevalent is to cross-train or combine jobs. Essentially, this means training employees to become proficient in more than one area, thereby making them more useful to the organization while broadening their skills at the same time. An excellent example of this is to have the staff of the reservations office use the telephone to prospect and qualify for the property during down times. This is ideal for our needs, and creates a situation in which everyone wins; the hotel gets the required information and the employee benefits from personal and professional growth.

The client's first impression of a salesperson sets the tone for future relations. The appearance, approach, professionalism, and perseverance of salespeople are their most significant attributes. And we must not forget that the same is true when the telephone is used as a sales tool!

The voice, the level of professionalism, and the overall approach of a salesperson can all be quickly evaluated by the prospect over the telephone. And, to make the most effective use of the telephone, the telephone salesperson, like the direct contact salesperson, must persevere!

"Good morning! This is the New York Hilton; Tom Baker speaking. How may I help you?"

At times it is necessary to put a caller on hold. "Hold" is not synonymous with "ignore." If a call cannot be routed or a question answered without leaving the line, the caller should be given an explanation of the delay. Instead of just saying "Please hold," the employee should say to the caller, "May I put you on hold for just a minute while I find that information for you?" If the caller is kept on the line for more than a minute, he or she should be given progress reports. The person waiting may be told, "Mr. McClendon, I'm still checking on your reservation. Do you mind waiting a little longer?" These progress reports assure the caller that he or she has not been forgotten, and may prevent the caller from getting angry or irritated. When the employee returns to the line, it helps get the caller's attention to begin with his or her name: "Mr. Sullivan, I have those figures for you now" or "Ms. Mercer, thanks so much for holding." This shows courtesy to the caller and may prevent having to repeat all or part of the information.

Sometimes the caller must be transferred. Far too often, the caller is transferred throughout the hotel before reaching the proper party. To avoid this situation, every attempt should be made to determine the purpose of the call and the person who can help. Then, the call can be transferred to the right party with a statement such as, "The catering manager, Mr. Philip Rodriguez, would be glad to take care of that for you. Shall I transfer you to Philip, or would you prefer to leave your name and number so he can call you?"

Incoming telephone calls that can lead to sales fall into three basic categories: reservations, responses to advertising, and inquiries.

Reservations

For years the telephone has played an important role in making reservations. Today, coupled with sophisticated computer systems, it is an even more effective sales tool. At small properties, reservations duties may be handled by a small reservations staff or the front desk agents, while at larger properties reservations may be handled by an extensive in-house staff.

Since the reservationist (or front desk agent) is often the public's first contact with the property, more and more emphasis is being put on the training of reservations personnel. Because of the sales-oriented nature of the position, reservationists must be trained in the importance of professionalism, product knowledge, and basic selling techniques.

Professionalism includes the ability to build rapport with callers. A voice that projects warmth is essential, as is the ability to listen to determine the potential guest's needs. Product knowledge not only involves knowing the property and the surrounding area, but also understanding and being able to communicate hotel policy regarding rates and booking procedures. Basic sales techniques include using the prospect's name often (especially during the close), selling the options available, and asking for the sale.

Central Reservations Systems. In addition to their own reservations personnel, many properties use a central reservations system (CRS), accessed through a

A hotel's in-house reservations staff is often the first point of contact between hotel and guest, so reservationists should be courteous and knowledgeable about basic selling techniques. (Courtesy of Opryland Hotel, Nashville, Tennessee)

toll-free telephone number, to facilitate bookings. This approach has proven so successful that many properties now operate two or more toll-free systems: one to serve the public and another for the exclusive use of travel agents or corporate meeting planners (see Exhibit 7).

A CRS, whether designed for a single property or a chain, includes a database that features such basic information as property facts (number of rooms, room rates, booking policy, etc.); information about area attractions and events; travel information (nearby airports, transportation available, etc.); and, in the case of chain systems, information on other properties in the chain.

One example of a chain-wide system is Westin Hotels' Central Reservations Office in Omaha, Nebraska. This system, considered one of the most sophisticated in the country, is linked to numerous airline reservations systems to better serve travel agents (travel agents account for 65% of Westin's bookings) as well as individual and corporate travelers. When a prospective guest dials the Westin toll-free number, a reservations operator asks which hotel he or she is interested in (a hotel is suggested if the caller desires that information), and the caller is given full information on the selected property (rates, availabilities, etc.) from data on the operator's computer screen. When the reservation transaction is completed, the information is transmitted to the appropriate hotel as a booking. This process takes just minutes, and the reservation is stored in the computer for future reference.

Since systems such as Westin's are extremely costly, it is important to utilize them fully. First and foremost, the information on each property must be kept up-to-date and complete. If there is a change in amenities or new room rates and weekend packages are offered at Property X, for example, the appropriate person

Exhibit 7   Toll-Free Numbers for Special Markets

at the CRS office must be informed. This information can then be included on the screen the CRS operators call up for Property X. (This screen can also be called up by someone at Property X, to make sure the information displayed has been updated.) It is important to include *all* information that may influence a sale—the property's proximity to an airport, the opening of a new recreational facility, or the staff's fluency in a foreign language, for example, can influence a buying decision.

In addition to highly trained personnel, computer technology, and toll-free numbers, there are other advantages to a CRS:

1. A CRS can help with yield management. Most of today's central reservations systems can be updated on-line to reflect changing market conditions and rooms inventory (as rooms are filled, rates can be changed on the screen). And the CRS can assist in filling rooms with the market segments most desirable to the property. If a property wishes to fill 85% of its rooms with business travelers and allocate only 15% to transient business, it can reflect this inventory on the computer screen.

2. A CRS is an effective tool for measuring sales and marketing efforts. Most systems provide detailed reports that show exactly where business is coming from—what types of rooms are being sold at what rates, how many rooms are being sold through travel agents, how many group bookings are realized, and so on. These reports can be used to evaluate promotional efforts and discover weaknesses in the property's marketing strategy. An absence of travel agent bookings, for example, may mean that there is a problem with paying commissions promptly.

3. A CRS can evaluate its own effectiveness—statistics generated can be used to calculate the "conversion factor"—the percentage of toll-free calls converted to sales.

4. CRS computer technology has not only made it easier to make reservations and track sales efforts, but, ironically, has increased personalization. Details of a past stay can be stored on the computer and called up to enable reservations personnel to "remember" the guest and facilitate the reservations transaction. This application alone makes a CRS a valuable sales tool (provided its data base is current). Chains have the added advantage of receiving outside assistance with room sales, being sent hard-copy confirmations of reservations mailed directly to guests, and having available a large volume of information on previous guest reservations.

To ensure that a CRS is providing good representation for your property, you should check the system periodically (at least quarterly) by calling the CRS and making a reservation at your property to check: (1) whether information given out by reservations agents about your property is up-to-date, (2) the selling techniques of reservations agents, and (3) how fast a reservations request is processed. In hotel-chain jargon, this is called "shopping your franchise."

Responses to Advertising

One of the most effective advertising methods used by hoteliers today is the listing of a toll-free telephone number in print ads. Since people are more likely to respond if the call is free, this method of advertising is an excellent source of immediate reservations and business leads and can generate a large number of calls.

Toll-free calls are often handled by a telemarketing staff that tries to get either a firm commitment for a reservation or information to pass along to a hotel salesperson. It is important that these calls be answered courteously and that sufficient information is available to enable telemarketers or salespeople to answer questions and get a commitment.

Inquiries

Excellent leads for prospective business come in the form of inquiries from people who call the property on the recommendation of friends, acquaintances, or business associates who are familiar with the property; or from people responding to advertisements, mailings, brochures, flyers, or other promotions (which were designed—often at a cost of hundreds or thousands of dollars—to generate this interest). While inquiries may generate a relatively small amount of business, many hotels fail to capitalize on these leads by either ignoring or mishandling them. Properly handling inquiries can result in a steadily increasing contribution to the property's guest base.

Since inquiry calls often come directly to the switchboard, switchboard operators should know where to place these calls. Individuals may be routed directly to a reservations agent; group accounts may be referred to the hotel's sales staff or the general manager. At small properties, telephone inquiries are often handled directly at the front desk. These calls may come in while front desk personnel are especially busy registering guests. Too often, there is a tendency to treat inquiry calls lightly. However, callers with inquiries usually want a room or seek information about accommodations, and they should be given prompt attention. If front desk personnel are too busy to handle the call, the caller should be transferred to another hotel employee (a salesperson, the sales director, etc.) who can give immediate attention to the call.

Once an inquiry call is received by the sales department, it should be handled in the same manner as other sales calls. The salesperson should be courteous and interested. Since no pre-call research has been done on the prospect, it is especially important to listen and ask open-ended questions to determine the caller's needs. Prices or rates should not be given until the exact nature of the business is determined, and the salesperson should discuss benefits rather than features. Handling an inquiry call also includes trying to close business at that time, but even if the call does not result in immediate business, it is important to follow up. Sending additional information by fax or mail—and keeping a trace card on the prospective account—may lead to business in the future.

Telephone Sales Operations

The telephone can be used in creative ways to boost sales. Two of the most common ways are telephone sales blitzes, which can be extremely effective for small to mid-size properties, and telemarketing, which is used primarily by large properties or properties with large sales budgets.

Telephone Sales Blitzes

Telephone sales blitzes are usually used to gather information, but they can also result in immediate sales. A telephone sales blitz is especially effective for properties that cannot afford expensive computers and other telemarketing technology; these properties are finding that they can still use the telephone "the old-fashioned way" to generate business.

Exhibit 8   Sample Sales Blitz Form

		BUSINESS			CLUBS, CHURCHES AND OTHER NON-PROFIT ORGANIZATIONS		
Person Contacted	Makes Reservations for Visitors	Makes Reservations for Company Banquets and Meetings	Uses Local Restaurants for Business Lunches	Makes Reservations for Visitors	Makes Reservations for Company Banquets and Meetings	Uses Local Restaurants for Personal Enjoyment
1. Name Title Phone						
2. Name Title Phone						
3. Name Title Phone						
4. Name Title Phone						

THE SALES BLITZ DECISION-MAKER IDENTIFICATION

This sales blitz form helps a salesperson or other hotel employee record the names of decision-makers and indicate what types of business they might book at the property. (Source: James C. Makens, *The Hotel Sales and Marketing Plan Book* [Winston-Salem, North Carolina: Marion-Clarence Publishing House, 1990], p. 217)

A successful telephone sales blitz begins with organization. The property's general manager or sales team usually targets a particular geographic area or market segment and develops a plan for contacting as many people as possible within a short period of time.

One advantage of a telephone sales blitz is that virtually any staff member can participate, since usually the prime objective is to gather information, not sell. And even if a blitz is designed to qualify prospects rather than gather information, reservations agents, night auditors, secretaries, and other staff members can easily be trained to use a script to ask specific questions and record the answers on a form for follow-up (see Exhibit 8).

Telemarketing Operations

In today's world of skyrocketing personal sales call costs, telemarketing is an effective sales tool that provides person-to-person contact, immediate feedback, and the flexibility of a variety of approaches without the costs of a personal sales call.

While telemarketing is often confused with general telephone sales, the two are worlds apart. Telemarketing is characterized by systematic use of the telephone, often by a special staff of highly trained telemarketers, along with computers and other technology that provides instant access to information.

A good telemarketer can speak to up to 50 decision-makers a day.[5] Using a carefully scripted message, telemarketers can simply gather information or present a sales message and close the sale.

Telemarketing should not be taken lightly. Hotels should refrain from pulling secretaries or clerks from other departments to attempt telemarketing duties. A highly trained staff, dedicated to the telemarketing function only, is the most cost-effective way for a property to use this form of selling.

All potential telemarketers have good communication skills; persistence; the capability to bounce back from rejection; good organizational skills; the ability to adapt to new situations and different types of clients; and, most important, the enthusiasm, friendliness, and flexibility that result in increased sales.

Telemarketing Scripts. Telemarketers use telemarketing scripts designed to communicate effectively with prospects and either make a sale or gather information necessary to follow up on the call. A telemarketing form can be completed and given to the property's sales representatives for evaluation and possible follow-up (see Exhibit 9).

Most telemarketing scripts begin with an introduction that breaks the ice and explains the purpose of the call: "Good morning, I'm Mary Kelly, representing Best Rest Inns. I'm calling to ask you a few brief questions regarding your company's use of meeting rooms and accommodations for your traveling salespeople. Any information you can provide will be extremely helpful. My first question concerns the number of meetings you hold each year." This type of introduction immediately involves the respondent.

The content of a telemarketing script will, of course, depend on the property's telemarketing objectives (see Exhibit 10). Is the script designed to gather information only? Is it designed to generate leads for follow-up by salespeople? Does it offer a benefit or special premium in return for a booking? No matter what the objective, a telemarketing script is usually:

1. *Short.* Long surveys or presentations may irritate prospects or cause them to lose interest. It is important not to take too much of the prospect's time.

2. *Specific.* The script should be to the point. Benefits should be spelled out early.

3. *Simple.* Long words and hotel jargon should be avoided to ensure that the presentation is readily understandable. Terms such as "comp," "guarantee," "rack rate," and "plus-plus" can confuse the prospect. It is better to ask, "Would you prefer a room with two double beds?" than "Would you prefer a double-double?"

4. *Structured.* The script should flow from general questions to more specific or sensitive areas. For example, it is far easier to build rapport with a prospect if the telemarketer begins by asking general questions about the prospect and

Exhibit 9   Sample Telemarketing Call Report

```
┌─────────────────────────────────────────────────────────────┐
│              TELEPROSPECT CALL REPORT                        │
│  DATE _____         │
│  ORGANIZATION _____        │
│  ADDRESS _____        │
│  _____ TELEPHONE _____        │
│  KEY CONTACT _____ TITLE _____        │
│  ADDITIONAL CONTACTS _____ TITLE _____        │
│  _____ TITLE _____        │
│  POTENTIAL      YES       NO           FREQUENCY             │
│        GROUP   [    ]    [    ]       [            ]         │
│   INDIVIDUAL   [    ]    [    ]       [            ]         │
│      MEETING   [    ]    [    ]       [            ]         │
│        OTHER   [    ]    [    ]       [            ]         │
│  HOTEL(S) CURRENTLY PATRONIZED _____        │
│  ACTION _____        │
│  TRACE _____        │
│  REMARKS _____        │
│  _____         │
│  _____         │
│  _____         │
│  _____         │
│  _____                                 │
│           SIGNATURE                                          │
└─────────────────────────────────────────────────────────────┘
```

Many telemarketers who prospect for leads use a form similar to this one to build an information base of organizations that may constitute potential business for the property. (Courtesy of L'Ermitage Hotels, Beverly Hills, California)

his or her type of business, instead of immediately starting off with questions about how much the prospect has paid for meeting space or accommodations.

A telemarketing script must keep the prospect on the line long enough to gather information, get a message across, or close a sale. To do this, the script must get the prospect involved and present a benefit of interest to the prospect. Eliciting reaction to one program versus another builds interest, as does asking for the prospect's opinions or including interesting stories and analogies that relate to the prospect's background.

Exhibit 10   Sample Telemarketing Follow-Up Survey

TELEMARKETING SURVEY

Hello _____ .

This is _____ from the Sheraton Naperville Hotel. I'm calling to thank you for staying at the Sheraton Naperville. I was hoping you would assist me by answering a few questions about our hotel so we can serve you better.

1. Which of the following describes your reasons for visiting Naperville?

    Corporate Business   Training   Convention   Sales Call   Other

    If other, explain: _____

2. Did you select our hotel personally, or was the reservation made by another individual? If by another person, then who (i.e.: secretary, travel agent, other)?

3. Was this your first stay with us?   Yes   No

4. Using the following scale, how would you rate your general impression of our hotel?

    Excellent   Above Average   Average   Fair   Poor

    Comments:

5. How would you rate our registration services?

    Excellent   Above Average   Average   Fair   Poor

    Comments:

6. What was the quality of our housekeeping services?

    Excellent   Above Average   Average   Fair   Poor

    Comments:

7. Did you dine in any of our restaurants during your stay?   Yes   No

    How would you rate them?

	Excellent	Above Average	Average	Fair	Poor	Did Not Use
Atrium Restaurant						
Banquet Service						
Beaubien Dining Room						
Cafe al Fresco						
LaSalle Drinkery						
Room Service						

    Comments:

8. Are you aware of any of the following special services we provide for our guests?

			Send Information
The Concierge Floor	Yes	No	——
Our Video Check-Out	Yes	No	——
The Guestroom Refreshment Bars	Yes	No	——
The Pool and Sauna	Yes	No	——
Our Sheraton International Club	Yes	No	——
The Meeting and Ballroom Facilities	Yes	No	——
Our Special Meeting Packages	Yes	No	——

    Would you like to receive information on any of these services?

(continued)

Exhibit 10   *(continued)*

---

9. Did you need or use information on the surrounding area?   Yes   No
   Comments:

10. Would you like the Sheraton Naperville to have any of the following services?

A Hotel Library	Yes	No
A Jogging Trail	Yes	No
Cable Television	Yes	No
Health Club Facilities	Yes	No

11. How often do you get to Naperville?
   More than once per month
   4 to 12 times per year
   1 to 3 times per year
   First visit
   What is your average length of stay?
   1, 2, 3, 4, 5, or more days

12. Would you choose the Sheraton Naperville for your next visit?   Yes   No

13. Can I make a future reservation for you at this time?   Yes   No

In appreciation for your taking the time to assist us in serving you better, we would like to send you a complimentary room upgrade or a certificate for a complimentary breakfast in our Cafe al Fresco. Which would you prefer? (Room Upgrade   Breakfast)

Our records show your address as _____ .
Is this correct?   Yes   No
(If incorrect, fill in correct address) _____

_____

What are the correct spelling of your name and your correct title?

_____ .

Thank you again for your help. We look forward to seeing you at the Sheraton Naperville again soon (or appropriate date if a reservation was made).

Many properties use telemarketing surveys such as this one to follow up on their guests. Information generated by the survey can be entered into a computer to determine areas of guest interest. The information can also be used to custom-tailor a letter or follow-up telephone call to the needs of the guest. Respondents to this survey receive a complimentary room upgrade or breakfast. (Courtesy of Sheraton Naperville Hotel, Naperville, Illinois)

Telemarketing Programs. Since telemarketing is so important, it is essential that a telemarketing program—whether established in a large regional or district office for an entire hotel chain, or headquartered at an individual property—be as disciplined as any other form of direct selling. There should be carefully developed production forms, professional training of telemarketers, continuing supervision, and tracking of results. If in-house staff is used to fill telemarketing positions, a training program should be implemented and an experienced telemarketing professional hired as either the program director or a consultant.

An example of a successful telemarketing program is the Days Inns' Automatic Telemarketing System (ATMS). This system was implemented after management considered the following telemarketing statistics:

- By the year 2000, there will be eight million telemarketing jobs.

- Telemarketing is already a $12 billion industry.

- 418 of the Fortune 500 companies are now testing telemarketing applications.

- The cost of an average out of town personal sales call is $220.

Days Inns' telemarketing operation focuses on three primary markets—the motorcoach business, group business, and the corporate market; and three secondary markets—travel agents, travel agent consortiums, and tour operators. The telemarketing program combines experienced telemarketing operators with a computer software package that includes prospect and guest tracking, an inventory of available literature and mailing materials, telemarketing representative productivity tracking, automatic telephone dialing, a program for rapid retrieval of booking information, guest booking histories, a room inventory, a directory of properties, complaint and complaint follow-up records, a program for developing effective telemarketing scripts, and marketing research functions.

In evaluating its program, Days Inns management found that 5% of telemarketing calls resulted in immediate bookings and 20% generated appointments with salespeople; 60% of the prospects contacted wanted to have further information sent in the mail; only 15% had no interest. The program was extremely cost-effective. In the first year of the program's operation, six telemarketing representatives were responsible for over $3 million in bookings.[6]

In addition to sales calls, telemarketers can use the ATMS for market research. Telemarketing surveys are used by Days Inns to monitor the needs of prospects. Survey results are entered into the computer system and the resulting profiles make it far easier for Days Inns to meet the needs of its clients and guests.

Any successful telemarketing program depends on a detailed marketing plan and a great degree of professionalism, but this tool provides an efficient answer to today's needs for pinpointing prospects, selling to serious buyers, and keeping in touch with regular clients and guests.

Endnotes

1. From a speech by Bruce J. Orr, AT&T National Market Manager for the lodging industry, at an AH&MA convention in Las Vegas, Nevada.

2. A helpful resource for building a "power word" sales vocabulary is Richard Bayan, *Words That Sell.* The book is available from Caddylak Systems, 60 Shames Drive, West Berry, NY 11590.

3. Jeff Erickson, "Telephone Techniques," *HSMAI Student Bulletin,* September/October 1990.

4. From a speech given at an AH&MA convention in San Francisco, California.

5. Robert A. Meyer, "Understanding Telemarketing for Hotels," *The Cornell Hotel and Restaurant Administration Quarterly,* August 1987, p. 26.

6. From a speech given by John Russell at a Hospitality Sales & Marketing Association International midyear workshop in Nashville, Tennessee.

Key Terms

appointment call

central reservations system

forced-choice question

promotional call

prospect call

public relations call

qualifying call

sales call

service call

telemarketing

telephone sales blitz

Review Questions

1. Why is telephone etiquette important?

2. What are three keys to good listening?

3. Outgoing telephone calls can be divided into which categories?

4. What is the objective of a prospect call?

5. What are the five steps of a telephone appointment call?

6. What are three techniques that can be used to get by intermediaries?

7. What is the main difference between an telephone appointment call and a telephone sales call?

8. What closing techniques can be used to get a commitment when making a telephone sales call?

9. How can a caller be put on hold in a courteous manner?

10. What are three types of incoming calls that can lead to sales?

11. What are some of the telemarketing statistics that caused Days Inns' management to establish a telemarketing program?

Chapter Outline

What Is Internal Marketing?
    Employee Empowerment
What Are Internal Sales?
    The Role of the General Manager in Internal Sales
        Hiring Sales-Oriented Employees
        Training Employees in Sales Techniques
        Motivating Employees to Sell
    The Role of Employees in Internal Sales
        Relationship Selling
        Employee Training
        Applying Sales Skills
        Employee Incentive Programs
Internal Merchandising
    Guest-Contact Areas
        The Lobby
        Guestrooms
        Elevator Floor Landings
        Elevators
        Restaurants and Lounges
        Barber and Beauty Shops
        Reservations or Convention Desk
        Cashier's Desk
    Back-of-the-House Areas
Special Services and In-House Promotions
    Special Services
    In-House Promotions

6

Internal Marketing and Sales

SELLING THE PROPERTY is everyone's business. Every employee, from the general manager to the bellperson, makes an impression on the property's guests—an impression that can leave guests looking forward to their next visit or send them packing in a hurry, never to return. In this chapter, we will discuss the vital areas of internal marketing and internal sales, and focus on how employees in every department can generate additional sales—and repeat business for the property— through suggestive selling, cross-selling, upgrading, merchandising, and promotional techniques.

What Is Internal Marketing?

Internal sales and internal marketing, while interrelated, are not the same; the major difference between the two is the target audience. Internal sales is a systematic plan to increase revenues by selling to guests already at the property; internal marketing seeks to sell employees on the property and their importance to its success.

When selling any product, complete product knowledge—and personal belief in the product—is crucial. But what about hospitality products? The hospitality product is an intangible, an experience—and the primary factor in guest satisfaction is the quality of service rendered. Since service is so important, every employee should understand the product and his or her role in the success of the operation. Management must sell employees on the hospitality product and the importance of each employee's role in generating guest satisfaction. According to the internal marketing concept, employees are just as important to please as guests if employees are to provide the levels of service needed to compete in today's marketplace.

Many hotel chains and independent properties are developing structured internal marketing programs. Bill Hulett, CHA, president of Stouffer Hotel Company, states:

> We endorse the thesis that management must become attuned to the value of the new generation of employees and managers who deliver our service. We believe our employees must be viewed from the same perspective that we apply to our guests. We are well aware that to attract and retain a strong, stable base of business we have to give guests what they want—and do it better than the competition. The same principle applies to how we treat our employees.[1]

Internal marketing begins with communicating the nature of the hospitality product, and focuses less on the "how" of specific job duties and more on the

197

"why." While the "how" is definitely important, knowing "why" helps employees see the value of their jobs in delivering the hospitality product to guests.

Marketing the property to employees consists of more than simply providing fact sheets about the features of the hotel or conducting guided tours; marketing to employees should include explanations about the importance of each hotel area, and should detail guest benefits. Employees should know not only their property, but also (1) current marketing campaigns, (2) current promotions and packages, and (3) VIP guests staying at the property.

Getting an overview of the operation—and each employee's importance in each area—promotes a sense of pride in employees that comes through in guest contacts. All employees, guest-contact and non-contact employees alike, must see their jobs as opportunities to promote guest satisfaction. A maintenance worker, for example, is not only fixing a television set—he or she is helping to ensure guest satisfaction. The dishwasher is not just preventing the return of a chipped glass to the dining room—he or she is making sure the property doesn't give a bad impression to a guest.

Improving employees' attitudes about the value of their jobs leads to better service. Many properties today are recognizing and rewarding employees who render the type of service that keeps guests coming back. Stouffer Hotel's quarterly magazine, *Impressions,* features a "Service with a Smile" column that recognizes employees who have made an extra effort to assist guests: a desk clerk who loaned her personal formal wear to a stranded client, a bellperson who rushed out to get an executive's glasses repaired, a restaurant worker who rounded up copies of a business publication for a meeting planner.

These employees saw a need and responded to it, but their actions had nothing to do with property policies; they did not bend rules to make a guest happy. But managers at an increasing number of properties are recognizing that sometimes it is necessary for employees to deviate from prescribed policy and solve problems on their own.

Employee Empowerment

Employee empowerment is a logical extension of internal marketing. Employee empowerment gives employees the authority to make on-the-spot decisions to respond to guest needs—decisions that were previously relegated to those higher in authority.

In addition to building employee morale, employee empowerment also benefits guests. Long waits while an employee checks with a supervisor are eliminated, and problems can be solved on the spot, greatly reducing guest frustration.

For empowerment to work for the good of all concerned, however, there must be clearly understood guidelines. In some hotels, for example, a front desk agent may be given parameters for changing guest bills. And, in most empowerment situations, decisions made are relative to the employee's responsibilities. A housekeeper, for example, could offer a reduced rate or other benefit in response to a guest's complaint about a room not cleaned satisfactorily, but would have no authority to respond to a guest complaint about dining room service.

Insider Insights

Mary Jean Bublitz, CHA
Co-Owner
Quality Suites
Flagstaff, Arizona

> *Mary Jean Bublitz started her hospitality career as a food server in her parents' restaurant while she was a high school student. Since that time, she has worked as a front desk agent, night auditor, bookkeeper, salesperson, maintenance person, and housekeeper—training that came out of necessity after she and her husband purchased a 20-room motel, then a 42-room motel, and, finally, their present 96-room franchised Quality Inn in Flagstaff, Arizona. She has served on the Convention and Meetings Committee of the International Operators Council (IOC), an organization of Quality Inns International licensees, and has served on the IOC Operations and Standards Committee. Bublitz earned her CHA certification in 1983, and recently opened a 102-unit all-suite hotel which is franchised as a Quality Suites property.*

The real joy of innkeeping is the challenge of promoting hospitality at its finest. Pleasing the hotel guest builds repeat business. I like comparing a hotel guest to a delicate crystal ball that will break and be ruined unless it is handled with tender care at all times. Every person choosing our hotel deserves the finest product we can provide, at the fairest charge possible; this can be accomplished by pricing our services competitively and by providing a friendly, well-trained staff of professionals who perform their jobs correctly.

My husband and I are involved in creating each job description and performance standard. We try to personally motivate our employees and train by good example. We treat employees as family members and have them participate in business decisions. And we emphasize that all employees should have two job titles on their name tags: General Manager/Sales Director; Guest Service Attendant/Salesperson; Maintenance/Salesperson; Room Attendant/Salesperson, and so on. This formula produces excellent results and is an exciting challenge to new staff people.

The best place to learn about the operation is still the front desk. It is still possible to learn more—and keep improving the bottom line—if I spend time at the front desk daily and listen to the guests' requests and comments. The non-smokers rooms idea evolved this way. Guests said, "We like your hotel. The rooms are immaculately cleaned and properly maintained, but wouldn't it be nice if you could get rid of those stale smoke smells!" My husband and I, being non-smokers, understood their comments since we had that same problem staying in hotel rooms. We decided we could do something about this, and began a non-smokers rooms program at our Flagstaff property. In June of 1984 I suggested the non-smokers rooms idea at a board meeting of the International Operators Council, an organization of Quality Inns International licensees. The IOC and Quality Inns International decided immediately to adopt the

(continued)

Insider Insights *(continued)*

program chain-wide, and mandated a minimum of 10% non-smokers rooms. That figure is now up to 15%.

We had introduced these rooms at the Flagstaff Quality Inn in 1980, and had kept a constant 100% occupancy in non-smokers rooms. In 1987, we set aside 25% of our rooms for non-smokers, and continued to enjoy the same occupancy rate! These statistics emphasize the importance of my crystal ball theory, an internal sales method that can work for any property that is willing to provide courteous, friendly service—and listen to its guests.

To promote effective employee empowerment policies, many properties develop "empowerment surveys" that seek employee input on such areas as frequent guest complaints, obstacles hindering employees from responding to complaints, and what authority employees need to better serve guests. Two major hotel chains, Marriott and Omni Hotels, offer seminars and employee training to ensure that employee empowerment policies are effective. Marriott's Total Quality Management (TQM) seminars help managers understand employee empowerment policies. Omni offers extensive employee training, including its "Power of One" program, which teaches employees how to manage service situations.

Employee empowerment is expected to play a major role in selling hospitality products in this service-oriented decade. As more properties discover that empowerment increases guest satisfaction, gives employees a sense of worth, and saves the property time and money, empowerment programs will become an essential component of good property management.

What Are Internal Sales?

Internal sales can be defined as specific sales activities engaged in by various employees of a property, in conjunction with a program of internal merchandising, to promote additional sales and guest satisfaction. The main objective of internal sales is to increase sales by promoting effective guest-employee relationships. Management can encourage these vital relationships in three ways:

1. Provide an environment conducive to good guest-employee relations

2. Instill pride (both in the property and in the value of their respective positions) in employees

3. Provide training that encourages employees to become more helpful to guests

The sales impetus must start with top management and filter down to employees. It is up to management to support and encourage employees in internal sales efforts, and to provide internal sales training, product training, and motivational programs. An enthusiastic management team can produce an entire staff that sells with enthusiasm.

There is a tremendous profit potential for internal sales, because in-house sales efforts are directed toward a captive audience. When selling to in-house guests, sales costs are minimal. Each additional dollar spent results in nearly pure bottom-line income. If every hotel guest could be induced to spend just $2 more per day, the additional sales for a 200-room property running at 80% occupancy (and an average per-room occupancy of 1.5 persons) would be $175,200 per year![2]

In order to be effective, in-house sales efforts must be continual. A one-month program is usually effective for only one month. Ideally, an internal sales program is tied to the marketing plan, is designed for the whole hotel (not just one department), and is a systematic yearly plan rather than a one-shot blitz effort. Internal sales, like external sales, should be planned for and directed to high-priority market segments and given special emphasis during periods when business is most needed.

The Role of the General Manager in Internal Sales

The attitude and direction of the general manager will greatly influence the success of an internal sales program. If the general manager is not sales-oriented, it is unlikely that the hotel staff will be highly motivated. A good general manager recognizes the value of guest satisfaction and sets goals to attain guest goodwill—and repeat business—by using effective internal merchandising and developing sales-oriented employees.

While internal merchandising will be discussed in greater detail later in the chapter, at this point it is important to note that a good internal merchandising program doesn't just happen; it is the result of planning, coordination, and careful evaluation of results. For maximum return, the general manager should see to it that an internal merchandising committee is made up of representatives from each hotel area who have an interest in promoting facilities and services, and that *one person* is given the responsibility for coordinating internal merchandising (it is advisable to select someone creative). This person not only should assist in training employees in sales techniques, but should supervise the production, placement, and storage of posters, displays, and other internal merchandising items.

A general manager can develop a sales-oriented staff by:

* Hiring sales-oriented employees

* Training employees in sales techniques

* Motivating employees to sell

Hiring Sales-Oriented Employees. Sales-oriented employees can greatly increase in-house sales. The human resources department at large properties, or the general manager at smaller properties, should develop sales-oriented job descriptions and be able to recognize sales-oriented applicants. When new employees realize that selling is part of their job and sales is the life-blood of the property, they will be more willing to learn sales techniques.

But while sales skills can be taught, personality can't, making it especially important to hire a staff that possesses attributes essential to selling a hospitality product. Many hotel managers "hire the smile and train the skill." Employees—

especially those who will have direct contact with guests—should be "sparklers," people who are sincere in their warmth, enthusiasm, and concern for guests.

Michael Hurst, a successful restaurant owner, uses an interviewing strategy to judge his applicants' enthusiasm and ability to interact with guests. His interviews always include the question, "What's the funniest thing that's ever happened to you?" If an applicant looks at him and says, "I guess I can't think of anything funny right now," Hurst knows that this is the way the applicant will come across to guests. If, on the other hand, the applicant becomes animated and tells a story with enthusiasm, Hurst knows he has a winner.[3]

Training Employees in Sales Techniques. Once an employee has gained a thorough knowledge of the property and the benefits the property offers to guests, training can help the employee learn the types of selling required for the position (upgrading, suggestive selling, cross-selling, etc.) and learn to recognize verbal and non-verbal clues from guests. These clues include tone of voice and body language; employees as well as salespeople should be well versed in how to "read" others. This knowledge will enable employees to better sell to a receptive guest, and help them know when not to approach a guest (perhaps the guest is angry, wants privacy, and so on).[4]

Motivating Employees to Sell. One of the ways the general manager can motivate employees to sell is by convincing them that they can, indeed, become effective salespeople. Armed with this confidence—and management encouragement—employees can put their skills to work to earn more money for the property. Many properties also offer incentive programs to employees to encourage sales. These programs may be similar to those offered to hotel salespeople, or may be inter-departmental, inter-property, or special promotional contests.

The Role of Employees in Internal Sales

Many employees make hundreds, even thousands, of guest contacts weekly, so involving employees in internal sales (and using their ideas and suggestions) is essential if a property wants to keep guests coming back. Twenty years ago, most guests didn't have much of a choice; perhaps there were only one or two hotels at their destination. Today, however, hospitality choices abound, and it is especially important to build guest loyalty to avoid losing even a small part of the guest base to competitors.

Relationship Selling. Most hospitality managers have concluded that it is less expensive to retain existing guests than to acquire new ones, and are focusing on building relationships with their current guests. Relationship selling (also called relationship marketing) can be defined as building guest loyalty by creating, enhancing, and maintaining a relationship with guests.

There are several ways for properties to learn more about their guests so they can build relationships with them. One commonly used method is the use of guest profiles. Guest profiles can be developed in a number of ways, from obtaining information from registration forms to conducting guest surveys. In order to be effective, however, guest profiles must contain information that will enable property personnel to determine individual guest needs.

Another, more personal, way to gain guest knowledge is using the input of property employees. Almost every employee, no matter how limited his or her actual guest contact, can assist in contributing guest information. Room attendants, for example, have access to "clues" such as special requests (extra towels, early turndown service, local morning newspaper). Food servers can glean invaluable information—food and beverage preferences, dietary restrictions, and so on—in casual, friendly conversations. This type of input makes it easy to provide favorite items for the guest's next stay—a thoughtful gesture that can build priceless goodwill.

Relationships can be enhanced and maintained through follow-up. Follow-up can be a telephone call from the general manager or a guest service representative, a thank-you letter, or a quarterly newsletter.

Employee Training. Employee training should include a number of areas that will enable employees to assist guests and build rapport. These areas include:

- Knowing the property

- Knowing the area

- Interacting with guests

- Using sales skills

Knowing the property. If employees do not know what the property has to offer, they cannot promote it. As part of the orientation process, every new employee should be given a complete tour of the property. All employees should learn an abbreviated form of the hotel fact sheet. They should also be informed of special promotional packages, special events, and other property happenings.

To sell effectively, hotel employees must sample the product. Food servers should taste every item on the menu so they can make a specific, personal recommendation if asked by a guest. Front desk agents will do a much better job of upselling if they have actually slept in the property's suites. It costs little to have employees stay at the hotel (employees can become "guests" on a slow Sunday night, for example), but the benefits of such stays can be great.

Knowing the area. Employee knowledge of the area surrounding the property can be helpful in two ways: employees can encourage guests to extend their stays by suggesting attractions to visit, and offering suggestions gives employees an opportunity to build good relationships with guests.

Employees should do more than just provide a brochure on an area attraction or quote from a fact sheet (especially if the employee is as unfamiliar with the attraction as the guest). Properties can ensure that their staff is well informed and helpful by (1) encouraging employees to keep abreast of area events and attractions (including hours, prices, and services); (2) holding training sessions that provide local area information and fact sheets that stress guest benefits; and (3) encouraging the staff to personally experience local attractions (most guests will ask the employee if he or she has been there).

Front desk employees are not clerks; they're sales representatives.

Because of the high potential for word-of-mouth referrals, many attractions offer complimentary tickets to hotel staff. Even if complimentary tickets are not available, management should still encourage employees—especially those in the sales and marketing departments and in guest-contact positions—to visit nearby places of interest so they can tell guests or potential clients about them. Royce Kardial, general manager of the Best Western Rancho Grande in Wickenburg, Arizona, takes her employees on field trips to museums and other local attractions.

Interacting with guests. Positive interaction with guests is crucial to making a good impression and generating repeat business.[5] One of the key departments for doing so at any property is the front desk. Front desk employees are not clerks; they are sales representatives. They are very often the first contact that a person has with a property, and a guest's entire perception of a property may be shaped by the way he or she is treated by front desk personnel.

Most properties recognize the value of retaining a friendly and competent front desk staff. Not only are operations smoother, but it is far easier to build a relationship with guests when the front desk staff is familiar to them. Many properties offer incentives to encourage employees to make a career of front desk operations, and front desk employees are often given the opportunity to add their input to improve operations. Through empowerment programs, front desk agents are given increased authority to make service decisions and otherwise resolve guest problems.

But front desk personnel are not the property's only representatives; every employee makes an impression, and should be trained in the areas of proper appearance, courtesy, and personal habits (food servers should be taught that it is not acceptable to touch their hair or mouths while serving guests, for example). Every employee should be reminded that each guest is valuable, and a friendly smile and a willingness to assist are vital in building rapport. It is especially important to make guests feel welcome. Employees should anticipate the needs of guests, learn details of previous visits if applicable, and call guests by name whenever possible.

Using names. Calling guests by name is one key to repeat business. Remembering guests' names shows a special caring—a respect for guests as individuals. In today's automated world, people appreciate recognition more than ever before, and there are a number of ways employees can learn and use names:

1. A list of names can be prepared to match room numbers. This list can be distributed to all the property's revenue centers, so that when a guest displays a key, the employee can match the room number to the guest's name and immediately begin calling the guest by name. In the lounge, for example, guests often place their keys on the table or bar. A server can note the room number, check it against his or her master list, and return with the drink—and a personal greeting: "Here's your manhattan, Ms. Clark."

2. New computerized telephone systems automatically display the room number and the guest's name on a monitor whenever a guest calls the switchboard from his or her guestroom. The operator can greet the guest by name: "Good afternoon, Mr. Herndon. What can I do for you?"

3. Before a guest registers with the hotel, the bellperson or porter can look for names on luggage tags.

4. The front desk agent gets guests' names upon receiving the completed registration forms. He or she can begin calling guests by name, and may ask the bellperson to "Show Mr. and Mrs. Lewis to their room, please." The bellperson can then begin calling guests by name also.

5. In restaurants, the host can greet the guest by name if the guest has a reservation, and pass the guest's name along to the food server.

6. Switchboard operators can use names when making wake-up calls. A cheery, "Good morning, Ms. Ricker. It's seven o'clock. Would you like room service to bring you a fresh pot of coffee and a danish?" is much more hospitable than "Hello, it's seven o'clock."

7. Any time guests use credit cards, there is an opportunity to learn and use names. Local patrons of the restaurant or lounge can be recognized in this way, or by simply asking them their names and welcoming them back to the property.

Name recognition works both ways. Not only do most guests appreciate the recognition accorded them by the property's staff, they also like to see familiar faces and greet staff members by name. Many properties use name tags displaying the employee's name and home state. These can be excellent conversation starters: "You're from Michigan? I went to school there—at MSU!"

Turning Mishaps into Marketing Opportunities

While every effort should be made to prevent problems, the unpreventable ones that do occur can present some invaluable opportunities. A good recovery can turn disgruntled guests into loyal ones—ensuring excellent repeat business potential as well as word-of-mouth referral business.

Consider the case of a group of vacationers who took off for a routine trip from New York to a Club Med resort, for example. Their troubles began when the flight took off six hours late, and it was downhill from there. The plane made two unexpected stops, had to circle for half an hour before it could land in Mexico, and—to make matters worse—food and drink supplies were exhausted long before the 2:00 A.M. landing—which was so rough that luggage (and the oxygen masks) dropped from the overhead compartments. Everyone aboard felt the vacation was ruined before it started. A lawyer on the plane began collecting names and addresses for a class-action lawsuit!

But, incredibly, this unhappy scenario had a happy ending. When Silvio de Bortoli, the general manager of the Cancun Club Med, heard about the horrendous flight, he took immediate action. He packed up half his staff, a supply of snacks and drinks, and a stereo system, and met the weary travelers at the airport with music and refreshments—and personal greetings, a sympathetic ear, assistance with luggage, and a chauffeured ride to the resort. But the fun didn't stop there.

Back at the resort, the other guests had been encouraged to wait up for the group. Those that did shared in a lavish banquet complete with champagne and a mariachi band. The party lasted until sunrise, and many guests said it was the most fun they'd had since college. The Club Med turned a negative experience into a positive one by using this opportunity to create a vacation that was memorable for everyone.

Source: Adapted from Christopher W. L. Hart, James L. Heskett, and W. Earl Sasser Jr., "Surviving a Customer's Rage," *Successful Meetings,* April 1991, pp. 68–69.

Handling complaints. There are times when it is impossible to please a guest. In some cases, a guest's unhappiness is justified—service may be slow, there may be an error in reservations or payment arrangements, or a guestroom may not be ready on time. Sometimes guests may simply be taking out their frustrations with other circumstances on the nearest available person. In either case, however, employees must respond to complaints in such a way that goodwill is restored.

An angry guest can be transformed into a loyal one if his or her complaint is handled efficiently and patiently. To do so, you must remain calm and determine the exact nature of the complaint. While it is natural to want to tell a guest to calm down, this approach should be avoided, because it may make the guest feel that you think the complaint is unimportant—which can make the guest even angrier. Instead, you should ask questions to determine the exact reason for the dissatisfaction.

Once you have identified the guest's complaint, take immediate action. If you cannot handle the situation personally, immediately contact a supervisor or other person in authority. In some cases, however, complaints cannot be handled on the spot—perhaps authorization has to come from the home office, or from a person who is not available. In this instance, you should make a definite commitment to the guest to follow up.

If a guest points out a problem with the property's products or services that the property resolves after the guest has gone home, the guest should be contacted by mail or telephone, thanked for bringing the problem to the staff's attention, and told how the property dealt with the problem. In many cases, guest complaints have led to the improvement of problem areas at a property—resulting in better service and increased guest satisfaction.

Since complaints can serve a useful purpose, guests should be given an opportunity to voice them. Some unhappy guests want to be heard, and have no qualms about writing a complaint letter, making a telephone call, or demanding to speak to the manager. Resolving problems for these "squeaky wheels" is far easier than dealing with the typical unhappy guest who never expresses his or her dissatisfaction; he or she just leaves the property to tell hotel "horror stories" to friends and business associates.

Property personnel can avoid this by trying to gauge guest reactions, or simply asking "How was everything?" when guests check out. In many cases, guests will volunteer information when asked directly. Or, to make it easy to complain without having a face-to-face confrontation, properties can offer a complaint hot line or toll-free number. These steps will help guests feel that what they think is important to your property and that you're willing to not only listen but to do something about their complaints.

Using sales skills. Sales skills help employees make the most of sales opportunities in their particular areas of guest contact. Most properties have features in common—swimming pools, in-room cable television, 24-hour room service, and so on—so what makes your property different? A guest usually needs help to visualize a tangible benefit, and that's where the guest-contact employee comes in. A benefits-oriented employee will not simply mention the property's lounge, he or she will offer a benefit: "You'll really enjoy the relaxing atmosphere after a long day of business meetings."

Once employees understand the benefits-oriented sales approach, there are several sales techniques they can use. Three of the most effective are upgrading or upselling, suggestive selling, and cross-selling.

Upgrading. Upgrading reservations is an effective way to increase revenues, but very few front desk or reservations staffs are trained to use upgrading techniques.[6] Although most hotels have several room types and prices, there is often no prescribed formula for selling rooms; employees simply quote a price and make no attempt to sell additional services or amenities.

One reason for management's reluctance to tell employees to try to sell rooms with higher rates is that they fear guests may be offended or feel pressured. However, a caller may be unaware of varying rates and amenities, and may appreciate the property's efforts to place him or her in a room that meets specific needs. Meeting specific needs is an important part of upgrading, and employees must be trained to listen to the caller and make suggestions for an appropriate accommodation.

Front desk and reservations agents should be trained to recognize when and how to upgrade a guest's request. Upgrading can be accomplished without pressuring a guest by using one of three methods:

- Top-down

- Rate-category-alternatives

- Bottom-up

The top-down method is used to encourage guests to reserve middle- or high-rate rooms. It begins with the front desk or reservations agent enthusiastically recommending the guestroom sold at the highest rate. The guest may either accept or reject the recommendation. In the latter case, the agent moves down to the next price level and enthusiastically discusses the merits of this accommodation. The guest may perceive the lower rate as a compromise on the part of the agent and be more open to accepting this recommendation. If the rate quoted is still unacceptable, the agent drops to the next-highest rate, continuing this process until the guest is satisfied with the price quoted.

The rate-category-alternatives method is an easy and effective way to sell middle-rate rooms to guests who might otherwise choose a lower rate. The front desk or reservations agent provides the guest with a choice of three or more rate-category alternatives, and puts no pressure on the guest. In most cases, people will attempt to avoid extremes: choosing the lowest rate could cause the guest to feel cheap, while choosing the highest rate might make the guest feel unnecessarily extravagant. Under these circumstances the logical decision would be to choose the middle rate.

The bottom-up method is used when a guest has already made a reservation or has requested a low-priced room. During the registration process, the front desk or reservations agent can suggest extra amenities or the merits of a more expensive room: "For only $10 more, you can enjoy a room with a view of the ocean," or "For an extra $25, you can have a deluxe room and two complimentary continental breakfasts." The higher rate must appear to be an attempt by the agent to enhance the guest's stay at only a small increase over charges anticipated by the guest.

It is much easier to show—and sell—the differences in rooms by using photographs. An effective sales tool for front desk personnel is a loose-leaf notebook of 8 × 10 inch color photos of the different types of guestrooms offered by the hotel. Simply telling a guest about an ocean-view room is not as effective as showing the room—and the view—in a photo.

No matter what method is used to upgrade a reservation, guests should *never* feel they are being pressured; sales pressure has no place in the hospitality industry. Rather, internal sales should be aimed at giving guests the opportunity to purchase additional products and services or to "trade up" from those already purchased. To do this, it is important to convey that guests are not just buying a room, but a home away from home, and that their needs are important to the property. By combining upselling techniques with a knowledge of guest needs, front desk employees can sell a pleasurable experience to guests while increasing revenues.

Upgrading can also be used in the food and beverage department. If a guest has ordered à la carte items, for example, the food server can suggest a complete dinner for just a small additional cost.

Suggestive selling. Suggestive selling is the practice of influencing a guest's purchase decision through the use of sales phrases.[7] Almost any employee can use

Insider Insights

Chad A. Martin, CHSE
Vice President of Marketing
Church Street Station
Orlando, Florida

Chad Martin says that he was fortunate to have been brought up around hoteliers, and that "this business has never not been fun." He held positions from pot washer to bellperson to outside salesperson for a hotel chain before joining the Ploss Hotel Group of 17 hotels on the Eastern seaboard. He was given an opportunity to add to his sales knowledge when Peter Ploss, the chain's president, sent him to Cornell University. His next position was with Mid-State Management, which was owned by Senator John Glenn and Henry Landworth, "the innkeeper to the astronauts." Landworth was responsible for increasing Martin's knowledge of making hotels profitable, an education that was invaluable in Martin's next position, at the 824-room Court of Flags resort in Orlando, Florida. After six years there, Martin joined Howard Johnson as regional director of sales, and most recently became vice president of marketing for Church Street Station.

Probably the most overlooked aspect of running a hotel is making sure the guest is warmly greeted and made to feel welcome by the people who work in hotels: the housekeepers, engineers, bellpersons, front desk agents, and night auditors. How much time is really spent with these employees: talking to them, telling them how important it is to have a smile on their faces, and that it's the person visiting the property—the guest—that's literally paying their checks?

In many cases, especially at small properties, the first person that guests see is the front desk agent. But now, in this age of automation, most of the time a guest will walk in and see only the top of the agent's head as he or she looks down at the computer, punches in information, and mumbles, "How do you want to pay for this?" or "How long will you be staying with us?" The guest doesn't even see the agent's face—or smile! We've got to get back to the fact that we are in the hospitality business; we've got to make front desk agents aware that they are in the sales business. The agents have to look up and say, "Good day, ma'am. How are you doing?" The guest should be welcomed, made to feel comfortable, made to feel that the hotel is a fun place to be!

This doesn't just happen. We must teach internal sales consistently, and we must spend the time to continually re-emphasize internal sales programs. I used to make it a point to go down to the housekeepers' office with a couple dozen donuts and talk with the housekeepers. I wanted our housekeepers to remember that when they saw me walking across the hotel with a client it was their job to smile and say "Good day, Mr. Martin," and look at the client and say, "Good day, sir." In other words, the housekeepers had to be trained not only to clean rooms properly, but to give the guest a smile, a greeting.

(continued)

Insider Insights *(continued)*

I always tell the story about the dishwashers at the properties. Many meeting planners and association executives want to see a property's kitchen; they want to know that it's clean, that their food is going to come out hot, and that they won't have to worry about having any problems from the kitchen. First impressions, in this case, can make or break business, so I always made it a point to speak to the dishwashers. I wanted to be sure they knew my name, and that when I walked through the door with a client they would smile and nod at me and say, "Chad, how are you doing?" And they would greet the client with the same courtesy and friendliness!

The reason people stay at our hotels—and especially the reason that they stay again at a particular hotel they've visited—is that they've been treated properly. They've been given good service, and they've been "sold." Internal sales is one of the most valuable tools we have. I believe that internal sales will bring guests back—and that's the name of our business.

---

this sales technique in most areas of the property. Suggestive selling may be used in all of a property's food and beverage outlets, for example. A host may inform guests of the special of the day after greeting them; a food server may suggest a cocktail before dinner, an appetizer, the special of the day, or a dessert; a bartender may suggest a specialty drink at a discount price. The power of suggestion is also a good way to introduce new menu items, promote low-overhead food items, and increase the server's tip base.

Food servers can follow these guidelines for suggestive selling:

- *Avoid asking questions that require a yes or no answer.* It is far more effective to give the guest a choice. For example, ask: "Which dessert would you like from our dessert cart?" rather than "Would you like dessert?" If the guest orders a steak, ask: "Would you like a red or a rosé wine with your steak?" rather than "Would you like a glass of wine with dinner?"

- *Suggest in specific terms.* Don't just suggest an appetizer, suggest a specific item such as fried zucchini, shrimp cocktail, or escargot. For even more effectiveness, paint a word picture for guests. It is far more effective to say: "Our catch of the day is rainbow trout stuffed with a delightful mixture of shrimp and fresh crabmeat, lightly floured and sautéed in butter, and garnished with fresh lemon and parsley," than to say, "Our catch of the day is stuffed trout."

Suggestive selling is only as effective as the verbal communication between the employee and the guest. Employees must be knowledgeable about the product or service and learn the art of making a sales approach. For a sales approach to work, you must be enthusiastic, considerate, and aware of how the sale will benefit the guest (see Exhibit 1).

Exhibit 1 Sample Sales Phrases

Situation	Suggested Sales Phrases
Front Desk	
Early morning check-ins	"Our valet service can have your suit pressed and returned to your room within an hour while you freshen up."
Early evening check-ins	"Do you enjoy Spanish music? We are featuring Carlos, one of the finest Spanish pianists in the country, in our La Mancha lounge."
	"Have you seen the exciting Hawaiian revue in our main showroom? It's almost like being on the Islands!"
	"If you'd like to have a refreshing drink to help you unwind, our Baron's Pub is located in the east wing near the coffee shop. Besides offering the best drinks in town, the Pub features continuous entertainment from 7:00 P.M. to midnight."
Late evening check-ins	"Our excellent room service is still available. Here's the phone number, sir."
Checking out	"Would you like me to make your return reservation for you now?"
	"Your next stop is Orlando, and our chain has another hotel there. Would you like me to confirm a reservation for you?"
Restaurants	
After taking the order for an entrée	"Would you care for a manhattan or a martini while you wait for your order?"
	"We've just received a new shipment of 1952 French champagne. Shall I bring you a bottle, or would you prefer to see our regular wine list?"
After the main course	"Would you like a B&B or a Drambuie to finish your meal?"
	"Would you care to try our new after-dinner coffee? We add a dash of brandy and top it off with whipped cream. We also offer Irish coffee."
Lounges	
While handing guests a drink list	"Exotic drinks are a house specialty. Perhaps you'd like to try a Scorpion, one of our most popular drinks."
In hot weather	"Would you like a nice, cool Tom Collins or would you prefer one of our refreshing fruit drinks?"
In cold weather	"Our bartender makes the best hot Tom and Jerry available anywhere. Would you care for one to warm yourself up?"
Room Service	
After delivering a meal	"Have you tried our Captain's Table restaurant yet? Tomorrow night they'll be featuring a special seafood buffet that I'm sure you'd enjoy."

(continued)

Exhibit 1   *(continued)*

When coming to clear	"Don't forget that we're available 24 hours a day. If there's anything else you'll need, you can reach us at extension XX."
Valet Parking	
Before parking the car	"Welcome to Complete Resorts. If you like Hawaiian cuisine, you'll love our Lanai Buffet. It's on the second floor above the pool area."
When delivering the car	"I hope you enjoyed your stay. Don't forget that we'll be having a special Western Barbecue next week. I'm looking forward to seeing you then."

Every guest contact presents an opportunity to sell additional features and services. Sales-oriented employees can greatly increase a property's profitability and build guest goodwill.

Suggestive selling can also be used in other revenue centers at the property. The health club attendant may suggest a relaxing massage after a workout; the golf pro can suggest a new set of clubs from the pro shop after a private lesson; the front desk agent can suggest a return visit during a special promotional period.

Of course, suggestive selling is used in the sales department also. Rather than simply taking room night orders during busy seasons, salespeople should suggest dates that best meet the property's needs. If Tuesday is a typical sell out or high occupancy night, for example, a salesperson might suggest another night of the week to clients. Monitoring competitors' bookings may also point to suggestive selling strategies. If the property is likely to sell out during a particular week due to overflow from a competitor's booking of a large convention, salespeople can suggest dates in the weeks before or after to maximize revenue potential.

Cross-selling. Cross-selling in advertising is simply using media in one area of the property to promote a different area of the property: a tent card in a restaurant may advertise another specialty restaurant or a sale in the pro shop, a poster at the front desk can promote the health facilities and spa, the matchbooks in the restaurant may advertise the property's lounge.

Registration and reservation confirmation forms also offer opportunities to cross-sell. A hotel might use its registration forms to tell guests about on-site restaurants, lounges, and other revenue centers. Reservation confirmations mailed to guests can remind them to bring workout clothes so they can use the hotel's health facilities.

Employees can also cross-sell: employees working at one facility may suggest that a guest take advantage of other facilities and services offered at the property. Employee cross-selling can begin at the front desk when the front desk agent recommends the property's restaurant. To assist front desk employees in promoting the restaurant, a special display might be posted within sight of the front desk, and copies of the restaurant's menu could be available for guests to examine. A sincere invitation to visit the property's facilities—along with display advertising or other aids to enhance the employees' presentation—can greatly increase revenues and make guests feel welcome.

Every employee must be thoroughly knowledgeable about all aspects of the property's operations before cross-selling can be fully effective. All employees, not just the food servers, should know the hours, specialties, dress requirements, and atmosphere of each of the property's restaurants. If a bellperson recommends the property's seafood restaurant, for example, it is not enough to mention the restaurant's name. What feature of the restaurant would make it worth the guest's visit? The food? A special buffet? The atmosphere? The low prices?

Employees should also be aware of special promotions (two-for-one coupons, discounts, weekend packages), pool and health club hours and services, live entertainment offered (if the property offers live entertainment, employees can be invited to hear the entertainment so they can give personal endorsements), and special services (valet, laundry, child care or baby-sitting services, secretarial assistance, complimentary transportation, and so on).

Applying Sales Skills. Most guest-employee contacts are potential sales situations. To ensure that employees learn about all the property's revenue centers and develop effective sales approaches, managers might have employees participate in role-playing and periodic testing. Employee sales skills can be evaluated and changed as necessary during these training sessions (and information kept current) to ensure that each guest-employee encounter will be productive.

What follows is a list of property areas and personnel that are particularly important to internal sales.

Switchboard. The switchboard operator is often the first contact that a prospective guest has with a property, so switchboard operators should answer calls in a pleasant manner that conveys a sense of welcome. Since the switchboard serves as an indicator of the property's efficiency as well as hospitality, calls should be answered promptly and transferred to the proper department without delay.

The switchboard operator can also direct guests to the property's revenue centers. A call from the operator in the late afternoon can recommend the hotel's dining room or room service. Since guests have to eat somewhere, this is often all it takes to keep them at the property. Operators can also make suggestions for restaurants or room service when they make wake-up calls.

Reservations. Since the basic function of the reservations department is to turn a prospect into a guest, reservations staff should be well-trained in sales and public relations. A pleasant and informed reservations agent, aware of upgrading and suggestive selling techniques, can increase the number of room nights sold at higher-than-standard rates.

While it is important that the reservations staff have a guest-oriented approach, equally important is a knowledge of room types, prices, special rates, and hotel packages. Staff members should have a complete knowledge of the property and an understanding of what determines the differences in price among the hotel's guestrooms. An ocean-view room, for example, may cost more than a comparable room on the other side of the hotel; the same guestroom may double in price during the "season." By following a policy of selling from the top down if the inquiry is from a new guest, or using the rate-category-alternatives or bottom-up approach if a reservation has already been made, reservations agents can increase revenues while providing service to guests.

When potential guests telephone for a room after the house is full, reservations agents should offer alternatives in an attempt to keep business. For example, the reservations department might adopt a waiting list system. The reservations agent can tell the caller: "I'm sorry, Mr. Jackson, we currently have no rooms available, but we often have last-minute cancellations. If you will give me your name and phone number, I'll call you immediately when a room opens up." If the reservations department is too busy to make call-backs, the agent might assign the guest a reference number and suggest that he or she call again after the 6:00 P.M. cut-off for holding reservations.

Suggesting that the caller change his or her arrival date is a selling technique that is seldom used, but could prove of immense value. While this certainly won't work with all guests, many business and leisure travelers will change their plans to stay in their "first choice" hotel. The reservations agent can make this option attractive with a statement such as: "Ms. Stewart, we are presently booked to capacity and have several names on a waiting list for Wednesday, November 30. But if you could change your travel plans, we have several attractive suites available on Thursday, December 1."

Front desk. Interacting with front desk employees is often the guest's first *personal* impression of the property, and it is here that hospitality begins.[8] Each guest should be greeted with a warm smile and a sincere, friendly welcome, *not* a curt, "Do you have a reservation?" A repeat guest should be greeted by name and a warm "Welcome back." From this point on, guests have *names*, not just room numbers.

The check-in function should be handled with a minimum of delay. To encourage guest loyalty, guests should be made to feel far more important than a computer screen or a few sheets of paper. Paperwork unrelated to registering the guest should be put aside until registration is completed. Additional help should be called if a long line forms.

Front desk personnel often have the opportunity to upgrade existing reservations. A low-key approach is best: "Since you made your reservation, two better rooms have opened up; one with a mountain view for $58, the other with a Jacuzzi for $62. Would you be interested in moving to one of these rooms?" Such an approach may increase room revenues and guest goodwill. The guest is being sold a better experience, not just a more expensive room.

This is also a good time to mention special coupons or discount offers and suggest hotel facilities and services. The front desk agent can ask if the guest would like a wake-up call, and use this opportunity to make sales suggestions: "Fine, Ms. Zimmerman. We'll call you at 7:00 A.M. Would you like room service to deliver our breakfast special of hot coffee, a cheese omelet, and freshly squeezed orange juice at 7:30?"

Another approach would be to inform the guest: "Mr. York, we have one of the best seafood restaurants in the city right here in the hotel, but it is generally very busy. I can arrange a reservation for you and Mrs. York now if you'd like, however. Would you like me to reserve a table for you for our early-bird buffet or for our regular dining hours?"

Insider Insights

Judi Del Ponte
Marketing Manager
Marriott's Brighton Gardens
Sun City, Arizona _____

> *Judi Del Ponte's introduction to working in hotels was through her work as a singer in a band that toured many states and many hotels from 1980 to 1985. It gave her a unique outlook because not only was she a temporary hotel employee, she was also a guest because the band stayed in the hotels it played.*
>
> *After leaving the band, Del Ponte started at the Holiday Inn Corporate Center in Phoenix, Arizona, in the food and beverage department. After two years, she moved to the front desk and learned the operations part of the business. At that time she was introduced to sales and marketing. Following her stint with Holiday Inn, she worked for the Sheraton Greenway for two years as a sales manager, then at the Ramada Hotel Downtown as a catering manager. In 1992, she made a switch from hotels to work as a marketing manager for a retirement community owned and operated by Marriott Senior Living Services.*

At the Sheraton Greenway Inn, where I worked as a sales manager, we operated with a small sales and marketing staff—about three in total. But our salespeople weren't the only sales experts on staff. The people behind the front desk played an extremely critical sales role that embraced much more than checking people in and out. Front desk agents knew important information about nearly every guest who stayed at our property—information that helped shape the guest experience. They knew what type of room the guest preferred, and whether the guest wanted a special service or convenience such as extra towels or a wake-up call. They were truly instrumental in ensuring the guests' comfort.

That's what made front desk people so excellent at sales and marketing. More than any other group of employees, front desk agents felt the pulse of the marketplace. They were there to greet guests walking in, and they were there when guests checked out. That gave front desk personnel a tremendous opportunity to make the positive impressions that kept guests coming back.

I can't emphasize enough how important it was for our sales staff and the front desk to work as a team—to really communicate with one another. That helped us avoid the mix-ups, dissatisfactions, and embarrassments that could have negatively affected our relationship with guests. We had weekly sales meetings with front office staff to make sure we relayed to front desk agents and reservationists all the information we had on a particular group or individual. I also tried to personally contact front office employees every day. Since our property was so small, I could generally speak one-on-one with individuals in the morning or at night, just to see how things were going or let them know what was happening in terms of sales and marketing.

(continued)

Insider Insights *(continued)*

Many times the communication snags we experience have to do with written communication—that memo that gets misplaced, misinterpreted, or read after the fact. It's very important to touch base with people in person as well as in writing, and to make sure people understand what's being communicated. I believe that daily communication—with a personal touch—kept our departments in tune with each other. It helped people on both the sales and the front desk sides understand *why* we were doing something a particular way.

Almost every group or individual reservation that came through the sales office had special requirements. For example, some groups wanted a special block of rooms, some needed a direct billing, and some scheduled a special dinner or activity. Whatever the case, it was critical for front desk agents to understand the arrangements we had made for a group or a person—and if they didn't understand, to give us a call.

Front desk agents were so integral to sales and marketing because they were the ones who provided and followed through on the services that made guests want to come back or recommend our property. Front desk agents were salespeople, not order takers. They sold everything from the restaurant to the bar to activities on and off the premises. And they had fun—because they were working with other employees to provide a quality guest experience.

Too often, hotel guests are unaware of what the property has to offer. Suggesting valet service, a light snack in the coffee shop, a relaxing swim or whirlpool in the health club, or room service—even if the guest declines—increases guest awareness, which may generate additional sales at a later time.

Food and beverage. Good service, which includes a friendly attitude and a timely delivery of the food or drink ordered, is the key to guest satisfaction and sales success in the food and beverage department.[9] In addition to increasing sales, good service ensures that the guest has a favorable experience and will want to return.

Food servers who share with guests their knowledge of the food, its ingredients, and preparation time (as well as the specialties of other property restaurants) add to guest involvement in the property, which can increase profits. A good sales approach by the server also results in spending less time answering questions, thus avoiding guest irritation.

Food and beverage service offers practically unlimited opportunities to make use of suggestive selling techniques. It is imperative that food servers offer enticing suggestions that describe a delicious item: "Have you tried our award-winning cheesecake, topped with fresh strawberries and a dollop of whipped cream?" is much more effective than "Would you care for anything else?" A food server can give the guest a choice of two or more items and state why the guest should choose one of them. For example, "Would you like a shrimp cocktail to start or would you prefer our freshly made onion soup? The shrimp arrived just this morning and are absolutely fresh, and the onion soup is excellent—the chef prides himself on making the best onion soup in the city." Suggestive selling benefits guests, food servers, and the property alike, as it can lead to increased guest satisfaction, increased tips for servers, and increased revenues.

Cross-selling can also be used by food servers. Room service personnel can suggest the dinner special in the main dining room or a special breakfast buffet for busy business travelers. A food server in the gourmet restaurant can ask guests if they have tried the "traveler's lunch" in the coffee shop. These soft-sell techniques are excellent methods of raising revenues and exposing guests to facilities they might not have tried (and might later recommend to friends).

Service personnel. Service personnel fall into two basic categories: guest-contact employees and back-of-the-house employees. A great deal of guest interaction is usual for the valet parking staff, door attendants, bell staff, and housekeepers, while guest contact is not as pronounced with maintenance crews and back office personnel.

Service employees with a great deal of guest contact have excellent opportunities for suggestive selling. If the hotel is near an airport, the hotel's limo drivers can sell the hotel's facilities and the local area as they drive guests from the airport to the property. A valet parker can welcome guests and ask if they have tried a particular property restaurant. A bellperson can promote the property's restaurants, lounges, laundry and valet services, and other amenities as guests are shown to their rooms. As guests leave, the door attendant or valet parker can suggest they return for a promotional event or special hotel package. In all of these guest contacts, it is important that the service staff be sincerely friendly without being pushy.

While employees who have less guest contact may be limited in their selling capacities, they "sell" the hotel by their appearance, attitude, and attention to small details. A friendly greeting from a pool attendant and the cheerful attitude of the maintenance crew can help make a guest's stay memorable.[10]

Employee Incentive Programs. Employee incentive programs can be an effective means of motivating employees to sell and tracking sales results. Management may establish an incentive program for front desk or reservations agents who upgrade reservations (see Exhibit 2), or may provide a bonus to split among the front desk staff for every night occupancy reaches a predetermined target. In the property's restaurants, management may promote contests to reward suggestive selling and give bonuses for most desserts sold. Other incentive programs may include a cross-selling contest with prizes to employees or departments sending the most guests to a specific restaurant. The bellperson who sells more laundry or dry cleaning services than average and the telephone operator who makes breakfast sales with morning wake-up calls can also be rewarded.

Incentive programs must include methods of tracking results. A discount coupon that bears the name of the food server who has recommended the lounge, a business card or coupon from the bartender that the guest can give to the host of the specialty dining room, a special two-for-one invitation to the lounge show from the bellperson—all three examples provide a means of tracking the effectiveness of both the promotion and the employee.

When developing any incentive program, management should realize that while incentives in the form of cash, merchandise, or trips are often used to

Exhibit 2   Sample Reservations Incentive Program

Schedule of Bonuses

Upgrade Bonuses

$10 Upgrade to Poolside	$1.00 per night
Upgrade to Bi-level or Fallback Rate	$3.00 per night
Upgrade to Bi-level or Rack Rate Suite	$5.00 per night

Booking Bonuses

Reservation booked under Rack Rate	$ .50 per night
Reservation booked at Rack Rate	$1.00 per night
Reservation booked at Poolside Rate	$1.50 per night
Reservation booked at Suite Fallback Rate	$3.00 per night
Reservation booked at Suite Rack Rate	$5.00 per night

This is a very liberal bonus program with lots of opportunities to increase your monthly take home pay by $50, $100, or even $200. Every time you upgrade or book a guest, just make a copy of the reservation with the appropriate information, and put the copy in your folder, located in the count room.

The person who converts the most room nights during the quarter will be eligible for a grand prize (to be determined) at the end of the year.

This is an excerpt from an incentive program developed by a Best Western property. Reservations agents are given bonuses for room conversions and upgrades monthly, and a grand prize is awarded at the end of the year. (Source: From a speech by Robert A. Rauch, CHA, at Best Western's annual convention in Las Vegas.)

motivate employees, recognition is as important as the reward for many workers. In the bartender's story above, for example, he was enthusiastic because he was distributing cards with his name on them; he began receiving recognition from his guests. Certainly one of the best forms of praise and commendation is public recognition. Honoring top-producing employees with photographs and plaques that are prominently displayed, writing up success stories in the property's newsletter, and even recognizing outstanding employees at a special ceremony or awards dinner can mean more to some employees than monetary rewards.

Internal Merchandising

Internal merchandising is the use of guest service directories in guestrooms, tent cards on restaurant tables, lobby display cards, elevator cards or posters, bulletin boards, and other promotional items to promote the property's facilities and services (see Exhibit 3).

Technology also plays a part in internal merchandising. The Hilton chain is one of several hospitality organizations that utilize a "video magazine." Video magazines may be shown in either the hotel's lobby (guests can watch the presentation on special monitors set up near comfortable chairs) or in guestrooms through the use of an in-house channel. The Hilton's one-hour video showcases the facilities and services of the host hotel as well as detailing the history and sights of the host city. The Hilton's video magazine changes monthly and is slightly

Exhibit 3   Sample Lobby Display Cards

Targeting in-house guests, these display cards promise a lively setting for singles to meet on Friday nights, a romantic and elegant atmosphere on Saturdays, and an elegant Sunday brunch with live entertainment.

		Annual Internal Merchandising Plan		
	Placement	Merchandising Piece	Message	Cost
Jan.	Lobby Display Front Desk/Counter	Poster/4-color Counter Display/4-color	Weekend Escape	$150.00
	Coffee Shop	Table Tent	Sunday Brunch	$ 75.00
	Elevator Entrance Elevator Walls	Display cards	Sunday Brunch Valentine's Day Special	$300.00
	Lounge	Wine Bottles Hanger Piece	Valentine's Day Special—Champagne Split with Dinner	$ 75.00
Feb.	Lobby Display Front Desk/Counter	Poster/4-color Counter Display with Flyers	Murder Mystery Weekend	$200.00
	Coffee Shop	Table Tent/	Conference Package	$ 95.00

Planning an Internal Merchandising Strategy

A marketing committee is important for ensuring that all areas of the property are represented in the marketing plan. While internal marketing can play an important role in generating revenue, it is an area easy to neglect. Too often, internal marketing takes a back seat to more aggressive forms of marketing, and efforts are piecemeal, resulting in outdated, worn, or poorly designed posters, tent cards, and guestroom directories.

In order to ensure that the property derives the greatest benefit from internal merchandising efforts, several steps should be implemented.

Step 1: Plan

An internal merchandising program should be planned on an annual basis, and tied to the marketing plan and marketing priorities. A review of occupancy and activity reports will indicate which areas need merchandising, when merchandising is most needed, and what type of promotional material will be most effective for reaching targeted guests.

Step 2: Coordinate

One person from the marketing committee should be responsible for coordinating and managing the internal merchandising plan. A planning chart, such as the one illustrated above, will (1) help to ensure that major traffic areas and revenue centers are covered, and (2) detail the costs of promotional pieces.

Step 3: Evaluate

Results should be evaluated throughout each promotion by charting and comparing sales before and after placement of merchandising materials. Each evaluation should include an assessment of the promotional costs in comparison to the profits realized. If problem areas are found, materials may need to be placed in alternate locations or redesigned for better results.

different for each property, but each video provides traveling tips; features geared toward the business traveler; and, most important, information on other hotels in the chain, with a suggestive selling message to book into one of these properties.

Internal merchandising should be carefully planned and controlled. All internal merchandising posters and print materials should be *professionally* done, and should be changed regularly. (There are few things less appealing than stained or torn tent cards or guestroom directories.) As a general rule, there should be attractive, persuasive internal merchandising media in each area of guest contact.

Guest-Contact Areas

The Lobby. Posters displayed in the lobby should promote all of the property's food service outlets and other property features. Lobby posters should be placed in high traffic locations. Posters on walls and columns where they can be illuminated are eye-catching. Many properties find that the use of transparencies—slide-like posters illuminated from behind—is especially effective.

Guestrooms. Essential information should be located in one attractive room directory whenever possible; the usual practice of cluttering a room with tent cards, folders, notices, and fliers does little to promote readership. Room directories should be attractive and small enough to be carried (directories make excellent promotional pieces). Most important, room directories should not only list services offered, but also include *complete* information, including telephone extensions.

In addition to the directory, the property may opt for a simple message placed on the television set or on the nightstand. One effective technique is the use of a message like the following, signed by the chef:

> My specialty tonight is beef Wellington. Please call 9049 to reserve a table.
>
> Chef Lambert

A sales technique used in guestrooms by the Grand Hyatt in New York is extremely effective. The management of that hotel designed a unique room service menu that is, for all intents and purposes, a picture book. The menu, which is left open on the guest's desk, features a photograph of the finished dish on one side of the page and a description of the dish and its ingredients on the other. Door hanger menus (completed by the guest and picked up at 2:00 A.M.) also serve to merchandise room service.

Elevator Floor Landings. Many guests walk out of a hotel to breakfast in an outside restaurant simply because they do not know their hotel serves breakfast. Attractive signs in a glass-framed cabinet located next to the elevator call button can feature the property's restaurants, bars, and lounges, and the services and hours of each. The elevator area can also be used to promote valet or laundry services, entertainment offerings, and special upcoming packages such as a family discount package, a ski weekend package, and so on.

One of the most effective restaurant display posters used near elevators is found in the Marriott Southeast in Denver. When the guest pushes the call button on the elevator, a display case on the wall next to the call button lights up. Almost without exception, guests immediately read the restaurant poster in the display case as they wait for the elevator to arrive.

Elevators. Many properties hang framed posters within elevators to advertise their restaurants. It is curious that some posters are placed in the rear of the elevator, since most guests face forward or look upward when riding. A sign in the rear gets a momentary glance—if the car is empty!

Attractive posters positioned on the elevator's side walls may be printed on both sides and should be rotated to reflect the meal(s) being served during a particular time period. To make the cards more appealing and persuasive, they should feature a mouth-watering photograph rather than just copy.

Restaurants and Lounges. Restaurant promotion can begin at the restaurant's entrance with an attractive poster announcing the day's specials. Inside the restaurant, well-designed menus can serve as promotional pieces, and tent cards (one per table is ideal) can promote specialty dishes or other restaurants on the property.

Lounges can be promoted through matchbooks, tent cards, attractive drink or snack menus, and souvenir items. For lounges featuring entertainment, a souvenir program or an autographed photograph of the performer mounted in a folder embossed with the property's logo makes an effective promotional piece.

Barber and Beauty Shops. Hotels with barber and/or beauty shops can sell the captive audience in these shops on the property's restaurants, bars, lounges, special facilities, and reservations services through the use of posters mounted in strategic locations.

Reservations or Convention Desk. Properties with a reservations or convention desk can have fliers, brochures, and other promotional material readily available in attractive displays. Local attractions might also be promoted to encourage longer stays by guests.

Cashier's Desk. Many properties provide inter-hotel reservations information and souvenir items (key chains, postcards, etc.) at the cashier's desk to encourage repeat or new business. Many properties offer such souvenir items as shoehorns, key chains, and garment bags, but neglect to imprint the property's telephone number on them. All giveaway items should have the hotel's name, address, and telephone number printed on them to make it easy for former guests to call the property to make return reservations. It is surprising how many people can picture a great hotel or a pleasant restaurant experience in their minds, but can't remember the name of the property after a short period of time.

Back-of-the-House Areas

Posters and bulletin boards in back-of-the-house areas that detail current sales promotions, selling suggestions, and incentive programs can stimulate employee selling and remind employees that they can powerfully influence a guest's decision to return to the property.

Promotional Idea Bank

The opportunities for promotion are almost limitless, and there are thousands of good ideas that can be used to generate additional business. Here are just a few:

Rooms

Suite & Surf Package—Includes a three-day, two-night stay in a spacious suite, a welcoming bottle of champagne, complimentary breakfasts, a voucher for renting beach equipment, and the use of a heated pool and spa.

Bed & Breakfast for the Business Traveler—Includes room accommodations and a choice of a continental breakfast or a self-serve breakfast bar.

Christmas Package Tours—Includes deluxe accommodations, tours of historic homes decorated for the holidays, complimentary wine and cheese on the tour, and a special Christmas party.

Festival Events—Features a special promotional package around a local festival—a harvest festival, the anniversary of the date the local community was founded, a "Rodeo Day," and so on—or a special event created by the hotel: "Chocolate Lover's Festival," "Wine Tasting Festival," and so on. Guests receive room accommodations, participate in festival activities, and are given a special souvenir.

Romance or Anniversary Package—Includes deluxe accommodations; welcoming champagne; and special amenities such as French perfume, breakfast in bed, whirlpool baths or hot tubs, and so on.

Food and Beverage Outlets

A Day with the Chef—Guests have the opportunity to watch the chef in action, ask questions, and taste the results. As an incentive, discount coupons or a complimentary meal ticket may be included.

Wall of Fame—Reward frequent lounge guests with their own pewter mug. Engrave the mugs with the guests' names, display them prominently on a shelf along the wall, and explain to other guests that they can have their own mug after, for example, 30 days of patronage over a 12-week period, or after bringing a certain number of guests to the lounge.

Monday Night Football—Attract guests and local visitors with a giant TV screen, free snacks, and complimentary drink tickets to backers of the winning team.

Suntan Contests or Amateur Nights—Contests and audience participation events are an excellent way to attract hotel guests and patrons from the local community. Invite guests or local celebrities to act as judges, and offer property amenities—free dinners, weekend packages, and so on—as prizes.

Cruising the Swimming Pool—Sell drinks and snacks through the use of a portable bar brought around to each poolside guest, or have food servers clad in swimming suits or Hawaiian dress provide tray service from a tropical poolside bar and snack stand.

Special Services and In-House Promotions

Special Services

Another effective way to sell the hotel to guests is to offer special services that will make their stays enjoyable and productive. Because of the large size of the business

The Omni Shoreham in Washington, D.C., developed a month-long food festival with a Paris theme to attract guests and locals to its charming Monique Café et Brasserie. The festival was publicized in-house with posters throughout the hotel and at the café's entrance.

traveler market, some hotels offer business centers—24-hour offices with personal computers, photocopiers, fax services, electronic mail capabilities, and secretarial services. Other properties may promote food and beverage service targeted at business travelers: continental or buffet breakfasts, designated business lunch hours to quickly and efficiently serve busy executives, and combination meeting/dining rooms.

To attract families, properties may offer supervised play activities, package tours to local attractions, in-house baby-sitting services, children's menus, and amenities such as cribs, high chairs, and play equipment.

Limousine service or transportation to and from airports, shopping centers, and area attractions are also services used to promote a property. Other special touches—free coffee, free newspapers, in-room closed circuit television, complimentary samples of local produce (apples, raisins, nuts, etc.) or products (wines, chocolates, and so on), and fresh flowers also play an important part in creating an atmosphere that will make a guest feel welcome and generate repeat business and referrals.

In-House Promotions

Many properties sponsor in-house promotions—special two-for-one coupons, contests and drawings, and special events—that make a stay more enjoyable and generate additional revenue.

One example of an internal promotion is a secretaries' club—a program that involves the secretaries of corporate guests in a number of planned activities. By guaranteeing corporate room rates, providing an exclusive telephone number or a direct contact person at the hotel, and ensuring VIP treatment for guests referred by these secretaries, a solid corporate business base can be built and maintained. To keep secretaries motivated, properties may offer health club privileges (or discounts), complimentary or discounted meals and drinks at food and beverage outlets, annual lunches or receptions, annual gifts (roses, chocolates, a free weekend getaway, etc.), and other amenities to secretaries participating in the program.

Other promotions designed to encourage repeat business may include frequent traveler programs—a point system that rewards guests who accumulate a certain number of points with gifts or room nights; promotional giveaways—all guests in the hotel are given a gift, but must fill out a redemption coupon to receive it (these coupons provide information that can help generate repeat business); and special packages for frequent guests or a specific target market.

The property's food and beverage outlets can benefit from in-house promotions such as two-for-one specials, discount coupons, special activities and contests, and "get acquainted" teas or cocktail hours.

The number of ways to promote to guests who are already registered (or guests who frequently return and already have a favorable impression of the property) are practically unlimited. By developing creative approaches and fun-filled activities, and awarding appropriate gifts or prizes, the property can greatly increase its base of business and leave its guests eagerly looking forward to the property's next special promotion.

Endnotes

1. From William Hulett's column in the Stouffer hotel chain's newsletter *Impressions: A Magazine for Stouffer Hotel Company Guests and Employees,* Summer 1991: Volume 8, Number 2, p. 2.

2. 200 guestrooms × 80% = 160 rooms rented × 1.5 persons per room = 240 guests per day × 365 days per year = 87,600 guests × $2 additional expenditure each = $175,200 per year.

3. From a lecture given by Michael Hurst at the University of Nevada, Las Vegas.

4. For tips on how to handle angry guests, see *Solving Guest Problems* (East Lansing, Mich.: Educational Institute of the American Hotel & Motel Association). Videotape.

5. Examples of positive employee-guest interaction are shown in *Guest Service: Putting the Guest First* (East Lansing, Mich.: Educational Institute of the American Hotel & Motel Association). Videotape.

6. Information on upgrading reservations is provided in *Suggestive Selling* (East Lansing, Mich.: Educational Institute of the American Hotel & Motel Association). Videotape.

7. Suggestive selling techniques are discussed in *Suggestive Selling* (East Lansing, Mich.: Educational Institute of the American Hotel & Motel Association). Videotape.

8. For a more detailed discussion of front desk procedures, see Michael L. Kasavana and Richard Brooks, *Managing Front Office Operations,* 4th ed. (East Lansing, Mich.: Educational Institute of the American Hotel & Motel Association, 1995).

9. Information on providing good food and beverage service is provided in *Food and Beverage Quality Service Skills* (East Lansing, Mich.: Educational Institute of the American Hotel & Motel Association), a two-videotape set; and *Food & Beverage Suggestive Selling* (East Lansing, Mich.: Educational Institute of the American Hotel & Motel Association). Videotape.

10. For suggestions on how to get all employees involved in guest service, see *Guest Service: Building a Professional Team* (East Lansing, Mich.: Educational Institute of the American Hotel & Motel Association). Videotape.

Key Terms

bottom-up method
cross-selling
employee empowerment
in-house promotion
internal marketing
internal merchandising

internal sales
rate-category-alternatives method
suggestive selling
top-down method
upgrading

Review Questions

1. How do internal sales and internal marketing differ?

2. Why do many companies hesitate to empower employees with the authority to respond to customer needs?

3. What is the role of the general manager in internal sales?

4. What is the three-part process for developing a sales-oriented hotel staff?

5. What are several techniques that might be used to establish relationships and dialogues with corporate travelers?

6. What are several ways employees can learn and use guests' names?

7. What are three internal sales skills?

8. What are three techniques for upgrading reservations? Distinguish among the three and suggest when each should be used.

9. Why are front desk personnel pivotal to the success of a property?

10. What two suggestive selling guidelines should be observed by food servers?

11. What is cross-selling?

12. How do employee incentive programs provide additional impetus to internal sales?

13. What are some examples of internal merchandising?

14. Add to the promotional idea bank on page 223. What outstanding internal promotions have you seen at hotels?

Chapter Outline

Positioning Restaurants and Lounges
    Positioning Research
        Trading Area and Guest Profile Research
        Situation Analysis
        Competition Analysis
        Current Trend Research
Merchandising Food and Beverages
    Creating Menus That Sell
        Image
        Price
        Message
        Design
        Supplemental Menus
    Other F&B Merchandising Methods
        Product Packaging
        Added-Value Alternatives
        Point-of-Purchase Materials
        Suggestive Selling
        Special Promotional Items
Promoting Restaurants and Lounges
    Types of Promotions
    Planning Effective Promotions
Building Repeat Business
    The Importance of Employees
    Guest Follow-up
Other Food Service Operations
    Room Service
    Limited-Service Operations

7

Restaurant and Lounge Sales

THERE WAS A TIME IN the not too distant past when hotel managers considered in-house restaurants to be a necessary evil. Today, however, hotel restaurants are being promoted and patronized more than ever before. Hotel restaurants have become "in" places that attract patrons from the surrounding community as well as in-house guests.

In this chapter, we will examine trends that are causing hoteliers to take a fresh look at the former stepchild of the hospitality industry. We will see how proper merchandising, creative promotion, and staff involvement can generate even more revenue from these increasingly popular facilities. (Because much of the following information can apply to both restaurants and lounges, unless otherwise noted the word "restaurant" will be used in this chapter to represent lounges as well.) While hotel restaurants and lounges are the focus of this chapter, much of the following information can be applied to free-standing restaurants as well.

Positioning Restaurants and Lounges

Since hotel restaurants may have to co-exist with other in-house food and beverage outlets (as well as room service and banquet service at some properties) and compete with local free-standing restaurants, the positioning of each restaurant becomes extremely important. For many years, hotel restaurants projected a tired, ordinary image. They existed as a token gesture to guests of the property, a boring alternative to eating out or eating alone in a guestroom.

Today's hotel restaurants range from the bright and cheery to the intimate and elegant; from coffee shops to lavishly decorated gourmet rooms. Despite improvements in hotel restaurants, some surveys continue to show that many hotel guests prefer to eat in an outside establishment. With dramatic changes taking place, why aren't more guests discovering and frequenting hotel restaurants more often?

The answer is found in positioning. Many guests don't feel that a hotel restaurant or lounge is as good as a free-standing restaurant or night spot. This view presents a challenge to hoteliers. Their food and beverage outlets must be positioned (in terms of physical location, atmosphere, and prices) to compete with free-standing eateries and lounges despite this negative view (see Exhibit 1).

Combating the negative physical positioning of a property restaurant (or restaurants) can be a fairly simple matter. Sometimes guests are intimidated when they have to walk through the hotel lobby to an elevator and ride up 20 floors to dine in a restaurant. Or, potential guests may not realize that hotel restaurants are open to the public (some resort hotels, for example, feature security guarded gates). In the latter case, the use of billboards can beckon potential guests; in the

Exhibit 1 Building the Image of Hotel Restaurants

This eye-catching promotion, featuring a wooden spoon attached to a brochure, was placed in guestrooms at The Summit Hotel in Hartford, Connecticut, to promote the property's restaurant, Gabriel's. This campaign is typical of those that try to upgrade the image of hotel restaurants in the minds of guests. The brochure was designed to convince guests that Gabriel's offered better food and service than what a guest would expect to find at a hotel restaurant. It also stressed the convenience factor. There was no need to drive or take a cab to find superior food; the restaurant was just an elevator ride away. (Courtesy of The Summit Hotel, Hartford, Connecticut)

former case, it is a matter of promoting restaurants and lounges as separate entities—dining or entertainment choices that just happen to be located in a hotel.

Several hotels have remodeled their restaurants to resemble free-standing establishments. Hotel restaurants with outside entrances, a canopy, and valet parking have seen their guest counts go up. Giving the restaurant a separate identity is a good way to enlarge the guest base. When Jim Nassikas managed the Stanford Court in San Francisco, for example, one of the most exciting and amusing compliments he received occurred when a guest came down from his guestroom and hailed a cab to the hotel's signature restaurant, the Fournous Ovens.

Creating a unique restaurant atmosphere can be more difficult than changing a restaurant's physical positioning. Years ago, property restaurants were usually built just as a convenience for in-house guests, and were often poorly designed and underrated in terms of potential profitability. Most of these restaurants have not done well, and must be repositioned to attract both in-house guests and local patrons.

For some properties, repositioning may mean dividing a large restaurant into smaller, more intimate rooms, or "theme" rooms. For other properties, repositioning may require other creative approaches—restaurant lighting can be varied and "props" (a portable salad bar, greenery, etc.) can be used to produce different atmospheres for different meals.

An important part of repositioning an ineffective food and beverage outlet is to find out who makes up the property's guest base, why they are dining out, and

Restaurant Positioning:
The Case of the Johnny Appleseed Restaurant

"A motel restaurant can be a tremendous drain on time, energy, and financial resources. If you don't have the expertise, don't get into the restaurant business—you'll be courting a financial disaster. What's more, if your restaurant's a mess, they'll stop lodging with you."

This is the opinion of Peter Watts, owner of an 88-room Best Western Motel and the adjacent (and enormously profitable) Johnny Appleseed Restaurant in Fredericksburg, Virginia. The restaurant provides a higher gross and a better return than his thriving motel, chalking up a volume of over $850,000 a year.

How?

First, Watts cites "certain basics." A prime location, right off busy Interstate 95, a key route to Florida. A unique name (it's now registered) that's "family-oriented and has a wholesome appeal—people love apples." And a "simple, inviting building" that won't deter those who associate frilly architecture with high prices. If there is any doubt about the nature of the place, a 14-foot replica of Johnny Appleseed near the entrance is enough to reassure the wary. "Hi, I'm Johnny Appleseed," says the replica when a visitor pushes a button, "and I'm so glad you're here. You'll love our apple fritters." It's actually the recorded voice of Peter Watts, who frequently assumes the Appleseed role—in complete costume—for promotional and goodwill appearances.

Inside, a rustic setting—provided by wood paneling, folksy art, and other homey effects—lends a casual, comfortable atmosphere. Long-gowned waitresses attend guests in private booths and free-standing tables.

For every breakfast and dinner patron, there's a free apple fritter, and for every lunch guest a free helping of popcorn. Service is virtually round-the-clock to help ensure maximum return on the facilities: hours are 6:00 A.M. to 10:00 P.M. daily.

Watts also places enormous emphasis on the quality of his staff. "Hiring the best people is the single most important thing the property owner can do to assure top efficiency and maximum profits. All other factors are secondary. You've got to have excellent people in managerial positions."

Source: Adapted from *Lodging Magazine*.

what would appeal to these guests (and attract additional guests). The best way to accomplish this is with thorough research.

Positioning Research

Positioning research should become an ongoing part of the operation of a restaurant. Positioning research falls into four basic areas:

1. Trading area and guest profile research
2. Situation analysis
3. Competition analysis
4. Current trend research

Trading Area and Guest Profile Research. Research into who guests are and where they come from is critical in restaurant positioning. An important factor often overlooked is the trading area (also known as the catchment area) from which business is derived. Usually the trading area for a restaurant is much smaller than that for a lodging facility, and it may vary from day to day. There may be an entirely different trading area on weekdays than on weekends, for example. The trading area may even vary by meal period. The lunch crowd, for example, might consist largely of businesspeople from within a 10 to 15 minute drive or 5 minute walk, while dinner guests may be residents within a 10 to 15 mile (16 to 24 kilometer) radius. Knowing exactly where guests are coming from and how they are getting to the restaurant can provide valuable insights into directing mailings, choosing media for advertising, and creating menus that will appeal to each trading area group.

Once the trading area has been determined, research into a guest's age, gender, type (new or repeat), and employment can also be helpful in restaurant positioning. Information for guest profiles can be more difficult to obtain in restaurants than at the front desk. If the restaurant patron is a guest of the hotel and charges his or her meal to the room, the patron's room number can be noted and information can be obtained at the front desk from the patron's registration form. In cases where a great deal of business consists of walk-in guests (whether local or traveling), there are a number of ways in which guest profile information can be obtained.

Personal conversation or observation. The host or food server can get information by conversing with guests, or by observing details such as an out-of-town driver's license used as identification when cashing a check, or a briefcase or business conversation that identifies a guest as a businessperson, and so on.

Special promotions. If the restaurant caters to a business trade, it can run a free-meal promotion and request the business cards of patrons as entry forms. One or more of the cards can be drawn on specified dates, and the winners given a complimentary meal. This type of promotion yields names, occupations, and telephone numbers, and is extremely cost-effective.

Guest surveys. Questionnaires or evaluation forms are excellent sources of information that can assist in menu planning and the planning of promotions for certain target markets. Questionnaires vary in content. A property targeting business lunch guests, for example, may use a questionnaire that asks questions relating to favorite food selections, speed of service, and other amenities that would make the restaurant more attractive to the business community. Or, a questionnaire can focus on food preparation (such as the trend from fried foods to broiled and steamed items), service (whether guests prefer buffets or table service), or general demographics (to get an accurate breakdown of market segments currently using the restaurant).

Completed guest surveys can assist the restaurant staff in serving present markets and give clues as to markets being missed. They can also aid management in making pricing decisions.

To encourage filling out questionnaires or other survey forms, a server can draw attention to the form and tell guests that they will receive a bonus gift or discount coupon if the form is filled out and presented when making payment. The restaurant can also provide conveniences to make filling out the form easier. This can include a complimentary pen, or providing an envelope for the completed survey. A guest who has received less-than-perfect food or service may feel intimidated when turning in an unflattering survey to his or her food server; an envelope ensures anonymity and may encourage more guests to respond. Still other food and beverage outlets provide stamped, self-addressed survey cards or questionnaires that may be filled out and returned at the diner's convenience.

Situation Analysis. Situation (or current business) analysis can be used to identify market segments. If a situation analysis shows that most of the property's lunch guests are businesswomen, for example, the property can appeal to that market segment with an eye-catching salad bar and specially priced small lunch portions for light eaters.

The singles market is a rapidly growing segment at many properties. Properties with a large singles clientele have developed a number of innovative ideas to profit from this lucrative market. One idea is the "Friendship Table." Friendship tables are designed to provide single diners with company and conversation if they don't want to eat by themselves (see Exhibit 2). While this idea has long been used on cruise ships, it is relatively new to the hospitality industry and has become a popular addition in many restaurants.

The senior citizens market may be important in a restaurant's positioning, especially if the restaurant is located in a hotel that is a favorite destination of seniors. Many hotel restaurants now have special menus, portions, and discounts for senior citizens.

Situation analysis also entails a look at statistics. Nearly all hotels make use of room occupancy statistics, but fewer have access to restaurant occupancy data such as total covers and table turnover ratios per meal. Tracking covers, for example, helps to identify slow, medium, and busy periods, and also helps to determine patterns of spending and menu choices. For best results, covers should be broken down into the six weekly meal periods or dining segments: weekday breakfast (Monday–Friday); weekday lunch (Monday–Friday); weekday dinner (Monday–Thursday); weekend breakfast (Saturday–Sunday); weekend lunch (Saturday–Sunday); and weekend dinner (Friday–Sunday).

Using these meal periods makes it easier to track such statistics as customer check average (dollars); entrée average (dollars); and number of beverages, desserts, and side items sold during each period. These statistics help managers to analyze strengths and weaknesses and take steps to increase sales, such as asking food servers to make a special effort to sell desserts during a typically slow dessert meal period. In addition, a breakdown by meal period provides invaluable information to assist in staff scheduling and tailoring service to the specific needs of guests.

Competition Analysis. While in-house research is extremely necessary, it is equally important to be aware of what the competition is doing. Areas that should be studied include the competition's:

- Menu items and prices

Exhibit 2   The Friendship Table

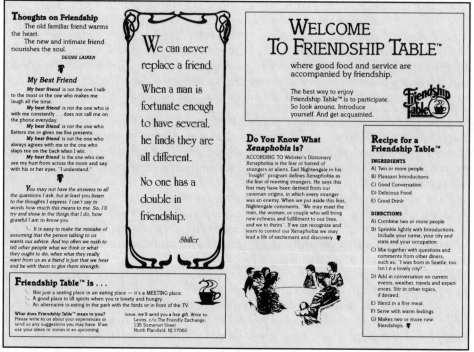

Friendship tables are relatively new to hotel restaurants but are rapidly gaining in popularity with singles, senior citizens, and business travelers who prefer not to dine alone. A newsletter such as this one can provide conversation starters. (Courtesy of Leon's Restaurant Services, North Plainfield, New Jersey)

- Facilities and services

- Mix (source and volume) of business

- Extra amenities—parking facilities, special menus or discount clubs for seniors, and so on

- Promotional efforts

Analysis of the competition should be used as it is by the rooms division—to determine property strengths and weaknesses and develop ways to differentiate the property's facilities from those of the competition. While questioning competitors and filling out forms is useful, it is far more effective to actually experience what the competition has to offer. Restaurant staff should visit competitors at various times (breakfast, lunch, and dinner; traditionally slow periods; and peak times) to get a complete picture of service and atmosphere.

Current Trend Research. Food and beverage managers should also examine current food trends and eating habits. Over the past several years, the trend has been away from heavy meals to lighter, healthier fare such as salads, fresh fruits and vegetables, and lean meats and fish. While some restaurants have been left behind by changing trends and have suffered financially, hotel restaurants can avoid this problem by supplementing traditional menu selections with trendy specialties. Menus can be changed each night to alleviate "menu boredom" for long-term guests, dining "adventures" (a sushi bar, a "select your own lobster" seafood buffet, meals prepared table-side, etc.) can be introduced, and special menus can be created for dieters and the health-conscious.

Merchandising Food and Beverages

Food and beverages can be merchandised by special packaging and pricing, promotional materials such as posters and table tent cards, and suggestive selling by food servers. But perhaps the most important merchandising tool is the restaurant's menu. A good menu, through the types of items offered and the presentation of those items, can enhance the image and increase the profits of any food and beverage operation.

Creating Menus That Sell

A menu must reflect the restaurant's positioning or image, provide information, and serve as a suggestive selling tool. While this may seem like a monumental challenge, it is actually quite easy when food and beverage managers follow a menu development cycle that includes image, price, message, and design.

Image. The menu development cycle begins with the restaurant's positioning or image. What image does the restaurant create? What type of ambience or atmosphere does it have? When people visit the restaurant, do they expect a romantic atmosphere or a casual dining experience? In other words, the restaurant's image refers to how the restaurant is perceived by its patrons, and the restaurant's menu must live up to their expectations (see Exhibit 3).

Since a restaurant's image is determined in part by the type of clientele the restaurant attracts (or hopes to attract), it is important to determine whether patrons are coming from inside or outside the property (or a mixture of both), and what market segments the restaurant serves. Does the restaurant cater primarily to the health-conscious? Do business travelers, who usually prefer rapid service during their lunch hours, make up the largest number of patrons? Or does the restaurant serve a great number of families and therefore need a more varied menu?

Price. Price information is a critical menu consideration. What prices do guests expect to pay for menu items? Will items be priced individually (à la carte) or as full meals? Will prices appear at all? Pricing strategy must be determined long before the menu is designed, and must correspond to the restaurant's positioning.

Determining prices. Unlike free-standing restaurants, which operate with established overheads, hotel restaurants often share facilities (kitchens, storerooms, etc.) with other arms of the food and beverage department, making it difficult to determine operating costs or to properly price menu items. For this reason, hotel restaurants price menu selections primarily on a cost-of-merchandise basis. Since cost-of-merchandise can vary significantly, it is impractical to use a

Exhibit 3   Sample Restaurant Menu

Menus should be designed to reflect the character or image of the restaurant. The headings in this menu from the Beef Barron are reminiscent of the Old West. Important dishes are encircled by lariats, and line drawings reinforce the Western theme. (Courtesy of Hilton Hotels Corporation)

general percentage for all items. Common cost of merchandise targets are 30% to 40% on food, 17% to 22% on bar drinks, and 33% to 50% on wines. Therefore, to determine the selling price of a menu item, you must divide the cost of the item by the desired cost percentage. Labor costs for certain items (oysters must be shucked, for example) should also be considered.

It is important to remember that you "can't bank percentages," and that a lower cost of merchandise percentage does not always mean higher profits. Exhibit 4, which lists Tuesday and Wednesday covers, foods costs, and revenue, shows how average gross profit per guest can differ substantially. Even though Tuesday shows the lower food cost percentage, it was the less profitable of the two days.

Menu pricing is also difficult because restaurants face the problem of changing market conditions, including fluctuating wholesale prices for merchandise and alterations in what the competition is offering and charging. Menu prices in most establishments must be monitored constantly and adjusted for seasonal and competitive changes.

Exhibit 4 Menu Price Analysis

Menu Item	Tuesday			Wednesday		
	Covers	Food Cost	Revenue	Covers	Food Cost	Revenue
Chicken	550	$ 1,650	$ 4,950	150	$ 450	$ 1,350
Prime Rib	200	$ 1,200	$ 2,800	400	$ 2,400	$ 5,600
Crab Legs	150	$ 1,350	$ 2,700	350	$ 3,150	$ 6,300
TOTAL	900	$ 4,200	$10,450	900	$ 6,000	$13,250
Food Cost %	$4,200 ÷ $10,450 = 40.2%			$6,000 ÷ $13,250 = 45.3%		
Total Gross Profit	$10,450 − $4,200 = $6,250			$13,250 − $6,000 = $7,250		
Average Profit/Guest	$6,250 ÷ 900 = $6.94			$7,250 ÷ 900 = $8.05		

The following factors should be studied in order to properly price menu items for hotel restaurants:

1. *Type of operation.* Is the hotel restaurant a coffee shop, a multipurpose dining room, or an elegant supper club? Does the restaurant offer a varied menu or are selections fairly consistent? Offering a consistent menu may keep costs down. If the restaurant caters primarily to hotel guests who stay for an extended period of time, however, a varied menu that could keep extended-stay guests interested in on-property food facilities may be more cost-effective.

2. *Guest perception.* How do guests perceive the restaurant? Do they expect to pay high prices for superior service and menu selections, or do they see the restaurant as a casual dining room and expect to pay low prices?

3. *Competition.* How many restaurants are nearby, and how do their prices compare with the hotel restaurant's? How do their food, service, and atmosphere compare? When a patron has a special occasion for dining out, does he or she have only a few acceptable restaurants to choose from or are there many high-quality restaurants in the vicinity?

Message. The menu's message—the written information it contains—is an important part of a menu's appeal. Will the menu simply list the foods and beverages offered, or will it also include the size of the item, the cooking method, the main ingredients, and methods of service? In addition to describing menu selections, will the menu be used to provide information such as restaurant hours, methods of payment, special dietary information, and cross-selling messages for other property facilities? A restaurant with historic significance may opt for menus featuring background stories; a "fun" restaurant (a restaurant that features zany decor or that involves guests in sing-alongs, for example) may feature offbeat information.

Menu copy should describe food in an honest and attractive manner. It is important that guests know exactly what they are getting ("served with your choice of soup or salad, vegetable of the day, and dinner roll or garlic toast"). The menu should feature the actual name of the item. "Steak and eggs," for example, is too vague; is it a sirloin steak, a T-bone steak, or a minute steak? Menu descriptions should also include:

- The cooking method ("deep-fried in vegetable oil," "broiled to your specification")

- Other main ingredients (descriptions can be kept brief, but should focus on the freshness and quality of additional ingredients)

- Descriptions of any sauces used ("brown butter sauce," "white clam sauce," etc.)

- Information about unusual presentations ("wrapped in parchment," "stir-fried at your table")

- Health-related information (information about fat, cholesterol, sodium, and calories is especially important to today's health-conscious consumers)

When writing menu copy or checking menu copy written by a menu specialist or advertising agency, it is important that the restaurant's image not be tarnished by the use of sexist language, negative restrictions ("Your credit card welcomed here" is far more diplomatic than "Positively no personal checks"), or poorly designed promotions. One of the most common errors—and a striking example of poor taste—is the lumping together of a senior citizens' menu and a menu for children: "For those under 12 and over 65."

Design. The menu's message is only part of the presentation. An attractive design will enhance the copy and draw guests to featured items and specials (see Exhibit 5). There are many styles of menus, from a simple blackboard on the wall to parchment paper tied with gold cord. The factors previously mentioned (image, price, and message) will play an important role in determining the menu's design. A restaurant with contemporary positioning and an emphasis on fresh foods, for example, may select a menu enhanced by color photography. A family restaurant or a coffee shop that caters to a variety of tastes may prefer using a menu divided into categories: a breakfast section, a light-lunch section, a "hearty fare" section, a dessert section, a "for the youngsters" section, and so on.

Good menus, no matter what the format, share the following design characteristics:

1. *Effective use of space.* The menu must be clean and uncluttered. Wide borders, space between selections, and large type are effective ways to increase the menu's readability.

2. *Effective layout.* The most popular items, or those that the restaurant wants to promote, should be placed at the head of a list, boxed, featured graphically, or otherwise set apart. Items listed first in each category sell best. If a two-page menu is used, the right page gets the most attention; with three-panel menus,

Exhibit 5   Basic Menu Layouts

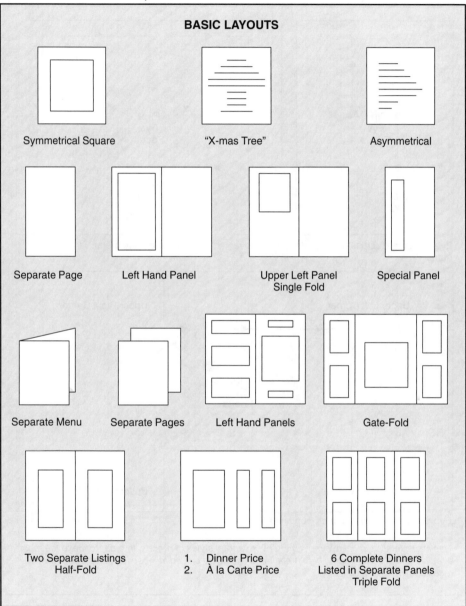

BASIC LAYOUTS

Symmetrical Square

"X-mas Tree"

Asymmetrical

Separate Page

Left Hand Panel

Upper Left Panel
Single Fold

Special Panel

Separate Menu

Separate Pages

Left Hand Panels

Gate-Fold

Two Separate Listings
Half-Fold

1. Dinner Price
2. À la Carte Price

6 Complete Dinners
Listed in Separate Panels
Triple Fold

the middle panel should be used for special promotions (see Exhibit 6). And last but certainly not least, prices should be placed at the end of each item (this can increase the check average by as much as 6%).[1]

Exhibit 6   Menus and Eye Movement

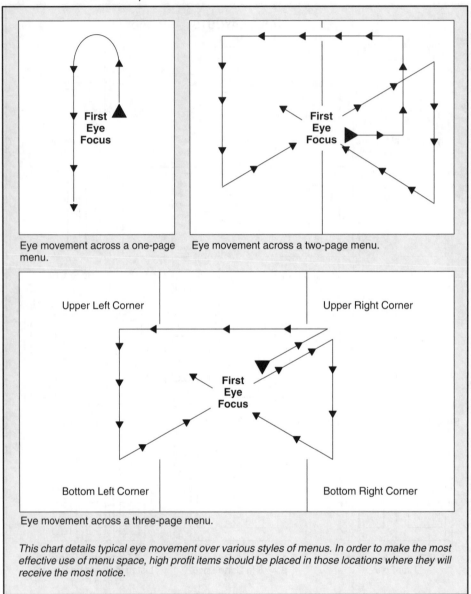

Eye movement across a one-page menu.

Eye movement across a two-page menu.

Eye movement across a three-page menu.

This chart details typical eye movement over various styles of menus. In order to make the most effective use of menu space, high profit items should be placed in those locations where they will receive the most notice.

3. *Eye appeal.* Good menus are attractive. The choice of paper, type style, and artwork is important. The color of ink and paper affects readability. Dark ink on light-colored paper is best, especially if restaurant lighting is dim.

Supplemental Menus. In addition to its regular menu, a restaurant may provide supplemental menus such as drink menus and wine lists, children's menus, and

Exhibit 7   Sample Children's Menu

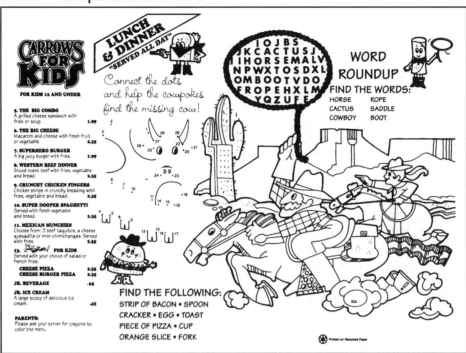

Children's menus are often designed to be entertaining. The games and activities on this menu help keep children occupied while waiting for the meal. Parents are invited to ask their food server for crayons if their children want to color the menu. (Courtesy of Carrows Restaurants)

dessert menus. Children's menus are often designed as colorful take-home items, and may feature games or stories to keep children occupied while waiting for the meal (see Exhibit 7). Dessert menus are an effective addition to the regular menu; by the time the meal is over, guests may have forgotten which desserts are available.

Clip-ons are used to avoid expensive reprinting when restaurants supplement the regular menu with daily specials, theme meals, or special menu items in season. If a restaurant plans to use clip-ons, appropriate space should be allotted in the menu's design. Perhaps a blank inside flap or a blank space in the center of the menu can be set aside so the clip-on does not obscure other entrées.

Other F&B Merchandising Methods

In addition to menus, restaurants can use merchandising methods such as the following to increase sales:

- Product packaging
- Added-value alternatives
- Point-of-purchase materials

- Suggestive selling

- Special promotional items

Product Packaging. In order to sell, product packaging relies on an appeal to the senses. Product packaging—both table setting and the garnishing of the food or beverage—usually involves producing a special visual impact that can turn something ordinary into a special delight.

Product packaging can begin at the restaurant's entrance—a display of wines, a tempting dessert cart, or an attractive display of fresh produce are all effective sales tools. A display of fresh produce not only whets the appetite but also conveys the message that the restaurant uses only the freshest ingredients. This message can be carried throughout the restaurant through salad bars and table decor.

Product packaging can inspire promotions that generate additional business. One restaurant featured an apple promotion that included theme posters, recipe brochures, bushel basket displays of apples, special menu items such as baked apples and apple bread, and a free apple with each deli soup and sandwich lunch.

Many food and drink items can be made special through product packaging. Colorful garnishes of fresh fruits or vegetables create a feeling of quality and abundance and can make even simple food and beverage items more appetizing and salable. A bowl of dry cereal, for example, becomes a more memorable breakfast when served with a choice of colorful fruits (bowls of bananas, strawberries, raisins, and so on). A simple salad can become a work of art when enhanced with skewers of fresh fruits or vegetables.

Unusual presentations can also be used for eye-appeal. A hollowed-out avocado can become a unique bowl for homemade guacamole, an impressive pineapple half may showcase a special chicken curry or salad, and a fresh, crispy tortilla bowl can hold a taco salad. Drinks, too, whether alcoholic or non-alcoholic, can generate impulse sales when presented in unique ways. An unusual glass; the addition of attractive garnishes, whether as simple as a few grapes placed in a glass of wine or as elaborate as artistically arranged skewered fruit in frosted glasses; and the use of specialty items (tiny umbrellas, unusual stirrers, or even a clay parrot or sombrero attached to a wooden skewer) can generate interest and sales.

Novelty service-ware might also increase food sales. Eggs served in cast-iron skillets, bread warm from the oven and offered on miniature breadboards, and soups brought to the table in small covered kettles are all examples of creative merchandising that sells.

Creativity is equally important in how the food is offered to guests. When every restaurant in town is serving prime rib, for example, why should a guest choose the hotel's? One answer might be the hotel's unique way of serving the meal. Perhaps the ribs are rolled to each table on a serving cart and the guest chooses his or her cut and watches it being sliced to order. Or, rather than making a salad in the kitchen, dousing it with salad dressing, and setting it unceremoniously on the table, a food server can prepare the salad at the guest's table, spinning the salad and sprinkling dressing over it as it spins. In either case, the difference is *entertainment value,* and dining becomes more than satisfying hunger. It becomes an experience to be enjoyed.

Sales can be increased by presenting a spectacular dessert early in the evening. A complimentary dish such as bananas flambé can be presented to one table of guests (the guests can be told they have been chosen to receive the dessert for any number of reasons), and sales of that item are almost guaranteed to increase as other guests are impressed by the flaming presentations. The ways that creative product packaging can be used to boost sales are almost endless.

Added-Value Alternatives. Not all guests are influenced by showmanship, however; there will always be guests who are most interested in getting value for their money. The principle behind added-value alternatives is simple—the guest is given an opportunity to purchase the greatest value among several alternatives. The ways in which to offer greater value are limited only by the imagination of the restaurant manager.

One way to provide value alternatives is to offer various sizes of items, whether the item is a cup of coffee or a steak. Salad items can be sold on different-size plates; steak can be sold by the ounce to appeal to those with small appetites. When large sizes are offered, it is important to note that although the cost-of-merchandise percentage rises, the contribution margin or profit per guest also rises.

Another option that will appeal to value-conscious guests is offering price alternatives—the choice of full meals or à la carte entrées, for example. Other examples of price alternatives are salad bars priced both with and without a dinner entrée, pie offered with or without ice cream, and drinks offered with or without appetizers. In order for this method to be effective, guests must see real value—an alternative that appeals to their lifestyle. Guests who never eat ice cream on their pie, for example, will appreciate not having to pay a higher price.

Prices also figure into another way to provide added-value alternatives: package pricing. This technique is often used in restaurants, and involves including a number of items in one selection; the price of the items, of course, would be higher if purchased separately. Examples of this type of alternative include offering a glass of wine with dinner; a sandwich served with a choice of soup or salad and beverage; a dinner entrée that comes complete with a choice of salad, vegetables, breads, and dessert; and so on.

Point-of-Purchase Materials. Sometimes guests are not influenced by either product packaging or value factors, and must be coaxed into making selections. Point-of-purchase merchandising can be used to promote specialty or high-profit items to best advantage. Merchandising at the point of purchase makes extensive use of display advertising such as posters, tent cards on tables (see Exhibit 8), and additional graphic reinforcement such as strategically placed salad bars, displays of wines, and dessert carts.

Some properties also use tabletop selling—for example, a bottle of wine labeled with a tag identifying it as the "wine of the month," or complimentary samples of appetizers or entrées that the restaurant is promoting. When using tabletop selling, the restaurant must make it clear whether the item is complimentary or for sale. If a bottle of wine is for purchase only, it must be clearly identified as such and

Exhibit 8   Sample Point-of-Purchase Display

Some point-of-purchase displays are as elaborate as this six-panel, full-color tent card promoting exotic drinks. Point-of-purchase materials are used to encourage impulse sales. (Courtesy of Flamingo Hilton and Tower, Las Vegas, Nevada)

guests must not feel obligated to buy. If a fruit basket contains complimentary fruit and is not on the table strictly for decoration or for sale, a simple banner ("With our compliments") can clear up any confusion and make guests feel more at home.

Point-of-purchase merchandising can lead undecided guests into making impulse decisions but, like menus, it has a limitation: it is a one-way communications medium. There is still a missing ingredient: people.

Suggestive Selling. Food servers and other restaurant personnel play an important part in merchandising food and beverages. One of their most effective merchandising tools is suggestive selling. Suggestive selling can begin from the moment a guest is seated. The food server can suggest a cocktail from the bar or a special appetizer to begin the meal. A group can be offered an appetizer sampler plate, and the food server can suggest several appetizers that can be ordered by various members of the group and shared. Entrées may be suggested or upgraded with a few suggestive-selling phrases. After the meal the food server can suggest a choice of desserts rather than just asking if anyone would like dessert. The chances of sales success are enhanced with the use of an attractive dessert cart.

Suggestive selling can also be used in a lounge. The bartender or cocktail server can suggest appetizers or specialty drinks: "We have a terrific new tropical drink

Dessert trays are often used by food servers to enhance their suggestive selling presentation.

that I know you'd enjoy. It's made with a blend of fresh pineapple juice and orange juice with our quality rum, and is served in a tall, frosted glass."[2]

Suggestive selling responsibilities should be part of a food or cocktail server's job description, and wait staff should be trained in the proper use of suggestive sales. Suggestive selling should never be perceived as an attempt to railroad guests into accepting items they really don't want, or as an effort to "bump up" a check. Instead, suggestive sales should be viewed as a part of good service, a way to serve the best interests of guests and make their visits more enjoyable.

Management should make sure that the staff understands the principles behind suggestive selling and the audiences that are most receptive to this sales technique. Leisure travelers, for example, may be more receptive to taking their time and trying new dishes than guests having a business lunch.

Special Promotional Items. Some restaurants use special promotional items such as recipe cards, postcards depicting drinks, and souvenir menus (see Exhibit 9). (If a menu is expensive to produce, a smaller-scale souvenir version can be designed to take home.) If the property is part of a chain, special promotional items may be available through corporate headquarters. They can also be specially designed by an advertising agency, freelance artist, or menu specialist. If outside sources are used, however, the food and beverage manager should approve the final design and ensure that the copy and design accurately reflect the positioning of the property.

Exhibit 9   Special Promotional Items

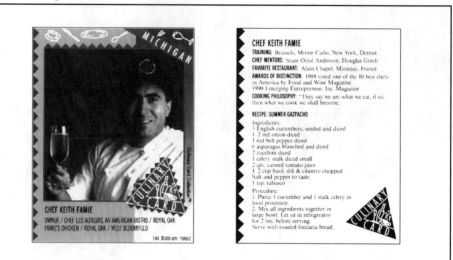

These collectible cards featuring Michigan chefs are the brainchild of Chef Keith Famie and General Manager John Messina of Les Auteurs, a restaurant in Royal Oak, Michigan. The cards have generated a lot of publicity for the restaurant, including a mention in USA Today and an interview on CNN (the cable television news station). "You beat your head against the wall marketing your restaurant, then do something crazy like this and get all sorts of national attention," says Messina. Plans are in the works to produce a set of cards for chefs in Chicago and New York City as well.

The cards are slightly larger than a baseball card; the front features a color photo of the chef, the back has information about the chef and a favorite recipe. A pack of 16 cards sells for $10.50, with 10% of gross sales going to the non-profit Rainbow Connection, which fulfills the wishes of terminally ill children.

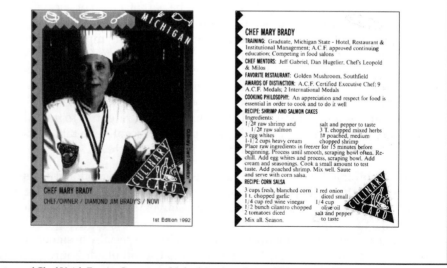

Courtesy of Chef Keith Famie, Owner, and John Messina, General Manager, of Les Auteurs, Royal Oak, Michigan (CREATORS OF THE CULINARY CARD COLLECTION)

Promoting Restaurants and Lounges

While word-of-mouth advertising lends exceptional credibility to a restaurant, it is usually not enough to properly promote the facility. Even if a restaurant has a popular menu, a good atmosphere, and an excellent staff, it won't be profitable if no one (or only a small group of loyal patrons) knows it's there. The restaurant must be promoted in order to attract guests and make a profit.

Types of Promotions

Sales promotions are useful for generating quick sales increases and can be targeted to times when business is most needed. Promotions can also be used to introduce new products or services (and stimulate trial purchases), to build excitement and entertainment for both guests and employees, and to build repeat business.

There are three basic ways to promote a hotel restaurant:

1. Personal promotions

2. In-house promotions

3. Outside promotions

Personal Promotions. Personal promotions include sales calls (both telephone and in-person) and sales letters to introduce prospective guests to the restaurant. Restaurant sales calls differ very little from sales calls made for rooms or banquet business. Whether the sales call is made by the restaurant manager or a member of the food service or sales staff, it should follow the basic presentation sales call format: an opening, getting prospect involvement, the presentation, overcoming objections, and closing the sale. Restaurant representatives should thoroughly familiarize themselves with these steps before attempting to make telephone or in-person sales calls.

Sales letters are another important phase of personal promotion, and may be used either as an introductory or follow-up tool to supplement telephone or in-person sales calls. Sales letters should be tailored to individual needs—a restaurant manager should not send the same letter to a business group and a bride!

In-House Promotions. In-house promotions range from coupons and contests to drawings and special events. The types of in-house promotions a restaurant engages in depend on the size, type, and staff of the restaurant as well as its typical markets and target markets. Promotions must be consistent with the positioning of the facility, and present a good reason for guests to patronize it. Creative promotions not only generate additional business, but also help to build guest goodwill and word-of-mouth advertising. In-house promotions that are cost-effective, build enthusiasm among the staff, and provide a benefit to guests (whether value or excitement) greatly enhance the image of the property as a friendly, comfortable place to eat and be entertained, and can help to overcome the stereotype of the boring hotel restaurant or dreary lounge.

Some of the most popular in-house sales promotions include:

"Four Walls" Sales Promotion

The three major purposes of sales promotions are to: increase guest traffic, increase the frequency of guest visits, and increase the average guest check.

While there are many ways to accomplish these goals, some of the best opportunities to increase business can be generated within the restaurant's own four walls.

Stimulating Lunch Business

Lunch business can be increased by offering "express" lunches (meals guaranteed to be served within 15 minutes or the meal is free) or by offering salad bars (this option not only provides variety, but allows guests to serve themselves).

Stimulating Dinner Business

One of the most effective ways to increase dinner business is by offering "early bird specials," dinners served at a reduced rate before the regular dinner crowd arrives (usually between 4:30–5:30 P.M.). Mike Hurst's 15th Street Fisheries in Fort Lauderdale, Florida, offers a $5 discount off any entrée during its "early bird" hours, attracting scores of retirees during a time that would otherwise be a slow period for the restaurant.

Special Promotions

Two other offers that generate additional traffic are birthday clubs and gift certificates. Birthday clubs usually offer the birthday guest a free item (from a dessert to a complete meal) or a meal at a reduced rate. The honored guest rarely comes alone—he or she will usually bring along at least one other person who will dine at regular prices. Similarly, gift certificates often result in additional sales. In many cases, the recipient will spend more than the gift certificate amount—and will usually not dine alone.

Increasing Guest Visits

Two popular options for increasing guest visits are the use of punch cards and bounce-back coupons. Punch cards usually consist of 5 to 10 boxes (depending on the length of the promotion) that are punched as requirements (purchase amounts, specific items, or number of visits) are met. Bounce-back coupons, which offer additional discounts at a later time, are a good way to build business during weak periods. If Tuesday dinner business is slow, for example, a weekend guest can be given a coupon good only on Tuesday night. An interesting—and profitable—variation to the bounce back is the "split meal" offered by hotels in the theater districts of London and New York. Dinner guests are given a dessert coupon to be used following the show, stimulating additional beverage sales (coffee, tea, liquor, cordials, wines, etc.) later in the evening.

Building Name Recognition

Giving guests something to take home often stimulates repeat sales. Popular items are calendars, pads of paper, pins or buttons, pens, matchbooks, and the business card of the manager.

- Coupons
- Premiums
- Sweepstakes, games, and contests
- Specials or special discounts
- Special-occasion clubs
- Gift certificates
- Sampling
- Food festivals and other special events

Coupons. Coupons are a popular way to offer a discount, introduce new items, or boost sales of a particular item. There are many types of coupons that can be used (see Exhibit 10). While all of the coupons listed in Exhibit 10 can generate immediate sales, it is important to note that coupons also have disadvantages. Some food outlets have "over-couponed," continually discounting the same item, leading guests to perceive the coupon price as the true value of the item so that they are reluctant to purchase the item at its regular price.

To avoid misunderstandings and ill-will, coupons should always be specific—the terms of the offer and any restrictions ("not valid on weekends," etc.) should be clearly spelled out, and each coupon should include an expiration date. Guest contact employees should always be informed of any coupon offers and redemption procedures.

Premiums. Premiums are items that are either given away free or sold at cost. The most successful premium promotions involve a series of items given out over multiple purchases—one item at each visit. McDonald's has been highly successful with this approach, as has Choice Hotels, which in 1992 sold a new character in a series of "Batman Returns" characters each week.

To be effective over the long term, premiums must reflect the positioning of the restaurant and appeal to the restaurant's target market. An upscale restaurant, for example, would not want to give away cheap toys or novelties; conversely, a budget family restaurant probably would not find it cost-effective to promote a top-of-the-line premium.

Sweepstakes, games, and contests. Sweepstakes, games, and contests are exciting ways to generate interest and build business (see Exhibit 11). Sweepstakes winners are chosen at random. There are no games to play and no skill is required—guests simply register or fill out a combination coupon and entry form. Games are similar to sweepstakes, but utilize game "pieces," such as match-and-win game pieces or scratch cards that reveal the prize contestants have won. Contests, unlike sweepstakes and games, require the entrant to demonstrate some skill in order to win.

Sweepstakes, games, and contests are even more effective if they require multiple visits. Holiday Inns, for example, offered a promotion that featured daily prizes, grand prizes, and bonuses for entrants, who were given another chance to win each time they visited. This type of promotion can be easily adapted for use by restaurants.

Exhibit 10 Types of Coupons

Buy-One-Get-One-Free (also known as Two-For-One)

No charge for an item or meal of the same or lesser value with the purchase of the promoted item.

Single or Multiple Item Discounts

A discount such as $1 off the purchase of two salad bars or half off one dinner.

Combination Meal at a Discount

A special price for a promoted meal (may include dessert and beverage, appetizers, and so on).

Discounts on Selected Sizes, or a Large Item for the Price of a Smaller Item

Discounts on a medium-sized item, a large coffee for the price of a smaller coffee, etc.

Discounts on Specific Purchase Amounts

Can be offered as percentages (20% off all checks over $25) or discounts ($1 off all purchases over $5).

Free Item with Purchase of Another Item

Free cup of coffee with dessert, free salad bar with dinner entrée, and so on.

Time-Fused Coupons

A series of coupons that are good during specific times of a particular promotion. Perhaps a different special each week, or a different individual item offered each week during the promotion.

Bounce-Back Coupons

Coupons that are given for future purchases. These are usually handed to guests when they leave, or they may be included on place mats or affixed to or inserted into "to go" packaging. Like time-fused coupons, bounce-back coupons can be used to stimulate business during otherwise slow periods—bounce backs should be good only on "slow" days or be for specific items that need increased sales.

Specials or special discounts. One of the most popular specials is the "Early Bird" dinner. This type of offer, which gives a discount to early diners, both satisfies guests who wish to dine early and builds business during what would otherwise be a slow time before regular diners arrive. Other discount options include offering discounts to seniors, students, and military personnel; offering free meals to children dining with their parents; and featuring discounts on a traditionally slow night (no coupon required).

Exhibit 11   Contests as In-House Promotions

Games, contests, and sweepstakes are often used to generate interest and build business. This contest, promoted by Marriott Hotels and Resorts, gives lounge customers the chance to win roundtrip tickets for two on Continental Airlines. (Courtesy of Marriott Hotels and Resorts)

Special-occasion clubs. Special-occasion clubs require a guest to register information regarding his or her birthday, anniversary, or other special occasion. An invitation, which offers a discounted or free meal or item, is then mailed to the guest in time for his or her "special day." Not only does this type of promotion build a mailing list, but additional sales are generated as well—rarely do recipients dine alone. At least one other person usually accompanies the "honored guest," generating additional sales at regular prices.

Gift certificates. Gift certificates can be issued in a variety of denominations or for specific meals (free dinner, etc.). As with special-occasion-club promotions, recipients will rarely dine alone, and, in many cases, the guest's check will exceed the certificate amount. In addition, gift certificates represent prepaid sales. In some cases, certificates are not redeemed, providing pure profit.

Sampling. Offering samples of new or specialty products is an excellent way to generate interest and build sales. Free samples give guests the opportunity to taste new items without having to pay for an entire dish. This type of promotion is especially effective if it includes some form of showmanship. Employees giving out samples of Swiss mocha cheesecake can be costumed in colorful Swiss outfits, for example.

Exhibit 12   Types of Advertising Used By Table Service Restaurants (By Check Size)

Types of advertising	Check Size in 1991*			
	Less than $8	$8 to $14.99	$15 to $24.99	$25 or more
Radio	55%	55%	57%	48%
Newspaper	81	80	81	75
TV	24	22	25	16
Restaurant Guide	42	59	66	63
Magazine	18	37	64	68
Billboard, Outdoor	44	29	27	18
Team Sponsorship	57	58	50	16
Community Event Sponsorships	56	58	61	55
Handout, Flier	40	49	54	40
Direct Mail	31	34	49	65
Press Release	17	25	36	57

This chart shows how the types of advertising used by restaurants differ depending on average check size. High-check restaurants, for example, reported using magazines, direct mail, and handouts or fliers as advertising vehicles, while making little use of the team sponsorship that is popular with many table service restaurants.

*1991 results for Tableservice Restaurant Trends, 1992, a survey conducted fall 1991.

Source: National Restaurant Association.

Food festivals and other special events. Themed events, ethnic nights, and other promotions, such as a "Meet the Chef" night or a "Chocolate Fantasy" festival, are excellent ways to generate interest and business. One restaurant staged a "Price Roll-Back" promotion to celebrate its 25th anniversary. Prices were reduced to reflect those on its first menu, and, while the promotion was initially costly, it generated tremendous crowds, and many guests returned after the promotion.

Planning ahead is the key to successful in-house promotions. Generally, major promotions should not run for more than four to six weeks and should be spaced with minimal intervals of two to three months. Maintaining a promotions calendar can help managers organize their promotions ahead of time, keep major holidays from sneaking up on them, and spark ideas for new promotions. April 29, for example, is celebrated as "Zipper Day" in Dunedin, New Zealand, to commemorate the invention of the zipper in 1913. Prizes are awarded for the most zippers on an outfit, and for telling the most outrageous "my-zipper-was-stuck" stories.

Outside Promotions. Outside promotions fall into two general categories: paid advertising and supplemental promotion.

Most restaurants, whether they are hotel outlets or free-standing facilities, make extensive use of a number of forms of paid advertising—both print (newspaper, magazine, direct mail, and so on) and broadcast (see Exhibit 12). Paid advertising offers the advantage of controlling the message to the consumer. Exhibit 13

Exhibit 13   Examples of Restaurant Advertising

provides examples of the types of creative advertising that can be used to promote a restaurant to both new and repeat guests.

Supplemental promotion includes the use of sales materials—discount coupons, fliers, offers of giveaways, and so on—and promotional pieces such as newsletters. A newsletter not only provides information about the restaurant's latest promotions or special offers, it also serves to keep the restaurant's name in front of the public. Since nearly everyone has an interest in food, this type of promotional literature is likely to be kept and referred to a number of times. And newsletters are usually extremely cost-effective in comparison with other print advertising.

Supplemental promotion also includes publicity. Publicity can play an important part in public awareness of a restaurant, and opportunities to receive free publicity are almost everywhere. Local newspapers may eagerly snap up news of restaurant expansions, special promotions and offers to local patrons, and feature stories about employees or special recipes.

Planning Effective Promotions

While sales promotions are used by many restaurants today because they stimulate sales, sometimes long-term guest loyalty may be sacrificed for short-term profit. Guests, faced with a myriad of discount options, may be more inclined to switch to the restaurant offering the best deal or postpone dining out until there is a "sale" or substantial discount rather than stay with a restaurant that has been satisfying in the past.

In order to combat this danger, sales promotions must be carefully planned and supportive of the overall marketing effort. To ensure that sales promotions are planned in a systematic way, management should:

1. *Analyze business patterns.* You should analyze records by volume and profit in as many ways as possible to determine areas that need promoting. Liquor versus food sales, lunch versus dinner volumes, and business by days of the week can be analyzed, for example.

2. *Identify profitable current business.* The direction of promotions will often depend on which areas are already most profitable; perhaps the gourmet restaurant is enjoying extensive local patronage or the coffee shop is attracting a large crowd for its Friday night clambake. Can profitable areas be expanded? Are potentially profitable areas being promoted to best advantage?

3. *Identify the audience.* What target market segments will the promotion be reaching? What types of promotions will appeal to the targeted segments?

4. *Set objectives.* Once you've identified the areas of greatest opportunity, you can set specific objectives, whether in terms of dollar volume, percentages, or number of covers or items sold.

5. *Evaluate promotion techniques.* A promotion may lend itself to publicity, paid advertising, internal merchandising, personal selling, or combinations of these techniques. Each of these techniques should be evaluated for possible use before actually creating a promotion.

6. *Determine an offer.* What types of items might be offered in a successful promotion? Prizes? Free meals? Discounts? Special dishes?

   When considering a promotion or offer, it isn't always best to offer discounts. If Tuesday is typically a slow night for a restaurant, simply lowering menu prices may not generate additional business. Instead, it might be a better idea to offer something special—a gourmet night, an ethnic night, or other themed event—at a higher price, which will still be perceived as a good value for the money. It is important to remember, however, that new promotions sometimes take several weeks to catch on; a promotion shouldn't be dropped just because it wasn't as successful as anticipated during the first week or two.

7. *Develop a budget.* The costs of the suggested promotion should be considered: printing costs, advertising costs, costs of incentive gifts for staff members involved in the promotion, costs of special offers, and so on. If not enough money is available to meet these needs, you may need to trim the promotion

to ensure effectiveness. A well-done small promotion is usually more effective than a poorly financed, half-hearted large one.

8. *Monitor the promotion.* An ineffective promotion can be discontinued if provisions are made to monitor results on a timely basis. If a restaurant is offering a half-price dinner special, for example, it is important to know the number of specials ordered, the number of regular dinners ordered, and the cost per person of the promotion.

9. *Involve the staff.* While this item has been listed last, it is certainly not least in its importance to a promotion's success. An enthusiastic staff can make an in-house promotion more successful than can paid advertising, and at a substantially lower cost. But the staff must be totally familiar with and sold on the promotion, especially if it involves special costumes or extra effort.

Building Repeat Business

Repeat business is a significant factor in the success of hotel restaurants. Therefore, it is important to cultivate guest loyalty.

The Importance of Employees

Guests do not buy just a meal or a few drinks; they buy a social experience as well. Social experiences always involve people. Food and beverage employees can help make dining or relaxing over a drink a pleasurable occasion. Well-trained employees dedicated to serving guests can make the difference between a highly successful operation and empty seats.

A good manager will make sure that his or her staff not only serves guests but makes friends of them as well. Managers should start with personable employees who are truly interested in each guest and eager to give guests the three free "gifts" that can make each visit memorable and build guest loyalty: recognition, recommendations, and reassurance.

Recognition. Recognition of guests is one of the most effective tools for building guest goodwill and repeat business. Almost everyone likes to hear his or her name and feel valued.

Name recognition should begin as soon as a guest walks in. This important part of guest relations can take a number of forms. In some restaurants, guests are greeted personally by the manager. If this is not feasible, a host can make guests feel welcome and introduce them to their food server, or give the food server the names of the guests before he or she waits on them. Food servers should use the guests' names often while greeting and serving them.

Recommendations. Recommendations are another part of the server's job that can help build repeat business. Good recommendations depend on both food and service knowledge. Servers should be fully informed about each item on the menu and should be ready to respond when guests ask for suggestions. Far too many servers are inadequate in this area. They answer questions about what's good on the menu with an evasive "Everything," and, if pressed about a personal prefer-ence, reply, "It's all good. I like everything."

These replies do not help the guest or increase the size of the check, so it is important that each food server know the ingredients in each dish, the method of preparation, and the approximate preparation time. In addition, each menu item should be taste-tested to enable the food server to answer questions about the dish's flavor, spiciness, consistency, and so on. For even better results, the restaurant's staff should occasionally eat at the establishments of competitors. If the server has dined at a competitor's restaurant, he or she can honestly tell the patron the differ-ence between the French onion soup offered by the competitor and the French onion soup served in the hotel's restaurant.

When food servers have this extensive knowledge, they find it far easier to as-sist the restaurant's guests in making selections, which helps build guest trust and loyalty.

Reassurance. Reassuring guests means making them feel at home. Food servers can use conversation and personal observation to tailor their service to each guest. A leisurely diner, for example, has time to talk to the server and taste-test different foods, linger over a meal that took time to prepare, and enjoy a dessert. A business-person, on the other hand, may want to place an order immediately and may pre-fer foods that can be prepared quickly. A group of guests engaged in an animated discussion may not want to be disturbed. In this case, the food server should sim-ply take the order and interrupt as seldom as possible.

Food servers should be sensitive to the special needs of certain guests. Diners eating alone, for example, may feel conspicuous, or families dining with small chil-dren may feel uncomfortable if the children become restless or cranky. In these cases, the food server can become a public relations ambassador by meeting the unique needs of these guests.

If a lone diner apologetically says, "There's just one today," for example, the host or food server can project a friendly image, be sure that the lone diner is not seated in an out-of-the-way location, and check back to make sure that everything is all right. Some restaurants offer a daily newspaper to guests dining alone, or (as previously mentioned) offer to seat them at a "Friendship Table" for company and conversation. Providing these special touches can prove to be enormously profit-able for the restaurant. Lone diners who are treated well are more likely to become repeat guests and may bring their friends to the restaurant as well.

In the case of a family dining situation, the food server can be friendly and at-tentive, and assure the family that the children are welcome. The food server should take the order promptly and, if possible, offer a light complimentary snack to the children to help prevent restlessness. Most children are satisfied when given a cracker, a piece of fresh fruit, or some type of "finger food" to occupy them while they wait for the meal. A little extra personal attention helps keep children (and parents) content.

Food servers can make all guests feel at home by engaging them in conversa-tion, truthfully answering questions, and involving them in the restaurant by shar-ing "trade secrets" or asking for feedback about the food or service. This usually

Insider Insights

Michael E. Hurst
Owner
15th Street Fisheries Restaurant
Fort Lauderdale, Florida

Mike Hurst is currently a professor at Florida International University's School of Hospitality Management in Miami, Florida, and is a director of the National Restaurant Association in Washington, D.C. He is a former regional (Southeast) chairman of the Culinary Institute of America and is past president of the National Restaurant Association. In 1991, Mr. Hurst received Industry Person of the Year honors from Pennsylvania State University and was the recipient of the Distinguished Alumnus Award from Michigan State University.

For food service students, there just could not be more exciting opportunities than at this time. You should prepare yourself to capitalize on these opportunities. If you lay the proper foundation, you should have an exciting and satisfying career.

My own foundation is based on five lessons I learned during my years in the food service business:

1. **Focus on people.** Early in my career, I was influenced by Ed Mirvish, then owner of Honest Ed's department store in Toronto, who achieved phenomenal business success due to his focus on people. Not only should you focus on your customers—you should also focus on the staff that serves your customers.

2. **Manage for your customers.** Another influence on my career was Paul Shank of the Tiffin Inn in Denver, who delivered food with runners to get the product to the guests hotter and faster. I asked Paul if he thought the runner system accounted for his success. Nope—his success was because he managed for customers: "Provide more service and you create customers."

3. **Dining is an experience.** Win Schuler's philosophy that guests thrive on recognition and friendliness was another important lesson. I learned that what people buy when they dine out is a pleasant experience, not just food. From remembering guest names, to remembering their favorite tables, to creating "Lover's Salads" and special appetizers and desserts, the philosophy of "giving to get" means exceeding customer expectations.

4. **Food can be fun.** The Coral Trout Restaurant in Brisbane, Australia, provided lesson number four: a specialty item—"Moreton Bay Bugs"—appeared on their menu. This fun dish proved to taste like lobster. I borrowed the idea and now serve a similar entrée at my restaurant in Florida—"Palmetto Bugs." I gave samples away and asked people to guess what was actually in the dish, creating a fun experience. Customers are willing to try a tasty, unusual item if you introduce it in the right way. Next time they will buy it because fun is precious at any price.

(continued)

Insider Insights *(continued)*

5. **Treat your employees as if your business depends on them—it does.** The guest experience is determined by the performance of your employees, and that truth has geared the way I manage. While recruitment and selection are important, I focus on making work exciting and fun, and on imparting a sense of worth to my employees. Giving the gift of friendship is as important or even more so than the good food, the decor, and so on. The lesson I took so long to learn is that the greatest compliment I can get is, "Where do you get the nice people who work here?"

These five principles, my "lessons of yesterday," are my game plan for tomorrow. Never forget that business is people. Playing the "game" of satisfying customers can be a non-stressful, fun game that, as a pro, you can win again and again.

---

enhances a guest's restaurant experience, and provides an excellent reason for the guest to return to "his" or "her" restaurant.

Guest Follow-up

One of the easiest and most inexpensive ways to build guest goodwill and loyalty is with a follow-up telephone call. Telephone numbers can be obtained from the reservations book or a guest survey card provided at each table. The call should be brief, but should express the fact that the guest is valued by the restaurant. Asking if everything was satisfactory can give guests an opportunity to express themselves and can provide the caller with the opportunity to handle complaints and obtain information to help serve guests better.

Keeping in touch with past patrons through the mails also helps to build repeat business. Personal notes or mailings are an excellent way to provide guest follow-up; notes may be sent after a telephone call or may be used to thank a guest for completing a guest survey. Another way to encourage guests to come back is to print a monthly calendar of events (see Exhibit 14). This type of general mailing can be used to announce special promotions, new menu items, or upcoming events.

Guests can also be given incentives to return, such as free meals after they have purchased a required number of dinners, prizes (food or merchandise) to frequent guests through drawings or special contests, and discounts on guestrooms or other property facilities for regular patrons.

Other properties make use of display items to recognize frequent visitors. Lounges may provide engraved mugs to regular patrons. Restaurants may even name a dish after a patron who has suggested the item or who is a frequent consumer of the selection.

Making sure guests are satisfied through guest follow-up is one of the most effective ways to build a loyal guest base and promote the restaurant. Satisfied guests are repeat guests and excellent sources of word-of-mouth referrals.

Exhibit 14   Sample Calendar of Events

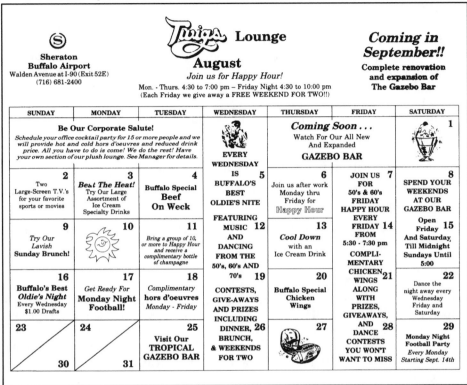

Calendars of events can be simple or elaborate, and may be printed in newspapers, distributed to local businesses, placed in guestrooms and on posters throughout the property, or used in a follow-up mailing to previous guests. (Courtesy of Sheraton Buffalo Airport Hotel, Buffalo, New York)

Other Food Service Operations

Room Service

Many properties, in addition to restaurants and coffee shops, offer room service for the convenience of their guests. Many managers consider room service a costly amenity because of the long and odd hours of operation and the impossibility of predicting the volume of business. Labor shortages and soaring overhead costs have also had a negative impact on room service operations. In terms of labor, for example, additional staff is required, including preparation cooks, stewards, order-takers, and delivery personnel, who must be willing to work the often inconvenient hours associated with room service operations. In addition, room service operations cannot take advantage of quantity cooking; meals must be prepared to order, which means a greater per-meal cost.

Nevertheless, many properties feel that room service is a key to keeping guests over the long term. To maximize effectiveness, room service operations, like other profit centers, require an individual budget and action plans to increase profitability.

Some of these action plans have brought about dramatic changes in the room service operations of today. The U.N. Plaza Hotel, San Francisco, for example, offers guests the opportunity to order food from a local McDonald's (the food is delivered on a silver platter by a bellperson). Other properties are opting for contracts with local pizza outlets, providing guests with a favorite food in the convenience of their rooms.

Other alternatives to traditional room service include:

- The addition of guestroom mini-bars with snack foods

- Microwavable items in guestrooms with mini-kitchens

- Hotel "delis," where guests can choose favorite foods and prepare them in their rooms

- Specialty kitchens that offer a single item, such as pizza, fried chicken, burgers, or sandwiches that can be ordered and delivered to the room

Limited-Service Operations

Limited service is a popular food and beverage option, especially with mid-priced properties and all-suite hotels. In a limited-service operation, one meal, typically breakfast, is offered to the guest at no (or a nominal) cost. In some cases, there is no table service—guests get their made-to-order breakfasts at a counter. At other properties, such as Budgetel Inns, a free continental breakfast is delivered to each guest's room.

Hotels have found that guests are enthusiastic about the free breakfast concept, both in terms of price and convenience, and many properties are featuring this option. But there are pros and cons to breakfast give-aways. The advantages are obvious: the guest saves money and time and receives an added value for the price of the room, the hotel can save money by providing meals or other food service without the overhead of a full-service restaurant, and free breakfasts enable mid-priced and budget properties to better compete with upscale properties that offer more amenities.

On the downside, the property may have to raise room rates to cover food expenses, additional workers may be needed to run breakfast bars or delivery services, and extra costs may be incurred for cleanup. But, overall, properties are finding that the benefits of serving "free" breakfasts far outweigh the disadvantages, and the "Breakfast Wars" may well continue through the 1990s.

In terms of generating guest relationships, free breakfasts are an ideal promotion. At Hampton Inns, for example, breakfast is served in a living room-type environment that brings guests together as "one big family." Mark Wells, vice president of marketing for Hampton Inns, states that guests not only get a high quality breakfast, but camaraderie is built among the people staying at the chain and the staff members servicing the breakfast—creating the potential for repeat business.[3]

Breakfast Wars

Some hotels are going to eggs-traordinary lengths to retain guests. The following hotels are among those competing in the free-breakfast market.

Budgetel Inns—Free continental breakfast (sweet roll and orange juice) is delivered to each guest's room; guestrooms are equipped with coffee makers.

Hampton Inn—Free continental breakfast, cereals, and fruit.

Hilton Suites—Complimentary cooked-to-order breakfast.

Embassy Suites—Complimentary cooked-to-order breakfast and express service (individual stations for coffee and hot and cold foods).

Park Inn International—Free continental breakfast in lounging area featuring giant screen television.

Holiday Inn Express—Free continental breakfast at limited locations.

Hilton Hotels and Resorts—Free continental breakfast as part of its "BounceBack Weekend" program.

Quality Suites—Complimentary cooked-to-order breakfast, including eggs, meats, juices, coffee, and hot and cold cereals.

Source: Edward C. Achorn, "Food Fight: The Free Breakfast War," *Lodging,* December 1990.

Endnotes

1. Herme Shore, "Money-Making Menus," *Restaurant Business,* May 1, 1990.
2. Serving alcoholic beverages properly is the subject of *Serving Alcohol with Care* (East Lansing, Mich.: Educational Institute of the American Hotel & Motel Association). Videotape.
3. Edward C. Achorn, "Food Fight: The Free Breakfast War," *Lodging,* December 1990.

Review Questions

1. What are four basic areas of positioning research?
2. In what ways can information be obtained for developing guest profiles for a restaurant?
3. What areas should be considered when assessing a restaurant's competition?
4. The "Friendship Table" appeals to what market segment?
5. How have eating habits and food preferences changed in recent years?
6. What are four elements of the menu development cycle?
7. What are some examples of product packaging used in restaurants?
8. What is package pricing?
9. What are three basic ways to promote a property restaurant?
10. What are nine steps for developing in-house restaurant promotions?
11. What are the three "gifts" that can make each restaurant visit memorable for guests?

Chapter Outline

The Catering Department
    Catering Department Personnel
    The Marketing Plan
Catering Sales
    Developing Leads
    Selling to Clients
    Planning the Function
    Managing the Function
    Following Up Accounts
Other Food and Beverage Sales
    Creative Refreshment Breaks
    Hospitality Suites
    Receptions
    Special Functions
    Off-Premises Catering
Meeting Room Sales
    Types of Meeting Rooms
    Meeting Room Setups
    Meeting Room Furniture
    Booking Meeting Rooms
    Managing Meetings

8

Banquet and Meeting Room Sales

IN LARGE PROPERTIES, THE PRIMARY profit center is guestrooms, with the catering department the second most profitable operation. The catering department of a hotel can produce additional, often high, revenues and generate positive guest relations through well-run banquets and other functions. Successful banquets can contribute greatly to the overall profitability of the hotel. The profit margin on sales for banquets often runs 35%, as opposed to 15% for hotel restaurants. There are several reasons for this difference:

1. Banquet sales volume often exceeds restaurant volume at a large hotel—in some cases two to one.

2. Banquets allow flexibility in pricing. Prime rib priced at $18 on the restaurant menu may bring $30 on the banquet menu. (Part of this increase is due to the cost of erecting and tearing down the banquet setup.)

3. Food costs are lower due to volume preparation. Also, no large inventory is needed for a banquet kitchen to function, since ordering can be done as needed.

4. Beverage costs can be controlled through pricing flexibility and volume purchasing.

5. Labor costs are lower. Since banquet servers can be supplemented by part-time employees on an as-needed basis, the regular banquet serving staff can be kept small. The cost of restaurant employees, in contrast, is largely fixed: restaurants operate on a continuous basis, and a regular staff must be maintained even during slow periods.

In this chapter, we will take a look at the dynamics of a successful catering operation—its staffing, responsibilities, and role in relation to overall sales—and learn how banquet and meeting room business contributes to a property's overall image and profitability. The chapter is divided into two parts. The first part will focus on the catering department. This department provides services for banquets, parties, and other business or social functions involving food and beverage. The second part will discuss the sale of meeting rooms, which, unlike banquet business, is most often handled directly by the hotel's sales office.

The Catering Department

Most catering departments have two basic responsibilities:

1. To sell food and beverage functions to businesses and individuals in the local community

2. To service in-house convention and group functions sold by the property's sales office

To plan and manage functions, catering department personnel must possess extensive knowledge of sales, service, the use of facilities and function space, food production, menu planning, and cost control.

The size and organizational structure of the catering department (see Exhibit 1) depends on a number of factors:

- Size of property and amount of function space available

- Types of catering to be handled

- The property's business mix

- Local and regional competition

- Departmental budgets

At most large properties, the catering department is an arm of the food and beverage department, while at smaller properties catering is often handled by a salesperson in the sales office. To be effective, this salesperson must be given extensive training in all aspects of the function business; selling food and beverages involves different strategies than selling rooms.

Catering Department Personnel

At large properties, catering is usually headed by a director of catering who supervises a banquet or catering manager, catering salespeople, clerical staff, and service personnel (food servers, buspersons, and so on).

The *catering director's* primary responsibilities are the sales and administrative aspects of the catering operation. As the hospitality industry becomes increasingly competitive, the catering director's sales responsibilities become more crucial; today's catering director may give a great deal of attention to soliciting or servicing accounts. The catering director is also responsible for the cost-effectiveness of the department, and works closely with hotel personnel (purchasing agents, chefs, and the marketing and sales department) to ensure that the catering operation falls within budget guidelines while still providing good service to clients (see Exhibit 2).

The *banquet* or *catering manager* is responsible for overseeing food and beverage functions and supervising service personnel, and may be directly involved in setting up function rooms. At large convention hotels, however, setup duties are often handled by a convention service manager, whose job is to manage the logistics of functions: the room preparation, setup, maintenance, and so on. Banquet managers also schedule personnel, prepare payrolls, and work with the catering director on special functions.

Catering salespeople are often employed by large properties to actively solicit business not brought in as part of conventions or meetings, such as weddings, Rotary luncheons, and similar local business. These salespeople should also be available to follow up on written, telephone, and walk-in inquiries. Catering

Exhibit 1   Sample Organization Charts

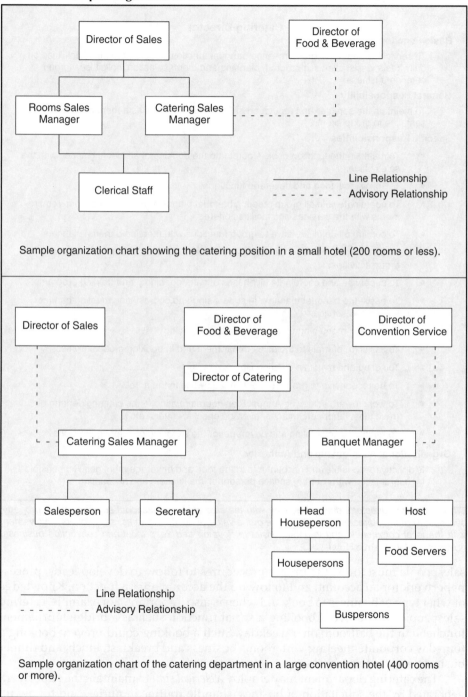

Sample organization chart showing the catering position in a small hotel (200 rooms or less).

Sample organization chart of the catering department in a large convention hotel (400 rooms or more).

Exhibit 2   Sample Job Description for a Catering Director

Catering Director

Basic Function

To service all phases of group meeting/banquet functions; coordinate these activities on a daily basis; assist clients in program planning and menu selection; solicit local group catering business.

General Responsibility

To maintain the services and reputation of Doubletree and act as a management representative to group clients.

Specific Responsibilities

- To maintain the function book. Coordinate the booking of all meeting space with the sales office.
- To solicit local food and beverage functions.
- To coordinate with all group meeting/banquet planners their specific group requirements with the services and facilities offered.
- To confirm all details relative to group functions with meeting/banquet planners.
- To distribute to the necessary hotel departments detailed information relative to group activities.
- To supervise and coordinate all phases of catering, hiring, and training programs.
- To assist the banquet manager in supervising and coordinating meeting/banquet setups and service.
- To assist in menu planning, preparation, and pricing.
- To assist in referrals to the sales department and in booking group activities.
- To set up and maintain catering files.
- To be responsive to group requests/needs while in the hotel.
- To work toward achieving Annual Plan figures relating to the catering department (revenues, labor percentages, average checks, covers, etc.)
- To handle all scheduling and coverage for the servicing of catering functions.

Organizational Relationship and Authority

Is directly responsible and accountable to the food and beverage manager. Responsible for coordination with catering service personnel, the kitchen, and accounting.

While a catering director's duties may vary with the size and organizational structure of the property, successful catering directors are fully aware of the value of telephone sales, sales letters, involvement with the local community, and in-person visits to develop and keep local and convention business. (Courtesy of Doubletree Hotels)

salespeople must know the proper procedures to follow to develop leads, process paperwork for an account, and follow up the account after a function. Knowledge of what type of business to book and when is also important. For example, catering salespeople should avoid booking a social function such as a bridge tournament luncheon in the ballroom on a weekday. Such a booking could prevent booking a four-day corporate meeting with rooms business and breakfast, lunch, and dinner business each of the four days.

The catering department may employ a *clerical staff* to maintain the paperwork generated by the solicitation of business, handle routine inquiries, and follow up

Exhibit 3   Catering Revenue as a Percentage of Total Food and Beverage Sales

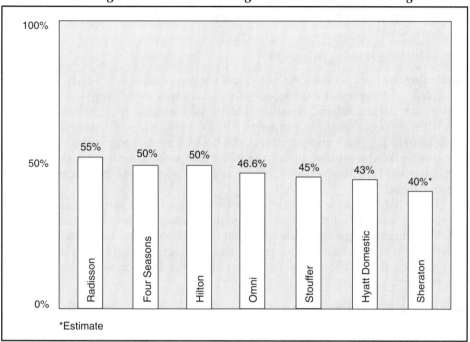

Source: Peter Niceberg, "Hotel Dining," *Restaurant Business,* August 10, 1990, p. 134.

on accounts. In large properties, a catering secretary may assist the catering director with administrative duties or manage the catering office.

Service personnel serve food and beverages, set up function rooms, and maintain banquet areas and equipment. Service personnel include hosts, food servers, buspersons, and maintenance or setup crews.

All of the employees just mentioned are involved in sales, whether they are actually selling banquets, servicing existing accounts, or simply projecting a friendly and hospitable image as they serve guests. This sales orientation is extremely important, especially since banquet sales at some properties represent 40 to 50 percent of the total revenue generated by the food and beverage department (see Exhibit 3). It is vital that members of the catering department see themselves and the department as important parts of the property's overall marketing and sales efforts.

The Marketing Plan

The catering department should have its own marketing plan, one that supports the property's overall marketing plan. The catering department's plan should include:

* Analyzing the competition
* Identifying key catering markets

- Setting goals

- Developing action plans and defining the roles of staff members in these action plans

- Evaluating results

Analyzing the Competition. An analysis of the competition is needed to determine the catering department's strengths and weaknesses in relation to competitors. Factors to consider include the location of the competitor, size of the function space available, aesthetic quality of function rooms, availability of equipment such as audiovisual equipment and portable dance floors, and the competitor's reputation. The use of a banquet competition and pricing comparison sheet can make comparison easier and provide invaluable information for positioning the property's facilities (see Exhibit 4).

While hotels, which can offer many services and have sufficient space to service events, generally have an advantage in the catering field, it is important for hotel catering managers to remember that there is non-hotel competition as well. Independent banquet and conference facilities, restaurant and banquet facilities, and mobile caterers should also be taken into consideration when analyzing the competition.

Identifying Key Catering Markets. Once the department's strengths have been determined and weaknesses corrected, key catering markets must be identified. There are three types of local business that can prove profitable: business from local corporate sources, business from civic and academic sources, and social business (see Exhibit 5). Local corporate business might include sales meetings, conventions, lecture-format breakfasts or dinners, and other meetings requiring the use of food and beverage service. Civic and academic business can include fund-raising banquets, conventions, annual parties, and special project events such as a hotel-based telethon or beauty pageant for such groups as the Jaycees. Social business includes weddings, parties, family reunions, and similar events.

For maximum effectiveness, leads should be qualified before a great deal of time is spent soliciting business. A potential client's creditworthiness can be checked through such organizations as TRW or Credit Bureau/Equifax, or may be checked in business financial listings such as Dun & Bradstreet. In some cases, a credit application may be extended to the potential client (see Exhibit 6). If the client's credit is approved by a hotel credit manager, a master account may be set up. If credit is denied, the client will be required to pay in advance. (One of the major reasons hotels are reluctant to extend credit except to large, established firms is that the services provided are completely consumed; they cannot be repossessed as can tangible goods.)

Setting Goals. After identifying potential sources of local business, the sales goals of the department can be set. When setting these goals, it is important to focus sales efforts on valley and shoulder periods. This is only possible when accurate information on function room usage is available. Useful function room statistics to monitor include:

Exhibit 4 Sample Banquet Competition and Pricing Comparison Sheet

BANQUET COMPETITION AND PRICING COMPARISON

HOTEL NAME	YOUR HOTEL HERE	HOTEL A	HOTEL B	HOTEL C	HOTEL D
LOCATION Address and Phone Number	(xxx) xxx–xxxx	(xxx) xxx–xxxx	(xxx) xxx–xxxx	(xxx) xxx–xxxx	(xxx) xxx–xxxx
BANQUET SPACE	# of Rooms/sq ft	# of Rooms/sq ft	# of Rooms/sq ft	# of Rooms/sq ft	# of Rooms/sq ft
Ballroom	1–7,050	1–5,500	1–4,000	1–15,000 / 1–4,578 blrm	1–2,178 / 1–3,608
Board Rooms	3–608			5	1–276
Meeting rooms	2–304		11–350 each / 2–1,200 each	6	10–5,779
Prefunction	1–1,218			1–3,044 Theater	
Other			a lot of pre-function space!		
PRICING	B L D	B L D	B L D	B L D	B L D
Lowest pkg	7.50 7.95 13.50	5.59 6.95 11.75	5.50 7.50 13.50	7.25 8.25 12.75	5.95 7.25 9.95
Highest pkg	11.50 12.75 22.00	8.95 9.95 16.00	8.50 12.95 25.00	13.50 14.25 23.75	8.95 10.95 18.95
Est Avg Ck	9.50 10.35 17.75	7.45 8.45 13.88	7.00 10.23 19.25	10.25 11.25 18.25	7.45 9.10 14.45
BEVERAGE	HOST CASH	HOST CASH	HOST CASH	HOST CASH	HOST CASH
House Brands	2.25 2.50	2.00	2.25 2.00	2.25 2.50	2.00
Call Brands	2.50 2.75	2.25	2.50 2.25	2.50 2.75	2.50
Premium Brands	2.75 3.00	Bottle avail.		1.75 beer 2.25 beer	Bottle only $48–$60 per bottle
Beer/Wine	1.75 2.00	1.50/1.75	1.75 1.75	13.50 bottle 2.75 wine	1.75
PERCEIVED POSITIONING	Highly social, Corporate rooms	Corporate 16% gratuity	Corporate 16% gratuity	group/convention some social	corporate/airport
PERSON CONTACTED AND TITLE		Linda Smith DOS	Don Marcos DOS	Mary Giesling SALES MANAGER	Ed Fisher SALES MANAGER

B = Breakfast   L = Lunch   D = Dinner

A banquet competition and pricing comparison sheet can be used to compare the property's positioning to that of competitors, and to record information that may be used to differentiate the property's catering services.

Exhibit 5   Sources of Local Business

LOCAL CORPORATE BUSINESS

Sources: Chambers of commerce, yellow pages, business section of the newspaper, trade journals, property staff members, competition's reader boards, referrals, past accounts.

Contacts: Sales managers, personnel directors, department or division officers or heads, key secretaries.

Types of events: Sales meetings (refreshment breaks, lunches, receptions); conventions (refreshment breaks, breakfasts, lunches, dinners, receptions); trade displays and exhibits (refreshment breaks); seminars and demonstrations (meals and refreshment breaks); retirement dinners; office and holiday parties; incentive vacations (meals included).

CIVIC AND ACADEMIC BUSINESS

Sources: Chamber of commerce listings; club directories; yellow pages; society, local news, and sports sections of local newspapers; competition's reader boards; referrals; past accounts.

Contacts: Organization officers, committee chairpersons, officers of alumni associations, social chairpersons of sororities or fraternities, coaches, key secretaries.

Types of events: Banquets; conventions (meals and refreshment breaks); annual parties; special project events (refreshments, beverage sales); class reunions (meals and refreshments); dances (refreshments, beverage sales); receptions.

SOCIAL BUSINESS

Sources: Society section of local newspaper; bridal fairs; mailing lists; personal contacts (jewelers, photographers, and so on); competition's reader boards; referrals; past accounts.

Contacts: Church secretaries, direct contact with the prospective client.

Types of events: Weddings (luncheons and teas, bridal showers, bachelor and bachelorette parties, rehearsal dinners, receptions); parties (holiday, anniversary, birthday, cocktail); family reunions (banquets, receptions); bar and bas mitzvahs; church-related functions (lunches, receptions).

These sources can be used to build catering sales. Since most competitors have access to the same sources, however, it pays to be creative. One successful catering manager, for example, visits local funeral directors twice a year, bringing wine, cigars, or other appropriate gifts along with information cards offering special rates for group dinners. His approach is rewarded by business from out-of-town families who are unfamiliar with area eating places.

- Function room occupancy by meal period
- Types of functions
- Pattern of unused times and days
- Use of guestrooms by function groups
- Popularity of individual banquet menu items

Exhibit 6 Sample Credit Application Form

CREDIT INFORMATION FORM

RETURN TO: RADISSON HOTEL ST. PAUL
CREDIT MANAGER
11 EAST KELLOGG BLVD.
ST. PAUL, MN 55101
(612) 292–1900

NOTE: TO BE CONSIDERED FOR DIRECT BILL PRIVILEGES, APPLICATION MUST BE FILLED OUT COMPLETELY!

NAME OF COMPANY _____

COMPANY ADDRESS _____

CITY _____ STATE _____ ZIP CODE _____ PHONE _____

NAME OF PERSON RESPONSIBLE FOR PAYMENT _____ POSITION _____

NAME OF BANK AND ADDRESS _____

ACCOUNT IN THE NAME OF _____ A/C# _____

REP. _____ PHONE _____

REFERENCE #1 (hotel or vendor) _____

CITY _____ STATE _____ PHONE _____

DATE OF FUNCTION _____

REFERENCE #2 (hotel or vendor) _____

CITY _____ STATE _____ PHONE _____

DATE OF FUNCTION _____

I HEREBY GIVE MY PERMISSION TO RADISSON TO VERIFY ANY OR ALL FACTS DISCLOSED AND UNDERSTAND THAT IF CREDIT IS ACCEPTED RADISSON'S PAYMENT POLICY REQUIRES ALL ACCOUNTS BE PAID IN FULL WITHIN (30) DAYS FROM THE CLOSE OF OUR FUNCTION. IN CASE OF A QUESTION OR ERROR IN BILLING, IT WILL BE THE ORGANIZATIONS RESPONSIBILITY TO CONTACT THE HOTEL ACCOUNTING OFFICE IMMEDIATELY TO CLEAR UP ANY PROBLEM.

ACCEPTANCE

IT IS AGREED BY THE PARTIES THAT THE FOREGOING WITH SUPPLEMENTS AS PRESCRIBED (if any) SETS FORTH THE ENTIRE AGREEMENT BETWEEN RADISSON HOTEL ST. PAUL

AND THE _____

TO PERFORM ALL POINTS CONTAINED HEREIN AND THAT THERE SHALL BE NO RIGHT OF TERMINATION FOR THE SOLE PURPOSE OF HOLDING THE SAME FUNCTION IN SOME OTHER FACILITY OR CITY.

THE PERFORMANCE OF THIS AGREEMENT BY EITHER PARTY IS SUBJECT TO ACTS OF GOD, WAR, GOVERNMENT REGULATIONS, DISASTER, STRIKES, CIVIL DISORDER, CURTAILMENT OF TRANSPORTATION FACILITIES OR OTHER EMERGENCY MAKING IT INADVISABLE, ILLEGAL OR IMPOSSIBLE TO PROVIDE THE FACILITIES OR TO HOLD THE FUNCTIONS. IT IS PROVIDED THAT THIS AGREEMENT MAY BE TERMINATED WITHOUT LIABILITY FOR ANY ONE OR MORE OF SUCH REASONS BY WRITTEN NOTICE FROM ONE PARTY TO THE OTHER.

ORGANIZATIONS CANCELLING FUNCTIONS OTHER THAN SPECIFIED WILL BE ASSESSED CHARGES AS PRE-SCRIBED HEREIN.

ACCEPTED AND AGREED TO:

ACCEPTED AND AGREED TO:

_____ (ORGANIZATION)

_____ (RADISSON HOTEL ST. PAUL)

_____ (ACCEPTED BY)

_____ (ACCEPTED BY)

_____ (TITLE)

_____ (TITLE)

_____ (DATE)

_____ (DATE)

In some cases, hotel catering operations offer credit to qualified buyers. To determine a client's credit-worthiness, a salesperson must fill out an application on the client and submit it for the approval of the hotel's credit manager. (Courtesy of Radisson Hotels International)

Action Plans: New Year's Eve in Vienna

As part of its action plan to generate publicity—and future bookings—for the property, the Hyatt Regency Grand Cypress in Orlando, Florida, puts on a special event called a "New Year's Eve in Vienna." This black-tie extravaganza transforms the property's ballroom into a "European palace" and the property's grounds into a winter wonderland. Sixty tons of snow are imported for the event, and guests are transported to the "Viennese ball" in horse-drawn carriages. The evening includes a five-course Austrian dinner served by food servers attired in traditional Austrian costume, and entertainment by members of the Florida Symphony Orchestra.

Creative promotions such as this one can be supplemented by strategically placed advertisements in local newspapers and in publications read by prospective guests in key feeder cities.

- Sales revenue per square foot of function space
- Average banquet check by type of function
- Average number of persons by type of function

Developing Action Plans. After sales goals have been set, action plans to reach those goals can be implemented. If a property has set a goal to increase wedding business by 65% over a specific three-month period, strategies might include the development of wedding brochures and planners; promotion of special wedding packages; attendance at local bridal fairs; and soliciting leads from local jewelers, photographers, and bridal boutique owners.

Action plans will vary with the goals set, target markets, budget available for promotion, and so on. Action plans may range from the simple to the elaborate. An action plan at one property might be to make 15 sales calls per week on local businesses to increase public awareness, while another property in the same city may stage a spectacular event for the same purpose.

Evaluating Results. Evaluating the results of sales and promotional efforts can reveal successful strategies as well as those areas needing improvement or new action plans. Action plans should be monitored on a monthly or quarterly basis. An "action calendar" is an effective way to keep track of activities and results. This calendar maps out sales, advertising, and public relations activities month by month. It allows the marketing and sales team to identify the time of year to approach each market. It also enables the sales manager to spread the workload and assign salespeople to specific solicitation dates. Periodic meetings of the catering sales staff will help ensure that goals and objectives are met for each market segment targeted.

Catering Sales

There are a number of different strategies used to sell food and beverages. While the majority of catering sales result from conventions and meetings sold by the property's sales office, catering department salespeople in midsize to large properties are

Action Plans: Theme Parties

Property banquet sales can be boosted with a little creativity. The Hyatt hotel chain, a leader in developing creative banquets, has developed several innovative approaches to boost banquet sales.

Theme-design sets have been introduced at the Hyatt Regency Cambridge across the river from Boston, Massachusetts. Three designs are available—Oriental, Mediterranean, and Caribbean—for a rental cost of $500 each. Meals to match these themes are available.

Theme parties are the specialty of the Hyatt Regency Maui in Hawaii. One of the favorite themes is a M*A*S*H Bash that features an elaborate set including an officer's club, a mess tent, an infirmary, and an operating room flanked by an assortment of jeeps, machine gun trolleys, and ambulances. The guests are issued dog tags and fatigues or surgical gowns and are hustled through a chow line featuring beef goulash, Yankee pot roast, fried chicken, and beans. Alcoholic beverages are available from IV tubes, a USO show is presented, and the highlight of the evening is the arrival of a helicopter flying in the "wounded" for treatment!

Additional parties offered by the Hyatt Regency Maui include a Great Gatsby Garden Party, a Shogun party, and a '50s party. Other Hyatt properties offer innovative parties such as the Chicago street party, an original creation of the Chicago Hyatt. The Chicago street party features a re-created Southside playground complete with a basketball court, break dancers, and music videos.

Any property regardless of size can come up with innovative ideas that will be popular with guests and employees alike, but it takes a team effort for a theme party to be successful. The chef must create a menu that will complement the theme, the beverage manager must plan drink specialties and novel ways to serve drinks, and the banquet manager must develop a setting—complete with props—that will be cost-effective as well as add to the atmosphere of the party.

---

responsible for selling to local meeting planners and other local clients (in conjunction with sales office staff). In this section we will look at the strategies used by catering department salespeople to increase food and beverage sales.

Developing Leads

A major factor in the success of catering department sales efforts is the development of leads. There are four basic ways to develop leads:

- In-person soliciting
- Telephone soliciting
- Sales letters
- Responses to inquiries

In-Person Soliciting. Personal selling involves contacting the owners of businesses frequented by members of a targeted market segment. The catering director may call on public relations firms to attract business from cultural organizations,

---

Action Plans to Attract the Bridal Market

There are many ways to attract bridal market business to your property. Here are just a few:

Stage a Bridal Show

Join forces with local wedding-related businesses and hold a bridal show or fair. When the Super 8 Motel in Saukville, Wisconsin, held its bridal show, invited businesses included local jewelry stores, bridal boutiques, florists, printers, bakeries, travel agents, and hair stylists. The property booked 15 weddings and over 300 room nights as a result of this promotion—as well as generating additional business from rehearsal dinners, receptions, bridal showers, bachelor parties, luncheons, and teas.

Offer a Wedding Booklet

While the menu may seem the most important consideration to a person booking a wedding or reception, following traditional etiquette is a prime factor in wedding or reception planning. Offering a booklet on wedding etiquette—especially one covering everything from pre-planning to the final toast—is usually greatly appreciated. The booklet should include fill-in charts, such as timetables, decorations needed, spaces for the names of printers, florists, etc., and should also promote the services offered by the property.

Larger properties or properties who do a large volume of wedding business might also consider either hiring a full- or part-time wedding consultant or contracting with an outside consultant and offering his or her services in the package price.

Create Deluxe Wedding Packages

Most people want to go first-class when it comes to a wedding, reception, or honeymoon, so hotels should not be afraid to prepare a deluxe package. Rather than offering the deluxe package first, it is best to present three options (deluxe, mid-priced, and budget). In many cases, purchasers will opt for the deluxe package for this "once-in-a-lifetime" occasion.

---

for example. Or, as mentioned previously, the catering director or a catering department salesperson may call on the owners of jewelry stores, bridal boutiques, or photography studios for wedding business referrals. Photographers are an excellent source of information regarding family reunions, wedding anniversaries, and other family social activities.

Property tours can be used in conjunction with an outside solicitation program to promote the property to local corporate sources and civic organizations whose members can provide future business (Rotary Club, Kiwanis, Chamber of Commerce, and so on).

Telephone Soliciting. Telephone soliciting is another excellent way to develop leads. Selling over the phone involves far less time than in-person visits. If the catering director has hired a sales-oriented staff, it can make most of these calls, freeing the catering director for other duties.

Insider Insights

Gus Moser
Director of Catering
Las Vegas Hilton
Las Vegas, Nevada

Gus Moser began his career at the Las Vegas Hilton at the age of 16. During his 21 years with the property he has advanced through ten different positions in six departments. He has held management positions within the steward, room service, convention setup, and banquet departments, and currently serves as the director of catering for the world's largest resort and convention hotel. In this capacity, Moser oversees more than 225,000 square feet of convention, banquet, and trade show space, and directly supervises a managerial staff that consists of two catering managers, two banquet managers, three convention setup managers, and a stage and sound department manager. These managers are responsible for the direction of over 350 food servers, 40 bartenders, 60 convention setup porters, 16 stage and sound technicians, and a full office staff.

Availability, creativity, and personal service will bring you the repeat business that every hotel strives for. The meeting planner of today is a sophisticated traveler who is continually encouraging his or her staff to surpass a previous year's convention program. The most difficult challenge for a catering director is to continually upgrade and be personally creative with a convention that books with the property year after year.

A catering director needs the human relations skills to make all clients comfortable with assigned rooms, but, at the same time, he or she must continue to upgrade menus, contribute to the uniqueness of each event, and create an occasion that will be long remembered. A catering career is diverse, with clients booking everything from early morning breakfasts and sales meetings to late evening receptions. And there's the ever-increasing market for special events, which range from boxing matches to concerts.

A catering director must be able to adjust to different clients from appointment to appointment—switch from the hard-driving sell required for a meeting planner or a training director, for example, to the gentler approach necessary for a nervous bride-to-be. The client that genuinely trusts the catering director and his or her staff will generate much-needed repeat business.

The Las Vegas Hilton may house as many as six separate, independent conventions occupying function space during the same time period. Well-organized office files prevent the catering director's nightmare—a double booking. If careful attention is paid to the initial meeting, pre-planning, setup, and eventual execution of service, however, the catering director derives the complete satisfaction of a job well done.

Sales Letters. Sales letters are another effective way to build business. Sales letters can be categorized as form letters or personalized letters. Form letters are most commonly used by the sales office to solicit out-of-town convention and meetings business, while the catering department usually writes personalized letters to solicit local business. Writing a personalized letter does not mean the property cannot use a format that is easily modified. Today's word processing capabilities make it easy to "personalize" a letter by changing names, adding a date, or mentioning facts gained through stories in the press or other sources.

A sales letter should be written with the prospective client's needs in mind. The requirements of a meeting planner will be far different from those of a wedding party, and letters should be prepared accordingly. But, no matter what target market is selected, the letter should attract the prospect's *attention,* create an *interest* in and then a *desire* for the product, and give the prospect a means to take *action* (a telephone number, invitation to stop by for a visit, and so on). This is known as the AIDA formula.

Responses to Inquiries. No matter what type of inquiry you receive, you should obtain pertinent information about the client, the client's organization (if applicable), and function needs *before* trying to make a sale. Inquiries are made in writing, by telephone, or in person.

Written inquiries. A written inquiry from a prospective client should not be answered in writing! A telephone call will reach the client (who has probably written to a number of properties) much faster.

Another reason for replying by phone is that letters from prospective clients are rarely specific. Few letters include the client's exact specifications. Will the function be formal or informal? What is the budget limit for the function? Does the potential client expect special services or setups? By talking with the client over the phone, the catering director or salesperson can determine exact needs, give details about function rooms and banquet menus, and negotiate terms. If a written communication is needed (a letter or proposal to be submitted to a board, for example), it can then be tailored to address specific needs.

Telephone inquiries. Telephone inquiries from clients must be handled quickly and efficiently in order to ensure that business is not lost. A potential client who is put on hold for too long—or is transferred from one department to the next—will usually try another property. To avoid this problem, the catering director can leave instructions with the switchboard that all calls should be put through without delay, and without asking the caller what the call is about. While this may be somewhat inconvenient at times, one of the catering director's primary responsibilities is to generate business—the director must be available at all times.

If it is impossible for the catering director to be available at all times, catering salespeople can handle banquet inquiries. At the very least, the clerical staff can be trained to take routine information (name of caller, type of function desired, preferred date, etc.) and assure the caller that the catering director will return the call as soon as possible.

In order for inquiry calls to be handled efficiently, the function book and other information (sample menus, room capacities, price lists, and so on) should be readily available. In addition, catering department salespeople must have the ability to obtain enough pertinent information over the phone from a prospective client to accurately quote prices, suggest serving styles, and book the request.

In-person inquiries. In-person inquiries should also be handled efficiently and hospitably. When someone drops in unexpectedly and inquires about function space, the following steps should be taken:

1. A member of the staff (the front desk staff if the person is asked to wait in the lobby, the catering staff if the person is shown to the catering department) should welcome the prospective client and offer him or her a seat.

2. The client's name should be taken and given to the catering director or a catering salesperson immediately. If there is going to be a wait (which many clients will expect due to the nature of walk-in calls), the client should be advised of the approximate time he or she will be seen.

3. The client should be offered coffee or tea and some reading material. The reading material should relate to the catering department—a photo album of previous functions, scrapbooks containing publicity features and photographs, brochures or information sheets, sample menus, etc. This type of material may answer some of the client's questions or give him or her a better idea of what is available.

Selling to Clients

The key to successful selling is putting yourself in the client's place. It is important to determine what area is most important to the client—menus, price, theme, and so on—and focus the sales presentation on that area. For example, a client who is staging a regional dinner and wants to impress company officials may be more concerned with the menu and the type of service than with the cost. The catering director could meet the needs of the client—and increase banquet revenues—by suggesting three different levels of service: "Mr. Rodriguez, our property offers three different types of functions—each featuring a superb sit-down meal. The difference is in the level of service. Our standard service is one server for every 20 persons, our first-class service provides one server for every 15 persons, and our regency or premiere service offers the ultimate in personal attention by providing one server for every 10 persons."

Since the client in this example has already expressed an interest in impressing company officials, chances are he will choose the regency service. This forced-choice suggestive selling can be used for all inquiries, whether the client's concern is primarily for upgraded or budget service. Given alternatives, the client will often "trade up," especially if alternatives are presented in the right way—that is, as answers to specific needs.

Another way to sell function space is to offer a tour of the facilities, preferably when the ballroom or an appropriate function room is set up. It is far easier for the client to picture a successful event if he or she has seen the facilities, decorations, and table service that will be used.

Experienced hoteliers report that less than 5% of catering sales are made on the first contact. Catering department salespeople will need to follow through with additional contacts to book business. Since new business is so difficult to come by, catering departments rely heavily on past business—clients who know the product and are satisfied. In many catering departments, sales efforts are focused more on these repeat clients than on developing new business, but, whatever the business mix, it is important to develop an efficient filing and trace system to service catering accounts.

Catering Sales Procedures. Like the guestroom sales department, the catering sales department should have clearly defined standard operating procedures (SOPs). A banquet sales manual should include instructions explaining how recurring catering activities should be handled, including catering filing and tracing procedures, solicitation and booking procedures, methods used to prepare banquet event orders and other planning sheets, dates and space reservations policies, confirmation procedures and cancellation procedures, meeting room rental rates and setup charges, deposits and refund policies, credit procedures, and guarantee policies.

All catering inquiries should be recorded on a catering inquiry form, whether the inquiry is from a new client or a previous one (see Exhibit 7). The top part of the form lists the name of the organization, the address, the telephone number, and the name of the contact person. Spaces are usually provided for recording the type of function, the date and time of the proposed function, and the number of people expected to attend. The middle portion of the form is used to determine the action to be taken: Does the client want additional information? Is he or she asking for a definite date? At the bottom of the form is a section that specifies the materials to be sent to the client (menus, additional information sheets, a confirmation letter, and so on).

Before taking action on a request or inquiry, it is necessary to check the function book to determine if space is available (see Exhibit 8). Since the function book is generally kept in the sales office, it is wise to have the catering department and sales office in close proximity. If the date of the function is tentative, the booking can be entered in pencil and an alternate date may also be penciled in. Information entered includes:

- Name and telephone number of the individual responsible for the function
- Name and type of function
- Hours of function
- Number of persons expected to attend
- Status (tentative or definite)
- Initials of the sales representative who made the booking
- Initials of the person making the entry in the function book and the date entered
- Type of setup(s) required and rates quoted
- Estimated time for setup, breakdown, and cleanup

In an automated sales office with a computerized function book, these time-consuming administrative tasks are easier to do. Automated systems provide up-to-the-minute information on the availability of function space, enabling salespeople to be more effective in selling space and providing customer service.

Exhibit 7   Sample Catering Inquiry Form

RMI   EXAMPLE

TIME: _____ 2:35 P.M. _____   SALES MANAGER: _____ SS _____

DATE: _____ 3/9/XX _____

CATERING INQUIRY

ORGANIZATION: _____ Carter/Hale Wedding _____

ADDRESS: _____ 1414 E. 14th St., Anywhere _____   STATE: _____ AZ _____   ZIP: _____ 81414 _____

NAME: _____ Mrs. Andrew Hale _____   PHONE: _____ 262-2626 _____

TITLE: _____ Mother of the Bride _____

BUSINESS POTENTIAL

TYPE OF FUNCTION: _____ Wedding Reception _____   TIME: _____ 7 P.M.–12:30 A.M. _____

NO. OF PERSONS: _____ 175 _____   DATE: _____ 8/22/XX _____

ALTERNATIVE DATE: _____ None _____

GUEST ROOMS: _____ 5 _____   ROOM RATE: _____ (current rack) _____

Have you ever used the Ramada Anywhere?   No, but neighbor
Where are/were functions held? _____   had her reception here last year _____

ACTION: _____ X _____   TENTATIVE BOOKING

_____   DEFINITE BOOKING

_____   FUTURE BOOKING

MENU ACTION:

    TO BE MAILED: YES _X_   NO _____   MENU: _____ Wedding package _____

    OTHER: _____

FOLLOW-UP BY: _____ 3/18 _____   HOLD SPACE UNTIL: _____ 4/9 _____

REPORT ON FOLLOW-UP—LOST DUE TO (check one)

    SPACE RELEASE POLICY _____

    PRICE _____   NO SPACE _____   SPACE NOT SATISFACTORY
                                                             (reason below)

    OTHER _____

    NO EXPLANATION GIVEN _____

CHECK LIST

ENCLOSURES REQUIRED FOR LETTER(S) CHECKED-OFF:

BUSINESS CARD	X
CATERING MENU BROCHURE	X
MENU PRICE LIST ONLY	
LETTER	X
CREDIT APPLICATION	
RACK BROCHURE	
AIRPORT TRANSPORTATION BROCHURE	
A/V SHEET	
WEDDING INFORMATION	X

Catering Administration Manual

This form can be used for all kinds of inquiries—written, telephone, or in-person—and serves as an information base for the client's file. Note that the form makes provision for potential business (tentative booking, definite booking, and future business) and provides a space for following up the account.

Exhibit 8   Sample Function Book

ROOM	A.M.		P.M.	
IMPERIAL ROOM	Organization		Organization	
	Function		Function	
	Time	Number	Time	Number
	Tentative	Confirmed	Tentative	Confirmed
	Engager		Engager	
	Booked By	Type Setup	Booked By	Type Setup
SALON ROOM	Organization		Organization	
	Function		Function	
	Time	Number	Time	Number
	Tentative	Confirmed	Tentative	Confirmed
	Engager		Engager	
	Booked By	Type Setup	Booked By	Type Setup
BOARDROOM	Organization		Organization	
	Function		Function	
	Time	Number	Time	Number
	Tentative	Confirmed	Tentative	Confirmed
	Engager		Engager	
	Booked By	Type Setup	Booked By	Type Setup
CONVENTION REGISTRATION OFFICE	Organization		Organization	
	Function		Function	
	Time	Number	Time	Number
	Tentative	Confirmed	Tentative	Confirmed
	Engager		Engager	
	Booked By	Type Setup	Booked By	Type Setup
THEATER OF PERFORMING ARTS	Organization		Organization	
	Function		Function	
	Time	Number	Time	Number
	Tentative	Confirmed	Tentative	Confirmed
	Engager		Engager	
	Booked By	Type Setup	Booked By	Type Setup
TOWER-CAMELOT POOL	Organization		Organization	
	Function		Function	
	Time	Number	Time	Number
	Tentative	Confirmed	Tentative	Confirmed
	Engager		Engager	
	Booked By	Type Setup	Booked By	Type Setup

The function book must be kept up-to-date to ensure that maximum use is gotten from function rooms. When a date is requested, a member of the catering department checks the function book for the day and time requested. If the inquiry date is open, an entry (either a tentative, a hold, or a definite commitment) is made in the function book for the date and time requested. In addition to the time the room will be in use, each entry includes the name of the organization requesting the room, the name of the contact person, the type of function, and the salesperson's name. When confirming or denying that function space is available, it is vitally important to check the times that the space is booked. A small function can often be booked between other functions.

After the inquiry has been noted and the function entered as tentative or definite in the function book, an account file is created for the client. This file includes all information pertinent to the account: details of telephone calls, written inquiries and return correspondence, contracts, etc. After functions have taken place, account files should be separated into "repeat" and "non-repeat" categories; the non-repeat files (weddings, companies that have gone out of business, etc.) should be placed in a "dead" file, but the repeat files should be organized into a tickler or trace file for periodic action. A tickler file is especially useful in catering sales since it may take four or five contacts with a new account to close a sale, and because past accounts are the backbone of catering sales.

Most past accounts should be approached several months prior to their previously scheduled function date. Many companies, associations, and clubs stage banquet functions at the same time each year, making it easier to set up a trace file for these accounts. You can call the past account's contact person, tell the client that the catering department is preparing a schedule of events, and ask if the client would like to rebook.

If the client responds negatively, it is important to find out why the account has been lost. If a specific reason is given, you should look into the problem. After a week or so you can send a letter thanking the client for his or her suggestions and informing him or her of steps taken to remedy the situation. The following week, a personal call should be made. At that time, you can again thank the client for his or her suggestions and invite the client to take a firsthand look at the improvements that have been made. If the client is still adamant about using another property, the account can be filed and followed up in another year or two.

Whatever the type of account—new or repeat business—no inquiry should be dropped without final resolution. If business is lost, a lost business report should be filed; if business is canceled, the tentative entry should be removed from the function book, and a lost business report filed; if business is booked, a definite status should be entered in the function book, a confirmation letter sent to the client, and further arrangements made.

Planning the Function

After a date has been confirmed, you must work with the client to plan the function. Most properties use a banquet/catering checklist to ensure that all requirements are met for both meeting and food and beverage functions (see Exhibit 9). This checklist can be used for telephone and in-person contacts, and will help build client confidence in the department's thoroughness as well as provide instructions for the proper management of the function.

The client should know just what is available: a dinner, for example, may be sit-down or buffet-style, formal or informal, set with round banquet tables (called "rounds") or rectangular tables. The number of people expected, the theme or atmosphere desired, and the client's budget will all play a part in the final decision.

If you put yourself in the client's place you can make use of suggestive selling to both increase revenues and ensure a successful function. A meeting planner, for example, may be worried that a luncheon won't finish on time; you can suggest a buffet or a simple menu so that the meal can be eaten quickly. Refreshment breaks a

Exhibit 9   Sample Banquet/Catering Checklist

BANQUET/CATERING CHECKLIST

— RMI

I.   MEETING

1. Time:_____
2. Location: _____
3. Expected Attendance: _____
4. Setup:
   - _____ Classroom
   - _____ Theater
   - _____ U-Shape
   - _____ Hollow Square
   - _____ Other _____
      _____
5. Speaker Requirements:
   - _____ Headtable
      - _____ Size
      - _____ # People
      - _____ Draping
      - _____ Other _____
         _____
   - _____ Tabletop Podium
   - _____ Standing Podium
   - _____ Risers
   - _____ Other _____
      _____
6. Audiovisual Requirements:
   - _____ Hotel Provide
   - _____ Client Provide
   - _____ Delivery Time
   - _____ Setup Time
   - _____ Screen(s)
      Size_____
      Price_____
   - _____ Projector(s)
      - _____ 16mm—Price
      - _____ 35mm—Price
      - _____ Lens Size—Price
      - _____ Overhead Projector—Price
      - _____ Acetate Roll—Price
      - _____ Grease Pencils—Price
      - _____ Other
   - _____ Other
   - _____ Microphones— _____ Stands
      - _____ Table
      - _____ Floor
      - _____ Lavalier—Price
      - _____ Handheld—Price
      - _____ Other
      - _____ Mixer—Price
   - _____ Flip Chart—Price
      (includes 2 markers and 1 pad)

_____ PA System (other than existing
         hotel system)
   - _____ Type _____
   - _____ Size_____
_____ Video Recorder/Player
   - _____ Type/Player-Recorder
      (circle one or both)
   - _____ 3/4" VTR—Price
   - _____ 1/2" BETA—Price
   - _____ 1/2" VHS—Price
   - _____ Other
_____ Monitor(s)
   - _____ Size
   - _____ Color _____
      _____ Price _____
_____ Advent Screen _____
   - _____ Size_____
      _____ Price _____
_____ Other _____
   _____

7. Registration Requirements:
   - _____ Time _____
   - _____ Setup_____
      - _____ Draped Table(s)
      - _____ Chair(s)
      - _____ Telephone
      - _____ Message Board
      - _____ Wastebasket
      - _____ Signage
      - _____ Other
8. Coffee Break Requirements:
   - _____ Times _____
      _____
      _____
   - _____ # People _____
   - _____ Location _____
9. Breakout(s):
   - _____ Time
   - _____ # People
   - _____ Location
   - _____ Setup
   - _____ Audiovisual Requirements
      _____
10. Meeting Room Charge: _____
11. Shipments: _____
12. Security: _____
13. Reader Board Posting Policy: _____
      _____
      _____

— Catering Administration Manual

This form is designed to aid the catering director or salesperson in determining specific client needs. It can be used when dealing with the client face to face or over the telephone, and can be customized to include pertinent details for individual properties.

Exhibit 10   Sample Creative Banquet Menu

INTRODUCTION

Fine food, superior service, cordiality and hospitality: this is what Sofitel is all about. In all things and in all ways it's l'amour toujours. Because at Sofitel we love what we do and we believe that we do it well. "It" is the business of serving you, your friends, your company, and your guests.

As the first French hotel company to enter the United States, Sofitel has created its own niche in the industry, built upon 20 years of fine service. "Classic Comfort with a French Accent" is our philosophy. At each Hotel in the U.S. you will find a consistent level of quality in service, accommodations, and cuisine...all with a distinctive French touch.

Meeting planners will be especially pleased to learn about creative accents that add sparkle to ordinary events. Having won a Gold Platter Award for superiority in food and beverage service, we think we can help. All food and beverage outlets are managed by master chefs from France. Sofitel's commitment to fine French cuisine is so distinct that in 1981 L'Hotel Sofitel School of French Culinary Skills was opened in Minneapolis. It is the only private Cooking School in the world certified by the French Ministry of Education.

Long ago, the French discovered that hospitality and gastronomy are both serious business. The chef even becomes part of the team to help customize your event.

Regardless of where you hold your next meeting, we would like to make your job a little easier. We created this guide after many planners told us that their principal concern is the planning and selection of their food and beverage activities.

Use this guide with our compliments.

John F. Lehodey

John F. Lehodey
Executive Vice President

THE FRENCH BANQUET GUIDE

Seeking to take away the mystery—but keep the mystique—of superb French food and beverage service, Sofitel Hotels has developed a banquet menu/beverage guide for meeting planners. This elegantly designed reference booklet, featuring a French Impressionist painting on the cover, not only suggests memorable themed events focusing on French foods and wines, but also contains such sections as "How Food Makes Your Meeting a Success," "Planning the Courses," and "Special Touches." A glossary translates French food and beverage terms into English to help meeting planners with menu planning. (Courtesy of Sofitel Hotels, a division of ACCOR)

couple of hours before the luncheon or serving dessert at an afternoon break are other time-saving suggestions that can (1) help build the meeting planner's confidence that the meeting will be successful, and (2) increase sales of profitable food items as well.

Menus. Providing banquet menus that are cost-effective yet appropriate for the function is an important responsibility of the catering director (see Exhibit 10). At some properties this is handled by the food and beverage director, although the catering director, working with the client, has the option of creating custom menus.

The catering director should try to sell banquet menus that can be prepared at different stations throughout the kitchen. A menu featuring cold hors d'oeuvres, cold salads, and deli plates puts the burden of preparation on one station; a combination of hot and cold hors d'oeuvres, a cold salad, and a conventional meal would spread the preparation around. For this reason as well as others, the catering director should try to sell banquet menus that have already been developed whenever possible. A variety of tempting menus can be created. With pre-developed menus, costs are already known, while custom meals may require extra staff and costly ingredients. If a custom menu is requested, however, the catering director should consult with the chef for suggestions to keep costs as low as possible. A food cost chart may also be helpful when customizing menus.

In order to keep food costs down yet still offer attractive menu selections, the following factors must be considered:

- Client preferences

- Food costs

- Labor costs

Client preferences. Knowing the regional food preferences of an area and having access to local foods can help keep costs low while providing palate-pleasing menu selections. It is also important to keep the client's preferences or background in mind. When serving Jewish groups, it is necessary to know about kosher laws and how they apply to menu planning and other aspects of food and beverage operations. Some senior citizens may have difficulty with a menu that features steaks, corn on the cob, and other difficult-to-chew food. And health-conscious groups may not want to indulge in rich desserts.

Food costs. When developing banquet menus, it is essential to choose foods that retain good flavor, texture, and appearance even when produced in volume. Inexpensive food items that can still be sold at a good retail price (chicken, vegetables in season, etc.) should be included in banquet menus.

Labor costs. Labor costs fall into two categories: food preparation costs and food service costs.

Food preparation costs can vary greatly. A filet mignon and a beef Wellington entrée may require the same amount of beef, but the latter dish requires extensive preparation time. It takes one person to put prime rib in the oven, set the temperature, and take the cooked meat out, while an elaborate chicken dish may require the skills of three chefs or assistants. Food preparation costs must be taken into account in all areas: appetizers (melons must be cut and seeded while tomato juice is merely poured); entrées (a chicken dish may keep costs down, but a simple beef dish may produce extra revenues); and desserts (fancy cakes require much more labor than a simple dessert like ice cream).

Food service costs vary with the type of service requested. The most common form of banquet service is *plate service*. Plate service requires a large kitchen and serving staff for a short service time. The food is plated in the kitchen. Cold food may be plated ahead of time and stored in large roll-in refrigerators or carts. Hot food must be plated at the time of service, and is sometimes served from a number of stations set up in the kitchen.

With *Russian service*, food is served from platters or other large dishes, and sufficient food for one table is placed on each platter. One food server serves the meat and sauce while another serves the potato and vegetables, so a large labor force is needed.

Buffet service is suitable for all types of meals and all types of functions—from informal breakfasts to formal dinners served in silver chafing dishes. Hot and cold foods are attractively displayed, and guests walk up and help themselves. Service personnel may be required to assist—carvers at dinner meals, omelet-makers at breakfast buffets, and so on—but labor costs are reasonably low.

Pre-set service is sometimes used for lunch meetings or for other occasions when time is short. The first course (a cold soup, salad, or appetizer) is set on the table before guests sit down; in some cases, the dessert may also be pre-set. While this type of service may be necessary at times, pre-set food is rarely as attractive as food that is set in courses during the meal.

Receptions or cocktail parties typically feature *butler-style service.* Hors d'oeuvres are placed on platters and circulated among the guests by servers.

A combination of service styles is often used for wedding receptions or corporate dinners. Many wedding receptions feature a buffet of appetizers and then a sit-down dinner. Another common combination is having the first course and dessert served by servers, with a main-dish buffet.

Seating arrangements may affect service style and prices and should be determined before plans are finalized. The typical seating arrangements for a banquet function feature either rounds (tables five feet [1.5 meters] in diameter are most commonly used) or eight-foot (2.4-meter) rectangular tables. Other factors that will influence the choice of service style include the size of the room, the size of the tables, the type of function, and the number of people attending.

Beverage Plans. In addition to food, alcoholic beverages are a part of many functions. Properties may use one or a combination of the following popular beverage plans to provide alcoholic beverages.

Cash bar. At a cash bar, guests pay cash to the bartender who prepares their drinks. Sometimes a ticket system is used at a cash bar for control purposes. With this system, guests pay a cashier for their drinks and are given tickets to present to the bartender. The food and beverage manager generally sets drink prices, which can be the same as or different from normal selling prices. Frequently, management will reduce drink prices from the normal lounge rates in order to attract beverage business.

Host bar. With a host bar, guests do not pay for drinks; rather, the host is charged, either by the drink or by the bottle. If by the drink, bartenders or cashiers must keep track of every drink served. This can be done by using tickets, ringing drinks up on a register, or keeping a tally sheet. If the host is charged by the bottle, the cost of every bottle consumed or opened is assessed to the host.

Charge by the hour. This plan involves establishing a fixed beverage fee per guest per hour. Obviously, arriving at an accurate estimate of the number of drinks guests will consume in an hour is extremely important. While an estimate that will apply to all groups is not easy to make (a health- or weight-conscious group will probably consume less alcohol than a fraternity, for example), a rule of thumb used by some major food and beverage departments is three drinks per person during the first hour, two the second, and one and a half the third. The number of drinks per person must be multiplied by an established drink charge to arrive at the hourly drink charge per person. As managers use the hourly charge system, they will obtain their own specific information that will assist them in setting hourly charges for future events.

Finalizing Arrangements. Once the menu, beverage plan, and other arrangements have been set, the catering director or salesperson must complete a banquet event order (BEO), also called a function sheet or banquet prospectus (see Exhibit 11). This sheet acts as a final contract for the client and serves as a work order for the catering department. The form includes the time and place of the function, physical arrangements of the function room, menu (foods are listed in the sequence in which they will be served), prices quoted for the menu items, beverage requirements, special requests, service notes (number of staff, special costumes, and so on), personnel required (servers, cashiers, checkroom personnel, and so on), tax and gratuity, payment arrangements, and guarantee clause.

A guarantee clause requires groups booking food functions to give the hotel a count of the expected attendance prior to the function—usually 72 hours in advance. This count is the minimum expected or "guaranteed" attendance; the group is charged for its guaranteed number even if actual attendance falls below the guarantee. Most hotels will agree to set tables for a percentage above the number guaranteed in order to accommodate additional guests. Many properties set for an additional 10%, others hold to 5%. The guarantee clause is important because it helps catering managers control labor and food costs.

Managing the Function

As noted earlier in the chapter, the banquet manager is primarily responsible for the management of the actual function, and supervises room arrangement, service personnel, and service procedures (see Exhibit 12). It is his or her job to see that the instructions on the function sheet are followed and that food is prepared and served at the designated time.

The banquet manager should make sure the function room is set up as far in advance as possible, and that extra or "dummy" tables for up to 10% over the guarantee are set up (if the number of guests exceeds the guarantee, time will be saved if tables are pre-set). A bulletin board in the service area outside the function room also helps to facilitate pre-function preparations. The bulletin board should list the name of the group, the time the function-room doors should be opened, the names of food servers and other service personnel needed, the menu that will be served, what items can be pre-set (if any), service assignments, and special notations (wait to clear tables until after the speaker has finished a presentation, dancing is scheduled between the dinner and dessert courses, and so on).

Just prior to the function, the banquet manager should check to be sure that the appetizers and dessert are ready to serve and that tables are properly set. He or she should also check with the chef to ensure that food preparation is proceeding on schedule, and advise the chef of any last-minute changes in the number of guests.

During the function, the banquet manager should be present to see that everything is going smoothly and the order of service is followed (see Exhibit 13). In some cases, the banquet manager presents the bill to the client. The banquet manager

Exhibit 11   Sample Banquet Event Order (BEO)

NOGA HILTON GENÈVE		BANQUETING DEPARTMENT

Address		Date
		Master N°:
		Telex:
		Telephone:
Name of the client:		Reservation N°:
INFORMATION BOARD:		Client:

Time	Type of Function	Rooms	N° Pers. guaranteed

CONFERENCE SET UP — Fr.
Room rental . . . .
Tables set up . . . .
School/Cinema Style . . . .
Minerals . . . .
Writing pads/pencils . . . .
Flip chart . . . .
Head table . . . . pers. . . . .
Stage . . . .
Speaker desk . . . .
Welcome desk . . . .

LUNCH/DINNER
Table set up . . . .
Host table . . . . pers. . . . .
Candlesticks . . . .
Table numbers . . . .
Stage . . . .
Dance floor . . . .

ORCHESTRA by hotel . . . .
by client . . . .
Police authorized by hotel . . h. . .
by client . . h. . .

TECHNICAL EQUIPMENT
Video . . . .
Screen . . . .
Overhead projector . . . .
Film/Slide projector . . . .
Large/small control center . . . .
Telephone . . . .
Microphone . . . .
Technician from . . . to . . . .

MENUS
Simple print by our self . . . .
Double print by our self . . . .
Print by client . . . .
Title: . . . .
. . . .

MENU: Fr.

COFFEE BREAK . . . .   Fr.
. . . .
. . . .
Croissant . . . . . Cake . . . .

BAR/APERITIF
Chips, peanuts, olives . . . . . .
International bar . . . .
Simple bar (without whisky, gin, vodka) . . . .

LUNCH/DINNER Fr.
Minerals . . . .
Wines . . . .

Liquors . . . .
Cigars . . . .
Drinks . . . .

FLORAL DECORATIONS
Round and long terrine . . . .
Arrangement . . . .
Green plant . . . .
By the client . . . .

WARDROBE ROOM
Stander . . . .
. . . . personne(s) . . . .

NH 6206   **IMPORTANT: SIGNATURE AND CONDITIONS ON THE REVERSE SIDE OF THIS PAGE**

A banquet event order is the basis of communication between property departments. Prepared for each meal and beverage function, copies are distributed to all departments involved about three weeks in advance of the catered function to provide ample time for scheduling, setup, and support activities. BEOs are usually sequentially numbered for easy reference. They contain such information as function date and type; organization's name, address, and contact person; rooms and setups to be used; beginning and ending time of the function; number of guests expected; menus; style of service; prices charged and billing instructions; and any special instructions needed. (Courtesy of Noga Hilton Genève, Geneva, Switzerland)

Exhibit 12   Sample Job Description for a Banquet Manager

Banquet Manager

1. Supervises and directs all catering food and beverage functions.
2. Supervises all banquet service personnel. May also supervise setup and mainte-nance staff if not supervised by a convention service manager.
3. Schedules service personnel for food and/or beverage functions.
4. Supervises room setups and implementation of special instructions from the ca-tering office.
5. Prepares payroll and maintains records for service personnel.
6. Inspects catering facilities and equipment as required.
7. Works with the catering director to implement innovative services or make changes in policies and procedures.

Unlike the catering director, whose job is primarily administrative and sales-oriented, the banquet man-ager is responsible for the actual management of functions scheduled by the catering department. Al-though a banquet manager's duties will vary with the size and organizational structure of a property, this excerpt from a job description outlines typical responsibilities.

Exhibit 13   Sample Order of Service

This is a typical order of service followed in serving a banquet. This order may vary in certain circumstances—the dessert may be served following a speaker's presentation, and so on—but service should always be handled as efficiently and quietly as possible.

1. The head table is always served first, no matter what type of service is ordered.
2. The appetizer should be placed on the table just before or as guests are seated. Appetizer dishes should be cleared away before salads are served if the party is small; for larger parties, service is faster if the salad is placed on the left side of the plate immediately after placing the appetizer.
3. All appetizer dishes, bar glasses, empty salad bowls, and salad dressings should be removed before serving the entrée. If cracker baskets were placed with the sal-ad course, they should now be replaced with bread baskets.
4. The entrée should be served, more water poured, and the beverage served.
5. Coffee can be served throughout the entire course of the meal.
6. Entrée dishes should be cleared from the table and water glasses filled.
7. Before serving dessert, all items not needed should be removed from the table. A dessert utensil, coffee spoon, glass of water, and beverage cup or glass should be the only items on the table when dessert is served.
8. The dessert should be served.
9. Dessert dishes should be removed, and additional coffee and water poured.
10. Ashtrays should be kept clean throughout the meal.

---

should be sure to thank the client for the opportunity to serve the group—this is the first step in following through on the account.

Following Up Accounts

Follow-up service is an important step in building a base of repeat clients. Immedi-ately following the function, a thank-you letter and an evaluation form should be sent to the client. A notation should be made in the tickler file and a follow-up note sent if the evaluation is not received within a specified length of time. While it is not a replacement for having checked on the success of the function in person, an evaluation form is an important source of feedback, both on the positive and negative aspects of service (see Exhibit 14). Any negative information can be used to correct flaws in service or avoid similar problems with other clients, while positive comments can be a source of encouragement for employees.

If problems occurred, adjustments in charges may have to be made; at the very least, a letter of apology is in order. The client should be given a reason to try the property again and recommend the property to business associates and acquaintances.

Other Food and Beverage Sales

While banquets are important sales, there are a number of other food and beverage functions that can increase catering department revenues. The following list suggests a few of the opportunities a creative catering director has to serve guests, create repeat business, and increase sales.

Creative Refreshment Breaks

Meeting planners may forgo lunch or dinner breaks and opt instead for refreshment breaks. The catering department can build business by offering a selection of creative refreshment break items rather than the usual Danish and coffee. The property can charge more for unique selections while building client goodwill.

Refreshment breaks are usually scheduled at mid-morning and mid-afternoon, and are intended to alleviate boredom and sharpen the attention and enthusiasm of meeting attendees. Typical refreshment-break fare includes a variety of hot and cold beverages, muffins and other types of bread and pastries, fruits (both fresh and dried), cut vegetables, and peanuts. Whatever the choices, speed is often a major consideration for refreshment breaks; menu items should include only those foods that attendees can pick up quickly.

An alternative to the typical refreshment break is a themed refreshment break. Examples include a New York Deli refreshment break featuring vegetable juice, lox and bagels, cream cheese, jellies, and cream sodas; and a Mexican refreshment break with exotic fruits and juices, Mexican pastries, and so on. Refreshment breaks can also feature unusual house specialties—hot spiced cider, a variety of breads, dried fruit and assorted nuts, and so on.

Hospitality Suites

Hospitality suites are often sold to sponsors of an event or to vendors or attendees as a place to do business and socialize. In many cases, a hospitality suite is set up in two or more guestrooms with connecting doors, or the hospitality suite may be located near the meeting area.

Most hospitality suites are open only in the evenings, but some may be set up as around-the-clock "open houses" which offer refreshment-break snacks during the day and another menu (that often includes liquor) in the evenings. Hospitality

Exhibit 14   Sample Evaluation Form

RAMADA®   — SERVICE CRITIQUE —

Group Name: _____   Date of Function: _____

Type of Function: _____

	Excellent	Good	Fair	Poor	Comments
REGISTRATION					
EMPLOYEES' ATTITUDES					
Banquet Staff					
Sales & Catering Staff					
Restaurant Staff					
Front Desk Staff					
Telephone Operators					
Bell Staff					
Housekeeping Staff					
RESTAURANT					
Food & Beverage Quality					
Food & Beverage Service					
LOUNGE					
Beverage Quality					
Beverage Service					
BANQUET FUNCTION					
Room Appearance					
Food & Beverage Quality					
Food & Beverage Service					
MEETING ROOM FUNCTION					
Room Appearance					
Equipment					
Lighting					
Temperature					
Reaction of your guests					

ADDITIONAL COMMENTS: _____

_____

_____

_____

A thank-you letter and an evaluation form should be mailed to the client as soon as possible after the function. An evaluation form helps the catering department determine the quality of service provided, uncover any unsatisfactory areas, resolve any difficulties, and compliment the staff on a job well done. (Courtesy of Ramada, Inc.)

suite charges must reflect not only the cost of the food and beverage, but also take into consideration any staff needed to service the function. Hospitality suites are not usually serviced by the catering staff; in many cases, they are handled by room service personnel.

Receptions

Receptions are an excellent way to generate revenues at a low cost. Most receptions involve a host or cash bar and simple hot or cold hors d'oeuvres. Such parties require little in the way of setup time (many receptions require only a few chairs around the room). When taking orders for receptions, the catering director should determine the purpose of the party, budget limits, and method of pouring drinks (measured or as requested).

Some receptions may be held during standard dinner hours, and are intended to take the place of dinner, giving guests a chance to both eat and socialize. If this is the case, a complete balance of food types must be offered to suit all tastes. A good solution is to locate several food buffet stations around the room. At functions where liquor is served, guests may either be served by circulating wait staff or get drinks from a bar. In all cases, there is a need for staff to be available to replenish foods, to oversee beverage service, and to remove soiled items and trash.

Special Functions

There may be occasions when special promotional packages are offered by the hotel's sales office for weddings, family reunions, and so on, and the catering director acts as a consultant for the client. While events such as weddings may not lead to immediate repeat business, a well-staged event may result in extensive word-of-mouth advertising. When planning a wedding, the catering director should offer options as part of the package: tuxedo rental services, limousine services, special dressing rooms for the bride and the wedding party, photography services, a complimentary honeymoon suite, and so on.

Other special functions may include requests for kosher service (see Exhibit 15) or requests for menus to meet dietary restrictions. When preparing for these types of functions, the catering director and kitchen staff must pay close attention to special requirements for purchasing and preparing foods.

Off-Premises Catering

Off-premises catering can be divided into two categories. The first, which is offered by many hotels, involves a function that is not held in the banquet rooms but is still on the property, such as a pool-side party or barbecue, a garden wedding, or a function held under tents pitched on the property's grounds. This type of off-premises catering is popular with many guests, and has the added advantage of being in close proximity to the hotel's kitchen and any equipment that is needed to service the function.

The second category of off-premises catering involves servicing functions away from the property, and is offered by far fewer hotels. One of the primary reasons for the reluctance to enter this area is the high initial start-up cost for

Exhibit 15   Kosher Service

Many hotels offer kosher service when requested for weddings, bar and bat mitzvahs, and other special occasions. This brochure, printed by the Hilton International in Sydney, Australia, details kosher services available at the property. (Courtesy of the Hilton International Sydney, Sydney, Australia)

transportation vehicles, equipment to keep foods at appropriate temperatures, and high inventory costs for other items such as tables, chairs, tents, and other items needed for functions. In addition, there are costs for labor (drivers, setup personnel), insurance (both for the vehicles and for liability), and health permits.

Meeting Room Sales

Meeting rooms are usually sold by salespeople in the hotel's sales office who sell group guestroom business to corporations and associations. At some large properties a separate convention department may solicit meetings and convention business. However meeting room sales are handled, it is important to understand the dollar value of meeting room space, and to keep these points in mind:

1. The amount of revenue that can be generated relates directly to the amount of space available. By arranging for the most effective use of meeting room space—for example, meetings following meetings in the same room rather than a banquet following a meeting—costs can be kept down and more space can be sold.

2. Selling the least desirable space first increases maximum space usage. If the least desirable space is sold, it is far easier to sell the desirable space at a later date. If the desirable space doesn't sell, the previously booked meetings can be moved into the prime space.

3. "Holds" that reserve space for all day or all evening should be questioned; few meeting planners need rooms for an entire day or evening, and a few hours of "dead" time can be used for another meeting.

4. Salespeople should concentrate on selling space during times when business is usually slow. Meeting rooms will practically sell themselves during peak periods, so sales activity should be aimed at valley and shoulder periods.

At large properties, a convention service manager may set policies on selling meeting rooms, while at a smaller property the sales director or manager may deal with this aspect. In either case, it is important to note that meeting rooms were often provided free of charge in the past if a banquet was involved; today, however, there is a trend to charge for meeting rooms even if the group uses banquet facilities. This makes it even more important to provide clients with the services they require.

Types of Meeting Rooms

Meeting rooms fall into three basic categories: exhibit halls, ballrooms for large meetings or banquets, and conference meeting rooms. The type of room used will depend on a variety of factors: the type of meeting, the number of people expected to attend, the size and layout of the room, and special requirements (audiovisual equipment, access to freight elevators, and so on). A meeting planner may also be interested in such room features as ceiling height, the location of electrical outlets, proximity to elevators, the location of exits, the number of doors and windows, and the presence of pillars or other potential obstructions.

Meeting Room Setups

There are various meeting room setups that can make the best use of space while still meeting the client's needs (see Exhibit 16):

Exhibit 16   Sample Meeting Room Setups

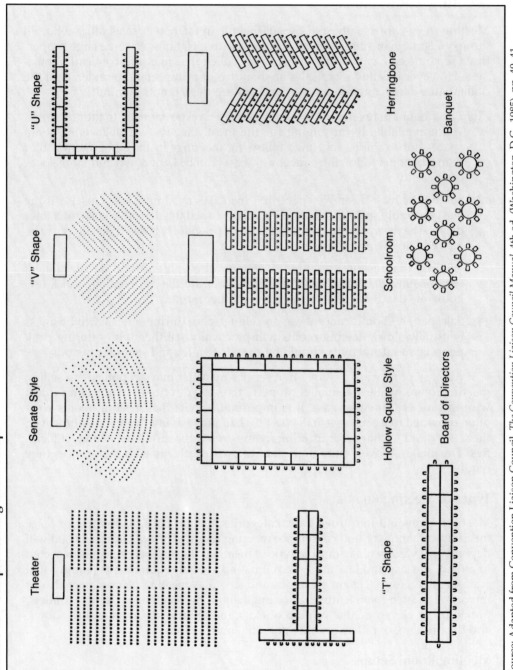

Source: Adapted from Convention Liaison Council, *The Convention Liaison Council Manual*, 4th ed. (Washington, D.C., 1985), pp. 40–41.

1. *Theater setup* (also known as a cinema or an auditorium setup)—Chairs are set up in straight rows (with aisles) parallel to the head table, stage, or speaker's podium.

2. *Senate-style setup*—Same as a theater setup, except chairs are placed in a semi-circle rather than in rows.

3. *V-shape setup*—Same as a theater setup except that chairs are placed in a V (the base of the V begins at the center aisle).

4. *U-shape setup*—Tables are set up in the shape of a block-letter U; chairs are placed outside the closed end and on both sides of each leg. This setup is also known as a horseshoe setup.

5. *T-shape setup*—Tables are set up in the shape of a block-letter T and chairs are placed around the outside.

6. *Hollow-square setup*—A series of tables forms a square with a hollow middle; chairs are placed around the outside.

7. *Schoolroom setup*—This is perhaps the most common setup. Tables are lined up in rows (one behind the other) on each side of an aisle. There are usually three to four chairs to a table (depending on table size), and all tables and chairs face the head table, stage, or speaker's podium. This is sometimes called a class-room setup.

8. *Herringbone setup*—This setup is similar to a schoolroom setup except that tables and chairs are arranged in a "V".

9. *Board-of-directors setup*—This is a popular arrangement for small meetings. It calls for a single column of double tables with seating all the way around.

10. *Banquet setup*—A meal-function setup that generally uses round tables. As mentioned, the most popular round is a five-foot (1.5-meter) table that seats eight to ten people. An eight-foot (2.4-meter) rectangular table may also be used, set in a "U" shape setup, "T" shape setup, or other setup that accommodates the needs of the group.

The type of setup used will affect the capacity of a meeting room, so it is essential that salespeople be knowledgeable about room capacities under all possible configurations. Most properties provide detailed scale drawings of each meeting room that include physical characteristics and room capacities (see Exhibit 17). The following are simple formulas for determining room capacities for three common setups:

- Theater—With this setup, a room's square footage should be divided by six. For example, if a room is 20 by 30 feet (6 by 9 meters)—a total of 600 square feet (56 square meters)—the seating capacity would be 100 persons.

- Schoolroom—A room's square footage is divided by eight with this setup. Total seating capacity may vary, however, if wide traffic aisles, exhibit space, or additional furniture is requested. In these cases, one square foot (or more, if a large exhibit area will be used) should be added per person—in other words, square footage would be divided by nine or more.

Exhibit 17   Sample Meeting Room Plans

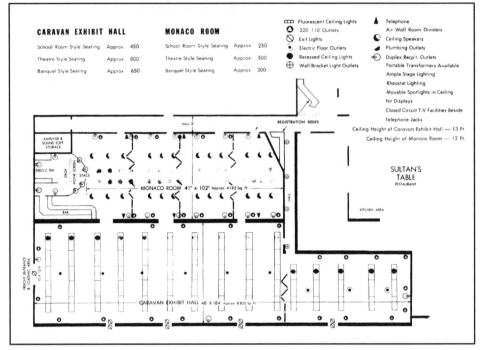

Meeting room plans showing such details as exits, electrical outlets, telephone jacks, lighting, door openings, and ceiling heights are often requested by experienced meeting planners, and are an aid in making a sales presentation. Note that this drawing also presents the room's capacities for schoolroom, theater, and banquet seating.

- Banquet—With this setup, a room's square footage should be divided by ten, whether the setup calls for rounds or rectangular tables. The resultant figure gives *maximum* seating capacity; in many cases, however, more room is desired per guest. This is especially true in the case of formal dinners, when additional place setting pieces and courses are required. For formal dinners, two square feet (.19 square meter) should be added per person—in other words, square footage should be divided by twelve.

Meeting room capacities are extremely important to meeting planners, and salespeople should be aware that the equipment required by a group often affects the room size and setup needed. Typical equipment offered by properties includes audiovisual equipment (microphones of various types, a PA system, overhead or slide projectors, and so on), speakers' equipment (flip chart stands, easels, blackboards), and accessory equipment such as portable stages and podiums.

Meeting Room Furniture

The choice of meeting room furniture is important to most meeting planners, and the types of furniture chosen will affect a room's capacity. While meeting room furniture can vary a great deal, there are certain types and sizes that are frequently offered by properties.

Chairs. Most chairs used for meetings are 18 inches wide by 18 inches deep by 17 inches high (46 by 46 by 43 centimeters). Stackable armchairs are slightly larger— usually 20 by 20 by 17 inches (51 by 51 by 43 centimeters). Most folding chairs are smaller, and not as comfortable as upholstered chairs; folding chairs are generally used for last-minute overflow accommodations.

Tables. A standard table has a height of 30 inches (76 centimeters) and a width of either 30 or 18 inches (76 or 46 centimeters). When seating is required on both sides of the table, the 30-inch-wide (76-centimeter-wide) table is used. In common schoolroom setups, in which people sit on only one side of the table, the 18-inch (46-centimeter) width is sufficient. The 30-inch-wide rectangular table is used most frequently for head table seating, even though people are seated on a single side, and is also used for displays and exhibits. The 30-inch-wide table is the most versatile of all tables available, as it comes in four-, six-, and eight-foot (1.2-, 1.8-, and 2.4-meter) lengths, making it easy to create a variety of total lengths by combining tables of different lengths.

Rounds are used for meeting sessions as well as for food functions, and are most often available in four-, five-, and six-foot (1.2-, 1.5-, and 1.8-meter) diameters. For the most comfortable seating, the four-foot table can accommodate 4 to 6 people; a five-foot table, 8 to 10 people; a six-foot table, 10 to 12 people.

Platforms. Folding platforms are often used to elevate the speaker's podium and the head table at banquets. The usual heights are 6, 8, 12, 16, and 32 inches (15, 20, 30, 41, and 81 centimeters); lengths fall into the four-, six-, and eight-foot (1.2-, 1.8-, and 2.4-meter) range, and widths vary from four to six feet (1.2 to 1.8 meters).

Booking Meeting Rooms

Once arrangements have been finalized, the salesperson can fill out a function book space request form detailing the client's meeting room needs. In some cases, space is placed on a tentative "hold" basis. It is important that a hold period does not extend beyond the time when the space can be sold if the commitment is not firmed up. To avoid this, an appropriate release date should be set.

Release Dates. When a large group such as a convention buys out the vast majority of the hotel's guestrooms, the group's request to hold all meeting rooms seems reasonable. But, in this case as well as in the case of smaller groups, a release date should be set in the contract. The reason for this is simple: many groups estimate requirements for meeting space a year or more prior to the actual event, based on a rough outline of the convention program. As the convention draws nearer, extensive changes may be made. With a release date (usually 60 or 90 days prior to the event), meeting rooms that are not needed can be released, and the hotel can then sell this space to other groups.

In many instances, another group can be given a tentative booking if, as in the example above, a group seems to have reserved more space than it will need. If the tentative booking cannot be filled because it turns out the first group does indeed need all the space it reserved, the second group must be notified immediately and a lost business report filled out.

Managing Meetings

While policies for managing meetings will vary from property to property, there are certain requirements that are followed almost universally. First, rooms are set up well in advance if possible. This allows for any last-minute changes. Setup teams vary with a property's size; small properties may use house attendants, medium-size properties may rely on crews supervised by the banquet manager, and large convention properties may have special setup crews.

Most properties provide general meeting room accessories. These include draped head tables, ashtrays, and pitchers of ice water with glasses. If the meeting is scheduled to run more than two hours, setup personnel or food servers usually freshen up the room by removing dirty or wet linens, straightening chairs, cleaning ashtrays, refilling water pitchers, and replacing glasses with clean ones.

Setup crews may also be involved in setting up exhibit booths or display areas. Many properties offer partitions that can be used to divide a room into smaller rooms or be opened to provide display or ballroom space. This option offers flexibility, and is popular with training directors who wish to divide meeting attendees into small groups after a general training session. Partitions also benefit the property by making possible better space control. Putting a meeting of 20 persons in a room built for 100, for example, wastes space and cuts into profits; with the use of partitions, the room can be divided to accommodate several small groups at a time.

After a meeting, follow-up should be taken care of promptly—a thank-you letter and an evaluation form sent and traced. Providing hassle-free meeting space and personalized service can help ensure repeat and referral business and keep the meetings business profitable.

Key Terms

banquet event order (BEO)	plate service
banquet setup	pre-set service
board-of-directors setup	release date
buffet service	Russian service
butler-style service	schoolroom setup
cash bar	senate-style setup
guarantee clause	T-shape setup
herringbone setup	theater setup
hollow-square setup	U-shape setup
host bar	V-shape setup

Review Questions

1. Why is the profit margin for banquets often greater than the profit margin for a hotel's restaurant?

2. What are two basic responsibilities of most catering departments?

3. What are the catering director's primary responsibilities?

4. What five steps should be included in a catering department's marketing plan?

5. Why should function room occupancy and activity statistics be tracked?

6. What are four basic ways to generate function sales?

7. The catering department usually writes what type of sales letter?

8. What steps should be taken with in-person inquiries?

9. What is the most common form of banquet service?

10. What are three popular beverage plans?

11. What is a guarantee clause?

12. What are some of the responsibilities of the banquet manager in managing a function?

13. Who usually sells meeting rooms?

14. Why should the least desirable meeting room space be sold first if possible?

15. What are some common meeting room setups?

Part III

Advertising, Public Relations, and Publicity

Chapter Outline

Why Advertise?
    To Whom Does a Property Advertise?
    Advertising Goals
    Advertising at Small Properties
Types of Advertising
    Outdoor Advertising
    Displays
    Collateral Materials
    Print Advertising
        Newspapers
        Magazines
        Directories
    Direct Mail Advertising
    Broadcast Advertising
        Radio
        Television
        Video
    Alternative-Media Advertising
Developing an Advertising Plan
    Deciding Where to Advertise
    Advertising Strategies
        Differentiation
        Segmentation
        Combination
    Advertising Characteristics
        Reach
        Frequency
        Consistency
        Timing
    Budgeting for Effective Advertising
Advertising Agencies
    Types of Ad Agencies
    Selecting an Ad Agency

9

A Guide to Effective Advertising

THERE ARE BASICALLY TWO METHODS of reaching potential guests and clients: direct selling and advertising. While direct selling is the backbone of hospitality sales, you should recognize the importance of advertising as a supplement to sales efforts. Advertising can assist you by making the prospect aware of the property *before* you make a sales call. It can produce a positive image of the hotel in the prospect's mind and generate interest in special services and promotions.

Advertising should employ the same principles as face-to-face selling: it should sell benefits, not just features; it should sell what the product does for the customer, rather than just the product; and it should be perceived as a "problem-solver," not just a product-seller.

Because advertising is becoming more widely used in the hospitality industry, and because today many salespeople assist in making advertising decisions, it is important that you have an understanding of the various types of advertising available, their advantages and disadvantages, and how advertising decisions are made. In this chapter we will discuss what makes advertising such an important sales tool.

Why Advertise?

There are several reasons for advertising:

- *Advertising reaches a vast audience.* Advertising—especially print and broadcast advertising—can reach thousands of potential guests and clients. Even advertising that is not aimed at a mass audience (brochures for meeting planners, for example) is seen by hundreds of people who may be sources for sales or sales leads.

- *Advertising is relatively inexpensive.* While printing, column space, and airtime costs are not cheap, the cost per reader or listener can be quite low. When figuring advertising costs, however, it is important to weigh one major disadvantage: not every reader or listener will be interested in your message.

- *Advertising can create a direct response.* Coupons, reply cards, and telephone numbers can be included in advertising to elicit responses. Invitations to call in or write for a reservation or more information get the reader or listener involved in the property and can open doors to future sales.

- *Advertising demonstrates a property's competitiveness.* Because other properties advertise, it gives the reader or listener an opportunity to compare benefits and features. A property that can present superior benefits or answers to a reader's or listener's needs can gain a competitive edge.

Advertising is an invaluable tool that can target those areas or audiences that have not yet been reached and offer additional information to those who already have a favorable impression of the property.

To Whom Does a Property Advertise?

The property's marketing plan lays the groundwork for determining the type of advertising the property will use and the target markets for the advertising effort. It is far better to concentrate advertising on targeted markets than to spread it out to a general audience that may not have a need for the property's products or services.

Before the first ad is designed or the first script written, management must address the following questions to obtain a clear picture of the market(s) that would be most suitable for a property's advertising:

1. *What is management's perception of the property?* Does management see the property's products and services as luxurious or as geared to middle-income travelers? What are the prime sources of income for the property? Business travelers? Leisure travelers? Group business? Does management have the statistics to back up these perceptions?

   Sometimes management's perception of the property can hurt sales. For example, a few years ago Hyatt's management positioned the Hyatt chain as a top-of-the-market chain, and reflected this positioning in its "A Touch of Hyatt" ads. Research two years later indicated that the positioning intimidated guests, causing them to think that Hyatt hotels were too ritzy for them. As a result of the research, a new ad campaign was developed to position the chain as a service- and value-oriented property. Public reaction, and sales, improved (see Exhibit 1).

2. *What is the marketplace's perception of the property?* Questionnaires and telephone surveys are excellent sources of information about the public's view of a property. In one instance, for example, a Chicago luxury hotel found that respondents thought the hotel was a private club or that it catered to "high-society dowagers." After discovering the public's perception, the hotel was able to alter its advertising to promote its convention facilities and luxury services for businesspeople.

3. *What is the property's positioning statement?* The property's positioning statement has a significant impact on the types and content of advertising and whom the property will advertise to. The positioning statement is an important part of the property's marketing plan, and must be consistent with what the property has to offer. The positioning statement can be used in advertising to reinforce the property's message.

Market segmentation is the basis for effective advertising. The media bombard consumers with hundreds of messages every day. This clutter produces so

Exhibit 1   The Importance of Positioning

This ad is an example of Hyatt's campaign to position itself as a service- and value-oriented property.

much advertising "noise" that consumers tend to tune out most messages. To break through the noise, hospitality firms must select market segments, research each segment's needs, and then carefully prepare the message and select the media that will most effectively reach target segments (see Exhibit 2).

Exhibit 2   Selecting Target Market Segments

When determining the most effective use of advertising, it is important to target key market segments. Hilton Hotels and Resorts selected five key target market segments and identified media choices for best reaching each segment.

Target Market Segment	Media Choice
Frequent Business Traveler	In-flight publications such as United's *Visa Vis*, USAir's *USAir Magazine*, American's *American Way*, Delta's *Delta Sky*, and Air Canada's *En Route*.
	Daily newspapers such as the *Wall Street Journal* and *USA Today*; weekly news magazines such as *Time* and *Newsweek*; and business publications such as *Forbes*, *Fortune*, and *Business Week*.
Leisure/Vacation Traveler	National and regional full-page consumer ads in *Conde Nast Traveler*, *National Geographic Traveler*, *Southern Living*, *Sunset*, and *Travel & Leisure*. Trade ads in *Travel Weekly*.
Corporate Meeting Planner	National trade publications such as *Meeting News*, *Meetings and Conventions*, *Successful Meetings*, *Gavel*, *Business Travel News*, and *Medical Meetings*.
Large Convention/Trade Show Customer	National and regional ads in targeted publications such as Customer *Convene*, *Best's Review*, *Association Meetings*, and *Association Management*.
Bounce Back Weekend/Summer Vacation Market	Local and regional newspaper and magazine ads; ads in national publications such as *USA Today*.

Market segments with the maximum potential to respond should be targeted for advertising efforts. If a property determines that 65% of its business comes from leisure travelers, advertising dollars should be spent accordingly.

Advertising Goals

Although advertising can take many forms, it is used to accomplish the following goals:

• Attract potential guests' attention and create product awareness.

• Create an interest in potential guests' minds. This is not the same as creating product awareness; potential guests must become interested enough to want additional information.

• Turn potential guests' interest into a desire to experience the property for themselves.

• Generate action on the part of potential guests. This is especially important in the case of hospitality properties, which sell intangibles. Consumers have the opportunity to inspect tangible products before they make a purchase; they can see for themselves whether the product will be suitable for their needs. When buying an intangible product, however, they must base their decision on someone else's word; they are literally buying promises that their experience will be a good one. A hotel's advertising must show potential guests the benefits available from the hotel and sufficiently motivate them to respond to the message.

Advertising at Small Properties

Many general managers or directors of sales at small properties feel that advertising goals can be achieved without the assistance of outside help, but, all too often, this just isn't the case. Effective advertising requires education and experience that few property managers have.

For best results, small properties should involve advertising professionals at some point to ensure that advertising dollars are not wasted. For some properties, this may mean retaining a free-lance advertising specialist to assist with special promotions or specific advertising materials such as brochures or posters. Other small properties may benefit from retaining a small advertising agency that would welcome the property's account and work hard to produce results.

Whether a property chooses to contract a free-lance advertising professional, hire a small agency, or employ the services of an agency with branches in several cities, the property should be knowledgeable about the different types of advertising and the advantages and disadvantages of each in order to work well with advertising professionals.

Types of Advertising

There are several types of advertising used in the hospitality industry: outdoor, display, collateral, print, direct mail, broadcast, and alternative-media. Each type has strengths that can be capitalized on for generating name recognition, selling property features and services, or opening up new markets, but each also has limitations that you should consider before developing an advertising plan for your property.

Outdoor Advertising

Outdoor advertising includes the property's sign and off-property billboards located along streets and highways. Billboards heighten awareness and recognition of the property, have a great deal of flexibility, and can attract impulse travelers. Disadvantages include the limited message that can be conveyed, the cost of production and maintenance, and the difficulty of measuring a billboard's effectiveness.

Displays

Displays include advertising materials such as transit cards and posters off the property in such places as buses and taxis, transportation terminals, and trade shows. This type of advertising is especially effective at airports and trade shows: at airports, deplaning passengers may make last-minute lodging decisions, while

---

Advertising a Small Property

Michael Handlery, CHA, general manager of the 93-room Handlery Motor Inn in downtown San Francisco (half a block from Union Square), emphasizes amenities in his advertising. The three most popular, according to guest comment cards, are: (1) free valet parking, (2) coffee makers in guestrooms, and (3) in-room food service. Other property features that find their way into advertising copy include the sauna and heated pool, in-room movies, remote control TV, electric shoe polishers, sun lamps, free morning newspapers, and special soap.

Handlery researches guest folios to find out where business comes from, then buys magazine advertising to reach the zip codes he wishes to target. *Time* magazine is a favorite medium—in regional editions, that is. He also advertises in regional editions of *Newsweek* and *TV Guide,* as well as, occasionally, the *Wall Street Journal.* Advertising in national magazines gives the message credibility, in Handlery's experience, and doesn't cost all that much if you can buy coverage for target markets only.

The following are four components in Michael Handlery's advertising program, with hints about how he rates each in effectiveness.

1. *Reciprocal Advertising.* Handlery uses reciprocal advertising with radio stations, concentrating on the Los Angeles/San Diego area and central California. Response: very good. And this advertising is inexpensive. Fewer than 50% of the room nights traded are used by the radio stations.

2. *Premiums.* Handlery, advertising in publications such as the *Los Angeles Times*, has offered special guestroom rates ($69.95 single or double with children free) plus gifts—a Parker pen/calculator set, for example—to guests during slow periods. Response: not worth it, considering the costs.

3. *Special Discount Rates.* Special discount rates during slow periods have been somewhat more cost-effective. But good recordkeeping is required to ensure that guests don't use the discounts when (1) business isn't needed, or (2) guests would be in the hotel with or without discount offers.

4. *Magazine, Directory, and Radio Advertising.* In addition to advertising in regional editions of the magazines mentioned above, Handlery advertises in regionally based travel publications such as *Sunset* and *Travel Age West.* Also used are national travel directories such as *Hotel & Travel Index* and *OAG TRAVEL PLANNER/ Hotel & Motel RedBook.* All radio and printed advertising is directed at zip code areas that represent lucrative present markets. Response to total advertising: good.

---

visitors to many trade shows (such as shows for travel agents or tour operators) are already in the market for lodging industry products and services. Displays do have disadvantages, however. For example, many people arriving at transportation terminals have already made a lodging decision. And the cost of producing quality, eye-catching displays is high when you consider their limited (and often uninterested) audience.

Exhibit 3   Sample Collateral Material

This poster was used by the Red Lion for in-house promotion.

Collateral Materials

Collateral materials include brochures, posters, fliers, and tent cards designed to promote the property's products and services (see Exhibit 3). Collateral materials may be used as in-house or off-property promotional tools, and can be designed for specific groups such as travel agents or in-house guests.

Key chains, shoehorns, and other specialty items that show the property's name (and, if possible, address and telephone number) are also considered collateral materials. Specialty items offer name recognition and a reminder of the guest's experience at the property. They also make excellent promotional pieces for travel agents, tour organizers, and meeting planners. A complimentary wall or desk calendar, for example, can keep the property's name in front of a meeting planner. One Holiday Inn that sought to book more honeymooners designed a special apothecary jar for travel agents. Imprinted with the words "Honeymoon Kisses" and the property's name, the jar was filled with chocolate kisses and distributed to travel agents at trade shows or delivered to their offices to serve as a decorative desk item—and a reminder to book newlyweds into the hotel.

There are disadvantages to specialty item advertising, however. In most cases, the small size of specialty items makes printing a long message impossible. Other

Exhibit 4   Sample Newspaper Ad

THIS WINTER, REKINDLE YOUR RELATIONSHIP.
SPEND A WEEKEND SOMEPLACE WARM.

If one of the greatest luxuries in life is time together, imagine how meaningful
that time can be in the very special warmth and elegance of The Ritz-Carlton.
Join us for A Weekend to Remember. The Newbury Street Spree. Who but Boston's
Five Diamond Hotel could offer A Weekend of Social Savvy for Children?
And of course, one of the nicest things about giving someone you love a weekend at
The Ritz-Carlton—you get to come, too. Call or write for our Weekend Catalog today.

THE RITZ-CARLTON
BOSTON

This newspaper ad won the top award for single entry newspaper advertising at the 31st Annual HSMAI Advertising Awards Competition. The ad was complemented by direct mail advertising (see Exhibit 6) promoting weekend getaway packages. (Courtesy of The Ritz-Carlton, Boston, Massachusetts)

disadvantages include the lengthy time required for production and delivery of the items, the difficulty in measuring their effectiveness, and the poor distribution rate (many items are thrown in drawers or kept by guests rather than being passed on to other potential guests).

Print Advertising

Print advertising media include newspapers, magazines, and directories.

Newspapers. Newspapers are used by the hospitality industry more than any other medium, and with good reason (see Exhibit 4). Newspapers are:

- *Widely read.* There are many cities and towns where one newspaper dominates, providing easy access to targeted markets in specific geographic areas. And, since newspapers are widely read, they are an ideal medium to reach the local community and can be a good source of word-of-mouth advertising. Special interest and ethnic newspapers can be used to open or penetrate markets.

- *Targetable.* Newspapers offer a variety of sections that can be used to target specific readers. In addition to the Sunday travel magazine or section (the most effective place for selling leisure travel), there are business sections in which to promote meeting facilities and corporate services, society pages to promote function space, and food and entertainment sections to promote the property's restaurants and lounges.

- *Flexible.* Newspapers offer a choice of ad sizes and the opportunity to place last-minute ads that promote newly created packages or special offers. It is also easy to change ad copy—sometimes a word or a line can even be changed between the morning and afternoon editions. Newspaper advertising is also easier to schedule—while broadcast advertising is restricted to a certain number of ads per hour, newspapers don't have limitations (more pages are added if there is an unusually large amount of advertising). And, because of the frequency of publication (dailies, for example, are published seven times a week), there are many opportunities to reach prospects over a short time period.

- *Inexpensive.* Last, but certainly not least, is the advantage of low advertising rates. Low rates permit frequent ad placement, which can generate name recognition. In addition, many local newspapers offer special local advertiser rates or bulk rates, enabling a local property to place more ads for less money.

With all these advantages, it may seem that newspapers are the perfect advertising medium. But there are drawbacks. Few people actually read the entire newspaper, so ads must be carefully placed. Newspapers can be cluttered with ads, causing some ads to get lost or be negated by placement next to undesirable advertising. Newspapers, for the most part, are thrown away, not saved—a disadvantage when even a great ad is usually forgotten after a day or two. Newspapers have a reputation for poor production quality: the paper stock is coarse, and color does not reproduce as well as in magazines or other publications. In fact, most newspapers rarely use color, and so are a less exciting medium visually.

Magazines. Magazines have the advantage of more readers per copy than newspapers. Most magazines are audited by an independent firm, and their publishers can provide a statement that gives information on circulation (broken down by paid subscriptions, number of copies available at newsstands, circulation of regional editions, and so on), subscription rates, advertising rates, and other information (see Exhibit 5). The Standard Rate and Data Service publishes a set of directories that also gives information on magazines—circulation, subscription rates, advertising rates, mechanical requirements for ads, and deadlines (these directories are usually available in public libraries). Such data can prove invaluable for properties. Knowing that subscription rates are fairly expensive, for example, enables the property to target upscale consumers; knowing the number of paid subscriptions versus newsstand copies can help a property determine whether the magazine is going to a specific audience or is being read by the public in general.

Magazines can provide a sophisticated, exciting format for promoting a property. Magazine advertising offers:

- *A specific audience.* Since most magazines target a specific readership, the property has a better chance of reaching its target audience.

- *Longer life.* Magazines, unlike newspapers, are generally read more than once, and are often shared.

Exhibit 5   Sample Publisher's Statement

VERIFIED
AUDIT CIRCULATION

13366 BEACH AVENUE, MARINA DEL REY, CALIFORNIA 90291-9990 • 213 306-1577

19 __

MAGAZINE
PUBLISHER'S STATEMENT

6   MONTH PERIOD

ENDING   6/30/

1.   HOTEL & TRAVEL INDEX
NAME OF PUBLICATION

2.   One Park Avenue   New York   New York 10016
ADDRESS   CITY   STATE

3.   Ziff-Davis Publishing Co. Inc.
PUBLISHING COMPANY   ADDRESS   CITY   STATE

4.   1937   5.   Quarterly   6.   (212) 555-5625
ESTABLISHED   FREQUENCY   TELEPHONE

7.   FIELD SERVED:

> HOTEL & TRAVEL INDEX serves owners, presidents, partners, managers, sales and other executives of retail travel agencies and wholesale tour companies, corporate travel managers and other corporate executives and departments requiring travel information; airlines, railroads, steamships,and other transportation companies; hotel reservations departments; hotel and motel representatives and other travel related services.

8.   AUDIT OF CIRCULATION

	PAID	CONTROLLED	TOTALS
Individual (subscriptions or controlled)	45,617		45,617
Group (paid only)		X X X X	
Association (paid only)		X X X X	
Single copy sales (paid only)		X X X X	
Bulk sales (paid or controlled)			
TOTAL AVERAGE (QUALIFIED) CIRCULATION PER ISSUE	45,617		45,617
TOTAL AVERAGE (NON-QUALIFIED) CIRCULATION PER ISSUE (advertisers, agencies, file, samples, etc.)			5,048
TOTAL AVERAGE COPIES PRINTED PER ISSUE			50,665

9.

> Verification of Accuracy of Circulation List and Receivership will be determined in the Annual Field Verification and Market Research being conducted presently on the SPRING 19___ issue and which will be made a part of the Annual Audit Report.

Publisher's statements provide a circulation breakdown to help a property's marketing and sales staff determine if the publication will reach targeted market segments. This publisher's statement also provides a circulation audit. Circulation audits, usually performed by a third party, are much more reliable than individual publication research, and break down circulation by qualified (paid) circulation and non-qualified circulation (free issues that are sent to advertisers, used as sample copies, and so on). Only the first page of the statement is shown here; other pages provide invaluable information about the publication's distribution.

If a publication is unfamiliar, it is a good idea to ask for a sample copy or a list of current advertisers. Just because the numbers look good in a publisher's statement doesn't mean that the publication will meet the needs of the property. Its pages, for example, might be cluttered with the ads of competitors, or the editorial content may not match your property's positioning and image. (Source: *Hotel & Travel Index.*)

- *Credibility.* Properties benefit from the image of the magazine in the minds of readers.

- *Quality and readability.* Most magazines make extensive use of quality color production that can be visually appealing to readers. In addition, readers are usually reading material that is of interest to them, and are generally more likely to be receptive to high-quality advertisements in magazines.

There are disadvantages to magazine advertising, however. Cost-effectiveness can be lessened through duplication of readership if a property advertises in more than one specialty or trade magazine. The national nature of most magazines means that much of the circulation paid for is wasted if the property's markets are limited geographically. Since magazines come out less often than newspapers, the property's ad is seen less often. There is much less control over positioning in a magazine than in a newspaper. Magazine readers are not necessarily looking for travel/hotel information as they are when reading through the travel section of the local newspaper.

Two production factors also create disadvantages: the high cost of production and the long lead time, which restricts last-minute advertisements. The use of color, photographs or illustrations, and special artwork or graphics greatly increases the cost of magazine advertising, yet the property's ad may be placed next to a competitor's and be overlooked. This fact, coupled with the average 45- to 60-day lead time needed by magazines, may play a part in a property's magazine advertising decisions.

Directories. Hotel and motel headings in the telephone directory yellow pages are referred to over 200 million times a year by people actively seeking information about a particular property or service. But while 85% of people "shopping" for a property through the yellow pages follow up with a phone call, letter, or visit, the high cost of this type of advertising may be prohibitive for some small properties.[1]

Business directories for the hospitality industry fall into two categories: hotel directories that list hospitality products and services, and trade directories that target such travel intermediaries as travel agents, tour operators, and meeting planners. Business directory advertising reaches a consumer actively seeking hospitality products and services, and is designed to give readers enough information to recommend the property or make a booking.

Direct Mail Advertising

This print medium goes directly to the property's target audience, something that cannot be guaranteed by any other medium (see Exhibit 6). The cost of sending a direct mail piece to a small target audience can be quite reasonable, even when the piece is a long illustrated message. Direct mail pieces, especially letters, fliers, and simple newsletters, can be relatively inexpensive to prepare even if color is used. They are also trackable. Pieces may be coded or sent with reply coupons that ensure measurability.

Although direct mail may be produced professionally, many people still think of direct mail as junk mail. Some people, in fact, are annoyed by direct mail advertising and may have a negative impression of a property that engages in it. In addition

Exhibit 6 Sample Direct Mail Package

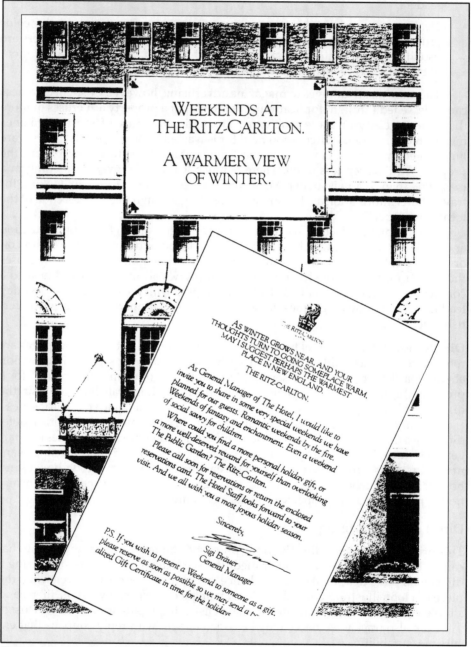

This direct mail package, which included a cover letter, direct mail piece, reservations/order form, and reply envelope, was used in conjunction with The Ritz-Carlton's newspaper advertising (see Exhibit 4) to promote winter weekend packages to upscale potential guests throughout New England and New York.
(Courtesy of The Ritz-Carlton, Boston, Massachusetts)

Exhibit 7   The Reach of Radio

Radio sets in use	507 million
Radio sets per household	5.4
Households with radios	99%
Automobiles with radios	95%
"Walk-along" radio users	18.3 million

Source: Radio Advertising Bureau.

to this "waste" factor, direct mail can become costly if it is used to blitz large target markets.

Broadcast Advertising

Broadcast media include radio, television, and video. For many years, this advertising avenue was overlooked by hoteliers for two reasons: cost and unfamiliarity. The cost factor included both the production of broadcast ads (especially for television) and the nature of the medium itself. Unlike print advertising, broadcast advertising is not a form of advertising that can be kept and referred to. Therefore, for the property's broadcast message to be remembered, it has to be repeated frequently, often over several stations. This repetition greatly escalates costs. Many hoteliers, accustomed to using print advertising, have hesitated to make a commitment of time and money to broadcast advertising.

This resistance to broadcast advertising is breaking down in today's highly competitive lodging industry. Many hoteliers are turning to broadcast media to reach a nation on the go, and radio, television, and video advertising is becoming more popular.

Radio. Radio's greatest advertising strength is that it is heard by over 83% of the public daily. Nearly everyone in America owns a radio. According to the Radio Advertising Bureau, most American households own at least five radios, making radio one of the greatest saturation media available to the hospitality industry (see Exhibit 7).

Radio has many advantages:

- It costs less to reach potential guests (on a cost-per-person basis) through radio advertising than through newspaper advertising.

- The relatively low cost of radio advertising allows for frequent advertising and image-building in the community.

- Radio can target specific audiences and is an extremely flexible medium.

- Radio is one of the most effective media in regard to instant recognition and retention of a slogan or message.

- Radio can be used to reach a variety of audiences during those time periods when the audiences are listening.

Radio also has several disadvantages. There are many radio stations and it is easy for a property's message to get lost among or become confused with other messages. There is no visual image to back up a radio ad; unlike print ads, radio ads cannot be saved and referred to at a later time. And, because of the widespread listening audience, radio messages must be broadcast over several different stations at frequent intervals for maximum effect.

Television. Through television, a property can give a total, "living" picture of the image it wishes to project. Since the message is both seen and heard, it is more likely to be retained by a segment of television's vast viewing audience.

While television is today's most popular saturation medium, many hoteliers forgo television advertising due to several disadvantages. First, there is the high cost of airtime and production. Unlike radio, which usually includes a bank of background music and announcers in the price of the advertisement, television costs are quoted for airtime only; the production of television commercials can add thousands of dollars to the price quoted. And, along with the high cost of a television commercial, it is impossible to accurately target the audience. While commercials can be aired in specific time slots, there is no guarantee that the message will reach the targeted audience.

Video. Since we are living in the television age, it is not surprising that many hotels now have videotapes to help sell their property. Many lodging properties use video brochures in addition to their printed brochures when soliciting travel agents and meeting planners. A video brochure is a short (usually four- to six-minute) presentation of the property's features and services. Some properties also have "video magazines," longer videos shown on television monitors in high traffic areas at the property such as the front desk. And some properties are finding that a videotaped interview with a satisfied client is a great sales tool.

Alternative-Media Advertising

In addition to these commonly used media, there are a number of more unusual avenues for getting a property's message across:

1. *Movie theaters.* Many movie theaters offer "commercial" time either before or between features. Using this medium can be especially effective prior to holidays (especially Christmas) and traditional eating-out days such as Mother's Day. Costs for this option include production expenses as well as actual airing time.

2. *Ballparks and other sports arenas.* Many ballparks and sports arenas offer a number of options for advertising. One of the most popular is the use of display boards along the perimeter of the stadium. These boards have the advantage of being in view during the entire event, unlike another option, electronic video screens, which flash messages periodically during the game (video screen messages, however, may seem more "catchy" to fans). Yet another advertising opportunity exists through participation in "special nights" (a seat cushion to the first 1,000 fans, etc.). This type of advertising puts the property's name before the public at a relatively low cost and generates community goodwill.

Display advertising at ballparks and other sports stadiums is an excellent way to attract sports fans to a property. In addition to the billboard-type advertising shown here, many stadiums and arenas also feature electronic video screens that can be programmed with graphics and special effects to enhance a property's message. (Photos courtesy of Richard Torento and the Las Vegas Stars baseball team, 1992)

3. *Parking meters and parking garages.* Display cards can be attached to the tops or bases of parking meters and display boards can be placed in parking garages.

4. *Bus shelters and park benches.* In many communities, advertising space is offered on bus shelters and park benches. The messages are viewed by large

Advertising on bus shelters and park benches is seen by passing motorists as well as patrons of public transportation. This eye-catching ad is for a show at a Las Vegas casino hotel. (Courtesy of Metro Display Advertising, Las Vegas, Nevada)

numbers of passing motorists as well as the "captive audience" waiting for public transportation.

5. *Inserts in billings.* Including advertising in billings can take two forms: individual and sponsorship. Individual advertising is done on the property's invoices, and may include a mention of an upcoming event or promotion. Many hotels today are teaming up with other hospitality related firms, such as car rental agencies, travel agencies, and credit card companies, inserting messages, special offers, and even entire newsletters in another business's billings or other mailings.

6. *In-flight and airport advertising.* This type of advertising includes ads on the backs of boarding passes, ads put up on the screen before the in-flight movie starts, and even ads inside sandwiches (the Meridien Hotel puts ads inside the wrapped sandwiches served on shuttle flights from Boston to New York City). Local hotels use video advertising in the baggage pick-up areas of some airports.

7. *Hot air balloons and other "high-flying" advertising.* Message boards on hot air balloons or banners pulled by airplanes, while costly, are excellent attention-getters. They are especially effective when used to promote special events.

8. *Retailer tie-ins.* Another popular option is advertising on cash register tapes—either on the back or directly on the front of each tape. Or, a property may team up with a store or other local retailer to have advertising printed on packaging or have fliers or coupons given away with purchases.

Advertising options are limited only by your imagination, but you should carefully evaluate any alternative-media advertising to make sure it fits the positioning and objectives of your property. An advertising option that is perceived as "cutesy," for example, may do more harm than good in the long run—as can teaming up with a firm that does not complement the property's image.

Developing an Advertising Plan

Because of the media clutter that exists today, you must give careful attention to both the purpose of advertising and the means that will most effectively communicate your property's message (see Exhibit 8). You should develop an advertising plan that will enable your property to reach its selected target markets within a predetermined CPM (cost per thousand)—the cost of reaching 1,000 households or individuals. Once each target market has been categorized according to its need for advertising, you must determine which advertising media will reach each target market, the best advertising strategies to pursue, and how much money will be needed to adequately advertise to each market (see Exhibit 9).

Advertising should always be considered a part or an extension of the property's overall marketing plan. The marketing audit, for example, will help in scheduling the property's advertising for maximum effectiveness; the positioning statement will help determine the content of advertising; and, of course, the overall marketing budget will play a key role in how much advertising is scheduled (and where). Once these factors have been analyzed, you can develop an overall advertising plan that will keep advertising consistent with property goals and resources.

Deciding Where to Advertise

Which media outlet you advertise in will depend on the outlet's ability to reach your property's target audiences. (A "media outlet" is an individual newspaper, radio station, television station, and so on.) It may be far less costly to place an ad in a local newspaper, but who will read the ad? Will it be read by locals who have limited needs for guestrooms, instead of by meeting planners whom the property hopes to attract? In this case, it would be far more cost-effective to place an ad in a trade journal or business directory, or develop a direct mail program for meeting planners.

To determine exactly where to advertise, you must know exactly how guests choose your property. If, for example, the majority of your guests make reservations through travel agents, you should advertise in travel agent directories. On the other hand, a highway property that attracts mostly walk-in guests will benefit most from billboard advertising or ads on local radio stations.

In many cases, print and broadcast media outlets can provide information on their readers and audiences that can assist a property in selecting the right outlets. Broadcasters can provide "reach and frequency" computer printouts that list the demographics of a radio or TV station's listeners. Most print media are able to

Exhibit 8   Sample Advertising Worksheet

ADVERTISING WORKSHEET

Property: Ritz-Carlton
Address: Newberry Street
          Boston, MA

Date: September 1
Telephone: 555-1564
General Manager_____
Director of Sales _____

A. Primary objective

To sell 200 more weekend room nights in December, January, and February.

B. Target audience (business people, families, diners, honeymooners)

Visitors traveling by car within three hours driving time; couples over 45 years old who no longer have to worry about baby-sitters or leaving their children. Primarily two-income families desiring to get away with other couples.

C. Unique selling points

Good value—offers several package alternatives including room, breakfast, and three-course dinner. Stress "weekend package" as an ideal gift.

D. Specify details to be included (prices, hotel facilities, location, nearby attractions)

Importance of spending time together. Complete attention, pampering. Relax in whirlpool, sauna, and exercise room. Complimentary breakfast in your room. Chilled bottle of Ritz-Carlton champagne awaiting arrival. Late check-out time on Sunday. Boston's only Five Diamond Hotel. Private Manager's Weekend Reception.

Theater district just steps away—Boston Pops Concerts. Historical attractions: Beacon Hill, Bunker Hill, The Tea Party Ship, Old North Church, Waterfront Marketplace, Charles River.

E. Suggested publications or stations (newspapers—local or urban area, radio, magazines, direct mail)

Suggested publications—local newspapers in urban areas within a radius of 200 miles. Advertisements should appear in the holiday/travel or amusement section of the newspapers. Place weekend break brochure in the envelope with confirmation slip to every business person booking a Thursday night stay. Message: "Why not spend a weekend break with friends." Direct mail to past guests in key geographic areas: Boston, New York, New England.

F. Dates advertising is to appear and frequency

Advertisements to appear once weekly beginning last week of December through end of February. Direct mail piece to be sent last week of November.

G. Direct response required

[X] Yes   [ ] No

H. Any other information

Direct response—telephone number and address for reservations. Coupon for weekend brochure request.

An advertising worksheet makes it easier to develop ads and other promotional material by stating the objective, targeting the audience, and listing unique selling points of each promotion. This worksheet was used by The Ritz-Carlton for its winter weekend campaign (see Exhibits 4 and 6).

Exhibit 9   Media Cost Comparison

Medium	Description of Advertising	Cost
Outdoor	12″ × 24″ 30-sheet poster in prime location	$800
	14″ × 48″ printed bulletin at same location	$3,000
Newspaper	Full page b/w ad in weekly edition of newspaper in major city	$6,000–$10,000
	Full page b/w ad in national edition of *USA Today*	$20,000–$30,000
Magazine	One-page, four-color ad in *Travel & Leisure*	$20,000
Directory	Full page four-color ad in *Hotel & Travel Index*	$7,500–$9,000
Direct Mail	Materials, production, and third class bulk mailing costs for a four-part mailer to 5,000 meeting planners	$2,350
Radio	30-second spot during morning drive time	$50–$75
Television	30-second spot during a popular prime-time program (local coverage) PLUS production costs	$500–$1,000 $400–$2,000

provide detailed statistics regarding readership, such as the publisher's statement shown in Exhibit 5. You can also study publications to determine who is already advertising in them. A firsthand look at consumer and trade magazines, for example, can give invaluable insights into their quality, content, and readership. Is the content such that the property's advertising would benefit from the publication's image, or is the publication a poorly produced, controversial vehicle that would detract from the property's advertising?

Before deciding where to advertise, you should consider a number of questions. Which advertising media:

- Reach the largest number of potential guests at the lowest cost per guest?
- Can deliver an adequate selling message?
- Sell the property rather than merely identify or announce it?
- Can repeat the property's message on a frequent basis?
- Are flexible enough for special promotions?
- Cover the property's targeted marketing areas or audiences?
- Offer the least "waste" coverage?
- Best fit the property in terms of image and prestige?
- Fall within the advertising budget?
- Are affordable without sacrificing other important media coverage?

Advertising Flow Chart

Client
Period
Date
Page _____ of _____ Pages

	JAN	FEB	MAR	APR	MAY	JUN	JUL	AUG	SEPT	OCT	NOV	DEC	Total
	3 10 17 24 31	7 14 21 28	7 14 21 28	4 11 18 25	2 9 16 23 30	6 13 20 27	4 11 18 25	1 8 15 22 29	5 12 19 26	3 10 17 24 31	7 14 21 28	5 12 19 26	
New York Times (Sunday Travel) SAU 10 @ $8,883						X X	X X	X X					$53,298
New York Times Magazine Page 4/C @ $23,040						X X	X						$69,120
Philadelphia Inquirer (Sunday Travel) SAU 10 @ $5,727.12						X X	X X	X X					$34,362.72
Philadelphia Magazine Page 4/C @ $5,360						X X X X	X X X X	X X X X X					$16,080
Washington Post (Sunday Travel) SAU 10 @ $7,946.40						X X	X X	X					$47,678.40
Washington Magazine Page 4/C @ $5,060						X X X X	X X X X	X X X X X					$15,180
													$235,719.12

KEY: SAU = Standard Advertising Units
     4/C = Four color

A media or advertising flow chart such as this one provides an overall view of what the property is doing in terms of advertising over a given period. Of course, media are not limited to newspapers and magazines. If the property is using radio spots or television commercials, or is involved in a direct mail campaign, these should also be included on the chart.

Source: Adapted from *HSMAI Marketing Review*, Spring 1983, p. 15.

When considering the last two questions, the property should take a look at three money-saving advertising resources: advertising agencies, reciprocal advertising, and cooperative advertising.

Advertising agencies offer expertise and experience in placing advertisements where they will be most effective. The agency fee (often 15%) is usually paid by the media in which the advertisements are placed. (Advertising agencies will be discussed in more detail later in the chapter.)

Reciprocal advertising, also called "due bill" or "trade-out" advertising, is the exchange of hotel rooms (and sometimes food and beverages) for outdoor, newspaper, magazine, radio, or television advertising (see Exhibit 10). Reciprocal advertising can be especially effective for properties with limited advertising budgets. Properties can control how many unsold rooms can be used and when. A property may receive an additional return on its trade-out because participants in a reciprocal agreement often spend money in the property's other revenue centers. A radio station manager, for example, who is given use of the property's health club may stay for lunch, or a newspaper executive given a free room for the weekend may buy meals and drinks at the hotel. There is an added benefit to reciprocal advertising—the endorsements of publishers, advertising executives, and broadcasters are influential, and their recommendation of the property to their business associates and friends can prove invaluable.

Cooperative advertising involves advertising in conjunction with another advertiser. There are two basic types of cooperative advertising: horizontal and vertical. Horizontal co-op advertising involves similar businesses, such as several hotels who pool resources to promote their destination city (see Exhibit 11). Vertical co-op advertising, on the other hand, involves several different types of businesses, such as when a hotel and an airline sponsor an advertisement that will benefit both parties (see Exhibit 12). Vertical co-op advertising is more common than horizontal co-op advertising.

There are many advantages to cooperative advertising: the costs of advertising are shared, identification with another prestigious product or firm may increase sales, and co-op advertising is available in a number of media.

Cooperative advertising also has disadvantages. In the case of the three competing hotels in Exhibit 11, the three properties may equally share advertising costs but they may not receive equal patronage. Some advertising partnerships may prove inflexible in terms of meeting each other's needs. Lastly, cooperative advertising agreements may have conditions that are less than ideal for one or more of the participating advertisers. Perhaps the contract limits the advertising to a specific medium, or the property must limit its message to specified areas—the property can promote its convention capabilities but not its weekend packages, for example.

Advertising Strategies

An important part of any advertising plan is deciding on advertising strategies. The three strategic options most commonly used are differentiation, segmentation, and a combination of the two.

Exhibit 10   Reciprocal Advertising

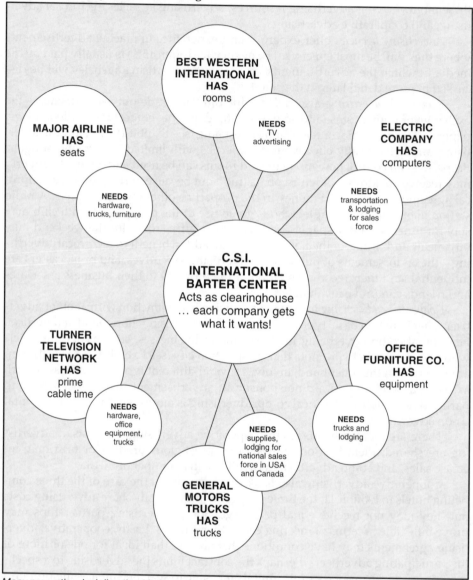

Many properties deal directly with the media to place reciprocal advertising, while others, including Best Western International properties, use a central clearinghouse to trade for advertising and other needs. (Courtesy of Best Western International, Inc.)

Differentiation. Differentiation emphasizes how your property is different from its competitors. In order to be effective, there must be meaningful differences—differences that are readily identifiable to potential guests. When using differentiation, however, you should steer clear of a disturbing trend that has clouded hotel

Exhibit 11   Horizontal Co-Op Advertising

Located within the heart of San Antonio's economic center, we can offer you a convenient convention.

It's not often that competitors call a truce, but we've done just that for you. With our combined forces we can supply your convention with over 500 rooms, meeting facilities up to 1,000, 5 restaurants, 3 swimming pools and 3 cocktail lounges. All within minutes from San Antonio International Airport. Our location also puts our triple treat in the middle of San Antonio's economic hub. There's all kinds of shopping available from giant malls to tiny one-of-a-kind boutiques. Plus banks, major office buildings and national corporate headquarters within easy reach. So take advantage of a convenient location and the services and facilities of not one, but three fine hotels.

In this example of cooperative advertising, three hotels have produced a brochure to attract convention and large-meetings business. The three properties, all located within minutes of the airport, together offer what one individual property could not; all will benefit from overflow guests from any one of the other properties. (Courtesy of La Mansión del Norte, San Antonio, Texas.)

advertising in recent years: ads that boost the image of one property while knocking the competition. Far too many properties are making use of advertising claims that either directly or indirectly derogate other hotels or destinations, a technique that may discredit the industry as a whole.

Getting the Most from Reciprocal Advertising

There are a number of guidelines that should be followed in order to receive the most from reciprocal or "recip" advertising:

1. Try to set up the exchange on a one-to-one basis; i.e., an equal dollar-for-dollar trade based on each party's retail price. You may have to give $1.50 in value for each $1 received in a high-quality print medium exchange, but generally one-to-one is the rule. Radio airtime can usually be negotiated at a more favorable exchange rate than television airtime or print ad space.

2. When possible, exclude your peak periods of occupancy in the exchange. The idea of barter is to exchange unsold room nights, so be sure your recip contract eliminates periods when you'd normally be doing full rack-rate business.

3. Consider making your recip arrangement good for group business only rather than individual room nights; you will have more control over what inventory is being used at what time. Most media are willing to go along with the group concept, since they have sales meetings, rallies, and staff seminars in which bulk space can be used.

4. Try to trade whatever costs you *least*—rooms instead of food and beverage, tennis or golf lessons, rental equipment, etc.

5. Consider a 50-50 deal, in which each recip dollar spent at your property is matched by a cash dollar. Thus, half the bill is paid in a media exchange, the other half in cash. This kind of arrangement can be negotiated when the media outlet needs you more than you need it.

6. Make sure the recipients (media personnel) of your recip program can't sell your "credits" to other people. Your trade should be limited to specific personnel (station manager, sales director, key executives, publisher, etc.), and they alone should be eligible to use your facilities.

There are three accounting methods for exchanges:

1. You can issue a "scrip" certificate that, when redeemed, entitles the bearer to use your services; e.g., one night's accommodations or a credit line of $100.

2. A special credit card can be issued with a ceiling set at the amount of the reciprocal agreement.

3. Monthly statements can be exchanged showing credits used and balances remaining.

Whatever method you use, seek the simplest format that protects you against credit abuses and does not require excessive time to administer.

Source: Updated and adapted from Howard A. Heinsius, "Reciprocal Advertising: Marketing Tool for the Eighties!" *Resort Management*, March 1982.

Headlines such as "Don't Book Your Convention into a Tourist Trap" or "Some Resorts Resort to Anything" do little to promote either a particular property or the industry in general. Classic ads that feature positive positioning statements,

Exhibit 12   Vertical Co-Op Advertising

In this example of cooperative advertising, Southwest Airlines and the Westin hotel chain have teamed up to present a promotional package. In this type of advertisement, the costs are shared by both advertisers, and each benefits from the prestige and following of the other.

a unique selling position such as an island location or guestrooms decorated with antiques or fine art, or themes that cast no aspersions on the competition are more effective in the long run.

Segmentation. A segmentation strategy can also be used to advertise your property. The basic premise of this advertising approach is that a target market can be carved up into smaller segments. The business traveler market, for example, can be segmented into women business travelers, businesspeople who travel on extended trips, meeting planners who book business for large groups, teams of business travelers rather than individual business travelers, and so on. Once a segment has been identified, advertising can be developed to appeal specifically to it. Advertising that attracts a woman business traveler would be totally different from advertising for a meeting planner, for example.

You should carefully assess each market to determine if a segmentation strategy would be more successful than a general advertising effort to the entire market. If your property is already attracting a large number of women business travelers, for example, it may not be necessary to advertise to this segment of the business traveler market; advertising dollars may be better spent on general business traveler advertising or on a segment of the business traveler market that is not staying at your property in acceptable numbers.

Combination. This strategy combines differentiation and segmentation. A specific market segment is selected to advertise to, and an attempt is made to differentiate your property from other properties by offering unique benefits that will be of interest to the selected segment. This strategy can work well for small properties, since they don't always have the wide range of products and services offered by larger properties or chain properties. A small property can focus on one of its assets (a rustic location, for example) and then advertise to a market segment that will be attracted to that asset. Market segments interested in a rustic location might include families, businesspeople who want to relax, and so on. This strategy can also work for any size property that has been rehabilitated or repositioned; the advertising strategy would focus on a particular aspect of the property (its restoration to its original condition, for example).

Advertising Characteristics

No matter what strategy is used, advertising must cut through the media clutter and promote the property in a memorable and cost-effective way. Four characteristics—reach, frequency, consistency, and timing—play important roles in all successful advertising strategies.

Reach. Reach refers to the number of different individuals or homes exposed to an advertising message at least once during a specified time period (a two-month promotion, for example). Generally, advertising costs will be higher as reach goals increase. Added reach will require more advertisements or the use of additional media outlets.

Frequency. Frequency is a measure of how many times the average person in the target market is exposed to the advertising message over a specified time period. It generally takes a number of exposures of a print ad or radio or television commercial to familiarize potential guests with the property's name or image and prompt them to respond. The frequency of a property's advertising will depend on the urgency of the property's message. A specific event or promotion, for example, will require a large number of ads placed within a relatively short amount of time to attract the attention of the public.

Many hotel marketing experts feel that frequency is more important than reach, due to the spur-of-the-moment nature of many decisions about where to lodge. Many people make reservations as late as the day before a trip, and advertising is more likely to be remembered if it was seen within the last week rather than a month or two previously. Peter Yesawich, president of Robinson, Yesawich & Pepperdine, Inc. (a marketing, public relations, and advertising firm), supports this philosophy:

> In media terms, the way to maximize the impact of your current [advertising] program is to trade reach (the total number of prospects exposed to your message) for frequency (the number of different times exposed). For example, rather than run an advertisement six times in six different publications, you should run twelve times in the three publications that deliver the most qualified (responsive) audience. The increased frequency will bring the audience to a "critical mass" of exposure faster, thereby producing quicker and better results.[2]

Consistency. A property's advertising is far more effective if it has a consistent look and, in the case of broadcast media, a consistent sound. A property that positions its print ad elements (headline, illustration, body copy, pricing, logo, etc.) in the same order and uses ads of the same size will be recognized more often than a property that tries a different look with each of its print ads. When broadcast media are used, time frames, jingles or other sound effects, the announcer, and the message should be similar for easier recognition.

Timing. Advertising should be scheduled for those times when it will be most effective. The Newspaper Advertising Bureau, for example, recommends timing advertising to coincide with seasonal sales patterns—promoting summer vacation packages just before the season, for example.

Advertising patterns can be varied to meet the needs and budget of a property. There are three basic patterns that may be used: continuity, pulsing, and flighting. Suppose the Quality Hotel wants to place 90 radio ads over a period of 30 days. If it follows a *continuity* pattern, it will schedule the ads evenly over the 30 days—it might schedule 3 radio spots per day for 30 days, for example. A *pulsing* pattern is an uneven scheduling of ads over a given time period. If the Quality Hotel follows a pulsing pattern, it might air one radio spot every day over the thirty day period, and feature additional spots on Thursdays, Fridays, and Saturdays to generate additional weekend business. *Flighting* means advertising only as needed over a given time period. If the Quality Hotel follows a flighting pattern, it might distribute all of its 90 ads on the Sundays and Mondays within the 30-day period to promote a Monday night dinner special.

Budgeting for Effective Advertising

Perhaps the most crucial part of an advertising plan is the budget. Advertising expenses are only a portion of the total budget for marketing and sales. While 3% to 6% of a property's revenues may be allocated to cover the total cost of the marketing and sales department, only about one-third of this amount will be spent on advertising.

(The rest of the money is spent on salaries, office expenses, and other expenditures that supplement the sales effort.)

Before establishing a workable advertising budget, you should be aware of a number of variables that will affect the kind of advertising budget used by your property:

- *The type of property.* The size of your property and the types of services and facilities it offers will greatly influence the amount of money necessary to effectively advertise it. Typically, it costs far less to advertise a standard highway property than a luxury resort.

- *The competition.* Although an advertising budget should not be established simply to match funds being spent by competitors, the level of your competition's advertising activity helps determine how much your property will have to advertise to receive a fair market share.

- *The property's marketing objectives.* The advertising budget should be tied directly to the property's marketing plan. If you want to expand your property's facilities or target markets, you may invest more in advertising. If your property enjoys a comfortable guest base and is generating a steadily increasing flow of new guests, you may want to concentrate efforts on direct mail or in-house promotions, usually far less expensive than broadcast or national print advertising.

- *Target markets.* The number and sizes of a property's target markets will affect the amount of advertising needed to reach potential guests. A hotelier targeting a regional market will spend less than the hotelier attempting to attract guests from across the country.

- *Cooperative advertising opportunities.* As mentioned earlier, this type of advertising enables advertisers to share costs and stretch advertising budgets. In some cases, a property may tie into a community or state plan that promotes an entire area and its services. A case in point is the successful "I Love New York" campaign.

You should consider these variables before developing an advertising budget.

Like the general marketing and sales budget, the advertising budget requires you to set objectives. Good planning ensures that advertising dollars are not thrown away in haphazard fashion. To get the most from advertising dollars, you should:

- *Make sure the advertising budget conforms to the property's marketing plan.* If one of the property's marketing goals is to increase weekend business by 45%, for example, more advertising dollars should be spent on newspaper and magazine advertising than on in-house brochures.

- *Target profitable market segments.* Some market segments bring more dollars into your property than others, and additional advertising expenditures for these profitable segments may be more cost-effective in the long run. Costly ads in consumer magazines that reach a small proportion of the property's guests are a poor substitute for a direct mail campaign that targets travel

Measuring Advertising's Cost-Effectiveness

There are three ways to look at the cost-effectiveness of your advertising:

1. Cost per thousand (CPM)
2. Cost per inquiry (CPI)
3. Cost per conversion

Cost per thousand refers to the cost for reaching one thousand potential buyers, and is calculated as follows:

$$\text{CPM} = \frac{\text{Cost of advertisement}}{\text{Vehicle circulation}} \times 1{,}000$$

Cost per inquiry can be used to evaluate both the response to a specific advertisement and the cost of soliciting each potential customer. CPI can be determined as follows:

$$\text{CPI} = \frac{\text{Cost of advertisement}}{\text{Total inquiries generated}}$$

Inquiries don't always result in sales, so to determine the actual value received for the cost of advertising, actual sales (conversions) must be measured:

$$\text{Cost per conversion} = \frac{\text{Cost of advertisement}}{\text{Total conversions}}$$

These formulas may be used to determine the effectiveness (or lack of it) of a particular advertisement or advertising campaign. If results do not prove cost-effective, you should analyze both the advertising and the media outlets used. Perhaps the advertising itself is not effective, or the ad is fine but the selected media outlets are not reaching the intended target audience.

For an example of how these three methods can help you evaluate an ad's effectiveness, let's look at three publications targeted to the vacation/leisure traveler:

Publication	Circulation	Cost of a 4-Color Ad
National Geographic Traveler	200,000	$10,000
Travel & Leisure	750,000	$30,000
Southern Living	1,000,000	$35,000

Using the formula for determining cost per thousand:

$$\text{CPM} = \frac{\text{Cost of advertisement}}{\text{Vehicle circulation}} \times 1{,}000$$

we find that the cost per thousand for *National Geographic Traveler* is $50, for *Travel & Leisure* is $40, and for *Southern Living* is $35. As you can see, although it costs more to place the ad in *Southern Living* ($35,000) than in the other two magazines, it actually delivers the lowest cost per thousand readers exposed ($35).

(continued)

(continued)

But CPM alone is not the only criterion used to determine cost-effectiveness; it is also necessary to evaluate cost per inquiry and cost per conversion to adequately analyze the best advertising value. If, for example, the property decides, based on the cost-per-thousand analysis, to advertise in *Southern Living* and *Travel & Leisure,* and the ad generates 3,000 inquiries and 2,500 inquiries respectively, it can determine the cost per inquiry using the cost-per-inquiry formula:

$$\text{CPI} = \frac{\text{Cost of advertisement}}{\text{Total inquiries generated}}$$

For *Southern Living,* the cost per inquiry is $11.66 ($35,000 ÷ 3,000); for *Travel & Leisure,* the cost per inquiry is $12 ($30,000 ÷ 2,500).

Perhaps the best measure of an ad's effectiveness is the number of sales or conversions the ad generates, however. In this example, the *Southern Living* ad led to 700 sales from readers who responded to the ad; the *Travel & Leisure* ad led to 600 sales. Cost per conversion, calculated using the cost-per-conversion formula:

$$\text{Cost per conversion} = \frac{\text{Cost of advertisement}}{\text{Total conversions}}$$

shows that for *Southern Living,* the cost per conversion was $50 ($35,000 ÷ 700); for *Travel & Leisure,* the cost per conversion was also $50 ($30,000 ÷ 600). As you can see, although the advertisement in *Southern Living* generated more inquiries at a lower cost ($11.66 versus $12), the *Travel & Leisure* ad was just as cost-effective in terms of delivering actual sales, its cost-per-conversion being the same as the *Southern Living* ad.

---

agents, meeting planners, and other travel intermediaries who can bring a great many guests to the property.

- *Promote benefits.* No matter what a property decides to promote—its most profitable services; special values (weekend packages, corporate rates, and so on); special services such as VIP limousines; or the property's location—in advertising, as in sales, the property should promote its benefits rather than its features.

- *Decide when to advertise.* Advertising costs are most effective when spread out into "campaigns." An advertising campaign is a series of messages on a given theme developed to reach audiences when they are most receptive to the property and what it has to offer. Preparing advertising budgets requires breaking down specific advertising campaigns and individual promotions into quarterly phases.

- *Research the budget options available.* There are a number of methods that can be used to develop a budget: percentage of sales, competitive parity, affordable funds, and zero-base. Each of these should be studied to determine which will work for the property.

No matter what budget method is used, it should be reviewed periodically. You should analyze advertising results on an ad-by-ad or campaign-by-campaign basis, and make adjustments if goals are not being met. An ad campaign's contribution to the bottom line will help determine whether shifts in strategies or media outlets used by the property are necessary.

Advertising Agencies

Since developing an overall advertising plan or creating a single ad campaign within a workable budget can be a complicated process, many properties seek assistance from advertising agencies. Advertising agencies can be extremely helpful in making media decisions that keep costs low. In addition, an agency will be expert in determining which media can showcase the property's message most effectively.

Types of Ad Agencies

There are several types of advertising agencies: full-service agencies, à la carte agencies, creative shops or boutiques, and media-buying services.

Full-service agencies are usually structured into four departments: the creative department handles the development and production of ads; the media department selects specific media and places the ads; the research department is the marketing arm that determines the characteristics and wants of the targeted audiences; and the business department handles the agency's business affairs. Many full-service agencies have developed relationships with other agencies (or have branches or affiliates) to provide coverage wherever their clients' products are sold.

À la carte agencies, also known as modular services, are usually full-service agencies that offer selected services on a negotiated fee basis. A property may use this type of agency for the production of an ad or radio spot or for a one-time placement of advertising.

Creative shops or boutiques are independent firms that offer creative services (the design and production of ads) on a free-lance, per-job basis. These agencies are usually staffed by free-lance artists and writers, and may develop into full-service agencies as their client base grows.

Media-buying services do not offer creative services, but specialize in the buying of radio and television time. Many media-buying services have found it difficult to compete with full-service agencies, since they do not provide any production or marketing services, but this type of agency can prove useful to properties with in-house advertising departments.

Most advertising agencies receive their compensation as media commissions, production commissions, and/or from negotiated fee arrangements. The most common compensation is the typical 15% media commission or rebate. If an agency places $30,000 worth of advertising in a particular magazine for a hotel, the agency is billed $25,500 by the magazine ($30,000 less 15%); the agency bills the hotel at the full $30,000, giving the agency a $4,500 commission. Media rebates are paid only to accredited agencies; the hotel would have been billed $30,000, not $25,500, had it bought the space independently. It is possible, however, for a property to save 15%

Insider Insights

G. Douglas Hall
Consultant
Four Seasons Hotels and Resorts
Toronto, Ontario
Canada

Douglas Hall began his business career with a Canadian advertising agency. After achieving the position of vice president there, he joined the Toronto office of Young & Rubicam, a multinational advertising firm. Hall was responsible for directing the advertising of such clients as General Foods, the Whitehall Laboratories division of American Home Products, Metropolitan Life, and Thomas J. Lipton (he spearheaded the successful introduction of Lipton Cup-A-Soup to the Canadian consumer) before acquiring Four Seasons Hotel Limited as a client. Hall, who had no previous hospitality industry experience, directed the development of the advertising that was ultimately to position Four Seasons as the leading luxury hotel group in North America. With this advertising, Hall won the coveted Adrian Award, the Hospitality Sales & Marketing Association International's highest honor for excellence in hotel advertising. It also brought him a job offer from his client, and today he serves as a consultant to Four Seasons.

Of course I believe in advertising. But the key is to use it properly. I'm a firm believer in research. It doesn't always have to involve a large, expensive consumer study; research is often just listening. Listen to your hotel guests, listen to your competitors, listen to the people who report to you. I get some of my best ideas from listening to others.

While I knew nothing about operating a hotel, I had used hotels for years, and my packaged-goods background had disciplined me to be consumer-directed; that's the basis of all marketing. Tell your customers about the benefits they'll enjoy, not just the features you offer. And don't let the fact that thousands of people will see your advertisement deter you from speaking directly to the customer as if you were selling face-to-face. Good advertising copy talks to one person: your ideal prospect.

Selecting the media in which your advertising will appear depends on your target markets and where they live. Start with a plan based on your budget. I'm a great believer in the rifle versus the shotgun approach. It isn't wise to scatter your advertising all over; you'll have so few exposures to any one target segment that you'll make no impression. It's far better to pick a few publications that reach the customers you've targeted and advertise in them with sufficient frequency to ensure that customers see and remember your ad.

If you're selecting an advertising agency, think of it as a potential partner in marketing. Share all the information you have about your hotel, your customers, and the times when you need business—and the times you don't. Your long-term success is the agency's success!

on ads it places on its own; it can license its in-house ad agency as a DBA ("doing business as") to receive media commissions.

Media commissions cover only the costs of space or airtime; ad agencies may charge production commissions on such services as typesetting, photography, copy-writing, and other production services. In addition, agencies may also charge fees for such marketing services as independent surveys, product testing, and research.

Finally, there may be other fee arrangements based on the type of work being done. This may include a negotiated flat fee for the development of an international ad campaign, for example.

Selecting an Ad Agency

Before you select an advertising agency, you should first understand your property's needs. Does the property need to create a new image? Are new ideas needed to reach present markets or to cultivate new target audiences? Is additional technical expertise required to develop effective, creative advertising?

Once needs have been identified, you can prepare a list of suitable agencies and begin the task of selecting one. A general questionnaire can help in the sorting-out process (see Exhibit 13). During the preliminary investigation, you should ask for:

1. The full name of the agency and its address and telephone number.

2. The names and titles of key agency personnel and the nature of the agency's nearest office. Is it a branch? If so, where is the agency's headquarters?

3. The length of time the agency has been in business and financial information (annual reports, financial statements, an accounting of gross billings, and so on).

4. The percentage of media billings for:

   a. Newspapers

   b. Magazines

   c. Directories

   d. Radio

   e. TV

Exhibit 13   Sample Advertising Agency Questionnaire

Background, Management Business Philosophy

1. When was your agency established? Is it part of a larger organization? If so, what is the name of the senior company and what degree of control does it exercise over your operations?

2. Please provide the names and titles of your principal officers and a brief résumé of each.

3. Do you or your organization handle advertising for any hospitality industry facility at the present time? If yes, please list the degree of involvement.

Personnel

1. Please submit an organizational chart of your agency showing its various departments and functions.

2. Provide the names of the people who would work on our account, including creative staff. Please submit a brief résumé of each and describe their talents.

Agency Size and Growth

1. What has been the growth rate in the past 5 years in terms of:

    (a) how many accounts you service that are in excess of $200,000 gross billings yearly?

    (b) percentage change since previous year?

    (c) sources of billings, i.e., percentage from old accounts and percentage from new accounts?

2. Please list your accounts according to:

    (a) the year account was acquired.

    (b) national or regional assignments.

    (c) which office handles these accounts.

3. Where is your main office located? Where are branch offices located?

4. Indicate, by percentage, the degree of emphasis you place on the various services carried out by your agency with your current accounts.

5. In the past year, how were your billings distributed in dollars and percentages among the following:

Dollars	Percentages	
_____	_____	Newspaper
_____	_____	Consumer magazines
_____	_____	Radio advertising
_____	_____	TV advertising
_____	_____	Outdoor advertising
_____	_____	Other

Public Relations

1. What services in the area of public relations have you provided for your clients?

2. Do you have specific staff who handle these activities? If so, please provide a brief background on the key people.

Exhibit 13 *(continued)*

Sales Promotion

1. Do you have a specific department or personnel to handle sales promotions?

2. What types of sales promotions have you prepared for your clients?

Marketing and Research Services

1. What ability does your agency have to plan and conduct target market surveys and other advertising research? Who are the key people in the research department and what are their backgrounds?

2. Describe the techniques of "advertising effectiveness research" that you have found to have been the most useful.

Compensation and Service Structure

1. What compensation structure would you prefer?

2. Please provide a copy of your agency-client contract with any changes or modifications you would suggest for our account.

3. Please provide a sample of contact reports and any other reports that you would provide to us on a regular basis.

---

    f. Outdoor advertising

    g. Other types of advertising (collateral materials, direct mail, and so on).

5. The number of full-time employees who work at the agency. Is the agency large enough to meet special needs and yet small enough that the property will not get lost in the shuffle? Has the staff had extensive experience in the hospitality industry?

6. The number of clients the agency currently serves. Are there any accounts that might present a conflict of interest? What is the typical size of an account? Can the agency provide the names of several of its accounts for reference purposes?

7. The media outlets the agency is advertising in. Can the agency provide a list of the media outlets it has used (radio and television stations, newspapers, and so on), the contact persons at each outlet, and statistics relating to each outlet's effectiveness?

8. Samples of advertising and collateral materials that have been used successfully in hospitality industry or other related industry campaigns.

    Using the information gained from the preliminary investigation, you can make a list of acceptable agencies. A selection committee composed of key property staff (the general manager, the director of marketing and sales, the sales director, the rooms manager, and so on) should visit each of these agencies rather than having agency representatives come to the property. This serves two purposes. First, it involves property employees in the choice of an agency; this involvement helps commit them to maintaining a successful relationship with the selected agency. Second, it provides property staff with the opportunity to observe how the agency conducts business, the quality of the agency's employees, and the agency's creative processes.

Although your first meeting with an agency should be informal, it is an important one. The following topics should be discussed during the visit:

- Who specifically would work on the property's account if the agency were selected? Does that person have hotel/restaurant experience?

- How willing is the agency to cooperate with the property in the things most important to the property: research, direct mail advertising, in-house promotions, and so on?

- Is the agency willing to stick to the property's budget? Is the agency experienced in reciprocal or cooperative advertising?

- How would the agency be compensated? Will the agency work for a fee, a commission, or a combination of both? Has the agency spelled out its rate schedule clearly and accurately? Are services and their costs covered individually?

Once the field has been narrowed to two or three agencies, a formal meeting with each of the top choices should be scheduled at your property. At these meetings, each agency should present its final advertising proposal and outline what it would do for the property. You should not expect this presentation to include actual ads or ad ideas for your property; it is unfair to ask for such without compensating the agency. Instead, the sample presentation should detail the types of advertising that the agency thinks will work best for your property, and include suggestions for brochures, direct mail pieces (if applicable), and other types of materials that the agency thinks should be used to promote the property. In many cases, this presentation is supplemented by examples of ads the agency has developed for other properties, services, or products.

At this time, it is important to tie up any loose ends: how the agency would handle emergency situations; who would cover the account if the property's agency representative was transferred or left the firm; and how communication will be maintained between the property and the agency.

In an ideal situation, the advertising agency you choose to work with becomes part of the property's sales team—familiar with the marketing plan, aware of the property's positioning statement, and willing to work with you to ensure that the property's image is presented as effectively and economically as possible.[3]

Endnotes

1. Barry Maher, "Do Your Hotel's Yellow Page Ads Talk to the Traveler?" *Florida Hotel and Motel Journal*, February 1992, p. 7.

2. Peter Yesawich, "Planting Seeds for Growth," *Hotel & Resort Industry*, January 1992.

3. Material in this section adapted from information provided by Tom McCarthy, owner, Tom McCarthy Associates, a hotel marketing consulting firm.

Key Terms

à la carte ad agency
advertising agency
alternative-media advertising
broadcast advertising
collateral advertising
consistency
continuity
cooperative advertising
CPI (cost per inquiry)
CPM (cost per thousand)
creative shop or boutique
differentiation
direct mail advertising
display advertising
flighting

frequency
full-service ad agency
horizontal co-op advertising
media-buying service
media clutter
media outlet
outdoor advertising
print advertising
publisher's statement
pulsing
reach
reciprocal advertising
segmentation
timing
vertical co-op advertising

Review Questions

1. Why do hospitality properties need to advertise?

2. What are four advertising goals?

3. What are the advantages and disadvantages of using newspapers? Magazines? Direct mail?

4. What are the strengths and weaknesses of radio and television advertising?

5. What are some advantages of using cooperative advertising?

6. What are three strategic advertising options discussed in the chapter?

7. What four characteristics are a part of all advertising strategies?

8. What variables may affect the size and structure of the advertising budget?

9. What are some questions a hotel should ask during its preliminary investigation of an advertising agency?

Chapter Outline

Outdoor Advertising
    Property Signs
        Reader Boards
    Billboards
      Location
      Size
      Design
      Copy
      Maintenance
      Contracts
Displays
    Transit
    Trade Show
    General
Collateral Materials
    Printed Items
      Fliers
      Tent Cards
      Brochures
    Specialty Items
Conclusion

10

Outdoor Advertising, Displays, and Collateral Materials

In today's highly competitive market, outdoor advertising, displays, and collateral materials are an important part of the sales efforts of properties of all sizes.

Outdoor advertising is a catchall term that includes a property's sign, billboards, and other methods used outdoors to put the property's name and image before the public. This type of advertising is especially well-suited to motels because motels rely on passing motorists for a great deal of their business.

Displays are used primarily indoors to attract guests to the property. In this chapter, we will take a look at several options for using this type of advertising, including displays in transportation terminals and at trade shows, conventions, and other gatherings.

Collateral materials cover a wide spectrum of advertising pieces—from rack brochures to intriguing specialty items. Nearly every property uses collateral materials to support the efforts of its sales force.

Outdoor Advertising

Although posters may sometimes be used for outdoor advertising, in this section we will focus on the two most common means of advertising a property outdoors: property signs and billboards.

Property Signs

A familiar property sign featuring the logo of a well-known hotel chain often is a welcome sight to an undecided tourist in an unfamiliar area (see Exhibit 1). In addition to identifying and calling attention to the property, a property's sign can advertise the property's restaurant, lounge, function facilities, and other revenue centers. It can also be an effective public relations tool when used to welcome groups or promote a community charity campaign.

It is important to note, however, that many properties have very little input into their property sign, especially if they are part of a chain or have a franchise agreement that requires standard signs. Some lodging chains, such as Best Western International, Choice Inns, and Holiday Corporation, offer their members a choice of several standard signs. But even these chains closely monitor property signs to ensure that members conform to graphic requirements and design specifications.

Exhibit 1   Sample Property Signs

Holiday Inn's "Great Sign," which featured a giant neon arrow (left), was originally designed to generate business from passersby on America's highways. During the 1970s and 1980s, however, the chain became more popular with business travelers and a change of image was necessary. An updated version of the sign (right) was designed. It cost 34% less than the Great Sign, used subdued backlighting (cutting energy costs by two-thirds), and was preferred by a consumer panel by a three-to-one margin. In addition to providing an updated image, the sign also reduced maintenance costs by 55%. Note the reader boards on both signs.

Uniformity in property signs establishes consistency and brand identification throughout the country and, in some cases, throughout the world.

Independent properties are most likely to create their own property signs. It is important that these signs fit into an overall marketing strategy. To develop the most effective property sign, managers of independent properties should consider the following factors (most of these factors should also be considered with billboard advertising):

1. What are the purposes of the sign? Will the sign only promote name recognition, or will it also advertise the property's revenue centers and provide other information such as the time or temperature?

2. A property sign's audience is most often in a moving vehicle, and the bigger the letters, the sooner the audience can read the message. Certain color combinations also make reading easier.

3. To be most effective, the property sign should complement the hotel's design and image. The sign's layout should be clean and uncluttered, and the sign itself should be attractive, well-maintained, and illuminated whenever possible. Signs can be electric, engraved, subsurface, movable, and so on.

4. A sign's design and complexity will affect the engineering needed to erect it. Before selecting a sign, you must consider climate, the structural strength of the proposed sign, maintenance, and local zoning codes.

5. Since a property sign is a long-term investment, care should be taken to select a manufacturer that will provide a quality product at a reasonable price. The property should also take into account the time needed to manufacture the sign, especially if the sign is to be used for a grand opening or is scheduled to be unveiled at a special promotional event.

6. Installation must comply with safety standards and codes, and should be accomplished at a time least inconvenient for the property's guests. Property management should check with the manufacturer or the firm actually doing the installing to determine installation time and costs.

7. Some properties have the option of leasing a sign rather than purchasing it, and may choose this option for the tax benefits and the maintenance contract included in the lease agreement. If a sign is purchased outright, the property must take maintenance costs into consideration.

Reader Boards. Some property signs feature a reader board—an area on the sign set aside for temporary messages.[1] Reader boards on property signs are an important part of a day-to-day promotional program. They are often a small hotel's most-read advertising. Properties large and small should take reader boards seriously. Messages should be changed frequently—every three days is not too often—and messages kept brief. To passersby, the outside sign indicates the quality of the inside operation, so the sign should be kept neat. Use reader boards to promote:

- Special rates or packages
- Special facilities or services: waterbeds, suites, saunas, continental breakfasts
- Community activities (this is an opportunity to build community goodwill and create a favorable image for the property)
- Whatever features or benefits separate your property from the competition

Reader boards can be creative or humorous too. Some examples from Super 8 reader boards include:

- BUY AND RAVE AT WHAT YOU SAVE
- HANDS UP! THIS IS A STEAL!
- OUR GUESTS ARE WISE; DON'T BE OTHERWISE
- WE WATCH OUR Ps AND Qs: PRICES AND QUALITY
- LAND HERE FOR DOWN TO EARTH PRICES
- THIS IS WHERE YOU COME IN

Insider Insights

Donna Hicks-Field, CHA, CHSE
Hospitality Consultant
Field's Unlimited
Madison, Wisconsin

Donna Hicks-Field was introduced to the hospitality industry when she worked as a wedding consultant. She served as director of sales at three diverse properties for over nine years. In addition to service at Inn on the Park and the Sheraton Inn and Conference Center in Madison, Wisconsin, and the Karakahl Inn in Mt. Horeb, Wisconsin, Hicks-Field has actively participated in the Wisconsin Society of Association Executives, Meeting Planners International, Toastmasters International, the American Marketing Association, the Hospitality Sales & Marketing Association International, Downtown Madison, Inc., and the Greater Madison Convention and Visitors Bureau. With a partner, Hicks-Field recently founded Effective Hotel & Motel Management. She is looking forward to putting her expertise in communications, advertising, and sales to work for a number of clients.

Is a billboard right for your property? The answer depends on your marketing objectives and the audience you plan on targeting with your message.

Special attention must be paid to billboard copy. Magazine and newspaper advertising has the advantage of being studied, while billboards are often seen with a fleeting glance. Billboard copy must be instructive but easily readable—and the audience should always be considered.

The cost of billboards will generally be related to the location and the number of people that pass that location on a daily basis. The higher the traffic count, the higher the cost. Lengths of outdoor contracts will also be a factor in determining monthly cost. Generally, a contract that can be negotiated for three to five years is most economical. However, the contract should allow for yearly review and include an escape clause that protects you against detours.

Billboards can offer imagery that's appealing and eye-catching. Brilliant colors are available for billboards, but it's important to consider changing climate conditions when choosing a billboard's background color. A white background would not be ideal for a billboard located in an area that has snow on the ground several months of the year.

The overall effectiveness of billboard advertising is difficult to measure. Effective monitoring is accomplished by TAB, the Traffic Audit Bureau, an impartial monitoring organization supported by advertising agencies and billboard companies. TAB verifies the number of billboards in a given market and their impact in that market.

Billboard advertising can be effective as a directional or informational sales tool, as in the case of two Madison hotels that I've worked with. The billboards we had for the Sheraton were located on the interstate and featured Sheraton's logo, the

---

Insider Insights *(continued)*

exit number, the number of miles to the property, and directions. A second directional billboard was located after the interstate exit and gave final directions to the Sheraton. Our target audiences were tourists and corporate travelers.

Billboards used by the Karakahl Inn had to be more descriptive. The inn's logo was familiar only to locals and past guests, so the billboards had to convey the size of the property and its amenities. The Karakahl Inn was bypassed when a new highway was built around the village of Mt. Horeb. Since our directional highway billboards were not yet complete, our tourist traffic dropped significantly. But when the billboards were completed, tourist traffic increased just as significantly.

Billboard advertising can be effective. It offers an advertising message all day long, every day of the year. As with any type of advertising, creativity is important. An advertising image must command attention, and a good billboard must be properly placed after being properly created to be an effective advertising tool for your property.

- TEED OFF ON YOUR DRIVE? PUTT IN HERE

- LUXURY FOR LESS

- SUPER 8—FOR THE BEST SURPRISE OF YOUR TRIP

For small properties, which often can't afford the expense of large billboards, a catchy reader board is one way to attract interest.

Billboards

There are several differences between property signs and billboards. One of the most obvious is that a property's sign is on property grounds, while billboard advertising is placed away from the property at strategic locations on well-traveled streets and highways.

The most common billboards fall into two general categories: posters and painted displays. Poster billboards are available in two sizes: a 24-sheet poster that measures approximately 9 by 20 feet (2.7 by 6.1 meters) and a 30-sheet poster that has 25% more copy area than the 24-sheet poster. In addition, a "bleed poster," which has a printed area extending all the way to the frame of the display and is 40% larger than the 24-sheet poster, is also available. Sheets are printed with the advertising message and then pasted like wallpaper on the display boards by the local outdoor advertising companies who own the boards.

Painted displays are usually more expensive, and fall into two sub-divisions: walls and bulletins. Painted walls are usually used only in cities, and consist of designs or copy painted directly on a wall rented by the property. Painted bulletins are generally much larger than poster billboards, with a typical size of 14 by 48 feet (4.3 by 14.6 meters). These billboards may be either hand-painted directly on-site, or may be created in the billboard company's studio and then transported to the

Painted Display Cost Guidelines

Here are the most important things you need to know before you sign a contract:

1. *Period of Purchase.* Normally, painted bulletins or painted signs or walls are bought for a minimum term of one year to a maximum of three (occasionally, five) years at a guaranteed rate, and payment is rendered on a monthly basis.

2. *Discounts.* Discounts are frequently offered for purchases extending for more than one year—most commonly, 5% for two years and 10% for three years.

3. *Cancellation Privileges.* Standard practice is that one-year contracts are non-cancelable, while second and third years may be canceled upon 60 days' notice prior to each anniversary of the initial completion date. If this notice is not given by the advertiser, the contract is not cancelable until the next anniversary date. The contract should clearly specify cost penalties for such cancellation.

4. *Initial Completion Date.* This is the day on which the sign is first completely painted and fully serviceable. This date establishes the effective date of the contract as well as any subsequent anniversary dates and the monthly billing dates.

5. *Painting.* A minimum of two complete paintings per year should be included in the monthly space charge. Under normal circumstances, the sign should be painted approximately every six months to keep the display in a bright and attractive condition, unless the sign faces within approximately 60° of true north, in which case it may be possible to get by with only one painting per year. Between paintings, the seller is obligated to maintain the painted surface in good repair without additional charge.

6. *Illumination.* The sign should be fully lit between 6:00 A.M. and sunrise, and between sunset and midnight. A cash credit of 25% of the daily cost is normally extended for any day on which illumination is not provided.

7. *Embellishments and Extensions.* Any requested special effects in the form of structural additions or embellishments to the face, top, bottom, or sides of the sign such as cut-out letters, neon effects, time/temperature modules, etc. will be charged for. These are normally billed on a one-time basis for fabrication and installation, and are the property of the advertiser. Frequently, a charge for monthly maintenance may be added.

Negotiating

Obviously, it helps if there are several sign companies operating in your area, since competition tends to keep prices down and produce wider availability. It also affords a chance to check on comparative pricing and invite competitive bidding.

Pricing of a sign is generally determined by several factors other than simply its basic cost to the operator:

1. Size of the sign's audience.

2. Size of the sign.

3. Visibility and impressiveness of the sign.

4. Exclusivity—how many other signs there are covering the same general area.

Item 1—the audience—is usually the most important single factor in the price. A painted bulletin ranging in size from 14 by 48 feet (4.3 by 14.6 meters) to 20 by 60 feet (6.1 by 18.3 meters) with a satisfactory approach should normally cost no more than about $1 to $2 for each thousand people who see it.

You can compute this cost yourself if you secure a vehicular traffic count for the primary approach artery (or arteries, if the sign can be clearly seen from more than one street). Take the traffic count, which is the number of cars passing the sign during a specified period of time—usually, a day—and multiply it by .83 if it is a two-way count on a two-way artery or 1.66 if it is on a one-way street (these figures are industry standards developed by the Outdoor Institute Association). Take that total and convert it to a monthly figure (by multiplying the daily count by 30, for instance). Next, divide the monthly figure by 1,000, and then divide that result into the monthly cost of the sign to get a cost-per-thousand-viewers figure. Here is an example:

Sign cost: $1,800 per month

Daily two-way traffic count: 200,000

$200,000 \times .83 = 166,000$ viewers per day

166,000 viewers per day $\times$ 30 days = 4,980,000 viewers per month

$$\frac{4,980,000}{1,000} = 4,980$$

$$\frac{\$1,800}{4,980} = \$.36 \text{ per 1,000 viewers}$$

Once you have arrived at an acceptable price, go ahead and contract for it, keeping in mind the relevant items above.

Source: Adapted from Sheraton Worldwide Advertising Manual, 1984, pp. 12–13. Courtesy of ITT Sheraton Corporation.

site and put up on the display board in sections. Depending on weather conditions, painted displays may have to be repainted two to three times a year to keep them looking attractive.

Factors to consider when purchasing billboards include:

- Location
- Size
- Design
- Copy
- Maintenance
- Contracts

Location. A good billboard location can mean the difference between increased sales and wasted advertising dollars. Before selecting a location—whether it be

Exhibit 2   Sample Directional Billboard

This directional billboard will be illuminated, since about 30% of a billboard's annual audience will pass the billboard between sunset and dawn. The billboard will have more visual impact at night (when the property is trying to attract business) than during the daylight hours.

Courtesy of ITT Sheraton Corporation

alongside a highway or a city street—a drive past the billboard should be made. This drive can disclose pertinent information on a billboard's potential. Factors to look for include the number of other billboards in the immediate vicinity, visibility (the closest distance at which the billboard becomes visible and then readable while traffic is moving at the maximum legal speed), and variable conditions such as tree foliage that might obscure the billboard at various times of the year. Another important factor to consider is highway construction. The highway department should be contacted to determine if any construction is scheduled near the billboard's location in the immediate future. A detour can mean drastically reduced readership for the billboard.

Before deciding on a highway billboard, it is important for city properties to determine which highways leading into the city are used more by traveling motorists than local commuters. Special in-city billboards featuring property restaurants, lounges, and other facilities may be designed to attract the latter group.

The number of a property's billboards will help determine their location on a highway. As a general rule, a property's billboards should be placed no less than two miles and no more than ten miles apart, although this spacing will vary with the size of the billboards, their proximity to the property, and the number of competing signs in the area.

Highway billboards can be complemented by in-city billboards that give directions to the property (see Exhibit 2). In-city billboards can also be used in key feeder cities and, as mentioned, to attract local patrons to the property.

Size. The optimum size for a billboard is usually based in part on the number of other billboards a property has on a given highway or street. For example, if a property is using only two or three billboards, they should be fairly large—14 by 48

Exhibit 3   Hilton's 3-D Billboards

The prestigious image of the Hilton chain is preserved in creative billboards which feature motion and three-dimensional images. This "Pot o' Gold" billboard is enhanced through the use of "gold coins" that rotate on the display area. (Courtesy of Donrey Outdoor Advertising, Las Vegas, Nevada)

feet (4.3 by 14.6 meters). If a property is using a number of billboards, the first two or three can be large, while the remaining billboards can be smaller in size.

Design. After the location of the billboard, its design is the most important selling factor. Today's designs offer a wide array of choices.

Whatever their type, billboards should be simple, readable, and designed to be read quickly from left to right. Colors should be bright and contrasting; lettering, simple and bold (see Exhibit 3). Fancy type styles, though sometimes appropriate in other advertising, do not work well on a billboard since they are often unreadable at traveling speeds. The type style should complement the billboard's overall design and be large enough to make an impression.

There are several design elements that can make a billboard more interesting. One is the use of *cutouts*. Cutouts can take many forms, but the most popular is an illustration that extends beyond the billboard itself. In addition to making the billboard more interesting, cutouts make billboards seem larger. Closely related to cutouts are *inflatables,* designs made of heavyweight nylon that add a three dimensional effect to billboards.

Today's computer technology has provided such high-tech special effects as *kinetic boards*—a series of two- or four-sided panels on a billboard that rotate to display different advertising messages—and computer-generated graphics that offer changing designs and messages.

A popular design often used by resorts is a billboard with a panel at the bottom that allows for easy copy changes. The bottom panel is used to advertise coming events, entertainment, or specialty restaurants on a rotating basis.

Most painted billboards are illuminated for best effect, but lighting is no longer limited to shining a few lights on the property's message. In many cases, special lighting that blinks or changes colors is combined with standard lighting, resulting in a display called a *spectacular.* This type of outdoor advertising is a common sight in such tourist attractions as Las Vegas, Atlantic City, and Times Square in New York City.

A fairly new form of lighting is *backlighting,* which makes the background of the display board "disappear" and makes the image seem to "pop out" against the night sky. Some advertisers are experimenting with *holography,* projecting a three-dimensional image either from or onto the display board.

Even if a property cannot afford these types of special effects, some type of lighting should be considered when designing a billboard. If the billboard cannot be illuminated, the property may want to have its name and one or two selling points treated with reflective material for increased visibility at night.

Many hotel chains have design and logo specifications for billboards that their properties must adhere to, although properties often have a choice as to billboard size. Chain requirements may include the shape of the billboard, colors, and a standardized logo. Individual properties can often "personalize" the sign with property information.

Copy. The key to successful billboard copy is to keep it brief. A billboard should convey one main idea: the most exciting and persuasive message will not work if it is too long to be read by passengers in a moving vehicle. Advertising experts suggest that copy be five to ten words long. A short, catchy phrase, one that both attracts attention and is memorable, works best.

Since most billboards feature artwork that conveys an immediate impression, copy can be kept simple. An illustration showing the size of a property is far more effective than using copy such as "150 rooms." Also, copy should not be wasted on advising travelers of services that they expect a property to have (air-conditioning, television, attractive rooms, and so on).

Billboard copy can be approached from a number of angles. It can notify travelers of the number of miles to the property, list amenities offered by the property, describe one special feature, or state the property's slogan. A slogan is especially effective if the property is part of a chain with name and value recognition.

Maintenance. No matter what type of billboard is used, it must be maintained on a regular basis. Peeling or cracked paint, rips in the design, or other damage can detract from a property's message and create a poor impression of the property. When contracting for a billboard, the property should determine maintenance responsibilities. Many contractors of painted billboards offer two or three repaintings as part of their service. Proper maintenance helps ensure that the property's billboards create the impression for which they were designed.

Contracts. Billboard space is usually purchased for one to three years. Space contracts are available in two forms: rotating or fixed.

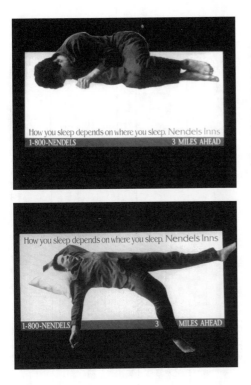

These three billboards, developed for Nendels Corporation, feature a man sleeping at various angles on the display and the chain's slogan, "How You Sleep Depends on Where You Sleep." Nendels Corporation, which offers three products—Nendels Inn, Nendels Valu Inn, and Nendels Suites—used billboards to build name and value recognition, devoting more than half of its 1992 marketing budget to its billboard blitz. Note the use of cutouts. (Courtesy of Nendels Corp.)

Rotating plans ensure that the property's message is seen in a number of areas; the display location is changed on a periodic basis (usually every thirty to sixty days). This type of advertising plan, which is usually sold on a six- to twelve-month contract, ensures that the message will be seen by more than one group of potential customers, and gives the impression that the property is advertising all over town.

Fixed or permanent plans provide billboard advertising at one location only. This type of plan is usually purchased when a billboard's location provides heavy coverage—on a freeway, for example. For maximum effectiveness, billboards limited to one location must be creative—even spectacular—and directly reach the target audience.

Most outdoor advertising companies provide rate sheets with detailed information about each type of advertising (see Exhibit 4). In addition to the typical plans just discussed, some outdoor advertising companies also offer a trial plan, ranging from three to six months (or available on a seasonal basis) to test the effectiveness of an outdoor advertising campaign.

Displays

Like billboards, displays are designed for use off the property's grounds in high-traffic locations. Unlike billboards, displays are used mainly indoors and, because they are less costly, are changed more frequently.

Exhibit 4   Sample Outdoor Advertising Rate Sheet

Las Vegas, Nevada

Mailing address: Post Office Box 4245 • Las Vegas, NV 89127-0245
Shipping address: 1211 West Bonanza Road • Las Vegas, NV 89106

Phone number: 702-382-5020
Fax number: 702-382-7088

Poster Rates and Allotments

Market/Populations (000)	#100 GRP/showing				#75 GRP/showing				#50 GRP/showing				#25 GRP/showing				Posting Dates
	Reg./Ill.	Total	Cost Per Month	Daily Eff. Circ. (000)	Reg./Ill.	Total	Cost Per Month	Daily Eff. Circ. (000)	Reg./Ill.	Total	Cost Per Month	Daily Eff. Circ. (000)	Reg./Ill.	Total	Cost Per Month	Daily Eff. Circ. (000)	
Las Vegas (784.6)	11/20	31	$14,355	784.7	9/15	24	$11,070	588.5	6/10	16	$7,695	392.3	4/5	9	$4,440	196.2	1, 5, 10, 15, 20, 25

Rotating Bulleting Rates

Market	Average DEC	12-month Contract	8–11 Months	4–7 Months	Unit Size
Las Vegas Metro	40,500	$1,910	$1,960	$2,100	14×48

Reno, Nevada

Mailing address: Post Office Box 10237 • Reno, NV 89510-0237
Shipping address: 4945 Joule Street • Reno, NV 89502

Phone number: 702-329-0220
Fax number: 702-329-7595

Poster Rates and Allotments

Market/Populations (000)	#100 GRP/showing				#75 GRP/showing				#50 GRP/showing				#25 GRP/showing				Posting Dates
	Reg./Ill.	Total	Cost Per Month	Daily Eff. Circ. (000)	Reg./Ill.	Total	Cost Per Month	Daily Eff. Circ. (000)	Reg./Ill.	Total	Cost Per Month	Daily Eff. Circ. (000)	Reg./Ill.	Total	Cost Per Month	Daily Eff. Circ. (000)	
Reno (196.0)—adults 18+	7/13	20	$8,400	196.0	6/9	15	$6,300	147.0	4/6	10	$4,200	98.0	2/3	5	$2,100	49.0	1, 5, 10, 15, 20, 25

Rotating Bulleting Rates

Market	Average DEC	12-month Contract	8–11 Months	4–7 Months	Unit Size
Reno Metro—adults 18+	21,000	$1,650	$1,810	$1,980	15×50

Outdoor advertising companies provide rate sheets detailing costs and requirements for poster billboards on rotating or fixed plans. This rate sheet also provides such important information as the number of regular (Reg.) and illuminated (Ill.) boards offered at the quoted price, the approximate daily viewership (DEC = Daily Effective Circulation), posting dates, and billboard sizes. (Courtesy of Donrey Outdoor Advertising, Las Vegas, Nevada)

Exhibit 5   Sample Outside Transit Advertising

Transit advertising space on taxicabs is generally sold on weekly or monthly contracts. Hotel advertisers must supply the advertising cards at their own expense.

Displays can be used for several purposes: transit advertising (advertising in or on buses, taxicabs, and—in some cities—the subway), trade show advertising (promotion of the property at conventions and trade shows), and general advertising (transportation terminal advertising, periodic displays at tourist attractions, local chambers of commerce, and so on).

Transit

Transit advertising falls into two separate categories: transit or inside cards and outside posters (see Exhibit 5). Transit advertising has several important advantages:

- *Low cost.* Transit cards offer excellent color reproduction at a relatively low cost. The advertiser pays only for the production of the transit card (design, typesetting, printing, etc.) and for the rental of the transit space. Rental fees for this space are usually quite low compared to the cost of advertising in newspapers or using billboards. Operators of transit systems realize their profits from the fares of users of the system. Renting space to advertisers is extra income, and reasonable fees are usually charged to attract as many advertisers as possible.

- *High readership.* Surveys show that readership of transit card advertising is high; many riders read transit advertising to relieve boredom. This is an effective medium with which to reach urban consumers, middle-to-lower income groups, and tourists.

- *Frequency.* People who take the same routes day after day are exposed to the transit card message on a regular basis. They can become guests or excellent word-of-mouth advertisers.

There are also some disadvantages to using transit advertising. It is not a prestigious medium; it does not target a specific audience; and, if there are numerous cards on a bus or if someone tries to read a poster as a bus or taxi goes by, the property's message may get garbled or be missed entirely. Still, a carefully planned, attention-getting message can make transit advertising worthwhile.

When planning transit advertising, it is important to remember that it can appear in two different locations—inside (buses, the subway) or outside (the subway, buses and taxis). Inside transit advertising is read by a captive audience and can contain more copy than a typical billboard; pads of coupons, which enable readers to take action on the property's offer, can be attached for a small additional charge. Outside transit advertising, however, must be designed to be read quickly, and artwork may play a more important role.

Trade Show

Trade shows are another avenue for displays. Trade shows are held for a variety of industries, trades, and professions, including such travel-oriented professions as travel agent, tour group operator, and meeting planner. A hotel may also wish to advertise at a trade show or convention that caters to a targeted market segment such as medical doctors, construction companies, the computer industry, and so on. Display posters are used to attract delegates to a property's booth, and may picture property amenities in detail.

General

General display advertising usually includes color posters of the property and its features, or posters describing special property promotions such as a Hawaiian week or a special two-for-one room rate. A poster can vary in size from the large 9-by-20-foot (2.7-by-6.1-meter) size to one-half to one-eighth that size. The size will vary with the intended use of the poster and the location. Some transportation terminals, for example, have fixed spaces for display posters, and the posters must fit into the frame or mounting panel.

Collateral Materials

Virtually all hotels use collateral materials in one form or another. Collateral materials include printed items (fliers, tent cards, brochures), and specialty items (matchbooks, shoehorns, key chains, and other giveaways). Collateral materials serve two purposes: first, they get the property's name in front of a great number of people; second, they can serve as "silent salespeople"—aids to supplement the message of the property's sales staff.

Collateral materials are usually given away either by salespeople or through other means such as in-house promotions, leaving the items in guestrooms, handing items to departing guests, and so on. Even though they are often given away, the value of collateral materials should not be taken lightly. Collateral materials are generally used to target a specific market segment desired by the property, and usually cost far less than mass-media advertising in terms of cost per inquiry and number of inquiries converted to sales.

Printed Items

Fliers. The simplest printed collateral items are fliers. Fliers can be used as envelope stuffers, direct mail pieces, or inexpensive promotional material. They can also be effective property fact sheets, especially when printed with photographs of the property, and may serve as an alternative to rack brochures. Fliers are especially useful for promoting special events or packages, since they can be quickly produced and usually cost much less than brochures.

For a flier to be effective, it must be attractive. The copy, if possible, should be prepared by a writer who has seen the property or the products it is offering, and should contain the following elements:

1. *A headline.* The attention-grabber.

2. *Headings.* Headings feature key points and break up copy for easier reading.

3. *Body copy.* The selling message. The copy should include prices if the property is offering a special package or promotion. The type should be large enough to be easily read.

4. *Art or photographs.* Artwork and photographs add interest to fliers. Photographs must be clear and sharp for good reproduction, and should almost always be captioned.

5. *Logo and signature.* The property's logo lends credibility to the flier, and the signature (the property's name, address, and telephone number) provides information a reader needs to contact the property.

Tent Cards. Tent cards may be simple three-fold cards or elaborate fold-together pieces that advertise restaurant specials, dessert menus, or other products and services offered by the property (see Exhibit 6). Tent cards advertising the restaurant may be placed in guestrooms as a suggestive selling tool, while tent cards featuring dessert specials or exotic drinks can be placed on restaurant or lounge tables.

Tent cards may be printed in one or two colors or, as is usually done, as full-color pieces. Tent card copy should be brief. A tempting dessert photograph will do far more than copy to sell desserts.

Many hotel chains offer tent cards or a combination package of tent cards and posters through corporate advertising departments. Individual properties can also design their own tent cards.

Brochures. Brochures are probably the most important collateral items and must be designed and written properly to be effective. When developing a brochure, a property should:

- *Set objectives.* What is this brochure meant to accomplish? For example, is the objective to attract banquet business or increase weekend occupancy?

Exhibit 6   Sample Tent Card

Tent cards can promote desserts, beverages, or property specialties. They may also be used as cross-selling tools to promote various property facilities. For example, tent cards may be placed in guestrooms to promote the property's restaurant or lounge. (Courtesy of Days Inns of America, Inc.)

- *Target the audience.* A property cannot effectively reach a number of different audiences with one brochure; trying to talk to everyone with one brochure is usually a waste of money. A brochure for business travelers is of little value to a family group; a brochure for convention planners has little meaning for a retired couple looking for a leisure vacation (see Exhibit 7). If a property wishes to reach several market segments, using several four-panel brochures is usually more effective than trying to cram everything about the property into a general eight-panel brochure.

- *List benefits.* Benefits should be listed for each target audience based on its needs. Each brochure must answer the question, "Why should I (the businessperson, the family member, the convention delegate, and so on) stay at this hotel?"

The amount of information and number of photographs or other artwork will determine the final length of a brochure. Brochures usually consist of four, six, or eight panels, although special brochures with additional panels or with reply cards may be designed.

No matter what type of brochure is designed and written, the property should never skimp on quality. It is far better to print a two-color brochure on quality paper

Exhibit 7   Sample Targeted Brochures

For best results, brochures should target individual market segments. Each of these Days Inns brochures was developed for a specific market: businesspeople, sports teams, government workers, educators, and senior citizens. Each has the advantage of addressing the specific needs of a group rather than attempting to "sell it all" in one general brochure. (Courtesy of Days Inns of America, Inc.)

than a four-color brochure on cheap paper that gives an image of shabbiness. If the property has done its job—created a brochure that lets readers know what the property can do for them—it should not then insult readers with a poorly produced piece.

Many chains provide generic or "shell" brochures to their properties. These brochures are usually full-color pieces with spaces provided for the property to add its own information (special amenities, packages, location, etc.) and photographs; others are fully printed pieces that describe chain-wide services and provide space on the back for the property's name and location. Shell brochures save properties a great deal of money, both in terms of production costs and printing expenses (even the paper has already been provided).

Design. When creating or reviewing a brochure's design, property managers or salespeople should keep in mind the following guidelines:

Match the brochure to the property. The brochure should reflect the personality of the property; it is the personality of the brochure that will distinguish it and the property from the competition (see Exhibit 8). If the property is a luxury hotel, a cheaply printed brochure would not convey the proper impression. A luxury hotel should use quality paper, distinctive type, and special touches such as embossing, foiling, or top-notch photography. In short, the brochure should exude elegance.

GRANDE BUTTE HOTEL

FUN
YEAR-ROUND

CRESTED BUTTE CO

CRESTED BUTTE'S ONLY SKI-IN/SKI-OUT, FULL-SERVICE HOTEL.

The cover of this brochure for the Grande Butte Hotel in Crested Butte, Colorado, features all the elements of an effective cover—the property's name and location, the promise of a benefit ("Year-Round Fun"), and a unique selling point ("Crested Butte's Only Ski-In/Ski-Out, Full-Service Hotel"). Action photos showing summer and winter sports activities add to the cover's appeal.

On the other hand, if the brochure is designed for a leisure resort, the personality of the brochure should be casual. The brochure for a dude ranch can use paper and artwork with a western look. If a resort is family-oriented, a brochure that features photographs of family "fun in the sun" is an effective sales aid. A brochure designed for families would not be written to appeal to a guest's need for status, as in the case of a brochure for a luxury property; instead, the copy would be more informal, focusing on what the property has to offer in terms of leisure options, scenery, and so on.

The brochure's cover is its most important selling point, and it must be designed to induce readers to read the rest of the property's message. Covers should include the name and location of the property, and should reflect the property's positioning and promise a consumer benefit. One large cover illustration is usually

Exhibit 8   Sample Rack Brochures

Although most rack brochures contain the same basic elements, designs differ to reflect the image and atmosphere of a property. This brochure reflects Outrigger's romantic location and features special packages for romantic weekend getaways. (Only three panels of the six-panel brochure are shown.)

more effective than several small ones, and photographs (especially those showing what the guest can expect to experience at the property) are far more effective than line drawings or similar illustrations.

Use photos to heighten the property's image and "sell" the property. Photographs must be chosen with an eye toward embellishing the property's image. The property may be known for a garden setting, for example; words would not portray the garden's beauty as well as a photograph. If a property is famous for unusual architecture, detailed close-ups of special architectural features may entice readers.

Showing special features is not enough, however. Photographs without people can appear cold and lifeless; photographs work best when they include people enjoying the property's amenities (see Exhibit 9). When preparing a brochure for a specific target market, it is important to show people that the brochure's readers can relate to. While professional models are often used, the models should reflect the brochure's target audience—families for a family-oriented brochure, businesspeople for a business-traveler brochure, and so on.

Properties can also use photos to promote tempting food specials; recreational facilities such as the property's golf course or tennis courts; nearby ski slopes,

Exhibit 9 Effective Brochure Photographs

THE SERVICE AND EXCELLENCE
YOU HAVE COME TO EXPECT

Hyatt offers the opportunity of dining or entertaining in style in a variety of elegant settings. You may choose the refined Langely Restaurant, the charm of the Brasserie, or perhaps the eastern delights of the Rama Thai. Cocktails in the Atrium Bar, Plain Street Bar or dancing till dawn in the exciting Kites Nightclub. If you plan to entertain a business contact, celebrate an occasion, dine with friends or simply enjoy a quiet drink or meal, Hyatt provides the ideal atmosphere, superb international cuisine and faultless service.

This brochure promoting the Hyatt Regency Perth (Australia) provides excellent examples of showing people in its advertising (rather than just the dining room) and using a close-up food photograph.

beaches, or parks; beautiful scenery; or other attractions. The property's biggest attraction should be featured in the largest photograph. If all photos are the same size, nothing stands out as being particularly significant.

Copy. The following are guidelines for writing or reviewing brochure copy:

1. *Position the property.* Every property should develop a short (ten words or less) positioning statement that can be used in all of its advertising. The positioning statement may represent a key benefit or a property philosophy, but it should be easy to understand and remember.

2. *Put the property's name and location on the cover.* If the property is located near a major city or recreational area, this information, along with the property's

Brochure covers should be as unique as the properties they represent. The rack brochure for the Sioux Narrows Lodge in Ontario, Canada, features a rustic design and a photograph of what the guest can expect to experience in close proximity to the property (the inside of the brochure carries out the outdoors theme). The directory brochure for Rank Hotels of Great Britain, on the other hand, reflects the upscale nature of the chain's properties. Although it does not contain a positioning statement or offer a benefit, this cover works because the chain is well-known in the area that it serves.

name, can be turned into an eye-catching headline. At the very least, the property's name should appear at the bottom of the cover.

3. *Use headings to highlight key facts.* Headings draw the reader to the property's key features. Even if the copy isn't read, the reader can still see the main points.

Fifteen Ways to Create Brochures that Sell

1. *Put your property's name and location on the cover.* Usually a property's name, unless it is well known, is not enough to sell a property to a traveler; most travelers choose a destination first and a hotel second. Be sure to include your city as well as your property's name, and never resort to simply using a picture of the property—no matter how attractive—on the cover.

2. *Put your selling message on the cover.* The cover of the brochure should establish the property's positioning and a unique advantage. If your property is the only four-star hotel in the area, say so!

3. *Promise the consumer a benefit on the cover.* Customers don't want to know how good the property is, they want to know what it will do for them. A meaningful and important consumer benefit will work harder for the property than a brochure that promises nothing.

4. *Identify your target audience on the cover.* Unless the brochure is a generic one, it should clearly spell out who it is addressing: business travelers, meeting planners, vacationers, seniors, sports teams, and so on. Not only should the brochure target its audience, it should also include a benefit ("The Rustic Inn: Where Vacationers Get Away From It All").

5. *Make the brochure reflect your personality.* Brochures should fit the property's personality. A sleek, modern hotel needs a stylish brochure to complement its image, while a rustic approach would more adequately showcase a dude ranch or mountain resort.

6. *Avoid the smiling chef and other cliches.* For maximum sales appeal, brochures should be fresh and lively. Don't rely on the old "stand-bys," such as a grinning bellperson or the couple posed in the bedroom. Instead, take a look around the property for unique features that will add excitement and interest to the brochure.

7. *Use photographs that stretch the reader's imagination.* In some cases, it pays to promote what is near your property as well as the property itself. If you are located near a major tourist attraction or "natural wonder," add photographs of what the guest might expect to see and experience.

8. *Demonstrate your point of difference.* If your catering department makes the most fantastic ice sculptures west of the Rockies, don't just tell readers—show them. The adage, "a picture is worth a thousand words," is particularly true when selling the intangible hospitality product.

9. *Show activities, not just scenery.* People are interested in people, and especially want to know what type of people they can expect to see at your property. Avoid showing just a feature; show people in the swimming pool, the coffee shop filled with diners, the lounge filled with couples.

10. *Photograph food in closeup.* Finished dishes—never just raw ingredients—should be photographed in close-up for maximum effect.

11. *Make picture captions sell your product.* Picture captions are the most-read element of a brochure after the cover. Caption all photographs with interesting copy that offers a benefit to the consumer.

12. *Use maps.* Most travelers love maps because they provide an easy to read graphic presentation to help them "get their bearings." Including a map that shows your property's proximity to transportation terminals, local attractions, and points of interest will greatly enhance the brochure's selling message.

13. *Give the reader helpful information.* If readers have never been to your property, the brochure may be the only information they have about the property. Make it easy on potential guests by providing useful information, such as what to wear ("formal dining," "come as you are," "casual atmosphere," "bring your jogging shoes," etc.), what to bring ("don't forget your sunscreen"), and what they can expect ("balmy weather year-round," "ski lessons available," and so on).

14. *Use the brochure to be helpful to special audiences.* Spell out any special services you offer to specific groups of travelers: "kids' camps" for families traveling with children; security locks for women business travelers; "Friendship Tables" for singles dining alone, etc. If you are trying to attract international travelers, indicate what languages are spoken by your staff and any special services and amenities (foreign language newspapers, traditional foods, etc.).

15. *Be alert to changing lifestyles.* Know what is going on in the world and keep your product up-to-date by advertising such features as light meals for dieters and the health conscious, exercise and jogging facilities, and other services that meet the needs of today's travelers.

Source: Adapted from an article by Jane Maas in *Lodging Magazine.*

4. *Highlight the property's most popular features and benefits.* Each brochure should highlight features and benefits that will appeal to the brochure's targeted market segment. This can be done in a number of ways, including devoting more copy to these features, setting copy in a different type style or size of type, and positioning the copy where it is most likely to be read (an advertising professional can make recommendations for optimum positioning). Special graphics can also highlight copy: copy can be placed in a box, enhanced with designs such as stars or bold lines, or be accompanied by catchy illustrations or photographs.

5. *Build credibility.* The property should back up claims and make use of testimonials for additional credibility. The property can develop a testimonial file by sending previous guests a token gift along with a survey card; the responses may provide hundreds of good quotes that can be used in brochure (and other) advertising.

6. *Tell the whole story.* Pack as much information as possible into each brochure.

7. *Urge the reader to take action.* Include invitations throughout the brochure to visit, call, or write. Then make it easy for the reader to do so by providing a reply card or a toll-free number.

These elements can be incorporated into any brochure, whether it is designed by an in-house staff, an advertising agency, or a chain property's corporate advertising staff.

The Staying Power of Specialty Advertising

Specialty advertising is not limited to serving as "reminder" advertising; it can be used to generate or boost sales as well if it is properly planned and enhances the property's other sales and marketing efforts. For example, when research done by the Holiday Inn in Richmond, Virginia, showed that 95% of the property's bookings were made by secretaries, a specialty advertising campaign was launched to make the most of this sales avenue.

The program began with the development of a list of approximately 250 administrative assistants and secretaries from local firms. These prospects were first visited by salespeople, who left a mug with the property's reservations number and the restaurant's logo. Their visits were followed up with a mailing that featured a pen imprinted with the property's name and reservations number. A buffet was also held, with another pen given as a take-home gift. This program was followed with another mailing—this time a key chain with the restaurant's logo, and a thank-you letter for business received to that date.

The result was that the hotel outperformed its competition consistently from Mondays through Thursdays, the typical strong nights for corporate business.

Campaigns such as this one can be extremely successful if they follow a clearly defined plan that includes the following steps:

1. *Define a specific objective.* Is the objective simply to get the property's name in front of the public? If so, a simple premium, such as a ballpoint pen (which can be purchased in large quantities for a relatively low cost) might be the answer. If the objective is to increase the number of business travelers, a calendar detailing promotional events and offering discounts or other incentives might be more effective.

2. *Identify the audience to be reached.* Is the target audience families with children? Consider a colorful toy; one, preferably, which will be easily recognized. Is it the business traveler? Try using a travel alarm clock embossed with the property's name and reservations number.

3. *Determine a workable distribution plan.* How will the premium be distributed? Will it be available at the check-out counter, in the property's gift shop, or by mail order? If the premium will be distributed in-house, is there adequate storage and display space?

4. *Create a central theme for the promotion.* Don't haphazardly order premiums that will clash with one another. If the theme is "getting away from it all," select related premiums (logo sunglasses, beach-related items, etc.) that will follow through on that theme.

5. *Develop a message to support the theme.* Enhance specialty items with a catchy message or memorable slogan. Or, promote a benefit that will result in increased bookings or covers. Be sure that all messages conform to the property's image and positioning.

> 6. *Select an appropriate advertising specialty*—preferably one that bears a natural relationship to the advertiser or theme. If your lounge features specialty drinks, consider giving away or selling unique glassware or coasters; if your property promotes an annual event each year, feature it on a number of specialty items—T-shirts, posters, keychains, and so on.
>
> A carefully designed, efficiently executed specialty advertising program can build customer goodwill as well as repeat business. Specialty items can keep your property and what it has to offer in front of present guests—and reach out to countless other potential customers who might never see a print ad or hear a radio ad.

Source: Adapted from Ken Koepper, "Specialty Advertising Has Staying Power," *Lodging,* March 1989.

Some brochures have different copy requirements than general rack brochures. In the case of a convention brochure, for example, detailed information is more important than fancy photography or scenes of leisure activities (see Exhibit 10). A convention brochure, in addition to listing the property's name, address, and telephone number, will usually include the following information: references from previous convention groups; guestroom information such as room block policy, reservations policy, a list of rates, and registration information; dining room information (names, types, and capacity); meeting room information (names, capacity for different types of functions, audiovisual equipment available); exhibit space (dimensions, scaled drawings, floor load, ceiling height); banquet and beverage service (capacities, types); special services and facilities (electronic mail, convention service personnel, contract photographers); transportation (distance to the airport or other travel terminals, parking facilities, tour facilities); auxiliary activities (spouse entertainment, and so on); and billing procedures.

Specialty Items

Specialty items, also called "premiums," are economical sales tools that can be remarkably effective. According to the Specialty Advertising Association (SAA), the recall factor with specialty items averages nearly 40 percent for as long as six months after the specialty item has been received.

A specialty item can be tied in with a holiday (such as giving out candles at Christmas time or beer mugs on St. Patrick's Day), given in conjunction with a property promotion (a beach bag or ball during a summer vacation promotion), or used as a promotion in itself (specialty items offered for "points" earned for room nights or meal purchases). Some specialty items such as glassware or such "signature" items as terry bathrobes or teddy bears become so popular that they are available for sale in a property's gift shop or through mail order.

Even a small property can afford high-use specialty items such as ballpoint pens and key chains, while other, higher-priced items such as coffee mugs, calendars, and T-shirts can be purchased by properties with larger advertising budgets. Wearable specialty items that mention a special property event or are embossed with a property's logo or slogan are extremely popular. The most sought-after

Exhibit 10 Sample Convention Brochure

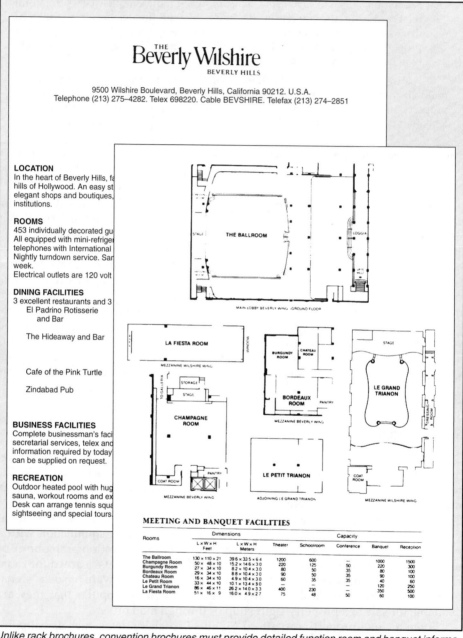

THE
Beverly Wilshire
BEVERLY HILLS

9500 Wilshire Boulevard, Beverly Hills, California 90212. U.S.A.
Telephone (213) 275–4282. Telex 698220. Cable BEVSHIRE. Telefax (213) 274–2851

LOCATION
In the heart of Beverly Hills, fa
hills of Hollywood. An easy st
elegant shops and boutiques,
institutions.

ROOMS
453 individually decorated gu
All equipped with mini-refrige
telephones with International
Nightly turndown service. Sar
week.
Electrical outlets are 120 volt

DINING FACILITIES
3 excellent restaurants and 3
   El Padrino Rotisserie
      and Bar

   The Hideaway and Bar

   Cafe of the Pink Turtle

   Zindabad Pub

BUSINESS FACILITIES
Complete businessman's faci
secretarial services, telex and
information required by today
can be supplied on request.

RECREATION
Outdoor heated pool with hug
sauna, workout rooms and ex
Desk can arrange tennis squa
sightseeing and special tours.

THE BALLROOM

LOGGIA

STAGE

MAIN LOBBY BEVERLY WING GROUND FLOOR

LA FIESTA ROOM

MEZZANINE WILSHIRE WING

BURGUNDY ROOM

CHATEAU ROOM

STAGE

STORAGE

STAGE

CHAMPAGNE ROOM

BORDEAUX ROOM

PANTRY

LE GRAND TRIANON

MEZZANINE BEVERLY WING

PANTRY

COAT ROOM

LE PETIT TRIANON

COAT ROOM

MEZZANINE BEVERLY WING

ADJOINING LE GRAND TRIANON

MEZZANINE WILSHIRE WING

MEETING AND BANQUET FACILITIES

Rooms	Dimensions		Capacity				
	L × W × H Feet	L × W × H Meters	Theater	Schoolroom	Conference	Banquet	Reception
The Ballroom	130 × 110 × 21	39.6 × 33.5 × 6.4	1200	600		1000	1500
Champagne Room	50 × 48 × 10	15.2 × 14.6 × 3.0	220	125	50	220	300
Burgundy Room	27 × 34 × 10	8.2 × 10.4 × 3.0	80	50	35	80	100
Bordeaux Room	29 × 34 × 10	8.8 × 10.4 × 3.0	90	50	35	90	100
Chateau Room	16 × 34 × 10	4.9 × 10.4 × 3.0	60	35	35	40	60
Le Petit Room	33 × 44 × 10	10.1 × 13.4 × 3.0	—	—	—	120	250
Le Grand Trianon	86 × 46 × 11	26.2 × 14.0 × 3.3	400	230	—	350	500
La Fiesta Room	51 × 16 × 9	16.0 × 4.9 × 2.7	75	48	50	60	100

Unlike rack brochures, convention brochures must provide detailed function room and banquet informa-tion for meeting planners. This sample convention brochure lists the property's location and general amenities on the second page, room layouts and capacities on the third. Other convention brochures may rely more heavily on photographs of function facilities. (Courtesy of The Beverly Wilshire, Beverly Hills, California) clothing and accessory items include T-shirts, sweatshirts, jackets, sun visors, baseball caps, tote bags, and beach towels. These items are often given away or sold at or slightly above cost. The investment is well worth it. The advertising message is seen each time the product is used or worn—at no additional cost to the advertiser.

Since many specialty items are small, the property should develop a message that is brief. In many cases, just the property's name, address, and telephone number appear on specialty items.

Sometimes specialty items are designed around a unique theme. For example, for the grand opening of the High Q Hotel in Orlando, Florida, a "First International Aerial Exposition Competition of the World" campaign was developed. Over six hundred businesspeople in the Orlando area were mailed parts of a balsa airplane. Wings for the planes were issued at the hotel's grand opening. Each of the participants was given a stylized name badge and escorted to the twenty-first floor to launch his or her plane toward a painted target in the parking lot. Winners were awarded special prizes. All participants were given a coffee cup imprinted with the hotel's name.

The coffee cups awarded by the High Q could be used on a daily basis and were a reminder of a fun experience at the hotel. Other specialty items that can be used daily include ashtrays, lighters, pens, and calendars. Unique or especially attractive specialty items, such as unusual ceramic or brass souvenirs, are more likely to be displayed rather than being thrown in a drawer and forgotten.

Another example of an unusual specialty item campaign is the placement of dictionaries in the rooms of the luxury Stanford Court Hotel on Nob Hill in San Francisco. This campaign is the result of an article by *New York Times* columnist William Safire, who wrote how nice it would be if hotels provided dictionaries. The president of Stanford Court at that time, James A. Nassikas, was a fan of Safire's and decided to do just that. Since early 1987, a copy of Webster's *New World Dictionary* has been placed in guestrooms alongside the familiar Gideon Bible. Although the dictionaries are not take-home items, they receive favorable guest response, and the hotel receives nationwide publicity for the "good words" placed in each room.

To ensure getting the most from specialty items, a property may wish to consult an advertising agency, or contact corporate headquarters if the property is part of a chain. Many chains offer specialty-item catalogs that feature everything from playing cards to clocks (see Exhibit 11). Items available from chain sources are more effective if they are imprinted with a toll-free reservations number.

Conclusion

The advertising discussed in this chapter ranges from gigantic billboards to matchbook covers. For this advertising to be effective, it must be carefully designed and coordinated to reflect the property's personality and make the property stand out in a crowd of competitors. Outdoor advertising, displays, and collateral materials—even in today's world of broadcast and high-tech advertising—still play a vital part in the successful marketing of a property.

Exhibit 11   Sample Chain Specialty Items

W. Tennis Balls The same **Dunlop** ®Championship tennis balls that are used in most major pro and amateur tournaments. Suitable for all types of courts. 3 Balls Per Can. **Minimum Order: 4 Cans**

X. Golf Balls Blue Maxfli® golf balls have been a favorite of country club business and professional golfers for over a generation. Super high energy cores give extra distance to every stroke and the exterior is covered by a tough-to-cut cover. 3 Balls Per Sleeve. **Minimum Order: 4 Sleeves**

Y. Days Inn Sewing Kit 6 colors of thread, a needle, buttons, and a safety pin to handle most mending emergencies. This is one room give-away your customers will surely use! **Minimum Order: 50**

Z. Luggage Tag Executive tag with plastic strap holds a business or identification card (included). Make a wonderful complimentary convention or conference gift. **Minimum Order: 50 Tags**

AA. Days Inn Emery Boards An inexpensive way to welcome your guests. Each board has a fine and a coarse side for neat manicuring. **Minimum Order: 100**

BB. Hand Lotion What a soft sell—Soothing Balm Argenta lotion in a **Days Inn** Logo bottle. Each ounce bottle holds 85 applications. **Minimum Order: 50**

CC. Survival Kit All life's little necessities in one neat kit! Includes: moist towelette, antiseptic, aspirin, antacid, adhesive bandage, and a HELP decal. **Minimum Order: 50**

DD. Plastic Coasters They hold any size glass, bottle, mug or cup—while protecting room furnishings! America's top-selling line of coasters. White Only. **Minimum Order: 50**

EE. Stadium Cup Employees and guests will enjoy this sturdy plastic cup for all their cold beverages. Holds a full 12 oz. Yellow or White. **Minimum Order: 50**

FF. Days Inn Coffee Mug Toast **Days Inn** round the clock with this mug that looks like ceramic but is ultra chip proof, break resistant plastic for both hot and cold beverages. Microwave and top rack dishwasher safe. Black Only. **Minimum Order: 12**

Chain hotels often have the option of ordering specialty items from a catalog prepared especially for the chain. This page from a Days Inns catalog shows a variety of items—from emery boards to tennis balls—that can be used as inexpensive promotional giveaways. (Courtesy of Days Inns of America, Inc.)

Endnotes

1. Much of the material in this section was adapted from *Lodging Magazine.* Used with permission.

Key Terms

backlighting
brochure
bulletin
collateral material
cutout
display advertising
fixed plan
flier
holography
inflatable

kinetic board
outdoor advertising
painted display
poster
rotating plan
shell brochure
specialty item
spectacular
tent card
transit advertising

Review Questions

1. What factors should be considered by an independent property before it contracts for a property sign?

2. What should be considered when scouting a billboard's location?

3. Advertising experts suggest that billboard copy be limited to how many words?

4. What are three types of display advertising?

5. What are two categories of transit display advertising?

6. What are the advantages of transit display advertising?

7. What are examples of collateral materials?

8. What factors should be considered when developing a brochure?

9. What key elements should be included in brochure copy?

10. What kinds of information are required in a convention brochure?

11. Why should a message designed for a specialty item be brief?

Chapter Outline

Newspaper Advertising
    Selecting Newspapers
    Placing Ads
    Positioning Ads
    Determining Ad Size
    Newspaper Production
    Designing Ads
    Writing Ads
        Headline
        Copy
    Evaluating Ads
    Advertorials
Magazine Advertising
    Types of Magazines
        Consumer Magazines
        Trade Magazines
    Designing an Effective Magazine Ad
    Creating a Statement with Photography
    Creating Effective Ad Copy
Directory Advertising
    Telephone Directories
    Business Directories
Measuring the Effectiveness of Print Advertising
Conclusion

11

Print Advertising

Pᴿᴵɴᴛ ᴍᴇᴅɪᴀ—ɴᴇᴡsᴘᴀᴘᴇʀs ᴀɴᴅ ᴍᴀɢᴀᴢɪɴᴇs in particular—are some of the most effective means of reaching potential guests and clients. Each day, millions of Americans pick up newspapers and magazines in search of information and entertainment. A well-placed advertisement can generate thousands of room nights for a property.

Unlike broadcast advertising, print advertising is unobtrusive. Potential customers can spend as little or as long as they like reading the ad and, since they chose to read the ad, they are often open to the advertiser's message. Unlike broadcast messages that are here and gone (and may be missed if a person is distracted or changing channels), print advertisements can be kept and referred to again and again—and passed along to other potential customers who may not even subscribe to the newspaper or magazine.

Print advertising can greatly assist you by making potential clients aware of your property prior to being contacted. If potential clients already know about the property, it makes selling easier. In this chapter, we will look at newspapers and magazines and how to make the most of these sales avenues. We will also discuss directory advertising and ways to measure the effectiveness of print advertising.

Newspaper Advertising

Newspapers are an excellent medium for selling hospitality products and services. Newspapers are considered an authoritative source of information, a source that is turned to when people seek information on vacation or business travel.

There are problems with newspapers, however. Most people don't read the entire newspaper, which means large portions may be skipped. In addition to this drawback, there is the problem of "clutter"—a large number of ads placed on a page. If a reader is thinking of taking a resort vacation, he or she will probably look at all of the resort ads, no matter how many are on the travel pages. But if the reader is not interested in a resort vacation at the time your ad appears, the ad may not even be glanced at.

Every ad must fight to get attention. You must be aware of the variety of factors that promote consumer buying, know how to write and position an ad that will generate sales, and set newspaper advertising goals. Newspaper ads are generally used to achieve three basic goals:

1. *Build awareness of the property.* While newspapers may have a disadvantage when it comes to targeting certain market segments, they can be effective in building a broad base of public awareness. Taxi drivers, for example, may not

Insider Insights

Neil W. Ostergren, CHSE
Vice President
Robinson, Yesawich & Pepperdine, Inc.
New York City

Neil Ostergren has been in the hotel industry since 1960. He held sales, marketing, and operations positions with Roger Smith Hotels, Hilton International, Americana Hotels, and Wyndham Hotels before assuming his present responsibilities as vice president with the advertising firm of Robinson, Yesawich and Pepperdine. Long active with Hospitality Sales & Marketing Association International, Ostergren served as president of HSMAI in 1987 and later as chairman of the HSMAI Foundation. He has also served as a marketing consultant, and is a regular contributor to industry publications. A Certified Hotel Sales Executive, Ostergren has received a number of awards, including the Albert E. Koehl Award for significant contributions to hotel advertising and Murdoch Magazines' Hotel Marketing Executive of the Year.

Throughout my career in the hospitality industry, it's been my belief that both consumer advertising and trade advertising are of great importance in reaching marketing plan objectives. Well-developed and properly targeted advertising is probably the most efficient sales component in any business, hotels included. Advertising is essential because it's the best way to create awareness, make product information available, and influence the consumer's buying decision. This is particularly true in print advertising.

Before any advertising decisions can be made, research is the mandatory first step. Only by knowing about the demographics and psychographics of consumers can a proper print advertising program be developed. Research must be continual so that advertising adjustments can be made when market changes occur.

Trade advertising to travel agents, meeting planners, and tour wholesalers should be looked at as a strategy designed and developed to support direct sales. In most cases, the ads alone will not sell anything. But good trade advertising, with the right message in the right media for the right target audience, can play a very influential role in persuading travel intermediaries to learn more about the property.

Consumer advertising in newspapers and magazines is somewhat different. Consumer ads should have less copy than most trade ads, but should clearly tell the reader what's being offered. Consumer ad copy can be about a package with a special price and a list of included features; it might be about the property itself, its location and its amenities; or, it might describe a guest benefit offered by the hotel. Consumer advertising should also be more visually attractive than a trade ad need be.

Marketing is nothing more than moving a product from conception to consumption. Well-planned advertising is important to the success of a lodging property, but advertising is not a science—it's very subjective. And hoteliers should keep in mind that advertising is just one part of the total promotion mix.

be potential guests, but they can exert a positive influence on those who are if they become familiar with a particular property through newspaper ads.

2. *Build rooms business.* Newspapers are an effective medium for filling guest-rooms on short notice. A simple newspaper ad can be prepared in hours, and can normally be scheduled in one to three days. If room sales are down, a timely newspaper ad placed in the major metropolitan newspapers of your property's key feeder cities could stimulate needed business.

3. *Build restaurant, lounge, and function business.* This advertising differs some-what from advertising used to build awareness of a property or attract guest-room business. For the most part, restaurant, lounge, and function business advertising is placed in the entertainment sections of local newspapers.

Before selecting a newspaper and designing and writing an ad, you must know exactly whom you are trying to attract and what you want to offer each targeted market segment (see Exhibit 1). Effective advertising must meet three criteria: it must have a clear-cut mission (increase the number of group meetings, for example); it must have an appropriate selling message geared to a targeted market segment; and there must be a logical plan of exposure. Will the ad be designed to stimulate weekday or weekend business? Will the ad be addressed to business travelers or to families looking for a vacation destination? Are there special packages or rates you wish to promote? These considerations will help determine the placement, size, design, and content of the ad.

Selecting Newspapers

You should consider three factors when selecting the newspapers that will best reach your property's targeted markets:

1. *Readership.* While total circulation is one factor to consider, it may not be the most important reason to advertise in a particular newspaper. To evaluate a newspaper ad's potential effectiveness, a newspaper's readership should be broken down into demographic groups. A large newspaper that serves a general audience of 1,000,000 may not generate as much business as a special interest newspaper with a circulation of 10,000 that serves a targeted market segment.

2. *Content.* The newspaper's content plays a part in successful advertising. Does it provide special sections, Sunday magazines, travel guides, and so on? Does it publish suburban or regional editions? Many large newspapers have regu-larly scheduled special interest sections for particular days—a special sports section on Mondays, business sections on Thursdays, weekend-entertainment sections on Fridays, and travel sections on Sundays are some examples. These, in effect, are publications within publications, and may be of particular inter-est to your property's target markets.

3. *Advertising rates.* Advertising rates are usually designed to stimulate advertis-ing by certain advertisers and limit advertising by others. This is accomplished by setting different rates for local, national, retail, classified, and, often, hotel and restaurant advertisers. Newspaper advertising rates are usually offered on

Exhibit 1   Sample Targeted Newspaper Advertising

Our weekday rates get better with age.

$43*
SENIORS
MID-WEEK SPECIAL

If you're 50 or older, you can get this low rate on a mid-week vacation in the heart of historic New England. The Sheraton Sturbridge gives you a great room, a full country breakfast, two tickets to Old Sturbridge Village (it's right across the street), and free use of the health club, indoor swimming pool and tennis courts. You'll also have plenty of places to shop, including antique shops, factory outlets and more. Call 1-800-325-3535 (in MA, dial 1-617-347-7393).

Sheraton Sturbridge Resort
The hospitality people of **ITT**
U.S. 20, opposite Old Sturbridge Village, 366 Main St., Sturbridge, MA

For the same low price, Host Farm Resort gives people 50 and over a great way to discover Amish Country. The rate includes your room, two tickets to an Amish Country tour and free use of the health spa, indoor swimming pool and outdoor tennis courts. There's also an 18-hole PGA golf course and outdoor tennis. And Host Farm's right down the road from historic Gettysburg and all kinds of factory outlets, too. For details, call 1-800-233-0121 (in PA, dial 717-299-5500).

Host Farm Resort
The most complete family resort in Pennsylvania Dutch Country.
2300 Lincoln Highway East, Lancaster, PA 17602

Per person, per night, 2 night minimum, Sunday through Thursday, by reservation only. Taxes not included.

This ad, published in regional senior-citizen publications, was designed to increase mid-week business by promoting a special weekday senior citizens' package. Note that this is a cooperative ad.

a flat or open basis; a flat rate is a fixed cost (no matter how much space is purchased or how often you advertise), while an open rate is subject to various discounts. Discounts may be offered for prompt payment or for providing camera-ready copy, for example. In many cases, frequency discounts are also offered to encourage regular advertising throughout the year.

These factors should be considered before selecting a newspaper. An overall picture of newspaper advertising opportunities and rates can be obtained through using a directory such as *Newspaper Rates and Data,* published by Standard Rates and Data Service and available either by subscription or at the local library.

Once you've selected a newspaper, you must decide on where in the newspaper the ad should be placed. Deciding where the ad should be placed may seem

Newspaper Advertising Rates

Advertising rates quoted refer to random positioning of the ad (termed "run-of-paper" or ROP). If a specific position is desired—whether the request is for placement in a specific section (travel section, food pages, etc.) or for a specific position on a page (upper right corner, bottom middle, etc.), there is an extra charge. Buying a specific position is called a "premium position buy." Regular and premium rates are usually listed on the newspaper's rate card.

There are also additional charges for advertising in special advertising supplements or the inserts offered by many newspapers. In some cases, inserts are produced by the newspaper as special sections (a winter sports section, a visitor's guide, a bridal section, etc.) that include articles and related advertising. Or the property can produce its own separate advertising piece and have it inserted into the newspaper by geographic location or on a general circulation basis. While this type of advertising attracts notice, it is far costlier than regular ROP or premium position buys within the newspaper's usual sections, and costs versus advantages should be carefully weighed.

One way to offset costs is to take advantage of the cooperative advertising opportunities offered by many newspapers. In some cases, the property can participate in the "sponsorship" of a public service or commercial ad (sponsorship boxes are sold to pay for the cost of the ad). The property can also join forces with other firms to produce an ad featuring their combined products or services. In many cases, national advertisers also sponsor co-op advertising. Co-op advertising opportunities can often be handled directly through the newspaper; most newspapers have a department—or at least a representative—to assist in setting up cooperative ads.

R.O.P. GENERAL RATES

A. OPEN

BLACK & WHITE RATES PER INCH

Daily	$35.00
Sunday	$36.60

BULK CONTRACT RATES WITHIN ONE YEAR

	Daily	Sunday
126″	$34.30	$35.87
250″	$33.95	$35.50
500″	$33.60	$35.14

In the event Advertiser fails to fulfill contract, a rate adjustment will be made to nearest contract rate actually earned or to the open rate.

B. REPEAT RATES

A 30% discount will be given for the second insertion of an identical ad run within a 6-day period. Discount is calculated on second run. Copy and ad size to be same. Subject to earned contract rate.

C. SPECIAL POSITION CHARGES

35% premium in addition to space charge—available daily & Sunday.

D. SPECIAL ADVERTISING RATES

	Daily	Sunday
Political Advertising (per column inch)	$35.00	$36.60

*Requires cash with space reservation

COLOR RATES—R.O.P.

Use Black & White inch print rate plus the following applicable flat costs for daily or Sunday.

Black plus 1 color	$650.00
Black plus 2 or 3 colors	$950.00 (min. size 31 1/2″)

---

premature, since the ad does not exist at this point in the process. However, an ad's design and copy are affected by the ad's placement, its position on the page, and its size. Therefore, placement, positioning, and size decisions should be made before design work is begun or copy written.

Placing Ads

Where your ad is placed will often mean the difference between whether the ad is read or ignored. For maximum effectiveness, you should place ads where they are most likely to be read by the target audience.

An ad's placement will depend on the type of traveler or local patron you wish to reach and the sections available in the newspaper. To reach leisure travelers, for example, a Sunday travel section is the best choice; if the paper has no Sunday travel section, however, alternatives such as local news or family sections have to suffice. Business travelers will be more likely to see ads placed in the business section or in the paper's first news section. Ads for "escape weekends" (see Exhibit 2) may be placed in the entertainment or media sections, or in the sports section if the escape weekend features sports activities such as golf or horseback riding.

When it comes to selling restaurants or function space, ads usually should not be placed in the Sunday travel section (see Exhibit 3). Many newspapers offer a "Restaurant Guide" to assist locals and out-of-town visitors in choosing restaurants. Since many people go to restaurants before or after attending a special event such as a concert or movie, restaurant ads can be effectively placed in the newspaper's entertainment section, or in the sports section if you are promoting a post-game buffet or pre-game dinner special.

It should be noted that dinner sales are much easier to promote than luncheon business. Traditionally, dinner is an "experience," and patrons are willing to travel for exotic foods or atmosphere, while lunches are usually eaten in close proximity to the home or office. Businesspeople looking for a prestigious lunch setting for entertaining clients may be reached by an ad in the business section or in the first news section.

The first news section is also an effective place to advertise special holiday promotions of both rooms and restaurants, since this is a newspaper's most widely read section. Function rooms for social events can be advertised in the society pages or family sections. Because business travelers frequently check the weather, the Stouffer hotel chain purchased ad space on the weather page of *USA Today* to reach this lucrative segment.

Positioning Ads

Once you've selected the newspaper section, the ad must be positioned on the page. There are several preferred positions, such as the top of the page alongside reading matter. This position is called *full position,* and may cost more in some cities, but the ad will be seen by more people than an ad placed next to other advertisements or buried at the bottom of the page. Most advertisers also try to avoid the "gutter"—the inside portion of the paper where the two pages meet—in favor of an outside position next to reading matter.

Another important positioning consideration is which days of the week to run an ad. This varies depending on what the property has to offer. As mentioned previously, the Sunday travel section is considered the best option for promoting leisure travel (see Exhibit 4). In determining other key days, you should take the newspaper's general makeup into consideration: Which days are typically light

Exhibit 2   Sample Ad for Weekend Business

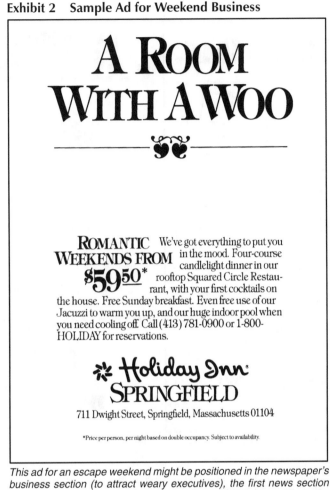

This ad for an escape weekend might be positioned in the newspaper's business section (to attract weary executives), the first news section (where it is most likely to be read by readers who do not read the entire newspaper), or in the entertainment or radio and television sections. Other ads offering different products or services would be positioned according to the product or service offered and the target market.

news days? What days are given over to supermarket ads? Which sections have the most readership, and on which day(s) of the week? By determining the answers to these questions, you can get a general idea of the best days to advertise. If a paper publishes a prestigious business section on Monday, for example, this would provide good positioning for the sale of business services or function space.

Determining Ad Size

The next step in creating newspaper advertising is determining ad size. As mentioned earlier, newspapers often are cluttered with ads promoting similar products

Exhibit 3   Sample Restaurant Ads

These ads for the Yarrow Resort Hotel & Conference Center offer both continuity and variety. The ads are the same size and the ad elements are positioned in the same sequence (headline, illustration, body copy, pricing, and signature). In addition, the same typefaces are used for the headlines, headings, and text, giving the ads a similar appearance. The consistent use of white space gives these ads an uncluttered look and separates them from adjacent ads.

or services on the same page or in the same section. Therefore it is often a large ad that will stand out in the crowd.

But is bigger always better? The answer depends on the ad's objective. In some cases a series of small ads placed frequently are better than an occasional large ad. The choice of a restaurant or night spot, for example, is often a last-minute decision, and most properties find that a series of small daily ads generates the most business. Two exceptions to this rule are (1) the promotion of special restaurant weekend events, which may be advertised with large ads on Fridays, and (2) holiday meal promotions, which should be published the week prior to the holiday to allow time for reservations.

Some advertisers recommend using a full-page ad. Many hospitality industry professionals think that large ads attract more readership than small ads, and that these additional readers are generally people who are not present users of the

Exhibit 4   Sunday Travel Section

Sunday is by far the best day to promote hospitality products to the leisure traveler, since most consumers enjoy the one-stop shopping option offered in the Sunday travel sections in most major newspapers. Travel sections typically are eight to sixteen pages and feature stories about attractions and travel. Because of the large number of hospitality ads published in this section—many placed by direct competitors—ads must be catchy and offer a unique bargain or benefit to stand out.

Stouffer Hotels Weather the Threat of Competition for the Business Traveler

After research showed that business travelers are especially concerned about the weather, Stouffer Hotel Company placed ads on *USA Today's* weather page. In addition to its advertising in *USA Today*, the hotel's advertising strategy also included advertising on the five-day weather forecast page in the Monday edition of the *Wall Street Journal*, and broadcast sponsorship on cable television's The Weather Channel.

property. A large, eye-catching advertisement has stopping power and may indeed grab the attention of the public, but it is important to remember that newspapers are not usually saved. Unless a person takes immediate action—or saves the ad—the property's message is usually quickly forgotten. In the final analysis, the decision on ad size must be based on your objectives and advertising budget.

Choosing the size of an advertisement is often difficult; unfortunately, newspapers contribute to this dilemma because the number of columns per page varies among newspapers. Newspapers can be printed with five, six, eight, or even nine columns. The number of columns per page will affect the width of each column and the number of lines it will take to print an ad. Copy that is 100 lines long in one newspaper might be 150 lines in another, for example. Advertisers often have to create two or more different-size advertisements to fit the different-size space offered by competing newspapers.

Newspaper advertising is usually offered by the column inch, an area one column wide by one inch deep. National advertising is quoted in terms of standard advertising units (SAUs), which have 14 lines to an inch and are one column wide. To figure a rate, advertisers must multiply the number of inches deep an ad would run, times the number of columns wide, times the cost per inch. For example, if an ad that is five inches deep and two columns wide costs $5 per column inch at a particular newspaper, the cost is $5 \times 2 \times \$5 = \$50$.

When figuring costs for ad sizes, it is important to remember that ads at most newspapers shrink somewhat due to the mechanical process used to make plates for printing the ad. You should either prepare a slightly oversize ad or reconcile billing charges to ensure that you are billed for the space actually used.

Once you have selected a specific ad size and shape, you should use it repeatedly. Rapid newspaper reading often precludes study of a property's ad copy, but name recognition can be generated if a reader's eye is drawn to the familiar size and shape of a frequently published ad.

Newspaper Production

Before you design or write an ad, you should know a few things about the mechanics of newspaper production. Newspaper production is worlds apart from sophisticated magazine production. The high-speed presses used by newspapers can distort images and type, the paper stock is coarse, color reproduction is usually mediocre, and production techniques limit the use of eye-catching graphics and condensed type.

When planning newspaper advertising, therefore, stick to simple techniques. Use line drawings instead of photographs unless the photographs are extremely clear and the ad is large. Special techniques such as reversed copy, in which the letters are white on a black background, should be used only occasionally. Condensed type should be avoided, especially in small ads.

Spot color—the use of one color (other than black) to enhance an advertisement—helps an ad stand out and generates greater reader response. The use of full color printing, or ROP (run-of-the-paper) color, often produces less than desirable results because, as mentioned, high-speed newspaper presses may distort.

Newspaper representatives can help you determine the production problems that may be inherent in a suggested ad, but you should limit a newspaper staff's involvement with your advertising to that kind of problem-solving. Many newspapers offer "pub-set" advertisements—ads designed, written, and typeset by the newspaper's staff. At first glance, pub-set may seem an attractive alternative to the high costs of in-house or advertising agency ad development. While costs may be lower, most pub-set ads are lower in quality and far less effective than a carefully planned ad developed by the property, its free-lance advertising personnel, or its advertising agency.

Designing Ads

Many advertisers find it better to design an ad before writing the copy for it. A distinctive design helps create an image for a property. Once a satisfactory design is developed you should use it for some time, departing from it only for special promotions.

The design process includes ad size and shape (discussed earlier) and graphic elements, including the property's logo, line drawings, and the use of white space (see Exhibit 5). White space is an important layout element in print advertising since the average newspaper or magazine page is so "heavy" with type. Generous use of white space separates or protects an ad from other ads on the page and make the headline and illustrations stand out.

As a rule, photographs only work well with large newspaper ads, so most newspaper ads should be designed around an eye-catching line drawing or headline instead of a photograph. Line drawings or photographs (if used) should show people in action around the product or enjoying the facility. Illustrations can be far more effective than copy in prompting readers to respond. Illustrations can also eliminate the need for a large amount of copy to tell your property's story.

Whether readers will read an ad depends in large part on the design. A catchy headline will not compensate for poor eye appeal, so the design should:

- *Be simple, but "flow."* The typeface selected should be bold and clear, and artwork—borders, logos, and so on—must reproduce well.

- *Include artwork or photographs.* Artwork and photographs can either break up the copy at strategic points or lead the reader's eye to additional copy.

- *Have captions under all photos.* While a picture is worth a thousand words, adding a few more words underneath it can prevent misconceptions and add information without cluttering the ad.

- *Identify the property.* The property's logo, preferably placed at the end of the ad as a signature, adds to credibility and name recognition.

- *Be appealing.* A poorly designed, unattractive ad will cast a negative shadow on the property, no matter how much it has to offer.

A simple factor such as the choice of type can make a vast difference in readership of and response to an ad, so you should give the design careful consideration.

Exhibit 5 Effective Newspaper Ad Design Elements

UP AND RUNNING.

The Ocala Hilton is now up and running. Like a real thoroughbred, we are eager to prove ourselves. And ready to take the lead as Ocala's most elegant hotel ever.

Months of planning, construction, decorating and training have gone into this exciting new beginning. And we invite you to share in celebrating our big start. Join us for a fine gourmet meal at Arthur's, an evening of entertainment at the Gentry Bar or a nightcap at The Lobby Court. Some are even considering a weekend stay for a chance to get away without leaving town. All of our guests will enjoy a heated pool with Jacuzzi, two lighted tennis courts and personal service from the warm welcome of our bellman to the attentive housekeeper. And for our most discriminating guests, our most luxurious accommodations are on the Tower Level.

For reservations and information regarding meetings, banquets, guest rooms and suites, call now, 854-1400. Find out what makes the Ocala Hilton an outstanding hotel. And a real winner.

Announcing The Birth Of A Thoroughbred.

OCALA HILTON

I-75 and S.R. 200, 3600 S.W. 36th Ave., Ocala, Florida 32674

This ad for the Ocala Hilton is an excellent example of a newspaper ad that successfully uses the basic principles of newspaper ad design. While the ad is fairly simple, it is striking in design, the type is large enough to read, and the copy is reduced to essentials. A good newspaper ad has an eye-catching headline or illustration (this ad has both), and makes good use of white space. The graphics used here increase the ad's image of sophistication.

Writing Ads

Because of the nature of newspapers—people look to them for news and information—newspaper ads that provide news (of new products, new prices, and so on) are usually most effective. The chances that a newspaper ad will be read are increased when ad copy includes a provocative headline, attention-getting claims or buyer benefits, and specific, believable offers.

Headline. The first consideration in writing a newspaper ad is to create a good headline. For best results, the ad's headline should offer a benefit, include news or information, and lead into the body copy. While it is extremely difficult to get all of

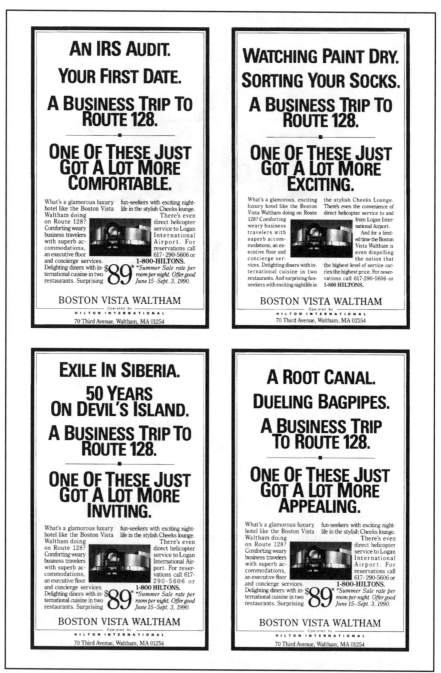

In newspaper advertising, a repeated ad format helps create name and product recognition. Note that this series of ads features large, humorous headlines, a unique benefit ("direct helicopter service to Logan International Airport"), and the property's full address. (Courtesy of Robinson, Yesawich & Pepperdine, Inc., Orlando, Florida)

Property Slogans

One of the most effective ways to identify a property in the public's mind is through the use of a memorable slogan. Listed below are slogans used by several prominent hotel chains. How many can you identify?

___	1.	A Welcome Change	a.	Best Western
___	2.	You Can Depend On Our Good Name	b.	Days Inns
___	3.	Twice the Hotel	c.	Embassy Suites
___	4.	When the Sun Goes Down... America Turns to Orange	d.	Hilton
			e.	Holiday Inn
___	5.	Wake Up to Us	f.	Howard Johnson
___	6.	America's Hotel Value	g.	Sheraton
___	7.	Service: The Ultimate Luxury	h.	La Quinta Inns
___	8.	We'll Leave the Light on for You	i.	Marriott
___	9.	As Individual As America Itself	j.	Motel 6
___	10.	Stay with Someone You Know	k.	Nikko Hotels
___	11.	Simply Everything. Simply.	l.	Radisson
___	12.	The Natural Choice	m.	Stouffer
___	13.	America's Business Address		

(Answers: 1-l, 2-m, 3-c, 4-f, 5-b, 6-h, 7-i, 8-j, 9-a, 10-e, 11-k, 12-g, 13-d)

these elements into one short headline, for maximum effect as many as possible should be included.

Copy. Once the headline has captured readers' attention, the ad's copy must give them a reason to respond. What does this property have to offer me?

Many different styles of newspaper advertising have been used by hospitality properties. Advertising copy can be serious, sophisticated, cute, innovative, or even instructional. The use of one or more of these styles is determined in part by the target audience and what the property is offering. Meeting the needs of customers should be the foremost objective of ad copy. According to Peter Warren of Warren-Kremer Advertising, Inc., "The trouble with most hotel advertising is that hotels talk to themselves instead of addressing customer needs and benefits."[1]

As a general rule, advertising copy should be brief and factual. Benefits should be offered *early*. Contrary to popular belief, the name of the property often is not the most important feature of a successful ad. If the hotel or restaurant has name recognition, that may give credibility to the message, but general image advertising has declined in recent years. Image advertising, which basically just tries to keep the

Nendels Inn uses a catchy headline to attract readers' attention.
(Courtesy of Nendels Corp.)

name of the property before the public, is not enough in tough economic times; promoting what the property has to offer will usually generate a better response.

Copy should be limited to one or two ideas. Too much copy might confuse or overwhelm readers. However, the copy must contain all the necessary information. You should always include the name, address, and phone number of your property. A map showing the property's location and a toll-free number or special offer can increase reader response. Prices should usually be included. Providing price information helps eliminate the inquiries that result when prices are not mentioned. And last but not least, you must ask for the sale. The copy should give reasons for readers to buy, then ask them to respond.

Evaluating Ads

After an ad has been designed and written, carefully check it to be sure the message is coming across as you intended. If the answer to "Will it sell?" is "Probably not," you must determine the reasons and redo the ad. Some common reasons a newspaper ad doesn't sell include:

1. *An ineffective headline.*

2. *Inappropriate copy length.* Copy length is a key factor in readability. Consider placing short ads in a newspaper's morning edition, when most people are more likely to be in a hurry, and long ads in the afternoon or evening editions. If long copy is required to get the message across, it should be broken up with headings or artwork.

3. *Meaningless benefits.* Whether benefits are included in the headline or in the copy, they must be meaningful to the ad's targeted market(s).

4. *Meaningless photographs or illustrations.* All photographs should be relevant and captioned.

5. *Incorrect style.* The copy should flow in a logical, interesting order and offer enjoyable reading. Hotel jargon, technical terms, and difficult-to-read copy turn readers off.

6. *Passivity.* The copy must involve readers. Verbs should be active, not passive. Ask readers questions, or ask them to imagine themselves in a particular situation.

7. *Lack of credibility.* Too many claims, promises, and extravagant descriptions can leave readers wary and unresponsive. Claims, limited to one or two, should be backed up by testimonials or statistics.

8. *Lack of urgency or immediacy.* The ad should urge immediate action and tell the reader what to do: "Call today," "Mail coupon now," or "Call our toll-free number for complete information." A promotional package should be accompanied by a telephone number or reply coupon to encourage quick action.

In addition to these considerations, how does the ad make people feel? Is it attractive and inviting? Does the ad project the image you intended? If these questions can be answered "yes," you have probably developed a good ad and should stick with it for an extended length of time. While modifications can be made from time to time, a well-placed, frequently appearing, recognizable ad is the key to success in newspaper advertising.

Advertorials

Before leaving newspapers, we should discuss another form of advertising: the advertorial. An advertorial is a combination of an advertisement and an editorial statement. Written by a member of the property's management team, an advertorial can enhance the property's credibility or promote the property's products and services. Advertorials are usually printed in a different typeface than the non-advertising copy on the page, and are distinguished further by the phrase "Advertisement" or "Paid Advertisement" at the top or bottom of the copy. An advertorial is usually enclosed in a box.

Advertorials have several advantages. An advertorial looks more like an article or an editorial than a conventional ad, so many readers will pay closer attention to the copy. An advertorial, since it often makes no use of graphics or illustrations, can present more information to the reader.

Exhibit 6   Sample Advertorial

(ADVERTISEMENT)

Las Vegas casino tests a radical slot machine; If it doesn't pay off, it gives back your money

---

LAS VEGAS—Lady Luck Casino Hotel has installed a bank of slot machines that can't win a penny for the house. They actually lose money.

The machines either give players a payoff up to $1,000.00, or give back the money the customer put in.

In the first few months of testing, 59 players hit $1,000.00 jackpots on the radical "Can't Lose" machines. The casino says "thousands" have hit smaller payoffs of $2.00, $5.00, $10.00, $20.00, $50.00, $100.00 and $500.00.

"Most dollar slot machines are set to hold 3% to 10% for the house," said Alain Uboldi, Lady Luck General Manager. "These new machines do the opposite. They're set to pay back 20% to 30% to the customer—or give back his money."

Each out-of-state customer with Lady Luck's "Best Casino Fun Book in Las Vegas" gets a pull on one of the special machines. And four times a day the casino holds drawings and lets the winners play for three minutes each.

"People were skeptical at first," said Uboldi. "They didn't believe we would give back their money on a losing pull. It was tough to convince some people they were risking nothing."

The machines are located in the casino's "Welcome Center." Besides the free pull, the casino presents players with their photos, free drinks, a free long distance call and a shrimp cocktail for 25 cents.

Lady Luck's unusual offers are part of a strategy to introduce a new 16-story highrise called the "luxury Tower," and two new restaurants.

"We took a look at Las Vegas fun books and found they all had one thing in common—they weren't fun," said Uboldi. The casino then produced its new "Best Fun Book in Las Vegas" as a satire, but Uboldi says the response has been "positively overwhelming."

The book is written in campy prose that brags about the hotel's "ferociously delicious" $2.49 buffet, offers a tongue-in-cheek "$8.00 for $10.00" slot tokens sale and admits the casino "must be crazy" for guaranteeing that a player's first card in blackjack will be an ace.

As a zany final touch, the casino rigged its parking payment machine to pay a $25.00 jackpot to every 2,000th user.

The "Best Fun Book in Las Vegas" is free to out-of-state residents, 21 years or older. Uboldi advises readers of in-flight magazines to "just tear out this page and bring it to our Welcome Center to get the book." Lady Luck is at 3rd & Ogden, downtown Las Vegas.

For a complimentary copy of the book by mail, send this story to "Best Casino Fun Book in Las Vegas", Lady Luck Casino/Hotel, P.O. Box 1060, Las Vegas, NV, 89125.

Or call free, 800-634-6580. ■

AMWE

Advertorials differ from typical newspaper and magazine ads in that they appear to be feature stories or editorials. This advertorial reads like a feature story, but note the word "Advertisement" at the top to distinguish it from editorial and feature material that appeared on the same page. (Courtesy of the Lady Luck Casino/Hotel, Las Vegas, Nevada)

Before opting to use an advertorial in newspapers, however, you should weigh the advertorial's potential effectiveness against the impact of your regularly placed newspaper advertising. In many cases, it is wiser to use advertorial advertising in magazines, since magazines are typically saved and read by people reading for enjoyment as well as for information (see Exhibit 6). Newspaper readers tend to be less inclined to read long ad copy.

Magazine Advertising

Magazines are another effective means of reaching potential business and leisure travelers. Magazine advertising offers the following benefits over newspaper advertising:

1. *Specific readership.* Most magazines are targeted to specific audiences or interest groups. Whether your property's target market is business travelers, family travelers, honeymooners, golfers, travel agents, or retirees, there is a publication available to reach that particular market.

2. *Longer life.* Magazines have a longer reading life than newspapers.

3. *Wider scope.* Since most magazines are national in scope, a magazine ad may be seen by more people.

4. *Quality of production.* Unlike newspapers, most magazines offer slick, high-tech production capabilities. Full-color photographs, multi-page spreads, and special effects (pop-up pages, fold-out sections, and so on) are commonly used in magazines.

There are also disadvantages to magazine advertising: long lead time precludes promotion of last-minute or short-term packages or services, magazine ads are significantly more expensive than newspaper ads, and—because of the national nature of this medium—advertising dollars are wasted if a property's markets are limited geographically. But magazines can provide an excellent avenue for hospitality advertising if you know who you are targeting, what you are offering the target market, and what type of publication will bring the most return.

Unlike newspapers, magazines do not sell space by the column inch; most magazines typically sell a portion of a page: a full, half, quarter, sixth, or eighth of a page (see Exhibit 7). The largest regular portion of space sold in a magazine is the *double-page spread* (called the *center spread* when it occurs at the center of the magazine). This spread is more expensive because the ad must be designed to "bridge" the gutter; no headline words can run through the gutter, and all body text must be on one side or the other.

Magazines also charge for the positioning of the ad; the back cover, inside front and back cover, and center spread are usually the most expensive. Additional costs are incurred for the use of color. Since many magazines do not offer pub-set services, ads must be presented camera ready—an additional cost to the property.

If there are a number of magazines directed toward a targeted market segment, you should not use every publication, especially if mass coverage would be at the expense of frequency or ad size. If ads are placed in too many similar magazines, there may be considerable duplication of readership. The best strategy may be to utilize two or three publications that are considered the best in the field, or that reach the most readers.

Study several publications aimed at specific target audiences before making a selection. Which magazine is most likely to enhance the property's image? Which one offers an attractive format that would complement what the property has to offer? Which publication offers the production capabilities required by the property (full-color, pull-out pages, reader response section, and so on)?

Types of Magazines

Magazines can be divided into two general categories: consumer magazines and trade magazines.

Consumer Magazines. Consumer magazines are excellent vehicles for reaching individual business or leisure travelers (see Exhibit 8). Consumer magazines fall into two broad categories: general interest magazines such as *The New Yorker* and *Better Homes and Gardens,* and special interest magazines such as *Car and Driver* and *Personal Computing.*

Exhibit 7   Magazine Space

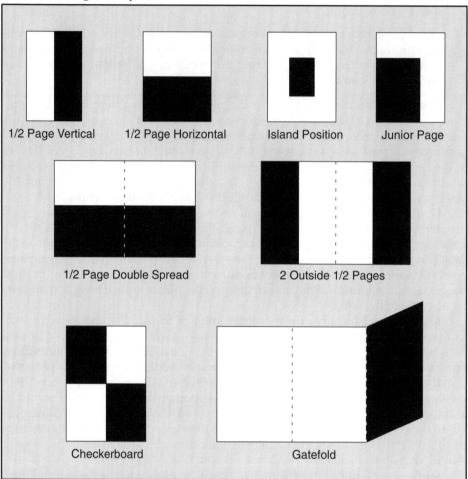

Magazine space is generally sold in terms of pages and fractions of pages. Some of the various ways space may be sold are illustrated above.

One of the advantages of consumer magazines is their format. Most use highly sophisticated production techniques and contain colorful, attractive ads. Consumer ads must be catchy, because most readers do not pick up a magazine for the express purpose of reading an ad about a vacation spot or hotel. It is for this reason that hospitality ads in consumer magazines are typically lush and inviting, with extensive use of photographs (see Exhibit 9).

Magazines also lend themselves to celebrity ads. Celebrity ads can feature "self-testimonials"—a pitch from the president, CEO, or general manager of a chain or property; or they can utilize celebrities—actors and actresses, sports figures, or other recognizable people—to promote the property. Properties may even be represented by a cartoon-character "spokesperson," such as Embassy Suites' Garfield.

Exhibit 8   Sample Consumer Publications

General Interest	**Business-Oriented**
Atlantic	*Business Week*
Better Homes and Gardens	*Dun's Review*
Harpers Bazaar	*Forbes*
McLeans	*Fortune*
New Yorker	*Inc.*
Saturday Review	*Nation's Business*
Southern Living	*Venture*
Sunset	
Town and Country	**Travel**
Vogue	*Holiday*
	Signature
Special Interest	*Travel and Leisure*
Brides	*Travel/Holiday*
Field and Stream	
Golf	**Outdoor Life**
Golf Digest	*Ski*
Gourmet	*Skiing*
Mature Outlook	*Tennis*
Modern Bride	
Modern Maturity	

These consumer publications are excellent for promoting hospitality products and services. When considering advertising in consumer publications, you should remember that publication schedules may differ—some magazines are published monthly, others weekly, and so on. The variety of magazines may seem tempting, but most properties should target a maximum of two or three publications and repeat ads rather than place one ad in a number of publications.

Many consumer magazines have a reader response card section or reply cards inserted in the magazine, making it easy for readers to respond to ads. Names taken from the reply cards that are mailed in can become the foundation of a mailing list for special promotions.

For many properties, the cost of advertising in a national consumer magazine is prohibitive. Some national magazines offer special regional or city editions that reach specific target areas or market segments. Many medium-to-large properties have found advertising in regional editions of national magazines to be a cost-effective way to reach key target markets.

Trade Magazines. Trade magazines are specialized publications that appeal to people in specific industries or professions. Examples of trade magazines that would be useful to the hospitality industry include *Travel Weekly, Successful Meetings,* and *Incentive Travel.* These publications are targeted to travel intermediaries such as travel agents, tour operators, and meeting planners. There are a number of other specialized trade magazines that target other businesses and professions (see Exhibit 10). These magazines are excellent opportunities to introduce the property's services to businesspeople who make their own travel decisions.

Trade magazine advertising differs from consumer magazine advertising in that it usually contains more copy and fewer photographs (see Exhibit 11). Business and group decision-makers are more interested in facts than fantasy, so trade ads generally provide more complete information.

Exhibit 9   Sample Consumer Ad

Robert, at the front desk, sent birthday flowers to my room — on behalf of the hotel staff!

That's why I call the Hay-Adams *my* hotel in Washington, D.C.

The Hay-Adams Hotel

Across from the White House
at One Lafayette Square

Washington, D.C.
(202) 638-6600, (800) 424-5054

This award-winning ad from the Hay-Adams Hotel in Washington, D.C., expresses elegance and personal service.

Designing an Effective Magazine Ad

Three factors—size, color, and bleed—are the most important to consider when designing an effective magazine ad.

Size is important for drawing attention. *CARR Reports,* a publication of Cahners Advertising Research (a nationally known advertising firm), showed that readership can be increased as much as 65% when an ad is doubled in size. Readership of two-page spread ads was 72% higher than that for full-page ads.[2]

Color ads, especially four-color presentations, are also attention-getters. A study by McGraw-Hill showed that color ads (which have increased in business publications by 600% over the past 20 years) grab attention regardless of where

Exhibit 10 Sample Trade Magazines

Users	Magazines
Travel agents, wholesalers, corporate travel managers, tour operators, special-interest-group organizers, airline executives, cruise-ship executives, tourist-board executives, hotel representatives, rental car executives	*ASTA Travel News* *Business Travel News* *Corporate Travel* *Corporate Travel Agent* *Courier* *Destination* *Hotel & Travel Index* *Jax Fax* *OAG TRAVEL PLANNER Hotel & Motel RedBook* *Official Airline Guide* *Official Hotel and Resort Guide* *Pacific Travel News* *Travel Age Network* *Travel Agent* *Travel Trade* *Travel Weekly*
Corporate meeting planners	*Medical Meetings* *Meetings & Conventions* *Meeting News* *Official Meetings and Facilities Guide* *Physician's Travel & Meeting Guide* *Successful Meetings*
Association and society executives	*Association & Society Manager* *The Association Executive* *Association Management* *Best's Insurance Convention Guide* *Insurance Conference Planner*
Incentive operators	*Corporate & Incentive Travel* *Corporation Meetings & Incentives* *Directory of Incentive Travel* *Incentive Marketing* *Incentive Travel* *Incentive World*
Training and development managers	*Training* *Training & Development Journal*
Corporate administrators and sales executives	*Sales & Marketing Management*

Trade publications and journals can be used to reach travel agents, incentive operators, motorcoach tour operators, corporate meeting planners, and administrators and executives in a variety of professions and trades. This is just a partial list of trade publications available to target specific market segments. (Source: Peter Warren and Neil W. Ostergren, "Trade Advertising: A Crucial Element in Hotel Marketing," *Cornell Hotel and Restaurant Administration Quarterly,* May 1986, p. 62.)

they are positioned in a publication.[3] Color is also a factor in heightening recall, creating a positive property image and increasing sales. A study conducted by the American Business Press and the American Research Foundation showed that sales nearly doubled when color was added to an advertising program.[4]

Exhibit 11   Sample Trade Magazine Ad

When it came right down to it, Bob Talley didn't care about our space.

Bob Talley, Manager, Association Services Division

"I could have gotten that anywhere. What I needed was experience."

Everyone who knows the business knows that the Sheraton Washington is one of the largest meeting and convention hotels on the east coast. 1,500 guest rooms and suites. 60,000 square feet of meeting and banquet space, including 34,000 square feet of ballroom area and 26,000 square feet of breakout meeting space. 95,000 square feet of permanent exhibit space. But that's *not* the main reason why Bob Talley's clients like the American Federation for Clinical Research meet here. No. They come to the Sheraton Washington because they're guaranteed something they can't find just anywhere. Experience.

"The people are what sold me. And the people are what keep me coming back."

You can tell the world that you've hosted every major group imaginable. *But*, if they don't come back, you've got nothing but an empty claim.

At the Sheraton Washington, they come back alright. Major associations. Fortune 500 companies. But not because of our 72-foot permanent registration desk. Or the ten separate loading docks we offer for easy access to our exhibit hall. No, they're coming back for one simple reason. Our people.

That's the way it should be. And that's why the first thing we do is assign every group their own personal meeting coordinator. One person who oversees everything. One person to call if you have a question. A request. Or even a problem.

"A convention is a big investment. I wanted mine well-protected."

A comfort level. That's exactly what we offer at the Sheraton Washington. A convention services staff whose experience combined, totals over 100 years. A staff of 1,000 who cater to large groups, day in, day out, year after year. And a hotel that's dedicated to only one thing. Successful meetings.

So, let's face it. You probably already know we've got the space. The amenities. Like seven different restaurants and lounges. Two huge outdoor pools. Even a Metro subway stop right on our grounds. But when all is said and done, the reason you should hold your meeting or convention at the Sheraton Washington should be what Bob Talley's was. Simply put, because we do what we do *so well*.

For more information, call John Hyland, Director of Marketing at (202)328-2000.

Sheraton Washington Hotel
SHERATON HOTELS, INNS & RESORTS WORLDWIDE

Circle #110 on Reader Service Card

Trade advertisements must promote business-oriented benefits such as profit, efficiency, or service. The credibility of this ad is enhanced by the photograph of a meeting planner and the quotes throughout the ad.

There are a number of ways to use color. One of the most effective is the "bleed" ad. Bleed ads are those that run all the way to the edge of the page, leaving no margin. These ads are designed to get extra attention, and may cost an extra 15

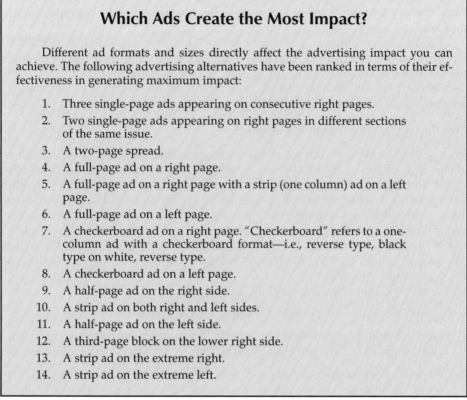

Which Ads Create the Most Impact?

Different ad formats and sizes directly affect the advertising impact you can achieve. The following advertising alternatives have been ranked in terms of their effectiveness in generating maximum impact:

1. Three single-page ads appearing on consecutive right pages.
2. Two single-page ads appearing on right pages in different sections of the same issue.
3. A two-page spread.
4. A full-page ad on a right page.
5. A full-page ad on a right page with a strip (one column) ad on a left page.
6. A full-page ad on a left page.
7. A checkerboard ad on a right page. "Checkerboard" refers to a one-column ad with a checkerboard format—i.e., reverse type, black type on white, reverse type.
8. A checkerboard ad on a left page.
9. A half-page ad on the right side.
10. A strip ad on both right and left sides.
11. A half-page ad on the left side.
12. A third-page block on the lower right side.
13. A strip ad on the extreme right.
14. A strip ad on the extreme left.

Sources: Starch Tested Copy, Starch INRA Hooper, Inc., as reprinted in "Advertising Positioning"; Magazine Publishers Association; CARR Reports.

to 20 percent, but the cost is usually worth it. Starch INRA Hooper, Incorporated, a research organization that regularly conducts tests to measure the visual impact and communication power of advertisements, reported that a four-color bleed ad scored 15% higher on readership scores than did a non-bleed, four-color page ad.[5]

Other production options include the use of multiple pages, gatefolds, and inserts. *Multiple page ads,* which are generally considered to be three or more ads appearing in the same magazine issue (in direct succession, on alternate pages, or randomly throughout the publication), greatly heighten advertising impact and reader recall. *Gatefolds*—oversized pages or portions of pages added to a regular page—are another excellent attention-getting device. Due to the requirements for their production and their expense, gatefolds are not offered by all magazines. When they are offered, they must be planned well in advance. Paper may need to be ordered, special production techniques may need to be employed, arrangements must be made for the folds, and so on. *Inserts* can increase ad readership or offer a convenient way for readers to respond to your advertising. Inserts may be simple (a business reply card) or elaborate (a full-page color section bound into the magazine). Reply cards may either be designed by the property, or, as in the case of many trade magazines, be produced by the publication and include reply numbers that correspond to the numbers assigned to the magazine's ads. This type of reply card is called a bingo card.

Production techniques, however eye-catching, are not all that is needed to capture attention and, most importantly, a sale. Magazine ads, especially in today's competitive market, must be carefully planned for maximum impact. In the next two sections we will look at how to make the most of magazine advertising by using effective photography and writing good ad copy.

Creating a Statement with Photography

Since so many magazine advertisers use photos in their ads, you should also use photos in your ads to attract attention to the property's message. Even properties with a limited advertising budget can use photographs if they plan carefully. It is often possible to schedule one photo session that will cover all of your print advertising needs. Shots of the property's exterior, grounds, recreational amenities, restaurants, lobby, guestrooms, and special features can be taken at the same photo session and used as needed for all types of advertising (see Exhibit 12). When scheduling a photo session, you should ask the photographer to bring both color and black-and-white film.

Whether color or black-and-white, all photographs should be:

- *Sharp.* The sharper the photo, the better it will reproduce.

- *Simple.* While photos employing special effects are sometimes used in ads, clear, simple photographs usually work best.

- *Relevant.* Photographs that depict rooms, restaurants, or the property's lobby do not belong with ad copy that describes the property's recreational amenities. Conversely, a campaign promising a romantic, secluded hideaway loses credibility if the ads feature photos of crowd scenes or a nearby metropolis.

- *Consistent with the property's image.* You can convey the property's image with photographs portraying a romantic, casual, outdoor, or sophisticated image. Photographs are also an excellent way to express such intangibles as impeccable service or a relaxing stay.

If you decide to have photographs taken at the property, carefully plan the photographer's schedule. Deliver copies of the schedule to department heads and, at large properties, to shop owners and concessionaires. To make sure the photographs project the desired image, select props and settings with care. Make sure the photographer signs the contract, and obtain model release forms from every staff member and professional model who appears in a photograph. Last, but certainly not least, orchestrate the shoot to create as little inconvenience as possible. Notify guests in advance of the photo shoot, provide a luggage cart for moving camera equipment, and schedule additional employees to provide assistance.

Creating Effective Ad Copy

Magazine advertising, like newspaper advertising, is not designed to entertain, it is designed to sell. While photographs or artwork can grab a reader's attention,

Exhibit 12   Sample Cost-Effective Photograph

Photo sessions should be set up to photograph property features in both color and black and white. This photograph from the Willard Inter-Continental in Washington, D.C., was shot in black and white for newspaper advertising and in color for full-color brochures, magazine ads, and posters. Its general nature makes it ideal for repeat use. (Courtesy of The Willard Inter-Continental, Washington, D.C.)

good copy is needed to convince readers that they would benefit from patronizing the property. Keep the following guidelines, very similar to newspaper ad guidelines, in mind when writing magazine copy:

1. *Use an effective headline.* More people read headlines than copy, and a good headline is essential to get your message or intent across.

2. *Be specific.* Provide enough specific information to permit readers to build accurate images in their minds of what a stay at the property or an experience at the restaurant or lounge would be like. Spotlight your unique differences.

Examining Your Ads

1. Do they say who you are and what you stand for? Do they create a mental picture?
2. Do they set you apart and show how you are different?
3. Do they preempt a benefit niche and capitalize on an advantage?
4. Do they turn any liabilities into assets?
5. Do they offer benefits to the target market you are trying to reach?
6. Do they provide tangible evidence or clues?
7. Do they feature the one or two things your target market wants most?
8. Are they consistent with your strategy?
9. Do they have credibility?
10. Do they make a promise you can keep?

Source: Robert C. Lewis, "Advertising Your Hotel's Position," *Cornell Hotel and Restaurant Administration Quarterly,* August 1990, p. 90.

> Are there industrial parks or historical attractions nearby? In most cases, an attraction within five miles of a property brings in guests.

3. *Keep it simple.* An ad for a leisure traveler shouldn't contain information about a property's meeting rooms or function space.

4. *Caption every photograph.*

5. *Include prices.* Include the price of guestrooms, special promotional packages, or other products and services offered in the ad. While some advertisers argue this point, including prices saves time for both the property and consumers.

6. *Ask for a response*—and provide a convenient means for doing so (reply card, fax number, etc.)

7. *Stick to a campaign that gets results.* This is perhaps the most important guideline of all. Repetition of an ad that gets results can mean more results; don't make changes just for the sake of change. The ad will always be new to some readers.

Directory Advertising

Another effective avenue for reaching buyers is directory advertising. While the list of directories grows yearly, directories can be divided into two basic categories: telephone directories (yellow pages advertising) and business directories.

Telephone Directories

The yellow pages section of the telephone directory is a popular advertising medium. Americans turn to the hotel and motel headings in telephone directories more than 200 million times each year, and 85% of those times the inquiry is followed up

Exhibit 13   Sample Yellow Pages Ad

This *Best Western* yellow pages ad has elements that can attract a potential buyer—an eye-catching graphic, a listing of the property's key features, and a map showing the property's general location. (Courtesy of Best Western International, Inc.)

by a phone call, letter, or visit.[6] In other words, yellow pages users are ready to buy, and a yellow pages ad can mean increased revenue (see Exhibit 13).

When considering yellow pages advertising, you must determine whether to place one large ad under the hotel and motel listing or a series of smaller ads under various categories such as restaurants, entertainment, resorts, and so on. If your budget allows you to place both types of ads, the small ads can refer readers to the large ad.

The property's name is very important in yellow pages advertising, since many yellow pages users already have a property in mind when they open the phone book. If the property is part of a chain, the chain's name or logo should be prominent in the ad.

If your property does not have great name recognition outside the local area, its name can be relegated to a lesser position (smaller type, bottom of the ad, and so on), while the property's benefits, products, and services can be highlighted. As in most advertising, the target market will determine what features and services you emphasize, regardless of whether the property is part of a chain or is an independent property.

It is important to give travelers an idea of the property's location, landmarks close to the property, and proximity to freeways and transportation terminals. Be specific. Advertising that the property is "centrally located" does not provide readers with enough information to make a buying decision. Instead, you should advertise "Only five minutes from the airport" or "Walking distance to Disneyland," etc.

In an age when many properties are offering similar amenities, a listing of special features and services (waterbeds, baby-sitting service, and so on) can make your property stand out from the competition. Your ad should give readers as many reasons to visit the property as possible: AAA approval, Mobil rating, awards, and so on.

Ask several questions when you evaluate a yellow pages ad. Is the ad uncluttered and easy to read? Does the artwork make the ad stand out, or does the ad fade into the background? Many chain properties have the advantage of using pre-designed or "shell" ads (see Exhibit 14). Small independent properties may choose to use the graphic arts services offered by yellow pages representatives. These representatives can help with graphics, typefaces, and even copy writing.

For best results, you should place an ad in the yellow pages of key target market areas and distant feeder cities as well as your property's own city. You should also place ads in the yellow pages of nearby cities, since travelers are often willing to go a little farther for additional amenities and services.

Business Directories

There are a number of general business directories for the hospitality and travel industries. Some of the major ones are: *Hotel & Travel Index, ABC Worldwide Hotel Guide, OAG TRAVEL PLANNER/Hotel & Motel RedBook,* and *Official Meeting Facilities Guide.* These directories are produced as resource materials for groups such as travel agents and meeting planners. The areas of the world each directory covers can vary. The *Hotel & Travel Index,* for example, is most widely distributed in North America, while the *ABC Worldwide Hotel Guide* covers markets in the United Kingdom, Germany, France, and the Asia/Pacific region. Most directories include a property's location and reservation information, rates, facilities, services, amenities, commission payment policy, and billing procedures, along with information on local area attractions.

In addition to advertising in hotel industry directories, you can advertise in business directories published for other industries and trades. One of the best of these is the American Society of Travel Agents (ASTA) membership directory. Travel agents are responsible for over 70% of the bookings at some hotels. Among other important directories to target are directories of meeting planners, executives, and key business and industry leaders. Advertisements in these directories will not follow the format of general consumer ads: as noted previously, travel agents, meeting planners, and executives want the facts.

Measuring the Effectiveness of Print Advertising ————

To determine if your advertising is producing the desired results, you must test it on a periodic basis. There are three basic categories of advertising measurement: number of inquiries generated, sales or conversions per inquiry, and communication impact.

Exhibit 14   Sample Chain "Shell" Ad

Some hotel chains provide individual properties with "shell" ads. For this ad, a property only has to list the price it wants to charge and its name, address, and telephone number. (Courtesy of Holiday Inns, Inc.)

The number of inquiries is an important indicator of an ad's effectiveness. If you have advertised in a publication but have received no responses, something is wrong. Either the ad is ineffective or the publication is not the best vehicle for the advertising.

Not all inquiries result in sales, so it is necessary to determine how effective the ad is at actually producing revenue. Determining the sales or conversions per inquiry gives you an indication of which publications provide the best value for your advertising dollar.

Communication impact measures the public's response to an ad. This measurement, often performed by professional testing services, tests the public's awareness of and attitude toward your property before and after an advertising campaign, and provides feedback to assist you in making any adjustments necessary to appeal to your property's target markets.

It is important to note, however, that testing and measurements are not always accurate. A number of factors—including weather, economic conditions, and so on—can affect sales. But you should still analyze which advertising is generating responses. There are a number of ways to determine where guests heard about your property. The front desk or reservations personnel can ask callers how they heard about the property. Or, the advertising itself can be designed to provide an easy way to track calls. For example, if coupons are included in an ad, they can be coded with numbers that correspond with the publication in which the ad appears. Or you may assign a special P.O. box, mailing address, department number, or contact person for each publication.

The telephone can also play an important role in response tracking. Some properties provide different toll-free numbers for each market segment, while others make use of remote call-forwarding systems. These systems, which are usually cheaper than setting up "800" systems, enable the property to receive calls from key feeder cities. Prospective guests dial a local number and the call is automatically forwarded to the property.

Some telephone companies offer another service—Advertising Response Tracking (ART)—that channels calls to the property's regular number when a "dummy" number published in an ad is dialed. The responses to each dummy number are counted and tracked by the telephone company, providing the property with an accurate picture of exactly what publications—and geographical areas—are producing the most responses.

The information gained from tracking inquiries and sales can help you make changes necessary to ensure that your advertising is effective (both in terms of cost and results). If, for example, an ad is pulling well on the East Coast but is generating little response in the Midwest, changes can be made in the copy to make the ad more appealing to the Midwest audience. If you find that one publication is pulling three times the response of another, you can drop the lower-producing publication and concentrate on additional advertising in the high-producing one.

Conclusion

While print advertising can be a valuable selling tool, it can also be complicated and confusing. The large number of marketing arenas (newspapers, consumer and trade magazines, and directories are just the most commonly used print media), technical elements (type styles, photography, and so on), and market segments that read print media can make the task of designing effective print advertising a difficult one. But there is help.

As mentioned previously, chain properties can take advantage of pre-designed corporate advertising that can be personalized for each individual property. This service saves considerably on the high cost of design.

Many properties depend on the expertise of a skilled advertising team, whether in-house or a contracted agency. In today's competitive market, this approach is often the most cost-effective, because chances are less that the property's advertising will be lost in a sea of similar, bland ads.

Small properties can make use of independent free-lance artists and writers, or small advertising agencies. After a successful ad has been developed, it can be used in a number of publications for maximum cost-effectiveness.

For the best results in print advertising, you must keep abreast of the latest developments in the field. Study the ads of competitors. Read books on the technical aspects of advertising, and request assistance from organizations that serve the hospitality industry, such as the American Hotel & Motel Association and the Hospitality Sales & Marketing Association International.[7] By studying trends, determining key newspaper and magazine markets, and developing advertising for targeted market segments, you can create print advertising that reaches thousands of potential guests, generates increased profits—and makes the sales job easier.

Endnotes

1. Marvin Perton, "Advertise to Revitalize," *Hotel and Resort Industry*, May 1991.
2. Marketing Effectiveness Studies, American Business Press; Laboratory of Advertising Performance Report, "High Impact Advertising," as reported in *Meeting Market Update*, Volume 2, Issue 2, 1992.
3. "The Impact of Business Publication Advertising on Sales and Profits," Performance Reports, Nos. 3020.5 and 3134 (New York: McGraw-Hill, 1992).
4. "Color … A Picture Perfect Advertising Opportunity," as reported in *Meeting Market Update*, Volume 2, Issue 2, 1992.
5. Starch Tested Copy, Starch INRA Hooper, Inc., Volume 1, No. 5, as reported in *Advertising Positioning*, Magazine Publishers Association.
6. Barry Maher, "10 Ways to Turn the Yellow Pages into Green Backs," *Lodging Magazine*, July/August 1992, p. 31.
7. *The Art of Hotel and Travel Advertising* (Margate, New Jersey: The Hotel Sales & Marketing Association International) is an attractive, four-color book illustrating award-winning collateral materials and print, brochure, and direct mail advertising.

Key Terms

advertising response tracking (ART)	insert
advertorial	multiple-page ad
bingo card	premium position buy
bleed ad	pub-set ad
consumer magazine	ROP color
double-page spread	shell ad
full position	spot color
gatefold	standard advertising unit (SAU)
gutter	trade magazine

Review Questions

1. Newspapers are generally used to achieve what three basic goals?

2. What factors should be considered in selecting a newspaper?

3. Where is a newspaper's "gutter" located?

4. What is spot color?

5. How can advertisers separate or "protect" their ads from other newspaper ads?

6. Should a property's name always be featured in a newspaper ad?

7. What are some common reasons why a newspaper ad doesn't sell?

8. What is an advertorial?

9. What are some advantages of magazine advertising over newspaper advertising?

10. How does trade magazine advertising differ from consumer magazine advertising?

11. What are some criteria for an effective photograph?

12. What guidelines should be followed for preparing effective magazine ad copy?

13. Why should a property advertise in the yellow pages?

14. What methods can be used to measure the effectiveness of print advertising?

Chapter Outline

Developing a Direct Mail Campaign
    Guest Profiles
    Types of Direct Mail Campaigns
        Series Mailings
        Single Mailings
        Timing Direct Mail
Mailing Lists
    Commercial
    General
    House
Direct Mail Pieces
    Types of Direct Mail Pieces
        Letters
        Newsletters
        Collateral Materials
        Specially Designed Direct Mail Pieces
    Guidelines for Direct Mail Pieces
        The AIDA Formula
        The Five Ps
    Posting Direct Mail Pieces
Measuring Direct Mail Campaigns
    Campaign Costs
    Reader Response
        Inquiry Handling and Fulfillment
Conclusion

12

Direct Mail Advertising

JUST A FEW YEARS AGO, direct mail advertising represented a 15% share of total advertising expenditures; today, that figure is over 30%, and direct mail is the third largest—and the fastest growing—of all forms of media marketing and promotion.[1] More and more properties are discovering that direct mail sent to selected potential guests can be one of the most effective means of advertising used in an advertising campaign. Direct mail has several advantages. Direct mail is:

1. *Targetable.* One of the major benefits of direct mail is that it enables the hospitality firm to pinpoint prime customers. Direct mail is known as a "rifle" medium—in contrast to other methods of advertising, which employ a "shotgun" approach. Unlike hit-or-miss efforts, direct mail is sent directly to prospects with the most potential. If the objective, for example, is to increase mid-week corporate meetings business, the hotel might obtain a list of companies with zip codes within a 200-mile radius, target companies with 100 or more employees, and address its mailing to executives in personnel, training, and sales or marketing. One hotel sales manager sums it up: "I go fishing with my advertising, but I catch fish with my direct mail."

2. *Personal.* A direct mail piece, unlike newspaper, magazine, and broadcast advertising, is directed to a specific individual. Automated word processing equipment can rapidly produce thousands of letters—each addressed to a different recipient—that have a "first copy" appearance. Today even printed signatures are so well done that it is often difficult to tell they are not hand-signed. Recipients are more apt to feel they are important to the property.

3. *Conspicuous.* A direct mail piece is not lost in the media clutter of ads in a newspaper or magazine.

4. *Flexible.* Direct mail offers flexibility in the types of pieces available, the timing of a mailing, and the types of mailings. While newspaper and magazine ads are limited by paper size and must be balanced in terms of editorial copy, and broadcast ads frequently are limited to 30- or 60-second spots, direct mail has fewer restrictions on space and format (see Exhibit 1). Direct mail can be any shape or size, as long as it meets postal codes, can utilize numerous types of paper, and lends itself well to such attention-getting features as pop-ups, scratch-off pieces, and even the inclusion of specialty items.

5. *Designed for prospect involvement and action.* Unlike what can happen when ads are broadcast over radio or TV, recipients do not miss key points of the message while they rush to get a pencil to jot down a name or telephone number.

Exhibit 1   The Flexibility of Direct Mail Pieces

Unlike newspaper and magazine ads, which are limited due to space and editorial considerations, the size of direct mail pieces can be extremely flexible—as long as pieces meet postal regulations. This postcard, promoting the Mobile Convention Center in Mobile, Alabama, is one of a series of four oversized mailings (the cards are 14 x 11 inches). Each postcard features a watercolor print of the convention center and the surrounding area, and advertises benefits for meeting planners on the reverse side. (Courtesy of the Mobile Convention Bureau, Mobile, Alabama)

All the information needed is contained in a single, convenient form, and reply cards and toll-free telephone numbers make responding easy.

6. *Easily cost-controlled.* Direct mail pieces are limited only by postal regulations
   and the property's budget. Expenses can be minimized by limiting mailings to
   qualified prospects or cutting the size of a direct mail piece. Also, to save
   money, parts of the direct mail promotion (a cover letter, for example) can be
   prepared by the property's staff rather than by an agency or graphic arts studio.

7. *Easily tested and measured.* The ability to accurately and quickly determine the
   success or failure of a direct mail effort is a great advantage and the biggest
   difference between direct mail and other advertising methods. As one advertiser once stated, "I know half of what I spend on advertising is wasted—I just
   don't know which half." Direct mail overcomes this problem, since direct mail
   pieces can be coded to track prospect response. A simple comparison of the
   number of names on a mailing list to the number and types of responses from
   that list also offers an effective measurement.

With all of these advantages, it is difficult to imagine why every property isn't
using direct mail advertising. While the advantages clearly outweigh the disadvantages, certain disadvantages must be considered when developing a direct mail
campaign or incorporating direct mail into the property's overall advertising plan:

- *Mailing lists can be expensive or may become ineffective quickly.* Unless a property
  uses the names of previous guests exclusively, it must purchase mailing lists,
  and costs can be prohibitive. Also, direct mail experts estimate that 15% to
  30% of the names or addresses on mailing lists change annually. This necessitates the evaluation, updating, and purging of lists on a regular basis.

- *Direct mail takes extensive planning and production time.* While direct mail pieces
  can be as simple as a letter or series of letters, many direct mail campaigns
  include four-color brochures, specially designed folders, or other collateral
  materials that require extensive production. Add to this the time involved in
  (1) preparing mailing lists if the lists are compiled in-house, or sorting through
  purchased mailing lists if the mailing is to go to a specific market group; (2)
  processing bulk mailings (folding, stuffing, addressing, sorting, mailing); and
  (3) responding to and recording inquiries, and costs can become prohibitive.

- *Direct mail may be viewed as junk mail.* A segment of the public views direct mail
  advertising as junk mail and may develop a negative image of a property that
  sends direct mail pieces. If a direct mail piece is relevant and attractive, it may
  dispel this image.

Developing a Direct Mail Campaign

When planning a direct mail campaign, you should differentiate between ordinary
correspondence and direct mailings.[2] While correspondence may fall into the sales
solicitation category, most correspondence is usually "one-on-one"—letters,
information sheets, or collateral materials are sent in response to specific customer
requests. Direct mailings, on the other hand, are planned solicitation efforts

Insider Insights

Jim Mastrangelo, CHA, CHSE
Director of Sales and Marketing
The Algonquin Hotel
New York City _____

Jim Mastrangelo began his career in the hospitality industry in 1962, working in a catering facility. Since that time he has received a Bachelors degree in Hotel and Restaurant Administration and a Masters degree in International Travel and Tourism. He is also a Certified Hotel Administrator and a Certified Hotel Sales Executive. During his career he has worked in a wide variety of properties, from a 150-room Caribbean resort to an 1,800-room New York City convention hotel. He is currently director of sales and marketing at The Algonquin, a New York City landmark. His responsibilities include marketing the hotel to worldwide accounts.

I've always been a strong believer in direct mail advertising. Direct mail advertising plays a very important part in the overall success of a hotel's marketing program. It's an excellent balance to outside sales calls and telephone sales. It presents your product to a client without the expense of a personal sales call. In addition, you're able to solicit many clients at one time—often many more clients than you'd be able to solicit individually—through direct mail.

A direct mail campaign can be either very successful or a complete disaster. All too often direct mail programs have little thought behind them. But direct mail should be as carefully planned as any other marketing or sales activity. Above all, there should be a central message or theme. Conveying one message successfully is much better than trying to clutter the communication with three or four thoughts, all of which are usually weakly presented.

Each direct mail campaign should be part of your overall marketing plan. If during a particular time of year you know you can expect a drop-off in business, for example, you can develop a direct mail campaign to bring in additional business. Such a campaign may involve offering free breakfasts to all business travelers, for example.

The promotional piece you develop for your direct mail campaign is as important as the message. It's critical that this piece include some form of response mechanism—a coupon so the client can request additional information, or a phone number for booking a meeting or making a reservation. To further stimulate inquiries, your campaign could offer a gift for each response.

The mailing list is another critical part of a direct mail campaign. You can develop a mailing list from your own hotel's sales department and catering department account files and reservations forms, or names can be purchased from outside sources. Before purchasing an outside list, it's very important to be sure it contains the names of potential buyers of your product. Many lists contain names of people who have absolutely nothing to do with making hotel travel arrangements or booking meetings. If you're soliciting meetings, the best source of potential clients are past clients.

Insider Insights *(continued)*

Another type of mailing list that may prove profitable is a list of residents within neighboring communities. This list can be used in a direct mail campaign designed to generate weekend business. Before choosing this option, remember that a direct mail campaign can be costly. You should compare the revenue you expect to generate to the cost of the program. In many cases, an advertisement in a local paper can develop more weekend business at a lower cost.

With direct mail, a property can remain in contact with its clients and generate new business. But, as with any successful marketing activity, direct mail campaigns must be carefully thought out, directed to a specific target market, developed around a strong theme or central message, and backed up by the capability to make good on claims. If your direct mail campaign meets these criteria, it could be one of the most profitable parts of your hotel's sales program.

---

targeted to specific market segments. The pieces are identical for each targeted segment, although different pieces may be developed for other market segments or sub-segments of the targeted market. And, in most cases, direct mailings consist of a series of pieces to increase exposure and enhance effectiveness.

Before developing a direct mail campaign, you should analyze your property's markets and determine what features and benefits are most important to its present and potential guests. One way to do this is to develop guest profiles. Guest profiles can be used to create relevant direct mail advertising materials and develop a list of potential direct mail recipients.

Guest Profiles

You can obtain accurate guest profile information in a number of ways. You can analyze data on previous guests. Guest registration forms, questionnaires, and even personal interviews can yield invaluable information on guests and what is most important to them.

You can also send questionnaires to potential guests in selected target markets. If you are planning to add a convention facility to your hotel, for example, you might send a questionnaire to meeting planners, group tour operators, and decision-makers in national or local associations. This type of questionnaire could provide input into the types of services required by the targeted market segments. It could also introduce your property and its facilities to the targeted market segment and provide a list of potential guests for the new facility. A future direct mail campaign could take questionnaire responses into consideration—a "you asked for it, you got it" approach.

Guest profiles of a hotel's previous guests should include the guests':

- Age (or age group)
- Sex
- Occupation

- Income

- Education

- Place of residence

- Source(s) of travel information (travel magazines, newspapers, travel agents, word-of-mouth, and so on)

- Reason(s) for travel decisions (influence of travel agents, friends, business associates; corporate policies; last-minute choice; and so on)

- Time(s) most likely to travel (season of the year, specific holidays, and so on)

- Number and length of previous stays

If a property finds that its average guest is a businessperson who typically stays three days during the week, for example, the property can mail out invitations for an extended weekend stay at a special rate. Or, a newsletter can be mailed monthly to business guests to keep them informed about special discounts, upcoming promotions, and other items of interest about the property.

Types of Direct Mail Campaigns

In addition to the direct mail pieces used (direct mail pieces will be discussed later in the chapter), there are two key elements to a direct mail campaign: (1) the type of campaign—whether it will be a series of mailings or a single mailing; and (2) the timing of the mailing of each piece.

The following factors help determine whether a campaign will be a series of mailings or a single mailing:

- *The purpose of the mailing.* Is the mailing designed to introduce new products, services, or facilities? Complement a current media campaign? Attract group business? Solicit inquiries? Solicit rooms or food business?

- *The target markets to be solicited,* and the potential return from each.

- *The property's budget* for direct mail.

Series Mailings. A campaign that involves a series of mailings has the advantage of keeping the property's name before the prospect: as most salespeople know, it is rare to make a sale on the first call. A series of mailings can address a variety of prospect needs, since each mailing in the series can offer one or two new benefits. In addition, a variety of direct mail pieces can be used in a series of mailings—postcards, full-color fliers or self-mailers, or even specialty items. This variety helps keep readers involved and looking forward to the next mailing.

When using a series of mailings, a thematic approach is especially important. The pieces must "tie in" and be mailed on a timely basis to encourage consumer recognition and involvement.

Single Mailings. A single mailing is handled differently. To avoid overwhelming the prospect, a single mailing is usually limited to one or two benefits, but the property should say all it has to say and ask for an immediate response. A single direct

The Bloomington Convention & Visitors Bureau in Bloomington, Minnesota, developed a series of mailings to introduce the bureau to meeting planners nationwide. Its mailings featured Executive Director Bonnie Carlson and her staff—the actual people who would be assisting meeting planners—and outlined some of the advantages of choosing a meeting site in Bloomington. (Courtesy of the Bloomington Convention & Visitors Bureau, Bloomington, Minnesota)

mail piece may take a number of forms—a letter, postcard, flier, or a combination of these in one package. Timing—the best time to mail the piece—becomes especially important with a single mailing.

Timing Direct Mail. The best timing for a direct mail piece varies with the type of piece being mailed, the lead time before a special promotion, the geographic locations of recipients, and other factors such as the mailing schedule of the local post office.

Whether the piece is a single mailing or part of a series of promotional pieces, you should avoid peak mailing periods when mail is likely to be delayed. These peak periods include the Christmas season, the period immediately preceding the deadline for income taxes, and special holidays such as Mother's Day, Valentine's Day, Father's Day, and so on. Direct mail pieces should also be timed to avoid periods when big bills are due (Christmas bills usually begin arriving shortly after January 1, and income taxes must be paid by April 15).

The intended recipients will also make a difference in the day a piece is timed to arrive. Sales letters to businesspeople, for example, should be timed to arrive on Tuesdays, Wednesdays, or Thursdays to avoid the Monday rush and the Friday cleanup of business for the week. When mailing to a home, a piece should be timed to arrive on Thursday or Friday so the family can discuss the property's offer over the weekend. For a weekend promotion, however, an arrival on the Monday or Tuesday preceding the weekend in question would be best (see Exhibit 2).

Direct mail pieces can be mailed at specific times of the year to target groups or individuals who are likely to want a relaxing vacation around that time—accountants after the tax season, ministers after the Easter or Christmas seasons, families during school vacations, etc.

Mailing Lists

Mailing lists are the heart of any direct mail campaign. Mailing lists fall into three basic categories: commercial lists, general lists, and house lists (see Exhibit 3).

Commercial

Commercial mailing lists are usually rented for a one-time mailing rather than purchased. Often, a property does not even see a rental list; the mailing is sent to the list owner's offices for labeling and distribution.

If a hotel buys a commercial list, the hotel has complete control over it and can use it as many times as needed; that particular list cannot be sold to any other property. Before purchasing a list, it is wise to test a portion of it. If a commercial list offers 150,000 names, for example, a property should buy perhaps 5,000 names. If the test mailing works well, the property can try an additional 10,000 names and continue to purchase if responses warrant the additional expense.

Types of Commercial Lists. Commercial lists, which are compiled from a wide variety of public information, generally fall into three categories:

1. *Resident lists.* Generated from telephone listings, car registrations, and other public records, resident lists contain individual names and can be broken down into geographic areas and selected on the basis of median income, home value, head of household, and other factors that would influence a hospitality buying decision. There is also a related list, an "occupant" list, which provides

Exhibit 2   Direct Mail Brochure for Weekend Business

BED & BREAKFAST
W E E K E N D

SUITE & LOVELY
W E E K E N D

Just the other day you said, "We're a sad case. If I get to work after 8 am, I feel guilty. And your only constant companion is that briefcase." Well, the Vista's got a simple question for you. Isn't it time the two of you spent some *real* time together?

Then it's time for our Bed & Breakfast weekend.

Your weekend includes an American breakfast in the Greenhouse Restaurant, or room service. Full use of the pool, sauna and fitness center, parking privileges, late check-out and much, much more. The real plus of this weekend is that it allows the two of you to spend some time together — to do what you want — or to do nothing at all. $69 per person, per night, double occupancy. For reservations call (212) 938-1990.

How long has it been since you've felt the excitement of "young love?" Or, rekindled a flame that was starting to dim? If you answered either question with "It's been so long, I don't remember," then it's time for a Suite & Lovely Weekend.

Your weekend includes either a duplex or one-bedroom suite — making the weekend ideal for honeymooners and other loving couples. Complimentary champagne, American breakfast in the Greenhouse Restaurant, or in your room. Full use of the pool, sauna and fitness center — and more. Best of all — you can get the Suite & Lovely "Weekend" *any* day of the week. $149.00 per person, per night, double occupancy. For reservations call (212) 938-1990.

Courtesy of Vista International Hotel, New York, New York.

addresses but not names. This type of list is not considered personal, but may be used in a general mass mailing—such as when introducing a new restaurant to the general population.

2. *Consumer lists.* Consumer lists are compiled from records of purchases or inquiries for products or services, and are useful when targeting markets with specific preferences or lifestyles. A property might target purchasers of ski equipment for a mailing about winter sports packages, for example.

Exhibit 3 Mailing Lists

COMMERCIAL LISTS

Sources: Magazine subscription lists; clipping bureaus (firms that search magazines and newspapers for items of specific interest to the hospitality industry; there is a fee for this service, but the leads that are provided are specifically targeted for the individual property or chain); membership lists of groups and associations (Meeting Planners International, the American Society of Association Executives, and so on). Commercial lists are available through a wide variety of services, including the Standard Rate and Data service, which lists over 25,000 direct mail lists. Lists can also be rented or purchased through association boards and commercial list brokers.

Advantages: Names targeted for specific markets; continually updated lists.

Disadvantages: Cost; possible duplication of names; use of same lists by competing properties.

GENERAL LISTS

Sources: U.S. Government directories and specialized publications; city and state directories; industry trade directories; credit rating books (Dun & Bradstreet, Standard & Poor's, and so on); local and national telephone directories.

Advantages: Low or no-cost; a large number of names at one time; availability of names from selected markets.

Disadvantages: These lists are untested and will result in a "hit or miss" effort; lists are often outdated—business and government executives often change positions; an extensive amount of time and research will be needed to cull out unwanted names.

HOUSE LISTS

Sources: Guest registration cards, surveys, responses to advertising, leads from the property's sales staff, referrals from guests and employees.

Advantages: Low cost; greater percentage of responses than from any other list.

Disadvantages: It takes time to develop a good house list; someone must frequently update the list.

---

3. *Business lists.* Lists of businesses can be generated from credit reports and other sources, including trade magazine mailing lists. In many cases, detailed information—such as sales volume, number of employees, and firm locations—is available, making it easy to target a specific market (a company with 200 or more employees and branches in the Midwest, for example). In all cases, businesses are identified by a Standard Industrial Classification (SIC) number. SIC numbers, assigned by the federal government, make it easy to reach related types of industries.

Commercial lists are also available with the names of people in particular professions, owners of certain makes of cars, and subscribers to various magazines. Costs vary with the type of list requested (see Exhibit 4). Rates usually run from $40 to $100 per thousand names.

Some commercial mailing list firms specialize in creating general lists of past and potential users of hospitality products and services. Names are often obtained from surveys, or by purchasing mailing lists from properties. This method of acquiring a list may seem to be the simplest and most cost-effective, but these "hospitality lists" fail to take a number of points into consideration.

Exhibit 4   Typical Mailing List Costs

Prime Target Marketing, Inc.

The Travel Industry's Resource for Focusing on the Right Buyers

BUSINESS TRAVEL LISTS PRICE SCHEDULE

Select business travel lists including corporate travel managers, transient business travelers, meetings and conventions managers and meeting planners. Buyer lists are available by geography, SIC, title, number of employees and sales volume. Traveler lists are available by lifestyle, geography and income. Free consultation.

List Name	Price per 10,000	Cost per Name
Corporations by Trading Area	$500	5 cents
Meetings and Conventions Planners	$950	9.5 cents
Smaller Companies by Trading Area	$500	5 cents
Transient Business Travelers	$1,300	13 cents
Travel Managers	$950	9.5 cents
Travel Agencies	$900	9 cents

List Selection Costs

Title Selection	$5 per thousand
Trading Areas/State/Zip/SCF Selection	$5 per thousand
Nth Name	$5 per thousand
Income	$5 per thousand
# of Employees Selection	$5 per thousand
Pressure Sensitive Labels	$7.50 per thousand
Phone Numbers	$25 per thousand
Magnetic Tape	$25
Floppy Disk	$10

SUMMARY OF TERMS AND CONDITIONS

1) All list prices include names delivered in mag tape or cheshire label format.
2) Minimum order varies for each list.
3) Prices are Net of commissions.
4) List delivery is 10 Working Days from receipt of order and payment.
5) All list rentals are for one-time usage.
6) Sample mailing piece required.

Please call 1–800–TARGETING (1–800–827–4384) for assistance

Prices effective February 1, 1992 and are subject to change.

945 CONCORD STREET, FRAMINGHAM, MA 01701
TELEPHONE: 508–879–9488   FAX: 508–879–0698   TELEX: 681759OHQWTC
CUSTOMER SERVICE: 1–800–TARGETING (1–800–827–4384)

This price list, similar to the rate cards used for newspapers, magazines, and billboards, gives the rates for commonly requested mailing lists. (Courtesy of Prime Target Marketing, Inc., Framingham, Massachusetts)

First, guest mixes differ from property to property. While a city property's ideal mix may be 80% business travelers and 20% leisure travelers, a resort may prefer to cater to a strictly leisure trade. Small properties along state highways would be more interested in individual leisure travelers than would properties with facilities for large groups. Since not all hospitality properties are the same, the names on a general hospitality list might not reflect market segments that your property is trying to attract.

Second, these lists do not provide a customer preference breakdown. Although a hospitality list may give the names of people who have stayed in hotels more than six times in one year, for example, it does not provide customer preferences. Does the guest prefer an upscale downtown hotel over an airport property? If so, an airport property would be wasting money on both the list and the expense of mailing. While more specific hospitality lists are available, they may prove to be too costly for a small property or a property that wishes to target a number of market segments.

Choosing a Commercial List. When shopping for a commercial list, you should consider the following factors:

- Does the list contain the desired market segments?

- How were the names obtained? Direct mail responses? Research?

- When was the list last updated?

- Who has tested this list?

- Who is using the list?

- What are projections for future names?

- What types of selections are available? Is the list broken down by zip code, age, income, occupation, job title, and so on?

- What is the cost for selections? Are separate charges incurred for the use of particular selection criteria (zip code, occupation, income, and so on)?

- What percentage of deliverability is guaranteed? Older lists will have more non-deliverable addresses; newer lists should offer up to 95% deliverability.

Many properties use list brokers to purchase commercial lists for selected target markets. List brokers, like real estate brokers, are extremely knowledgeable about the market, and bring buyers (hospitality properties) and sellers (list compilers) together. List brokers do not compile the actual lists, but work with list compilers to select the best list for your property.

If you decide to use the services of a list broker, the broker should work closely with you throughout the entire direct mail process. He or she should have a thorough understanding of your property's needs.

General

General lists are usually obtained in two ways: through business directories or through the membership rosters of associations.

Business directories can provide good lists of key decision-makers. If the property is seeking convention business, for example, a publication such as the *Directory of Corporate Meeting Planners* can prove invaluable. Other publications, such as the *Encyclopedia of Associations,* can also provide the names of group decision-makers.

Another excellent tool for creating a general list is the membership roster of associations to which the property's salespeople belong. Many hotel salespeople are members or associate members of associations relating to the hospitality industry, such as Meeting Planners International (MPI), the Society of Corporate Meeting Professionals (SCMP), the American Society of Travel Agents (ASTA), the National Tour Association (NTA), and the American Society of Association Executives (ASAE).

House

House lists are prepared by staff members at the property itself, usually from information gathered from registration cards. House lists can also be compiled from responses to surveys, responses to advertisements, leads from the property's sales staff, referrals from the property's guests, and names supplied by the property's employees.

House lists are the most effective of all lists available. Many properties have received up to a 30% response using house lists, as opposed to an average 2% response obtained from a "cold" mailing to names purchased from a commercial list broker. One disadvantage of house lists is that they usually take time to develop.

House lists should be subdivided by market segment because the sales approach and promotion will usually be different for each market segment. House list divisions might include:

- Customers who paid full rack rate

- Business travelers with an average stay exceeding five days

- Guests traveling with their families

- Meeting and conference planners

- Travel agents

- Catering clients (non-repeating clients, such as wedding planners, might be omitted)

- Restaurant and lounge customers

- Special markets such as users of fitness clubs and other recreational facilities

- Purchasers of weekend specials or other packages

Once the type of campaign has been determined and mailing lists developed or purchased, the property's staff can begin the process of creating successful direct mail pieces.

Direct Mail Pieces

Direct mail pieces represent the property, so it is important that they be creative but relevant and consistent with the property's image.

Before developing a direct mail piece, you should consider the following questions:

- What does the property want to accomplish with the piece?
- Who is the target audience?
- What type of piece will convey the property's message most effectively?
- How much money is available to develop the piece?
- How many pieces will be needed? Will the mailing be a single mailing or a series of mailings?
- How long will it take to complete the pieces needed?

To address these concerns, you might hold a brainstorming session with the property's marketing and sales staff, and with the ad agency if one is employed by the property. Studying successful past campaigns can also provide good ideas.

Types of Direct Mail Pieces

Types of direct mail pieces include letters, newsletters, collateral materials, and specially designed direct mail pieces.

Letters. By far the most common and simplest direct mail pieces are letters (see Exhibit 5). Letters have several advantages:

- They are simple to prepare.
- They can be used for a variety of purposes—announcements of packages, products, or services; follow-ups; introductions to collateral materials sent in the mailing; and so on.
- They can be personalized to involve the reader in the property.
- They can invite immediate action.
- They are relatively inexpensive to produce and mail.

A letter must give the reader a reason to read it and respond. Personalization is often used today to try to ensure that the letter doesn't end up in the wastebasket unread. Personalization may be as simple as addressing the letter to a specific person and using that person's name throughout the letter, or as complex as mentioning details of past stays (obtained from the guest history card) or other personal information (hobbies, preferences for specific locales, etc.) that have been obtained through referrals, surveys, and so on. Computers make it possible to produce personalized letters efficiently, quickly, and economically. But the property's efforts should not stop there. Letters to important guests or clients, especially meeting planners who can bring in thousands of dollars of business, should be *hand-signed*, as time-consuming as it might be. It is surprising how many people examine a signature to see if it is real or printed.

To further increase the chances that letters will be read, letters and envelopes should be of high quality stock, and a dateline should be included to prompt a quick response.[3] (Datelines tend to personalize a letter and give a sense of urgency.)

Exhibit 5   Sample Direct Mail Letter

The
STANFORD COURT

EXECUTIVE OFFICES

Dear Mrs. Smith:

I would like you to send me your husband.

I promise to return him intact, extravagantly well fed and cared for, and a very happy man.

I work for the brand new STANDORD COURT HOTEL here in San Francisco. It's my job to convince Very Important People to try us just once, the next time they're in San Francisco.

And it occurred to me that the quickest way to convince your Very Important Husband is to convince his Very Important Wife, namely you, that the STANFORD COURT is perfect for him.

To do that, I've come up with the attached questionnaire. Please look it over. When you finish it, you might be surprised to find out how much more it's taught you about your husband.

And when you've finished, if you're convinced that he'll like us, please let him know. And suggest that he try us, just once.

Ninety-nine times out of a hundred, he'll come home so pleased with himself for having "discovered" a beautiful new San Francisco experience, he'll bring you back with him to share the joys on his next trip.

And in all the questionnaire results I've ever tabulated, I've never seen anyone turn down a trip to San Francisco.

Sincerely,

Gail Jones

Gail Jones
Sales Representative

GJ/sd

NOB HILL · SAN FRANCISCO · CALIFORNIA 94108 · 415-989-3500

Letters are the most common form of direct mail. They can be used alone, as a cover accompanying brochures or other collateral items, or to introduce a guest survey. (Courtesy of Stanford Court, San Francisco, California)

Mail with postage stamps will generally command more attention than metered mail. Properties mailing in large quantities, of course, may have to opt for metered mail in the interest of saving time and labor, but many properties find the more personal look achieved by using postage stamps worth the extra time and effort.

Design. The design of direct mail letters (as well as other direct mail pieces) will depend in part on the design and type of the property's other advertising. Direct mail is far more effective if the targeted audience can identify it with other advertising—newspaper ads, radio spots, and so on. This kind of "thematic" approach lends credibility as well as name recognition.

A major portion of the cost of a direct mailing is the components of the piece. Using non-standard paper weights and envelopes can substantially increase costs (with no guarantee of increasing effectiveness). You should take the following factors into consideration when designing a direct mail piece:

1. *Stationery size.* While a smaller size might offer eye appeal, it is far more practical to use the standard $8^1/2 \times 11$ inch stationery or the slightly smaller $7^1/4 \times 10^1/2$ inch Monarch style. The property's letterhead may take up considerable space on smaller-size stationery, limiting the length of the message or necessitating the use of two or more sheets of paper.

2. *Stock color and finish.* Standard white stationery is effective and conservative, and is used primarily for corresponding with groups and businesses. For individuals, a neutrally colored paper stock (buff, tan, gray, etc.) is acceptable (neutral stocks convey a conservative, businesslike image), particularly if the color fits into the property's overall advertising image. Regular bond finishes are normally used for all colors.

3. *Letterheads.* A one-color letterhead is most commonly used, and the same color can usually be used for both white and colored stocks. The letterhead should include the property's name, street address, telephone number, and fax number; a logo is also an effective eye-catcher. If desired, the property's slogan or the name of a contact person or the general manager may be included as part of the letterhead.

4. *Envelopes.* Most properties use standard business-letter envelopes that can accommodate $8^1/2 \times 11$ inch stationery and a rack-size brochure. The most commonly used envelopes are the *Monarch* ($3^7/8 \times 7^1/2$ inch envelope with $7^1/4 \times 10^1/2$ inch letterhead), *Number 10* ($4^1/8 \times 9^1/2$ inch envelope with $8^1/2 \times 11$ inch letterhead), and *9 × 12 inch* (9×12 inch envelope with $8^1/2 \times 11$ inch letterhead). The property's name, address, and logo or slogan should appear in the upper left corner of the envelope. Envelope and stock colors should match—white envelopes with white stock, and so on.

5. *Addressing.* There are two basic types of addressing—manual and mechanical. Manual addressing can be accomplished by hand or with a typewriter. This form of addressing should always be used on a personalized letter, and is also often used for small mailings that don't merit the time and expense of printing computerized labels.

   Mechanical addressing is done by computer, and usually involves generating labels. Labels come in two basic formats: pressure-sensitive (peel and stick) and Cheshire (1×3 inch strips of computer paper that are usually printed four across; a Cheshire high-speed machine then cuts the labels and glues them onto the mailing pieces). Computerized labeling can greatly reduce the costs of sorting bulk mail, as labels are usually printed in zip code order. This type of addressing is often used for first-time mailings and mailings of "generic" pieces, such as non-personalized postcards and self-mailers.

An attractive envelope will help ensure that the letter is opened, but this is only half the battle. The format and copy of the letter will determine whether it is read and acted on or tossed in the wastebasket.

Format. An attractive format can make a letter more inviting. The block letter format is used most often, but there are a number of variations. Unusual formats can be used as a sales gimmick as long as they are tied to a specific promotion or market segment. For the most part, business executives prefer a conservative format rather than a gimmick. The typeface used should be in keeping with the format and content of the letter. Conservative type is more suitable for standard business letters, while script type can be used for "personal" invitations.

Copy. While people may open attractive letters, few make buying decisions without having a good reason. Direct mail letters should begin with an interesting first sentence to grab the reader's attention. Often, a headline in the form of a question ("Does Your Spouse Deserve a Break?") can serve as an attention-getter to prompt reading on.

Addressing the needs of the reader is of utmost importance, and the first paragraph should do just that. The letter should be customer-oriented; rather than talking about the hotel, it should address consumer concerns and how the hotel and staff can help solve them. Many business letters start out with the same trite phrases; these letters often don't get read. Readers should not have to read half the letter before they know what the property is expressing or offering. Direct mail letters must be informative and interesting, complete but not repetitious.

The body of the letter should be written in clear, concise statements that inform the reader of property benefits. Avoid long sentences, fancy words, and industry jargon. The letter should get the reader involved. Avoid beginning sentences with "I" or "we"; begin sentences with phrases such as "As you can see," "Knowing how you feel about," and so on. Emphasizing "you" focuses on the reader and his or her personal interests. "You can enjoy a workout or a tennis game no matter what the weather" is far more involving than saying "We have a complete indoor gym and tennis courts."

An action-oriented conclusion, such as "Return the attached postal-reply card today to take advantage of this special program, available only through April 30th," should be included to stimulate a response. You should give the reader a convenient way to respond; a toll-free telephone number or a reply card, postcard, coupon, or certificate can be a part of or be included with the letter.

Letters are effective only if they are read. A professional presentation, interesting copy, and reader involvement will ensure that the property gets the most from the letters in its direct mail campaign.

Newsletters. Newsletters are often used to solicit business for a property (see Exhibit 6). While some properties limit the use of their newsletter to public relations campaigns, this sales tool also can be used to entice potential guests, travel agents,

Exhibit 6   Sample Newsletters

Newsletters are a good way to keep in touch with previous guests and announce new services and packages. For best results, a property's newsletter should reflect its positioning and, whenever possible, be targeted to specific market segments. The Sheraton chain, for example, publishes three separate newsletters—Convene for meeting planners, Agency Dialogue for the travel industry, and The Sheri Club for past guests. (Courtesy of ITT Sheraton Corporation)

How to Write an Effective Sales Letter

Think before you write. Many people start writing before they know what they want to say. That's always a mistake. An important factor in business writing—indeed, in any kind of writing—is advance thinking. Before you write a word, ask yourself these questions:

- What am I trying to convey? Clearly define your purpose. Write it in a few words at the top of your rough draft and stick to it.

- Who is my reader? Think in terms of one person, even if you're writing a letter that will ultimately be addressed to 100 persons. Firmly visualize that person in your mind.

- How can I make this letter truly readable? Imagine that the intended recipient has just walked into your office and is sitting across the desk from you. Write to him or her as you would talk to him or her in person.

The best way to become proficient in writing is by observing certain rules—and practicing. Here are eight steps to get you started:

1. Jot down notes in advance on what you want to cover in your writing. Decide which is the most important point and put it up front.

2. Express your thoughts clearly and concisely. Avoid redundant expressions and long, involved sentences. Use personal words—such pronouns as I, my, ours, theirs (as you would in talking to someone).

3. Use concrete words that involve seeing, tasting, touching, feeling, and hearing. For example, avoid abstract terms such as "recreational activity" in favor of concrete words that can be visualized such as "tennis, golf, swimming." Don't say "meeting facilities" if you can truthfully say "12 meeting rooms on the mezzanine."

4. Keep your reader's vocabulary in mind. Although not everybody knows what a "familiarization tour" is, anybody would respond to "Visit us as our guest and see our facilities for yourself." Avoid trite expressions and slang.

5. Keep it active, not passive. For example, "Our staff will prepare the dinner" is better than "The dinner will be prepared by our staff." Place the person doing the action—the doer—before the verb. "The manager invites you to use the pool" is better than "Guests are invited to use the pool."

6. Keep sentences short (15 words or less), and limit paragraphs to one to four short, crisp sentences to ensure easy reading. If you have several key points to stress, bullet them to make them stand out.

7. Be explicit when making requests. State "We'd appreciate your reply by August 28th," rather than "Respond as soon as possible" or "Contact us at your earliest convenience." Dates and deadlines get results.

8. Always stress benefits rather than features. While mentioning "Express Check-in and Check-Out" points out an important feature, adding copy that promises a benefit ("No more waiting in long lines") allows the reader to visualize what the feature actually means to him or her.

Source: Portions of this material were adapted from Robert D. Lilien, "How to Write a Better Letter," *Lodging,* August 1982, pp. 55–59.

and meeting planners to purchase the property's products and services. Like letters, newsletters can be fairly inexpensive to mail and are excellent sources of information about the property.

When using newsletters as direct mail pieces, keep the following in mind:

- *Appearance.* While white paper is adequate, colored paper attracts more attention. Artwork should be kept simple, photographs (if used) should be sharp and clear, and the type should be easily readable. Since readers' eyes can only take in so much copy at a time, most newsletters should be set in two columns. Copy that extends across an entire page tends to be hard to read.[4]

- *Layout.* The reader should be led from one article to the next through the use of bold headlines or enticing artwork. White space should be used skillfully to make the newsletter more attractive and readable.

- *Identification.* The property's logo, name, address, and telephone number should appear on every page of the newsletter. This information can be prominently displayed in a box, or at the bottom of each page, or can appear somewhere in the copy on each page. This repetition makes it easier for the reader to respond to attractive promotions or packages.

While newsletters may cost more than letters to produce and mail, they have the advantages of a longer reading life (many are passed on to friends and acquaintances) and more room for illustrations. The problem of timing may also be solved with newsletters. Most newsletters are produced on a regular basis, and seasonal special editions can be included to coincide with peak buying times.

Collateral Materials. Whether used separately, in conjunction with letters, or enclosed in bills or business correspondence, collateral materials play an important role in direct mail. For example, the Denver Inn used collateral materials creatively in a direct mail campaign that featured a teddy bear theme. For the first mailing, travel agents were sent a colorful direct mail piece with a tiny teddy bear attached. Responding travel agents were sent a second mailing that included a small, stuffed teddy bear wearing a Denver Inn banner with the property's toll-free reservations number printed on it.

Some collateral materials such as fliers are inexpensive to produce and can be used most effectively in a general mailing or as envelope stuffers in routine correspondence to previous guests. Another inexpensive option is the inclusion of flattering press releases—most people enjoy reading about hotels and restaurants they have visited.

Some collateral materials, such as four-color brochures, are expensive to produce and should not be sent out as a general mailing. It is far more cost-effective to save four-color materials for responding to inquiries.

If the property has a substantial advertising budget, distributing a property magazine is another good way to get the word out about the property, its services, upcoming events, and other news of interest to present and potential guests. Magazines can be as simple as an expanded newsletter or as elaborate as any glossy, full-color magazine found on a newsstand. Properties that wish to take advantage of this effective way to advertise can either make their own publishing arrangements

Exhibit 7   Sample Postcard

Postcards are an economical way to advertise—both in terms of costs of production and mailing—and can be as simple or elaborate as a property desires. This postcard targets meeting planners. (Courtesy of AMC Convention Center Sales, Atlanta, Georgia)

or contact the several printing companies that offer "shell" magazines—four-color presentations that include articles of general interest and space for the property to add its own articles, schedules of events, or advertising. The property may purchase the entire amount of space available—which usually consists of several full pages—or can contract space out to related businesses to help cover expenses.

Specially Designed Direct Mail Pieces. Specially designed direct mail pieces are often used in direct mail campaigns. There are a number of formats or styles that can be used. One of the most popular is the four-page letterhead: a personally typed letter on the first page with three pages of illustrations or descriptive materials following.

Another widely used form is a full-color postcard with a reservation reply card attached (see Exhibit 7). Because of the relatively low costs to produce and mail them, postcards are an attractive option—especially when used for short messages, such as to announce the opening of a restaurant or to solicit inquiries about a package. And postcards require a minimum of handling. In many cases, a bulk mail permit is printed onto the postcard, eliminating the need for stamping.

A postcard is like a mini-billboard; space is limited, making it essential that the message be short yet complete. For best results, you should use sentence fragments whenever possible and bullet or highlight key points. As with any other direct mail piece, the postcard should include the property's name and logo and a way to respond (a toll-free number, for example).

Still other properties use a self-mailer: a specially printed piece that advertises a special promotion or the property itself. A self-mailer saves a property both time and money—there is no need for the piece to be inserted into an envelope and the mailer can be sent third-class.

Even properties on a limited budget can take advantage of using specially designed direct mail pieces. As with other media, there are often cooperative advertising opportunities available, either through promotions with travel-related firms, other properties, or through area or regional tourist entities (see Exhibit 8). As with other co-op efforts, there are potential disadvantages: your business may not benefit as much as the other businesses, or the piece may not be specifically targeted to a desired market segment. But using co-op direct mail may be a viable option for attracting potential consumers that the property could not have reached using its own resources.

Guidelines for Direct Mail Pieces

The following guidelines can be used when creating all types of direct mail pieces.

The AIDA Formula. For best results, many properties use the AIDA formula. AIDA stands for *Attention, Interest, Desire,* and *Action:*

- *Attention.* As mentioned previously, before a direct mail piece can be effective, it must first get the reader's attention, whether that attention is gained through an intriguing teaser on the envelope, a clever caption or drawing on the mailing piece, or the copy itself. The main point of the property's message should be presented at the beginning of the piece. To get read rather than discarded, direct mail pieces must capture attention immediately.

- *Interest.* Once the reader's attention has been captured, it is important to offer the reader the promise of a reward. In other words, his or her interest must be kept through offering an answer to the question, "What's in this for me?"

- *Desire.* If the prospect's interest has been maintained, he or she may then begin to desire to experience what the property has to offer. But doubts may still exist ("Can anything be this good?" "Is there a catch?"). Additional creative copy can both dispel these doubts and enhance the reader's desire.

- *Action.* Just because readers have a desire to respond does not mean they will; the property's message should *ask* for action. If a reply card is enclosed, a postscript may suggest: "Interested? Mail the convenient, postage-paid reply card today!" Or, the copy may note the property's toll-free reservations number.

In order for the AIDA formula to work, the emphasis should be on the consumer; he or she will respond far more favorably when the piece is directed to meeting personal wants and needs. Secondary attention should be placed on considerations such as availability and price. An exception is the direct mail piece designed for travel agents—then availability and price become more important.

The Five Ps. Another approach to developing a direct mail piece can be called the Five Ps. No matter what type of direct mail piece is being designed, with this approach the message should first form a *picture* in the prospect's mind. The prospect should get involved in what the direct mail piece has to offer.

The second part of the message should offer a *promise* and show how the property can fulfill that promise. This portion of the message should clearly define products and services that can make the promise a reality. Features and benefits

Exhibit 8   Sample Co-Op Direct Mailer

Sale Away With Super Hotel Deals!

Long Beach hotels are "sailing away" with great new incentives and value rates if you book rooms July 1, 1992 through December 31, 1993.

Best Western Golden Sails Hotel
Golf & Conference Center
6285 E. Pacific Coast Hwy,
Long Beach, CA 90803
Jeff Horn, GM
310/596-1631
800/762-5333
$59 single/double occupancy. Meeting facilities for up to 1,000 people. Seven-acre courtyard setting on the marina. Private golf course. Located a short 20-minute drive from Disneyland.

Doubletree Hotel & Marina
Los Angeles Worldport
2800 Via Cabrillo Marina
San Pedro, CA 90731
Mary Ann Woods, DOS
310/514-3344
Located on the water overlooking Cabrillo Marina with 10,000 sq. ft. of space. Free parking and area shuttle. Includes one complimentary room night for every 30 room nights booked. Special group rates available.

Holiday Inn Long Beach Airport
2640 Lakewood Blvd.
Long Beach, CA 90815
Kelvin Nanney, DOS
310/597-4401
800/235-9556
"Sale Holiday Inn" package includes sleeping room, meeting space with 25 consumed rooms and Continental breakfast, $49 per room. Special lunch prices available. $59 per room January 16-April 15, 1993. $55 per room April 16-December 31, 1993.

Holiday Inn Long Beach Convention Center
500 E. 1st St.
Long Beach, CA 90802
John McNaughton, DOS
310/435-8511
One complimentary guest room and function room with minimum of 25 guest rooms booked. Complimentary hospitality room and hosted welcome reception with minimum 50 rooms booked.

Hyatt Regency Long Beach
200 South Pine Ave.
Long Beach, CA 90802
Carolyn Austin, DOS
310/491-1234
Walking distance from Shoreline Village and a short water taxi ride to Catalina terminal. All sleeping rooms offer views of the water. $69 per room, 1992; $72 per room, 1993.

Long Beach Airport Marriott
4700 Airport Plaza Dr.
Long Beach, CA 90815
Haley Powers, DOS
310/425-5210
Accommodations and breakfast for two, $69 per room, double occupancy. One complimentary room with every 20 booked.

Ramada Inn Long Beach
5325 E. Pacific Coast Hwy.
Long Beach, CA 90804
Diane Dagostino, DOS
310/597-1341
Complimentary meeting space with minimum 15 guest rooms booked per night. Includes Continental breakfast and unlimited coffee service. Special group rates available.

Ramada Renaissance Long Beach
111 E. Ocean Blvd.
Long Beach, CA 90802
Gary Tate, Dir. Assoc. Sales
310/437-5900
Includes choice of complimentary meeting room or hospitality suite with every 35 rooms booked per night. $85 per room, single or double occupancy.

Sheraton Long Beach
333 E. Ocean Blvd.
Long Beach, CA 90802
Joan Cantarelli, DOS
310/436-3000
$89 per room, double occupancy. Complimentary suite above the 1/40 comp. room policy. Free meeting space if at least 50% of attendees are registered guests. Complimentary Continental breakfast first day of meeting.

Travelodge Hotel Resort & Marina
700 Queensway Dr.
Long Beach, CA 90802
Ian Gee, GM
310/435-7676
"The Best For The Least On The Bay!" Deluxe bayside rooms, meeting space, two meals and complimentary audio visual aids included in your full-service package. $69 per room, double occupancy.

All special offers listed above are subject to availability. Complimentary meeting space will be proportionate to group size.

Look What's Waiting on the Shore!

World-class hotel and meeting facilities await you in Southern California's Long Beach... plus, five-and-a-half miles of oceanfront beach, sunny weather year-round, watersports like windsurfing and parasailing, theater, dinner cruises, the Queen Mary/Spruce Goose and the Toyota Grand Prix! Long Beach's central location makes getting to Disneyland, Knott's Berry Farm, Universal Studios, Hollywood and picturesque Catalina Island a breeze.

Take advantage of these outstanding hotel offers and book your next meeting today.

NO POSTAGE NECESSARY IF MAILED IN THE UNITED STATES

BUSINESS REPLY CARD
FIRST CLASS PERMIT NO. 4947 LONG BEACH, CA
POSTAGE WILL BE PAID BY ADDRESSEE
Long Beach Area Convention and Visitors Council, Inc.
One World Trade Center #900
Long Beach, CA 90831-0300

This mailer, developed by the Long Beach Area Convention and Visitors Council, Inc. of Long Beach, California, promotes the accommodations and attractions of the city to meeting planners. The piece highlights ten area hotels, and includes a business reply card so readers can request additional information on specific properties. As with all co-op advertising, there is no guarantee that the advertisers in this ad will benefit equally. (Courtesy of Long Beach Area Convention and Visitors Council, Inc., Long Beach, California)

should be carefully spelled out. You should never assume that everyone knows what your property stands for and what services it offers.

Next, the message should *prove* what the property is claiming is true. Testimonials, endorsements, success stories, and statistics can be used to support the property's claims.

The fourth part of the message should provide a *push*—tell the prospect exactly what the property wishes him or her to do: fill out a reply card, call a toll-free number, or answer a questionnaire. Because it is so important, the push should be included in the last paragraph or part of a message, and may also be included in the first part. The push should be specific and directly relate to what the direct mail piece has to offer.

The final part of the direct mail piece is a simple *postscript*. When reading a direct mail piece, many people first glance at the top (the letterhead) and the bottom (the signature, and the P.S. if there is one). An interesting postscript can generate reader involvement.

Posting Direct Mail Pieces

There are three basic ways to send direct mail advertising:

1. *First class*—Personal letters and postcards.

2. *Third class single piece*—Booklets, brochures, catalogs.

3. *Third class bulk*—newsletters or other pieces mailed in quantity.

Third class bulk is the most inexpensive way to mail, although it takes longer than first class mail. As of January, 1993, properties using bulk mail must pay an annual fee of $75 for the privilege, in addition to $75 for a mailing permit. Permits are issued for an indefinite period, provided the property mails under the permit at least once during a twelve-month period.

Six criteria must be met for a mailing to qualify for the third class bulk rate:

1. The mailing must consist of a minimum of 250 pieces, or the total weight of the mailing must be 50 pounds.

2. The pieces must be identical in size and weight.

3. The address of each piece must include a zip code.

4. Pieces must be presorted and bundled or sacked according to zip code.

5. The pieces must be separately addressed to different persons and must carry postage permit imprints, meter stamps, or pre-canceled stamps.

6. The mailing must be deposited at the post office which issued the bulk mailing permit, or at a location designated by the postmaster.

These restrictions and additional steps make third class bulk mailings a little more work than first class mailings, but many properties find the savings worth the extra effort. At the current rate, direct mail pieces can be bulk mailed for almost half the cost of first class mail for the first 250,000 pieces mailed in one year.

Insider Insights

John J. Patafio, Jr.
Vice President—Marketing
Ambassador Mail Advertising Company, Inc.
Long Island, New York

John J. Patafio, Jr., has held a number of positions in the direct mail field, including serving as an account executive for John Mather Lupton Advertising Agency and the national advertising manager of Direct Marketing *Magazine. He has held various positions—including sales representative and sales manager—for Ambassador Mail Advertising Company, Inc., one of the largest mail advertising production organizations in the country. Patafio has also served as president of several industry organizations, among which are the Association of Advertising Men and Women (New York City), the Long Island Advertising Club, and the Long Island Public Relations Association.*

What is direct mail advertising? Direct mail advertising is any advertising sent through the governmental postal or other mail delivery system at a time decided by the advertiser, to a list of names controlled by the advertiser. This definition sets direct mail advertising apart from advertising in trade magazines, which are also delivered through the postal system. Trade magazines are mailed at a time decided by the publisher to a list of names controlled by the publisher.

Direct mail advertising is a medium exclusively controlled by you, the advertiser. Using the mail, you become your own publisher. You control who will receive your advertising messages, when and how often your messages will be sent, what format they will take, and how much they will cost. When you advertise in another medium you must accept that medium's audience. That audience is never 100% your audience. In direct mail, you control your audience, because you control your mailing list.

For direct mail to be most effective, it should be part of your annual marketing program. It may be produced professionally by your advertising agency, if your agency has a direct mail advertising capability. If your agency does not (and many agencies don't), direct marketing agencies and mailing services should be looked into. It's quite all right to have a general advertising agency, a separate public relations agency, and an independent direct mail facility, if your general advertising agency lacks public relations and direct mail expertise.

The producers of direct mail advertising quite often have special creativity as well as excellent production capability. Mailing services that offer printing, mailing, data processing, and fulfillment service quite often can provide you with considerable assistance with copy, artwork, and even with selecting your mailing list, resulting in a single-source organization to work with you. Your communication management team would then consist of your advertising agency, your public relations agency, and your direct mail agency. All three should be involved in planning sessions if they are to put their best efforts into your marketing program.

Measuring Direct Mail Campaigns

The cost-effectiveness of a direct mail campaign can be measured by comparing campaign costs with the level of reader response.

Campaign Costs

To address the first consideration, let's look at the classic four-part direct mail package—a mailing envelope, a letter, a brochure or other piece of collateral material, and a reply form. In developing this direct mail package, there are a number of costs involved:

- Material costs: paper, envelopes, collateral materials or specialty items used as collateral materials

- Production costs: ad agency or freelance personnel costs (if used); typesetting, artwork or photographs; printing costs

- Labor costs: costs of compiling the mailing list if it is created in-house; costs of inserting, sorting, stapling, and so on; costs of record-keeping (responses, updating lists, etc.)

- Other costs: mailing list fees, postage

Many properties employ mailing services or lettershops to reduce labor costs and save time. The mailing list and the components of the direct mail package are delivered to the mailing service, which stuffs the envelopes, sorts the mail, and meters and mails the finished pieces. Using a mailing service is often more cost-effective than hiring additional office staff or burdening the property's regular staff with a large mailing.

Reader Response

The success of any direct mail campaign is measured primarily by reader response. To measure reader response, a response code or number should be printed on direct mail pieces. If a piece is being sent to the Midwest, the South, and the Northeast, for example, the mail for each of these areas can be coded with a particular number that allows for tabulating the responses. In the case of pieces that invite response via a toll-free number, a particular operator's name or number can be used for tabulation—respondents in the Midwest might be directed to ask for Operator 1, for example. Responses can be tabulated to determine which list is most effective, which market segment is responding most favorably to the promotion, and which areas seem most profitable for follow-up promotions.

A test mailing is sometimes used to measure reader response. With a test mailing, you mail inexpensive pieces to targeted audiences—audiences defined by occupation or geographic location, for example. The response to this test mailing gives you an idea of the number of responses you can expect from a regular mailing. You can send out more expensive direct mail pieces to a particularly responsive market segment or geographic location.

It is also possible to measure the potential of two similar package promotions by split-testing a direct mail list. If, for example, you want to test whether a $10

Some Important Direct Mail Do's and Don'ts

DO

- Keep in mind that direct mail is a pinpoint or "rifle" medium that is most effective when used to reach specific markets.
- Compile or purchase mailing lists with utmost care. The mailing list is the single most important element of a mailing. List brokers are professionals; use their knowledge. Tell them your objectives and let them suggest the best list(s).
- Keep lists up-to-date. Lists deteriorate at a rate of 20% or more a year, and "dead" names cost money. You can use a mailing service to computerize your house list if it is not already on computer.
- Use the reader's name whenever possible; direct mail is the only medium in which you can.
- Spell names right. A person's name is his or her most important possession.
- Insist on quality production and careful attention to details. The impression readers get from your mailing is the impression they get of your hotel. Make sure that first impression says "I care."
- Make your copy interesting and persuasive. But, most of all, make it sincere and believable. Promise only what you can deliver—and deliver what you promise. A sales letter is not business correspondence; for best results, you may wish to use the services of a professional copywriter.
- Be consistent. Repeat your important sales points often.
- Tell readers exactly what you want them to do. Ask for the sale.
- Follow up inquiries fast. Be sure requested information is furnished.

DON'T

- Try to say too many things in one mailing. Make one or two important points clearly and completely.
- Make it hard for your readers to reach you. See that your address and phone number appear on every major element of your mailing.
- Mail duplicate pieces to the same person. Duplicates cost money for printing and postage and create an impression of management carelessness and disinterest.
- Forget to plan and prepare for following up leads. Make sure that literature and employees are available in sufficient numbers to handle responses.
- Tire of a good theme or program before your readers do. They pay a little less attention to your promotion than you do. Only *results* can tell you when a good idea is wearing thin.
- Quit after one or two mailings. Good salesmanship and good advertising require patience and persistence.
- Try to "do it yourself." Direct mail is a complex medium, and a qualified consultant can help you in two ways—by maximizing results and minimizing production and postage costs.

Source: Adapted from information provided by John J. Patafio, Jr., Vice President of Marketing, Ambassador Mail Advertising Co.

Direct Mail Costs

Typical costs per direct mail piece are as follows:

LIST	$.065
COMPUTER	.005
LABEL	.005
LETTER	.025
BROCHURE	.040
RESPONSE DEVICE	.020
ENVELOPE	.020
LETTERSHOP	.020
POSTAGE	.120
TOTAL	$.320

The following formula can be used to determine the costs per response of a direct mail effort:

$$\frac{\text{Cost per piece} \times \text{number of pieces mailed}}{\text{Number of responses}} = \text{Cost per response}$$

Assuming the cost per piece is $.32, and that 2,500 pieces were mailed and generated a response rate of 4%, the cost per response would be calculated as follows:

$$\frac{\$.32 \times 2,500 \text{ pieces}}{100 \text{ responses}} = \$8$$

While the $8 figure calculated in this example may seem high, it is important to remember that this cost is a *front-end cost* only. "Front-end cost" refers to the cost per response from the initial mailing. Over a period of time, the respondents to the initial mailing will likely respond to additional offers. Therefore, the property will make money on the *back-end*—the subsequent responses—in addition to having acquired each respondent for a house list (an additional savings on the back-end; the property no longer has to purchase these respondents' names).

If the piece was mailed to meeting planners and achieved a 1% sales rate, that means that the direct mailing produced 25 meetings (2,500 × .01 = 25). If the dollar income from these meetings is tracked, the return on the direct mail investment can be determined with the following formula:

$$\frac{\text{Total income from the 25 meetings}}{\text{Cost of direct mailing}} = \text{Return on direct mail investment}$$

Continuing with our example, if the cost of the direct mailing was $800 (2,500 pieces × .32), and the 25 meetings generated $25,000 in income, then the return on the direct mail investment for this campaign was $31.25 for every dollar spent.

---

reduction on a weekend package would produce enough additional business to justify the cost, you can mail two equally numbered batches of letters to prospects; one mailing would promote a $145 rate, while the other would offer rooms at $135.

The response would quickly indicate whether the lower price produced enough additional business to justify the price reduction. A split test assigns every other name from the mailing list to one promotion, the remaining names to the other. Whichever promotion draws the most responses is the better package, and the one that will be used in future mailings.

The audience that receives the mailing influences cost-effectiveness in terms of sales per direct mail piece. You may send out 2,500 letters to individuals and 2,500 letters to travel agents and group meeting planners, for example, and even though the initial cost of production and mailing is the same, the resulting sales may vary greatly. It is likely that more business will be generated by the travel agents and the meeting planners, so their mailing will probably be more cost-effective. While this fact may lead you to send out more direct mail pieces to sources of group business, a property's desired guest mix also has to be considered. You may need to continue sending direct mail pieces to individual potential guests in order to maintain your property's desired guest mix.

When monitoring responses, keep in mind that it may require six to eight mailings before the public is ready to buy. In many cases, a campaign begins slowly, but response increases with each mailing; a famous advertising man put it this way: "Continuous direct mail advertising, like continuous work, is the most effective. If there is any enterprise a quitter should leave alone, it is direct mail advertising." This does not mean that every campaign has to be a series campaign; as mentioned previously, single mailings can be used to announce special events or services, and may also be sent to coincide with major holidays and other times when specific major market segments may be planning their vacations.

Inquiry Handling and Fulfillment. To make the most of direct mail responses, inquiries should be answered at once. Many direct mail pieces are offers of additional information; the key to an actual sale is the prompt mailing of the material requested. The cost of additional office help to accomplish this should be figured into the direct mail budget. Before initiating a direct mail program, you should detail exactly how leads will be followed up, particularly if requests will be coming in from widely dispersed geographic areas. It may make more sense to rotate the distribution of mail by geographic area, allowing adequate response time for inquiries to come in from one area before distributing direct mail pieces to another.

Many properties, unfortunately, do not prepare adequately to respond to inquiries. The results are wasted advertising dollars and lost business (both at the time of the inquiry and in the future). Therefore, to ensure cost-effectiveness and customer goodwill, it is essential to establish a system for responding *before* the advertising or mailing appears.

While different markets will require different approaches and materials, all inquiry packets—mailings to prospects that have requested information—should include the following elements:

- *A fast response.* Responses to inquiries should be mailed first class within a week of receiving the inquiry. If the property does not have adequate staff to handle this, it may opt to hire temporary help or the services of a lettershop.

- *A cover letter.* Whether it is a personalized letter (which is preferred) or a form letter addressed to specific target markets, a cover letter should always be sent with the inquiry packet. The cover letter should thank the respondent for taking the time to respond and explain what is included in the inquiry packet.

- *Printed literature.* Professionally produced and up-to-date literature should always be included in the inquiry packet. Materials should be targeted to the correct market segment, and include only those materials relating to the advertisement or offer that generated the inquiry. (It is a waste of time and money to send leisure-oriented materials to a meeting planner or banquet information to a family group.) Packets should include only the printed literature needed to make the sale.

- *An action element.* An inquiry packet should include a means for the recipient to request additional information—either by mail or by a visit from a salesperson—or provide a toll-free number to enable the prospect to respond immediately. Including an additional or special offer ("Respond by December 15 and receive a 10% discount") may stimulate a buying decision.

Following these guidelines—especially when it comes to a prompt response—may give your property an edge over the competition. How you respond to a potential guest's request for information provides his or her first impression of the property's service.

Conclusion

Direct mail, when properly planned, managed, and followed up, can be an excellent source of future referrals, rooms and facilities business, and repeat business. By using a good mailing list, designing attractive direct mail pieces, offering appropriate benefits to each targeted market segment, and promptly following up on responses, a property can build an excellent guest base at a relatively low cost.

Endnotes

1. Direct Marketing Association's Statistical Fact Book, 1990–1991.
2. The Hospitality Sales and Marketing Association International Foundation publishes actual samples of hospitality direct mail programs. *Marketing Your Hotel Through Direct Mail* can be ordered by writing: HSMAI, 1300 L Street, Suite 800, Washington, DC 20005.
3. *Direct Mail and Local Media Advertising Guide,* prepared by TWA, p. 22.
4. *Direct Mail and Local Media Advertising Guide,* p. 37.

Key Terms

AIDA
business list
commercial list
consumer list
direct mail advertising

general list
guest profile
house list
inquiry packet
lettershop

list broker

mailing list

occupant list

resident list

rifle approach

self-mailer

shell magazine

shotgun approach

split test

test mailing

Review Questions

1. What are the advantages of direct mail advertising?

2. What drawbacks must be considered before incorporating direct mail into a property's overall advertising plan?

3. What information should a guest profile contain?

4. What are some of the factors that help determine whether the direct mail campaign will be a series of mailings or a single mailing?

5. What are three basic categories of mailing lists? Which list is most effective?

6. What factors should be considered before purchasing a commercial mailing list?

7. What are some questions that should be considered before developing a direct mail piece?

8. What are some advantages of direct mail letters?

9. What is the AIDA formula?

10. What are six criteria that must be met for a mailing to qualify for the third-class bulk rate?

11. What costs are involved in developing a typical direct mail package?

Chapter Outline

Radio Advertising
    Selecting Radio Stations
    Developing Radio Ads
        Types of Radio Ads
    Radio Ad Costs
        Buying Radio Airtime
    Measuring the Effectiveness of Radio Ads
Television Advertising
    Selecting TV Stations
    Developing TV Ads
        Types of TV Ads
    TV Ad Costs
        Buying TV Airtime
    Measuring the Effectiveness of TV Ads
Video Advertising
    Video Brochures
    Video Magazines

13

Broadcast Advertising

Until the twentieth century, advertising was limited largely to the printed word. Today, however, through radio, television, and video advertising, a property has many exciting alternatives available to get its message to thousands, even millions, of potential guests at one time.

Radio Advertising

Radio is an excellent saturation medium: that is, radio is a medium that allows a property to repeat its message with considerable frequency to reach a large number of people. There are over 7,000 radio stations in the United States, and 500 million radios in homes, offices, and automobiles.[1] Radio's reach is everywhere, and, best of all, radio is a selective medium. Unlike commercial television, which is programmed for a mass audience, radio stations generally appeal to a more focused audience. There are rock, top-40, country, classical, all-talk, all-news, and ethnic music stations. Before planning a radio strategy, you should know the demographics of a station's audience, and the best times to advertise a particular message.

To reach the teen audience, top-40 and rock stations offer the most exposure. Many properties overlook this important market, but teenagers are generally an affluent group and are excellent prospects for restaurant and special local promotion advertising. In addition, teenagers often influence the family's choice of vacation spots, so this market may well be worth the advertising dollars spent.

To reach people in the 18-to-30 age bracket, progressive rock, soft rock, adult contemporary, and golden-oldie stations are effective avenues. Most people in this age group either work or go to school, so the best times to reach them are drive times (6:00 to 10:00 A.M. and 3:00 to 7:00 P.M.), in the evening after 7:30 P.M., and on weekends after 10:00 P.M.

If the target audience is families, messages can be offered on golden-oldie, adult contemporary, country, all-talk, and all-news stations. Surveys have shown that radio stations reach their largest family audiences between 6:00 A.M. and 7:00 P.M. on weekends. A large audience of upscale families and working women can also be reached between 7:00 P.M. and midnight.

Selecting Radio Stations

You should consider several factors when selecting the radio station or stations that will best get your property's message across to its targeted audiences. Demographics, costs, a station's image, and special promotions offered by radio stations to attract advertisers will all play a part in the selection process.

Almost all radio stations offer demographic information on their listening audiences, but before making a final selection, a property's marketing and sales staff, advertising staff, or ad agency representative should listen to each station. Important factors to note are the number and frequency of ads. Are there ads from competitors? Are ads lumped together or are they spread out over each hour? How many ads does the station run on an average day? A property's message might easily get lost if ads are run too frequently, or if a competitor can afford to advertise more often during a certain time period.

Before deciding on a station, it is important to determine:

- *Reach.* How many households are reached by the station? What are the demographics of the audience in specific time periods? Early morning audiences may not be the same as late evening audiences, for example.

- *Frequency.* How often will a property's message be aired? Will it be aired during the target market's prime listening time?

- *Cost per thousand (CPM).* How much will it cost the property to reach 1,000 listeners?

- *Target market group(s).* Does the station reach the specific audience or audiences targeted by the property? If not, is there another station that does? If the target market is spread out over a large area, how cost-effective would it be to split advertising between two or more stations?

Information that can help you choose the right station(s) can be found from two major sources: Arbitron Ratings Company and Birch Radio. Arbitron Ratings, the nation's largest ratings service, independently monitors radio stations and offers a number of reports relating to listener statistics, including the Local Market Report; Arbitron Information on Demand (AID), a report that can be accessed by computer to provide information on such variables as demographics, listening patterns at various times of the day, etc.; and an Arbitron Radio Ratings Ethnic Composition Report, which can assist properties desiring to reach specific ethnic groups. Arbitron's competition, Birch Radio, is a monthly service that issues reports based on telephone recall interviews (audience response to messages previously heard). This service can assist a property in determining the effectiveness of an ad.

The decision-maker for selecting radio stations varies from property to property. At small properties the general manager may be ultimately responsible for choosing radio stations. At midsize properties, these decisions may fall to the marketing director, who may request recommendations from the property's advertising staff or ad agency. In the case of large properties, recommendations are usually given by ad agencies, and final decisions may be made by the marketing director or by another designated member of the property's management team, such as the director of advertising.

Selecting a radio station can be confusing, but there is a way to make the selection process easier and at the same time promote your property to the stations that will be advertising its products and services: a "Radio Day."

Michael J. Dimond
Corporate Vice President of Marketing
Gaylord Entertainment Company
Nashville, Tennessee

Michael Dimond held a number of positions within the Hyatt Hotels Corporation from 1962 to 1973, including serving as national sales manager for the chain's New York City properties during his final three years with the firm. He has also served as the national sales director for Doral Hotels of Florida, and was vice president of marketing for Opryland Hotel from 1975–1985. In 1983 Dimond was named chairman of the corporate marketing committee for Opryland USA, Inc. He later served as vice president of the Boca Raton Hotel and Club, as general manager of Saddlebrook Resort, and as senior vice president of marketing for Caesars Palace in Las Vegas before assuming his present duties as corporate vice president of marketing for Opryland Hotel in Nashville, Tennessee. Dimond is an active member of many industry organizations and has served as vice president of external affairs for Meeting Planners International and as the first vice president of the Hospitality Sales & Marketing Association International. Dimond has also won a number of awards, including Salesman of the Year (Insurance Conference Planners), Supplier of the Year (Meeting Planners International), 1984 Marketing Executive of the Year (HSMAI), and recognition as one of the nation's 25 top travel executives in Business Travel News.

Television delivers a message immediately to large numbers of people. Although areas of programming such as sports or special-interest subject matter allow television to be targeted to fairly narrow groups, most television programming is designed to appeal to the largest possible audience.

Frequency is important if the TV ad's message is to be thoroughly understood and remembered. Cost will depend on the length of the commercial. The primary unit of commercial length is 30 seconds, although 10-, 15-, and 60-second lengths are also common. A 60-second spot generally costs twice as much as a 30-second spot; however, a 10-second spot is 50% to 60% of the cost of a 30-second spot, and a 15-second spot is about 75% of the cost of a 30-second commercial.

Television requires a fairly lengthy lead time in terms of commercial production. Commercial production and purchase of time must be planned well in advance to assure the ad's exposure during programming that will best contribute to a property's image.

One of the best uses of television is to purchase time during programs whose content ties in with the property or its message. A special program on Las Vegas, for example, would be an excellent vehicle for a Las Vegas property's commercial. Or, long-term sponsorship of a local sports team can stimulate community goodwill and provide local identification for a property.

(continued)

Insider Insights *(continued)*

Radio is used more for frequency than for high reach. You must buy time at a lot of radio stations in order to reach a mass audience, since radio offers such a wide variety of stations. But radio is useful when the property wishes to closely target a particular audience segment. Radio is also used to announce special events or promotions as they arise, or to boost sales on an as-needed basis.

Production of radio spots can be quick and inexpensive. In fact, an advertiser can choose to have copy read live by a station announcer and avoid expensive production costs. The most common length for radio commercials is 60 seconds, although 30-second spots are available at 80%—or more—of the 60-second costs. Rarely are radio spots under 30 seconds. The rates for radio commercials are highly negotiable and are based on a combination of audience size, ratings, and supply and demand.

The concept of a Radio Day is simple. Each radio station is contacted by phone and follow-up letter and asked to come to the property and give a 30-minute presentation on what the station has to offer. Each station is told which target markets the property wishes to reach, and asked to bring demographic data, information on marketing strategies, and a sample tape of typical programming (see Exhibit 1).

At the conclusion of the presentations, all of the station managers or salespeople can be invited to a complimentary reception or buffet. The station representatives may be told the date of the final decision at that time.

Selecting radio stations in this way prevents executive wear and tear, and gives the property's marketing or advertising staff an opportunity to review all pertinent data in a relatively short time. It is also an excellent way to develop rapport with the local media.

Developing Radio Ads

Once you've selected a station, the next step is to decide how to best present what the property wants to promote.

For the most part, a radio ad should keep to one general idea. Ads should be tailored to specific market segments. Background music, sound effects, and method of announcing are very important. Some properties opt for a local disc jockey or celebrity to announce the ad. This technique can give the ad credibility, especially when the announcer has a large following. But no matter what the property's choice, it is important to create an ad that will stand out from the rest (see Exhibit 2).

Since radio advertising cannot make use of the visual impact common to print and television ads, radio spots must be creative. Since a radio ad can only be heard—leaving behind nothing for the listener to use as a reference should he or she have a question—the message must be memorable. Products and services should be mentioned often.

Exhibit 1   Sample Radio Media Kits

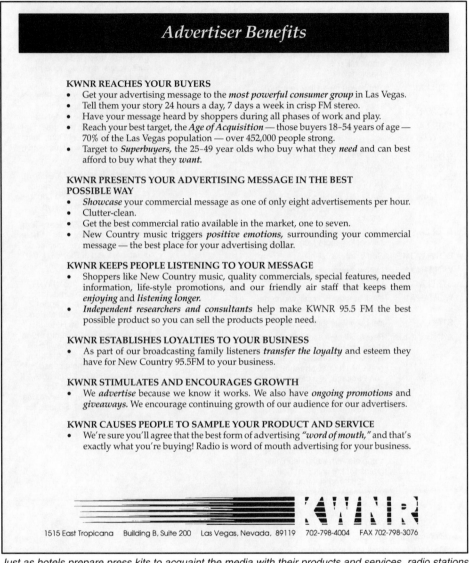

Advertiser Benefits

KWNR REACHES YOUR BUYERS
- Get your advertising message to the *most powerful consumer group* in Las Vegas.
- Tell them your story 24 hours a day, 7 days a week in crisp FM stereo.
- Have your message heard by shoppers during all phases of work and play.
- Reach your best target, the *Age of Acquisition* — those buyers 18–54 years of age — 70% of the *Las Vegas* population — over 452,000 people strong.
- Target to *Superbuyers,* the 25–49 year olds who buy what they *need* and can best afford to buy what they *want.*

KWNR PRESENTS YOUR ADVERTISING MESSAGE IN THE BEST POSSIBLE WAY
- *Showcase* your commercial message as one of only eight advertisements per hour.
- Clutter-clean.
- Get the best commercial ratio available in the market, one to seven.
- New Country music triggers *positive emotions,* surrounding your commercial message — the best place for your advertising dollar.

KWNR KEEPS PEOPLE LISTENING TO YOUR MESSAGE
- Shoppers like New Country music, quality commercials, special features, needed information, life-style promotions, and our friendly air staff that keeps them *enjoying* and *listening longer.*
- *Independent researchers and consultants* help make KWNR 95.5 FM the best possible product so you can sell the products people need.

KWNR ESTABLISHES LOYALTIES TO YOUR BUSINESS
- As part of our broadcasting family listeners *transfer the loyalty* and esteem they have for New Country 95.5FM to your business.

KWNR STIMULATES AND ENCOURAGES GROWTH
- We *advertise* because we know it works. We also have *ongoing promotions* and *giveaways.* We encourage continuing growth of our audience for our advertisers.

KWNR CAUSES PEOPLE TO SAMPLE YOUR PRODUCT AND SERVICE
- We're sure you'll agree that the best form of advertising *"word of mouth,"* and that's exactly what you're buying! Radio is word of mouth advertising for your business.

1515 East Tropicana   Building B, Suite 200   Las Vegas, Nevada, 89119   702-798-4004   FAX 702-798-3076

Just as hotels prepare press kits to acquaint the media with their products and services, radio stations prepare media kits to sell potential advertisers on the benefits of advertising on their radio stations. Types of information prepared for radio media kits usually include program schedules, special programming and events information, advertising information and rates, demographics, ratings information, and testimonials from satisfied advertisers. This page from KWNR's media kit outlines benefits advertisers will enjoy when they advertise on KWNR. (Courtesy of KWNR, Las Vegas, Nevada)

A typical radio ad includes:

- *An attention grabber.* It is essential to reach listeners immediately, before they switch to another station. This can be done with sounds or music as well as copy.

Exhibit 2   Sample Successful Radio Advertising

SAWGRASS Radio :60	PIER 66 Radio :60
(office sounds in background)	
WOMAN #1: Stella, you notice anything weird about Mr. Hastings?	TOM: Boy, it's good to be home again. I wonder who called? *SFX: (Click, rewind phone message machine)*
STELLA: Ahhh, you mean like wearing sunglasses in the office?	RAY: *(telephone voice, beep)* Tom. It's Ray. I'm going to spend the weekend at Pier 66. Meet me there. They've got this great Get Acquainted Summer Deal. Just 25 bucks a day if we share the room.
WOMAN #1: Well, ya.	
STELLA: Mmmm, mmm.	
WOMAN #1: And look at his feet.	
STELLA: He's wearing golf shoes.	
WOMAN #1 Right.	JONI: *(second message; SFX/Beep)* Tom, this is Joni, Sally's friend. Meet me at the Pier Top Lounge at Pier 66 Friday night. Bye.
STELLA: Uh!	
WOMAN #1: You know at the coffee area, he asked me if he could play through.	RAY: *(third message; SFX/Beep)* Tom, Ray again. Sunday night. Where have you been?! You missed a great weekend at Pier 66. I met this terrific gal named Joni.
STELLA: Oh, well, listen, I caught him at his desk, hanging ten, yelling	
BOTH WOMEN: Surf's up!	DON PARDO: *(SFX soap opera music)* Will Ray find out about Tom and Joni? Will Joni find out about Tom and Ray? Find out at Fort Lauderdale's Pier 66 Hotel and Marina, the 22-acre island resort on the Intracoastal. They'll be talking about it around the pool, on the courts, in the jacuzzis, at the restaurants and high above it all in the revolving Pier Top Lounge. Make your reservations now. Call 525-6666. So long for now from Pier 66.
WOMAN #1: I know, I heard that.	
STELLA: Mmmm, mmm.	
WOMAN #1: Well, at least he's still wearing a tie.	
STELLA: Ya, but with a tennis outfit?	
ANNOUNCER: People all over Jacksonville are driving themselves to distraction. A beautiful distraction. Sawgrass. With our Commuter Vacation Package, you can go from desk to dunes in 30 minutes or less. Stay in the Sawgrass Resort Village, play golf, tennis or just relax on the beach after work and be back in the office the next day. Give your family a week or weekend at Sawgrass, complete with supervised programs for the children. Call 285-2261 and say you want to drive yourself to distraction. No one at work will know you're on vacation, unless you get carried away.	
(office sounds in background)	
WOMAN #1: Stella, what's he doing in the secretarial pool?	
STELLA: I don't know. Looks like a half gainer.	
(springboard)	
STELLA: Stand back.	
(splash)	

Both of these award-winning radio spots use an attention grabbing statement, both use a humorous approach to keep the listener's attention, and both give the listener an opportunity to act on the property's offer. (Source: *The Art of Hotel & Travel Advertising, A Look at the Past—A Guide to the Future* [Washington, D.C.: Hotel Sales & Marketing Association International, 1987], pp. 53-54.)

- *A message.* An ad's message should focus on one idea only and should be clear and direct; unnecessary information should not be included. The property's name should be mentioned early and often. Once name awareness has been built, the ad should stretch the listener's imagination: word pictures, references to current events, imaginative sound effects, and music can all add to the impact of the message. Since the ad cannot be retained to be reread, important points should be repeated. Listeners should be given reasons to call or visit rather than be overwhelmed with a barrage of property facts.

- *A call to action.* Radio is an excellent tool for building urgency, and you should not neglect to ask for the sale. The ad should urge the listener to "Call for reservations now," "Drop by for a visit today," or "Call our toll-free reservations line." Since it is not as easy to get a response with radio as it is with print advertising (there is no way to include a coupon, you can't display the name, address, and phone number of your property, and so on), the ad should make it as convenient as possible to respond. Many advertisers, however, do not use telephone numbers in radio advertising since they are difficult to remember (many people who are listening to the radio are in their cars or otherwise occupied, making it difficult to jot down numbers). To combat this problem, some stations offer the option of calling the station for additional information. If this is not possible, repeating the property's name at the end of the message makes it easier for listeners to remember the property and look up its number in the telephone directory.

After radio copy has been written, it is not enough to read it; it must be *listened to* in order to judge its impact on radio listeners. The ad should be judged in terms of clarity and interest, and for compatibility with the station's format or programming. Properties can get help in this area from the radio station itself. Most radio stations can provide background music, sound effects, and technical assistance (most of these services are offered as part of the ad price). If the property is part of a chain, the property may use special "donut" ads that have been prepared by corporate offices (see Exhibit 3). Donut ads are either 30- or 60-second prerecorded ads (usually music and a voice-over) that leave room for individual property messages. The prerecorded tapes are taken to the radio station along with individual property copy for final production.

Types of Radio Ads. There are several types of radio ads that can be used by a property:

1. *Straight announcement.* This type of ad simply lists the benefits of the product offered and asks the listener to act. In most cases, little or no background music is used. Straight announcements can work well for a property, but the copy must be interesting to attract and keep the listener's attention.

2. *Musical.* Musical ads rely heavily on jingles or a musical background to promote a product or service. There are several ways that music can be used. In some ads, the entire message is sung. In others, jingles are interspersed throughout the message—the ad may begin and close with a jingle, for example. Still other ads use background music that the advertiser hopes listeners

Exhibit 3   Sample Donut Ad

Sample 60 sec. "Come to Sheraton" w/36 sec. donut	
SINGERS: (MUSIC/VOCAL — approx. 15.5 seconds)	When you plan a trip you know Excitement's in the air Any place in the world you go You want it all right there.
SAMPLE LOCAL ANNCR: (Music under) (Approx. 36 sec.)	Come to Sheraton you'll love the life Next time you're going to New York for business, bring your family and stay through the weekend! Taste a Sheraton holiday in the Big Apple! The Sheraton Centre is right in the heart of the city. so it's perfect for business and a great family weekend! Here's our Big Apple weekend package—3 days and 2 nights of wining, dining and entertainment. A Continental breakfast every morning … delicious prime rib accompanied by fine wine for dinner and an evening of entertainment and dancing. Just call the Sheraton Centre at 581-1000 or ask your travel agent.
SINGERS: (MUSIC UP)	Come to Sheraton you'll love the life You'll love the life at Sheraton.

LEGAL REQUIREMENTS/RESTRICTIONS

As part of Sheraton's agreement concerning the use of this recording, we are legally required to quote the following:

"This commercial has been produced under the provisions of AFTRA National Code of Fair Practice for Transcription for broadcasting purposes, and its use is governed thereby. Accordingly, the dealer (Sheraton Manager) is granted a limited license to use this commercial only as a local program or commercial on local non-interconnected stations."

Please note that this commercial is not cleared for use in all countries. Currently, this Radio Donut is for use in the United States and Canada only.

This donut ad, from the Sheraton Corporation, provides a music/vocal background with a 36-second gap for individual property information. Note legal information at the bottom of the suggested ad copy. (Courtesy of ITT Sheraton Corporation)

will begin to associate with the product. A classic example is Coca-Cola's use of "I'd Like to Teach the World to Sing" in many of its ads in the early seventies. Many people who hear the song associate it with Coca-Cola.

3. *Slice of life or problem solution.* This is an ad in which characters discuss a problem and propose the product as the solution. While these ads can be either factual or humorous, they must quickly present the problem—a dilemma over which restaurant the family should choose, for example—and quickly propose

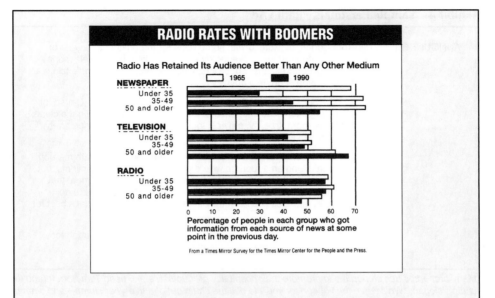

RADIO RATES WITH BOOMERS

Radio Has Retained Its Audience Better Than Any Other Medium

☐ 1965   ■ 1990

NEWSPAPER
Under 35
35-49
50 and older

TELEVISION
Under 35
35-49
50 and older

RADIO
Under 35
35-49
50 and older

0   10   20   30   40   50   60   70

Percentage of people in each group who got
information from each source of news at some
point in the previous day.

From a Times Mirror Survey for the Times Mirror Center for the People and the Press.

Targeting Baby Boomers with Radio:
How Radio Worked for an Arizona Resort

When the Westin La Paloma resort near Tucson, Arizona, wanted to boost its summer occupancy, it turned to radio advertising. The result was a record-breaking 16,000 room nights sold over what was generally an off-season period.

The resort's first step was to consult with Western Media Corporation of San Diego, California, a firm that works strictly with the hospitality industry. The firm's president, Phil Goodman, is a nationally recognized expert on—and advocate of advertising to—the baby-boomer generation. He planned La Paloma's advertising to reach this lucrative 25- to 54- year-old market.

The property's campaign, "Summer Magic Getaway," featured a special price of $69 and stressed that the price was a "limited offer." Ads were aired on Tucson and Phoenix radio stations that broadcast to the targeted baby-boomer market.

The result was 16,000 room nights sold (compared to 8,500 the previous year). The resort sold out all but one weekend between Memorial Day and Labor Day, proving Goodman's belief that the baby-boomer generation represents one of the most lucrative markets in the country.

According to Goodman, who publishes *The Boomer Report* newsletter and advises hospitality firms regarding the mind-sets and needs of baby-boomers, boomers earn over $985 billion annually, and spend money whether they have it or not, making them prime candidates for the hospitality product. In addition, boomers like radio, making it an extremely cost-effective medium to reach them (see chart above).

Baby-boomers are particularly fond of "oldies-all-the-time" formats. (According to the March 15, 1991, issue of Goodman's newsletter, the number of radio stations that play oldies is up 166% since 1985.) For maximum effectiveness, Goodman suggests that ads should be geared toward women, who make 80% of the buying decisions for this market segment.

Exhibit 4   Sample Personality Radio Ad

ANNOUNCER:	Hi, Tom Bodett for Motel 6 with some relief for the business traveler or anyone on the road trying like the dickens to make a buck. Well, money doesn't grow on trees and I'm probably not the first person who's told you that, but maybe I can help anyway.
	Why not stay at Motel 6 and save some of that money? 'Cause for around 22 bucks, the lowest price of any national chain, you'll get a clean, comfortable room, free TV, movies, local calls, and long distance ones without a motel service charge.
	No, we don't have a swinging disco or a mood lounge with maroon leather chairs and an aquarium where you can entertain your clients, but that's O.K. I got a better idea. Take the money you save and meet that client in town. Besides, they probably know all the best places to go anyway. Let them tell you what they know best and you do what's best for business.
	Call _____ for reservations at Motel 6. I'm Tom Bodett for Motel 6 ... and we'll leave the light on for you.

Many properties use celebrities to promote their hospitality products. Motel 6 used Tom Bodett (and the chain's slogan, "We'll leave the light on for you") to pull the chain out of a five-year slump—and catapult its radio spokesperson to national prominence. (Tom Bodett ad courtesy of Motel 6 and the Richards Group [an advertising agency])

the solution: "At XYZ Hotel, there's a restaurant for every taste under one roof."

4. *Personality.* Personality ads rely on the talents of the announcer to promote the product (see Exhibit 4). In many cases, a local celebrity, disc jockey, or talk show host is chosen. Some hotels hire a professional actor or a prominent figure to lend credibility to the property's product. This can be especially effective if the personality has influence over the target audience.

Radio Ad Costs

There are a number of factors that will affect radio ad costs. First, you must decide whether the ad will be live or taped for presentation. A live ad usually requires less work—the script and background music or special sound effects (if any) are brought to the station and the only costs incurred are for airtime (unless a celebrity has been hired to read the script) and the script.

In the case of a taped or recorded ad, costs of production have to be considered. Since many hospitality professionals are not familiar with broadcast media, it is often necessary to hire an agency to develop the ad. Development involves writing the script (costs may be lower if there is someone on the property's staff who can write an effective message), casting an announcer or an entire cast for the production, finding background music (this may entail acquiring taped music or hiring musicians or singers), and recording the ad several times. In most cases, the music, sound effects, and vocals are recorded separately and mixed on a final master tape. This master tape is then duplicated (the duplicate tapes are called "dubs") and sent to the radio station(s) for broadcast.

Celebrities Tout Hospitality Products

Celebrities have been a staple of print ads for a number of firms, and the hospitality industry is taking advantage of the attention celebrities attract by featuring well-known figures in their print and broadcast advertising. Choice Hotels International, for example, featured a series of "suitcase ads" with celebrities that included Vanna White, Joe Frazier, Eva Gabor, Evel Knievel (a scene from the TV commercial featuring Evel Knievel is used in the print ad pictured at right), Tom Landry, Tip O'Neill, Dick Weber, and Mrs. America. Other hospitality chains and their celebrity spokespersons include:

"Next Time You're On The Road, Save 30% At Choice Hotels."

- Best Western—Yakov Smirnoff

- Econo Lodge—Tim Conway

- Holiday Inn—John Larroquette

- Motel 6—Tom Bodett

- Ramada—John Madden

- Red Roof Inns—Martin Mull

While celebrities can be persuasive, there are disadvantages to using them. They may overpower the product, or they may not be considered credible sources. Many people perceive them as participating "for the money"; if the celebrity endorses a lot of products, that can also hurt credibility.

Some properties stay away from celebrities and select company officials, such as the president or CEO, to be spokespersons. Marriott's ads, for example, feature Bill Marriott, while Hilton uses Barron Hilton to promote its chain.

No matter what option a property or chain selects, its spokespersons must be credible or their participation can hurt the property's image. Leona Helmsley, for example, used to appear in ads for her New York hotel, but is now in jail for tax evasion—which has caused considerable negative publicity for the property.

Evel Knievel ad courtesy of Choice Hotels International

Exhibit 5   Sample Radio Rate Cards

KNEWS 970 RATE CARD NO. 9	KNEWS 970 RATE CARD NO. 9

30 Second Announcements
MORNING DRIVE
5 AM − 10 AM

FREQ.	1 WK	4 WKS	13 WKS	26 WKS
1 − 14X	$37.00	$35.00	$33.00	$28.00
15 − 19X	36.00	32.00	30.00	27.00
20+	33.00	28.00	27.00	24.00

MIDDAY
10 AM − 3PM

FREQ.	1 WK	4 WKS	13 WKS	26 WKS
1 − 14X	$22.00	$21.00	$19.00	$17.00
15 − 19X	21.00	20.00	18.00	16.00
20+	19.00	18.00	16.00	15.00

AFTERNOON DRIVE
3 PM − 7PM

FREQ.	1 WK	4 WKS	13 WKS	26 WKS
1 − 14X	$27.00	$25.00	$23.00	$21.00
15 − 19X	26.00	24.00	22.00	20.00
20+	23.00	21.00	20.00	16.00

30 Second Announcements
1/3 TOTAL AUDIENCE PLAN (TAP)
5 AM − 7 PM

FREQ.	1 WK	4 WKS	13 WKS
1 − 14X	$26.00	$24.00	$22.00
15+	22.00	20.00	18.00

1/4 TOTAL AUDIENCE PLAN (TAP)
5 AM − 10 PM

FREQ.	1 WK	4 WKS	13 WKS
1 − 14X	$24.00	$22.00	$18.00
15+	20.00	18.00	16.00

7 PM − 10 PM   LATE NIGHT
$13.00   MIDNIGHT − 5AM
$8.00

For 60 second rates, add 30% (multiply by 1.3).

10 second rates on request

PROGRAM RATES ON REQUEST

All schedules paid in advance receive 10% in bonus commercials.

Contracts earning consecutive week discounts or weekly frequency discounts cancelled or reduced prior to end date are subject to short rate.

Radio stations receive their revenue from the sale of airtime, and rates vary widely—even in the same market. Most radio stations issue rate cards that provide advertising information and the station's rates for advertising spots at various times of the day. (Courtesy of KNEWS, Las Vegas, Nevada)

Buying Radio Airtime. While prices vary from station to station (see Exhibit 5), and even at the same station (discounts during slow periods, and so on), there are several basic ways to buy radio airtime:

1. *A "fixed position" spot.* The property's message is run in a specific time slot every day over the contract period. Since this method prevents the station from selling additional spots in that time period, it is usually the most expensive way to buy radio time.

2. *A weekly plan.* Weekly plans usually consist of ten to forty spots per week, and can be set up in a number of ways:

   a. *Total Audience Plan (TAP).* The broadcast day is divided into four basic time periods: morning drive time (6:00 to 10:00 A.M.), daytime (10:00 A.M. to

3:00 P.M.), evening drive time (3:00 to 7:00 P.M.), and nighttime (7:00 P.M. to 6:00 A.M.). A TAP spreads announcements throughout this broadcast day. This plan ensures that the message is heard in each time period, but it is important to note that it may be heard by different audiences, not just the target audience, at different hours of the day.

   b. *Run-of-Station Plan (ROS).* Announcements are aired in different time slots as time is available. This is one of the least costly plans.

   c. *Best-Time-Available Plan (BTA).* Like the ROS plan, the times for the property's announcements are chosen by the station and costs are fairly low. The difference between BTA and ROS is that a BTA spot may be run at the same time each day, while an ROS ad is aired in a variety of time slots.

3. *A monthly plan.* Monthly plans charge a flat rate for a fixed number of ads no matter what time slot is selected.

4. *Bulk or annual rates.* This method of purchase is often the cheapest way to purchase radio time. If your property runs 250 or more ads a year, you can sign a contract in advance to ensure the lowest possible rate.

5. *Co-op.* Like cooperative print advertising, co-op radio advertising involves two or more businesses that advertise together. All parties share in the cost of the ad, and all may benefit from the prestige and following of the other advertiser(s).

6. *Radio sponsorship.* This is another good way to build on someone else's prestige and following, but in this case, a property is associated with a radio program or personality. The property pays for a certain amount of airtime and receives mention throughout the program ("This program is sponsored by ABC Resort").

7. *Reciprocal advertising.* Reciprocal advertising is a method of bartering for reduced advertising fees. The property exchanges rooms, meals, or services for all or part of the advertising bill. This method can be extremely cost-effective for the property, especially when rooms are designated for use during slow business periods.

Before leaving the subject of time and costs, it is important to mention that the cost of a radio ad will also depend on the length of the ad. Most radio ads fall into the 30- or 60-second category, although some stations may sell shorter or longer ads. In most cases, 60-second ads do not cost twice as much as 30-second ads and may be the better value. Sometimes 30- and 60-second ads sell for the same price! It pays to shop around for the best radio buys.

Measuring the Effectiveness of Radio Ads

The final test of a radio ad is its effectiveness. There are several ways to measure the success of a radio ad:

- Listener participation promotions
- Premium offers
- Survey cards

- Monitoring sales

Listener participation promotions involve offering a special product or discount in return for action on the part of the listener. An excellent example of this type of monitoring is the radio coupon. Some years ago, selected McDonald's franchises ran an advertising promotion that encouraged listeners to make their own dollar-bill-size coupon and bring it to the nearest McDonald's for a free soft drink with the purchase of a Big Mac. The response was phenomenal—thousands of coupons poured in, sales increased 15% to 17% at all participating outlets, and the promotion saved the corporation thousands of dollars in printing costs.

Radio coupons can also be effective for the hotel industry, and can be used to promote special room packages, restaurants, lounges, and special events. To ensure greater measurability, listeners can be asked to write the call letters of the radio station on each coupon.

Premium offers are similar to radio coupons in that they invite listeners to take advantage of a giveaway when they mention the ad or the call letters of a particular station. In many cases, restaurants offer a free glass of wine or a complimentary dessert. If the hotel or restaurant advertises on more than one station, the premium advertised at each station can be different in order to help measure listener response.

Survey cards can also be used to measure a radio ad's impact. Front desk agents or restaurant hosts can ask guests how they heard about the property or a special offer. If radio is the answer, call letters can be entered on the card to determine which radio station is reaching which markets most effectively.

Monitoring sales before and after a radio promotion is another way of measuring radio effectiveness, although it may be less accurate than direct monitoring. A property restaurant may experience an increase in sales after a radio promotion, for example, but the promotion might not be the only factor: increased suggestive selling by food servers may have played a part in the increased sales.

California's Inn at Saratoga (a three-star property in the Santa Cruz mountains) tested the effectiveness of its radio advertising program by developing two-week campaigns at various times throughout the year. Advertising was placed in newspapers, on radio, and during prime time television programming. At the end of the campaigns, which featured a package price with limited availability, the radio spots resulted in 14 calls per day with a 35% booking rate, the newspaper ads generated 7 calls (with 50% booking), and, while the television spots generated 25 to 30 calls per day, less than 5% actually booked. The radio spots, then, were termed most effective in generating actual sales.

Whatever the method used to measure results, you should remember that name recognition takes time. Give promotions a chance to work. Canceling all radio advertising simply because sales have not increased dramatically may be a mistake; often, a great deal of repetition is required before a significant impression is made on radio listeners. If a particular radio promotion has not paid off after a reasonable length of time, however, you should consider changing it. Radio is a flexible medium that lends itself to a variety of approaches—perhaps a contest, or a series of ads focusing on trivia questions or famous facts would spark interest.

Radio is an excellent medium for reminder messages, and, used properly, radio can give a property the reach, frequency, selectivity, and efficiency available in no other medium. And radio, a part of almost everyone's daily life, can often get the property's message across at a fraction of the cost of print and other broadcast media.

Television Advertising

Like radio, television is a saturation medium. Millions of people watch commercial and cable television every day. Television offers the advantage of appealing to the eye as well as the ear. The audience can see and hear the message and become familiar with the property long before they visit it.

People spend considerably more time watching television than they do reading magazines, newspapers, or their mail. Television advertising can seem more believable than print advertising, a fact that is extremely important considering recent studies indicating that the average consumer spends more than six hours per day in front of a television set.

With these advantages, it would seem that properties would be eager to make television part of their advertising plan. However, television has a number of drawbacks that greatly limits the use of this medium:

- *General audience.* Because of high viewership levels, it is difficult to target specific market segments. As a general rule, people with above-average income and education (often the market that a property wishes to target) watch less television, although more higher income families are watching cable television.[2]

- *Decreasing viewership.* Advertisers on commercial television are not getting the huge audience they used to. With the advent of cable television, commercial television's viewing share has dropped to under 68% of the total market.[3]

- *High costs.* Although it is relatively easy to buy local and national coverage, messages are restricted by time segments (the 30-second spot is most common), and television costs can be extremely high. In most major cities, a 30-second prime time ad with local coverage costs between $500 and $1,000. In addition to airtime fees, production costs for TV ads have risen dramatically.

Selecting TV Stations

Properties wishing to use television advertising have a wide variety of options. In addition to the three major networks (ABC, CBS, and NBC), FOX also offers nationwide coverage, and time may also be purchased on the local affiliates of these networks. There are also independent local stations, over thirty nationwide cable networks, local cable systems, specialized commercial broadcast services, and "super stations" that offer broadcast time. The largest cable networks include Cable News Network (CNN), the Nashville Network (TNN), Music Television (MTV), and the Entertainment and Sports Programming Network (ESPN). Super stations, whose programming is carried by satellite for pick-up over a far-flung area, include WTBS-TV (Atlanta), WGN-TV (Chicago) and WOR-TV (New York).

Before selecting TV stations, you must decide whether to advertise nationally as well as locally. Some target audiences may be effectively reached through local advertising alone, while other target audiences may require the use of national advertising. In the long run it may be more cost-effective to advertise in distant key feeder cities or nationally, even though initial costs may be higher.

To select the station or stations most likely to give your property the most exposure to its target markets, you have to look at the available stations and compare audience coverage. There are three basic measurements that can be used to determine the best advertising buy: ratings, gross rating points (GRP), and households using television (HUT). *Ratings* represent the percentage of individuals or homes tuned to a particular program. (Closely related to ratings is *share of audience,* or *share,* which indicates the number of households watching a show to determine how the show is doing against its competition.) *Gross rating points (GRP)* is the rating a program achieves multiplied by the number of times the advertisement is run. For example, if a program has a rating of 16 (16 percent of all TV households have their sets tuned to that program) and if a commercial is run three times on that program, the advertiser would expect to receive 48 GRPs. *Households using television (HUT)* indicates the size of the audience available in a particular market. HUT measures the percentage of homes using television (not watching a particular program) during a particular hour, and will vary with the time of day, day of the week, season of the year, and area of the country.

Like radio stations, television stations take periodic surveys of their audiences and pay close attention to their total number of viewers and the ratings of specific programs. These factors are important when selecting a time slot, especially if the television station uses viewing measurement services (Arbitron, Nielsen, etc.) that provide a detailed, accurate survey of the viewing habits and demographics of the station's audience.

Most reputable stations have their audience estimates audited by a third party to ensure accuracy. Ratings for television (and radio) stations are usually audited quarterly, and the reports generated are made available to advertisers to support advertising claims made by the station.

Commercial television is watched primarily by middle- or lower-income families, although television specials or popular programs can attract a greater—and more affluent—audience.[4] As mentioned previously, commercial television also has the drawback of being viewed by a general audience. It is extremely difficult to determine the demographics of general viewership, and advertising dollars can be wasted if there are not enough of the targeted viewers in the general audience. On the positive side, local advertising for general products or services can usually be purchased for a moderate sum, especially if the airtime purchased is not during prime time. Of course, if prime time is not purchased, you must consider: Is the property sacrificing audience for the sake of spending a few less dollars?

Properties wishing to attract a more affluent audience are turning more and more to cable television. Cable television can reach specific target segments through special stations such as CNN and ESPN. Another advantage of cable television is that cable subscribers watch more hours of television than do watchers of commercial television.

The number and type of announcements aired also play a part in station selection. Many stations suffer from media clutter—too many announcements run

Television Measuring Systems

There are two primary measuring systems used to determine television viewing habits: The A. C. Nielsen Company's Nielsen Station Index (NSI) and the Arbitron Company (ARB). The Nielsen Station Index uses a method known as *designated market areas* (DMA), while Arbitron, the company that introduced this method of measuring, uses *areas of dominant influence* (ADI). In both of these surveys, geographic areas are broken down into counties or cities, and the public's viewing habits are monitored to give a rating for local television viewership.

The Nielsen ratings are derived from Audimeters, complex electronic instruments attached to the television sets of 1,200 scientifically selected households. The Audimeter reports time of day the set was used, total amount of set usage, and station tuning; the information is relayed to a central computer where it is analyzed.

The Arbitron system uses diaries in which families record television viewing habits for each set in the home. The diaries are analyzed to determine stations watched, programs watched, time periods of viewing, and demographics of the viewers. Arbitron uses electronic meters in New York, Chicago, Los Angeles, and San Francisco.

No matter what method is used, the data is used to determine a number of viewing statistics:

TVHH (TV households)—the number of households that own television sets (over 98% of the households in the United States have at least one television set). This statistic is used to gain a sense of the market.

HUT (Households using television)—This statistic refers to the number of households with television sets actually in use at a given time. If there are 2,000 television sets in a small town and 1,000 are turned on, the HUT figure would be 50%.

Program ratings—The program rating is figured by dividing the number of people actually tuned in to a television program by the number of television households in the test area:

$$\text{Rating} = \frac{\text{Number tuned to specific station}}{\text{TVHH}}$$

Share of audience—This statistic is calculated by determining how many HUT homes are viewing a specific program. A program watched by 500 viewers in an area that has 1,000 HUTs will garner a share of 50%.

Total audience—the total number of homes reached by a program (even if a portion of those homes watched only a part of the program).

back-to-back during commercial breaks or between programs. The frequency of advertising and the type of advertising can make the difference between a property's expensive ad being effective or being tuned out.

Certainly an important factor in selecting a station relates to costs. Costs may vary widely with the station, time slot, and time of the year. Like radio, television offers co-op advertising to help cut costs, and it is another medium that lends itself well to reciprocal advertising. Television stations give prime consideration to an advertiser who is willing to pay cash for airtime (as do radio stations), but reciprocal advertising can play a role in negotiating final terms.

Developing TV Ads

As with any other form of advertising, it is important for your property to develop a TV ad that will attract the attention of the audience. A creative approach is essential. If attention and interest are not captured during the first few seconds of the ad, viewers may either change the channel or head for the kitchen.

A successful television ad should:

1. *Grab the viewer's attention.* The viewer should immediately be given an incentive to watch and listen. This can be done through the use of interesting visual images or creative audio approaches such as unusual speech (accents, rapid talking, and so on), playing a jingle, etc.

2. *Be visual.* In television, the picture should tell the story—many viewers will remember more of what they see than what they hear. Since the message should be told visually, a storyboard is often used to judge a proposed ad. A storyboard is a panel or series of panels with small rough sketches depicting the important scenes of an ad. To help anticipate audience reaction, planners should look at the storyboard sketches and determine if the whole story is given in the visual images.

3. *Be uncomplicated.* Television thrives on simplicity. An ad should be built around one frame, called a "key visual," that tells the whole story simply and directly. A simple "name-claim-demonstration" format has proven to be the most effective; if more time is available, the key point should be repeated rather than additional points added. A storyboard can help show if an ad is too complicated. Television screens are not movie screens, and crowded, fast-moving ads can confuse viewers.

4. *Have an identity all its own.* Each ad should have its own personality, one that reflects favorably on the products and services offered. The tone or image of the ad should give viewers an idea of what to expect when they visit the property. Once that image has been established, it should be a part of all future TV advertising.

5. *Avoid wordiness.* A 30-second ad gives the advertiser approximately 60 words or less to get the message across, so it is essential that the verbal message be clear and concise. An ad should use the simplest, most memorable words and avoid clichés, flowery adjectives, and ambiguous statements.

6. *Create name recognition.* The ad must register the name of the property in the viewer's mind, whether this is done by words, visuals, or, ideally, a combination of both. For maximum effect, a combination of spoken words, visual

---

Martin Mull Promotes Red Roof Inns

Red Roof Inns wanted to stress its chain's consistency and value, and decided humor was needed to attract price-conscious travelers. The property selected comedian Martin Mull to appeal to their targeted audience with television ads such as this one:

MULL: What do $60-a-night motel chains offer you that you can't get at Red Roof Inns? Let's add them up and see.

This handy shower cap, 59 cents; shampoo-ette, $2. Ah, dental floss, always a plus.

Ooh, we're still spending $27 a night more than at Red Roof Inns.

Uh, wait a minute. I forgot the mint.

VOICE OVER: Don't pay too much, hit the roof, Red Roof Inns. Call 1-800-THE-ROOF.

MULL: It's a good mint.

It's not worth $27, but it's good.

In another ad, Mull throws a businessman's wallet into the canyon at Hoover Dam because "people who don't stay at Red Roof Inns are throwing their money away." These TV ads have been extremely popular.

---

images (perhaps the property's sign or logo), and a superimposed graphic of the property's name can be used during the message.

Types of TV Ads. There are several general types of television ads:

1. *Straight announcement.* This is the oldest type of TV ad. It can be effective if the announcer is convincing and the script is well written. A straight announcement ad is also relatively inexpensive, since it consists simply of an announcer giving a message as a slide or film is shown. Few ads of this type are made today.

2. *Demonstration.* In demonstration ads, products or services may be shown in use, competing with another product or service, or in before-and-after situations. A property may use this type of ad to show a first-class chef in action, for example. Demonstrations should relate to a viewer's needs.

3. *Testimonial.* Most people are more influenced by a TV ad that features a third-party endorsement than by a property saying something good about itself. Satisfied guests can be excellent testimonial spokespersons, as can local or national celebrities.

4. *Slice of life or problem solution.* While ads that try to portray a real-life situation may be less believable for consumer products (do people really spend their

days admiring their reflections in a waxed floor?), slice of life ads can be highly effective for the hospitality industry. The key to success is to show believable situations and people: a family checking in, receiving a warm welcome, and taking a relaxing dip in the pool after a hard day on the road, for example. But creating believability requires professional talent.

5. *Lifestyle.* This type of ad, which can also be highly effective for the hospitality industry, focuses on the consumers of a product or service. For example, a lifestyle ad would show the "beautiful people" enjoying dinner at the property's restaurant or relaxing around the pool. The emphasis would be on the type of clientele the property wishes to attract rather than on product benefits.

6. *Animated.* The use of cartoons, puppets, or animated demonstrations is an effective way to capture interest, especially if a property's message is complex. The entire ad can be animated, or animation can be used to accentuate specific parts of a more conventional ad. Production costs for this type of advertising are often prohibitive.

TV Ad Costs

Before deciding on the type of ad you want to present, you should consider the following costs:

- *Preproduction.* All work done prior to the actual filming: casting, arranging for locations, hiring a production company, props, costumes, etc.

- *Production.* The actual filming or videotaping. This includes equipment, lighting, salaries for actors and crew, etc.

- *Postproduction.* The work done following the filming or taping of the ad: editing, processing, recording sound effects, mixing the audio and video, and duplicating the final film or tapes.

When considering costs, you should find out what assistance is offered by the television station. Many stations, especially on the local level, offer production facilities at relatively low rates, usually charging only the amount required to cover costs incurred by the station. The station may recommend a local production company that will work within your property's budget—and may even work on a reciprocal basis.

Buying TV Airtime. One of the most expensive options is buying network time. Because of the high cost, network advertising is currently dominated by relatively few advertisers, and is bought on a negotiation basis. Network buys begin in late May, with up-front buys by the largest network advertisers and advertisers who have time or seasonal considerations; the remaining space is sold on an "as available" basis. Since network buying is done on such a large scale (the top ten TV advertisers alone account for over $2 billion in airtime), only the largest hotel and restaurant chains are able to buy network time. Most of this is sold on the basis of programming—advertising during a highly watched sporting event or popular prime-time series.

Since many hospitality industry advertisers cannot afford network advertising, they usually opt for local coverage in selected markets, either in the property's own market area or in key feeder cities. There are basically three ways for a property to buy advertising time on local television stations: sponsorships, participations, and spot announcements.

Sponsorship means that an advertiser presents a program as the sole advertiser or in cooperation with other advertisers. Sponsorships are usually quite expensive, and sole sponsorship is usually limited to television specials and sporting events. Hallmark, for example, sponsors the "Hallmark Hall of Fame" programs.

Most television advertising is sold on a *participating* basis. With participations, several advertisers purchase 30- to 60-second spots within a specific program. For example, several different advertisers can purchase advertising in a situation comedy that is aired nationally on a weekly basis. Under a participation arrangement, an advertiser can choose several options: to advertise on the program once, to advertise on a regular basis (once a week, once every two weeks, and so on), or to advertise on a sporadic basis—when the property is having a special promotion, for example.

Properties that do not choose to sponsor or participate in a program or programs can also purchase *spot announcements* on both local stations and the networks. Spot announcements are usually grouped together and run between programs, and are far less expensive than the other two options. The most common length for spot announcements is 30 seconds, although they may also be sold in 10-, 15-, and 60-second segments. Because of high costs, the 15- and 30-second commercial spots are most commonly used—unlike radio, where 60-second ads are typical.

Time of day is also a factor when purchasing television time. While radio's prime hours are usually defined as being morning or evening "drive times," television's most popular (and most expensive) times are in the evening. An ad scheduled for the early evening, for example, will be far cheaper than an ad scheduled during TV's prime time—7:30 P.M. to 11:00 P.M. But the property should not automatically opt for the lowest rate. Is its target audience watching during the non-prime-time hours?

Measuring the Effectiveness of TV Ads

Television advertising is expensive, and properties using it should develop a plan for measuring its effectiveness. When airtime is purchased, the station draws up a contract listing the dates, times, and programs on which the ads will appear; this contract also details the length of the ads, the rate per ad, and the total amount of ad time purchased. After the contract has been completed—that is, the ads have been aired—the station returns a form to the client that states when the spots were run. This form, called an affidavit of performance, is the client's guarantee that he or she got what was paid for.

Comparing the information on the contract and the affidavit with the number of viewer responses can help you determine how much money was spent per viewer response and whether television advertising is cost-effective for your property. Many of the techniques used to measure listener response to radio ads can be used to measure viewer response to TV ads: monitoring sales before and after television promotions, using survey cards, and using premium or discount offers.

Video Advertising

In addition to radio and television, a great many properties are taking advantage of a relatively new form of advertising: video brochures and magazines (see Exhibit 6). Video can be used both in-house and off-property, and has the advantages of being relatively inexpensive and versatile. Video is an especially attractive medium if it is not being used by a property's direct competition.

Video Brochures

One of the most effective uses of today's new video technology is video brochures.[5] A video brochure, unlike a printed brochure, has the advantage of not just telling prospective guests about the property but of actually showing the property, often at various times of the year. The sound, color, and action characteristics of video brochures have made them an extremely effective sales tool when selling to travel agents, group tour organizers, and central reservations systems agents who might not have the opportunity to visit the property in person. The flexibility of video enables portions of the video to be changed as necessary, providing travel intermediaries with up-to-date information. Videos can be used in face-to-face presentations or they can be mailed out as supplements to printed brochures and other collateral materials. Yet another new twist for video brochures is playing them for "captive audiences" on motorcoaches, 75% of which have VCR equipment.[6]

A video can assist travel intermediaries in choosing a particular property in a number of ways. A video can show:

1. *Property facilities at their best.* While site visits can be disastrous if a banquet or meeting room has recently been used and is in a state of disarray, a video can show each dining facility, banquet room, and meeting room in its most attractive state.

2. *A variety of setups.* Prospects can see exactly what the different types of setups look like in the property's banquet and meeting rooms. A meeting room, for example, can be shown with a theater setup, a V-shape setup, a schoolroom setup, and so on—all on the same tape.

3. *Seasonal attractions.* If a meeting is planned for the spring, a site visit might take place in the fall; a video could give the meeting planner the opportunity to see the hotel's gardens in bloom. A summer visitor might not be aware of the winter sports opportunities nearby; a video could show the property's facilities year-round and generate business in other seasons.

4. *Remodeling or expansion.* A video may eliminate the necessity for a meeting planner or travel agent to make an additional site visit, if the site was selected before a remodeling or major renovation. The video can also serve as a reminder of property amenities and services.

Exhibit 6　Sample Video Brochure Transcript

OUTRIGGER HOTELS Video 5:00
(Hawaii Five-O theme music and under)

JAMES
MCARTHUR: Book 'em Dano. That's how we usually ended our shows on Hawaii Five-O. Book 'em. And that's probably how you'd like to end any story in your business too. Let's book 'em. I'm Jim McArthur, and this is Waikiki. We filmed a lot of shows right here. And in the last few years there's this tall, good lookin' guy with a moustache who's filmed quite a few more. Those shows have helped to give Waikiki its image as the world's most exciting and varied beach resort. But it's not just an image. It's the truth.

(ukulele music and under)

There is literally something here for everyone, from anywhere, something for every taste.

For every appetite.

For every age.

For every station in life.

For every level of fitness.

For every level of curiosity.

For every level of intelligence.

For every demand for pleasure and entertainment.

For every sense of excitement.

Waikiki. There's something here to appeal to any, and every client that comes to your desk. But this very diversity, this sweeping appeal, does give you a problem. Many different kinds of people want to come to Waikiki. How can you be absolutely confident, that your client with a twenty-two dollar a day room budget, and your client with a two hundred dollar a day room budget, will both come back from Waikiki happy. The answer is when you book 'em, book an Outrigger. Outrigger is by far the largest hotel chain in Waikiki offering you and

your clients 18 hotels to celebrate the sun.

(piano music background and under)

The accommodations range from clean and reasonable.

To luxuriously elegant.

From family convenience.

To indulgent opulence.

With a broad selection of banquet and convention facilities.

No other host in Waikiki can produce such a range of price and luxury.

Yet, it is just not the number or the accommodation that sets Outrigger Hotels Hawaii apart.

These are two of Outrigger's senior vice presidents on a regular walking tour. It's policy that senior management at Outrigger personally visit every one of their hotels several times a week. Senior management of any national chain couldn't begin to make such a claim.

While it's the largest hotel chain in Waikiki, Outrigger is still a family headed group. The pride they share in their enterprise is infectious. It doesn't matter at which hotel an Outrigger employee works, or what the rates are, or whether the hotel is economical or prestigious, the services your clients have paid for at any Outrigger will be excellent. In fact, most Outrigger employees can move from one property to another, and back, and not miss a beat. Thank you Karena.

Outrigger likes to say that its service ranges from excellent to excellent. So when your clients want Waikiki, and nearly all of them do sometime, give them the confidence of being with Waikiki's largest chain and the genuine warmth you get only in a family hotel. Book 'em in an Outrigger. Aloha.

(Wrap—Hawaii Five-O theme music up)

This award-winning video brochure for Outrigger Hotels Hawaii features a "Hawaii Five-O" theme. The brochure was developed for travel agents and ran five minutes. (Source: *The Art of Hotel & Travel Advertising, A Look at the Past—A Guide to the Future* [Washington, D.C.: Hotel Sales & Marketing Association International, 1987], pp. 71–72.)

5. *Third party endorsements.* Portions of favorable television coverage of the property or interviews with satisfied guests (including meeting planners, leisure travelers, travel agents, etc.) can add credibility to the video presentation.

6. *Tag lines.* A tag line (which should appear on the screen at least 30 seconds) can provide the viewer with the property's name, address, and telephone number and any other pertinent information to make responding easier. In addition to the tag line, the business card of a salesperson should be attached to each video brochure, and the video itself (both cover and tape) should have the property's name, address, and phone number on the labels in case the business card is lost.

The optimum length of a video brochure is four to six minutes. This allows adequate time to present the property without losing the viewer's interest. Since time is short, it is important to present the property's best points. This means you should plan the video brochure before asking for ideas and advice on the video's actual production.

To ensure the best video brochure possible, you should consult with video experts, especially firms that specialize in hotel videos. While these firms might be somewhat more expensive than a general video production company, a hotel specialist will have more experience in putting hotel videos together without causing undue inconvenience to property employees and guests during the filming process.

It is especially important to consult with experts when marketing on an international level. There are three primary—and incompatible—VCR systems used worldwide, so it is not simply a matter of obtaining a translation and doing a new voice-over when targeting foreign markets. The United States, Canada, Mexico, the Soviet Union, and the Pacific Rim countries (Japan, Korea, and Taiwan) use the NTSC system, while most of Europe and the United Kingdom use the PAL system.

As video becomes more and more common, there will be few properties that do not make use of this dynamic sales tool. In fact, some experts predict that soon hotels that do not have at least one video brochure will be as rare as a property that does not have a printed brochure today.

Video Magazines

Video magazines, unlike video brochures, are primarily designed for in-house viewing. While a few video magazine presentations may be found at airports or other transportation terminals, most hotels show video magazines on-site over in-room TV or lobby TV screens. A typical video magazine takes a guest on a tour of the property's facilities, promotes the various restaurant and entertainment offerings, and provides information on reservation services, special upcoming packages, and other promotions. Some video magazines, like those produced by the Hilton chain, feature tours of local attractions, general travel tips, and promotions of other properties within the chain in addition to specific property information. Video magazines are also used to educate guests on topics such as casino gaming. The Flamingo Hilton in Las Vegas, for example, offers guests gaming lessons via video in the comfort of their guestrooms.

Like video brochures, video magazines are perhaps best produced in association with a hotel video specialist, or, if the property is a chain property, through the chain's corporate headquarters.

An interesting, lively video magazine that changes monthly (as does the Hilton's) is an excellent sales tool that can help make guests feel at home and promote additional sales by showing the various services offered at the property. The use of video in this manner continues to grow, and video magazines will no doubt play an important role in the future advertising plans of many hotels.

Endnotes

1. Some of the material in this section was adapted from Ted E. F. Roberts, *Practical Radio Promotions* (Boston: Focus Press, 1992).
2. *Nielsen Report on Television 1980,* A. C. Nielsen, Chicago, 1980, pp. 1–9.
3. Susan Sewell, *Advertising Made Easy* (Los Angeles, Calif.: Tern Enterprises, 1990), p. 46.
4. Nielsen, *Television 1980*, pp. 1–9.
5. Some information in this section was adapted from R. Scott Lorenz, "A Guide to Video Marketing," *HSMAI Marketing Review,* Winter 1991/1992.
6. Susan Sewell, *Advertising Made Easy* (Los Angeles, Calif.: Tern Enterprises, 1990).

Key Terms

animated ad
best-time-available plan (BTA)
bulk or annual rate
demonstration ad
donut ad
drive time
dubs
fixed position spot
gross rating points (GRP)
households using television (HUT)
lifestyle ad
master tape
monthly plan
musical ad
participations
personality ad

prime time
problem solution ad
radio coupon
ratings
run-of-station plan (ROS)
saturation medium
slice of life ad
sponsorship
spot announcement
storyboard
straight announcement ad
testimonial ad
total audience plan (TAP)
video brochure
video magazine
weekly plan

Review Questions

1. Which is a more selective medium, radio or television? Why?

2. What types of radio stations would be effective in reaching people in the 18-to-30 age bracket?

3. What factors should a hospitality firm consider before making a final decision on whether to advertise on a particular radio station?

4. What is a "Radio Day?"

5. What are four types of radio ads?

6. What are basic ways to buy radio airtime?

7. What is the difference between an ROS plan and a BTA plan?

8. How can a radio ad's effectiveness be measured?

9. What are the advantages and disadvantages of commercial TV advertising?

10. What factors should a property weigh before selecting a particular television station?

11. What are some elements of a successful television ad?

12. What are several general types of television ads?

13. What are the advantages of a video brochure?

Chapter Outline

Public Relations
   The Public Relations Plan
   Selecting a PR Staff
   Contracting for Outside PR Services
   Measuring PR Performance
Publicity
   Publicity Planning
   Developing Promotional Materials
      News Releases
      Press Kits
   Travel Writers
      Qualifying Travel Writers
      How to Maximize a Travel Writer's Visit
Press Relations
   News Media Interests
   Personal Interviews
      TV Interviews
   News Conferences
   Sensitive Subjects
   When a Story Contains Errors

14

Public Relations and Publicity

WHILE ADVERTISING IS A POWERFUL sales tool, especially since the content and timing of the message can be controlled, advertising alone is not always enough to keep the property's name before the public. But advertising, public relations, and publicity can form a powerful partnership to reach the property's target audiences.

In this chapter, we will look at public relations, publicity, and press relations. We will see how public relations and publicity can enhance a property's image, and why good press relations are important to a property's public relations program.

Public Relations

In today's hospitality industry, the term "public relations" is often bandied about, but there are varying opinions on just what it means. While there may be many definitions of public relations, most hoteliers agree that a public relations program supplements sales efforts and is necessary to a property competing in today's marketplace.

We will define public relations as the process of communicating favorable information about a property to the public in order to create a positive impression. Public relations is much more than merely getting a property's name in the newspaper or on the TV screen; the purpose of public relations is to create a good image, a positive aura, a favorable public perception of the property.

Public relations is everybody's business; it is not the exclusive domain of the general manager or public relations director. Public relations starts with the guest's first contact with your property—the switchboard operator who answers a call, or the front desk agent who welcomes an arriving guest. From the moment a guest or potential guest becomes involved with the property, the property is involved in public relations.

Public relations starts at the property itself, but it is probably most useful in the "outside world." News releases, news conferences, special events, and community service are some of the ways a property seeks to communicate favorable information about itself to the "outside world" of the local community, current and potential guests, and other properties and professionals throughout the industry (see Exhibit 1). Ideally, public relations can result in favorable media attention for the property, attention that can be much more effective than advertising because the favorable message is coming from a source other than the property itself.

The Public Relations Plan

For any public relations effort to be successful, it must start with objectives and a plan of action. A good public relations plan does not simply seek publicity for

Exhibit 1   Award-Winning Public Relations Efforts

The following are examples of public relations efforts that were given awards by the American Hotel & Motel Association at its "1992 AH&MA Stars of the Industry" national awards program.

Omni Shoreham Hotel, Washington, D.C.

In recent years, Rock Creek Park, a scenic section adjacent to the hotel, had fallen into disrepair because the National Park Service did not have the budget or the employees to maintain it. Omni Shoreham employees took it upon themselves to contract with the Park Service for a long-term, grassroots clean-up campaign of a portion of the park. More than 150 hotel employees committed to 8,000 labor-hours over a 12-month period. The hotel contributed food and beverages for a picnic for workers the day the cleanup began.

Omni Shoreham employees were among the first groups to join in preserving and enhancing the national parks under the "Save Our Parks" program. Besides providing a community service, the project also promoted a spirit of cooperation among the hotel staff and instilled the need to be environmentally conscious.

Treasure Island Inn, Daytona Beach Shores, Florida

Treasure Island Inn's "First Mates" organization consists of volunteers representing every department of the hotel. First Mates involve themselves—and the hotel—year-round in community and philanthropic activities. First Mates help with such charitable endeavors as United Way fund-raisers and membership drives, American Cancer Society walk-a-thons, American Red Cross blood drives, and the March of Dimes. First Mates are also active in a "Christmas for the Needy" project.

Other activities of First Mates:

- First Mates collected items for care packages for U.S. personnel serving in the Persian Gulf during Operation Desert Shield/Storm.

- To assist in improving the environment, First Mates pick up litter from road and beach areas near the resort, and take part in a voluntary recycling program.

- First Mates and other hotel employees promote the arts in the local community by hosting a number of fund-raising events and dinner theater performances at the hotel.

Through the efforts of First Mates, Treasure Island Inn has become a model for other businesses in the community of how to become involved in public health, arts, and environmental awareness programs.

Sheraton New Orleans Hotel, New Orleans, Louisiana

For the opening of its new Waterbury Conference Center, the Sheraton New Orleans sought to emphasize the center's historic site. The state-of-the-art conference center is located on the former site of the Waterbury Drug Store, a long-time New Orleans landmark.

To promote the grand opening of the center, the hotel mailed press kits and invitations to key media people. A week before the event, "medicine bottles" were hand-delivered to media representatives as a reminder of the event, calling further attention to the historic significance of the new center's location.

The grand opening was well attended by local media as well as many local corporations. The event resulted in numerous stories in local and national publications, written from several perspectives, such as the artwork being done by Louisiana artists, the rooms named for Southern writers, and the historic nature of the conference center's location.

The Carlton Hotel, Washington, D.C.

Many of the guests who stay at The Carlton Hotel arrive by cab. The hotel designed a promotion to thank the "ambassadors of Washington"—the cab drivers—for their friendly, efficient work. Valentine's Day was chosen as the day for the promotion. The D.C. Taxi Commission assisted the hotel by distributing a flier announcing the event—framed in a Valentine's Day heart—to all of the city's cab companies.

Exhibit 1 *(continued)*

> Between 11:30 A.M. and 2 P.M. on Valentine's Day, The Carlton Hotel gave each cab driver who stopped by a free carry-out box lunch and gifts. The gifts were a manifest clipboard with the hotel's logo and address on it (suggested by a hotel employee and part-time cab driver), and a packet of cab receipt notepads with a promotional message to the passengers on the back, urging them to visit The Carlton Hotel.
>
> More than 450 cab drivers were given lunch and gifts during the promotion. The cabbies were very appreciative of the gesture, one commenting, "No one has ever done something like this for us before."
>
> The hotel plans to make the Valentine's Day cab driver promotion an annual event each February.

Source: Adapted from *Saluting the Best of the Best: the 1992 National Awards Program,* a booklet published by the Communications Department of the American Hotel & Motel Association, 1992.

publicity's sake. Just because your hotel was mentioned numerous times by various media throughout a given year does not mean your public relations efforts have been successful. To be effective, a public relations plan should be integrated into the overall marketing plan, targeted toward important market segments, and timed to reduce occupancy soft spots. When public relations efforts are aimed at solving particular marketing problems and meeting particular marketing objectives, the results are far more productive than those obtained through unorganized publicity seeking.

A written public relations plan can allow for a review of objectives, eliminate waste of time and money, ensure better (or at least measurable) results, and involve all of the property's key people in a concentrated effort. A public relations plan should be kept simple and should integrate six major factors:

1. *Goals.* Goals should be specific. The more defined goals are, the more effective the public relations plan is likely to be. A typical goal might be: "Submit three press releases to local media during the first quarter of the year. These press releases will highlight our guestroom renovations, and will be aimed at the individual business traveler market."

   The time and effort proposed for each targeted market segment should be in direct relationship to the importance of that segment. It may be helpful to assign priorities and allocate funds to each market segment in relation to its potential return.

2. *Audience.* The best public relations plan will do little for a property if it is not reaching the people who are in the best position to buy the products or services offered. The public relations plan should target specific markets or promote specific revenue centers as set forth in the marketing plan.

3. *Media.* Once market segments have been selected, it is vital that the public relations plan identify the media that can best reach those segments.

4. *Message.* Once a medium has been selected, the public relations staff can begin developing ideas for feature stories or news spots, keeping in mind that these ideas must appeal to the medium and its audience. The staff should look at the

Using Public Relations to Reach Key Market Segments

Public relations and publicity should be planned for each market segment and included in sales action plans. In 1990, the Loews-Ventana Canyon Resort near Tucson, Arizona, sought to promote its premier golf resort to the Japanese market, and began its efforts by traveling to Tokyo for meetings with USTTA, key tour/travel operators, and the media.

As a result of these meetings, property management found that the Japanese:

- Did not know Loews Hotels—or the proximity of Tucson, Arizona, to the Los Angeles airport

- Travel to "confirm," not "explore," but see new destinations

- Rely heavily on word-of-mouth recommendations

- Book largely through travel agencies

- Desire a continual flow of information (they are voracious readers of the 3,000 magazines published monthly in Tokyo)

While this study determined that advertising an unknown destination would be a waste of money, it pointed out the need for a public relations campaign to penetrate this market. In 1990/1991, $30,000 was allocated for a public relations campaign to achieve at least 50 media exposures. The objectives of this campaign were to establish an image of the Loews-Ventana Canyon Resort as "a golfer's paradise; an upscale, full-service destination resort in a unique, natural setting and desert environment." This campaign, which would later be expanded to reach honeymooners, would also build destination awareness by presenting the proximity of Arizona to the West Coast, and would promote state and local attractions to build additional interest.

To accomplish these goals, the principal golf, trade, and consumer magazines of Japan were identified, and personal visits with journalists in Tokyo, Los Angeles, and New York City were scheduled. Television exposure was sought through the broadcast of golf tournaments. In addition, site visits for individuals and groups were arranged, and a network of contacts with principal Japanese governmental agencies, travel wholesalers, airlines, department store travel services, corporate travel agencies, and incentive companies was established. In-house Japanese language collateral materials and training programs were provided for the staff to ensure that Japanese visitors were properly served during their stays.

As a result of this campaign, the property received over forty gratuitous mentions in Japanese publications, as well as four television spots and one radio airing, and generated a number of tour packages that would ultimately result in word-of-mouth advertising and repeat business. Despite the sluggish economy and the Gulf War, the public relations campaign enabled the Loews-Ventana Canyon Resort to triple the number of room nights from Japanese visitors as compared to the previous year!

Source: Adapted from the Loews-Ventana Canyon Resort entry to the Hospitality Sales and Marketing Association International's Golden Bell Award in Public Relations.

property through the eyes of the specific medium (a TV station, for example) to determine what information would appeal to that medium and its audience while accomplishing the property's goals.

Exhibit 2 Sample Community Service Event

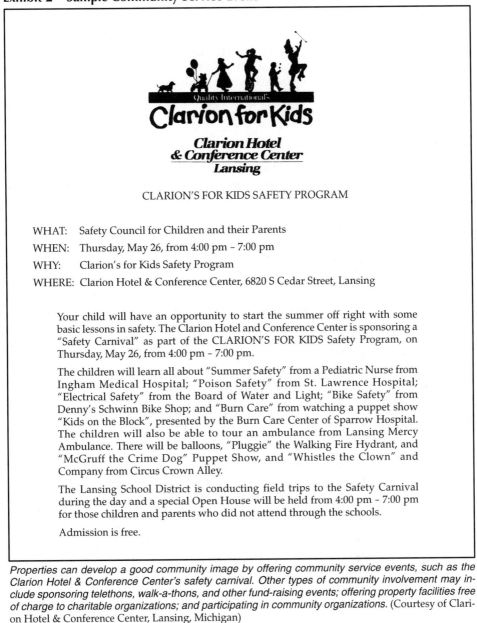

Quality International's

Clarion for Kids

Clarion Hotel
& Conference Center
Lansing

CLARION'S FOR KIDS SAFETY PROGRAM

WHAT: Safety Council for Children and their Parents

WHEN: Thursday, May 26, from 4:00 pm – 7:00 pm

WHY: Clarion's for Kids Safety Program

WHERE: Clarion Hotel & Conference Center, 6820 S Cedar Street, Lansing

Your child will have an opportunity to start the summer off right with some basic lessons in safety. The Clarion Hotel and Conference Center is sponsoring a "Safety Carnival" as part of the CLARION'S FOR KIDS Safety Program, on Thursday, May 26, from 4:00 pm – 7:00 pm.

The children will learn all about "Summer Safety" from a Pediatric Nurse from Ingham Medical Hospital; "Poison Safety" from St. Lawrence Hospital; "Electrical Safety" from the Board of Water and Light; "Bike Safety" from Denny's Schwinn Bike Shop; and "Burn Care" from watching a puppet show "Kids on the Block", presented by the Burn Care Center of Sparrow Hospital. The children will also be able to tour an ambulance from Lansing Mercy Ambulance. There will be balloons, "Pluggie" the Walking Fire Hydrant, and "McGruff the Crime Dog" Puppet Show, and "Whistles the Clown" and Company from Circus Crown Alley.

The Lansing School District is conducting field trips to the Safety Carnival during the day and a special Open House will be held from 4:00 pm – 7:00 pm for those children and parents who did not attend through the schools.

Admission is free.

Properties can develop a good community image by offering community service events, such as the Clarion Hotel & Conference Center's safety carnival. Other types of community involvement may include sponsoring telethons, walk-a-thons, and other fund-raising events; offering property facilities free of charge to charitable organizations; and participating in community organizations. (Courtesy of Clarion Hotel & Conference Center, Lansing, Michigan)

5. *Special projects.* Ways in which the property can create news through special projects or community service can then be developed (see Exhibit 2). Seminars, workshops, and special functions that are worthy of news stories can be

held. These projects should be integrated into the marketing plan and, ideally, should be scheduled to take place during the property's slow periods.

6. *Measuring results.* Results of public relations strategies should be checked often. You can monitor how many stories are submitted to the media and how much print space or broadcast airtime is given by media outlets, for example. By measuring results, you can see which medium is more effective and which media outlets are not as interested in using your property's public relations releases.

Selecting a PR Staff

A public relations plan is only as good as the staff that implements it (see Exhibit 3). No matter what the duties, or what size the property, it is best that a *professional* public relations person or staff be employed or contracted. Small properties may rely on one person or an outside agency; larger properties may engage a staff with diverse capabilities or work with an outside agency.

An in-house public relations staff may have many responsibilities: developing local promotions, contacting the media with news releases, writing promotional literature, sending thank-you notes to past guests, and so on. Since maintaining good relations with the media is important, there may be a staff member that meets with at least one member of the media each week. Another staff member may write a weekly column for a local publication.

In those cases where it is impractical to hire an in-house public relations staff, or at those properties where public relations duties are new or overwhelming, a public relations agency may be the answer.

Contracting for Outside PR Services

Before hiring a public relations agency, there are several factors to consider that are very similar to those considered when hiring an ad agency:

1. *Location.* Is the agency headquartered in the property's locale? Is the local office a branch office? If so, where is its corporate headquarters?

2. *Longevity.* How long has the agency been in business? What is its track record with clients?

3. *Effectiveness.* How can the agency benefit the property locally? Do the agency's representatives know local media representatives? What is the agency's working relationship with the local media? Does the agency employ writers, researchers, and media-contact specialists?

4. *Experience.* Does the agency specialize in the travel industry or related industries? Specialization can save start-up costs and time.

5. *Fees.* How does the agency charge for its time? Is the agency working on a fixed retainer, or will you be charged on an hourly or daily rate? Or does the agency expect a minimum fixed guarantee, billing the property for any extra hours of personnel time?

Exhibit 3   Typical Duties of a Director of Public Relations

1. Develop, implement, promote, and publicize programs or special events designed to attract and meet the needs of markets targeted by the marketing and sales department.

2. Publicize special rates and packages to markets through story placement, direct mail, brochures, flier distribution, etc.

3. Package special events to build awareness of the hotel and its facilities in order to bring potential guests into the hotel.

4. Create and develop sales aids to be used by the property's sales team, such as slide presentations, photographs of the property and various events it has hosted, and scripts that can be used by telemarketers and other members of the property's sales force. Scripts may also be developed for other property employees, such as front desk agents and food servers.

5. Compile and update direct mail lists for all special interest groups to sell special packages, events, and weekend rates.

6. Assist major meeting planner clients in press contacts; place stories for key convention groups.

7. Develop, implement, promote, and publicize programs or special events to increase food and beverage and catering sales and gain maximum publicity for the hotel.

8. Formulate plans and a strategy for a promotional calendar of events.

9. Maximize press relations by:
   - Seeking story placement in local and national media
   - Soliciting media coverage for all special events and programs
   - Generating publicity for new facilities, entertainment, services, and functions of the hotel through news releases, memos, and story solicitation of the news media
   - Initiating and placing hotel or hotel personnel stories in local media that will add to the awareness and prestige of the hotel
   - Placing photos of officers or meeting planners of important groups, along with key hotel personnel, in places where other meeting planners may see them, such as insurance, banking, electronics, and manufacturing publications
   - Acting as a liaison between the hotel and the press to answer all media inquiries

10. Assist with the property's newsletters, whether they are written in-house or by an advertising agency.

11. Administer the department by:
    - Developing long-range plans and goals for public relations
    - Preparing monthly reports of activities
    - Supervising subordinates

Source: Adapted from Chad A. Martin, "Public Relations: It Works For You," *HSMAI Marketing Review,* Fall 1986, p. 20.

6. *Other factors.* Does the agency represent clients that would present a possible conflict of interest?

You should request a proposal outlining how the agency would support the property's marketing objectives (see Exhibit 4). Proposals enable you to weed out agencies with unsatisfactory plans or exorbitant rates.

It is also important that management meet with the agency representative who would be assigned to your property. Since a good working relationship between the

Exhibit 4 Agency Proposal Checklist

> Before deciding on a public relations agency, a property should ask for a detailed proposal. A good proposal should include:
>
> 1. An outline of an overall public relations plan for your property.
>
> 2. Examples of specific story ideas, promotions, special events, and media-oriented activities that will be created for your property under a three-month, six-month, or one-year contract.
>
> 3. The amount of time the agency will spend on your account every month.
>
> 4. Names of media contacts who will be approached on your behalf.
>
> 5. A meetings schedule. A good agency will request frequent meetings with property representatives for input and review.
>
> 6. A specific review period. A good agency will want to review its work and its relationship with you, usually after three months.
>
> 7. The agency's fee schedule. Always compare fees with similar agencies to make sure fees are competitive.

Source: Adapted from Tom McCarthy, "Selecting Your Public Relations Agency," *Hotel and Resort Industry*, May 1985, p. 26.

property's staff and the representative is essential, there are several questions that should be answered before making a final decision. The potential representative should be asked:

1. How long have you been with the agency? How long have you been in your present position?

2. What other accounts do you handle? If you were transferred or if one of your other clients had an emergency requiring your services for several days, who would handle our account?

3. If we had an emergency, how much time could you devote to our account? Could you focus your energies on our account for several days?

4. What are the names of some of your other clients? May we ask them for references?

Once a public relations agency has been selected, you should work closely with it. An employee can be appointed to keep the agency representative posted on happenings at the property. For closer contact (and better results), the representative should be invited to sit in on important staff meetings, treated as a member of the marketing and sales team, and expected to provide monthly or quarterly reports on the results of the agency's efforts.

The agency representative should review your property's marketing plan so he or she can allocate time and effort to the market segments and time periods that are priorities to the property. The representative should make sure hotel personnel are the first to know about any public relations activities planned for the hotel. A notified staff is not necessarily an informed staff, however. The staff needs to know more than just when an event will take place. It should know the purpose behind a particular public relations event in order to help promote and sell the hotel.

Measuring PR Performance

Whether public relations efforts come from an outside agency or an in-house staff, every public relations plan should include a periodic audit. It is important to measure the results of the public relations plan against the goals that were set. The plan should be monitored at least every six months (at shorter intervals during the plan's initial implementation) to determine progress.

Measuring the impact of public relations is extremely difficult. Public relations cannot be measured in terms of how many sales leads or room nights are generated. While responses to advertisements and direct mail pieces can be tracked, it is difficult to determine how many guests checked into the hotel because they read a glowing article in a national magazine or a favorable story in a newspaper, although the staff can be instructed to ask guests how they decided to stay at the property.

Public relations has to be measured in terms of media space and "value equivalencies." Measuring media space in print media can be as simple as keeping a log of publications that articles have appeared in, the date of publication, the number of column inches featuring the property, and the circulation of the publication (see Exhibit 5). While this type of measurement does not help track reservations or sales, it is a good indicator of the amount of recognition and awareness (and, one hopes, goodwill) that public relations is generating.

The second measurement, value equivalency, is a means of measuring the dollar value of the publicity received by your property. Value equivalency is determined by auditing the exact amount of space or airtime given to your property over a specified period of time, and determining the value of the exposure in terms of what it would have cost to purchase the space or airtime for advertising purposes. For example, if your property gets a full-page editorial in a travel magazine that charges $8,400 for a page of advertising space, the equivalent value would be $8,400. It should be noted, however, that this figure represents a *conservative* estimate of value; the actual value includes credibility that is priceless.

Since free space or airtime may be worth many times the equivalent advertising space or airtime, it is essential that your property's management team evaluate public relations efforts often, and review and revise plans and strategies to maximize their return.

Publicity

Public relations and publicity, while closely related (and often grouped together) are actually two different activities. In their book, *Marketing Leadership in Hospitality,* authors Robert C. Lewis and Richard E. Chambers offer this description of the difference: "Publicity is different from public relations in that events are created.... Public relations tells the story of the product, while publicity makes a story for the product."[1] Publicity, then, is a part (one technique) of public relations, and can have a strong impact on public awareness of a property or program.

Publicity is one of the most effective promotional tools available to the hospitality industry, yet few properties include publicity in their marketing plans. But publicity—the media's gratuitous mention of the property, its staff, and special

Exhibit 5   Measuring Public Relations

Publication	Story and Reporter	Day, Month, Year	Column Inches	# of Photos	Circu-lation
The Washington Post	"Personalities" Chuck Conconi	Tuesday September 30	4.00		728,857
Business Review Vienna, VA	"Design Elements Seen Aiding Willard Office Building Success"	Monday September 29	1.50		17,000
Swimming Pool Age & Spa Merchandiser Atlanta, GA	"Accommodations in Nation's Capital Range From Economical to Luxurious"	October	7.00		15,000
New York Air Skylines	"Metropolitan D.C." Karen R. Heuman	October	1.00		400,000
The Washington Post	"Personalities" Chuck Conconi	Wednesday October 1	4.00		728,857
The Daily News Newport, RI	No Title	Thursday October 9	1.50		16,450
The Examiner Chronicle San Francisco, CA	"Dining at the Willard Recalls the Best of Washington's Past" Paul Lasley & Elizabeth Harryman	Sunday October 19	22.00		711,560
San Diego Union	"Commercial Real Estate Outlook Poor"	Sunday October 19	3.00		391,100
Madison Avenue Magazine	"Menus and Venues" Vanessa Duchesne	November	2.75		32,000

While it is difficult to put a dollar figure on the value of public relations, properties can measure the amount of publicity generated with the aid of charts such as this one used by The Willard Inter-Continental in Washington, D.C. (Courtesy of The Willard Inter-Continental, Washington, D.C.)

property events—can reach thousands of potential guests at little cost to the property.

Publicity should not be confused with advertising. With advertising, a hotel buys media space or time and controls the message; with publicity, the media provide the space or time, and the media—not the property—control the message. This apparent "drawback" is the real strength of publicity. With advertising, the property extols its own virtues, but when the property, through successful public relations efforts, receives favorable publicity, someone else is praising the property—which results in greater believability.

Publicity, while it is not advertising, *supports* advertising. The public may respond much more readily to advertising messages after reading of the property's community involvement; its special programs such as safety fairs, bike rodeos, and business seminars; and its contributions of cash or services to charities, scholarship funds, or other community organizations.

Publicity can be unplanned. A celebrity might stay at the property and talk about his or her stay during an interview; this could be good publicity even though

Using Sponsorships to Generate Community Goodwill

Sponsorships involve promoting a community event or program either wholly or in part. Sponsorship contributions can come in the form of cash funding, or can involve the donation of facilities, food, or other services. A property's involvement in community and charitable affairs can enhance its image and result in invaluable free publicity, as evidenced in the two following examples.

In the District of Columbia, the Ramada Renaissance Washington Tech World adopted a neighborhood school, Thomson Elementary. Not only does the property donate funds to the school, it also offers opportunities for students to be exposed to different management positions within the hotel. It promotes contests and provides exhibit space so that students can display their creative abilities in the arts. Music workshops; safety, cooking, and etiquette classes; and seasonal activities are also offered by the property.

This program has received extensive local and national media coverage, and resulted in the property being awarded the Gold Key Public Relations Award for Community Service by the American Hotel & Motel Association of Washington, D.C., and the Partners in Education Award given annually by the District of Columbia Public Schools.

The Plaza San Antonio Hotel's sponsorship campaign came as a result of its involvement in the Fiesta San Antonio, a community event held each April. The Fiesta, which attracts more than 3 million visitors, involves 150 events run by 50,000 local volunteers. The Plaza San Antonio Hotel, seeking to increase its public visibility, created a program to honor the Fiesta's volunteers during the Fiesta's centennial year.

The hotel developed "The Faces of Fiesta," a volunteer recognition program honoring 100 of the thousands of volunteers. The Fiesta Commission and the *San Antonio Express-News*, the leading local newspaper, were invited to be co-sponsors, and the *Express-News* kicked off the campaign by running nomination forms explaining the program and soliciting nominations.

One hundred days before the Fiesta, a reception was held for all nominees, and, on each of the hundred days leading up to the event, an honoree was recognized with a story of his or her contributions (each write-up mentioned the hotel), and received a framed certificate of recognition.

According to a spokesperson for the property, the program was a success on several levels:

> Our investment of approximately $1,300 for the reception and the certificates gave us newspaper space equal to more than $40,000 in advertising, based on our regular advertising rates, and daily visibility for three months. Since our "Faces of Fiesta" stories were recognized by readers as editorial stories, not ads, we also received the extra benefit of the public's perception of the hotel as a good corporate citizen and an important partner in the Fiesta Centennial celebration. Publicity done through local television stations increased our visibility even more. The project also brought us approximately $20,000 in business from the Fiesta San Antonio Commission—business that had not come to us in previous years. We also strengthened our ties with the *San Antonio Express-News,* who will be a strong promotional partner for us in the future. In addition, through our contact with the individual honorees, we made some good contacts who are spreading the word about the Plaza throughout the community, and strengthened our ties to the Fiesta Commission for future promotions.

Source: Adapted from entries to the Hospitality Sales and Marketing Association International's Golden Bell Award in Public Relations.

it was unplanned. A restaurant reviewer might give the property's restaurant a bad review; a property might counteract this bad publicity by making adjustments in its menu or service and inviting the reviewer to return.

Other unplanned publicity includes natural disasters, labor disputes, mishaps at the property, and so on. Several years ago, for example, heavy flooding was reported in the area of Phoenix, Arizona. While this flooding did not affect resorts in nearby Scottsdale, extensive media coverage gave the impression that everything was under water, and the resorts had to convince soon-to-arrive vacationers and other guests that the resorts were still operating. The Wigwam, for example, called everyone with a reservation, while Marriott's Camelback Inn sent Mailgrams. In other emergencies—a fire at a property, for example—more extreme measures are needed to counteract unfavorable publicity; these measures will be discussed later in the chapter.

Publicity can fulfill a variety of marketing needs, but publicity can also backfire. The difference between successful and unsuccessful publicity programs is *planning*.

Publicity Planning

Publicity is most valuable when it communicates a favorable message to people with whom the property wishes to communicate. A well-developed plan can lead to favorable publicity, which can attract new business, remind previous guests about the property, and build community goodwill.

The plan begins with knowing what the property has to offer. This includes becoming aware of everything there is to know about the property—its history, facilities, services, staff, and marketing and sales goals. There is a wealth of stories under a property's roof—an exciting marketing concept, an upcoming event sponsored by the property, and employees who have excelled in special fields (see Exhibit 6). Many media representatives recognize that hotels are full of interesting stories and people. Unique staff members, upwardly mobile management personnel, and VIP guests may generate reams of publicity for the property.

Once the staff compiles a background or inventory of what the property has to offer, the next step is to get to know the media. What are the most appropriate media outlets for the property's publicity? Who are the journalists, columnists, and broadcasters who can assist in getting the property's message across? What materials must be developed in order to facilitate the publicity process?

Developing Promotional Materials

One way to interest the media in the property is to distribute promotional materials that will make a journalist's job easier should he or she choose to write about the property. Promotional pamphlets and brochures are excellent examples of materials that provide useful background information. Previous articles are also effective because they show the property has been newsworthy and provide background on what has already been done in print.

Newsletters can bring news of the property, its staff, and its services to the attention of the media as well as the public. Newsletters range from typewritten copy on property letterhead to slick full-color presentations. No matter what the

Exhibit 6   Publicity Opportunities

- The opening of new facilities (property, wing, restaurant, bar, lounge, health club, tennis courts, etc.). These are considered especially newsworthy if features such as unusual architecture, special technology, or unique benefits are promoted.

- Expansions, renovations, or relocations are usually of interest. Even the acquisition of a new piece of equipment—a super computer system, a high-tech lawn maintenance system, improved cooking facilities—can result in free publicity, especially if the improvement will result in better guest service.

- Restaurant reviews are popular with the public, and can be solicited upon the opening of a new restaurant, the addition of new specialty dishes or drinks, or the addition of new styles of service (new lunch buffet, outdoor dining, and so on).

- If the property features live entertainment or special programs, these can be announced or reviewed. For best representation, background information on the entertainer(s) or special program (dinner theater presentation, poetry reading, etc.) should be provided.

- Special events, such as a property anniversary celebration, a promotion to celebrate the opening of another property in the chain, a "celebrity" cooking class, a food festival, or other special events are usually considered newsworthy.

- Employee appointments or promotions, employee awards and special recognition (25 years of service, "Employee of the Month," etc.), and the outside activities of the staff (Boy Scout leader, coordinator of a charity event, volunteer teacher of disabled people, and so on) provide innumerable opportunities to recognize achievements, build employee morale, and garner publicity for the property.

- Celebrities and VIPs who visit the property can also provide opportunities for press and broadcast coverage *if* the celebrity is willing to participate. In many cases, a celebrity is on a promotional tour, and will welcome the opportunity to be interviewed by the local media, but requests for privacy should always be honored.

- Public service activities such as sponsorships of community events; donations of funds, facilities, or services to charitable organizations; and community service seminars are always newsworthy—and are excellent vehicles to build community goodwill as well as name recognition.

treatment, the important point is getting the newsletter into the right hands so it can generate favorable publicity about the property and its employees. Although not specifically prepared for them, newsletters may be sent directly to print and broadcast journalists.

Promotional materials especially prepared for the media include news releases and press kits.

News Releases. A news release is a news story about a special event, celebrity guest, new promotional program, or other interesting item that is sent to the news media in hopes that it will generate an article, interview, or photograph (see Exhibit 7).

Before writing a news release, the marketing and sales department or the property's public relations specialist or staff must know the media and their needs. What may seem newsworthy to the owner of a property may be of little interest to

Exhibit 7   News Release Do's and Don'ts

DO

- Write clearly in plain language, using short sentences and paragraphs.

- Be brief. Rarely should a story be longer than 500 words (about two pages).

- Give your news release a professional appearance. Always show the name and address of a person to contact for more information.

- Respect media deadlines. Learn radio, TV, and print media deadlines and allow as much lead time as possible when submitting material.

- Establish a reputation for honesty. If you do not have the answer to a question, tell the media representative. Credibility is basic to good press relationships.

DON'T

- Request or expect news space simply because your property or chain is an advertiser.

- Expect writers or broadcasters to report only the good news about your property and its personnel. Their job is reporting all the news—good, bad, or neutral. Don't expect your friends in the media to play down a negative story.

- Try to manage the news. Let the editor decide if your story merits space or time.

- Assume you know what media representatives want. Instead, make it a point to find out how you can be helpful.

- Ask to review a reporter's story or notes. If you believe a reporter is misinformed, discuss it.

---

a busy television producer, for example. The challenge is to "create" news that is really news, not just a publicity stunt.

If a particular story seems most appropriate for a newspaper, the public relations staff should check with a local newspaper to find out which department (food, entertainment, travel, business) may be interested in the story. If there is sufficient time, the staff may write a letter about the story to the department's editor. Ideas, statistics, and photographs that would enhance the story might be included with the letter to help the editor decide on the story's value.

While it is best to send a specific story to only one media outlet, there are times when news of a general nature can be written up in a general news release and sent out to many media outlets. This enables each outlet to determine the release's value —and allows each to develop its own individual story. General news releases may be sent out when a property books a new act in the lounge, plans new restaurants or meeting facilities, redecorates or expands, implements new energy conservation programs, or participates in community service events (see Exhibit 8).

How to write a news release. Releases should be double-spaced on a "News Release" form or on paper with the property letterhead. Many properties use a specially printed news release form that includes the words "News" or "News Release" on the top of the page. White stock is usually used to facilitate the copying of

Exhibit 8   Sample News Release

MAYFAIR
SUITES

FOR MORE INFORMATION:
Peggy A. Gredington or
Todd E. Vasel

Background Information: AMESBURY LTD.
(314) 863-5054

MAYFAIR SUITES: A HISTORIC LANDMARK

The doors of Mayfair Suites reopened in downtown St. Louis
in July 1990, following a $20 million renovation that restored the historic
hotel's original charm and elegance.

The 320-room Mayfair Hotel—as it was originally named—opened
in 1925 under the ownership of Charles Heiss, a former busboy from
Heidelberg, Germany. Today, the European charm Heiss brought to the
hotel remains evident in the hotel's service, accommodations and
restaurants.

Added to the National Register of Historic Places in 1979, Mayfair
Suites now has 184 guest units, a result of room enlargements and
renovations over the years. Most are one-bedroom suites complete with
parlors, dressing areas and baths. Four 18th-floor penthouse suites
offer living and dining areas; baths with jacuzzis, showers and dressing
rooms; fireplaces; and, magnificent cityscape views.

– more–

806 St. Charles Street / St. Louis, Missouri 63101-1507 / 314-421-2500 / 1-800-444-3313
Member Preferred Hotels Worldwide

*This is the first page of a news release for Mayfair Suites in St. Louis, Missouri. Note that the release is
typed on property stationery, starts roughly a third of the way down the page to leave room for an editor's headline, and includes the name of someone a journalist can contact for more information. (Courtesy of Mayfair Suites, St. Louis, Missouri)*

news releases. A release date (the date on or after which the story can be published
or "released") should be given unless it is the same as the dateline. The name and
phone number of the property's media contact person should be included.

Exhibit 9   Sample Video News Release

(videotape included)

WEEKEND LEISURE TIME SURVEY
Video News Release (TRT: 1:03)

A VNR is a ready-to-air television news story. News programs often provide a local lead-in announcement and then use a VNR in its entirety — including the Hilton credits.

This VNR will extend the Hilton BounceBack Weekend message to your local news programs. The VNR highlights the results of the Hilton survey and positions Hilton as the expert on weekend leisure.

Visuals	Audio
	NARRATOR:
Men raking leaves	WE'RE FACING A LEISURE TIME CRISIS TODAY. ACCORDING TO A
New York street scene	RECENT NATIONAL SURVEY COMMISSIONED BY HILTON HOTELS,
Woman putting child in grocery shopping cart	WEEKEND RELAXATION IS ON ITS WAY OUT.
Man climbing ladder	IN FACT, WE SPEND ALMOST HALF OUR WEEKEND DOING CHORES,
Two men carrying briefcases	INCLUDING WORK BROUGHT HOME FROM THE OFFICE.
Women entering revolving door of office	THE RESULT? WE GO BACK TO WORK MONDAY MORNING FEELING NO
Man slowly walking down street	MORE ENERGETIC THAN WE DID ON FRIDAY.
	DR. HANSON:
Dr. Hanson in office	
	"One of the best prescriptions I've ever written is to tell people to try to get away for an occasional weekend to recover — or bounce back — from their stresses."
Man buying movie ticket Men playing golf	"My first principle of stress defense is to pamper yourself. And never underesti-
Dr. Hanson in office	mate the value of your spare time. Let someone else do the cooking and the cleaning, for example, and you'll find it could make a real difference."

Weekend Leisure Time Survey VNR
Page 2

Visuals	Audio
	NARRATOR:
Guest signing in at hotel registration desk	THE TRAVEL AND HOSPITALITY INDUSTRIES ARE RESPONDING TO THIS NEED WITH A VARIETY OF SPECIAL PACKAGES.
	MICHAEL RIBERO:
Ribero on camera	"The hospitality industry is in a unique position to help people to get away for the weekend. The key is, to make it easy and affordable."
	NARRATOR:
Women reviewing hotel literature rack; cut to guest driving up to entrance, doorman open jeep door and takes bag	BY TAKING ADVANTAGE OF SPARE TIME TO DO A LITTLE ADVANCE PLANNING, IT SEEMS IT IS POSSIBLE TO BRING BACK THE WEEKEND. THIS IS CHRISTOPHER MICHAELS REPORTING.

# # #

Start the news release about a third of the way down the first page (this leaves room for an editor's headline), and begin with a paragraph detailing the who, what, when, where, why, and how of the article. The release should be accurate and complete, with names spelled correctly. The release should also be brief and factual; avoid opinions or editorials. Direct quotes of the general manager or other authorities may enhance the impact of the release.

You must realize that whether or not your news release or special event is reported in the media will depend on its merit. You should not pressure an editor or broadcaster for space or airtime just because your property buys advertising, but it is permissible—and even advisable—to follow up to ensure that the release has been received and ask if there are any questions.

Video news releases. A new wrinkle on the news release theme is the video news release (see Exhibit 9). In addition to writing traditional news releases, some properties also produce short videos and send them to television stations for possible airing. To be considered news rather than commercials, these videos must present something that a TV news editor might consider newsworthy.

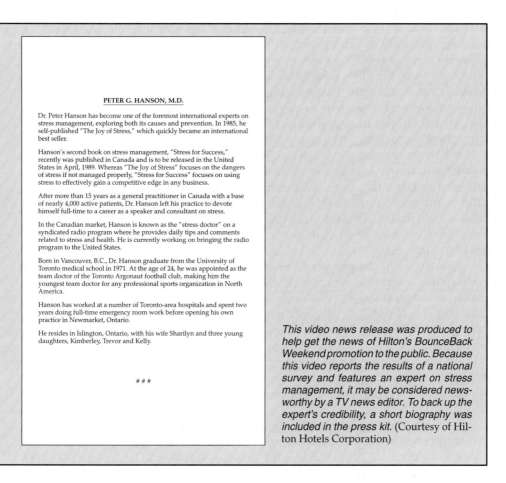

PETER G. HANSON, M.D.

Dr. Peter Hanson has become one of the foremost international experts on stress management, exploring both its causes and prevention. In 1985, he self-published "The Joy of Stress," which quickly became an international best seller.

Hanson's second book on stress management, "Stress for Success," recently was published in Canada and is to be released in the United States in April, 1989. Whereas "The Joy of Stress" focuses on the dangers of stress if not managed properly, "Stress for Success" focuses on using stress to effectively gain a competitive edge in any business.

After more than 15 years as a general practitioner in Canada with a base of nearly 4,000 active patients, Dr. Hanson left his practice to devote himself full-time to a career as a speaker and consultant on stress.

In the Canadian market, Hanson is known as the "stress doctor" on a syndicated radio program where he provides daily tips and comments related to stress and health. He is currently working on bringing the radio program to the United States.

Born in Vancouver, B.C., Dr. Hanson graduate from the University of Toronto medical school in 1971. At the age of 24, he was appointed as the team doctor of the Toronto Argonaut football club, making him the youngest team doctor for any professional sports organization in North America.

Hanson has worked at a number of Toronto-area hospitals and spent two years doing full-time emergency room work before opening his own practice in Newmarket, Ontario.

He resides in Islington, Ontario, with his wife Sharilyn and three young daughters, Kimberley, Trevor and Kelly.

# # #

This video news release was produced to help get the news of Hilton's BounceBack Weekend promotion to the public. Because this video reports the results of a national survey and features an expert on stress management, it may be considered newsworthy by a TV news editor. To back up the expert's credibility, a short biography was included in the press kit. (Courtesy of Hilton Hotels Corporation)

Press Kits. Somewhat similar to sales kits, press kits are designed to give journalists background material about a property.

The following materials are typically found in a press kit:

- Letter of introduction
- Summary sheet
- Property fact sheet(s)
- Basic property news release
- Photographs of the property
- Biographies and photographs of key personnel
- News clippings
- Advertising materials

A *letter of introduction* simply explains that the press kit contains promotional materials and gives permission to use them. A letter of introduction should be typed on property letterhead and include the name and telephone number of the property's media contact person.

A *summary sheet* lists what is contained in the press kit, enabling the recipient to tell at a glance exactly what materials he or she has received.

Fact sheets are written in a non-narrative style and include information about the general design and appearance of the property, guest services, food and beverage outlets, parking facilities, safety features, and names of key property personnel.

A *basic property news release* is a short, general article (usually no more than 500 words) in narrative form about the property. Written on a news release form or hotel letterhead, this two-page (maximum) article highlights the range of special facilities and services available at the property (including weekend and other promotional packages); unique features of the property (unusual architecture, murals, fountains, and so on); and other basic information about the property that may be of interest.

Photographs of the property's exterior from a number of angles, and interior photographs of guestrooms, dining facilities, and special services should be included in the press kit. All photographs should be black and white, and no smaller than 5 × 7 inches (13 × 18 centimeters). The sharper the image, the better the photograph will reproduce, so hiring a professional photographer is often a good investment.

All photographs should be identified by a title or caption that is written or typed on a separate sheet of paper and then attached to the photo. At no time should a title or caption be written directly onto the back of a photograph, as this may damage the photo.

For best results, photographs should include small groups of people in unposed, natural situations. A release must be obtained from each person pictured. This release need not be included in the press kit, but should be kept on file at the property in case the photograph is published.

Brief *biographical sketches* detailing the experience and expertise of key property personnel may lead to feature stories (see Exhibit 10). Profiles should be short, factual, and interesting. A biography's appeal is enhanced by a sharp black and white photo of the subject.

News clippings, if available, should also be included in a press kit (see Exhibit 11). Previously printed articles may lead to additional stories (perhaps with a different slant), and let members of the media know that the property has been considered newsworthy in the past.

Full-color brochures, pamphlets, fliers, and other *advertising materials* provide additional information and appeal.

Since media personnel may receive hundreds of press kits each year, it is important that your property's press kit make a positive first impression. All materials should be attractively presented in a sturdy folder that features the name, logo, address, and telephone number of the property. All materials within the folder should be clearly marked in case the folder is dropped or mishandled.

Exhibit 10   Sample Biographical Sketch

HOTEL *Bel-Air*

701 STONE CANYON ROAD • LOS ANGELES, CALIFORNIA 90077 • 213/472-1211

GEORGE J. MAHAFFEY
EXECUTIVE CHEF

George Mahaffey joined Hotel Bel-Air in 1987, and was named executiv chef of the hotel in August of 1989, after serving as executive sous chef.

Prior to joining Hotel Bel-Air, Mahaffey gained valuable experience with The Cloister Hotel, Sea Island, Georgia; Hotel Hershey in Hershey, Pennsylvania; and the Marriott Crystal Gateway Hotel in Crystal City, Virginia.

Mahaffey has accumulated many awards and honors through culinary competitions in several catagories, such as pastry and garde manger work. Included among these are several "First Place" awards and a "Best in Division" award from The Virginia Culinary Arts Competition. In addition, Mahaffey trained young culinarians for "show work" and competition in Virginia, New York, Georgia and Pennsylvania.

After having received a B.A. in philosophy from Virginia Commonwealth University, Mahaffey attended the American Culinary Federation Eductional Institute.

Courtesy of the Hotel Bel-Air, Los Angeles, California.

Travel Writers

Another way you can encourage publicity at a reasonable cost is to invite travel writers to your property. Travel writers write about modes of transportation, hotel accommodations, and business and vacation destinations.

Qualifying Travel Writers. Because travel writers vary in their styles, abilities, and markets, it is wise to develop guidelines to ensure that any travel writers given discounts to stay at the property are qualified journalists. (Discounts normally apply to room costs, exclusive of food and beverage and incidental expenses.) While

Exhibit 11   Sample News Clipping

THE NATION'S NEWSPAPER   FRIDAY, JUNE 29, 1990

USA TODAY

BONUS SECTION
THE BEST OF THE USA

TRAVEL EXPERTS PICK THEIR BESTS

	Harold Evans	**Barbara Fairchild**	**Pamela Fiori**	**Robin Leach**	**Andrew Harper**
There's no place like home, but for those who travel there's nothing like finding creature comforts on the road. A look at where to find peace and quiet, fun and adventure—or service with a smile.	Editor in chief of Conde Nast Traveler, he often relies on readers' choices when choosing his favorite destinations.	Executive editor of Bon Appetit, a magazine of fine food and travel, she travels frequently, speaking to writers' groups and professional organizations.	Former editor of Travel & Leisure, she is now editorial director and executive vice president for American Express Publishing Corp.	Executive producer of Lifestyles of the Rich and Famous, he travels at least 250,000 miles a year. His 1990 World's Best TV special airs in July and August.	The pen name of the editor of the Hideaway Report: A connoisseur's guide to peaceful and unspoiled places. He travels anonymously to evaluate destinations.
Best hotel	The Hotel Bel-Air, Los Angeles. Lush with 11 acres, gardens and beautiful outdoor pool and cottages. 213-472-1211	The Hotel Bel-Air, Los Angeles. Beautiful environment, excellent service, absolute privacy. 213-472-1211	The Hotel Bel-Air, Los Angeles. Stands out for sheer beauty, level of service and luxury. 213-472-1211	The Hotel Bel-Air in Los Angeles. The most romantic and elegant. 213-472-1211	The Boulders, Carefree, Ariz. Golf and tennis resort captures dramatic desert surroundings with style. 800-553-1717

Intimacy meets elegance at the Bel-Air

By Arlene Vigoda
USA TODAY

So what's the nation's best hotel — at least according to most members of our travel panel — really like?

Los Angeles' Hotel Bel-Air is unpretentious, private and tasteful.

"The elegance and quiet are incredible," says panel member Barbara Fairchild, editor of Bon Appetit magazine. "It's in the middle of the glitziest city in the country, yet there's absolutely nothing glitzy about it. It has an air of tradition that's rare in L.A."

From the lavishly landscaped grounds nestled in the valley of Stone Canyon, to the casual elegance of the two-story mission-style bungalows, there's a magical quality, the travel experts say.

"Even our employees are coached for excellence," says Paul Zuest, the hotel's general manager.

With only 90 rooms, including 32 suites, the hotel's bungalows — connected by archways and passageways —have an intimate, casual ambiance, more like an estate's luxurious guest house rather than a hotel. All rooms have skylights or French doors opening

PREMIUM PRIVACY: The lobby at the Hotel Bel-Air shows its guests understated elegance in the middle of Los Angeles glamour.

onto private landscaped patios, some with Jacuzzis.

They're furnished in a Southwestern motif, using "lots of terra cotta and desert colors that are relaxing and easy on the eye," says Fairchild.

The price: $245-$385 a night for double occupancy; suites can run up to $1000 a night.

While guest amenities include the often-standard 24-hour room service, cable TV and valet parking, the hotel goes a step further. It also offers complimentary shoe shines, current magazines in every sitting room or bath-

room, phones in every bathroom, and a large selection of automobiles for guests' use upon request.

A restaurant is on the grounds. "You can have three phenomenal meals a day there and never have to leave, even though you're in a seven- to 10- mile radius of trendy L.A. restaurants," says Fairchild. The provincial-style California cuisine features fresh and grilled vegetables, pastas, fish and salads.

"People love that we're in a little canyon away from the hustle and bustle," says Zuest. "Privacy is what we really sell here more than anything else."

The Hotel Bel-Air included this news clipping from USA Today *in its press kit.* (Courtesy of the Hotel Bel-Air, Los Angeles, California)

there are relatively few writers who take vacations at a property's expense, making sure travel writers are qualified will ensure that the writers entertained by your property have the expertise to make the most of their visits.

Travel writers fall into two basic groups: staff writers and free-lance writers. Staff writers work for specific publications, and assignments are often arranged through an editorial staff. Free-lance writers are harder to qualify. Many belong to professional organizations such as the Society of American Travel Writers as either active or associate members.[2] Some free-lancers dislike group memberships, however, and you must rely on the writer's reputation for qualification purposes.

If your property is part of a large chain, a call to the corporate public relations department can facilitate the qualification process; most corporate offices keep request logs (a list of writers requesting to visit a property), clippings, or media directories. Independent properties can also refer to media directories. If questions arise, it is permissible to verify a writer's assignment by contacting the publication he or she is writing for. As a last resort, clippings or tear sheets of previous work may be requested from the writer.

How to Maximize a Travel Writer's Visit. Although travel writers are guests of your property, they are also critics obligated to present an impartial view of their stay. There are several things you can do, however, to create a favorable impression and enhance a travel writer's visit:

1. *Be prepared.* Preparation is essential to a positive experience for the travel writer. Both the writer and the property's managers should know what to expect during the visit. What is the writer's itinerary? What will be provided on a complimentary basis? What does management expect in the way of publicity?

2. *Don't overtax the writer.* The needs of the writer should be taken into account. Specially scheduled events and appointments should not cut excessively into the writer's time. A travel writer needs the opportunity to see the property through the eyes of a *guest.*

3. *Don't overdo.* When conducting tours of guestrooms or facilities, show only one in each category. It is also important to entertain travel writers when the property's schedule is relatively free. Combining a writer's visit with property openings or social events may leave little time to discuss the project at hand, and can leave the writer with a bad impression of management if he or she is ignored.

4. *Follow up.* It is generally a bad idea to load down the travel writer with materials as he or she is leaving, so press kits or other informational materials should be sent to the writer following the visit if they were not sent in advance of the trip. After the visit, a short note expressing the hope that the writer enjoyed his or her stay is appropriate. A few weeks after the visit, you may call the writer's editor to get an idea of the coverage the property will receive. After reviewing the finished article, you should send a letter of thanks to the writer, even if the story contains negative elements. After all, public relations includes enhancing the property's image with everyone, even an unhappy travel writer.

Press Relations

It is easier to establish or maintain an effective public relations program if your property enjoys a good relationship with the press. A property's chances of receiving positive publicity are enhanced if it can build an image as a place that makes it easy for reporters to do their work.

Never underestimate the power of the press. A few well-placed stories can propel an unknown property into the public eye as nothing else can; even established properties can benefit from—or be damaged by—the press's "third party" credibility. Therefore a good relationship with the media is vitally important.

News Media Interests

To develop good media relations and get the most from media coverage, you should consider several factors. First and foremost, your property's public relations person or staff must understand media interests. Just as property employees must sell the benefits of the property to guests, newspapers and magazines must generate reader interest and increase circulation; radio and TV stations must appeal to their audiences and increase ratings. Publishing or airing interesting features or news stories is one way the news media seek to appeal to audiences.

Good public relations staffs are aware of the elements required for a good news story. They are also aware of the problems faced by the media. Excellent press relations can be maintained by following a few simple guidelines:

1. *Prepare news releases properly.* A news release should be well thought out, written in the particular medium's typical style, and double-spaced to allow for editorial revisions. A who, what, when, where, why, and how paragraph should be included.

2. *Avoid duplication.* With the exception of general news releases (news of expansions, new entertainment offerings, and so on), properties should resist the temptation to submit the same story to a number of media outlets. Instead, the property should write the story from a number of angles. If a well-known performer is staying at the property, for example, the property can send out stories relating to the performer's past career, other performers who have stayed at the property, the history of the suite in which the performer is staying, and so on. In this way, the property can offer a measure of exclusivity, without seeming to show favoritism to one or two media outlets.

3. *Be honest.* If questions arise, the property's staff should be candid and straightforward. Inquiries should be dealt with quickly.

4. *Respect deadlines.* Deadline pressure is a fact of life for most news media representatives, and a prompt response to a question may mean the difference between a story that is "killed" and one that influences thousands of potential guests (see Exhibit 12). News releases and conferences should be timed with deadlines in mind.

It is important to get to know the local media. The property's public relations coordinator should make an effort to establish and maintain contact with radio and television reporters and program producers; he or she should also contact local newspaper offices and obtain a list of columnists and reporters who may be interested in material the property has to offer. Food, travel, and business editors at newspapers and local magazines should be cultivated. The property's public relations staff should get to know newspaper and magazine editors and their needs, perhaps by inviting them to the property.

Exhibit 12   Media Deadlines

Morning newspapers	3 P.M. to break the following day. Reach the editor the morning before.
Afternoon newspapers	9 A.M. that day. Reach the editor the day before.
Sunday newspapers	Wednesday (some sections 1–2 weeks ahead).
Sunday magazines	4 weeks in advance.
News magazines Weekly newspapers (based on Thursday publication date)	Monday. (Stories are written or rewritten Tuesday; printing and delivery take place Wednesday.)
Monthly trade magazines	Either the 1st or 15th of the month preceding cover date.
National monthly magazines (e.g., *National Review, Vogue, Atlantic*)	Either the 1st or 15th of the month preceding cover date. However, these magazines generally work on a three-month lead time (so, in April, they're working on the July issue).
Television news	2 P.M. that day for 6 o'clock edition. Most TV news conferences take place at 10 A.M.
Television features, talk shows	Book 2–5 weeks ahead of time (except in the case of big celebrities). Differs for each show, so check with the producer.
Radio news	Anytime. All-news stations are a particularly good bet.
Radio talk	Roughly 2 weeks ahead but, again, it varies from show to show. Check with producers.

A property must adhere to media deadlines in order to receive timely coverage of property news and features. This exhibit gives general guidelines for various print and broadcast media.

By developing good relations with news media personnel, unfavorable publicity concerning the property might be played down at a future time.

Personal Interviews

There may be times when a journalist asks you for a personal interview. It is almost always a good idea to comply with interview requests, whether they come from print or broadcast journalists. If an interview is refused, a reporter may try to piece together a story from outside, often uninformed, sources, or the reporter may ignore the property at a future time. Interviews can generate good exposure for the property and serve as a powerful public relations tool.

Insider Insights

Debbie Geiger
President, Geiger & Associates
Tallahassee, Florida

Debbie Geiger began her career in the hospitality industry at the Florida Division of Tourism as director of the state's publicity bureau. In 1985 she formed her own media marketing agency. Her agency represents a wide range of domestic and international tourism clients, including state divisions of tourism, convention and visitors bureaus, resorts, attractions, airlines, cruise lines, hotel and motel associations, and historic preservation groups.

Public relations—specifically media marketing—is a promotional strategy receiving more attention these days as hoteliers search for alternatives to the high cost of paid advertising. Forget those outdated notions that public relations is just being nice to your guests and fostering good will. Done correctly, public relations is a highly specialized marketing strategy with a measurable impact.

A full-page, four-color ad in the travel section of many large urban newspapers costs more than $40,000. That same ad could cost between $50,000 and $60,000 in many glossy travel and lifestyle magazines with a national circulation. Few hotels can afford that kind of advertising. Yet you can generate many times that amount of free editorial coverage in those publications if you know what to do to interest those editors in the newsworthiness of your property and its promotions.

As with sales activities, planning is the key to successful public relations. Your plan for public relations should take into account all the media outlets that reach potential guests. You should develop a press kit tailored to each media outlet. An ongoing series of press releases can announce your property's real news. You can also discuss potential stories with journalists either face-to-face or over the telephone. You can invite journalists to the property individually or put together a group press tour.

Once you decide to supplement your advertising and sales operations with a public relations effort, you must decide who will handle public relations activities. Your options include giving a current staff member public relations responsibilities, hiring a full-time public relations staff person, or contracting with a public relations agency.

If you decide to work with a public relations agency, ask agency representatives a lot of questions before you enter into a contract. The most effective agency will be one that offers media marketing for the hospitality industry, not advertising, as its primary business. The agency should be willing and able to provide numerous references from other clients, as well as from journalists who work for the publications or broadcast outlets in which you are seeking publicity. You should ask for examples of the kind of media coverage the agency has generated for other clients. It should also provide proof of its bility to negotiate complimentary air transportation to fly journalists in to see your property for editorial research. Of

---

Insider Insights *(continued)*

course, an understandable breakdown of the agency's fees, activities, and time frames is a must.

Finally, there should be chemistry. You should feel comfortable with the agency's personnel and believe you can trust them with your reputation. Monitor the agency's work on a monthly basis to ensure you are getting the service you are paying for, but let agency employees use their own judgment to do the job you hired them to do.

If you have an idea of the general purpose or direction of the interview, study pertinent information and develop answers to questions that may be raised. Avoid giving off-the-record information or taking potshots at competitors. Above all, be honest; a "no comment" response projects a negative image. It is usually best to answer questions briefly, but it is permissible to volunteer information that will help clarify the topic.

Keep in mind that the journalist is running the interview, and that clearance of the article or broadcast material that results is seldom offered. Most reporters will use a tape recorder to ensure accuracy, especially in cases where the material is of a complex or technical nature. In the majority of cases, a story or broadcast based on an interview will be correct and unbiased.

TV Interviews. A TV interview is slightly different from a print or radio interview in that the public will have a visual image of the property and/or its personnel. Obviously, appearance is important. If you are asked to give a TV interview, it is essential that you look and feel your best. Conservative clothes work best for television; stark white and bold patterns should be avoided. Flashy jewelry should also be avoided. You should project an image of credibility and stability.

What is said during a TV interview is also important, of course, especially if the broadcast is live. Being well-prepared is a must. You must be absolutely certain of the information you are giving. If asked a loaded question, deal with your objection first before answering the question. It is not necessary to pretend to be an expert in areas outside the hospitality field. In areas where you have no expertise, admit that fact or give an opinion and label it as such.

It is especially important to stay alert during a TV interview. You should follow the interviewer's instructions regarding the cameras and always assume the cameras are on until the interviewer says the interview is over.

Although a television experience can cause some nervousness or anxiety, you can learn to enjoy time before the cameras. TV interviews can be exciting opportunities to promote the property to a large, potentially profitable audience.

News Conferences

There may be times when a news release or an interview with one member of the media is not adequate. Perhaps the property has experienced a labor dispute or a disaster, and it is important that the facts be presented to all of the media to avoid speculation or misrepresentation. If there is sufficient cause for a news conference, these guidelines will help to increase its effectiveness:

1. *Schedule appropriately.* Except when the time of a news conference is dictated by a disaster or emergency, try to select a day and time convenient to the schedules of the news media. Most television and newspaper staffs need sufficient lead time to prepare stories or edit film, so an early morning news conference (9:00 to 10:00 A.M.) is usually best.

2. *Be prepared.* Special press kits relating to the presentation should be available. The speaker(s) should be adequately prepared—background or fact sheets should be studied, and answers to possible questions rehearsed.

3. *Keep the conference brief and to the point.* Presentations should be limited to around fifteen minutes and be followed by a question-and-answer session.

4. *Be aware of media requirements.* Make sure the room in which the news conference is held (whether on or off the property) is adequate in terms of space for the reporters and their equipment. If the news conference will be televised, there must be adequate electrical wiring and outlets, sufficient room for television equipment, and easy access. Also, do not use white backdrops or table covers. Make it easy on the press by displaying the property's logo on the lectern or conference table, and by providing biographies of the principals involved (the property's general manager, safety engineer, and so on).

5. *Maintain good press relations.* Be sure there is adequate parking and that someone from the property greets press members. If time permits, provide coffee or refreshments.

6. *Provide press kits to media members who were unable to attend the conference.* This should be done the same day, if possible, and immediately after the conference in emergency situations.

Sensitive Subjects

Bad news about the hotel may create lasting memories and negatively affect the property's image well after the disaster, labor dispute, or financial crisis is over. It is important, therefore, for a property to develop a public relations strategy to handle emergencies or other situations that can generate bad news. Proper planning can limit potentially negative publicity and reinforce a positive public image.

One of the most important elements in handling sensitive subjects is the naming of one spokesperson. This helps minimize conflicting reports and misrepresentations of facts. The entire staff should be aware of this policy and refer all questions from the media to a spokesperson who is fully briefed on the situation.

In most sensitive situations, information should be given to the media at a scheduled news conference so that each media outlet receives the same information at the same time. The spokesperson can then answer questions and describe positive actions being taken by the property. This often results in a more sympathetic press.

Four Common Negative Situations and How to Deal with Them

A Guest Commits Suicide or Is a Victim of Violent Crime

In the case of a suicide, the hotel itself is rarely responsible; your response should be low-key, and the media referred to the local police. In the case of a violent crime, especially when the hotel may share in the responsibility, you may overcome potentially damaging publicity by stressing the security measures the hotel had in place to protect its guests (roving security patrols, surveillance cameras in elevators, electronic door locks, and so on).

A Public Figure Engages in Illegal Activity at the Property

You are never obligated to answer questions about either the individual or the incident, but you should obtain the name of an authorized spokesperson to enable media calls to be referred to the proper party.

The Area Is Hit by a Natural Disaster

If the hotel is not damaged, you should issue a statement to that effect. If guests are taken in from hotels damaged in the disaster, media interviews with the guests will reinforce the message that all is well at your property.

If the hotel has been damaged, you should issue statements regarding the property's efforts to assure the safety and comfort of guests, and issue updates on the restoration of services or projected re-opening plans.

A Controversial Guest Prompts Demonstrations

If a demonstration takes place, you should issue a press statement to the effect that the hotel has no involvement in the demonstration. You should notify the local police if protesters must be removed from the property.

To avoid potential problems, you should obtain the name and telephone number of the guest's authorized spokesperson, to whom inquiries can be directed, and make arrangements to keep the visit as low-key as possible (get the guest in and out as quickly as possible, avoid connections to the property—e.g. property logos on podiums at press conferences, and advise the switchboard to handle inquiries as routinely as possible).

Source: Adapted from Stephen M. Agins, "How to Survive Bad Publicity," *Lodging Magazine,* January 1991.

The press may raise difficult questions, including how or why the problem or accident occurred, the name(s) of the person(s) involved, and estimates of damage. The spokesperson should never reply to these questions with a "No comment," but should provide a reason if he or she is unable to answer the question with specifics. It may be illegal to answer questions, especially when next-of-kin must be notified or in cases where only an insurance company can make an assessment of damages. The spokesperson can truthfully say that he or she cannot speculate on the cause of a disaster—the cause will be revealed after an investigation by the proper authorities.

The important part of crisis public relations begins long before there is an emergency. Managers and employees must be aware of property policy and their roles in dealing with the media. By following a well-directed comprehensive plan, the positive aspects of a property's press relations can combat any negative feelings the press and public may have toward the property because of the crisis.

When a Story Contains Errors

There may be times—no matter how good press relations have been—when a newspaper or magazine article, radio spot, or television report is slanted or contains misleading or incorrect information. In some cases, the property's image may be such that the negative story will not affect business and it is best to let the story die. In other cases, however, the negative publicity may be damaging and the error must be dealt with.

The best way to deal with an error is to contact the writer or broadcaster responsible and discuss it. Never appear to be trying to manage the news, but do present the property's case—backed up by facts—in a friendly, professional manner. If the journalist does not offer a satisfactory solution, the next step is to contact the editor or station manager and ask for a correction, retraction, or apology. Most media representatives are as anxious as hotel managers to maintain good public relations, and will generally cooperate by offering rebuttal time or an additional story to correct errors.

It is extremely important in these cases, no matter what the outcome, to avoid discussing the error with other media representatives or to attempt to discredit the offending journalist. It is important to maintain a good public image and build a reputation for fairness with the press.

Endnotes

1. Robert C. Lewis and Richard E. Chambers, *Marketing Leadership in Hospitality* (New York: VNR, 1989), p. 451.
2. The Society of American Travel Writers membership directory is available from the Society of American Travel Writers, 1120 Connecticut Ave., N.W., Suite 940, Washington, D.C. 20036.

Key Terms

news release

press kit

publicity

public relations

travel writer

value equivalency

video news release

Review Questions

1. What is public relations?
2. What are six factors to consider before developing a public relations plan?
3. What factors should be considered when hiring a public relations agency?
4. What are two ways public relations efforts can be measured?

5. How does publicity differ from advertising?

6. What are two examples of promotional materials especially prepared for the media?

7. What should be included in a press kit?

8. What can a hotel do to maximize a travel writer's visit?

9. What guidelines should be followed to maintain good press relations?

10. What guidelines should be followed if a news conference is required?

11. What is the best course of action if a story contains errors?

Part IV

Marketing

Chapter Outline

Business Travelers
    Frequent Business Travelers
        No-Frills Travelers
        Cost-Plus Travelers
        Extroverted-Affluent Travelers
    Women Business Travelers
    Types of Stays
        Overnight
        Extended
        Relocation
        Vacation
Meeting the Needs of Business Travelers
    Executive or Business Floors
    Business Services
    Health and Fitness Centers
    Special Amenities
    In-Room Refreshment Centers
    Frequent Traveler Programs
    All-Suite Properties
Reaching Business Travelers
Conclusion

15

Marketing to Business Travelers

T HE BUSINESS TRAVELER MARKET is the major market segment in the hospitality industry today, accounting for over half of all room revenue.[1] As the number of business travelers escalates each year, lodging properties are taking a number of steps to attract this lucrative market. In this chapter, we will discuss different types of business travelers and how properties are meeting their needs.

Business Travelers

While statistics on this market vary from year to year (and from source to source), one survey of U.S. business travelers reported that:

- 92% of all business travelers spent at least one night away from home on their most recent trip;

- 73% stayed in hotels or motels;

- the average length of stay was 4.3 nights; and

- more than half paid $50 or more per night for their accommodations; 11% paid $100 or more per night.[2]

These statistics explain why more and more properties are developing special amenities and services to attract business travelers.

Of all the different types of travelers, business travelers are perhaps the most knowledgeable and sophisticated, and they have definite preferences regarding the selection of a hotel:

1. *Convenient location.* Approximately 78% of all business travelers rated this factor as the prime reason for choosing a hotel.

2. *Clean, comfortable rooms.* This factor came in second (67%), and was in all probability influenced by the growing number of women travelers, who rate cleanliness high on their list of priorities. Several years ago, cleanliness was low on the list of selection factors—although it remains consistent as a primary factor in determining whether someone returns to a hotel.

3. *Room rates.* Over 55% of all business travelers cited room rates as a factor in hotel selection, although this priority is likely to change with the new influx of upwardly mobile, more affluent travelers entering the business traveler market.

Meeting the Needs of Business Travelers

As part of its ongoing effort to monitor the needs of business travelers, Wyndham Hotels & Resorts commissioned a nationwide poll of 2,000 men and women to determine the "Pet Peeves of American Business Travelers." The responses were as follows:

1.	Rooms that smell stale	70%
2.	Inefficient and unfriendly front desk personnel	64%
3.	Late or missed wake-up calls	62%
4.	TIE: Showers with low water pressure	60%
	Unfriendly or inefficient service personnel	60%
5.	Not being able to get an outside telephone line	59%
6.	Room keys that don't work	54%
7.	Cheap, uncomfortable pillows	53%
8.	TIE: Too long to check out	43%
	Thin, poor-quality bath towels	43%
9.	Inflexible check-out times	40%
10.	Too long to check in	38%

Courtesy of Wyndham Hotels & Resorts

4. *Recommendations of friends and colleagues.* Over 87% of business travelers make their own decisions regarding accommodations, and many (35%) base their decisions on the recommendations of colleagues or friends rather than on the recommendations of travel agents (11%); 22% make a choice based on corporate or company policy.

5. *Previous experience with the property.* Previous experience with a property or a chain figured as a selection factor with 33% of the business travelers surveyed. The respondents favored chain properties for their consistency and predictability; 41% said chains offered better service and 16% preferred chains for ease in making reservations.

6. *Facilities.* Meeting facilities influenced 33% of the respondents, while restaurants and food service were important to 22%. Restaurants and food service tend to be more important to business travelers who travel frequently, especially to women business travelers. Women business travelers were more likely to select hotels on the basis of extended-hour or 24-hour room service.

7. *Frequent traveler programs.* Although many properties place a great significance on these programs, this factor played a part in selection decisions for only 2% of those surveyed. Prospective guests were often much more concerned with the availability of services and amenities than with saving money through frequent traveler programs.[3]

Business travelers can be divided into two general categories: occasional and frequent. Frequent business travelers are responsible for approximately 50% of all business generated by business travelers and are more easily targeted than occasional business travelers. Many of the programs and services developed for frequent business travelers can also be used by occasional business travelers. Therefore, in this chapter we will focus on frequent business travelers and learn how properties are tailoring amenities and developing unique marketing strategies to reach this lucrative segment of the business traveler market.

Frequent Business Travelers

Frequent business travelers spend an average of 21 nights a year away from home on business and use hotels or motels 76% of the time. They are typically employed in managerial, sales, or professional positions, are well-educated (67% hold four-year college degrees), and affluent (67% earn over $35,000 per year, while 44% earn more than $50,000 annually).[4] While this group is largely male, an increasing number of frequent business travelers are women. This statistic should lead to increased hotel revenues because women tend to use in-house food and beverage services more than men do.

Several independent surveys have helped hotels design services for frequent business travelers. A MasterCard survey,[5] for example, asked the question, "Assuming that the primary considerations of location, room price, and cleanliness were comparable, what other factors are most important in making a lodging selection?" The following factors are accompanied by the percentage of frequent business travelers who found them important:

- Restaurant on premises (32%)
- Quality service (22%)
- Room appointments (14%)
- Sports and recreational facilities (14%)
- Ambience (11%)
- Entertainment on premises (10%)
- Prior knowledge (10%)
- Safety and security (3%)

The survey further revealed that there are three distinct groups of frequent business travelers: no-frills travelers, cost-plus travelers, and extroverted-affluent travelers. By studying the requirements of each group, you can create or revise amenities and services to attract one or all of them.

No-Frills Travelers. The largest group in the MasterCard survey (36%), no-frills travelers, is made up largely of middle- to upper-management men and women primarily interested in a clean, comfortable, and quiet room at a fair price. No-frills travelers show little interest in hotel-sponsored social events. In fact, the business-people in this group are almost hermit-like in their business travels. They are not as

Selling Economy Lodging to the Business Traveler

After the Marriott hotel chain took a look at the no-frills business traveler segment, it decided to provide a product that would meet the needs of business travelers who typically take six or more business trips per year, expect to pay $30 to $50 per night, and pay for their own lodging (no expense accounts).

The chain's economy product, Fairfield Inn, is the result of extensive independent research undertaken to determine the needs of economy-minded business travelers. As a result of the research, Fairfield Inn was developed to include a number of amenities requested by frugal business travelers while remaining in the $30 to $40 price range:

1. *King-size beds.* Room options include one king-size bed (preferred over queen-size beds) or two double beds.

2. *Free cable television.* Top-line cable programming was a preference; a satellite dish at each property brings in three premier cable channels (HBO, ESPN, and CNN) as well as local programming.

3. *Television remote controls.*

4. *Thick towels.* A top guest preference over the standard "postage-stamp size" towels found at other economy properties. Fairfield Inn's towels are the same as those found at more expensive Marriott properties.

5. *Free local phone calls.*

6. *A comfortable chair.* Recliners have complicated parts and are difficult to maintain, so upholstered chairs and ottomans are provided for relaxation.

7. *Large desk.* Business travelers' rooms must also serve as work spaces, so Fairfield Inn provides large desks. Guests can spread out papers and still have plenty of room to work.

8. *Alarm clock.* Since many business travelers worry about a missed wake-up call, alarm clocks are provided along with the wake-up service option.

9. *Coffee and tea in the lobby.* Rather than the more expensive individual hot water dispenser, coffee is brewed every morning and served in the lobby. This option gives guests a chance to circulate.

10. *Swimming pool.* Although swimming pools were included mainly for weekend leisure guests, business travelers may take advantage of this recreational option.

11. *Inside or outside room entry.* While some business travelers prefer the convenience of parking their cars next to their guestroom doors, others prefer the security of an inside entry. Fairfield Inn provides both types of guestrooms at all of their properties.

12. *Smoking or no-smoking rooms.* Again, guests requested a choice, so 25% of Fairfield Inn rooms are no-smoking.

13. *Long-cord telephones.* Long cords allow business travelers to make calls while working or moving around the guestroom.

14. *Separate vanity.* This amenity helps speed up morning activities if there are two or more people in a room.

15. *Meeting room.* A meeting room off the lobby is available on a first-come, first-served basis.

16. *Vending machines.* Vending machines provide snacks, juices, and soft drinks. Other machines dispense valet items that guests may have forgotten to bring.

In addition to marketing the physical amenities, stressing the quality of service is an important part of marketing Fairfield Inn properties to business and leisure travelers.

Source: Alan L. Dessoff, "Marriott Research Creates a Fresh Amenities Mix," *Lodging,* June 1988, p. 15.

interested as the other two groups in meeting people, staying where they are known, staying at fashionable hotels, or socializing.

Although they have higher budgets than cost-plus travelers, no-frills travelers are also likely to stay at budget properties. Properties that do not have facilities such as swimming pools, saunas, tennis courts, and putting greens, and properties that do not feature large bars or organized social activities have an excellent opportunity to attract this group. No-frills travelers were the only group to express a definite preference for a particular property atmosphere. Properties wishing to meet the needs of this group must convey a sense of peace and quiet—the atmosphere most desired by no-frills travelers, and one they are willing to pay for.

Cost-Plus Travelers. This is the next largest group of frequent business travelers (34%). Like no-frills travelers, these travelers are extremely cost-conscious, often to the point of forgoing convenience in favor of a lower room rate. Although cost-plus travelers—typically salespeople and middle-management executives—are often on strict expense accounts, many pride themselves on their ability to find bargains, and look for amenities at no-frills prices.

Cost-plus travelers are more interested in being sociable than no-frills travelers. A restaurant's operating hours, the availability of hospitality suites or lounges at which to meet peers, and no-cost amenities are important to cost-plus travelers.

Cost-plus travelers are generally more loyal or brand-oriented guests than the other two groups. Cost-plus travelers are more apt to belong to frequent traveler programs—both because of the value offered, and because of their loyalty to a property. Although cost-plus travelers are more likely to stay in a mid-price property on an interstate highway than in a first-class downtown hotel, they can be attracted to other properties if the price is right.

Extroverted-Affluent Travelers. This group, which made up 30% of the frequent business travelers in the MasterCard survey, holds the promise of generating higher sales per room than either of the other two groups. Extroverted-affluent travelers are typically young, affluent, and either self-employed, top-level executives, or professionals. They demand the best in amenities and service.

Extroverted-affluent travelers are not concerned with saving money (either on business or pleasure trips), and demand fashionable properties. More than the other two groups, extroverted-affluent travelers put a high priority on amenities. Recreation facilities, live entertainment, and restaurants offering the finest decor and cuisine are important to extroverted-affluent travelers, and having a good time is more important than the expense. This group is also more likely to add vacation time to a business stay.

While these travelers make their own decisions when selecting a property, they are more likely to be influenced by the suggestions of friends and colleagues than any other group. Extroverted-affluent travelers are also more likely to have travel agents or corporate travel managers book their reservation.

Women Business Travelers

Women are an important segment of the business traveler market. This segment is growing at a phenomenal rate: only 1% of business travelers were women in 1970;

today, 37.4% of business travelers are women, and this figure is expected to top 50% by the year 2000.[6] Women already constitute 50% of business meeting attendees and 51% of all meeting planners; therefore, you should take a close look at the wants and needs of these travelers.

Although businesswomen express many of the same preferences (location, rates, etc.) when making a hotel selection as their male counterparts, they appreciate different things when they travel. In one study, two out of three women mentioned cleanliness and attractiveness of hotels as reasons for booking, while only half of the men cited these factors as selection criteria.[7]

Since women tend to be more loyal repeat guests than men, it is especially important that a property provide the features most important to women travelers:

1. *Security.* Women tend to be more security-conscious than men. A study of women business travelers by Choice Hotels determined that a property's location/neighborhood was an important factor when women selected a property.[8] Most women consider door chains, dead bolt locks, and door "viewports" or "peepholes" essential guestroom features. Many women prefer hotels with a single entrance close to the front desk and an atrium, where all rooms open into a central, well-lighted area. Women also prefer hotels that feature an inside restaurant, room service, and a well-lit lobby. Valet parking or a brightly lit parking garage are other security essentials.

   A property can add to a woman's feeling of security by following security procedures in place for all guests, such as making sure front desk agents, restaurant staff, and valet parkers do not call out room numbers; refusing to give out room numbers to callers or visitors; and instructing bell staff to leave the room door open and check the room before leaving the guest. Of course, proper guestroom key control is a must.

2. *Comfort and service.* Women, like men, appreciate clean, attractive, well-lit rooms and friendly, courteous service. Amenities such as full-length mirrors and skirt hangers are popular with women (see Exhibit 1).

   Women are more influenced by good service than men; an unsatisfactory experience in this area will irritate women business travelers and make them less likely to return. Hotel staff should be trained to treat women in a courteous and businesslike manner. Many women will react negatively to overly familiar terms such as "honey" and "dear."

3. *Convenience.* Most businesswomen prefer to have a space set aside in their guestrooms for work or meetings. This is one reason suites are finding increased popularity with women—the bed is in a separate room, away from the business area. When suites are not available, foldaway beds are sometimes used, although these meet with mixed reactions. At the very least, a woman business traveler should have a desk with a telephone and good lighting.

4. *Facilities.* Because women tend to stay on the property more than men do, facilities such as swimming pools and fitness equipment are attractive to them.

Since businesswomen take more mini-vacations than businessmen, typically spend 25% more in restaurants than men do, and often meet with associates while

Exhibit 1   Amenities for Women Business Travelers

1. 24-hour room service
2. Laundry service and one-hour emergency pressing
3. Well-lit desk space
4. A morning newspaper and the opportunity to order breakfast via room service the previous night
5. Shampoo, detergent, and sewing kits
6. Upgraded lighting in bathrooms
7. Makeup mirrors, hair dryers, and ironing boards
8. Additional electrical outlets for grooming appliances
9. Adequate closet space and closet bars hung high enough to accommodate formal gowns
10. Skirt hangers and full-length mirrors
11. Sufficient towels and washcloths
12. 24-hour fitness and sauna services

While women business travelers cite the same general preferences for selecting a hotel (location, cleanliness, etc.) as their male counterparts, they have different requirements when it comes to amenities. A survey by Best Western International showed that the amenities listed above were most important to women business travelers. This list can serve as a guide to properties wishing to attract this growing market segment. (Source: Griffen Miller, "The Corporate Woman: Satisfying Her Travel Needs," *Business Travel Management*, November 1989, p.12.)

at the property, it is important that properties provide the security, comfort, and service that will appeal to this growing market segment (see Exhibit 2).

Types of Stays

Business travelers, no matter what type or gender, generate the following types of stays:

- Overnight stays
- Extended stays
- Relocation stays
- Vacation stays

Overnight. Overnight stays are probably the most common, and may include food and beverage sales as well as guestroom business. Quick check-in and check-out; clean, comfortable rooms; and easy access to quick food service are the keys to attracting overnight business guests.

Extended. Extended stays may be a combined business and vacation trip, a longer stay for a conference or study program, or a sales trip. Business travelers on extended stays typically require more amenities and services than do overnight travelers. Extended-stay business travelers look for on-site restaurants, entertainment, recreational facilities, and business services. Extra amenities such as suites, in-room bars, and kitchenettes may offer added appeal to this market segment.

Relocation. Relocation stays are becoming increasingly important to hospitality properties, particularly all-suite hotels. Many all-suite hotels provide additional services, such as city tours and baby-sitting services, to guests.

Vacation. Vacation stays are often an offshoot of business travel, either occurring at the end of a business trip or later when the guest returns to the property (either

Exhibit 2   Selling to Women Business Travelers

THE TRAVELING WOMAN . . .

THE TRAVELING WOMAN'S BILL OF RIGHTS

These are among a few of Ramada's policies that make a woman's trip problem-free. They are the heart of Ramada's employee training program designed to meet the specific needs of traveling women.

1. You have the right to a room that fits your needs for security or convenience to facilities.

2. You have the right to expect that your room number will be handled in a most confidential manner.

3. You have the right to have a bellperson check your room for security, and to make sure that all towels and amenities are in full supply.

4. You have the right to a good table in the dining area where you are assured privacy, yet aren't singled out as being alone.

5. You have the right to refuse cocktails sent gratis — and your server or bartender should not serve you an unrequested drink, or pass a note to you.

6. When arriving alone by car at a hotel without valet parking, you have the right to have a bellperson drive with you to the parking area, or meet you there, and accompany you back to the hotel with your luggage.

7. You have a right not to be addressed in a casual or familiar manner by employees.

8. And like any guest, you have the right to be treated with courtesy and to receive prompt, attentive service.

WHAT MAKES RAMADA SPECIAL TO WOMEN TRAVELERS

Ramada inaugurated its Traveling Woman Program and spearheaded the movement in the hospitality industry to provide women travelers with the utmost in security and comfort.

Ramada has set the industry standard in providing courteous, conscientious, and efficient service to traveling women by responding to their unique needs and the problems they encounter. By undertaking an extensive employee training program throughout the country, every member of the hotel staff is trained to respond to the problems and discourtesies encountered by women travelers. Ramada has instituted property-level improvements and provides room amenities to accommodate the particular needs of women travelers such as installation of skirt hangers, increased lighting, and added security measures.

Today, Ramada is leading the industry by addressing the more sophisticated needs of the woman traveler, who now represents a full 37% of the business traveling public. As a traveling woman, you will feel more comfortable at Ramada, whether you're traveling with business associates or alone, because Ramada understands your needs.

Ramada took the lead in addressing the needs of women business travelers years ago with its Traveling Woman Program. This program taught employees to be sensitive to the needs of women travelers. (Courtesy of Ramada, Inc.)

alone or with family members). In most cases, vacationers will require recreational facilities or easy access to recreational opportunities in the immediate vicinity.

Meeting the Needs of Business Travelers

Properties are meeting the needs of business travelers in a number of unique ways, including the introduction of women-only floors, executive or business floors, business services, health and fitness centers, special amenities, in-room refreshment

Insider Insights

Raymond E. Schultz
President and Chief Executive Officer
Hampton Inns, Inc. and Homewood Suites, Inc.
Memphis, Tennessee

Raymond Shultz is president and chief executive officer of Hampton Inns, Inc., a mid-price hotel chain, and Homewood Suites, Inc., a growing chain of extended-stay hotels. Prior to being named to his present position in 1983, Shultz held various senior management posts within former parent company Holiday Corporation's Holiday Inn Hotel Group. He was responsible for the group's franchise development, system marketing, product services, and business development. Shultz began his 20-year tenure with Holiday Inns, Inc., as vice president of information systems.

Before entering the hospitality industry, Shultz held several key positions in the IBM Corporation, including industry marketing manager. Shultz is a graduate of Pennsylvania State University, and holds a bachelor of arts degree in labor-management relations. He was named the "1991 Economy Lodging Council Person of the Year" by the American Hotel & Motel Association for his contribution to the growth of the hotel industry.

Homewood Suites, owned by the Promus Companies, believes the extended-stay segment is the fastest growing in the lodging industry. The first Homewood Suite opened in 1989; there are now 23 in 15 states.

In the hotel business, success often can be measured in the number of times a guest returns to one of your hotels. But based on our experience at Homewood Suites, there's no greater compliment than a guest who simply won't leave.

Pete Flannigan, a systems installer for AT&T, is one of those guests. When he checked into our hotel outside Hartford, Connecticut, his plans were to complete his three-month field assignment and head back to his home on Long Island. Before his three months were up, he reported that he was feeling right at home, and, thanks to an increase in business, extended his stay at our hotel—to a year and a half!

This feeling of being "right at home" is what extended-stay hotels such as Homewood Suites are all about. Extended-stay hotels balance the convenience and service of a traditional hotel with the comfort and atmosphere of a home or apartment. Our formula for achieving this balance is a careful blend of tangible attributes—a residential-style complex consisting of two- or three-room suites—with the intangible, the feeling of home that keeps our guests coming back, or, in cases like Pete Flannigan's, keeps them from leaving.

Who are extended-stay guests? By definition, extended-stay hotels cater to the sector of the traveling public that books a hotel room for five nights or more. These guests typically are in a given city for business seminars, training programs, corporate relocations, sales trips, or other temporary assignments.

(continued)

Insider Insights *(continued)*

Each Homewood Suites hotel has been developed with the idea that guests will use not only their suites, but the property overall, as a temporary home. So each of our hotels features a "community" concept, with residential-style suites built around a central hospitality center and swimming pool/recreation area.

We know that physical amenities—no matter how comprehensive—are just one part of making guests feel at home. So we've wrapped these physical facilities in a service culture so complete that we're able to guarantee every aspect of a guest's stay through our 100% Satisfaction Guarantee—or that night is free.

The feeling of home begins when a guest makes a reservation (800-CALL-HOME). When checking in, guests notice that our service teams are professional, but don't stand on formality. Each member of the service team wears a name tag bearing the employee's first name only, and the name of the employee's hometown. Our research reveals this small touch is one way to break the ice and make guests feel more comfortable about their extended stay.

We've empowered every employee—from the front desk agents to the housekeeping staff—to make guests feel at home. Whether it's baking a cake for a guest celebrating a birthday away from home, or working with the local school district to schedule a temporary bus stop at the hotel for a relocating guest's child, it's this attention to service that has helped achieve occupancy levels that currently lead the segment. Our recent Guest Satisfaction Study bears this out: we have an industry-leading overall rating of 96 percent, and an intent-to-return rating of 97 percent.

centers, frequent traveler programs, and all-suite properties. Most of these services have met with wide approval, especially the concept of executive or business floors. An exception is the women-only floor; many women travelers prefer not to be segregated.

Executive or Business Floors

Executive or business floors are designed to provide a secure, comfortable environment in which to meet peers, conduct business, or relax after a busy day. Double-tree Club Hotels, for example, offers Compri Clubs—5,000-square-feet facilities that include lounge areas, intimate bars, libraries stocked with books and periodicals, work desks complete with credit-card telephones, and large-screen televisions. Certain floors are set apart strictly for the use of VIPs and executives. The Club Floor at the Biltmore Hotel in Los Angeles offers a library, television center, game room, billiard room, and bar.

Executive-floor guestrooms are designed for an increasing number of executive travelers who want such amenities as special soaps and shampoos, terry bathrobes, turn-down service, and complimentary chocolates.

Executive floors require special promotion. Hotels use direct mail, press releases and other forms of publicity, and advertisements in airline magazines and such newspapers as the *Wall Street Journal* to reach upscale business travelers.

Word-of-mouth advertising and personal calls on corporations have also generated business for these special floors. Properties hope these floors will help change the image of businesspeople from harried travelers to pampered executives relaxing in facilities as comfortable and secure as their own homes.

Business Services

Business services are becoming important to—and expected by—business travelers. Secretarial services, copying machines, fax machines (both public and in-room), telex and cable services, computer terminals, and electronic mail are just some of the business services now offered by some properties for the convenience of business guests. At many properties, for example, a business traveler can call the secretarial service, dictate over the phone, and have his or her materials delivered the following day. Business travelers staying at the Chicago Hilton and Towers can request that a voice machine be hooked up to their guestroom telephone to provide an answering service. Guests are given a beeper to take with them when they leave the hotel; the beeper alerts them when they get a message. They may then call the hotel, ask for their room, access the tape with their beeper, and get their message.

Health and Fitness Centers

An increased awareness of stress—and its impact on productivity—has led many business travelers to pursue more healthy lifestyles, including dietary changes and a commitment to regular exercise. While properties have offered the standard swimming pool for years, it is not unusual today for properties catering to business travelers to offer a complete array of exercise options. These may include tennis courts, jogging trails, or complete health clubs featuring state-of-the-art exercise equipment, whirlpools and saunas, and even exercise instructors or personal trainers.

Special Amenities

Some special guestroom amenities for businesspeople have already been mentioned. For both overnight and extended-stay business guests, many properties feature guestroom work areas (some complete with personal computer hook-ups or special writing desks), and executive check-in/check-out programs, some of which are available via computer or through an in-room television screen. Other special amenities include complimentary copies of the *Wall Street Journal* or other daily papers, cable television featuring news and business stations, and even telephones and televisions in bathrooms to enable busy executives to keep up with the daily news while getting ready for the day.

In-Room Refreshment Centers

While in-room refreshment centers (also called minibars) have been standard amenities in European hotels for years, only recently have American properties offered this convenient—and highly profitable—service to guests. Minibars, which a hotel can purchase or lease, provide a convenient way for guests to refresh themselves or entertain in the comfort of their rooms. Favorite minibar items include light beer, spring water, soft drinks, peanuts, and scotch. Other items, such as juices, snack foods, and other mixers and liquors are usually stocked as well. Minibars are often linked to the hotel's computerized billing system for immediate posting of charges.

Frequent Traveler Programs

The growing number of business travelers has also prompted the development of frequent traveler programs that offer discounts, premiums, and hotel services to corporations or guests booking a specified number of room nights. The Holiday Inns' Priority Club, Hyatt Hotels' Gold Passport, Marriott Hotels' Honored Guest, Ramada's Business Card, and Sheraton's International Club are all examples of these programs. Properties should carefully weigh the expense against the results before heavily promoting a program, however. As mentioned earlier, only 2% of business travelers said they felt that a frequent traveler program was important when deciding on a hotel. Location, cleanliness, and rates remain the key factors in hotel selection.

While many frequent traveler programs are available at no cost, some chains, such as Sheraton, charge a nominal membership fee to cover startup costs. Chains and properties often offer elite levels in their frequent-traveler programs to pamper their best customers; those on elite levels (usually 5% or less of frequent travelers) enjoy such amenities as complimentary upgrades to suites, private club rooms, and complimentary transportation to the airport.

All-Suite Properties

All-suite properties also play an important role in serving business travelers. These properties are ideal for businesspeople who are relocating. Residence Inn by Marriott, for example, caters to businesspeople who stay seven or more nights, and offers monthly as well as daily rates to guests. Guests staying at Hawthorn Suites enjoy a living area, full kitchen, and separate bedroom. Hawthorn Suites also offers free breakfast buffets and hospitality hours, grocery shopping services, free daily newspapers, and outdoor recreational amenities.

Residence Inn has identified four areas of importance to today's transferees and their families:

1. *A home-like atmosphere.* A home-like atmosphere is important to 58% of this market segment. To address this need, Residence Inn properties are designed as a "neighborhood" of two-story, residential-style buildings.

2. *Residential-style housing.* Buildings that look residential are important to 36% of this segment. Residence Inn meets this need by offering both single-story studio and two-story townhouses surrounded by landscaping and recreational facilities.

3. *Price.* Of those surveyed, 32% listed price as an important consideration. Residence Inn's suites are priced competitively with hotels, and offer a sliding rate scale based on the length of stay.

4. *Reduced relocation stress.* Residence Inn helps lessen relocation stress by offering grocery shopping services, arranging for baby-sitters, and providing orientation activities.[9]

Exhibit 3   Hotel Reservations for Business Travelers

Source: Doreen Bell, "Frequent Travelers Speak Out," *Lodging Hospitality*, February 1990, p. 60.

Reaching Business Travelers

Business travelers are relatively easy to locate. Some, in fact, might be vacationers staying at the property who will be traveling on business sometime during the year. But in today's competitive market, you cannot rely on repeat guests or word-of-mouth referrals to reach business travelers. You must actively solicit specific business traveler market segments. Properties must first find out who makes business reservations, and then target those sources (see Exhibit 3).

Business traveler business—meals, functions, and rooms—can be obtained from corporations in the immediate vicinity of your property. Local corporations are often the sources of national business from traveling salespeople or state, regional, and national meetings. These corporations can be identified through a number of sources:

- Office building locator boards
- Chamber of commerce listings
- Competitors' function boards
- Local newspaper articles
- State and regional publicity materials

Business travelers throughout the nation can be targeted by obtaining the names of corporations and decision-makers through:

- Business publications and directories
- Travel publications
- State industrial commissions
- Mailing list brokers

This unusual ad was successful for Red Lion Hotels & Inns. (Courtesy of Borders Perrin and Norrander Inc., Portland, Oregon)

- National trade conventions

Potential business leads obtained through these sources should first be screened to determine market potential before any costly sales efforts are initiated. This screening may be done in the form of a direct mail questionnaire or a telemarketing survey, and a computer can be used to categorize responses.

As in all sales efforts, a direct approach will probably be the most effective for reaching potential business guests. You may employ sales letters, telephone calls, and even personal sales calls. Some properties locate a potentially profitable area and use a sales blitz to saturate the market and obtain business. A sales blitz can be

Targeting the Corporate Travel Manager

There are an estimated 4.2 million corporations in the United States, and these corporations spend a yearly average of $2 million on travel and entertainment (a half million dollars on lodging alone). To manage corporate travel growth and control costs, an estimated 30% of these corporations have corporate travel managers whose job it is to make travel arrangements for company employees. The number of corporate travel managers is estimated at 1.3 million, an increase of 132% since 1986.

To determine the characteristics of this group, *Hotel & Travel Index* commissioned Market Probe International to survey corporate travel managers (800 responded) to determine their characteristics and what influenced their travel buying decisions. Some of the responses were as follows:

1. Corporate travel managers list their leading duties as: (1) contacting travel agents for transportation or hotel bookings (68%), (2) making travel arrangements for company management (64%), and (3) making travel arrangements for travel staff and self (62%).

2. Corporate travel managers' personal involvement in travel planning activities for company employees included recommending (80%) and booking (76%) hotels, booking air or surface transportation (71%), negotiating corporate rates with travel suppliers (57%), and coordinating bookings for employees with travel agents (55%).

3. Nearly all corporate travel managers (96%) use travel agencies. Eighty-two percent use travel agencies for air bookings, 71% for car rentals, and 67% for hotel bookings.

4. More than half (52%) of hotel bookings made for company employees are made directly by corporate travel managers.

5. More than one third (37%) of corporate travel managers have computerized reservation systems (CRS), and 87% of these managers use hotel directories when making hotel bookings on the CRS.

6. Nine out of ten travel managers say information on the location of hotels is important when booking hotels for company employees. Other important information includes locator maps showing hotels and attractions (88%), the hotel's telephone number (86%), and the hotel's distance from the airport (81%).

Source: *Corporate Travel Manager Survey: A Study of the Characteristics and Hotel Bookings of Corporate Travel Managers* (An Independent Survey Prepared by Market Probe International for *Hotel & Travel Index*); Reed Travel Group, 1990.

effective if it is properly planned and monitored, and if collateral materials, follow-up information, and personal contact supplement the blitz.

In addition to contacting business travelers directly, properties can reach business travelers through a variety of other sources:

- Corporate travel managers
- Secretaries' clubs

- Travel agents

- Tour operators (group leisure travelers might have an occasion to revisit the property on company business)

- Real estate agents and relocation services

- Hotel representatives in key cities

Corporate travel managers often plan travel for company executives, and are excellent sources of referral business. Many corporate travel managers are members of such professional organizations as the National Business Travel Association (NBTA). This association serves the travel managers of over 400 corporations and business organizations and may prove to be an excellent source of business leads. Hotels may join the NBTA as allied members.

Secretaries' clubs are another effective way to reach business travelers and build repeat business. Secretaries' clubs are primarily social organizations. A property may offer annual parties, familiarization tours, the use of recreational facilities, and other rewards or incentives to secretaries who refer guests to the property. The Sheraton Meridian's Inn-Siders Club, for example, offers discounted food and drink tickets, the use of recreational facilities, and quarterly prizes to secretaries who provide the most bookings.

Travel agents and tour operators influence the lodging choices made by business and leisure travelers. Real estate agents and relocation services may be sources for leads regarding people in the local community who will be moving, or people new to the community who need a place to stay temporarily. Hotel representatives may serve to build both new and repeat business.

Properties can also target business travelers through advertising, promotion at trade shows, and public relations and publicity.

Advertising can take a number of forms, depending on the business traveler segment you are targeting.

Print advertising can be especially effective, as long as ads are designed to show benefits and amenities that will attract the targeted segment: no-frills approaches for the no-frills traveler, elegance and impeccable service for the extroverted-affluent traveler, and cleanliness and security for the woman business traveler (see Exhibit 4). Ads can be placed in local newspapers, regional newspapers of targeted cities, business and trade magazines, and travel and in-flight magazines.

You can use billboards to attract business travelers on the road, and direct mail promotions to promote to specific market segments. You can also use radio and television spots to reach business travelers. Radio is most effective at reaching businesspeople during the early morning and late afternoon drive times and on all-news stations.

Trade shows can be excellent opportunities to promote a hotel's facilities and services to businesspeople. Trade shows are most often used to reach association and corporate meeting planners.

Public relations and publicity are also excellent ways to reach the business community. You can get business press for expansions, promotions within various departments, and announcements of special business plans or amenities.

Exhibit 4 Sample Print Ads Targeting Business Travelers

Courtyard by Marriott targeted business travelers with a series of ads that featured the theme "designed by business travelers for business travelers." Each of the ads provides solutions to problems business travelers face on the road, and includes a photograph of a Courtyard property. (Courtesy of Courtyard by Marriott)

Public relations efforts can include sponsoring a business seminar, donating money for business scholarships, or organizing a "Career Day" at which representatives from a variety of businesses meet with students. The business community can also be cultivated with special "Business Appreciation Days," receptions or tours, and special discount rates for food and beverages, health club facilities, or other recreational amenities.

Conclusion

While business travelers spend over $100 billion dollars annually for transportation, accommodations, and meals,[10] studies have shown that business travelers are still faced with confusion—and a good deal of misinformation—due to today's many travel choices. When Marriott Business Travel Institute (MBTI) conducted a study in 1990, for example, it found that many business travelers didn't know what services were offered in a number of hotels or that airlines offer over one million fare choices (with over 160,000 of them changing daily). To help business travelers make cost-effective travel choices, the MBTI published a 28-page report, *Business Travelers: The Choice Is Yours (A Guide to Travel Options that Benefit the Travel Planner, Business Traveler and Bottom Line)*. This publication details travel options in transportation, lodging, and other travel-related fields.

As a result of surveys and studies such as Marriott's, many hospitality properties are developing special programs and services to appeal to business travelers. Executive or business floors, business services, executive check-in/check-out programs, frequent traveler programs, and all-suite properties are just some of the new facilities and services that have changed the nature of the hospitality industry. Most hoteliers feel that the change has benefited properties and business guests alike.

Endnotes

1. *Trends in the Hotel Industry,* USA Edition, 1992, PFK Consulting.
2. These statistics are a part of the 1985–1986 Survey of Business Travelers conducted by *Travel Weekly* and the U.S. Travel Data Center.
3. The statistics in this section are a part of the 1985–1986 Survey of Business Travelers conducted by *Travel Weekly* and the U.S. Travel Data Center.
4. MasterCard International Frequent Business Traveler Study. Prepared by MasterCard International, New York, NY 10106. Sample size: 344 telephone respondents.
5. MasterCard International Frequent Business Traveler Study.
6. U.S. Travel Data Center Survey of Business Travelers; reprinted in *Lodging,* December, 1991, p. 11.
7. This statement and some of the other material in this section on women business travelers were adapted from "The Woman Traveler: A Special Report," *Lodging Hospitality,* and Joan Moulsdale, "What Do Women Business Travelers Want?" *HSMAI Marketing Review,* Winter 1985.
8. Susan Bard, "Special Report: Women Travelers Sold on Safety," *Hotel and Motel Management,* August 20, 1990, p. 50.
9. The statistics in this list were gathered from Residence Inn's sales literature for prospective franchisers.
10. Brian P. Tierney, "More Than $100 Billion Worth of Untrained Business Travelers Are on the Road," Marriott Business Travel Institute News Release, 1991.

Key Terms

cost-plus traveler
executive floor
extroverted-affluent traveler
in-room refreshment center
no-frills traveler

Review Questions

1. What do business travelers cite as the prime reason for choosing a hotel?

2. How many nights during the year does the average frequent business traveler spend away from home on business?

3. The study on frequent travelers discussed in the chapter revealed what three distinct groups of frequent business travelers?

4. Which group of frequent business travelers expressed a definite preference for a particular property atmosphere?

5. Which group of frequent business travelers will probably generate higher sales per room than either of the other groups?

6. Women made up what percentage of business travelers in 1970? What is that percentage today?

7. What are some security measures hotels can follow to meet the security needs of women business travelers?

8. How are hotels meeting the needs of business travelers?

9. What sources may be used for locating local and national business travelers?

Chapter Outline

Individual Leisure Travelers
    Families
        Meeting the Needs of Family Travelers
        Finding Family Travelers
        Reaching Family Travelers
    Seniors
        Meeting the Needs of Seniors
        Finding Seniors
        Reaching Seniors
    Baby Boomers
    Others
        Business/Leisure Travelers
        Single Leisure Travelers
Group Leisure Travelers
    Tour Intermediaries
        Negotiating with Tour Intermediaries
    Types of Tours
        Motorcoach Tours
        Airline Tours
        Amtrak Tours
        Property Package Tours
Leisure Travelers and Small Properties
Conclusion

16

Marketing to Leisure Travelers

Y̲OU CAN INCREASE ROOM OCCUPANCIES and food and beverage sales by attracting leisure travelers as well as business travelers. Over 65% of all Americans take an annual vacation; Americans spend some $73 billion on leisure travel each year![1] The leisure traveler market can be divided into two segments: individual and group. In this chapter we will take a look at the needs of each of these segments and show where they can be found. We will see how you can reach leisure travelers through advertising, direct mail, travel intermediaries, and other avenues. Finally, we will discuss how properties are meeting the needs of leisure travelers through discounts, unique marketing methods, and special packages and programs.

Individual Leisure Travelers

Individual leisure travelers can be defined as non-business guests who are traveling independently rather than with a group on a pre-arranged tour. They can be divided into four general categories:

- Families

- Seniors

- Baby boomers

- Others

Families

Today's hospitality industry targets a diverse base of family travelers: married couples (who may travel with or without their children), single parents, and grandparents and other family members traveling with children. Families take mini-vacations (weekend trips and other stays of less than a week) and extended-stay vacations, and are also excellent sources of function business for such occasions as reunions and birthday and anniversary dinners.

Families—especially those with children—are generally cost-conscious. Many married couples without children are also cost-conscious, but they tend to place more emphasis on quality. They can afford to spend a little more on a vacation, since in many cases both the husband and wife work. Married couples without children do not always travel alone; they often travel with other couples.

While in the past husbands were usually the decision-makers for families, today women make almost 90% of their families' vacation travel decisions.[2]

Meeting the Needs of Family Travelers. Families will usually shop around when looking for lodging. They often prefer resorts or properties that are near a number of attractions. Properties seeking to appeal to families can offer special rates (no charge for children staying with their parents, for example), low-cost recreational amenities (swimming pools and arcade games rank highest in popularity), and kitchenettes (to enable the family to save money on meals). Other conveniences attractive to families include ice and soft drink machines, parking close to the guestroom, and laundry facilities.

Other ways properties are meeting the needs of families include special services, weekend packages, and advance-purchase discounts.

Special services. Special services can make a difference in a family's decision to visit or return to a property. Many properties provide families with free cribs, extra towels, and information of interest to parents, such as the names and telephone numbers of local pediatricians. Items for children in the gift shop, children's menus, and discount coupons for meals and attractions are other special services properties may provide.

Some properties provide recreational facilities designed specifically for children. The Westin Hotel in Winnipeg, for example, offers a weekend child-care center equipped with furniture and play equipment for children between the ages of two and eleven. The center is staffed by professionals and has proven to be a business-builder for the property.

Still other properties offer special "camps" and "clubs" for young visitors. Hyatt Hotels, for example, offers Camp Hyatt, featuring planned activities for children, with a frequent-stay program for kids. The Embassy Suites Resort Hotel in Palm Beach Shores, Florida, provides children's activities in its Fat Cat Beach Club.

Hilton Hotels offers youth programs at the Las Vegas Hilton and the Flamingo Hilton and Tower in Las Vegas, the Anaheim Hilton in California, the Hilton at Walt Disney World Village, and the Fontainebleau Hilton in Miami Beach. Activities range from breakfast with Mickey, Goofy, and Donald to pool and playground activities, movies, and arts and crafts. At both Las Vegas properties and at Walt Disney World Village, Hilton offers Youth Hotel dormitories for naps and overnight stays.

Weekend packages. While families are sources of business for extended stays, they are also taking more weekend trips, usually within 200 to 300 miles of home. This can be explained by the increasing number of two-income families. Statistics have shown that the number of two-income households has risen dramatically—from 28.5% in 1960 to 49.0% in 1985. This figure is projected to rise to 75% by 2000.[3] While this trend does provide more discretionary income, it results in less leisure time. Properties are taking advantage of this by creating special weekend packages offering quality accommodations and access to a wide range of facilities and recreational amenities.

Weekend packages can be action-packed or relaxing, budget or luxury. The Stouffer Hotel Company, for example, offers weekend "Breakations," special packages that range in price from $49 to $279 per night. Properties have taken a number of other creative approaches to attract families and other weekend travelers. Weekend packages for couples, for example, are often more successful

Selling to the Family Market

Because of the growing number of families traveling, many hospitality chains and properties are researching this lucrative market to determine how to attract it. The Holiday Inn Family Holiday Survey and the Hilton Report on Children and Travel revealed a number of family preferences—and ways for hospitality properties to meet the needs of the traveling family.

Special Rates

While many properties have offered a "Kids Stay Free" option for some time, more and more properties are offering special amenities—cribs, baby-sitting services, planned activities, etc.—at special family rates. In some cases, the family rate includes two adjoining rooms—one for the parents and one for the kids.

Supervised Children's Activities

No longer are parents limited to on-call baby-sitters. Many properties offer licensed child-care services, which provide such supervised activities as crafts, swimming, and off-site excursions to mini-hotels for children. Children's clubs (some with frequent visitor discounts and amenities) are also growing in popularity, with many offering club products and services (tee shirts, monthly or quarterly newsletters, and so on).

Special Children's Menus

Many properties offer children's menus with favorite foods such as tacos, pizza, hamburgers, fresh fruit, and healthy snacks in child-sized portions. At many properties, children eat free when accompanied by an adult.

Family-Oriented Services and Products

Many properties have teamed up with local attractions to offer discount rates, special children's excursions, and learning activities. In addition, property gift shops are stocking up on items popular with traveling families—activity books, crayons, comic books, and toys. Properties are adding video arcades to appeal to young guests.

No matter how a property decides to present its product and services to families, it is especially important to be aware of local and state guidelines (especially regarding child care) and to ensure the safety of parents and children alike.

Source: Peggy Palmer, "How to Sell to the Family Market," *HSMAI Marketing Review,* Spring 1991, p. 28; Lynn O'Rourke Hayes, "The Family Comes into Focus," *Lodging Hospitality,* October 1991, p. 99; and "Surveys Find Children's Opinions Count in Marketing Family Vacations," *Hotel and Resort Industry,* May, 1990.

when promoted as a getaway for groups of four to eight friends, rather than individual couples.

Theme weekend packages range from food or event-related festivals to elaborate murder mystery weekends (see Exhibit 1). Hyatt has had great success with its

An increasing number of properties are offering special family-oriented services and amenities to attract families with children. The Fat Cat Beach Club is promoted in a brochure targeted to children, while a quarterly newsletter from The Ritz-Carlton in Boston keeps kids and their families up-to-date on special activities.

Hyattfest Weekends, which are designed around such themes as wine tastings and ice cream festivals. Hyattfest Weekends include accommodations, participation in festival events, and discounts on meals and recreational amenities. Murder mystery weekends involve the guest in a dramatized "murder" and subsequent "investigation." At the end of the weekend, guests gather to determine who has correctly solved the mystery. This type of package includes accommodations, meals, and the fun of playing detective.

Sports weekend packages are popular with guests who want an active weekend. The Woodlands Inn, located 27 miles north of downtown Houston, is a good example of how a suburban property with appropriate recreational facilities can attract city-dwellers. The Inn's "King of Aces" sports package includes breakfast, unlimited golf on the property's renowned golf courses, use of the tennis facilities and health and fitness center, and a seasonal gift.

Shopping weekend packages can be used by downtown hotels to boost weekend business. In many cases, properties provide gift certificates and transportation to

Exhibit 1   Murder Mystery Weekends

Date	Location
January 13th/14th	BLOSSOMS, Chester.
February 3rd/4th	BEECH HILL, Windermere
March 2nd/3rd	ROYAL ALBION, Brighton
March 9th/10th	NEW CLIFTON, Blackpool
March 16th/17th	PRINCE OF WALES, Southport
May 25th/26th	PRINCE OF WALES, Southport
June 29th/30th	PRINCE OF WALES, Southport
July 13th/14th	IMPERIAL, Blackpool
August 3rd/4th	IMPERIAL, Blackpool
August 17th/18th	GOLF HOTEL, Woodhall Spa
September 7th/8th	PRINCE OF WALES, Southport
October 5th/6th	PRINCE OF WALES, Southport
October 26th/27th	ROYAL ALBION, Brighton
November 2nd/3rd	ROYAL ALBION, Brighton
November 9th/10th	PRINCE OF WALES, Southport
November 16th/17th	CAIRN, Harrogate
December 7th/8th	NEW CLIFTON, Blackpool

Other Murder Weekends for Private Parties can be arranged. For any further information contact:

Prince of Wales Hotels,
72 King St., Southport,
England. PR8 1LG.
Tel: (0704) 37700

To attract weekend guests, some properties offer murder mystery weekends. For one inclusive price, guests receive accommodations, meals, and the opportunity to play detective after a dramatized "murder." This concept, which is extremely popular in Britain, is also gaining popularity in the United States. (Courtesy of Prince of Wales Hotels, Southport, England)

leading department stores or shopping malls, in addition to discounting guest-room or restaurant charges. This type of weekend may also be combined with theater tickets or tickets to other special events—all for one inclusive price.

Escape weekend packages can vary greatly in price and scope. Often properties simply discount guestrooms and offer the use of the property's recreational facilities (swimming pool, health club, golf course, and so on) for the cost of the room (see Exhibit 2). Other escape packages may include special amenities such as breakfast in bed, champagne, and gourmet meals. Whether simple or luxurious, an

Exhibit 2   Sample Escape Weekend Package

OUR SECRET TO A MEMORABLE THANKSGIVING IS IN THE DRESSING.

Warm Up To Our Thanksgiving Package, From $87.50 Per Night.* Avoid the blustery weather and Aunt Jane's jellied salad this Thanksgiving. Start a new and elegant tradition at The Boca Raton Hotel and Club. We offer Five Stars, Five Diamonds and one dazzling experience on the Gold Coast.

Our special Thanksgiving rates include accommodations, breakfast and dinner daily, unlimited golf greens fees and tennis and lots of festivities. All for $87.50 per person, per night, based on double occupancy. Write P.O. Box 225, Boca Raton, FL 33429, see your travel agent or call toll free 800-327-0101.

And feast your senses at the most tasteful resort in all the world.

The Boca Raton Hotel and Club
QUITE SIMPLY THE BEST®

This weekend package, which invites prospective guests to escape "blustery weather and Aunt Jane's jellied salad," includes meals and recreational amenities. (Courtesy of The Boca Raton Hotel and Club, Boca Raton, Florida)

escape weekend package must be perceived as a real value and targeted to audiences within a reasonable distance from home. Some properties have pushed back check-out time to 4:00 P.M. to allow a more leisurely departure day (see Exhibit 3).

A property's target markets, facilities, and in-house amenities, as well as local attractions, will greatly shape the nature and success of packages offered. If your property has an 18-hole golf course, for example, a golf package is a logical choice. But if a hotel across town also has a golf course, your golf package should offer something more, either in terms of value or extra amenities.

Advance-purchase discounts. The family or budget traveler's interest in value has led to a new trend in the hospitality industry: discounts based on advance purchase of rooms. Ramada, for example, offers a discount of 30% off rack rates when travelers book 30 days in advance, while Holiday Corporation's discount rate program, "Great Rates," offers discounts of 20% to 40% at its Holiday Inn and Crowne Plaza properties. These programs are patterned after "Super Saver" airline fares, and certain restrictions may apply (and will vary from chain to chain). For example, Great Rates cannot be used in conjunction with any other discount, must

Exhibit 3   Marketing to the "Short Break" Traveler

In response to today's trend toward more frequent, but shorter, vacations, chains such as Hilton Hotels are promoting getaway weekends to attract this lucrative market segment. In this ad for travel agents, the chain promotes its special weekend package, which includes later check-out times, a free Continental breakfast, and an information service on happenings in 30 major cities.

Targeting the "Short Break" Market

One of the fastest growing and most lucrative segments of the leisure traveler market today is the "short break" traveler. The trend toward shorter, more frequent vacations can be attributed to the time crunch experienced by two-income families or busy executives, the recognition of the need for short breaks to prevent burnout, and the increasing costs of travel to distant locations.

According to the 1991 Hilton Times Values Survey and research by the Daniel Yankelovich Group, there is a growing number of travelers who are taking an average of four vacations a year, with 55% lasting three days or less, and half taken over a weekend.

Most of these travelers are looking for a convenient, nearby location that offers varied options—an opportunity to sample local culture, a choice of both indoor and outdoor activities, and opportunities for leisure and relaxation. Some travelers seek a planned agenda; others may wish to be on their own. In either case, the package offered by the property must be perceived as a real value. It may include lower priced accommodations, extended check-out times, discounts to area attractions or recreational facilities, and so on.

Short break or getaway weekends are an excellent way to boost weekend business. Since most short breaks are taken less than 500 miles from home (with the majority within a 250-mile radius), getaway vacations can be promoted through three of the least expensive advertising vehicles—local newspapers, radio, and direct mail campaigns.

Source: "Study Shows Executives Value Time-Out Vacations," *Hotel and Resort Industry,* September 1992, p. 8; and "Surveys Report Short Getaways Are Long on Appeal," *Hotel and Resort Industry,* May 1991, p. 37.

---

be guaranteed by credit card, and must be made at least one week (but not more than four months) in advance; any cancellation made within 72 hours of the arrival date results in a $25 fee.

Advance-purchase discounts, also offered by Hyatt, Marriott, and Days Inns of America, are aimed at families, leisure travelers on a fixed budget, and value-conscious travelers who often make airline reservations in advance to save money. While most of these programs are available at any time during the week, Hyatt's program is specifically targeted to the weekend market.

Finding Family Travelers. It is generally more difficult to obtain the names of individual leisure travel prospects than it is to find group leisure travelers, but families can be contacted through lists of names from mailing list brokers, membership lists of family-oriented organizations such as the YMCA and YWCA, and from referrals, direct mail questionnaires, and previous guest registrations. The most effective way to contact this market may be through travel agents.

Reaching Family Travelers. Family travelers can be reached through a number of avenues: direct mail; advertising in newspapers, magazines, and travel guides; collateral materials; radio and television advertising; and public relations efforts.

Direct mail can be especially effective if a member of the family has already visited the property on business or vacation. He or she will appreciate the opportunity to return to the property for a special promotion at a special rate. Direct mail can appeal to first-time visitors as well, especially if the direct mail effort follows a recent promotion or publicity-generating event at the property.

Advertising in newspapers, magazines, and travel guides can also get the word out to family travelers. When advertising to families, however, it is important to remember two things. First, most families are not just seeking a hotel; they are seeking a "vacation experience," whether the trip is for the weekend or for an extended period of time. Advertising must communicate the type of experience the family desires, whether it be an active-leisure experience or a quiet getaway. Second, many families make impulsive vacation decisions. While some families may plan their vacations for a year or more, many families decide on the spur of the moment to take mini-vacations or weekend trips. This makes advertising in newspapers especially important because frequent newspaper advertising keeps the public informed of special packages and events that may stimulate impulse getaways.

Magazine advertising can reach a vast audience (see Exhibit 4). Since many family vacation decisions are made by women, advertising should be placed in both general interest magazines and women's magazines. Ads can also be placed in special interest publications (such as golf magazines) that relate to property facilities.

Travel guide advertising can also be an effective way to reach family travelers. Many families seek recommendations from sources such as AAA and Mobil travel guides. Along with providing locator maps, these guides list a property's accommodations and services, but do not offer the opportunity to advertise special, short-notice promotions.

Collateral materials designed for families may be placed at bus, train, and airline ticket counters, at car rental counters, and at chambers of commerce in key feeder cities. These materials can also be distributed through direct mail packages, travel agents, or organizations that cater to families.

Radio and television advertising is used by many properties to reach family leisure travelers. While television is usually too costly for the average small to mid-size property, these properties can use radio to announce family promotions.

Hotels can also reach family travelers through public relations efforts. A special family-oriented weekend such as a tennis clinic can generate favorable publicity, both in terms of press coverage and word-of-mouth recommendations. In addition, a property can offer special rates that might interest the news media. Offering adjoining rooms for a single price or rolling back to 1950s prices in conjunction with a '50s promotion may make newsworthy copy that generates family leisure business.

Seniors

Seniors are a growing—and highly profitable—part of the leisure traveler market. Statistics show that one out of every five Americans is over the age of 54; this age group accounts for nearly one-third of all hotel business.[4] The average household income for Americans between the ages of 50 to 65 is almost $30,000, nearly 20%

Exhibit 4   Sample Magazine Ad for Family Travelers

This magazine ad appeals to family travelers by promising low rates and activities for the kids.

higher than the national average. Seniors control nearly half of the nation's discretionary income—an estimated $150 billion (see Exhibit 5).

Our nation's older population is healthier and more active than ever before. According to the American Association of Retired Persons (AARP) and the U.S. Travel Data Center, older travelers account for:

Exhibit 5   The Seniors Market

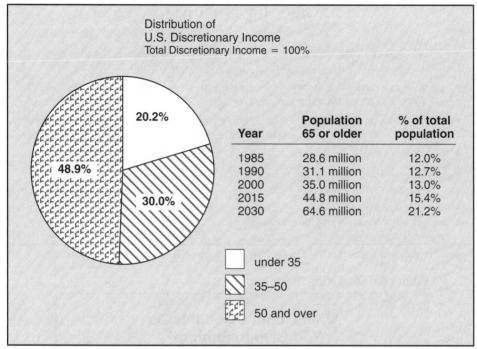

Distribution of
U.S. Discretionary Income
Total Discretionary Income = 100%

Year	Population 65 or older	% of total population
1985	28.6 million	12.0%
1990	31.1 million	12.7%
2000	35.0 million	13.0%
2015	44.8 million	15.4%
2030	64.6 million	21.2%

□ under 35

▨ 35–50

▥ 50 and over

In the coming years, that portion of the U.S. population that is 65 or older is expected to dramatically increase. What does this mean to the hospitality industry? Seniors already control nearly half of the discretionary income in the United States, and with the growing number of seniors with more money and leisure time, the hospitality industry is in an excellent position to capture more of this discretionary income in the future. Older travelers can be more flexible about when they travel than families, making seniors an excellent potential source of business for the off-season. (Source: U.S. Census Bureau projections, and "Midlife and Beyond: The $800 Billion Over-Fifty Market," Consumer Research Center.)

- 30% of all travel
- 30% of air trips
- 32% of nights spent in hotels and motels
- 72% of trips in recreational vehicles
- 44% of adult passports issued

Seniors are especially important to the lodging industry. Many older people have the time and money to travel more often, stay longer, and, if retired, travel more easily at any time of the year. Seniors are also frequent users of in-house restaurants, and can be extremely loyal, generating both repeat business and word-of-mouth referrals.

Meeting the Needs of Seniors. Like family travelers, many older travelers are value-conscious. Many properties now offer clubs or other programs that provide special rates or services to mature travelers (see Exhibit 6).

Older Traveler Trivia

- Polls of Americans over 55 revealed that this age group rejects the idea of being old, and dislikes being grouped together as "senior citizens."

- Older travelers take three or more vacation trips a year, which average 20% longer than those taken by younger travelers.

- More than half of older Americans enjoy traveling together and are largely responsible for the 10 to 12 percent annual growth of the group travel industry.

- Americans between 55 and 64 eat out an average of three times a week.

- The number of parents who feel obligated to leave as much money as possible to their children has dropped from 80% to 27%.

- *Modern Maturity* magazine reaches 18 million households; the net worth of the average reader is more than $159,000.

Source: "Myths and Facts of the 50+ Market," *Courier Update on Travel*, October 1990, p. 95.

Exhibit 6   Marketing to Seniors

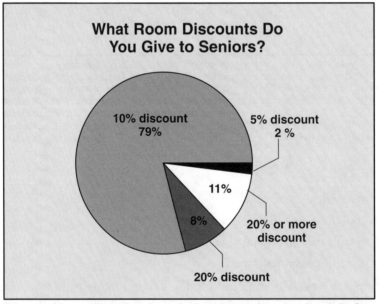

What Room Discounts Do You Give to Seniors?

- 10% discount 79%
- 5% discount 2%
- 11%
- 8%
- 20% or more discount
- 20% discount

Because of the emphasis placed on value by older travelers, more hospitality firms are offering discounted rates (on both accommodations and food) to attract seniors. (Source: *Lodging Hospitality* research.)

Days Inns of America's September Days Club offers travelers aged 50 or above a 10% discount on room rates, gift items, pharmaceuticals, and dining at nearly 300 properties across the country. In addition to these discounts, the $10 annual membership fee also entitles older travelers to discounts on rental cars and on travel by bus, airplane, and cruise ship.

Hilton Hotels' LXV (65) Club offers unlimited lodging for two for $999 per year. This fee entitles the member to share a room with another person (who does not have to be over 65) at over 215 hotels and inns in 42 states. Members cannot exceed five nights per trip or 15 nights per year to any one destination area, cannot stay within 100 miles of home, and can only get rooms on a "space available" basis for such special events as the Kentucky Derby and the Super Bowl.

Omni Hotels offers a special program for AARP members that includes 50% off room rates any night of the week (based on space availability) in 23 luxury hotels nationwide. A complimentary continental breakfast is provided to the guest and the guest's registered companion, and a 15% discount is offered on food and non-alcoholic beverages at Omni Hotel restaurants. To qualify for these benefits, guests have only to show their AARP membership card at check-in.

Other properties offering discounts or special services to seniors include Hampton Inns (Lifestyle 50 program), Sheraton (Retired Persons Plan), Marriott (Leisure Life Program), TraveLodge (Golden Guest Program), Choice Hotels (Prime Time), and Ramada (Best Years). Age limitations and membership fees, if any, vary somewhat in each of these programs.

Many older travelers are value-conscious, but they also insist on quality and service. Clean, comfortable rooms and public areas are important to them. Many of these travelers prefer rooms with two beds, and look for well-lit public rooms for conversation and card playing. Seniors are interested in safety and security, and generally prefer guestrooms on the ground floor or near elevators, smoke detectors in guestrooms, and light-colored carpets (especially on stairs).

Older travelers are also influenced by personal attention. A property's staff can build guest loyalty if it takes the time to talk to and listen to seniors and meet their specialized needs. One of these needs is personalized service in the dining room, and, since many older guests prefer to dine early, it is often easy for restaurant staff to provide this extra personal attention.

The front desk staff should take advantage of other opportunities to extend special service. Front desk agents should be trained to offer general information about hotel services and the local area. Since many older guests are interested in exercise, the staff can make a favorable impression by recommending nearby walking or jogging routes and other exercise facilities.

Information is so important to older travelers that Choice Hotels has produced a 40-page booklet, *Tips for Travelers Over 60*, as part of its Prime Time program. This publication lists brief descriptions of hotel types (luxury, all-suite, etc.), their price ranges, and addresses and telephone numbers for major travel associations and senior citizens' organizations. It also gives tips on how to select and work with a travel agent; how to travel by car, airplane, boat, bus, and train; and how to find a property that can meet the needs of older travelers. Such a publication can prove invaluable to seniors when they are making travel decisions.

Finding Seniors. As with family travelers, it is difficult to solicit individual seniors. You can reach seniors through mailing list brokers, membership lists of senior

Exhibit 7   Senior Citizens' Organizations

These are some of the major organizations serving America's senior citizens. While many of these organizations will not provide the names and addresses of their members, they will offer advice to properties who wish to serve senior citizens, and some produce publications that accept travel advertising.

The American Association of Retired
  Persons & The National Retired
  Teachers Association
1909 K St., NW
Washington, DC 20049
(202) 872-4700

Mature Outlook
P.O. Box 1205
Glenview, IL 60025
(800) 336-6330

The National Council of Senior
  Citizens
925 15th St., NW
Washington, DC 20005
(202) 347-8800

Catholic Golden Age
1012 14th Street NW
Suite 1003
Washington, DC 20005
(202) 737-0231

National Association for Mature People
P.O. Box 26792
Oklahoma City, OK 73118
(405) 523-5060

citizens' organizations (see Exhibit 7), referrals, direct mail questionnaires, and previous guest registrations.

It may be more cost-effective for you to target older travelers through in-house promotion of your property's senior citizen program. Older travelers are not always aware of these programs, and a point-of-purchase display may lead seniors to sign up immediately to take advantage of discounts. Their pleasurable stay at substantial savings may lead them to recommend the property to others.

Reaching Seniors. Besides in-house promotions, you might consider promoting to seniors through religious groups and private associations such as local community centers where seniors gather for recreation and friendship. Many of these organizations are delighted to work with hotels to help arrange low-cost vacations for their members.

Print advertising to reach this market may be placed in local and feeder city newspapers and in various magazines. While such organizations as the AARP, the National Council of Senior Citizens, and the Catholic Golden Age will not release the names of their members, they do offer publications that accept travel advertising.

In order to effectively sell to seniors, you should customize advertising or other promotional efforts. Value is often of utmost importance, for example, but this doesn't mean that rates have to be slashed; offering an upgrade or a free amenity (such as a complimentary breakfast or tickets to a local cultural event) often results in increased sales. Promotional material should reflect seniors as they perceive themselves—active and healthy—and should stress service, convenience, and reliability as well as savings.

You can also advertise to older travelers in travel guides. In addition to the AAA and Mobil guides, seniors turn to publications available at most local libraries such as *OAG TRAVEL PLANNER/Hotel & Motel RedBook* and *Hotel & Travel Index.*

Collateral materials that promote special packages for older travelers can be distributed through direct mail campaigns, travel agents, senior citizens' clubs, chambers of commerce, and so on.

Baby Boomers

The baby-boomer market consists of the 77 million Americans born between 1946–1964, and covers a wide spectrum. Baby boomers include single adults, two-income couples without children, couples with children, and blended families. This lucrative group, with an average income of $53,000, takes more trips, travels more for both pleasure and personal reasons, stays longer, and accounts for nearly 53% of today's hotel guests.[5]

Baby boomers, which will account for 66% of the U.S. population by the year 2000, are interested in value and quality. Special package prices appeal to all segments of this group, while parents tend to look for facilities and programs that will give them opportunities to spend quality time with their children.

Baby boomers generally have little time for television and rarely read the entire newspaper, making advertising in these vehicles less cost-effective if you are trying to reach the baby-boomer market. A combination of radio spots and outdoor advertising is usually the best approach to reach this group. Ads should stress value, quality, and the unique experience offered by the property.

Others

Other individual leisure travelers include business travelers on extended business/leisure trips and single travelers who may be traveling alone or with a group of other singles.

Business/Leisure Travelers. Many businesspeople who extend their stays are interested in some form of self-improvement. A property that offers special programs—from tennis clinics and fitness weekends to language classes and financial seminars—may attract this type of traveler.

There are a number of ways to reach business/leisure travelers. Convention attendees, for example, can be asked to stay after the convention, either indirectly by providing the meeting planner with information about local attractions and special hotel packages, or directly by talking to the delegates as they arrive or at appropriate times during the convention. Delegates, especially association delegates who are attending on a voluntary basis, will often respond to a personal invitation.

You can also reach business/leisure travelers by direct mail. If a businessperson makes a Thursday reservation, for example, you can send with the confirmation notice a brochure or flier that invites the traveler to extend the stay through the weekend. You may decide to place ads in the business pages of local and feeder-city newspapers (see Exhibit 8). Radio spots on all-news stations are excellent ways to advertise weekend promotions to business travelers who are looking for worthwhile mini-vacations.

Exhibit 8   Discount Weekend Rates

Stay a whole weekend. Get half off.

For a limited time only, you can stay at the Watergate Hotel for a weekend getaway and get away with a great price. Our half-price Watergate Weekend includes Continental Breakfast for two and parking. Reserve your room or suite for Friday, Saturday or Sunday night. Call right now. Availability is limited.

The Watergate Hotel

CUNARD
A Family of Distinctive Hotels

2650 Virginia Ave. NW
Washington DC 20037
For reservations, call (800) 424-2736
or (202) 965-2300.

Many properties that cater to the business traveler during the week face low occupancies over the weekend. To help fill rooms, many properties offer special rates for guests staying over the weekend.

Single Leisure Travelers. Many single leisure travelers look for personal enrichment while on vacation, and, like the business traveler on an extended stay, may enjoy hotel-sponsored activities such as unique food events or personal enrichment seminars. Such activities provide the opportunity to meet other singles, as do recreational facilities.

The singles market, however, is not made up solely of unmarried adults. The increasing number of two-income households has made it difficult for married couples to take time off together. A growing market segment, made up of married individuals traveling without their spouses, travels in small groups to destinations or activities such as historical or cultural events, sporting events or tournaments, business or personal enrichment seminars, etc.

You can reach single travelers with print ads. A getaway package, for example, can be offered in the entertainment or business section of a key feeder-city newspaper. Many single travelers are attracted to sophisticated consumer magazines, which make excellent vehicles for promoting packages or programs for the single traveler. Broadcast media advertising can also be effective.

A number of single travelers join travel groups. The formation of a singles program within a chain or at an individual property could attract this market segment, as could offering singles' packages through travel agents or direct mailings.

Group Leisure Travelers

Group leisure travel business can greatly benefit a property. First and foremost, groups can be scheduled during soft business periods, generating much-needed room occupancies and revenues. Groups are easier to plan for than individual guests, since you know exactly when the group will arrive, how many people are in it, what services it will require (meal functions, baggage handling, and so on), and the duration of the stay.

Although group leisure travelers are sometimes thought of as simply groups of people taking pre-arranged vacations, they are actually part of a complex travel and tour system. Group tour packages range from transportation, accommodations, and baggage handling to more extensive arrangements that include such add-ons as meals, sight-seeing, entertainment, and admission to attractions. Since group tour packages are usually arranged by a travel intermediary, it is important to understand the various types of travel professionals involved.

Tour Intermediaries

Travel professionals who arrange tours include tour brokers, tour wholesalers, and retail travel agents.

Tour brokers, also known as motorcoach brokers or tour operators, are licensed by the Federal Interstate Commerce Commission to put together package motorcoach tours in the United States and, in some cases, Canada. While tour brokers do not actually provide the transportation, they contract with certified carriers such as Greyhound or Continental Trailways for the buses required, and with hospitality properties for accommodations or meals. Many tour brokers operate travel agencies through which tours are sold. Motorcoach tours can also be sold by motorcoach companies or travel companies. Tours include motorcoach transportation, room and tax, baggage handling, and tickets to attractions (when applicable).

The tour broker assumes responsibility for the success of the tour. He or she does not work on a commission basis. If seats are not sold, the tour broker must take a loss on the deposits paid out to properties, attractions, etc.

Tour wholesalers, like tour brokers, put tour packages together, but typically work with airlines rather than ground transportation. Most tour wholesalers contract with hotels, airlines, and other travel and lodging suppliers months in advance, and put packages together that are sold through retail travel agents, incentive travel companies, or their own travel agencies. These packages include air transportation, hotel or motel accommodations, and such extras as meals, sight-seeing, and entertainment, all at prices lower than those a traveler would pay on an itemized or individual basis.

Pricing Rooms for Tour Groups

While many lodging operators believe that tour business is undesirable due to high discount rates, selling rooms to this market segment can be profitable. Look at the following example of a hotel charging $60 rack rate for a single, $70 rack rate for a double:

Typical Revenue from a Commercial Traveler	$ 54.00 (Single)
Less 10% travel agent commission:	− 5.40
Less 4% credit card cost:	− 2.16
NET:	$ 46.44
Typical Motorcoach Tour Revenue	$ 70.00 (Double)
Less 20% discount:	− 14.00
NET:	$ 56.00

In this example, it is more profitable to sell motorcoach doubles at $56 each than to sell commercial singles at $46.44. As in this case, most group tour rates will be equal to or greater than the average daily rate.

Retail travel agents are intermediaries who sell tours offered by tour brokers and wholesalers, as well as tour packages developed by properties.

Negotiating with Tour Intermediaries. Companies that package tours buy "in bulk" from hotels, sight-seeing businesses, and transportation companies, and then add a markup to all the tour's elements to reach an all-inclusive price. Because they block a number of rooms, these tour intermediaries often try to negotiate a significant reduction off the hotel's room rates. Hotel salespeople, therefore, must be well versed in negotiating skills to effectively represent the hotel's interests, while continuing to maintain a good working relationship with tour intermediaries.

The first rule in negotiating is to be prepared. You must have a clear view of your own situation and an understanding of the other party's needs. This type of a foundation results in a climate conducive to negotiating a "win-win" situation for both parties.

Most properties strive to build a base of both transient and group business. The number of rooms set aside for group and tour business is commonly called the *group sales allotment,* and, although these rooms are often sold at discounted rates, they can be an important source of revenue. While it may not seem cost effective to discount rooms at the normal discount of 20% off rack rates, guestroom sales to tour groups can actually result in higher revenue than sales to individuals.

Once you clearly understand your property's position, it is easy to go into a negotiating session with a commitment to one's product. By clearly understanding the value of what your property has to offer, it is far easier to overcome the tour intermediary's price objections. However, it is equally important for the negotiator to understand the travel intermediary's point of view. By listening carefully and understanding the other party's needs in terms of services, rates, space, and policies and procedures, you can more easily offer compromise solutions that will be mutually beneficial.

Types of Tours

There are four types of tours commonly taken by group leisure travelers: motorcoach tours, airline tours, Amtrak tours, and property package tours.

Motorcoach Tours. Motorcoach or bus tours fall into two general categories: the overnight or non-destination tour and the destination tour.

Overnight tours are stops en route to another destination. These tours are an opportunity for your property to increase food and beverage revenues as well as guestroom revenues, provided you can give the quick service motorcoach tour groups require for baggage handling and meals.

Overnight tour guests have usually been traveling for many hours and appreciate special services upon arrival. Many properties offer refreshments and an information session while guestroom keys are being distributed to the tour escort and baggage is being unloaded. Depending on departure time, brief local tours may be arranged for overnight guests, but, in any case, group travelers should be familiarized with the property's attractions and facilities.

Overnight tour guests appreciate having a wide variety of food choices available. Buffets and cafeteria-style service are popular. Many motorcoach tours cater to older travelers who appreciate light fare or room service. Breakfast service on the morning of departure should be handled quickly. As a precaution, restaurant staff should be increased to handle the demands of the group on a timely basis.

Destination tour guests are those who will be staying a minimum of two nights to either take advantage of a property promotion or to use the property as a base of operations to tour local attractions. Often these travelers have also been traveling for a long time, and may appreciate a tour of the facilities upon arrival, both to get acquainted with the property and to stretch their legs.

While technically not motorcoach tours, since travel intermediaries and special packages are usually not involved, motorcoach charters are another potential source of group business for properties. Motorcoach charters are groups of people traveling together who select a destination and then contact a motorcoach company to charter or rent a bus to take them to their destination. Overnight stops and the destination property may be decided on by the group; in other cases, the group will ask for the motorcoach company's recommendations.

In order to attract groups traveling on a charter arrangement, you should approach groups or organizations that typically arrange charters. (Charters are not limited to motorcoach companies; airplanes and trains can also be chartered.) Contact persons for this type of business can be found in both the corporate and association meeting planner categories.

Meeting the needs of motorcoach tour travelers. Most motorcoach tour groups enjoy being welcomed by a greeting on the property sign's reader board and a reception or happy hour either before or after their orientation tour. A welcoming party hosted by the property's manager or another hotel representative

Insider Insights

Chaney Ross
Director of Sales
Holiday Inn
Hammond, Louisiana

Chaney Ross worked as night manager in the advertising department of a local newspaper while attending the College of Journalism at Ohio State University, and later accepted a position as production manager in one of the city's largest advertising agencies. On both of his jobs, Chaney worked closely with salespeople. It didn't take him long to realize that his fate and income were in their hands, since the financial future of both businesses depended on the salespeoples' talents and ability to produce revenue. He wanted to place his future in his own hands, so he embarked on a career in sales, selling everything from pots and pans, appliances, and automobiles to approximately ten million dollars' worth of real estate! When the opportunity arose to put his sales experience to work in the hotel industry—an industry that had long fascinated him—Chaney jumped at the chance. As a director of sales, he feels that selling hotel rooms and services—especially to the tour market—is one of the most exciting, challenging, and competitive occupations one can find.

It requires an all-out, disciplined effort over a long period of time to get a share of the tour market segment. There are many "musts" to be followed to meet tour market goals.

Tour and motorcoach operators like to do business with hotels that provide good service to their clients, and the entire hotel staff must act in concert to establish this atmosphere. All groups must be met, all rooms must be pre-assigned, express check-in and smooth baggage handling must be a part of the service, and guests must feel they're wanted and are being attended to in a courteous and efficient manner. In addition to serving guests, the property must be flexible enough to meet the needs of tour operators. Operators have unusual problems from time to time, and they need and appreciate assistance. Sometimes bending the rules is necessary!

The property must be consistent and honest, and must take the good with the bad. A hotel sales representative can't tell tour operators that their business is wanted only on weekdays, not weekends; or their business isn't wanted during the hotel's peak season because their lower group rate adversely affects the average daily rate. The arrangement between the hotel and tour operators must be equally satisfactory and profitable to both. The hotel's promises should be "good as gold." Nothing destroys a relationship faster than a property's failure to keep its word.

One of the ways a property can tap into the tour market is by maintaining memberships in industry associations such as the American Hotel & Motel Association, the Hospitality Sales & Marketing Association International, the National Tour Association, the American Bus Association, the Travel Industry Association of America, and local and state tourist commissions. In addition to these affiliations, clients can be met face to face through participation in trade shows and seminars.

Insider Insights *(continued)*

No matter what sales avenue is chosen, it must be part of a property's long-range marketing plan. Market segments must be targeted and worked in depth; efforts should not be so thinly spread that they become diluted and ineffective. It's important to build lasting relationships with tour and motorcoach operators, and these relationships can only be built slowly and carefully.

The consistent theme behind the "musts" I've been talking about is *salesmanship.* You are constantly selling yourself, your property, and your services. Hotels can do many things in an attempt to gain the public's attention. A hotel room, amenity, or service can be advertised, promoted, romanced, and hyped, but nothing really happens until some talented salesperson *sells* it!

Selling. That's where the action is; that's where the thrill is. I invite you to try it.

can make a favorable impression on guests and increase the property's chances for repeat business. Guests may also be impressed by such special features and services as a game room for cards, checkers, and chess; free coffee in guestrooms; free maps of the local area; discount coupons for local attractions; and excursions to nearby points of interest, escorted by a property staff member.

Both overnight and destination tour travelers look for clean, comfortable rooms and friendly service. Plenty of guestrooms with two double beds should be available, along with a few singles for the group's tour escort, bus driver, and tour guests desiring to room alone. All rooms should be equipped with basic amenities such as telephones, televisions, and full baths, and should be blocked together for group security and the supervision of children, if any. When blocking rooms, consider the nature of the group. For example, older travelers, as previously mentioned, usually prefer ground floors.

Attention to safety is considered a prime factor in booking groups. Hallways should be well-lit, elevators should have emergency telephones, and simple directional signs should be posted throughout the property. An attractive exterior and interior appearance is also important to both tour operators and guests.

In addition to meeting the needs of motorcoach tour guests, you must provide for the needs of the tour operator or escort, the bus driver, and other staff who may accompany a group, such as an interpreter or a physician. You should provide ample parking for motorcoaches and have all guests preregistered for rapid check-in and distribution of room keys. It is also helpful to make available one staff member to assist the tour escort in dealing with any last-minute changes or problems that might arise during the group's visit. Offering property-sponsored activities (theme weekends, movies, or other entertainment) will also ease the responsibilities of the tour escort. Making the escort's job easier can help generate repeat business, since the property's initial customer is the tour broker, not the individual guests.

Finding motorcoach tour brokers. Hotels can find the names of motorcoach tour brokers in a number of ways (see Exhibit 9):

Exhibit 9   Sources for Motorcoach Tour Business

American Bus Association (ABA)
1015 15th Street, N.W.   (202) 842-1645
Washington, DC 20005   (800) 422-1400

     Hotels and motels can become travel industry members of ABA. Resources and services of this association include the *ABA Directory*, which lists nearly 600 major bus operators and key sales contacts, and an annual convention that matches bus operators with lodging properties in their touring areas.

National Tour Association (NTA)
P.O. Box 3071
Lexington, KY 40596   (606) 253-1036

     Hotels and motels can become allied members of NTA. Resources and services include the *NTA Directory,* which lists tour brokers and the areas they service, and an annual convention which features computerized matching of allied members with tour brokers.

Ontario Motor Coach Association (OMCA)
234 Eglinton Ave. E., Suite 604
Toronto, Ontario M5P 1K5   (416) 488-8855

     Hotels and motels can become allied members of this organization, which, like ABA and NTA, publishes a directory and holds an annual trade show.

United States Tour Operators Association (USTOA)
211 E. 51st Street, Suite 21B
New York, NY 10022   (212) 944-5727

     Members of the United States Tour Operators Association are the largest tour companies. The organization's membership includes both motorcoach and air transportation tour companies.

American Society of Travel Agents (ASTA)
1101 King Street
Alexandria, VA 22314   (703) 739-2782

     ASTA works with tour brokers and publishes *Motorcoach Touring,* a manual that provides an excellent overview of the motorcoach industry to hotel/motel operators. This manual includes a state-by-state listing of ABA and NTA companies.

Travel Industry Association of America (TIA)
Two Lafayette Center
1133 21st Street, N.W.
Washington, D.C. 20036   (202) 293-1433

     TIA publishes the *Discover America Package Handbook.*

Official Domestic Tour Manual
2 West 46th Street
New York, NY 10036   (212) 575-9000

     This manual, published quarterly by *Travel Agent* magazine, lists sources for motorcoach tours in the United States and Canada. Price: $15 annually.

- Lists from professional associations such as the National Tour Association (NTA) and the American Society of Travel Agents (ASTA)

- Bus associations such as the Ontario Motor Coach Association and the American Bus Association

- Sources from the U.S. Travel Service and domestic airlines

- Travel trade journals such as *Travel Weekly, Travel Trade,* and *ASTA News*

- Incentive tour operators such as E. F. MacDonald and Maritz

- Recommendations from personal contacts and hotel representatives

Before attempting to sell to motorcoach tour brokers, however, you should determine exactly what your property has to offer—a location near an airport or major highway, proximity to a number of popular attractions, facilities for large groups, etc.—and contact those brokers who handle the types of tours best suited to the property.

Reaching motorcoach tour brokers. You can reach motorcoach tour brokers directly by sending representatives to motorcoach trade association meetings to promote your group packages and rates, and by participating in motorcoach trade shows.

Direct mail is one of the most popular avenues of selling to motorcoach tour brokers, because it is a way to get answers to a number of questions efficiently and inexpensively. All correspondence with tour brokers should include a discussion of the following issues:

1. *The property's rates.* Special group rates are often a deciding factor in booking motorcoach tour business. Some properties have developed group rate directories that detail group rates at various seasons of the year (see Exhibit 10). Since many tours are prepackaged, it is important for the motorcoach tour broker to know the total cost of the property's rooms and meals. Is tax included in the rate quoted? Does the property offer an inclusive group rate for meals? Are the rates commissionable? This last question is very important if the motorcoach tour will be sold through travel agents.

2. *Comps and discounts.* You should advise tour brokers about the availability of complimentary rooms or meals to the tour escort and driver, or of special commercial rates available to tour bus drivers.

3. *Services.* You should list preregistration services (putting keys in envelopes with guests' names and room numbers on them, for example), baggage handling services (very important to tour brokers), and special features such as a welcoming party or a departure gift.

4. *Facilities.* Your ability to handle group business must be emphasized. You should "sell" your property's large banquet facilities or restaurants, its extra-large swimming pool or numerous recreational amenities, and its other group facilities—lounges, meeting rooms for card games or conversation, and so on.

5. *Location.* The property's location may be a deciding factor for a motorcoach tour broker. Roadside properties are ideal sites for overnight tours or meal stops, especially if the property is near the entrance or exit of an interstate or major state highway, while downtown hotels located near a number of attractions are ideal for destination tours.

Direct mail letters can be accompanied by brochures detailing what the property has to offer. These brochures should feature photographs of groups being served at the property. A brochure should be developed for each group package offered and should speak directly to the needs of motorcoach tour brokers. A

Exhibit 10   Sample Group Rate Manual

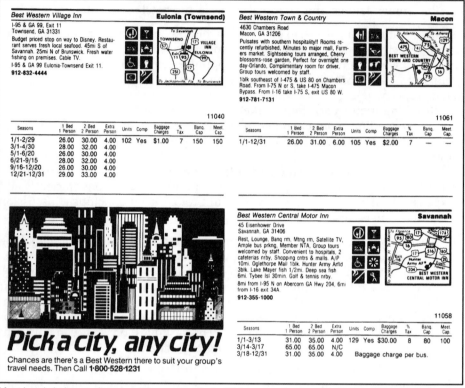

Seasons	1 Bed 1 Person	2 Bed 2 Person	Extra Person	Units	Comp	Baggage Charges	% Tax	Banq. Cap.	Meet. Cap.
1/1-2/29	26.00	30.00	4.00	102	Yes	$1.00	7	150	150
3/1-4/30	28.00	32.00	4.00						
5/1-6/20	26.00	30.00	4.00						
6/21-9/15	28.00	32.00	4.00						
9/16-12/20	26.00	30.00	4.00						
12/21-12/31	29.00	33.00	4.00						

11040

Best Western Village Inn — Eulonia (Townsend)
I-95 & GA 99, Exit 11
Townsend, GA 31331
Budget priced stop on way to Disney. Restaurant serves fresh local seafood. 45mi S of Savannah. 25mi N of Brunswick. Fresh water fishing on premises. Cable TV.
I-95 & GA 99 Eulonia-Townsend Exit 11.
912-832-4444

Best Western Town & Country — Macon
4630 Chambers Road
Macon, GA 31206
Pulsates with southern hospitality!! Rooms recently refurbished. Minutes to major mall. Farmers market. Sightseeing tours arranged. Cherry blossoms-rose garden. Perfect for overnight one day-Orlando. Complimentary room for driver. Group tours welcomed by staff.
1blk southeast of I-475 & US 80 on Chambers Road. From I-75 N or S, take I-475 Macon Bypass. From I-16 take I-75 S, exit US 80 W.
912-781-7131

Seasons	1 Bed 1 Person	2 Bed 2 Person	Extra Person	Units	Comp	Baggage Charges	% Tax	Banq. Cap.	Meet. Cap.
1/1-12/31	26.00	31.00	6.00	105	Yes	$2.00	7	—	—

11061

Best Western Central Motor Inn — Savannah
45 Eisenhower Drive
Savannah, GA 31406
Rest., Lounge, Banq. rm., Mtng rm., Satellite TV. Ample bus prkng. Member NTA. Group tours welcomed by staff. Convenient to hospitals. 2 cafeterias nrby. Shopping cntrs & malls. A/P 10mi. Oglethorpe Mall 1blk. Hunter Army Arfld 3blk. Lake Mayer fish 1/2mi. Deep sea fish 6mi. Tybee Isl 30min. Golf & tennis nrby.
8mi from I-95 N on Abercorn GA Hwy 204, 6mi from I-16 exit 34A.
912-355-1000

Seasons	1 Bed 1 Person	2 Bed 2 Person	Extra Person	Units	Comp	Baggage Charges	% Tax	Banq. Cap.	Meet. Cap.
1/1-3/13	31.00	35.00	4.00	129	Yes	$30.00	8	80	100
3/14-3/17	65.00	65.00	N/C						
3/18-12/31	31.00	35.00	4.00			Baggage charge per bus.			

11058

Pick a city, any city!
Chances are there's a Best Western there to suit your group's travel needs. Then Call **1-800-528-1231**

Most hotel chains produce group tour manuals that list group rates (usually 10% to 30% off) and special weekend rates for tour groups. Group rate manuals are distributed annually to bus companies, tour brokers, and tour wholesalers through direct mail efforts or at travel trade shows. (Courtesy of Best Western International, Inc.)

brochure that features a locator map of the property and a toll-free number will often get more attention than one that simply describes the property.

You can also acquaint motorcoach tour brokers with your property by offering familiarization tours. These complimentary tours, which can be scheduled for slow business times, allow brokers to experience the property firsthand. The Radisson Hotel High Point in High Point, North Carolina, offered motorcoach tour brokers a Motorcoach Month promotion that featured two room nights, a complimentary breakfast, and a packet of informational materials. The program generated a favorable response from the participants and increased the hotel's tour business.

Motorcoach tour brokers can also be reached through print advertising in travel guides and trade publications. Tour brokers often use *OAG TRAVEL PLANNER/ Hotel & Motel RedBook* and *Hotel & Travel Index* to obtain information about properties in a specific area, although the information within these publications is not usually geared to motorcoach tour brokers. To provide the information most important to motorcoach tour brokers, you may wish to advertise in trade publications such as *Bus Tours Magazine, Bus World, Courier, Destinations, National Bus Trader,* and

Exhibit 11   Advertising to Tour Brokers

Tour groups take a front seat at The Fort Magruder Inn, Williamsburg.

Book your next Williamsburg group into the Fort Magruder Inn — just two minutes from the historic area and The Old Country/Busch Gardens.

Our 304 room, luxury hotel has lots of little extras your group will enjoy: a pool, hot tub, sauna, fitness room, lighted tennis courts, balcony rooms, live entertainment in the lounge, and nearby golf.

Most important, our professional and cooperative staff will make sure that the hospitality and service your clients get from us is as good as the tour they've gotten from you.

For tour booking information, call Alexis: 800-446-4082 (in Virginia: 800-582-1010).

Fort Magruder Inn
& CONFERENCE CENTER
Your Special Place In History.
Route 60, Box KE, Williamsburg, Virginia 23187

Ads such as this one, which appeared in Courier *(a trade magazine for tour brokers), can be used to promote group leisure travel. While this ad primarily stresses property benefits, other print ads may include such booking information as group discount rates, property tour policies, and special amenities such as complimentary rooms to the tour guide and driver, discounts to nearby attractions, and so on.*

Tours, using ads that provide pertinent tour information, the property's contact person for bus tours, deposit requirements, cancelation policies, and other information (see Exhibit 11).

You can also generate repeat business and word-of-mouth referrals by providing special services. Some properties clean the interior and windows of the bus, while others offer welcome gifts such as fruit baskets or a local product to the tour escort and bus driver. These gestures demonstrate that you care enough about the tour operators and guests to warrant repeat business.

Airline Tours. Airline tours are another excellent source of group business. Airline tours are usually arranged by airline tour wholesalers, who not only contract with properties and attractions, but also promote the tours they develop. This takes a good deal of responsibility for advertising away from the property.

Like motorcoach tour brokers, airline tour wholesalers seek to provide a complete vacation experience for their clients. Properties located in or near popular destination cities or in close proximity to a number of attractions (Disneyland, Knott's Berry Farm, and Universal Studios in southern California, for example) are attractive to airline tour wholesalers, but a property that can offer an extensive rec-reational package may also be able to sell to this market.

If a property is not located close to an airport, an intermodal tour can often be arranged by an airline tour wholesaler. An intermodal tour makes use of more than one form of transportation (air-motorcoach, air-sea, air-car, and so on), and is often used to promote golf vacations, honeymoon trips, and extended group trips such as fall "color" tours. Intermodal tours may include air transportation to the tour's departure city, motorcoach transportation to several points of interest, and even a ferry or boat trip.

Airline tour wholesalers also package group tours that may include cruise ship travel. Air transportation to the port of departure, hotel accommodations and meals while in port, and the cruise itself can be included in one package price. Properties located in popular ports or near international air terminals have an excellent opportunity to take advantage of this year-round business, especially if they can handle the demands of group travelers.

Amtrak Tours. Other opportunities to capture a portion of the group leisure traveler market can be found through contacts with Amtrak. Amtrak develops and pro-motes a variety of rail tours each year. Once a group has booked a reservation on Amtrak, an Amtrak representative can book hotel reservations at the destination. Groups booking through Amtrak receive lower rates than if they made their own reservations independently. Properties wishing to book groups traveling by train can contact Amtrak directly through its local or regional offices.

Property Package Tours. In addition to selling special group rates and services to tour brokers and tour wholesalers who develop tour packages, you can also develop your own tour package (see Exhibit 12). Before you take such a step, however, you must first familiarize yourself with the tour industry and determine what type of tour (either an independent package or a package in conjunction with other travel suppliers) would work best for your property. An aid in learning about the tour market is the *Discover America Package Tour Handbook,* published by the Travel Indus-try Association of America. This handbook gives an overall view of the extensive package tour market, and provides the names of contacts for assistance or sales leads.

There are several reasons why you should consider developing your own package tour. Property packages can:

- Increase sales by offering consumers convenience and value

- Bring in business when you need it most, such as off-season or shoulder periods

- Encourage property recognition, especially if the package is innovative or a real bargain

Packages can be simple or complicated. One property may opt for a simple package of one or two room nights with a complimentary continental breakfast, while another property may put together a package that includes recreational ame-nities (golf, tennis, swimming), meals, discounts in the gift shop or discount cou-pons to nearby attractions, and turn-down and valet service. Properties that wish

Exhibit 12   Property Package Tours at a Glance

What:	Property package tours are group tour packages put together by an individual property or a chain. Property package tours offer several travel elements for one price, and may include lodging, meals, baggage transfers, recreational facilities, local guided tours, attractions, and entertainment. Properties that opt to include other travel suppliers—airlines, rental car companies, bus lines, and so on—can also offer transportation as part of the package.
Why:	Property package tours are popular with travel agents and consumers because they can be purchased for one inclusive price. For consumers, this makes it easier to budget. For travel agents, property package tours mean guaranteed availability and lower booking costs—the agent does not have to book the individual components separately.
When:	Property package tours can be developed for those times when business is most needed. They can also be developed to coincide with local events such as rodeos, food festivals, and county fairs.
How:	Property package tours can be developed in a number of ways. The property can package its own services (rooms, meals, entertainment, recreational facilities, etc.) and promote the package through advertising to travel agents and directly to consumers. Many properties, however, have found that developing a package in conjunction with another attraction or travel supplier offers the benefit of the experience of the other package participant(s) and generates a wider customer base. Selling the package to tour brokers after it has been developed is also an excellent way for the property's package to reach a wide base of potential guests.

to provide complete vacation packages or weekend getaways can include other travel suppliers (airlines, rental cars, local bus operators, or limousine services) and attractions (amusement parks, historic sites, etc.) in their tour packages.

While developing a tour package can be profitable, it also requires knowledge. You must first determine which markets you will target. Tour packages developed for older travelers may differ greatly from those designed for downhill skiers, for example. Since the needs of each market segment will be different, you have to determine which segments you can best serve.

When promoting tours, it is important to determine the type of group to whom the advertising is being directed. Tour groups can fall into active or passive categories. A description of the property's facilities, amenities, and services should appeal to the type of group visiting the property. An active group, for example, responds to copy promoting the exotic, sensual, and adventurous, while a passive group would be more comfortable with copy that stresses the traditional, well-known, and charming. Having a group profile beforehand will help you better attract and serve each group.

Once a package is developed, the next step is to promote it. You can sell the package to tour wholesalers, travel agents, or the public. If sold through tour wholesalers or travel agents, the package should be made commissionable and given an IT (inclusive tour) number. IT numbers are codes used on the hotel's tour folders to assist travel intermediaries in identifying and booking packages.

In addition to direct contact with tour wholesalers and travel agents, property packages can be promoted to them through direct mail and print advertising. Advertising in trade journals will reach many of these travel professionals. Ads should be designed to promote the benefits of the property's tour package to the wholesaler or agent as well as to guests. You can also advertise in the *Consolidated Tour Manual,* a publication sponsored and published by participating U.S. airlines. The manual, which is distributed free to member airline sales offices and certain travel agents, offers hotels a full-page listing in the manual for a fee.

Properties that choose to include other travel suppliers in a tour package may enjoy the benefits of cooperative advertising and the consumer bases of these suppliers. Packages can be promoted through print advertising and by direct sales efforts on the part of not only the property, but also the other travel suppliers involved. Air-ground-rooms packages, for example, may be promoted through colorful brochures at airline ticket terminals, at the offices of participating bus lines, and at the property's front desk. Or, the participants in the package could sell the entire package through tour wholesalers, saving on advertising costs.

Whatever option you choose, it often takes time for a property's tour package to reach consumers. It may take more than one season for a package to consistently fill rooms. You must make sure that a sparsely used package has been properly promoted before deciding it is unsuccessful. Group leisure travelers often book their reservations on a long lead time (up to two years in some cases), and may not be able to take advantage of a particular package when it is first offered. Before dropping a package, you should measure the effectiveness of the promotional campaign and talk to tour wholesalers about their response to the package.

Leisure Travelers and Small Properties

While many of the strategies discussed in this chapter are most applicable to large properties, small properties can also tap into the leisure market—both individual and group—in a number of creative ways. While their promotional budgets may be far smaller than those of large properties and chains, small properties may still take advantage of low-cost advertising in local and regional directories, and can reach potential leisure travelers through radio spots and a combination of public relations and promotional activities.

Combining public relations and promotion is an extremely cost-effective way to promote a small property. For example, Bud Schramm, who owned the 31-room Buffalo Trail Motel in Winner, South Dakota, employed several creative and inexpensive ways to keep his property in the public's eye. One of Schramm's promotions was to place jars of red and white mints in gas stations and restaurants in the community. The jars were located by the cash registers, and featured signs that said, "You're worth a mint to us," and "Compliments of Buffalo Trail Motel." Not only did the jars provide promotional benefits, but they helped to establish contacts with people in the community who could help sell rooms for the property. Another idea that involved community support was the printing of "appreciation cards" offering a discount at the motel. These cards were given to public contact people—store clerks, food servers, mechanics, and so on—who handed them out to people passing through town. When enough of the cards were redeemed, the public contact people were eligible to win a free weekend stay for two at the motel, giving them an added incentive to hand out as many cards as possible.

Small properties can sell the uniqueness of their local areas in promotional pieces. They can also join groups or networks that help small properties boost business. The Independent Motels of America, Inc., is a network of more than 130 independently owned motels and inns that publishes a directory (complete with reservations numbers) of its members. The American Hotel & Motel Association (AH&MA) has a committee on small properties that runs seminars throughout the country. Small properties that belong to AH&MA can also take advantage of AH&MA's Information Center, which provides research assistance and help with marketing and promotion to members.

Conclusion

The leisure traveler market is a large, complex, and valuable source of business for lodging properties. Growth in this market is expected to continue through the 1990s and into the next century due to extended holidays, four-day work weeks for a growing number of employees, the increase in the number of dual-career families, longer life expectancies, and increased discretionary income.

Leisure travelers look for ease and convenience in travel and find special packages like the ones discussed in this chapter particularly attractive. Many packages designed for leisure travelers are sold through travel intermediaries. You should be aware of opportunities to build good working relationships with such travel intermediaries as tour brokers, tour wholesalers, and travel agents.

Endnotes

1. From *The Nationwide Travel Trends Survey,* commissioned by American Express and Arthur D. Little, 1992.
2. *The Nationwide Travel Trends Survey.*
3. Marvin Cefron, "The American Renaissance in the Year 2000: 74 Trends That Will Affect America's—and Your—Future," 1992.
4. These facts and others cited in this section are from an October 1990 study, *Discover America: The Mature Market,* commissioned by the Travel Industry Association of America and prepared by the U.S. Data Research Center.
5. Phil Goodman, "Boomer Lust," *Marketing Management,* Winter 1992, p. 6.

Key Terms

airline tour

Amtrak tour

group sales allotment

Independent Motels of America, Inc.

intermodal tour

motorcoach charter

motorcoach tour

tour

tour broker

tour intermediary

tour voucher

tour wholesaler

Review Questions

1. Individual leisure travelers can be divided into which three general categories?

2. How are properties meeting the needs of family leisure travelers?

3. What are some of the ways families can be reached?

4. Senior citizens control how much of the nation's discretionary income?

5. How are properties meeting the needs of mature travelers?

6. What is a tour broker?

7. What are four types of tours commonly taken by group leisure travelers?

8. How are properties meeting the needs of motorcoach tour travelers?

9. What are some resources for finding motorcoach tour brokers?

10. What should correspondence with motorcoach tour brokers include?

11. What is an intermodal tour?

12. Why should a property consider developing its own package tour?

Chapter Outline

Travel Agencies
    Types of Travel Agents
    Travelers Served
Meeting the Needs of Travel Agents
    Property Information
        Airline Reservations Systems
        Hotel Directories
        Information Packages
        Familiarization Tours
    Service
        Toll-Free Numbers
        Travel Agent Clubs
        Commission Payment Plans
        Serving Clients
Finding Travel Agents
Reaching Travel Agents
    Hotel Directories
    Trade Magazines
    Direct Mail
    Trade Shows
    Personal Sales
    Public Relations
Conclusion

17

Marketing to Travel Agents

Not too long ago, the relationship between hotels and travel agents was shaky at best. Many properties had a careless attitude toward serving travel agents, and travel agents had many complaints about the way they were treated: long waiting times on the telephone, properties failing to honor their reservations, and properties negligent about paying them promptly, to name a few. Today, however, this relationship is changing. Travel has become more complex. More and more, business and leisure travelers are turning to travel agents for help in making travel plans and reservations, and properties are recognizing that travel agents and hotels make an ideal sales team. In this chapter we will take a look at today's travel agents and the types of travelers they serve. We will also learn what properties are doing to meet the needs of travel agents.

Travel Agencies

The concept of an individual assisting other individuals with travel plans can be traced to 1841, when a British Baptist minister named Thomas Cook signed up 570 people to accompany him to a temperance meeting. Cook got the group a rate of a shilling per person for the 22-mile round trip from Leicester to Loughborough, and included a picnic lunch and entertainment as part of the "package." His tour proved so popular that by 1856 the enterprising Cook was advertising a "Grand Circular Tour of the Continent." In 1869, Cook introduced his "middle class conducted crusades" to the Holy Land.

Most American travel agencies began as "mom and pop" establishments operated on the same principles as Thomas Cook's original tours. Tours were often "guided" by the owners of the travel agencies, based on personal experiences at the destinations. These early operations are a far cry from the travel agencies and travel agents of today.

There are more than 43,000 travel agencies, staffed by over 250,000 travel agents, in the United States and Canada. The complexity of the travel market has led to the modernization and computerization of travel agencies, and travel agents have become highly trained and sophisticated professionals. It is estimated that U.S. travel agents sell 70% of all domestic air flights and 80% of international air flights, and account for 90% of all package tours, 50% of car rentals, 37% of rail sales, and about one-quarter of U.S. hotel reservations.[1]

The changing face of travel agencies has not escaped the notice of the lodging industry. Hotel operators are aware that travel agents are, in effect, sales representatives for a host of travel suppliers, including hotels. Hotels increasingly depend on travel agents to serve as a part of their sales force—salespeople who work at no overhead costs to a property. According to Bill Hulett, CHA, president of Stouffer Hotel Company:

> Hoteliers must re-examine their strategies for communicating with travel agents, employing special marketing programs that turn agents into more fully integrated extensions of their sales arms. The percentage of our business booked through agents has virtually tripled—from approximately 15 percent to some 40 percent.[2]

Other leading hoteliers support Bill Hulett's view. Michael A. Levin, president of Franchise Hotels Division, Holiday Inn Worldwide, says, "The travel agent has become a major counselor of the traveler. So, essentially, you've added to your sales staff thousands of agents." Bill Grau, CHA, president of Ramada International Hotels and Resorts, refers to travel agents as "the ultimate conduit to our customer, generating more than 30 percent of our company's annual sales," while John Norlander, CHA, president of Radisson Hotel Corporation, views travel agents as "key partners" in his corporation's global expansion.

Types of Travel Agents

Travel agents can be grouped into three basic categories:

- Retail travel agents
- Wholesale travel agents
- Agents who work for consortiums or chains

Retail travel agents act as agents for airlines, cruise lines, railroads, bus lines, hotels, car rental firms, and, sometimes, wholesale travel agencies. Retail travel agents work directly with clients, supplying information on a wide array of travel services and making reservations or bookings.

Wholesale travel agents differ from wholesale tour operators in that wholesale tour operators work almost exclusively with group leisure travelers. A wholesale travel agent, on the other hand, specializes in putting tour packages together for individual business and leisure travelers. These tours are marketed to the public through retail travel agents or the airlines. Wholesale travel agents do not deal directly with clients unless their travel agency has a retail department (many of the large wholesale travel agencies have such departments).

Agents who work for consortiums or chains can be retail travel agents or wholesale travel agents. Consortiums and chain travel agencies are associations or networks of travel agencies that have banded together to share information and take advantage of bulk purchasing and cooperative marketing. The travel industry has become more complex, and there is a greater need for sophisticated technology, technology that is often too costly for individual agencies. A consortium allows agencies to pool their resources.

No matter what category a travel agent is in, he or she has one basic product: information. With today's unprecedented competition in the airline and lodging industries, the average traveler is faced with a bewildering array of services and facilities. Today's travel agent must sell more than just travel. He or she must sell information—and back that information with service.

Travelers Served

Generally speaking, travel agents serve three types of travelers:

- Business travelers
- Leisure travelers
- International travelers

In 1986, 25% of all business travelers and 44% of frequent business travelers used the services of a travel agent. Today, business travelers represent over one-half of all business generated by travel agents. Each month, over four million business travelers book rooms through travel agents or through corporate travel planners who use travel agents.[3]

In addition to individual business travelers, more travel agencies are also serving business groups. In 1986, over 70% of the nation's travel agencies booked business group travel, 51% booked conventions, and 41% were involved in planning and directing incentive trips for their clients. This trend has led to the development of agents or separate departments within travel agencies that specialize in business meetings and groups.

The fastest growing segment of the business group market is the small meetings segment (meetings for 25 or fewer people). Over 43% of travel agents surveyed felt that small meetings would eventually become the backbone of business-travel revenue for most travel agencies, especially since many large corporations are consolidating travel purchasing. IBM, for example, consolidated the number of travel agencies it does business with from 1,200 travel agencies to 3! And IBM is not an isolated case. In 1986, the needs of the Fortune 500 companies were handled by 8,800 travel agencies; today, fewer than 500 agencies assist those companies. Consolidation has led more and more travel agencies to focus on the small meetings market and individual business and leisure travelers.

Leisure travelers often need more assistance in planning their travel than business travelers. Business travelers usually have a predetermined destination and are often restricted in their choice of hotels, but less than half of all leisure clients know precisely where they want to go. Eighty percent of all individual visitors to resort destinations such as Hawaii, Las Vegas, the Bahamas, and Bermuda use a travel agent to help plan or book their vacations. Over 70% of all leisure travelers ask for an agent's help in selecting a hotel.[4]

To increase their leisure traveler business, many hotels are teaming up with travel agents by creating commissionable weekend packages. Travel agents are big sellers of weekend packages, especially in such markets as New York, Boston, New Orleans, and Washington, D.C. They are attracted to the inclusive-price and easy booking features inherent in many packages (see Exhibit 1).

International travelers can be business or leisure travelers. It is important to note here that the number of foreigners traveling to the United States is increasing substantially. To promote a property to international travelers, travel agents must have adequate information. Special services, such as the availability of on-property translators, can help attract international travelers to a property.

Exhibit 1   All-Inclusive Pricing

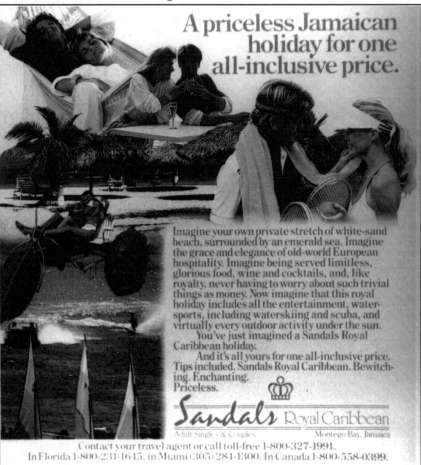

All-inclusive pricing is popular with travel agents because it allows them to offer a complete vacation to clients—meals, tips, recreational amenities, and special entertainment—without the hassle of having to negotiate for the various components offered.

Meeting the Needs of Travel Agents

Since travel agents deal with such a wide range of clients, you must understand what a travel agent needs in order to successfully promote your property. These needs can be broken down into two general areas: information about the property, and good service—to travel agents as well as their clients.

Property Information

Airline reservations systems, listings and ads in hotel directories, information packages, and familiarization tours are some of the ways properties meet travel agents' need for property information.

Airline Reservations Systems. Hotels can provide basic reservation and rate information to travel agents through computerized airline reservations systems. Travel agents use computers to access these systems. The major airline reservations systems are:

System Name	Airline(s)
Abacus	A Singapore-based computer reservation system (CRS) formed by Cathay Pacific, Malaysian, Philippine, and Singapore Airlines.
Amadeus	A European CRS formed by Air France, Iberia, Lufthansa, and SAS Airlines.
Apollo	The airline reservation system hosted by United Airlines.
Datas II	The airline reservation system hosted by Delta Airlines.
Galileo	An international consortium data-base network supported by Alitalia, Swiss Air, British Air, and KLM.
Gemini	A Canadian-based CRS owned by Air Canada and Canadian Air.
Pars	The airline reservation system hosted by TWA, USAir, and Northwest Airlines.
Sabre	The airline reservation system hosted by American Airlines.
System One	The airline reservation system hosted by Continental and EDS.
Worldspan	A partnership of Delta, Northwest, and TWA.

While 95% of the nation's travel agencies are equipped with computer terminals, studies have shown that many travel agents do not use them to book hotel reservations. The reluctance to use airline reservations systems stems from the fact that booking hotel accommodations is much more complicated than booking airline seats or rental cars. Besides price and availability, a number of other factors figure into hotel bookings, including location, hotel features, guestroom size, amenities, restaurants, special rates, and credit card policies. Airline reservations systems do not supply this type of information, and they are not programmed to answer questions or make alternative suggestions.

Though hotels have lagged behind the airlines in computerized reservations systems, globalization has led many hotel chains to establish their own CRS networks. Sheraton, for example, has linked 17 of its reservations centers around the world and provided toll-free telephone numbers in 44 countries.

Several hotel chains, including Best Western, Days Inns, Hilton, Holiday Inns, Hyatt, Inter-Continental, Marriott, Ramada, Sheraton, Forte Hotels, and Westin, are taking advantage of Ultraswitch, a system that links hotel reservations systems with those of the major airlines. This arrangement makes it easier for travel agents to provide complete travel packages to their clients, and is expected to generate additional hotel bookings from travel agents.

Hotel Directories. Hotel directories provide the detailed information travel agents need to properly service clients. An agent can compare one property's costs, location, amenities, facilities, and activities with another's, and make recommendations to clients based on much more extensive information than that found in airline reservations systems.

Insider Insights

James P. Tierney, CHSE
Vice President, Marketing
Amelia Island Plantation
Amelia Island, Florida

> *Jim Tierney is a native of Pennsylvania, where he received his Bachelor of Science degree in education from West Chester State College in 1966. After college, Tierney completed the U.S. Navy's Officer Candidate School in Newport, Rhode Island, and served as a naval officer from 1967 through the middle of 1970.*
>
> *In September 1970 he started his hotel career as manager of the convention center at Boca Raton Hotel and Club in Boca Raton, Florida. A variety of sales manager positions followed in Illinois, Missouri, and Florida. Tierney joined the Marco Beach Hotel and Villas as sales manager in the summer of 1977 and was promoted to director of sales in 1979. In 1980 he returned to Boca Raton Hotel and Club as director of sales, then became vice president, sales and marketing of South Seas Plantation Resort and Yacht Harbour in August, 1981. In September 1991 Tierney assumed the position of vice president, sales and marketing for Indian River Plantation Resort and Marina. He is currently vice president of marketing for Amelia Island Plantation.*
>
> *Tierney has been a member of the Hospitality Sales and Marketing Association International since 1973. In 1983 he was co-founder of the Southwest Florida chapter of HSMAI, serving as president for two and a half years. He was elected to the executive committee of HSMAI in 1985; in 1988 he was elected vice president. He served as president-elect throughout 1989, and became HSMAI's president in November, 1989. In January 1991 he passed the gavel on to the new president, but continues to serve as a member of HSMAI's board of directors.*

One of the properties I worked for in the past, South Seas Plantation Resort and Yacht Harbour in Captiva Island, Florida, attracted a market that was dramatically different from any other large Florida resort. While other properties are almost totally dependent on conference or convention business, South Seas Plantation's mix was 70% individual leisure travel and only 30% group business. Of the leisure travel business that we enjoyed, 35% came through travel agents. At certain times of the year, their contribution to this market approached 50%! Therefore, we spent a good deal of time and effort in encouraging travel agents to recommend South Seas Plantation to their clients.

Being a travel agent has to be a unique and sometimes frustrating experience. Travel agents are required to work hard to make less money! Clients look for the least expensive airfare, the most economical tour package, and the best possible room rate. In finding these deals, the agent makes less commission. And the agent is held personally responsible if anything goes wrong with the client's vacation or travel arrangements.

In order to make the travel agent's job easier and increase leisure traveler business, South Seas Plantation launched a major travel agency marketing program in

Insider Insights *(continued)*

1982. This program included travel trade advertising, a public relations program, attending travel trade shows, a direct mail program, a toll-free number for travel agents, agency familiarization trips, and the initiation of the King's Crown Club promotion. Weekend familiarization packages included tours of the resort, meetings to update agency owners and managers about the resort's facilities, food and beverage functions, and plenty of time for recreation. In 1982 more than 400 travel agents toured the property, with another 250 to 300 following in 1983. The results were almost immediate. Our leisure travel business jumped substantially in each of those years and steadily increased thereafter.

The King's Crown Club was an important factor in our success. This incentive program was designed to reward top-producing travel agencies. In order to get into the club, agencies in 1982 were required to produce a minimum of $10,000 in rooms revenue from individual leisure travelers. If the agency also produced group business, the membership minimum was $20,000. Agency bookings were tracked on an annual basis, and once an agency reached the target, we increased its commission from 10% to 13% for additional revenue produced through the balance of the year. While only one agency qualified for the club in 1982, within five years we had 47 agencies qualify—even though we had raised the minimum requirements to $12,500 for leisure business and $25,000 for group business.

Part of the reason that membership in the King's Crown Club was so desirable was the Annual Celebration Weekend. This was held from Thursday to Sunday in the spring, and everything was on us. The weekend included a recognition breakfast at which plaques were presented, photographs taken, and information about new things going on at the property was provided to the agents. Receptions, first-class dinner functions put together by our food and beverage department, and lots of recreation time were also included. These efforts paid off in happier travel agents—and increased bookings.

Three of the most widely used guides are the *Hotel & Travel Index,* the *Official Hotel Guide,* and the *OAG TRAVEL PLANNER/Hotel & Motel Redbook.* Each directory lists over 30,000 properties worldwide and provides information on hotel locations, accommodations, number of rooms, size of property, rates (including special packages), amenities, and number of restaurants. All three directories include property ads as well as a listing of properties.

A survey of travel agents found that 4% use the listings in hotel directories to select a property, 6% use a hotel's ad, and 90% use both to select a hotel.[5] It would be wise, then, for you to purchase a directory ad if possible. To attract attention and get your message across, choose the largest ad you can afford. Some chain properties are eligible for a special discount rate.

When polled about which elements of an ad they use, travel agents rated a toll-free number the highest (96%), information on the hotel's location second (92%), and a map of the property's location third (88%).[6] These elements make it easier for an agent to select and book a property.

There are a number of hotel directories. It is important for you to choose a directory that will reach a large number of readers. The cost of a directory may be an indication of its popularity.

Information Packages. In addition to providing information through hotel directories, many properties also offer information packages to travel agents. These packages may include a property fact sheet, photographs of the property, a description of property amenities, and information about booking procedures, commission payments, and special travel agent programs. While some properties include rate sheets in their information packages, as a rule travel agents do not use them. Most agents call a property directly to obtain current rate information.

A property can also include a large quantity of brochures for agency clients in its information package. These brochures should be consumer-oriented and have a blank space for the travel agent's stamp. Other collateral materials, such as colorful posters, can also be sent to travel agents. Agents should be provided with order forms, especially for brochures. Order forms can be included in the information package or mailed with the agent's commission check.

Familiarization Tours. Many properties offer familiarization or "fam" tours to travel agents. These tours can be conducted during slack periods and are an effective way to promote the property.

For fam tours to be successful, you must first look at your objectives. What percentage of travel agents are expected to send business to your property following a fam tour? How many room nights do you expect to pick up? If measurable objectives are not set, there will be no way to determine what type of fam tour should be offered and no way to determine a tour's success.

Planning a fam tour includes determining the ideal size of the tour group. Hosting too large a group will not allow the property to show itself off to best advantage. You must also determine exactly what you have to sell and the best way to showcase your property's products and facilities. If your property is noted for its recreational facilities, for example, you should allow the travel agents plenty of opportunity to use them.

Once you've planned a fam tour, you must invite the right travel agents to participate. Travel agents serve different types of clients. A property that caters primarily to leisure travelers will not benefit from inviting travel agents who specialize in business travel. The best prospects for fam tours are agents who have recommended clients to the property in the past, and those who serve clients in key feeder cities. Travel agents can be solicited by direct mail or by telephone and should be given a reasonable amount of advance notice (usually four to six weeks). Let agents know exactly what the tour involves: the duration of the tour, what is included (meals, transportation, and so on), whether the event is open to spouses or guests, and other pertinent information.

When the travel agents arrive for the fam tour, each should be greeted personally and given a schedule of events. Most properties assign staff members to handle the on-site details of the tour. A well-planned, well-executed tour will usually result in increased business from the travel agents involved.

While the travel agents' initial reactions to the tour may serve as a general barometer of the tour's success, it is also helpful to obtain an evaluation of your efforts a week or two after the tour. Questionnaires can be sent to participants to determine their perceptions of the strengths and weaknesses of the tour and the property. Of course, the real success of the tour will be measured in the number of bookings it generates.

Service

The kind of service agents receive from a property is an important factor in whether they will recommend that property again. Service to travel agents includes service to their clients also (see Exhibit 2). Travel agents are often blamed for bungled reservations, specific requests that are not met, and any number of details not handled to the guest's satisfaction at the property. It stands to reason that agents will be far more likely to recommend a property that has treated them and their clients well than a property that has been lax in its dealings with them and their clients. Toll-free numbers, travel agent clubs, commission payment plans, and good service to clients are just some of the ways properties can provide good service to travel agents.

Toll-Free Numbers. Most travel agents prefer to book hotel space over the telephone, and providing a toll-free number continues to reign as the most effective way to ensure travel agent bookings. A toll-free number encourages travel agents to call if they have questions. Agents can explore various options and rates, find out about special events that may interest clients, ask about special services, and receive immediate confirmation of reservations.

A toll-free number serves the property as well as the agent. Property representatives are given the opportunity to sell extra services. In addition, these calls are an excellent way to bring travel agents up to date on property information. The property also can better control its room inventories; rooms may be pushed during slow periods and alternate dates can be suggested for business that cannot be booked due to a full house.

Since travel agents generate so many bookings, some hotels go a step further; they dedicate a special toll-free number for the exclusive use of travel agents. This number is not available to the public and is promoted only through press releases to travel agents or through direct mail and other advertising directed to the travel trade.

Travel Agent Clubs. Another effective way you can provide service and build rapport with travel agents is through travel agent clubs. Club members are informed of property events and special programs and discounts through direct mail or a club newsletter. Some clubs give prizes to travel agents who book a certain number of room nights at the property. An agent with 100 room nights or "room credits" may earn a watch, for example. Most clubs offer travel agents such travel-oriented promotional items as tote bags, travel alarm clocks, and baggage tags imprinted with the property's logo and the travel agent's telephone number. Travel agents can use these items to stimulate business for themselves and your property.

Exhibit 2   Providing Service to Travel Agents

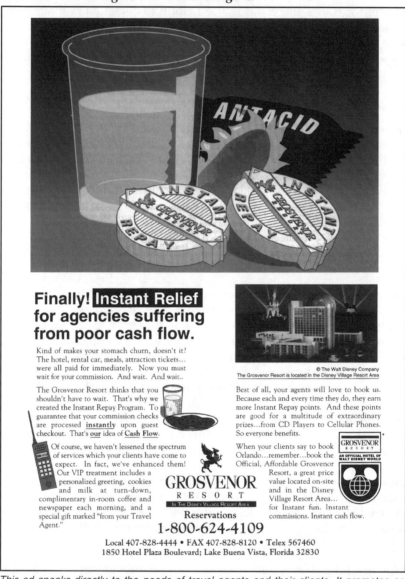

This ad speaks directly to the needs of travel agents and their clients. It promotes an instant commission payment plan, a personalized greeting—and special gifts—to the agent's clients, and a travel agent club that offers prizes for bookings.

Commission Payment Plans. A very important way that properties are serving travel agents is through commission payment plans. In the past, getting paid was difficult for many travel agents. Their number-one complaint was that the check that was "in the mail" never arrived. But properties have taken giant strides to

Exhibit 3   Travel Agent Commission Payment Plans

Our travel agent recognition program will make your job so easy you'll think you're on vacation yourself.

Hyatt's commitment to making travel agents' jobs as easy as possible is the driving force behind our new Special Agent Recognition Program, which includes our Golden Rules for Travel Agents. Key commitments include:

- Commission checks mailed within 72 hours of guest departures
- Guaranteed 10-day response on any late commission notices
- Commissions paid on any additional nights a guest stays
- Commissions paid for any guests relocated with previously confirmed reservations
- 10% commission on all published rates
- Non-commissionable rate information at time of booking
- Written notification if there is a guest no-show or a reservation change
- Commissions deducted in advance from deposits or prepayments sent to Hyatt®
- Special HYschool educational programs
- Preferred treatment while staying at Hyatt
- A toll free Travel Agent Hotline at 1-800-423-2400 to answer any questions concerning commissions, travel and Hyatt programs

The Hyatt CRT code is HY. For more information and reservations call

Hyatt Hotels and Resorts worldwide at **1-800-233-1234.**

**HYATT
SPECIAL AGENTS**ᴿᴹ
THERE'S NO ONE   QUITE LIKE YOU.ˢᴹ

HYΛTT
HOTELS & RESORTS ®
Feel The Hyatt Touch.®

Go USA!

Hyatt Hotels and Resorts encompasses hotels managed or operated by two separate groups of companies–companies associated with Hyatt Corp. and companies associated with Hyatt International Corp. ©1992 Hyatt Corp.

Prompt payment of commissions is an important consideration for travel agents. This ad outlines the Hyatt Hotels & Resorts' commission policy, designed to attract bookings from travel agents. Note also that the ad features a toll-free number and other services for travel agents only.

ensure that travel agents receive commission checks on a more regular basis (see Exhibit 3).

One of the reasons for the sporadic payment of commission checks was that individual properties were responsible for generating the checks. In many cases, a property did not have the technical capabilities to track bookings, and chains that did have these capabilities charged travel agents a fee.

In 1981, the Holiday Corporation changed all that with the introduction of a centralized commission payment plan. Instead of receiving checks from each property in the chain, travel agents received one monthly check issued automatically through a computer in the chain's corporate office. Travel agents were no longer charged a fee. The program was subsidized through fees charged to individual hotels, but the hotels still saved money since they no longer incurred the administrative, stationery, and postage costs involved in paying travel agents.

Many chains have followed this lead with similar systems. Hyatt, for example, guarantees commission payments within 72 hours of the client's departure. Hilton's policy is to pay commissions within three weeks of check-out. Checks are mailed out on a weekly or monthly basis, and agents can deal directly with the corporate office if checks are not received. Along with the commission check, many hotel chains mail a statement of guest histories for the month, any changes made in a reservation after it was booked by the travel agent, and information relating to new hotel facilities or policies.

To further alleviate commission payment problems, an industry-wide computerized system was established late in 1991. This automated system, the Hotel Clearing Corporation (HCC), is used by 16 major hotel chains, including Best Western, Hyatt, Ramada, Sheraton, and Westin. Travel agents pay a $100 initial fee for three years of service, and 5 to 10 percent of their commissions (based on their annual hotel commission totals). HCC provides monthly commission payments to travel agents, rather than sporadic individual commission checks. The centralized idea, which shifts the debt risk from the travel agent to the hotel, is popular with travel agents—over 5,000 signed up in the first few months the service was offered—and the idea is catching on in Canada, too.

Many properties give increased commissions to agents who book clients during off-season periods or during certain special package promotions (see Exhibit 4). Properties can also award special bonuses or free accommodations or trips when an agent exceeds a quota of room nights in a given period, or offer other incentives, such as contests and sweepstakes, to generate additional bookings (see Exhibit 5).

Serving Clients. Providing good service to travel agents means providing good service to their clients as well (see Exhibit 6). It is very important to travel agents that their clients be well treated, since a client's experience at a property will likely affect the client/agent relationship. If the client has an enjoyable stay, he or she will be more likely to use the services of the travel agent again. If, on the other hand, the stay does not meet the client's expectations, the agent will lose credibility—and possibly a client.

Guests booked into the property by a travel agent should be greeted by a friendly staff, and their stay should be made as pleasant as possible. Some properties pamper their travel-agent-booked guests with complimentary wine, fruit baskets, or local specialties delivered to the guestroom with a welcoming note and a card that gives the travel agent credit for the gift.

Exhibit 4   Travel Agent Bonuses

100% PERFECTION. 15% COMMISSION.

The Boca Raton Hotel and Club has always been the perfect resort for your most discriminating clients. With a stunning beach, glorious golf, sensational tennis and seven magnificent restaurants. But now we've found a way to improve on perfection.

We'll pay you a 15% commission on all individual guest bookings made for the period of January 3rd through April 30th. And we're also offering a limited number of rooms at a very special rate – only $95 per person, per night.* For reservations, call toll free 1-800-327-0101. Treat your clients to perfection, while the percentages are even more in your favor than usual.

The Boca Raton Hotel and Club
QUITE SIMPLY THE BEST®

Per person, per night, double occupancy. Limited availability in The Cloister. Taxes and service charges not included. Not available to groups. From January 22nd through April 7th, stay will include M.A.P. at an additional $35 per person, per night. Boca Raton, Florida 33429

Many properties offer bonuses to make off-season or slow-period bookings more profitable for travel agents. Properties may also award bonuses to agents for booking a certain number of room nights or for maintaining a certain level of bookings.

7You can easily give special treatment to guests booked by travel agents if these guests can be readily identified. Check guest registrations to determine which guests are commissionable to travel agents. The first time an agent sends a client to your property, you should call and thank him or her. Such actions deliver a powerful message that agents' clients will be well cared for, and may encourage agents to recommend the property to other clients.

Checking guest registrations can also lead to identification of travel agents who come to the property, unannounced, to see what the guest experience is really like. These agents are usually the owners or managers of top-producing agencies. When you identify these travel agent guests, a welcoming phone call can let them know that you care about travel-agent-related bookings and are receptive to the needs of the travel agency market.

Finding Travel Agents

There are five resources that can help a property identify travel agents and agencies it may want to do business with:

1. The *Official Airline Guide (OAG)*
2. The *World Travel Directory*

Exhibit 5 Sweepstakes for Travel Agents

EVERY TIME YOU MAKE A HOLIDAY INN® RESERVATION THROUGH YOUR CRS DURING JUNE, YOU'LL BE ELIGIBLE TO WIN ONE OF 51 DAILY PRIZES!

One Daily Grand Prize: Every weekday during June, we'll be awarding a fabulous trip for two to a "mystery" destination of

NORTHWEST AIRLINES

our choice. Trip winners will enjoy six nights accommodations at one of our 1,600 hotels worldwide, roundtrip air transportation courtesy of Northwest

Airlines, and use of a Hertz rental car.

Where in the world will you be going if you're one of our lucky grand prize winners? You'll have to figure that out...for yourself! (See following pages for details.)

A $500 BONUS PRIZE FROM

VISA

BOOK A HOLIDAY INN BEST BREAKS™ PACKAGE AND YOU'LL *DOUBLE* YOUR CHANCES OF WINNING! GUARANTEE RESERVATIONS TO THE VISA® CARD, AND YOU'LL *TRIPLE* YOUR CHANCES!

This summer, like never before, your clients are looking for ways to make their vacation dollars go farther.

So tell them all about the Holiday Inn *Best Breaks* package. It includes a comfortable room as well as a breakfast coupon for up to $12*...kids 19 and under stay free in their parents' room... and kids 12 and under eat free off the kids' menu with a dining parent. (Limit: Four kids per family**) *Best Breaks* packages are available through September 7, 1992 at participating U.S. and Canadian hotels.

For the first time ever, you can book our *Best Breaks* packages directly, through your automated reservations system. *Every Best Breaks reservation you make for stays completed by September 7 will earn you two automatic sweepstakes entries!*

And any reservation guaranteed to a client's Visa® card earns you three automatic entries!

If you guarantee your grand prize-winning reservation to your client's Visa® card, you'll win a bonus—$500 in Visa® travellers checks to take on your trip!

50 Additional Prizes, Every Day! Each weekday, in addition to the grand prize trip, we'll be awarding two first prizes ...and 48 second prizes! (See following pages for details.)

MEET CARMEN SANDIEGO, STAR OF THE HOTTEST, HIPPEST GAME SHOW ON TV!

WHO IN THE WORLD IS CARMEN SANDIEGO?

She's the star of *"Where In The World Is Carmen Sandiego?"*® Broderbund's popular computer software game, which educates youngsters 6–14 about geography. The software is also the basis for a popular children's game show, seen daily on PBS, sponsored in part by Holiday Inn.

Carmen has a band of crafty thieves who circle the globe, stealing the Mona Lisa or swiping the torch from the Statue of Liberty. Luckily, every day, they get caught... by contestants who decipher clues, requiring knowledge of geography, that lead to the thieves' hiding places. Every Carmen fan finds out fast that crime doesn't pay...but geography knowledge *does!*

SHE'S ALSO THE STAR OF HOLIDAY INN HOTELS' SUMMER PROMOTION!

This summer, Holiday Inn is the Official Hotel For Family Fun℠ All summer long, participating hotels in the U.S. and Canada will be giving away a free gift to families who stay with us— a colorful activity book, based on the adventures of Carmen Sandiego and her gang of outlaws.

There's a super-exciting sweepstakes, too, plus a free Carmen Sandiego travel game by mail for clients who charge their stay to their Visa® card.

SIMPLY BOOK A HOLIDAY INN RESERVATION THROUGH YOUR CRS. IT'S THAT EASY TO WIN!

During June, every Holiday Inn reservation you make through your CRS will earn you one automatic entry into our sweepstakes.

Every Holiday Inn *Best Breaks* reservation you make will earn you two automatic entries!

And every Holiday Inn reservation you guarantee to the Visa® card will earn you *three* automatic entries!

To be eligible, you must enter the following information in each Holiday Inn reservation booking segment:

/SI-BB-FIRST INITIAL LAST NAME
Examples:
   /SI-BB-RSMITH
   /SI-BB-RJONES

Do not leave a space between your first initial and last name.

Note: Reservations must be for stays completed by 9/7/92. You need not make a reservation in order to enter. See official rules for alternative means of entry.

This sweepstakes, promoted by Holiday Inn, offers travel agents prizes for booking Holiday Inn reservations for clients via computer.

Exhibit 6   Serving the Clients of Travel Agents

You can encourage additional travel agent bookings by providing good service to travel agent clients staying at your property. This advertisement promotes ANA Hotels International's service to guests, promising travel agents that their clients will be pampered while they enjoy the facilities of a world-class hotel.

3. In-house records

4. American Society of Travel Agents (ASTA) mailing lists

5. Travel industry trade shows

The *OAG* lists all airline activity between domestic and international cities, and provides valuable information on the flow of airline traffic into a property's locale. While this guide does not specifically list travel agents or agencies, it does target the key cities from which air traffic originates. You can then find out the names of travel agencies in those cities and contact them.

The *World Travel Directory* can be purchased for under $100 and lists the names of travel agencies and agents, the size of agencies, what type of business each agency specializes in, and where agencies are located. A listing of wholesale tour operators is also included. This book can be an excellent source for travel agent leads.

In-house records provide a history of commission payments to travel agents and can help you target agents who have recommended the property in the past. In-house records can also help identify an agent's specific needs. For example, has an agent most often booked individual business or leisure travelers, or does the agent primarily serve the small meetings market?

You can also use in-house records to develop a travel agent mailing list. The in-house mailing list can be expanded through the purchase of outside lists. ASTA mailing lists are some of the most useful. ASTA provides national, regional, and state lists on a cost-per-thousand basis.

Some properties use industry trade shows as opportunities to meet travel agents. These shows (which will be discussed later in the chapter) allow you to communicate with individual agents and determine specific travel agent needs. Information on these shows can be obtained from ASTA or from trade publications.

Reaching Travel Agents

You can reach travel agents through hotel directories, trade magazines, direct mail, trade shows, personal sales, and public relations.

Hotel Directories. Perhaps the most effective way to reach travel agents is through advertising in hotel directories. Hotel directories are used by travel agents to book eight out of ten leisure traveler bookings and six out of ten business traveler bookings. Hotel directories are used extensively even when a computerized system is available: 67% of all travel agents said they consulted a hotel directory as well as a computerized system.[7]

Since travel agents receive an average of 80 to 100 directories each year, a property's directory ad must attract attention. The headline should include the property's chief benefit, and the ad itself must clearly convey the hotel's name and image. Ads should appeal to a travel agent, not a potential guest.

In addition to the standard print directories, many of today's properties are taking advantage of computerized visual hotel directories that provide a full-color "look" at thousands of participating properties. Jaguar's SABREvision, for example, offers a number of options, ranging from a single screen with color graphics to a maximum of 12 screens featuring visuals, rate information, and maps (see Exhibit 7). Travel agents and their clients love pictures, and these exciting visuals help sell a property far more effectively than a computer screen offering only printed information.

Exhibit 7   High-Tech Hotel Directories

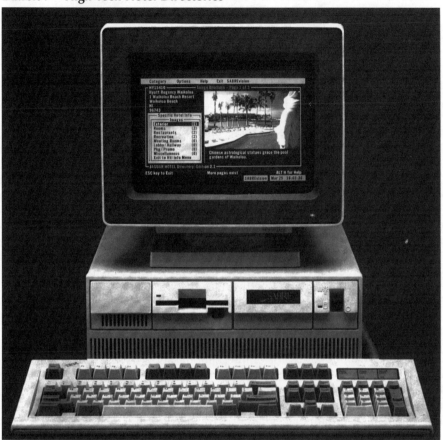

No longer are hotel directories limited to print; today's computer technology puts property informa-tion—and photographs—at the travel agent's fingertips. This program, JAGUAR on SABREvision, offers 12 image and data screens. (Source: JAGUAR, Secaucus, New Jersey)

Trade Magazines. In addition to directory advertising, many properties also advertise in travel trade magazines such as *ASTA Travel News* and *Travel Agent*. Unlike consumer ads, trade ads are often lengthy, since information is so important to travel professionals. Copy should include:

1. *Pertinent location information.* Indicate proximity to major highways and airports or other transportation terminals, distances to popular attractions, mileage to nearby industrial complexes or downtown business areas, and availability of complimentary transportation (airport limousine, hotel courtesy van for trips to shopping malls or attractions, and so on).

2. *Rate information.* List regular rates, group rates, and special rates such as "children free," along with special packages (rates, availability, what is included) and special discounts available for off-season bookings.

3. *Booking information.* Provide toll-free reservation numbers, credit card policies, and other pertinent booking information (such as travel agent guarantees).

4. *Commission information.* Provide information about payment policies and special incentives.

You can use photographs in addition to copy to grab attention and introduce your property to travel agents. Exterior shots, lobby photographs, and photographs of guestrooms or function areas are examples of appropriate photos.

Direct Mail. Another way to reach travel agents is through direct mail. Direct mail includes sales letters, collateral materials, promotional giveaways, and newsletters. Collateral materials can be used to introduce new facilities or packages; they can be as simple as printed fliers or as elaborate as full-color folders and special advertising gimmicks. Newsletters are an excellent way to keep in touch with travel agents and inform them of price fluctuations, new promotions, and efforts to better serve travel professionals. Since travel agents receive so much mail, direct mail pieces must be attractive to avoid being thrown away unread. To reinforce the property's message, a series of direct mail pieces is often effective. Series mailings keep the property fresh in the travel agent's mind, especially if they are developed along a theme or are otherwise attention-getting (see Exhibit 8).

Trade Shows. Another, more personal, way to reach travel agents is through attendance at industry trade shows. As mentioned previously, trade shows give you the opportunity to talk directly to travel agents and learn their individual needs. Trade shows fall into two categories: major international shows, which are organized and coordinated corporately, and traveling "marketplace" shows, which run for several days in selected cities. The most well-known trade shows are the International Tourism Bourse (ITB) in Germany, ASTA conventions, the Travel Industry Association of America's semi-annual conference, Travel Age West, the Henry Davis Travel Show, and the Foremost trade show.

Travel agents visiting trade shows can be reached through sales presentations and the use of visual aids, including video brochures. Video brochures can be almost as effective as a personal tour of the property. When a video brochure is not available, presenters can use printed brochures and attractive posters—both travel-agent-oriented and consumer-oriented—to help the sales presentation.

Personal Sales. A property may wish to contact local, potentially high-volume travel agents through personal sales calls (see Exhibit 9). Many travel agencies are staffed by agents who have specialized areas or client followings, so it may be necessary to deal with a number of agents at each agency. Since travel agents are usually busy, it is best to call ahead for an appointment. Avoid calls on Mondays and Fridays, when business volume is heaviest.

Presentations should be brief. Travel agents offer a complex array of properties to clients; therefore, the presentation should clearly differentiate the property from competing properties. A familiarization tour or invitation to view the property's video can be offered. Getting to know travel agents and getting them to learn about the property and its management is one of the keys to success.

Exhibit 8   Series Mailings

"AND LITTLE JENNY WAS SO HAPPY WHEN WE FOUND HER LOST DOLLY AND MAILED IT TO HER," SAYS GM.

"Every day, it seems like our housekeeping staff finds something of value left in one of the rooms. To Jenny, that little doll is priceless. It's no longer surprising to us that so many things get misplaced during a guest's visit. Since we completed our 2 1/2 million dollar renovation, people stay around the hotel for much longer periods. Everything looks so new now... the rooms, lobby, restaurant, entertainment lounge, pool and tennis areas... all first-class.

And when they do venture out, they discover how convenient the hotel is to any of the attractions, beaches, golf courses, shopping centers and business parks. Being located at Orlando's two main traffic arteries provides guests with access to any and all of the area's Magic. With everything that there is to do, on and off property, you can see how it might be easy to lose track of things once in a while."

Give us a call at 1-800-242-6862. Your clients will appreciate the convenience and warm, friendly service. And they can always check their dolly at the front desk.

1-800-242-6862

Holiday Inn®
ORLANDO / ALTAMONTE SPRINGS

"BUT HE ALWAYS ORDERS A MANHATTAN," SAYS BARTENDER AT THE WHY NOT LOUNGE!

"It's amazing what a 2 1/2 million dollar renovation can do for a property! Rooms. Lobby. Restaurant. Meeting Space. And of course the Why Not. Inside and out...it all looks new! And ever since we completed the renovation, people check in and never want to leave. We're close to the beaches and golf courses. It's an easy route to any of the attractions. But does anyone go? No! Instead, the lobby's always busy, the pool is packed, the restaurant is full and the Why Not rocks all night long. Sure, business is great. But it would be nice to see some new faces for a change."

Give us a call at 1-800-242-6862. We'll do our very best to squeeze your clients in here and make you a hero. But please, tell them to leave the hotel sometime.

1-800-242-6862

Holiday Inn®
ORLANDO / ALTAMONTE SPRINGS

A series of direct mail pieces is often effective in getting your message across to travel agents. These two pieces were developed by the Orlando/Altamonte Springs Holiday Inn to promote its $2.5 million renovation, proximity to popular attractions, and special travel agent toll-free reservations number.

Exhibit 9   Guidelines for Working With Travel Agents

1. Let agents know you want and value their business. Help them sell your property by providing a checklist of what you want them to know. This checklist should include facts about your location, reservation system, accommodations, facilities, rates, packages, meeting and convention facilities, commission policies, and local attractions. If possible, list specific sales points, using actual quotes from a third party to add credibility.

2. Make the hotel easy to book. Advertise the toll-free 800 reservations number. For additional convenience, provide agents with another number to call for information they are unable to obtain from the reservationist. Above all, keep reservationists informed about your property.

3. Honor agents' reservations and avoid overbooking. Lost reservations and overbooked hotels are two of the most frequent agent complaints. If possible, guarantee the reservation with the client's credit card or an agency check.

4. Have the client's room ready when he or she arrives and add a special touch such as a welcoming note.

5. Pay commissions promptly. Brightly colored checks and promotion gimmicks aren't necessary, only the money.

6. Provide familiarization trips or special rate discounts so that agents can get a firsthand view of the hotel.

7. Make personal contact with agents whenever possible by attending trade shows or making calls and visits.

8. Educate the hotel staff so that it recognizes and knows how to handle agent reservations and vouchers.

9. In advertising the hotel, remember that agents receive 400 or more pieces of mail a week and discard 90% of it. Fliers, brochures, and other advertising pieces are more trouble than they're worth, agents say. They rely instead on the listings and advertisements in hotel indexes.

10. When promoting the hotel, for best results include not only pictures of the hotel but also of the immediate area. Aerial shots of the hotel and the surrounding landscape are especially desirable. Include details which will help the agent sell the property to a first-time client.

11. Consider giving agents incentives such as special commissions for booking business during slow periods.

12. Above all, be consistent. Build the property's reputation for good service and your reputation for dealing with agents fairly.

Source: Adapted from *Texas and Southwest Hotel-Motel Review,* April 1980.

Public Relations. Good public relations may do more to reach travel agents than all the advertising in the world. For example, you might invite travel agents to learn about the inner workings of your property's reservations system. Inviting travel writers to visit the property may lead to travel trade articles that are read by travel agents. Properties can also provide news releases to trade publications that appeal to travel agents. Another public relations idea is to host a "travel agent day" honoring exceptional travel agency partners.

Conclusion

The growing variety of transportation and lodging choices makes travel decisions more complicated than ever before. Travel agents can be expected to handle even more business and leisure travel in the future. Meeting the needs of travel agents and maintaining a positive attitude toward travel agencies can mean increased bookings and revenues for your property—at a fraction of the cost of in-house sales efforts.

You should strive to develop excellent working relationships with travel agents. Travel agents appreciate the value of hotel bookings, and hotels have come to view travel agents as an extension of their sales staff—salespeople who do not ask for payment until they have produced business.

Endnotes

1. "Louis Harris Hotel Market Survey of U.S. Travel Agents," a study conducted by Louis Harris and Associates for *Hotel & Travel Index*, 1991.

2. William N. Hulett, "The Hotel-Travel Agent Relationship Must Be Cultivated for Mutual Benefit," *Hotel and Resort Industry*, July 1989, p. 44.

3. Information in this section is based on five studies: "1991 *Travel Weekly* U.S. Travel Agency Survey," conducted by Louis Harris and Associates; the "1990 North American Travel Agent Usage Study," conducted by Market Probe International; "Business Travelers' Use of Hotels," 1990, "U.S. Meetings Market," 1991, and the "1990/91 Corporate Travel Manager Survey," underwritten by *Hotel & Travel Index*.

4. "Louis Harris Hotel Market Survey of U.S. Travel Agents," a study conducted by Louis Harris and Associates for *Hotel & Travel Index*, 1991.

5. "An Analysis of the Hotel Selection Process for Business Travelers," an article based on personal interviews conducted with travel agents by the Harvey Research Organization, Inc. for *Hotel & Travel Index*.

6. "An Analysis of the Hotel Selection Process," *Hotel & Travel Index*.

7. "Louis Harris Hotel Market Survey of U.S. Travel Agents," a study conducted by Louis Harris and Associates for *Hotel & Travel Index*, 1991.

Key Terms

retail travel agent
wholesale travel agent
familiarization (fam) tour

Review Questions

1. How many travel agencies are there in the United States?

2. What is the difference between a retail travel agent and a wholesale travel agent?

3. What are some of the ways properties are meeting travel agents' need for property information?

4. Why are travel agents reluctant to use airline reservations systems for booking hotel rooms?

5. Who are the best prospects for a property's fam tour for travel agents?

6. What are some of the ways in which properties can provide good service to travel agents?

7. What are the advantages of a centralized commission payment plan?

8. What are five resources that can help a property identify travel agents and agencies?

9. What is perhaps the most effective way to reach travel agents?

10. Trade magazine ad copy should include what types of information?

11. What public relations efforts might be used to develop travel agent business?

Chapter Outline

The Group Meetings Market
    Associations
        Types of Associations
        Types of Association Meetings
        Planning Factors for Association Meetings
        Whom to Contact
    Corporations
        Types of Corporations
        Types of Corporate Meetings
        Planning Factors for Corporate Meetings
        Whom to Contact
Finding Association and Corporate Group Business
Reaching Association and Corporate Meeting Planners
    Personal Sales Calls
    Sales Blitzes
    Trade Shows
    Print Advertising
    Other Sales Tools
Conclusion

18

Marketing to Meeting Planners

Pᴇʀʜᴀᴘs ᴛʜᴇ ʜᴇᴀʟᴛʜɪᴇsᴛ ᴀɴᴅ ᴍᴏsᴛ growth-oriented part of a hotel's total guest mix is the group meetings market. Jet transportation, generally rising incomes, and increased leisure time all contribute to this market's expansion.

Group meetings business can benefit a property in a number of ways:

1. *Additional revenue.* Because group meeting guests are more or less a captive audience, they not only provide guestroom revenue, they also spend more in the hotel's other revenue centers and on hospitality suites and food and beverage functions than do other guests. Spouses are accompanying meeting and convention attendees more than ever before. This typically increases business in gift shops, health clubs, and other revenue centers.

2. *Ease in filling slow periods.* Group meetings are an excellent way to generate business during your property's slow periods.

3. *Ease in employee scheduling.* With groups, the length of each guest's stay is usually predetermined. You can schedule employees more efficiently and reduce labor costs.

4. *Repeat business.* Group meetings can result in repeat business from the group organizing the meeting and from individual attendees who are introduced to the property during the meeting. Individuals may later visit the property as business or leisure travelers, and can recommend the property to friends and business associates.

There is yet another benefit to targeting the group meetings market. Group meetings business frequently increases during periods when leisure travel is on the decline due to a struggling economy. A poor economy actually stimulates group meetings business by creating the need for more direct contact among business associates.

The group meetings market can be a consistent revenue-producer for properties large and small. In this chapter we will take a close look at this market and learn how to meet the needs of the men and women who plan group meetings for associations and corporations. We will explore each segment of the group meetings market in terms of size, the types of meetings held and the requirements for these meetings, the cycle and pattern of meetings, and the duration of meetings. We will also learn how to obtain leads, work with decision-makers to generate business, and use sales and advertising techniques to build a property's group business.

The Group Meetings Market

According to recent industry-wide studies, nearly 15% of U.S. hotel guests are meeting attendees. Of course, for major convention hotels, this figure is significantly higher. Complexes such as the Opryland Hotel in Nashville (2,011 rooms), the New York Marriott Marquis (2,028 rooms), and the Las Vegas Hilton (3,444 rooms) attribute as much as 80% of their total sales volume to convention business.[1]

A common misconception is that all group business meetings and conventions are large gatherings of thousands of people. In reality, there are many more small meetings than large ones. Research conducted by industry trade publications shows that 75% of all corporate meetings have fewer than 100 people in attendance.[2] This means that group meetings are a potential source of business for lodging properties of all sizes.

The group meetings market can be divided into two segments: associations and corporations. While the needs of these two segments may be the same in some areas, they are quite different in others, and the many organizations within each segment have needs that vary greatly. In fact, it is rare that a single organization's requirements are the same from one meeting or convention to the next! For this reason, each segment—and the organizations within each segment—must be examined separately.

Associations

An association is an organization of persons having a common interest or purpose. There are many associations throughout the country and the world, and their sizes, natures, and purposes vary greatly. The Council on Education for Public Health has a membership of 2; the National Association of Realtors has a membership of 720,000. There are associations for doctors, bankers, and lawyers. There are also associations for magicians, beekeepers, hospital purchasing agents, horseshoe pitchers, fruit growers, and urethane foam contractors. The American Hotel & Motel Association is an example of an association in the lodging industry.[3]

Types of Associations. Associations can be divided into at least seven general categories:

1. Trade associations

2. Professional and scientific associations

3. Labor unions

4. Educational associations

5. Fraternal and service groups

6. Ethnic associations

7. Religious associations

Trade associations are made up of individuals, companies, or corporations that have similar business needs or concerns. These associations are usually considered the most lucrative source of group meetings business because their memberships

Insider Insights

Jonathan Tisch
President and Chief Executive Officer
Loews Hotels
New York City

Jonathan Tisch was a cinematographer/producer for WBZ-TV in Boston before joining Loews Hotels in 1979 as a sales representative. In 1983 he became executive vice president, responsible for coordination of domestic and international hotel development. Tisch was named president of Loews Hotels in 1986. In January, 1989, he also assumed the role of chief executive officer. In addition, Tisch has served as a member of the Board of Directors of Loews Corporation since 1986. Loews Hotels consists of 14 properties, 13 in the continental United States and Canada and one—Loews Monte Carlo—in Europe.

Tisch is actively involved in many community activities. He is a member of the New York Convention and Visitors Bureau's Executive Committee, the Board of Trustees of Tufts University, The Gunnery School in Connecticut, The Robert Steel Foundation for Pediatric Cancer Research at Memorial Sloan Kettering Cancer Center, and the Board of Pediatrics AIDS Foundation. He is also a member of the Urban Land Institute and was recently appointed to the Dean's Advisory Council for the School of Hotel Administration at Cornell University. He also serves as director and treasurer of the New York Giants football team.

There's no question we operate our hotels with group business in mind. We count on the meetings market for a large share of our revenues. So a lot of our attention is paid to making sure our meeting space, as well as the accommodations and other amenities, suits the needs of meeting planners.

The meeting planner is our client, whom we try to please. But the planner has a client to please, too, whether that be the company's CEO, president, or some other senior officer. And it's this person who has to be pleased with the outcome of the meeting. What we're looking to create is a win-win situation for all the parties concerned. If the senior officer is happy, then the planner's happy, and if the planner's happy, we've done our job.

To serve the meetings market we start with the physical structure. It's foolish to think you can conduct effective meetings at a site with insufficient or inadequate meeting space. In building new hotels, we've gone so far as to stop construction and redo the plans if we think the meeting space should be enhanced. And the same applies when we're taking over existing properties; the meeting space is critical.

To keep tuned to changes in the meetings market, I attend industry meetings. You have to attend trade shows. I'll even work the booth. We can't expect to understand planners' needs if we don't ask them about their concerns.

The booming 1980s are over and the hotel industry is facing a much more sobering future. In a slow economy, the meetings business becomes even more crucial for hotels. With transient bookings shrinking, group business becomes a source of

(continued)

Insider Insights *(continued)*

stability. We are also seeing lead times getting shorter, which just means we have to be more client-sensitive than ever.

At all our hotels, we try not to take ourselves too seriously. We want our hotels to be user-friendly, both from the perspective of the meeting planner and the meeting attendee. This isn't to say that the meetings won't be productive, because they will. We'll provide the highest level of support at our disposal to make that happen. But when the meeting's over for the day, people can relax and enjoy themselves.

---

consist largely of successful executives. Many trade associations hold conventions in conjunction with trade shows, such as the trade show staged by the National Restaurant Association. Restaurant and kitchen equipment suppliers exhibit at this annual convention, which draws more than 100,000 delegates to Chicago.

Professional and scientific associations are closely related to trade associations, but differ in regard to meeting frequency. Most professional and scientific associations have regular meeting schedules, but it is not unusual for special meetings to be called if a major discovery affects a particular association. Many of these associations are affiliated with national and international associations, and these groups are typically very large. Examples of professional and scientific associations include the American Bar Association, the International Association of Dental Students, and the American Statistical Association.

Labor unions meet only at hotels that are unionized, and typically generate high food and beverage revenues because several social functions are usually included in the convention program. Examples of labor unions include the International Brotherhood of Electrical Workers, the Teamsters Union, and the United Steel Workers of America.

Another important source of group business is the non-profit organization segment. This non-profit segment has been given the acronym SMERF, because of its make-up of social, military, educational, religious, and fraternal groups. SMERF is now a major market segment for many properties. It shares three characteristics: meeting attendees are usually price sensitive, most SMERF groups book their meetings during the property's off-season, and most meetings are arranged by non-professional meeting planners, who may change from year to year. Specific needs of some of the SMERF groups are as follows:

Educational associations are groups of teachers or other education professionals and supporters. Although expenses are generally paid by the educational institutions involved, these groups tend to be very cost-conscious. Examples of educational associations include the National Education Association, the Modern Language Association, and the Council of Hotel Restaurant and Institutional Educators.

Fraternal and service groups are made up of individuals who have a similar area of interest, whether it be of a scholastic, philanthropic, or social nature. Members who take part in fraternal or service group meetings typically pay their own expenses. Meetings usually include family participation. Examples of fraternal and service groups include the Benevolent Protective Order of Elks, the Fraternal Order of Eagles, and Soroptimist International.

Ethnic associations provide a common denominator based on race or national origin. Like fraternal associations, ethnic associations are family-oriented, and meeting attendees pay their own expenses. Examples of ethnic associations include the National Association for the Advancement of Colored People, the German-American Club, and the National Association of Latin Americans.

Religious associations can be divided into two groups: vocational and avocational. Vocational groups include associations of ministers or other clergy; avocational groups include educational and charitable religious groups. Religious associations as a whole are very budget-conscious. Examples of religious associations include the National Conference of Christians and Jews, and Gideons International.

Types of Association Meetings. With this wide diversity of associations, it is evident that association meetings will vary. Associations generate several types of group meetings business:

- Annual conventions
- Regional conventions
- Conferences
- Seminars and workshops
- Board and committee meetings

Annual conventions are held by associations of all types. Some conventions are huge affairs attracting between 20,000 and 30,000 people, while others may have an attendance of fewer than 100. The average convention has 400 attendees.[4] Most annual conventions have a main session for all delegates, supplemented by a number of smaller meetings sometimes called "breakout" meetings. Almost half of all annual conventions are held in conjunction with a trade show or with exhibits.[5] In some cases, trade shows may be held without a convention program; these functions are called exhibitions or expositions, and may be sponsored by an association or by individual entrepreneurs or companies for the benefit of the association.

Since annual conventions vary widely, it is necessary to look at the convention needs of the different categories of associations.

Trade associations usually have complex convention programs that include many meetings and social activities. These associations usually make extensive use of sophisticated audiovisual equipment.

Professional and scientific associations also make use of sophisticated audiovisual equipment. Scientific and medical associations typically hold several breakout meetings, and the availability of a number of meeting rooms is more important than provision for social events.

Labor unions require the use of large properties, especially when the general session is the focal point of the convention. Labor union conventions usually last longer than most other association conventions and feature a great many social

Insider Insights

Michael K. Hausman, CHSE
Director of National Accounts
Marriott Corporation
New York City

Michael Hausman graduated from Temple University in 1966 and began his career in the hospitality industry that same year. His first position was with the Philadelphia Convention and Visitors Bureau. He worked for a number of hotel companies before his current twelve-year stint with Marriott Hotels and Resorts. Hausman is a past vice president of Meeting Planners International and also served as a vice president for Hospitality Sales & Marketing Association International. He has received numerous honors during his career. He was inducted into the New York chapter of Meeting Planners International Hall of Fame, named Associate Member of the Year by the New York Society of Association Executives, and selected as Supplier of the Year by the International Association of Meeting Planners International.

Of all market segments, the association market is the most apt to book more than several years out. Some associations book 15 or more years out because they use virtually all of a city's hotel rooms and convention facilities. When doing long-term room rate and financial projections, knowing that several associations have made commitments with the property can be quite reassuring for the lenders, the property's owners, and corporate headquarters.

The association market covers myriad associations. Not only are you soliciting large, city-wide associations, which are generally coordinated through a city's convention and visitors' bureau, you're also soliciting association meeting business of under 500 rooms. This includes regional, state, board of directors, and a variety of other types of association meetings. This means that virtually any hotel can solicit some part of this important market segment.

Association decision-makers may vary, but in most cases the executive secretary or executive director has a great deal of control. Very often, particularly in the case of large annual meetings, there is a board of directors or a site committee that must stamp its approval on the executive director's recommendation. It's helpful if members of the board of directors or site committee can be solicited for their support. If there is a local chapter of an association in your area, the chapter president often becomes an important contact.

As mentioned, most city convention and visitors' bureaus are in the business of soliciting major associations, and an effort should be made to coordinate your property's interests with their efforts. Often, the property can tie together an attractive package with the convention and visitors' bureau, but if there are associations that the property wants to target on its own, a number of techniques can be used.

Various encyclopedias and directories list vital information on the size and type of association meetings and the names of key executives. A phone call or letter to a decision-maker should elicit a response, but nothing is more effective than

---

Insider Insights *(continued)*

meeting with association executives. Trips to major association cities such as Washington, D.C., Chicago, and New York can be most rewarding—if planned in advance with set appointments. Other avenues include attendance at various trade shows, including the American Society of Association Executives, the National Association of Exposition Executives, Professional Conventions Managers Association, and a whole alphabet of other organizations. Many of these organizations have city and state associations that let you target markets in close proximity.

While the association market is exciting because of its vast size and the dollar value it represents to a hotel, a coordinated effort that involves selling to a number of market segments is vital to the success of a hotel. A property's percentage of association market business can vary from year to year, making soliciting other market segments a necessary addition to association selling.

---

and food and beverage functions. These conventions often take on a political atmosphere. Prominent political speakers, signs, banners, and buttons are usually part of the program.

Educational associations maximize meetings and minimize social functions at their annual conventions. Meetings are usually scheduled at night as well as during the day. Most educational association conventions are organized around a large general session (often featuring a political speaker), but a number of breakout rooms are usually needed as well.

Fraternal and service groups usually have annual conventions built around large general sessions. Attendees often combine vacations with convention attendance, so properties should offer recreational activities. There should also be sightseeing areas and entertainment facilities nearby.

Ethnic associations typically prefer annual conventions with elaborate social programs. Since most of their annual conventions are family-oriented, there is a high percentage of multiple occupancy in this group, and recreational and sightseeing opportunities are important.

Religious associations require varied facilities, depending on the nature of the religion. Conservative religions tend to look for fewer but larger meeting halls, while liberal religions are more interested in a sufficient number of breakout rooms.

Regional conventions are smaller in scope than annual conventions, and are further limited by geographic restrictions. Although some members elect to fly, most members attending regional conventions drive to the convention site. Therefore, airport properties do not necessarily have an advantage when soliciting regional conventions.

Conferences are usually staged to supplement a convention program. A conference supplies information related to new developments of interest to the association's members. Conferences are more common in professional, scientific, and educational associations, although other associations may book conferences following breakthroughs in their fields, changes in tax or corporate law, and other events that would affect the association's members.

Seminars and workshops are similar to conferences but are smaller in scope. They are generally used to train and educate association members. Many seminars are developed by independent seminar consultants who travel around the country presenting special programs of interest to association members, while other seminars may be developed by the association's paid staff.

Board and committee meetings are the smallest association group meetings in terms of attendance. They are often set in beautiful locales to attract outstanding people to serve on the board or committee, or to reward unpaid association officials. Board or committee meetings may range in size from fewer than 10 to up to more than 100 persons, and are ideal for almost any size property. Even a very small property can usually handle a meeting of ten or fewer. A large property may use the success it has with board and committee meetings to generate support for its selection as a convention site.

Planning Factors for Association Meetings. Obviously, there is a wide variety of associations and association meetings. You must identify the individual association's needs and determine ways to meet them if you want your property to be selected as that association's meeting or convention site. However, you should be aware of some factors that all associations must consider when planning a convention or group meeting. These include the timing of meetings, lead time, geographic patterns, geographic restrictions, attendance, and site selection.

Timing. Most association conventions—whether national, state, or regional—are held during the same month each year. Some associations, in fact, hold their annual convention during the same week of the same month each year.

Lead time. Most associations plan conventions well in advance. The average lead time is 2 years, although this varies from as little as 1 to as many as 15 or more years, depending on the convention's size. This lead time, though frustrating to hoteliers, is necessary for associations to select a site and plan their convention.

Geographic pattern. Many association conventions follow a definite geographic pattern. Often a convention is rotated among three or four cities. Some associations alternate between the East and the West in site selection; a popular variation of this pattern is to select a Midwestern city every third year.

The time of year a convention is scheduled may influence which area of the country is chosen. If a Midwestern location is chosen for a winter convention, for example, attendance could suffer in the event of a blizzard, an ice storm, or other inclement weather. Most meeting planners try to avoid weather problems through prudent scheduling. This is why the most popular months for conventions are October, May, April, June, and September, in that order.

Geographic restrictions. Some associations are limited to a site selection in their own states or within a specified mile limit. This is especially true of small or regional associations. However, there is a growing trend to bend these restrictions and choose a site that appeals to the majority of association members no matter where it is located.

Attendance. Attendance at most association meetings is voluntary. Since the option to attend is the member's, an association meeting planner must *attract*

Exhibit 1   Boosting Association Meeting Attendance

Since meeting attendance is voluntary for a number of groups, especially non-profit associations, it is often necessary to offer an incentive for members to attend. This advertisement, developed by the Hawaii Visitors Bureau Meetings & Conventions Department, promotes Hawaii as a popular location for meetings.

members to the meeting—and may try to do so with an appealing price, an interesting location, or special programs or events (see Exhibit 1).

Site selection. While the primary needs for conventions and group meetings are adequate meeting space, a sufficient number of guestrooms, and the services of

Exhibit 2 Special Packages for Meeting Planners

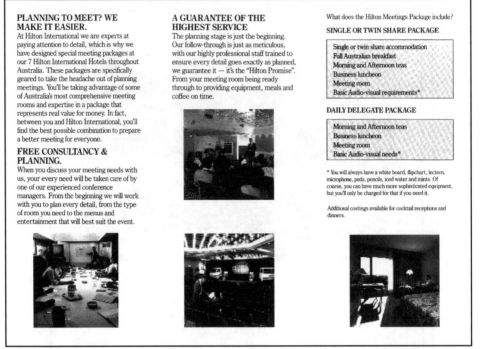

PLANNING TO MEET? WE MAKE IT EASIER.

At Hilton International we are experts at paying attention to detail, which is why we have designed special meeting packages at our 7 Hilton International Hotels throughout Australia. These packages are specifically geared to take the headache out of planning meetings. You'll be taking advantage of some of Australia's most comprehensive meeting rooms and expertise in a package that represents real value for money. In fact, between you and Hilton International, you'll find the best possible combination to prepare a better meeting for everyone.

FREE CONSULTANCY & PLANNING.

When you discuss your meeting needs with us, your every need will be taken care of by one of our experienced conference managers. From the beginning we will work with you to plan every detail, from the type of room you need to the menus and entertainment that will best suit the event.

A GUARANTEE OF THE HIGHEST SERVICE

The planning stage is just the beginning. Our follow-through is just as meticulous, with our highly professional staff trained to ensure every detail goes exactly as planned, we guarantee it — it's the "Hilton Promise". From your meeting room being ready through to providing equipment, meals and coffee on time.

What does the Hilton Meetings Package include?

SINGLE OR TWIN SHARE PACKAGE

- Single or twin share accommodation
- Full Australian breakfast
- Morning and Afternoon teas
- Business luncheon
- Meeting room
- Basic Audio-visual requirements*

DAILY DELEGATE PACKAGE

- Morning and Afternoon teas
- Business luncheon
- Meeting room
- Basic Audio-visual needs*

* You will always have a white board, flipchart, lectern, microphone, pads, pencils, iced water and mints. Of course, you can have much more sophisticated equipment, but you'll only be charged for that if you need it.

Additional costings available for cocktail receptions and dinners.

Price is a primary consideration for many meeting planners. This four-color brochure describes the special meeting packages Hilton International developed for meeting planners in Australia and New Zealand.

experienced hospitality employees, associations do consider other factors when selecting a specific site for a convention or group meeting.

Transportation is an important factor in selecting a site. If members must fly to the convention or meeting site, an airport property is most convenient; if they usually drive to the convention, a location near an interstate highway is a good choice.

Another factor in site selection is price. Most association conventions average two to four days, and since many delegates pay their own expenses, guestroom rates must be within the reach of association members (see Exhibit 2). In some cases, an association meeting planner will select a property that offers the lowest cost accommodations; in other cases, the finest accommodations are necessary, and resort or upscale properties will be the meeting planner's first choice. In other words, there is no one right price level. The price an association is willing to pay for guestrooms will depend on the nature of the association and its members' ability to pay.

Whom to Contact. Because of the many factors involved in planning a convention or group meeting and selecting a site for it, the planning and selection process an association goes through is a lengthy and often complex one. It is important for you to become involved in this process as soon as possible. That means getting to know the decision-maker. Who is the decision-maker for an association? Depending on the type of association and/or the type of meeting, he or she may be one of the following:

- Professional meeting planner

- Association executive

- Site committee chairperson

- Board of directors chairperson or member

- Local association member

Some associations employ a *professional meeting planner* who is responsible for recommending meeting sites. Many employ an *association executive* who may be given a title such as president, executive vice president, or executive director. No matter what the title, the association executive is usually the key to your sales efforts. He or she is ordinarily involved in the initial screening and final selection of a convention or meeting site. The association executive may either visit prospective sites in person or delegate this responsibility to others. He or she may have an administrative staff that assists with convention planning.

Small associations often cannot afford a full-time association executive, and may use a multiple association management firm. These firms serve an association as needed, selecting a site and planning a convention at costs the association can afford.

A *site committee chairperson* may be involved in screening convention sites or deciding on the final site, depending on the size and structure of the association. Chairpersons of other association committees may also be involved with the selection of sites for seminars, especially if the seminar will deal with matters important to their particular committees.

A *board of directors* is not usually involved in the decision-making process until the time for the final site selection. Many boards immediately accept the recommendation of the association executive. Others may take more time, but in the end most boards of directors agree with the association executive's recommendation.

In many associations, especially professional and scientific ones, local chapters bid for the honor of hosting the national group. In these cases, you can approach a *local association member* and offer assistance in planning a convention or meeting if it will be held at your property. When taking this approach, however, you must demonstrate your property's convention and meetings expertise.

Once the key decision-maker has been identified, the job of selling begins. Techniques for selling to association meeting planners will be discussed in detail later in the chapter.

Corporations

Corporations can be a highly lucrative source of group meetings business. Most corporate meeting planners average 14 meetings or conventions in a single year.[6] The short lead time required for most corporate meetings makes it easier for you to book corporate meetings during slack periods. Corporate groups can be an important source of revenue to small properties as well as large, since, as mentioned

Insider Insights

Robert C. Mackey, CHSE
Vice President, Sales and Marketing
Sofitel North America
Scarsdale, New York

Robert Mackey, an Ohio native, received his B.A. in psychology from Ohio University in 1972 and worked in the insurance industry from 1972 to 1977. In 1977, he began his career in the hotel industry as a room clerk at the Waldorf-Astoria. Mackey progressed through the ranks to convention manager and sales manager before leaving the property in 1979 to join the pre-opening office for Vista International New York as a sales manager. With Vista International Hotels, he served as assistant director of sales, director of sales, and director of marketing. Today he is vice president, sales and marketing for Sofitel North America, the luxury division of France's Accor chain. Mackey is a Certified Hotel Sales Executive and a past president of the New York chapter of the Hospitality Sales & Marketing Association International. Mackey has been a guest lecturer at the New York City Technical College and has contributed articles to Marketing Review.

It can be very difficult to identify and reach decision-makers in the company meetings segment. According to *Successful Meetings Magazine*, 80% of the company meetings planned each year are planned by non-professionals. A non-professional meeting planner is someone who devotes less than 50% of his or her time to planning meetings. An example of this could be a senior vice president of the human resources department who takes on the responsibility of planning a meeting for all the personnel managers in the company. Anyone at a company can become a meeting planner and thus a potential client. All that's required is that the person be assigned to organize a meeting.

The best way to reach non-professional meeting planners is through the judicious use of your own in-house mailing list. Although it's often impossible to predict who within a company will become a meeting planner, it's certainly reasonable to assume that someone who's contacted you in the past might become a client in the future. Contacts within a company can also be helpful. For example, the travel manager whom you work with for individual corporate business travel may be aware of employees in other departments who have been—or will be—involved in planning meetings. Another, but more expensive, method of reaching meeting planners is through consumer advertising in local newspapers and magazines. A potential meeting planner within a company may see your ad and recall your hotel when assigned to arrange a meeting.

Like all kinds of selling, selling to the corporate meetings market involves identifying a client's needs and communicating what your product or service will do to meet them. The ideal salesperson in the company meetings segment isn't a salesperson in the traditional sense, but rather a problem-solver. With non-professional meeting planners, that's often exactly the kind of salesperson they need!

previously, 75% of corporate meetings average an attendance of fewer than 100 persons.

Types of Corporations. Corporations vary greatly in size and purpose. There are local, state, national, and international corporations that sell products, services, or both. Whatever their size and type, at one time or another most corporations hold group meetings that require lodging facilities.

Types of Corporate Meetings. Corporations hold many types of meetings:

1. National or international sales meetings
2. Regional or district sales meetings
3. Training and development meetings
4. Distributor and dealer meetings
5. Executive conferences
6. Product presentations or launchings
7. Stockholders' meetings
8. Board meetings
9. Management development seminars
10. Incentive travel meetings

National or international sales meetings are the oldest type of corporate meeting. Attendance is usually restricted to senior salespeople and supervisory executives; spouses are not usually invited. Average attendance is 183 persons, and meetings last an average of 3.6 days.[7] Meeting requirements and site selections are varied. If a national sales meeting is scheduled to introduce new products, for example, it is important that the meeting be held at a site that provides easy access for product delivery. If a sales meeting has been called to develop a new advertising campaign, usually the site is chosen based on ease of access by the participants. The average per-person expenditure is generally above the usual meeting average. Participants tend to stay close to the property and dine in the property's restaurants or make extensive use of room service.

Regional or district sales meetings are usually smaller than national meetings, averaging 54 persons. Ordinarily these meetings are shorter than national or international sales meetings, although programs are often of the same type. With lower budgets, smaller attendance, and geographic restrictions, the per-person expenditure at regional or district sales meetings drops to the medium level.

Training and development meetings average an attendance of 30 persons, and may last from one to seven days. This is a no-nonsense type of meeting—there is a high level of double occupancy of rooms and meetings are often set up school-room-style. Since the budget is a prime consideration for this type of meeting, especially when training entry-level employees, the per-person expenditure drops to the low-to-medium level. Training and development meetings are well-suited to small properties regardless of location, especially when a "conference center" atmosphere can be provided.

Distributor and dealer meetings are conducted to show new products or motivate dealers. These meetings are usually open to spouses and vary in length from one to three days. Top executives often attend, and meeting attendees are given the best in accommodations, cuisine, and entertainment. Elaborate food and beverage functions and entertainment events make these meetings the cream of the corporate meetings market.

Executive conferences can also yield high per-person expenditures, since this type of meeting requires the finest accommodations available. These meetings are usually arranged on a short lead time, attendance may vary, and spouses are often invited. Additional revenue can be generated through programs for spouses and the sale of first-quality food and beverages.

Product presentations or launchings average from two to five days and may be public or private functions. A private or trade event will have the same general requirements as those for a distributor and dealer meeting. Product presentations or launchings usually require a large ballroom or exhibit area, elaborate staging or setup, and labor and time for dismantling exhibits. These meetings may inconvenience other guests at the property.

Stockholders' meetings are the lowest income-producers of all corporate meetings, since the purpose of the meeting is to conduct business as quickly as possible. Stockholders' meetings almost always last one day, and there are no planned food or beverage functions. A property's revenues will come strictly from the rental of a large ballroom or meeting room, room accommodations for a few executives, and meals for some of those coming from out of town.

Board meetings average under 20 in attendance, but the top executives and corporate officers who attend these meetings generate a high per-person expenditure for guestrooms and food and beverages. Board meetings are usually conducted at city properties or resorts.

Management development seminars are similar to regular training and development meetings except that the per-person budget is higher. These meetings vary in attendance and length.

Incentive travel meetings generally run from five to eight days in length. Spouses are usually invited. Since incentive meetings are rewards for jobs well done, the destination is an important consideration. Almost all trips are to exotic locations (see Exhibit 3). Incentive meetings are best suited to resorts or properties in popular getaway spots, although for other properties there is the potential for overnight stays at the point of departure and the point of return if the incentive travel program includes cruise ship or overseas travel.

There are many details to attend to before an incentive meeting gets off the ground. Many large corporations that sponsor incentive travel have their own travel managers who make all travel and hotel arrangements for the group. Smaller companies that do not employ a travel specialist often call on outside incentive travel companies, sometimes referred to as "motivational houses," to coordinate their incentive meetings. Incentive travel companies include E. F. MacDonald, S. & H. Travel Awards, Maritz, and Top Value Enterprises. These companies assist corporate meeting planners with all stages of the travel incentive program, including

Exhibit 3   Sample Incentive Ad

Why Is This Man Smiling?

An incentive planner sent him to the Lucayan Beach Resort & Casino on Grand Bahama Island. Now he's got time to relax. Recharge his batteries. Take his mind off business. Hard work does have its rewards.

And the rewards? Golf, tennis, sailing, scuba. Deep sea fishing from our 150 slip marina. Craps, roulette, blackjack, baccarat and slots. 20,000 square feet of gaming action at the only casino on the beach in Grand Bahama. A dazzling cabaret in our Flamingo Showcase Theatre. Four restaurants, four bars, entertainment, and more. Or just soaking up the Bahamian sun on two miles of white sand beach.

Put a smile on someone's face. Contact the Lucayan Beach Resort & Casino U.S. Sales Office at 1610 S.E. 10th Terrace, Fort Lauderdale, Florida 33316. Or call us at: (800) 772-1227.

Lucayan Beach Resort & Casino
GENTING INTERNATIONAL RESORTS AND CASINOS
• Kuala Lumpur, Malaysia • Adelaide, South Australia • Perth, Western Australia • Lucaya, Grand Bahama •

Properties located in exotic locations or popular destination cities have special appeal for the lucrative incentive travel market.

negotiating with hotels; packaging transportation, lodging, and meeting accommodations; and arranging for meals, tours, and entertainment.

Planning Factors for Corporate Meetings. As with associations, you should be aware of several planning factors common to all corporate group meetings.

Timing. Unlike many association conventions or meetings, there is no particular "time cycle" for business meetings. Most meetings are scheduled as needed and may occur at any time throughout the year.

Lead time. Lead time is far more flexible for corporate meetings than for association meetings. While annual conventions or sales meetings are usually planned a year or more in advance, training meetings and seminars may be set three to six months in advance, or with even less lead time if the meeting is called to deal with a crisis. Executive conferences and board meetings also may be called on short notice.

Geographic pattern. Corporate meetings are held where they are most needed —close to corporate headquarters, near the field office, or—in the case of an incentive travel meeting—at an attractive location. Training and development meetings, executive conferences, board meetings, seminars, and so on are not rotated among a few locations, as are some association conventions. This lack of a geographic pattern opens the door for almost any property, no matter what its location or size, to land corporate meetings business.

Geographic restrictions. Geographic restrictions usually affect only incentive travel meetings. As mentioned, an incentive travel meeting must offer a desirable destination—Hawaii is a popular choice, as are resort destinations like San Diego, Las Vegas, Miami, and the Caribbean. Some companies may offer trips to exciting cities such as New York or San Francisco.

Attendance. Although there are some exceptions, attendance at business meetings is usually mandatory. Therefore, corporate meeting planners do not have to work as hard as association meeting planners to attract meeting attendees.

Site selection. Companies select the specific site or property for a business meeting because of its meeting facilities and services. Recreational amenities are a secondary consideration.

A resort is an obvious choice for incentive meetings, but may also be chosen for a training and development meeting by a corporate meeting planner who wants meeting attendees to be free of city distractions. An airport location is ideal when convenience and speed are important. A suburban hotel may be best for attendees arriving by automobile or chosen because of its proximity to the home or field office. Budget or mid-price downtown hotels may be the choice of a meeting planner who wishes to save money; another meeting planner might choose a luxury downtown hotel to house visiting executives in a posh first-class environment.

Transportation is also an important factor in site selection, especially for annual conventions. For this reason, cities that are transportation hubs are often selected for annual conventions. Many companies return to such locations as Chicago and Dallas year after year because of the convenience factor.

If you want your property to be selected for a convention or group business meeting, you must provide adequate meeting space, guestrooms, security, and service—including convention or meeting planning services if necessary. In many cases, exhibit space will be needed, especially for meetings that launch new product lines. In other cases, a combination of exhibit or large meeting space and breakout rooms will be needed. Many companies prefer to have breakout rooms conveniently located near the large hall or ballroom used for the general session or group meeting.

Whom to Contact. No sales effort succeeds unless it is directed at the person or persons with the authority to make the final site decision, and the convention sales picture is no different. Your sales pitch is useless unless it is presented to the right person.

In order to find the right person, a hotel salesperson has to ask the right questions. "Who coordinates your meetings?" is not a good question; the person who coordinates the details of a meeting may not be the decision-maker. It is far better to ask, "Who is responsible for deciding which hotels your company uses for meetings?" With this approach, you will be able to save valuable time and effort by making immediate contact with the decision-maker.

Another approach may require slightly more time and effort but may also prove profitable: start at the top of a company and work downward. Speaking with the president of a company may not result in an immediate booking, but the contact can prove valuable in two ways: you won't be referred to someone below the decision-making level, and a referral "from above" is an excellent door opener.

A salesperson who can say, "Your president, Mr. Sanchez, suggested that I contact you" has an edge on someone making a cold contact call.

Once the key contact is determined, you should also pay attention to tomorrow's decision-makers. As the account is worked, and information is obtained on the organizational structure, "peak performers" should be identified, and relationships with them cultivated. Knowing the people who are likely to succeed decision-makers when they are promoted or retired can pay big dividends in the future.

As with associations, decision-makers for corporate group meetings vary, and can include:

- A full-time meeting planner

- Key executives, such as a president or vice president

- A corporate travel manager

- Division or department heads

- A secretary or associate

Often large corporations employ *full-time meeting planners* to oversee the organization and implementation of company meetings and conventions. This is ideal for a property because full-time meeting planners are experienced, usually know what they want, and know how to go about getting exactly what they need for each type of meeting.

Many companies, however, rely on *key executives* (a president or vice president, the chairperson of the board, etc.) to plan meetings and conventions. These executives will never be listed in meeting planner directories, and they do not think of themselves as meeting planners. But since they call meetings, decide where they will take place, and sometimes plan them, these executives are important to the hotel sales staff. Key executives may or may not have meeting planning experience.

According to The American Express 1991 Survey of Business Travel Management, corporate business travel and entertainment expenses have escalated to $125 billion annually. In an attempt to manage escalating travel costs more effectively, many corporations have appointed or hired *corporate travel managers.* Corporate travel managers may arrange for a number of trips, from management meetings to incentive trips, and are important contacts for booking a large variety of group meetings (see Exhibit 4).

Division or department heads such as training directors, personnel directors, and advertising managers may also make decisions regarding meetings, seminars, or conferences. Like higher-level company executives, these staff members may or may not have much experience at planning meetings, but are important contacts for the property's sales staff.

Other companies may have *secretaries or associates* plan meetings. Again, it is important to remember that they may not be experienced meeting planners. Although meeting planning may be part of their job descriptions, many secretaries or associates do not know what is required for a successful meeting. They tend to worry about small details while sometimes missing the big picture (see Exhibit 5). In these situations a property's meeting planning experience can be a deciding factor. A property that will help the secretary or associate plan a successful meeting is

Exhibit 4   The Importance of Corporate Travel Managers to Booking Group Meetings

Source: *Hotel & Travel Index* Corporate Travel Manager Survey.

more likely to book the meeting than a property that just sells meeting space (see Exhibit 6).

Finding Association and Corporate Group Business

Group meetings business for associations and corporations may be pursued locally (at a very small cost) and nationally. A local effort can start at the property. Account files of previous group meetings business can be checked for opportunities to serve associations or corporations again. At the front desk, agents can search local newspapers for news of associations and corporate groups. In addition, property salespeople can check the yellow pages of the local phone book and the phone book of the state's capital city (many associations have headquarters in state capitals). Salespeople may also obtain leads from the reader boards of competitors or through word-of-mouth referrals.

Other opportunities can be found at the property level. Suppliers of products or services such as the local dairy operator or insurance agent are potential sources of group meetings business. Even if your property's suppliers do not require meeting space for themselves, many belong to trade, professional, civic, social, or religious organizations. Your suppliers could recommend the property as a meeting site for these organizations.

Exhibit 5   Solving Problems for Meeting Planners

Many meeting planners worry about small details. This ad featuring Holiday Inns' "No Excuses" Meeting Guarantee assures meeting planners that their meeting or convention will proceed as planned and that Holiday Inn can handle any problems that arise.

The property's employees may also be good sources of meetings business. Many employees belong to organizations that meet regularly or need meeting space for special occasions. Property employees could influence an organization to choose "their" property.

Local and state chambers of commerce, convention and visitors' bureaus, and industrial commissions can provide leads for local group meetings business. For

Exhibit 6   Assured Meeting Agreement

Assured Meeting Agreement

TO: _____ REPRESENTATIVE OF: _____

For Meeting To Take Place At _____ On: _____
(Hotel)   (Date)

This is to certify that the management and staff of the above named Radisson Hotel are dedicated to providing the finest in facilities and services to assure the quality and success of your meeting. We attest that the Radisson Assured Meeting^{SM} Program, including our unique 54-point checklist, is a comprehensive program designed to meet your most demanding requirements for a quality meeting. Further, it is pledged that if any items specified below should not be fulfilled properly, you will be promptly compensated or credited as indicated.

• Meeting rooms will be ready on time	OR your master account will be credited $50	• Guaranteed banquet menu prices six months in advance	The price increase will be absorbed by the hotel and not passed onto you
• Refreshment break will be served promptly	OR the refreshment break will be complimentary	• Room rates will be guaranteed one year in advance	You will pay no more than the quoted rate in the signed contract even if rates do increase
• Meal functions will be served as scheduled	OR your master account will be credited 5% of the meal cost	• No preassigned meeting room outlined on signed event orders will be changed without your approval	OR the hotel will credit your master account $50
• Meeting rooms will be refreshed during refreshment and luncheon breaks. (Does not include exhibit halls).	OR your master account will be credited $50	• The hotel will honor all guaranteed payment reservations	OR we will place the room at the closest, comparable, available hotel and pay for transportation to those accommodations and back to the hotel the next morning. We will pay for your first night's lodging at the alternative hotel and pay for the first 3 minutes of a phone call home.
• Meeting and banquet rooms will be set up according to your written specifications	OR your master account will be credited $100		
• The convention service manager or management representative will respond to any problems you may have within 15 minutes of notification	OR you will be provided with a complimentary room night		

Thus stipulated and warranted this _____ day of _____ , 19 _____

_____
For Radisson Hotels

_____
General Manager

Acknowledged and Affirmed by:

_____ Front Office Manager _____ Sales Director

_____ Banquet Manager _____ Food and Beverage Director

The Radisson Hotels

This certificate is part of Radisson Hotel Corporation's program to put meeting planners at ease. It demonstrates the corporation's awareness of the concerns and needs of meeting planners and is an excellent way to build client confidence—and repeat business. (Courtesy of Radisson Hotel Corporation)

national and international associations and corporations, the sales staff can consult trade periodicals and directories for leads and the names of key decision-makers.

Another good way to develop leads is to visit and exhibit at trade shows, make contacts at annual conventions, and join professional associations—especially those that are users of hospitality industry products. If the property is part of a chain, the regional or corporate office may be able to provide leads.

Reaching Association and Corporate Meeting Planners

Many properties try to reach association and corporate meeting planners haphazardly. They buy a mailing list of meeting planners and send direct mail pieces to

Since many meetings are organized by novice meeting planners, hospitality firms often attract group meetings business by promoting their expertise and willingness to help stage a successful meeting. These print ads, developed by the San Francisco Hilton, were part of an advertising campaign to promote the property's experience and commitment to making meeting planning easier.

everyone on the list, for example. While this technique may produce some results, it is far better to do thorough research and aim selling efforts at a small group of 30 to 40 "hot prospects."

This is not to say that you cannot make use of a mailing list or place ads in trade periodicals, but most properties find it more effective to know something about the person they are trying to sell to. If you opt to use a mailing list, you should send out questionnaires to research the needs of those listed before sending an expensive, full-color convention brochure to meeting planners whose requirements you may not meet (see Exhibit 7).

Hotels can also do research locally. The property's staff can gather marketing information by speaking to guests about their businesses or professions. It is estimated that one out of every ten guests has the potential to generate group business. It is far less costly for a hotel to pursue leads right under its roof than to spend considerable time and money on mailing lists, out-of-town trips, advertisements, and sales blitzes.

The most effective way to sell to association or corporate meeting planners is face-to-face. As we have noted, some meeting planners are not trained professionals.

Exhibit 7   Sample Questionnaire

ALADDIN
HOTEL

CONVENTION QUESTIONNAIRE

Name _____   Title _____

Firm or Association Name _____

Street Address _____   City _____

State _____   Zip _____   Phone _____

Meeting sites are selected by:

☐ Me   ☐ Board of Directors

☐ Committee   ☐ General Membership

☐ Other (Please specify): _____

Has your organization ever met in Las Vegas?   ☐ Yes   ☐ No

How do you classify your Las Vegas meeting?

☐ National/Annual Convention   ☐ Regional Convention

☐ Sales Meeting   ☐ State Convention   ☐ Board Meeting

☐ Incentive Trip   ☐ Pre- or Post-Convention

Estimated Attendance: _____   Rooms Required: _____

May we send you a written proposal for your consideration?   ☐ Yes   ☐ No

Are you planning a Las Vegas visit this year?   ☐ Yes   ☐ No

If so, what month? _____

Questionnaires like this one are often included with direct mail pieces. The information provided by respondents helps qualify them and lays the groundwork for personal sales calls. (Courtesy of Aladdin Hotel, Las Vegas, Nevada)

A face-to-face presentation provides the opportunity for you to answer any questions the meeting planner might have and reassure the meeting planner that your property is experienced at staging successful meetings.

Face-to-face selling can be accomplished in three ways: personal sales calls, sales blitzes, and attendance at trade shows. The first method, personal sales calls, focuses on selling to individuals, while a sales blitz and attendance at trade shows involve prospecting and selling to a larger number of people over a short period of time.

Personal Sales Calls

Personal sales calls are the best way to sell to meeting planners. You can schedule an appointment call to meet the meeting planner and learn his or her needs. After determining the meeting planner's needs, you can develop a presentation tailored to meet those needs and set up a presentation sales call.

Sales Blitzes

A sales blitz is essentially an intensive survey of a given geographic area over a specified time period. This time period is usually very short—one to three days is typical. Although the purpose of a sales blitz is largely to gather information, immediate business may be generated.

Planning is the key to a successful sales blitz. Most properties begin planning at least 30 days before the effort. If the blitz concept is new to you, you might plan a one-day blitz as a learning experience before undertaking a more extensive one.

A city directory is essential for planning a sales blitz, since sales routes should be carefully planned for the most effective use of time. Once sales routes have been mapped out, you can write on index cards the names and addresses of individuals or companies to contact and give the cards and a street map to blitz participants. In most cases, each person is assigned around 30 calls per day and makes approximately 90 to 100 calls over a three-day period.

It is essential that participants have an adequate supply of survey sheets (see Exhibit 8) and such collateral materials as convention brochures and key chains or other low-cost specialty items. All specialty items should be imprinted with the property's name and telephone number.

Property salespeople, other members of the property's staff, or outsiders can take part in a sales blitz. A recently rediscovered and increasingly popular approach is to use hotel or marketing students to blitz an area. Nervous students can often get through doors that are closed to experienced salespeople. You should give students a training session and incentives for making calls. Incentives can range from reimbursement for out-of-pocket expenses (gas, parking, meals, etc.) to prizes or cash awards. Hiring students to blitz an area frees the property's sales staff to pursue other business or follow up on leads generated during the blitz.

Trade Shows

Just as a sales blitz may be an effective prospecting and selling tool for properties large and small, attendance at trade shows can help build a client base for all types of properties.

There are generally two types of trade shows. An exhibit show features booths that enable exhibitors to distribute materials and talk to buyers. A marketplace show offers a structured environment of scheduled appointments between buyers and sellers. Some of these shows are sponsored or attended by local convention and visitors' bureaus, and it may be possible for you to share booth space and expenses with your local bureau.

Trade show selling should begin long before the show actually starts. You should set goals such as a specific sales volume or number of pre-arranged appointments. You should target specific prospects, and at least a week to ten days before the show you should send a direct mailing to them. Address this mailing to a key contact, and include a personal invitation to visit the property's booth, a preview of what the booth will be offering, and a response mechanism. Many trade

Tailored Sales Presentations

When selling a hospitality product, you should gear your presentation toward meeting the needs of the meeting planner. It is especially important to sell value rather than price. While price is often a prime consideration for meeting planners, the meeting planner who says, "Your price is too high" may actually be saying, "Your value is too low." You can overcome this objection by showing how your property offers value and service to the meeting planner, as shown in the following dialogue:

Jean: Good morning, Mr. Webb. My name is Novello, Jean Novello. I'm the sales manager of the Regency Hotel, just two miles down the road from here.

Webb: Yes, I pass it on the way to work. Please have a seat. What can I do for you?

Jean: Well, Mr. Webb, I understand you hold a lot of meetings in your board room here.

Webb: Yes, we do.

Jean: And many of them last all day?

Webb: Yes, that's correct.

Jean: Could you tell me about your problems in holding these meetings?

Webb: Problems? What do you mean?

Jean: Well, as an example, are there interruptions—when someone gets a telephone call, or there's a problem in the factory?

Webb: (Thoughtfully:) Yes, we do. In fact, there's always at least one person who seems to get telephone calls throughout the meeting.

Jean: I suppose this affects the whole flow and productivity of the meeting.

Webb: (Emphatically:) It certainly does. Pretty costly interruptions—even if it's just ten minutes. The salaries I pay!

Jean: Can I ask you, Mr. Webb, whether your meetings are creative, in the sense that they're about looking for ways to reduce costs or increase sales?

Webb: That's the idea—yes.

Jean: Well, Mr. Webb, this is what I'd like to do for you. Try one of your next meetings in our redecorated meeting rooms and I'll do two things. First, I'll see that the meeting is not interrupted unless it's really urgent. That should increase the meeting's productivity. Second, I believe that by moving some of your meetings to a new environment in the Regency Hotel, your employees will produce more ideas for making or saving money. A different environment will help your employees focus their attention on the meeting at hand, not on what's happening at the factory.

Webb: Well, it's worth trying. But how are we all going to get there?

Jean: I've already thought about that problem. Most of these meetings will be booked in advance, and I'd be happy to have our hotel mini-bus pick you all up first thing in the morning at your factory.

Webb: That sounds fine, but how much is this going to cost?

Jean: (During the last few minutes, Jean has moved to a trial close. She brings out her diary and opens it.) Before talking about your investment in holding some of your meetings at the Regency, could I suggest you make a provisional booking for your next meeting? You can stop in within the next few days to show me exactly how you want the room set up. I'll have it set up that way, and show you our special executive conference package. What is the date of your next meeting, Mr. Webb?

Webb: (Looks at his diary.) Tuesday, October 19th.

Jean: (Looks at her diary and frowns.) I'm sorry, Mr. Webb, but all three meeting rooms are already booked on that day and I gather your dates are fixed. When is your next meeting?

Webb: Yes, they are fixed. The next one is Tuesday, October 26th.

Jean: (Looks at her diary again.) That's fine—I'll book it provisionally for you. (Scribbles a note in her diary.) I've taken up a lot of your time. All we have to do now is fix a time for you to see the room and discuss how you want it set up.

Webb: Well, I'm pretty busy today. What about on my way home tomorrow at, say, six o'clock?

Jean: Fine, ask for me at the reception desk—Jean Novello. Here's my card. I'll leave another one with your secretary on my way out.

Webb: Okay, Jean.

(They shake hands.)

Jean: Thank you for your time, Mr. Webb. See you tomorrow.

Webb: Thank you. Six o'clock then. Good-bye.

Source: Adapted from Melvyn Greene, *Marketing Hotels Into the 90's* (New York: Van Nostrand Reinhold, 1987), pp. 263-264.

show attendees prefer to plan their itinerary beforehand to visit "must see" booths, and allowing them to make a pre-show appointment may result in sales. Qualified prospects may also be attracted by pre-show publicity and advertising.

At trade shows, a property's booth and personnel must accurately reflect the property's image and professionalism. The people who staff the booth should always be courteous, friendly, and informative, and the display should be arranged to involve prospects. Many exhibitors make the mistake of setting tables across the front of their booths; it is usually more effective to place tables at the sides and back of the booth to draw people into the display. In addition, many exhibitors give too

Exhibit 8   Sample Sales Blitz Survey Sheet

Sales Blitz Survey Sheet

Organization _____

Address _____

_____ **Zip** _____ **Phone #** _____

Contact _____ **Title** _____

Contact _____ **Title** _____

1. How many meetings do you have a year? _____ When? _____
    Size? _____ Who plans them?

Contact _____ **Title** _____

When is your next meeting? _____

Where are meetings usually held? _____

2. Do you have incoming visitors that require sleeping accommodations?
    Yes _____ No _____ How many per month? _____

    If yes, where are they housed? _____

    Do you reserve the room? Yes _____ No _____ (If not, who does?)

Contact _____ **Title** _____

3. Does your organization plan such things as:
                     —Christmas Parties   —Retirement Dinners?
                     —Award Dinners?   —Other Social Events?

    Are you the organizer, or is there a social chairman?
    Yes _____ **No** _____ **Contact** _____

4. Are you, or any of your associates, affiliated with any other organizations or associations that might have need for meeting or banquet space? Yes _____ No _____

Name _____ **Contact** _____

Comments:

Taken by: _____ Date Taken _____

Survey sheets are used to obtain information that will be used for personal sales calls if the prospect warrants a follow-up. An experienced sales blitz participant can complete approximately 30 of these forms a day, generating information that may produce future business for the property. (Source: Howard Feiertag, "Blitzes and Sales Calls: Indispensable Selling Tools," *HSMAI Marketing Review,* Winter 1987, p. 24)

many items away. Since most buyers want to travel light, it may be better to show a video brochure or other audiovisual presentation and give prospects just a business card or small brochure.

A property's trade show representatives should make the best use of the time and money spent on the property's exhibit. In other words, you should greet all prospects who walk into the property's booth, but quickly *qualify* them. Qualifying prospects ensures that you won't spend too much time on browsers.

You can begin the qualifying process by asking questions: "What types of meetings do you hold throughout the year?" or "Has your company ever booked a meeting at our hotel?" These inquiries can lead to other questions that will help you determine the prospect's needs and influence over a meeting site decision. Additional questions may include: "How many people usually attend your meetings?" "What types of facilities do you need for your meetings?" "How do you decide where to hold meetings?" and "Who determines the location of your meetings?"

If the prospect's needs are compatible with the products and services your property offers, and the prospect has some influence over the decision-making process, you should pursue the conversation further or invite the prospect to fill out a questionnaire. If the prospect is just looking, however, you may want to terminate the conversation as politely as possible and move on to another prospect.

Your sales efforts should not end when the trade show closes. For maximum effectiveness, leads must be followed up quickly or business may be lost to competitors. To prevent lost business, deadlines for follow-up should be established before the trade show. Personnel should be designated to handle follow-up, ensuring immediate response to inquiries.

Trade show booths and presentations should be directed to meeting planners rather than consumers. Meeting planners, like travel agents, need information. Guestroom sizes, types of accommodations, group rates, and convention services are the types of information important to association and corporate meeting planners.

Print Advertising

In addition to personal selling, properties also use print advertising to reach meeting planners (see Exhibit 9). You can place ads in trade journals or magazines, or in the business or social sections of newspapers in key association and corporation feeder cities. In some instances, you may be able to participate in advertising planned by your local convention and visitors' bureau. An entire destination area is usually featured in this type of advertising. You may increase your property's exposure by placing your own ads near the bureau's.

Other Sales Tools

The information theme should be carried through in direct mail and collateral materials (see Exhibit 10). Meeting planners are not looking for romantic photographs; convention brochures and other direct mail pieces should feature room layouts and capacities, special services, and reservations information. In an attempt to provide necessary information, many properties and chains publish full service meeting guides (see Exhibit 11).

Since personal experience is a major factor in site selection, familiarization tours and public relations activities can also be effective sales tools.

Many meeting planners will not book a meeting before seeing the site. You can maximize site visits in a number of ways. First, schedule tours when the property is busy; full hotels, restaurants, and banquet rooms legitimize claims of quality.

Exhibit 9   Sample Print Ad for Meeting Planners

WHY PAY AN ARM AND A LEG IN FLORIDA?

TEXAS WINS HANDS DOWN.

Thinking about another meeting in the Sunshine State?

Maybe that's not such a bright idea. In fact, in light of the recession we're in, you need to watch your bottom line closer than ever. Otherwise, you could lose your shirt over Florida's glaring meeting costs.

But just because the economy's down doesn't mean you have to be. You can be a star and convene in the Lone Star State. At Del Lago, the biggest, most complete resort in the Southwest.

Just check out this chart. For what you'd shell out in Florida, we give you all these extras with a little change left over. Even Texas taxes are lower. And if you take the time to add it all up...well, it all adds up.

We're equidistant to the coasts. Convenient.

Less than an hour from Houston Intercontinental Airport. More convenience.

And with championship golf, tennis, full-service marina and fresh water beach, we're a whole lot of fun, too. So think about it and give us a call. Or better yet, come see for yourself.

We'll make you look good.

WHAT YOU PAY & WHAT YOU GET:

	Florida	Texas
a room	$165*	$159**
lake-view suite		
breakfast		
lunch		
dinner		
coffee breaks		
golf		
tennis		
health club		
AV package		
meeting room		
tax	8–12% tax	6% tax

*Based on high season group rates at comparable Florida resorts.
**Per Suite, slight occupancy. High season.

DEL LAGO
RESORT & CONFERENCE CENTER

Just North of Houston on Lake Conroe.
For information and availability, please call
800-833-3078
600 Del Lago Blvd., Montgomery, Texas 77356

Operated by Hospitality Management Corporation, Dallas, Texas

This two-page print ad, promoting the Del Lago Resort & Conference Center near Houston, Texas, was directed to meeting planners. It promotes the property's facilities and the cost-effectiveness of booking a meeting at the resort rather than at better-known Florida destinations. This national campaign, printed in trade magazines, increased inquiries from meeting planners by 200%.

Exhibit 10   Sample Direct Mail Pieces

To reach meeting planners, the International Association of Conference Centers uses a newsletter promoting the centers within its network. The Sheraton Colony Square Hotel in Atlanta, Georgia, opened a line of communication to meeting planners by sending a direct mail letter explaining a special property promotion and a colorful brochure outlining meeting facilities and services.

There should also be ample time for personal attention to the planner; he or she should be able to meet the staff who will be assisting with the meeting, sample menus, and experience the property on a "guest" level.

The tour itself should include only those items of interest to the planner. State-of-the-art audiovisual equipment may be impressive, but can be a waste of time to a planner who is arranging a largely social function. Meeting and banquet rooms are most effectively sold when they are shown in use (this helps the planner to visualize his or her own function) or, if this is not possible, shown in four-color photos accompanied by third-party endorsements. Rooms should be shown from the "bottom up"—standard, then luxurious, then suites. Sell the benefits of facilities and amenities as well as their features: "The ballroom is adjacent to the break-out rooms" (feature), "so that attendees can move quickly from the general session to the workshops, saving time and keeping the meeting on schedule" (benefit).

Public relations activities may include meeting planning seminars and social functions staged for various types of associations. "Ethnic days" or food festivals may draw local association members and meeting planners.

Conclusion

Although meeting planners can bring much-needed group meetings business to a property, dealing with them can sometimes be challenging. There are many

Exhibit 11 Sample Meeting Guide

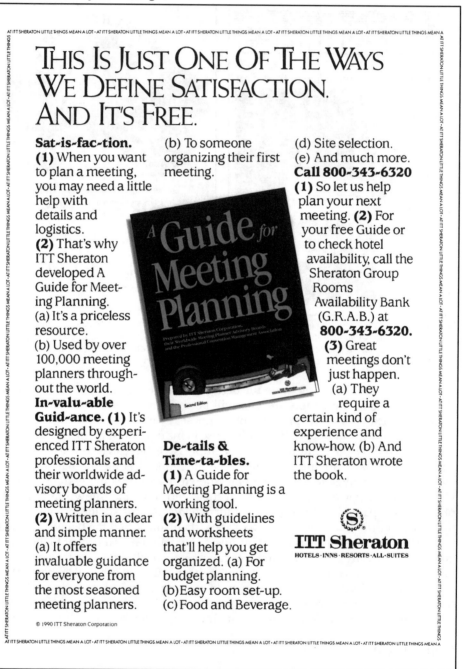

THIS IS JUST ONE OF THE WAYS WE DEFINE SATISFACTION. AND IT'S FREE.

Sat-is-fac-tion.
(1) When you want to plan a meeting, you may need a little help with details and logistics.
(2) That's why ITT Sheraton developed A Guide for Meeting Planning.
(a) It's a priceless resource.
(b) Used by over 100,000 meeting planners throughout the world.
In-valu-able Guid-ance. (1) It's designed by experienced ITT Sheraton professionals and their worldwide advisory boards of meeting planners.
(2) Written in a clear and simple manner.
(a) It offers invaluable guidance for everyone from the most seasoned meeting planners.

(b) To someone organizing their first meeting.

De-tails & Time-ta-bles.
(1) A Guide for Meeting Planning is a working tool.
(2) With guidelines and worksheets that'll help you get organized. (a) For budget planning.
(b) Easy room set-up.
(c) Food and Beverage.

(d) Site selection.
(e) And much more.
Call 800-343-6320
(1) So let us help plan your next meeting. **(2)** For your free Guide or to check hotel availability, call the Sheraton Group Rooms Availability Bank (G.R.A.B.) at **800-343-6320.**
(3) Great meetings don't just happen.
(a) They require a certain kind of experience and know-how. (b) And ITT Sheraton wrote the book.

ITT Sheraton
HOTELS·INNS·RESORTS·ALL·SUITES

© 1990 ITT Sheraton Corporation

Sheraton developed a booklet for meeting planners, "A Guide for Meeting Planning," which it promoted in trade magazine ads such as this one.

professional meeting planners who are relatively easy to work with because they know the requirements of a business group and what it takes to put on a successful meeting. Other meeting planners are inexperienced, and some individuals—ranging from key executives to secretaries or associates—are called on to plan a meeting with no experience at all.

Almost all meeting planners, experienced or not, tend to be anxious about the meeting or convention they are responsible for. With their professional reputations at stake, it is understandable that most meeting planners are very concerned about a property's ability to stage a meeting and respond successfully to problems that may come up (many veteran meeting planners would change this to "problems that *will* come up"). That is why properties that sell their meeting planning experience and expertise, rather than just their meeting space, will be the most successful at selling to meeting planners.

Endnotes

1. Milton T. Astroff and James R. Abbey, *Convention Sales and Services,* 3d Edition (Cranbury, New Jersey: Waterbury Press, 1991).
2. "The Meetings Market Report 1992," *Meetings and Conventions,* 1 March 1992.
3. Associations and facts cited in this paragraph were found in Karin E. Koek and Susan Boyles Martin, editors, *Encyclopedia of Associations,* 22nd ed., vol. 1 (Detroit, Mich.: Gale Research Company, 1988).
4. "The Meetings Market Report 1992."
5. "The Meetings Market Report 1992."
6. "The Meetings Market Report 1992."
7. This statement and many of the facts cited in this section are from "The Meetings Market Report 1992."

Key Terms

incentive travel
meeting planner
SMERF

Review Questions

1. In what ways can the group meetings market benefit a property?
2. The group meetings market can be divided into which two segments?
3. Associations can be divided into what seven general categories?
4. What types of meetings business do associations generate?
5. What are some planning factors common to all association group meetings?
6. What is the average lead time for an association's annual convention?
7. Who are possible decision-makers for an association?

8. What are ten types of meetings corporations hold?

9. Who are possible decision-makers for corporate group meetings?

10. What are some ways hotels can pursue local group meetings business?

11. Who can participate in a sales blitz?

Chapter Outline

International Travelers
    The Decision-Maker
    Meeting the Needs of International Travelers
    Finding International Travelers
    Reaching International Travelers
Honeymooners
    The Decision-Maker
    Meeting the Needs of Honeymooners
    Finding Honeymooners
    Reaching Honeymooners
Sports Teams
    Football Teams
    Baseball Teams
    Basketball Teams
    Other Teams
Government Travelers
Disabled Travelers
Other Special Segments
Conclusion

Marketing to Special Segments

Business and leisure travel (by both individuals and groups) are still the backbone of the hospitality industry, but more and more properties are finding that they must solicit additional or special market segments to ensure consistent occupancy. Going beyond the major market segments and soliciting the "mini" or special segments is necessary for most properties to maintain a consistently high level of occupancy. Reunion groups, juries, out-of-town wedding or funeral guests, truckers, sports teams, and movie crews are just a few examples of the small or special market segments that many properties are now targeting.

Your property's ability to appeal to these segments will vary depending on its products, services, and location. In this chapter, we will take a look at some special market segments that can prove financially lucrative if you are willing to spend the time and money to research them and modify your property's products and services to meet their needs.

International Travelers

One of the fastest growing and most profitable special segments is the international traveler market (see Exhibit 1). International travelers are travelers originating from points outside the United States, and are usually divided into three categories: North American travelers, European travelers, and other international travelers (Asian, Australian, African, and so on). According to the United States Travel and Tourism Administration (USTTA), travel and tourism is now the United States' number one services export earner, ranking ahead of agricultural goods, chemicals, and motor vehicles. Also, for the first time in history the United States is expected to register a travel surplus in the 1990s. Foreign visitors to America will spend more money traveling in the United States than Americans will spend traveling abroad.[1]

It is difficult to give a general profile of the international traveler. Visitors from different countries are interested in different attractions and have varying needs. But it is possible to define several patterns in this market:

1. *Point of origin.* Approximately 60% of international travelers visiting the United States come from Canada or Mexico, but this influx of North American travelers is on the decline, and the market may soon be dominated by Asian and European travelers. The most significant increases will be from the United Kingdom and Japan.

Exhibit 1   The International Traveler Market at a Glance

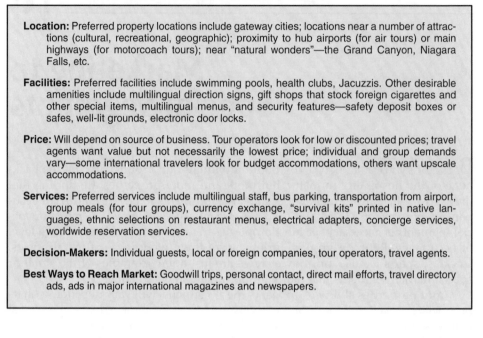

Location: Preferred property locations include gateway cities; locations near a number of attractions (cultural, recreational, geographic); proximity to hub airports (for air tours) or main highways (for motorcoach tours); near "natural wonders"—the Grand Canyon, Niagara Falls, etc.

Facilities: Preferred facilities include swimming pools, health clubs, Jacuzzis. Other desirable amenities include multilingual direction signs, gift shops that stock foreign cigarettes and other special items, multilingual menus, and security features—safety deposit boxes or safes, well-lit grounds, electronic door locks.

Price: Will depend on source of business. Tour operators look for low or discounted prices; travel agents want value but not necessarily the lowest price; individual and group demands vary—some international travelers look for budget accommodations, others want upscale accommodations.

Services: Preferred services include multilingual staff, bus parking, transportation from airport, group meals (for tour groups), currency exchange, "survival kits" printed in native languages, ethnic selections on restaurant menus, electrical adapters, concierge services, worldwide reservation services.

Decision-Makers: Individual guests, local or foreign companies, tour operators, travel agents.

Best Ways to Reach Market: Goodwill trips, personal contact, direct mail efforts, travel directory ads, ads in major international magazines and newspapers.

2. *Reasons for travel to the United States.* In recent years, the United States has been the most popular destination for British, French, and German travelers who planned to leave Europe for vacation.[2] These travelers cited the quality of nightlife, shopping, and accommodations as reasons for visiting the United States. The devalued dollar also played a part in bringing European and Asian travelers (mostly Japanese) to the United States, although the United States is considered a travel bargain regardless of the dollar's strength. Most international travelers cite the lower costs of U.S. goods and services as an important factor in choosing to travel in this country.

3. *Destinations.* European and Asian travelers have distinct preferences in destinations. The Japanese, for example, often prefer large cities and like to stay in one spot rather than visit a number of cities. The French also tend to stay put, but favor cities that offer cultural events (theater, opera, etc.) and nightlife; California, Florida, New York City, and New Orleans are favorite destination spots for French travelers. Most other Europeans prefer smaller cities or vacation destinations featuring a number of attractions. The British favor destinations like the Grand Canyon and the Rocky Mountains. German visitors often tour a great deal or take beach vacations; Hawaii, Florida, and New York are among the destinations most often selected by these Europeans.

4. *Length of stay.* The length of stay will depend on the type of international traveler. Stays for individual leisure travelers usually range from three days to two weeks. Individual business travelers often travel on expense accounts,

generating high expenditures per person. They usually stay from one to seven days, and often take vacation time at the conclusion of the business portion of the trip.

Group leisure travelers may account for short trips or long stays. First-time international visitors often travel in groups and usually prefer a two- to three-day stay. Seasoned international group travelers typically stay longer—sometimes two weeks or more.

Group business travelers generally stay from five to seven days and may bring spouses along if the purpose of the trip is to attend a trade show or convention. Group business travelers may also include delegations touring factories or farms, groups traveling to international seminars, and groups stopping over en route home.[3]

The Decision-Maker

Since the international traveler market is so diverse, a property must appeal to a number of different decision-makers, including individual guests, local or foreign companies, tour operators, and travel agents.

Individual guests usually make travel decisions based on the purpose of the trip. If the trip is for business, the destination is predetermined, and only a property must be chosen. International business travelers tend to choose the familiar. They are likely to choose a chain property that operates in their home country over an independent resort or hotel. Individual leisure travelers, on the other hand, are more likely to choose a property close to interesting attractions. Price is often less important to individual leisure travelers. These travelers are willing to pay higher rates for special amenities or services or for a location close to attractions.

An important trend within the individual travel segment is *foreign independent travel* (FIT). FIT travelers want the convenience and price of an arranged tour (without traveling in groups), usually buy packages at home, and travel unescorted to prearranged destinations. Most FIT travelers have visited the United States in a group, and return on their own. They usually travel individually or in twos, may be either business or leisure travelers, and are looking for a travel "experience"—shopping, sight-seeing, and so on—in addition to low hotel rates.

Properties in key destination cities are the mostly likely to attract FIT travelers. Since most FIT visitors use the services of travel professionals, a property wishing to boost occupancy with this segment must solicit associations with tour operators and wholesalers, airlines that plan their own ground packages, and retail travel agents who specialize in the international market.

Local or foreign companies are often the decision-makers for individual or group business travelers. Local companies frequently make their decisions on the basis of credit arrangements; they will house foreign visitors in properties at which they have charge accounts. Foreign companies prefer to do business with familiar properties. They book into chain properties that operate in their home country, or seek a recommendation from the American company with whom they are doing business.

Tour operators usually make the lodging decisions for group leisure travelers. Tour operators look for a convenient location and good service. Locations easily accessible from main highways (for motorcoach tours) or airports (for air/ground

Exhibit 2   Japanese Traveler Profile

- Over 3.1 million Japanese are expected to visit the United States annually.

- Typical Japanese travelers have a family income of over $50,000 per year. Thirty percent are first-time visitors to the United States; 87% book air transportation and lodging through travel agents; 87% use travel agents as information sources.

- Their visits are characterized by a short stay, with 79% returning to Japan within 10 days.

- They are probably the highest spenders per day of all international visitors.

- The average adult visitor is around 31 years of age; 56% are between the ages of 18 and 44, with the largest percentage (35%) in the 25 to 34 age bracket.

- Japanese travelers are very security conscious and many cite their fear of crime and violence as a deterrent to selecting the United States as a travel destination.

- Fear of AIDS is fast becoming a major deterrent to the Japanese in selecting the United States as a country to visit, especially among parents of student travelers.

- The largest number of Japanese visitors arrive in August (some 11% of the annual total), followed by July, December, and September, with April recording the lowest number.

- The highest percentage (62.7%) visit only one state, followed by 21.4% visiting more than three states and 15.9% two states.

- Japanese travelers are discovering more destinations beyond the Rockies.

- The majority of Japanese outbound travel originates from the metropolitan Tokyo/Kanto areas (46%), with the Osaka/Kansai region producing some 17% and the Nagyo/Chubu district 11%.

Source: The material in this exhibit has been adapted from Marjorie L. Dewey, "How to Develop the Japanese Market for Your Hotel," *HSMAI Marketing Review,* Fall 1990; and Laurence Price, "Selling and Serving the Japanese Traveler," *Lodging,* July/August 1987, p. 53.

packages) and areas that offer a number of attractions within a day's driving distance are favorite choices. Tour operators also want good service, and usually will return to a property that serves group meals promptly, blocks off rooms for the group, and offers discounts or all-inclusive rates.

Travel agents are influential in making lodging decisions for individual and group business and leisure travelers. Travel agents also look for a good location, but price plays a lesser part in selection. Since most travel agents work on a commission basis, they won't necessarily seek out the absolute lowest price, but their clients must feel they are getting value for their money. Travel agents insist on good service, and can serve as excellent sources of repeat business if previous clients have been treated well.

Tour operators and travel agents look for U.S. properties with amenities such as swimming pools and saunas (features not common in European hotels). Security may also play a part in their decision to book with a property. Operators and agents who cater to the Japanese market, especially, look for security. The Japanese are very concerned about their personal safety, and look for hotels that offer safety deposit boxes or safes, well-lit grounds, and other security measures (see Exhibit 2).

Meeting the Needs of International Travelers

The needs of international travelers vary widely, but there are several areas of common concern:

- *Making reservations.* Whether reservations are made by an individual traveler or by a tour operator or travel agent, easy booking is important. You can meet this need in a variety of ways: establish field offices in key feeder cities (Tokyo, London, Paris, Mexico City, etc.) that offer worldwide reservations services, use Telex machines and toll-free numbers, and create tie-ins with foreign air services.

  The importance of handling international bookings has led Radisson Hotels International to establish a toll-free reservations system in over a dozen foreign countries. All calls from the countries served ring directly into Radisson's reservation center in Omaha, Nebraska, but calls are answered by reservationists who speak the native language of the caller (a call on the German line, for example, will be answered in German). This system should make it easier for international guests to book reservations, and will be expanded into other markets as the need arises.

- *Language barriers.* Many international travelers have difficulty communicating in English. While some international guests speak English quite well (Japanese businesspeople, for example, are usually fluent in English), others have trouble with our language, especially with slang. Hotels that cater to international guests can ease this problem by hiring a multilingual staff and providing multilingual menus and in-house signs. Other useful and appreciated solutions are "survival guides" with text in several languages. These booklets or brochures can serve as a directory of hotel services; give instructions on the operation of the phone system, television set, and air-conditioning unit; and give additional information that may make the visitor feel welcome.

  Today's technology is also being used to eliminate language barriers. Two major translation networks are now available to hotels catering to international guests—the AT&T Language Line Services and the Japanese Assistance Network (JAN). AT&T's Language Line Services links guests to interpreters fluent in more than 140 languages and dialects, while the JAN provides Japanese translation for business and leisure travelers. Both services are available 24 hours a day, and can be directly accessed from the concierge desk or from guestrooms.

- *Transportation to the hotel.* First-time international guests traveling by air often have difficulty getting from the airport to the hotel. Many properties offer complimentary limousine service or arrange to have taxis pick up international guests.

- *Methods of payment.* Many international visitors are unfamiliar with the American policy of prepayment for rooms. If possible, you should explain payment policies before the trip.

  You should willingly accept foreign traveler's checks or currency. Properties that accept foreign currency or provide currency exchange services, either

Insider Insights

Paddy Fitzpatrick
Owner and Managing Director
Fitzpatrick Hotel Group
Dublin, Ireland

Paddy Fitzpatrick began his hotel career at the age of 18, when he took a practical hotel management course at the Gresham Hotel (where he subsequently became assistant manager). He later served as general manager of the Old Ground Hotel in Ennis, Ireland, and the managing director of the Talbot Hotel in Wexford. Before opening his own hotel in 1971, Fitzpatrick also worked as general manager of the Doyle Group of Hotels. He is currently owner and managing director of Fitzpatrick Castle Hotel, Fitzpatrick Shannon Shamrock, Timesharing Ireland Limited, and Castle Transport & Marketing Services—the general sales agent for TWA in Ireland. His time-share complex was recently given the prestigious "Resort of International Distinction Award." Fitzpatrick has a worldwide reputation as Ireland's number one hotel ambassador.

It is only when you study the trends of American marketing and sales that you realize the significant difference between the American and European approach. European hotels must look for business from the rest of the Continent and the world. Dealing with different languages and customs is a significant part of planning.

It's my impression that until recently the average American marketing and sales manager showed interest only in travelers originating from neighboring states. But with the development of air transport, and with the increasing number of international travelers coming to American shores, it's extremely necessary for American hotel salespeople to focus more attention on the international market.

What do international travelers look for in European hotels? The American visitor loves the mystique of history, and is fascinated by castles and the tracing of his or her ancestry. The English and Germans want outdoor sports and scenery; the French want luxury as well as scenery, fishing, and gourmet food. The Japanese come with their cameras, but thousands of them are also interested in playing golf and gambling.

Serving the international market requires a knowledge of the needs and expectations of many different types of visitors. The ability to attract this lucrative market is limited only by the salesperson's interest and imagination.

in-house or through an agreement with a local bank, can realize a 6% to 10% profit as well as offer a much-needed service to their guests. Hotels can either employ an exchange specialist who daily determines the value of foreign currency or arrange for this service through local banks. Foreign currency usually is sent to a bank each day and a check is returned to the property the following day.

Insider Insights

Jim McAllister
Assistant Director of Sales
Sage Hotel Corporation
Boston, Massachusetts _____

To reach and service the international market, sales and operations personnel alike must be of the same mind-set. As the Japanese and most Europeans have done already, we must learn a world view. Only with the proper attitude will we be able to effectively attract and host the growing numbers of international visitors. This means learning new cultures, attempting new languages, and trying to understand the way these guests think.

The international market, most notably the Japanese segment, is still an underdeveloped market. A recently released report by the United States Travel and Tourism Administration says Japan, West Germany, the United Kingdom, and France are generating upwards of 14 million international travelers, and the numbers will only increase as we move through the 1990s.

Knowing what attracts—and repulses—this huge market, and determining similarities and differences among the various segments, will largely determine what percentage of the international market hoteliers can attract. To be effective hosts, we need to know and care about our guests. Abroad, we sometimes have the reputation of being ugly Americans; it's time to dispel this image at home.

- *Special appliances.* International travelers who bring such small appliances as electric shavers, hair dryers, and travel irons on their trips often have trouble with U.S. voltage. Hotels can help by providing adapters in the room or stocking the gift shop with adapters and small appliances for sale or rent.

Above all, hotels should make international guests feel at home. While some international travelers want a taste of adventure, others feel more comfortable with the familiar. They appreciate ethnic menu items and staff members who speak their language.

The Hilton Hotels Corporation is the leader in catering to Japanese travelers. The chain offers special amenities such as green tea for its Japanese visitors. Hilton realizes the importance of staying in touch with Japanese guests, and sends cards or letters to Japanese visitors to build guest loyalty.

The Sheraton Carlton Hotel in Washington, D.C., hosts a wide variety of international travelers. Located just two blocks from the White House, the hotel is situated in a popular destination area for travelers worldwide. The hotel's international flavor is enhanced by prominently displayed international time clocks. Foreign language newspapers, multilingual information brochures, and multilingual

Insider Insights

John B. Richards
Senior Vice President—Marketing
Four Seasons Hotels and Resorts
Toronto, Ontario
Canada

John B. Richards is responsible for the overall sales and marketing effort of Four Seasons Hotels and Resorts' 23 hotels in North America, England, the Caribbean, and Japan, as well as for new properties under construction in Hawaii, Mexico City, and California. Previously, Richards served as vice president of marketing and planning for Royal Viking Cruise Lines, where he built a marketing organization and developed and implemented award-winning advertising and direct sales programs. He is a 1976 graduate of the Wharton School of Business at the University of Pennsylvania, from which he has received an M.B.A.

The travel industry today faces a tremendous challenge. We not only have to anticipate and respond to the evolving needs of the communications-oriented business traveler and the emerging new values of the traveler at large; we also face the challenge created by an explosion in international travel. With the globalization of the world's economy, lowered airline rates, and increased flight schedules, more people than ever before are traveling from abroad for both business and pleasure. Hoteliers must respond by changing the way they think, act, and operate. It is essential that hospitality management maintain existing standards of service and, at the same time, be ready to accommodate the present and future needs of the international traveler.

One of the ways Four Seasons Hotels acknowledges its international guests is by having on staff a number of multilingual concierges who speak a range of languages, including French, Spanish, German, Italian, and Japanese. In addition, a number of senior-level hotel executives are multilingual. Those who are from Europe, in addition to being fluent in a variety of languages, are more sensitive to other cultures because of their own backgrounds. Several general managers, also of European background, are able to provide their employees with firsthand knowledge of appropriate customs and protocol for the variety of international guests that visit their hotels.

Hoteliers located in international business centers find it imperative that they not only provide excellent service, but that they address the special needs of international guests. The smallest gestures can sometimes mean the most—whether it's greeting a guest in his or her native language, or having a guest's hometown newspaper available with the morning coffee. Hotel restaurants also must cater to the needs of travelers from abroad. This special attention can range from serving cheeses at just the right temperature to offering a selection of wines from the world's leading wine regions. Other extras might include offering a selection of European mineral waters, liqueurs, and beers.

Insider Insights *(continued)*

One of the biggest changes affecting the hotel industry is the continued influx of Japanese guests. Japan's increasing role in the global marketplace has had a great effect on our industry, influencing both business and leisure travel. And as Japanese investments in the United States increase, more Japanese will be traveling to the major North American business centers.

Many hoteliers are responding to the increased business from this segment with the introduction of special services designed for Japanese travelers. For example, at a number of Four Seasons properties, a traditional green tea service is offered to Japanese guests on arrival. Japanese slippers and *yukatas* (Japanese-styled cotton bathrobes, sometimes called "happy coats") are placed in the rooms of many of our hotels. Japanese-speaking concierges are on staff, and hotel literature is also printed in Japanese. Our hotel in Beverly Hills even provides a Disneyland brochure translated into Japanese.

One Four Seasons hotel has introduced a baby-sitting service with Japanese-speaking women, as well as an authentic Japanese breakfast. (I might add that this breakfast has become quite popular even with non-Japanese guests.) It's a combination of steamed rice, *miso* soup with tofu, grilled fresh salmon, *tamagoyaki* (a Japanese omelet), seaweed, pickled Japanese vegetables, and green tea. This platter, a brainchild of one of the hotel's sales managers, will soon be offered in all our hotels.

At other hotels, Japanese guests are welcomed with a note in their native language from the general manager, along with *otenguai* towels (oversized wash cloths). In addition, all Four Seasons hotels accept the Japanese credit card, JCB.

One of the most innovative and creative ways to better serve our Japanese clientele was to acquaint our employees with the basics of Japanese protocol. A series of workshops at The Pierre in New York trained the staff on how to communicate with, and effectively serve, Japanese guests. This kind of experience not only benefits the guest, but also gives staff members confidence that enhances their performance.

These sessions were led by an expert on Japanese protocol and focused on basic social customs and on the most commonly used Japanese phrases. The Pierre staff learned how to properly greet a guest in the Japanese fashion (there's more to it than just a bow), how to present a business card, and how to negotiate on an executive level. Techniques in entertaining Japanese clients were also covered. We will soon be conducting similar sessions at other Four Seasons hotels.

The demands being made on our industry are not simple, but they can be met with common sense, understanding, and quality products. Travel and tourism will continue to flourish in the 1990s and into the next decade. Hoteliers will thus continue to be faced with the challenge of catering to international travelers who expect excellent service and welcome the added touch of "a bit of home."

---

menus help travelers feel comfortable. The hotel also offers concierge service (a service prevalent in Europe) and provides on-call multilingual limousine drivers for its international guests.

Another property that depends on international visitors is the Registry Hotel in Minneapolis, Minnesota. Minneapolis is home to several large international companies (3M, Pillsbury, Control Data, etc.), and attracts a number of individual and group business guests from abroad. Registry employees must be fluent in at least one foreign language. The Registry's international guests are further served by multilingual signs, the availability of electrical adapters, and a staff that is sympathetic to their needs.

The Sundial Beach and Tennis Resort on Sanibel Island, Florida, has a "Welcome Mat" program for international travelers that includes a dedicated fax line for international travelers and travel agents, international language symbols throughout the resort, a currency exchange, restaurant menus in several languages, electrical adapters in the gift shop, a listing of second and third languages spoken by employees, and an international welcome packet that includes information on area attractions, shopping, the environment, and other facts important to tourists. Questionnaires help keep services relevant by asking international guests for feedback and suggestions on how to make them feel more comfortable.

Finding International Travelers

As we have mentioned, familiarity is important to many international travelers, so sometimes these travelers do not need to be solicited—they contact a U.S. hotel chain property after exposure to the chain's product overseas. Chains such as Holiday Inn, Quality Inns, and Sheraton are well-known abroad, and their worldwide reservations systems make it easy for international travelers to book into U.S. properties. Other properties have joined such consortiums as Preferred Hotels Worldwide to reap the benefits of international recognition.

Most independent or small properties cannot boast this advantage, however, and must seek out international travelers. Sources of international business can sometimes be found in a property's own community. Many schools, colleges, and universities bring foreign exchange students or special study groups into the country. These institutions can also assist a property by providing translators and information about foreign customs.

Other local sources of prospects include service and fraternal clubs that may bring in international guests. The local chamber of commerce can provide information on local companies that do business with foreign firms. Many communities have "Sister City" programs that involve international visitors. Other cities may invite international guests for information exchanges, political symposiums, and so on. Properties can contact local ethnic groups to request the names of potential visitors such as students on scholarships or guest speakers from abroad.

On the state level, a property can often obtain information and potential contacts from state tourist agencies or from convention and visitors' bureaus. On the national level, a property has a number of resources: the United States Travel and Tourism Administration (USTTA), the Travel Industry Association of America (TIA), the American Hotel & Motel Association's International Travel Committee, and a number of industry associations. The names of other organizations that are involved in international travel are available in the public library in such references as *Encyclopedia of Associations* and *National Trade & Professional Associations*.

Exhibit 3   Cooperative Advertising to the International Traveler

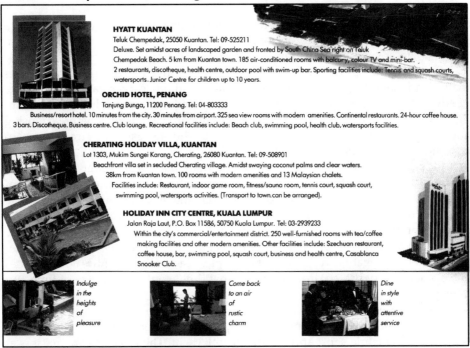

HYATT KUANTAN
Teluk Chempedak, 25050 Kuantan. Tel: 09-525211
Deluxe. Set amidst acres of landscaped garden and fronted by South China Sea right on Teluk Chempedak Beach. 5 km from Kuantan town. 185 air-conditioned rooms with balcony, colour TV and mini-bar. 2 restaurants, discotheque, health centre, outdoor pool with swim-up bar. Sporting facilities include: Tennis and squash courts, watersports. Junior Centre for children up to 10 years.

ORCHID HOTEL, PENANG
Tanjung Bunga, 11200 Penang. Tel: 04-803333
Business/resort hotel. 10 minutes from the city. 30 minutes from airport. 325 sea view rooms with modern amenities. Continental restaurants. 24-hour coffee house. 3 bars. Discotheque. Business centre. Club lounge. Recreational facilities include: Beach club, swimming pool, health club, watersports facilities.

CHERATING HOLIDAY VILLA, KUANTAN
Lot 1303, Mukim Sungei Karang, Cherating, 26080 Kuantan. Tel: 09-508901
Beachfront villa set in secluded Cherating village. Amidst swaying coconut palms and clear waters. 38km from Kuantan town. 100 rooms with modern amenities and 13 Malaysian chalets. Facilities include: Restaurant, indoor game room, fitness/sauna room, tennis court, squash court, swimming pool, watersports activities. (Transport to town can be arranged).

HOLIDAY INN CITY CENTRE, KUALA LUMPUR
Jalan Raja Laut, P.O. Box 11586, 50750 Kuala Lumpur. Tel: 03-2939233
Within the city's commercial/entertainment district. 250 well-furnished rooms with tea/coffee making facilities and other modern amenities. Other facilities include: Szechuan restaurant, coffee house, bar, swimming pool, squash court, business and health centre, Casablanca Snooker Club.

Indulge in the heights of pleasure

Come back to an air of rustic charm

Dine in style with attentive service

The high cost of marketing to international travelers forces many properties to work with other properties, travel-related services, and other firms that cater to the tourist trade. This page from a full-color booklet published by Malaysia Airlines promotes several local hotels.

Reaching International Travelers

Since the international traveler market is so far-flung, an individual effort may be far too costly for a small to midsize property. Even larger properties may want to consider a cooperative effort when targeting international travelers, such as joining with a travel supplier (airline, tour group, etc.) or an entire destination area's effort to reach overseas visitors (see Exhibit 3).

Affiliation with a travel supplier such as an airline may involve a number of options—from joint advertising to cooperatively offering complete package vacations or business trips. Some properties can offset the price of this type of promotion by supplying space or services to the travel supplier (convention rooms for a company convention, discounted rooms to airline crews, and so on).

Destination area efforts may be local in scope or part of a state or national campaign to attract international visitors. USTTA maintains regional marketing offices overseas. You can often promote your property through these outlets at a cost that is far less than an individual effort. State tourist agencies may also have programs to attract foreign visitors to a state or area; you can advise these organizations of your interest in reaching the international market. Destination area efforts to reach international travelers may also include goodwill tours to "Sister

Cities" overseas by municipal governments, convention and visitors' bureaus, or chambers of commerce.

Individual property efforts to reach international travelers typically involve many of the methods used to reach other markets: personal selling, participation in trade shows, advertising, direct mail, and public relations.

Personal selling often involves a hotel representative or "rep" who specializes in international sales. This rep may maintain a field office overseas, or may make goodwill tours to foreign travel agencies, corporations, and trade shows to promote your property. You must be well-versed in national customs before choosing a rep to send to certain countries. In parts of the Middle East, for example, a property should always send a male representative.

Face-to-face contacts with potential international guests differ greatly from the face-to-face presentations common in our country. Whenever possible, presentations and written materials should be in the language of the country in which the presentation is taking place; business cards should show titles and other pertinent information in the prospect's native tongue. This is particularly important to the Japanese. Appointments are a must in many countries, especially with tour wholesalers and travel agents. In France, for example, practically the entire country goes on vacation in August, so drop-in calls at that time would be a waste of time and money.

There are other factors to consider when selling in person to international travelers. Spaniards and Italians, for example, often linger over negotiations, so it is unwise to schedule short appointments with them. The Japanese are masters at negotiation, and have the patience to wait long periods of time in order to have their demands met. In many cases, it is wiser to contact potential international guests indirectly, through referral services or professional travel agents.

Another way to reach international travelers is through *participation in trade shows* such as the Discover America International Pow Wow (sponsored by TIA) and the National Tour Association Marketplace. The latter show offers opportunities to reach tour brokers who arrange trips for international travelers. Travel agents can be reached through world congresses of the American Society of Travel Agents or through the International Tourism Exchange held annually in Berlin. TIA and USTTA attend the International Tourism Exchange. The names and locations of other shows can be obtained from USTTA or trade publications such as *Meetings & Conventions* and *Travel Weekly*.

Advertising in international markets can be extremely expensive. Some resorts find it cost-effective to offer collateral materials, such as rack brochures, in a variety of languages (see Exhibit 4). International print advertising, however, is far costlier. Large properties do most of the consumer advertising overseas. Small properties may find it feasible to advertise overseas if they advertise to the travel trade. Specialized "Visit USA" publications are targeted toward travel agents and tour brokers in a number of areas: *El Travel Agent Internacional* reaches travel professionals in Mexico, Central America, and South America; *Visit USA Guide* reaches travel professionals in Western Europe, Japan, Australia, South America, Mexico, and Canada.

Exhibit 4   Rack Brochures for International Travelers

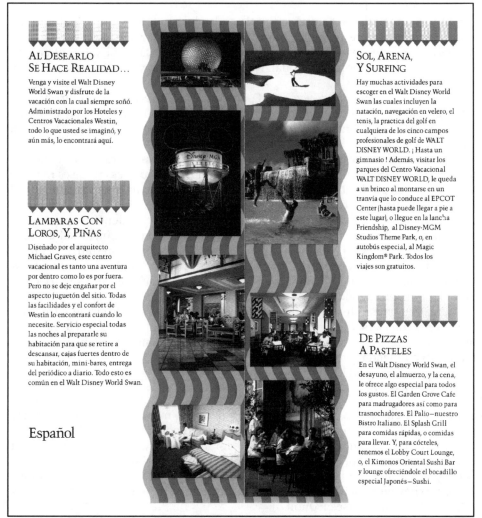

AL DESEARLO SE HACE REALIDAD...

Venga y visite el Walt Disney World Swan y disfrute de la vacación con la cual siempre soñó. Administrado por los Hoteles y Centros Vacacionales Westin, todo lo que usted se imaginó, y aún más, lo encontrará aquí.

LAMPARAS CON LOROS, Y, PIÑAS

Diseñado por el arquitecto Michael Graves, este centro vacacional es tanto una aventura por dentro como lo es por fuera. Pero no se deje engañar por el aspecto juguetón del sitio. Todas las facilidades y el confort de Westin lo encontrará cuando lo necesite. Servicio especial todas las noches al prepararle su habitación para que se retire a descansar, cajas fuertes dentro de su habitación, mini-bares, entrega del periódico a diario. Todo esto es común en el Walt Disney World Swan.

Español

SOL, ARENA, Y SURFING

Hay muchas actividades para escoger en el Walt Disney World Swan las cuales incluyen la natación, navegación en velero, el tenis, la practica del golf en cualquiera de los cinco campos profesionales de golf de WALT DISNEY WORLD. ¡ Hasta un gimnasio ! Además, visitar los parques del Centro Vacacional WALT DISNEY WORLD, le queda a un brinco al montarse en un tranvía que lo conduce al EPCOT Center (hasta puede llegar a pie a este lugar), o llegue en la lancha Friendship, al Disney-MGM Studios Theme Park, o, en autobús especial, al Magic Kingdom® Park. Todos los viajes son gratuitos.

DE PIZZAS A PASTELES

En el Walt Disney World Swan, el desayuno, el almuerzo, y la cena, le ofrece algo especial para todos los gustos. El Garden Grove Cafe para madrugadores así como para trasnochadores. El Palio—nuestro Bistro Italiano. El Splash Grill para comidas rápidas, o comidas para llevar. Y, para cócteles, tenemos el Lobby Court Lounge, o, el Kimonos Oriental Sushi Bar y lounge ofreciéndole el bocadillo especial Japonés—Sushi.

This rack brochure, for Westin's Swan Resort at Walt Disney World, has been printed in three foreign languages—Spanish, Portuguese, and German—to promote the property to international travelers. (The one shown is in Spanish.) This type of collateral material is extremely cost-effective; the brochure's photographs and other graphic elements are designed first, and separate printings in specific languages can be ordered as needed.

Hotels can also reach overseas travel professionals through directory advertising in such publications as *OAG TRAVEL PLANNER/Hotel & Motel RedBook* and *Hotel & Travel Index.* European travel agents seeking information about lodging facilities use hotel directories more than any other information source. Your listing or ad should include specific information such as the proximity to your property of an international airport or gateway city (a city with an airport that handles direct flights from other countries). Such information makes it easier for the agent to make a recommendation.

If you have a large enough advertising budget to target individual international travelers, there is the option of advertising in foreign newspapers. The names of these newspapers are usually available in the local library. It is often best to have advertising for international travelers developed by an advertising agency in the targeted country.

Like advertising, *direct mail* efforts are more cost-effective when directed toward groups or travel professionals. Direct mail material should always be in the language of the recipients, preferably translated by a native of the country to which the letter will be sent.

Public relations can be an effective way to acquaint overseas travel professionals and individual travelers with your property. You may send press releases to trade and consumer publications or offer familiarization trips to international travel writers. Another way to get publicity is to promote the specialized services you provide for international travelers. One hotel chain received extensive press coverage when it introduced an international traveler program that included 24-hour translation and telex services, a currency exchange, a multilingual staff, and multilingual directories and telephone information. A property might also hold educational seminars or "international days" to promote its facilities and services and build foreign guest goodwill.

Creating goodwill seems to be the key to ensuring repeat business from international travelers. If a property can make international visitors feel at home, it may receive one of the most valuable forms of advertising available: word-of-mouth recommendations from satisfied guests.

Honeymooners

Since almost all newlyweds plan a honeymoon, this market can be an extremely profitable one for the hospitality industry. Honeymooners are often loyal guests. Many return to their honeymoon property for anniversary visits or recommend it to friends. Favorite honeymoon destinations include Florida, Hawaii, California, Pennsylvania, and New York. Properties in other areas can appeal to this lucrative market if they offer facilities that will help create shared memories—the chief purpose of a honeymoon (see Exhibit 5).

Today's newlyweds are older (the average bride is 24 years old, bridegrooms 26), more sophisticated (many have traveled together before and are looking for something different), more affluent (many couples have been earning two paychecks for several years), and interested in activity as well as privacy. The fact that many couples are earning two incomes also means that honeymoons tend to be shorter, a trend that lends itself to special honeymoon weekend packages.

Another trend that can prove profitable to properties interested in attracting this market is the "destination wedding." Many couples are opting to travel to a specific location for both the wedding ceremony and honeymoon. Walt Disney World in Lake Buena Vista, Florida, has a complete Fairy-tale Weddings department that offers theme weddings, such as Cinderella and Prince Charming. The Westin Maui has, in addition to several wedding packages, a "director of romance"

Exhibit 5   The Honeymoon Market at a Glance

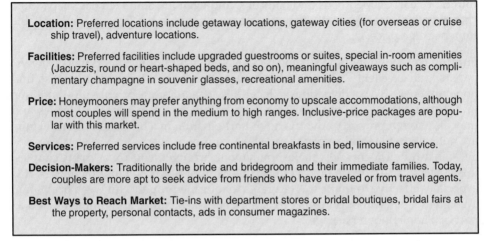

Location: Preferred locations include getaway locations, gateway cities (for overseas or cruise ship travel), adventure locations.

Facilities: Preferred facilities include upgraded guestrooms or suites, special in-room amenities (Jacuzzis, round or heart-shaped beds, and so on), meaningful giveaways such as complimentary champagne in souvenir glasses, recreational amenities.

Price: Honeymooners may prefer anything from economy to upscale accommodations, although most couples will spend in the medium to high ranges. Inclusive-price packages are popular with this market.

Services: Preferred services include free continental breakfasts in bed, limousine service.

Decision-Makers: Traditionally the bride and bridegroom and their immediate families. Today, couples are more apt to seek advice from friends who have traveled or from travel agents.

Best Ways to Reach Market: Tie-ins with department stores or bridal boutiques, bridal fairs at the property, personal contacts, ads in consumer magazines.

who handles all the details and takes the stress out of wedding planning. As this trend continues, more properties may be hiring or contracting with professional wedding planners to offer hassle-free weddings and honeymoons.

The Decision-Maker. The honeymoon decision-maker is almost always someone in the wedding party itself. The bride and bridegroom play the most significant role, but they listen to suggestions from their families and other members of the wedding party. Most honeymooners use the services of a travel agent.

Meeting the Needs of Honeymooners. The average honeymoon trip lasts one to two weeks. Some honeymoons last more than two weeks; some are as short as a weekend. No matter what the length of stay, however, the typical honeymoon couple is looking for a romantic atmosphere, privacy, and a lot of activities at an affordable price.

Special packages are appealing to many honeymoon couples on a budget. All-inclusive packages—meals, accommodations, entertainment, sporting equipment, tips, etc. included in one price—are attractive to newlyweds who do not want to be bothered with details. You should keep in mind that couples usually book honeymoon reservations months in advance. You should plan honeymoon packages on a yearly schedule so that they may be promoted in plenty of time for honeymooners to consider them.

"Adventure" honeymoons have gained popularity. Many couples take art tours of Europe, archeological trips to Mexico, and safari in Africa. You might still receive business from these couples if your property is located in a gateway city or in the city or town in which the wedding takes place. An overnight package with breakfast, complimentary champagne, and transportation to the airport or cruise ship can attract couples who will be honeymooning abroad.

The honeymoon market has long been a mainstay in such places as the Pocono Mountains and Niagara Falls. In the lavish, four-season resorts of the Poconos, couples are treated to breathtaking scenery and rooms that feature plush carpeting, round or heart-shaped beds and bathtubs, and even in-room Jacuzzis shaped like champagne glasses. Most of the honeymoons offered in the Poconos are available for a package price.

Finding Honeymooners. Watching for engagement announcements in local news-papers is an excellent way to develop honeymoon market leads. You can also find honeymooners by participating in local department store or specialty boutique bridal promotions. These sources can provide names of prospective brides and may also accept property advertising or participation in a bridal fair. If bridal fairs are not held in the local area, you can stage your own event.

Since travel agents now make honeymoon arrangements for so many couples, it is essential that you do not overlook these important travel intermediaries. It is especially effective to invite travel agents to tour the property during a bridal fair. This gives agents an opportunity to experience the facilities and dining offered as part of a honeymoon package.

Reaching Honeymooners. The two most effective means of reaching the honey-moon market are direct mail and advertising. Direct mail includes letters of congratulation to couples whose engagement announcements have appeared in newspapers, and invitations to special events at the property. You can also send direct mail pieces to travel agents. These pieces are more effective if they include all-inclusive honeymoon packages.

Advertising in newspapers and magazines can build a property's honeymoon business (see Exhibit 6). If the property is located in a popular destination spot, ads can be placed in newspapers in key feeder cities. Special interest magazines such as *Modern Bride* are excellent for attracting this market.

Other ways to reach the lucrative honeymoon market include letting the cou-ple experience the property for themselves during a "Champagne Brunch" or giv-ing them a personal tour of the property. Inviting the society writers of local newspapers to property functions encourages good coverage of the property and may lead to personal recommendations. Creating a unique honeymoon package or offering a special honeymoon package as a prize in local or national contests or on game shows may also generate publicity for the property.

Sports Teams

Another way to meet the challenge of filling guestrooms is to target sports teams. Professional, college, or local sports teams can provide a year-round opportunity to properties that can meet the needs of these groups (see Exhibit 7).

Janna Mugnola, national sales manager for the Westin Galleria and Westin Oaks in Houston, says that attracting baseball teams is the property's biggest coup, resulting in 5,000 room nights per season, but other sports teams can also boost busi-ness. Bill Bohde, director of marketing for the Marriott in Greenbelt, Maryland (the official hotel of the Washington Bullets basketball team and the Washington Capitals hockey team), says other sports teams are also lucrative because they provide winter

Exhibit 6   Sample Honeymoon Ad

Sweet. Secluded. Seductive. Your romance continues on the waterfront at The Lodge of Four Seasons on beautiful Lake of the Ozarks, Missouri. (Featured on Lifestyles of the Rich and Famous.)

We make your escape heavenly with a honeymoon package which includes a four-star dinner, a free monogrammed bath robe for each person, and complimentary champagne on arrival. Plus, you'll be served a special breakfast each morning before you spend the day enjoying our many sports activities and guest amenities.

Call 1-800-THE-LAKE now.
All you need is your honey.
We'll provide the moon.

the Lodge OF FOUR SEASONS
Celebrating 25 Years of Hospitality.

business, fill rooms over the weekends, spend heavily on food and beverage, and boost revenue by drawing fans.

Football Teams

Visiting high school teams in town for one night, college players in league games or tournaments, and professional teams in regular season games or the Super Bowl are all sources of football team business. The most important factor in attracting any of these teams is location. If a property is within 20 to 30 minutes of the playing field, it has a good chance to sell to this market. After this need has been met, others can be addressed. For most professional teams, this means service, food, and rates, in that order.

Exhibit 7   The Sports Team Market at a Glance

Location: Preferred locations are within a 20- to 30-minute drive of the sports arena; close proximity to airport or major highway.

Facilities: Preferred facilities provide guestroom blocks; group function rooms; small meeting rooms; 24-hour room service or late-night restaurants; extra amenities such as game room, sauna, or swimming pool; secure storage facilities for equipment.

Price: Non-professional teams usually look for low rates; professional teams will pay higher rates. Professional and amateur sports teams look for group rates and complimentary rooms for the head coach and business manager.

Services: Preferred services include discount clubs; preregistration; late check-out; maps of shortest route to playing site; complimentary newspapers; ability to meet dietary requirements and serve group meals on time; availability of box lunches for teams traveling by road; team welcome, including signs or banners (with permission of head coach); bus parking if needed; wake-up service; bill ready at time of departure; after-stay follow-up.

Decision-Makers: Coaches, athletic directors, athletic business managers.

Best Ways to Reach Market: Personal contacts, direct mail, advertisements in college magazines, consumer newspaper advertising to attract fans.

Professional football teams expect the best in service. Properties that serve this market (Marriott, Holiday Inn, and Ramada lead the field) have identified several key needs:

1. *Personal greeting.* Most properties assign someone to meet the team and attend to any special needs. This service not only makes the team feel welcome; it also makes a good impression on the head coach (who doesn't need additional hassles).

2. *Efficient registration.* Most properties receive a rooming list within five days of the team's arrival. The team is usually housed in one wing or in a quiet area away from other groups. Guestroom keys are made available to the head coach or someone else on the coaching staff for distribution to the players.

3. *Team functions.* Most professional football teams require an arrival dinner and several other meals (pre-game meal, post-game meal, breakfast, and so on). You should make arrangements for these meals well in advance to allow for special dietary requirements. In addition to following instructions for menus, you should serve ample portions and allow extra space at tables because of the large size of the players.

4. *Meeting rooms.* Most professional football teams require at least three meeting rooms and a room for taping the players before the game. There is usually a meeting of the whole team at which a film of the competition is shown. This may be followed by two smaller meetings (usually groups of 35 to 50 people) of the offensive and defensive squads.

   The taping room can be set up the morning of the game, and should be equipped with two eight-foot tables approximately 12 inches off the floor. This can be accomplished by placing wooden blocks under tables whose legs are left folded up. This arrangement eases the strain on the trainers, and is a gesture that will usually be appreciated and remembered.

5. *Other services.* Many properties welcome the team with an outside sign or a sign on the lobby function board, but this must be approved by the head coach. It is also wise to check with the head coach to determine if players may have phone calls or visitors, and if there are any food restrictions (no food after 10:00 P.M., and so on). Many properties also offer a complimentary room to the head coach, provide daily newspapers to coaches and players, and offer box lunches to teams that are traveling by bus or car.

College football teams have similar requirements, although they do not expect the VIP treatment extended to professional teams. Rates may be more important to these teams than service, since many college football teams operate on a limited budget. But college football teams can generate good business, especially when the property offers fan packages to supporters traveling to cheer their team on.

Football teams can be a good source of revenue, but it is important to contact the decision-makers well in advance of the season. Most collegiate schedules are available in January. Properties can contact coaches, athletic directors, or athletic business managers by obtaining names from the National Directory of College Athletics or making contacts at the annual College Athletic Business Managers' Association convention in January. You must be a member of the association to exhibit at this meeting. Professional teams can be contacted by phone or direct mail, or through inquiries to the respective leagues.

Baseball Teams

Professional football teams play approximately 20 games each year; in contrast, American League and National League baseball teams play 162 regular season games each year. Because baseball games are often played in a series, teams usually stay in hotels an average of two to four nights at a time. Baseball teams usually return several times to play the home team again later in the season. Football teams, on the other hand, travel once to a city during the regular season and stay just one or two nights. The professional baseball leagues are actively involved in hotel negotiations and recommend certain hotels after a bidding process has been completed. Although baseball teams make their own lodging decisions, most teams follow the recommendations of their league. You can also tap into the business generated by minor league teams.

The needs of professional baseball teams differ from those of professional football teams. While most football teams focus on group functions and meals, group functions for baseball players are rare, and most of the time players are on their own when it comes to meals. Properties that offer 24-hour room service and a number of restaurants are popular with baseball teams, as are properties that are close to other restaurants and attractions.

College baseball teams, in contrast, often request group meal functions, which vary depending on the time of arrival and the game schedule. As with football

Where to Write for Team Addresses

Professional Football:	National Football League 410 Park Avenue New York, NY 10022
Professional Baseball:	Major League Baseball 350 Park Avenue New York, NY 10022
Professional Basketball:	National Basketball Association 645 Fifth Avenue, 10th Floor New York, NY 10022
Professional Hockey:	National Hockey League 650 Fifth Avenue, 33rd Floor New York, NY 10019

College Sports:	National Collegiate Athletic
	  Association
	Box 1906
	Mission, KS 66201
	
	National Directory of College
	  Athletics
	Box 7068
	Amarillo, TX 79144

teams, there may be dietary restrictions before a game, and it is best to have pre-arranged menus when serving this group.

Baseball teams may be solicited through minor and major league offices and through the athletic departments of colleges and universities. You can advertise package deals for fans through travel agents or in the visiting team's hometown newspapers.

Basketball Teams

While basketball teams typically use fewer rooms than football or baseball teams, they still offer the potential for increased room occupancies, especially when tournament play is involved. Tournaments are held on the professional, collegiate, and high school levels, and typically involve extended team stays as well as rooms and food and beverage business from fans.

When targeting basketball teams, it is important to remember that the average basketball player is well over six feet tall and may require an oversize bed, high ceilings, and additional leg room at tables when meetings are a part of the team's stay.

Basketball teams can be solicited through league offices (schedules are available in June) or through collegiate athletic departments.

Other Teams

Major universities and colleges participate in a number of other sports—hockey, soccer, tennis, cross country, and track. There are professional teams in a number of these sports as well. Most of these sports teams require guestrooms when they visit other cities. Properties that wish to sell to these teams can contact the appropriate professional leagues or college athletic offices.

Still other opportunities to tap into America's fascination with sports include servicing tournaments—both amateur and professional—in such sports as bowling, tennis, boxing, and swimming. You can obtain information on events and dates by writing to sports associations such as the United States Tennis Association and U.S. Swimming Inc.

Many properties find the sports teams market so lucrative that they are developing clubs that offer discount rates to teams and fans alike (see Exhibit 8). Days Inns, for example, offers a Sports Plus Club that includes team discounts, rental car discounts, free local phone calls, late checkout, and room blocks, and invites athletic administrators and coaches to join its sports advisory board. Winegardner & Hammons, Inc., a hotel management company, promotes a "We Promise" sports program available at such properties as Holiday Inn, Quality Suites, Radisson hotels, and Comfort Inns.

Government Travelers

Federal, state, and local governments provide numerous opportunities for properties to increase room occupancies throughout the year. Thousands of government agencies require out-of-town travel to conduct business.

One of the factors that has held many properties back in the government traveler market is the complexity of soliciting government business. Another is the assumption that every piece of government business automatically goes to the lowest bidder. By law the federal government must give every potential supplier a hearing, but the final decision is not made on the basis of cost alone. The final decision is also based on the property's ability to contribute to the efficiency and effectiveness of government operations. In other words, government officials are not necessarily looking for the lowest rates. They want value, but they are also looking for quality accommodations and service.

Before bidding for government business, you should be aware of the requirements involved in establishing a business relationship with the government. You should also be aware of how expense money is allocated to government travelers.

Straight per diem is a dollar figure allocated to cover lodging, meals, local transportation, and gratuities when government employees travel on official business. This is the most common type of per diem. The amount of money allocated is based on the Consumer Price Index of the city or area the government employee is traveling to. This amount will vary from year to year.

Actual and necessary per diem is a maximum amount that can be spent regardless of location, and is usually equal to or higher than the straight per diem rate. This rate is usually given to upper-level government employees.

Exhibit 8   Discount Rates for Sports Teams

Some hotel chains offer discount rates for sports teams, coaches, recruiters, and fans. This flier for Holiday Inns' Sports Rate program details the benefits of the program and provides an application form. (Courtesy of Holiday Inn Worldwide)

Sources for Government Travel Business

Federal Travel Directory—$8 per copy
    Source: Superintendent of Documents
                U.S. Government Printing Office
                Washington, DC 20402
                (202) 783-3238
                Stock # GPO 722-006-00000-3

United States Government Manual—$20
    Source: Superintendent of Documents
                U.S. Government Printing Office
                Washington, DC 20402
                (202) 783-3238
                Stock # 069-000-00015-1

**List of Government Cost-Reimbursable
Contractors:**

GSA Federal Procurement Data Center
    4040 N. Fairfax Drive, Suite 9001
    Arlington, VA 22203
    (703) 235-1326

Society of Government Meeting Planners
    1213 Prince Street
    Alexandria, VA 22314
    (703) 836-3855

Society of Travel Agents in Government
    6935 Wisconsin Circle, N.W.
    Washington, DC 20815
    (301) 654-8595

**Government Services Administration
Traffic and Travel Zone Offices:**

EASTERN ZONE
Federal Supply Service Bureau
75 Spring Street, S.W.
Atlanta, GA 30303
(404) 331-5121

CENTRAL ZONE
Federal Supply Service Bureau
1500 East Bannister Road
Kansas City, MO 64131-3088
(816) 523-6029

SOUTHWEST ZONE
Federal Supply Service Bureau
819 Taylor Street
Ft. Worth, TX 76102
(817) 334-2737

WESTERN ZONE
Federal Supply Service Bureau
525 Market Street
San Francisco, CA 94015
(415) 974-9292

NATIONAL CAPITAL ZONE
Federal Supply Service Bureau
7th and D Streets, S.W.
Washington, DC 20407
(202) 472-2003

Source: Adapted from Lyn Matthew, "Guidelines for Developing the Government Market," *HSMAI Marketing Review*, Winter 1989, p. 7.

Contract per diem is the most complex of the pricing arrangements, and incorporates the total cost of accommodations, meals, gratuities, travel expenses, etc. For example, a government agency might want to use a hotel to stage a training program. The agency would put out the program requirements for bid. Private companies or consultants act as intermediaries between the government agency and travel suppliers, similar to the way tour wholesalers operate. These companies or consultants contact several hotels for bids and submit a final bid for the entire estimated costs.

Per diems offered to state and local government employees are often less than those offered to federal government employees. State and local employees often incur more non-reimbursable expenses, and will be more likely to choose a property that offers low rates.

Insider Insights

Victoria Dunn
Consultant
It Shall Be Dunn
Alexandria, Virginia

Victoria Dunn is a principal partner in It Shall Be Dunn, an Alexandria, Virginia, consulting firm with expertise in government and military travel services. Dunn has 14 years of experience in the government arena. She was a founding member of the Society of Government Meeting Planners and has served on SGMP's national board for six years.

You have to do your homework before pursuing the government market. What follows are some proven strategies for success.

Assign a dedicated salesperson to the government market, someone who will become educated about the types of government travelers and the policies and regulations that pertain to government travelers and your hotel. This government-specialist-in-training should be regarded as an essential, long-term investment. All too often, properties assign their least experienced staff members to the government segment and promote them just when they start to become effective.

Focus on specific sectors of the government market rather than all of it. If you determine that meetings are the mainstay of your government business, join the Society of Government Meeting Planners. SGMP's monthly chapter meetings, national newsletter and directory, and annual conference are invaluable. If you find out the transient sector is dominant, join the Society of Travel Agents in Government (STAG). STAG hosts two national meetings a year, both in Washington, D.C.

Make sure your government rates and programs information is accurate and up to date in all airline computer reservation systems that carry it. List your property in the *Federal Travel Directory (FTD)*, a monthly federal government publication (no advertising is accepted), and the *OAG BUSINESS TRAVEL PLANNER,* a quarterly publication that covers lodging, car rental, and per diems for government and military travelers and travel coordinators (advertising accepted). Subscribe to, and consider advertising in, other publications that reach government travelers.

Educate your entire hotel staff, especially front desk employees, about the value of government business. For too many years, government and military travelers were the Rodney Dangerfields of hotel guests, but they're savvy now and expect good treatment. Educate yourself on the latest regulations binding the hotel industry, including the Hotel and Motel Fire Safety Act and the Americans with Disabilities Act.

If you really want to make the most of government business, think beyond hit-and-miss approaches. Government travelers recognize and appreciate consistent efforts to meet their needs. Your property's commitment to government travelers will be rewarded with repeat business.

Exhibit 9   Sample Ad for the Government Market

If you are interested in selling to this market, you have several options. The first, of course, is direct mail contact with various government agencies and officials (names and addresses may be located in government directories available in libraries). A direct mail package should contain a government rate sheet or brochure or offer an opportunity for a member of the agency to visit the property.

Advertising can also be used to reach government agencies and officials (see Exhibit 9). The Sheraton chain, for example, launched a successful ad campaign in *The Government Executive* magazine, but only after more than three years of research.

Exhibit 10   The Disabled Traveler Market at a Glance

Location: Preferred locations depend on reason for traveling.

Facilities: Preferred facilities may depend on the type of disability:

- *Mobility impaired travelers* prefer nearby parking spaces, ramps into property, self-opening doors into lobby, grab bars in hallways and in restrooms, wider doors to rooms, swimming pools adapted for disabled individuals.

- *Hearing impaired travelers* prefer telecommunications systems adapted to their needs; amplified phones; Visual Alert Systems (VAS) to signal telephones ringing, visitors at door, or emergencies.

- *Visually impaired travelers* prefer braille labels on elevators, menus, and directories printed in braille; property information available on audiocassette.

Price: Like other guests, the price disabled travelers are willing to pay for accommodations will vary depending on the reason for travel and other personal factors.

Services: The most important service properties can offer is a staff sensitive to the needs of disabled guests but not solicitous.

Decision-Makers: Individual guests, corporate meeting planners, tour operators, travel agents.

Best Ways to Reach Market: Typical avenues used to reach any guest. Consumer or trade advertising may mention special facilities for disabled guests. Public relations efforts may include tie-ins with organizations that assist the disabled, such as Easter Seals and the Muscular Dystrophy Association.

Another important starting point for advertising is the *Federal Travel Directory*, published by the General Services Administration (GSA) and the Department of Defense. This directory lists government contract airports and airlines, recommended ground transportation and car rental agencies, and includes a directory of domestic hotels and motels, extended-stay apartments, and international lodging facilities. Listings in the directory must fall within government per diem requirements (and reflect a 10% discount on rack rates). To advertise in the directory, hoteliers must request an application form from the GSA.

Disabled Travelers

It is estimated that slightly more than 15% of the U.S. population can be defined as disabled.[4] There are three main divisions of this group: the mobility impaired (defined as people who use wheelchairs), the hearing impaired, and the visually impaired. These physical impairments do not prevent the disabled from traveling. In 1984 it was estimated that over half of the disabled population traveled on vacation.[5] That number is expected to increase as the hospitality industry becomes more aware of the needs of this market (see Exhibit 10) and complies with the Americans with Disabilities Act (ADA), which became effective in 1992.

Title III of the ADA, a civil rights statute, requires that all public facilities be accessible to disabled people. It calls for the removal of architectural barriers that

ADA Guidelines

Renovations that properties may have to make to comply with ADA guidelines include the following:

1. Installing ramps.
2. Making curb cuts in sidewalks and entrances.
3. Lowering shelves.
4. Rearranging tables, chairs, vending machines, display racks, and other furniture.
5. Lowering telephones and installing telecommunications devices for the deaf (TDDs) in a number of guestrooms and at the front desk.
6. Adding raised letter markings on elevator control buttons.
7. Installing flashing alarm lights.
8. Widening doors.
9. Installing offset hinges to widen doorways.
10. Eliminating a turnstile or providing an alternative accessible path.
11. Installing accessible door hardware.
12. Installing grab bars in toilet stalls.
13. Rearranging toilet partitions to increase maneuvering space.
14. Insulating lavatory pipes.
15. Installing a raised toilet seat.
16. Installing a full-length bathroom mirror.
17. Lowering the paper towel dispenser in a bathroom.
18. Creating a designated accessible parking space.
19. Installing an accessible paper cup dispenser at an existing inaccessible water fountain.
20. Removing high-pile, low-density carpeting.
21. Modifying vehicle hand controls.

Source: Harvey Jacoby, AIA, "What Hoteliers Need to Know About ADA Requirements Effective This Month," *Florida Hotel and Motel Journal,* January 1992, p. 18.

may limit access to those with disabilities, and provides 21 guidelines for compliance. While it may be costly to modify existing properties, most hoteliers believe that making properties more accessible to disabled travelers will lead to additional bookings.

The needs of disabled travelers vary, of course. There are, however, two basic ways in which hospitality operations can meet the needs of all disabled travelers: removing physical barriers and improving employee training.

The removal of physical barriers does not necessarily mean just adding ramps and widening doors. While these improvements will help the mobility impaired, they mean little to hearing impaired or visually impaired guests. Visually impaired guests can be better served through directories and menus printed in braille, raised room numbers, and braille labels in elevators. Visually impaired guests will also appreciate having the housekeeping staff clean around items that the guests have left in the room.

Properties are meeting the needs of hearing impaired guests by offering amplified phones, special telecommunications services, and Visual Alert Systems (VAS). VAS includes sound-sensitive lights that let hearing impaired guests know when someone is at the door, or that the telephone is ringing, or that there is an emergency such as a fire.

Disabled travelers can also be attracted by a courteous and thoughtful staff. Employees should be sensitive but not solicitous when dealing with the disabled. Chains such as Holiday Inn, Sheraton, Hilton, Best Western, Ramada, and Hyatt have implemented employee training programs, but a property does not have to be a member of a chain to train employees in the proper way to serve disabled guests. Information is available from organizations such as the Society for the Advancement of Travel for the Handicapped, or from local organizations for disabled people.

There are several ways a property can reach disabled travelers. The employees of many properties find it personally rewarding to affiliate themselves with such organizations as Easter Seals, United Cerebral Palsy, and the United Way. These employees can make important contacts while serving the community. You can indicate your property's ability to serve disabled travelers in your consumer ads to business and leisure travelers and your trade ads to tour operators and travel agents. Other options include direct mail (names can be obtained from directories of associations for the disabled in key feeder cities or from referral sources) and public relations and publicity. For example, properties that sponsor events (fund-raisers, Special Olympics, and so on) with the United Way and other organizations may receive favorable publicity. A property can also contribute a lump sum to organizations that help the disabled or donate a contribution based on a special sales promotion.

Other Special Segments

In this section we will take a quick look at other special markets that can increase occupancies and revenues: reunion attendees, travel crews, truckers, movie crews, military personnel, and sequestered juries.

The fast-growing *reunions* market consists of family, class, and military reunions. Recent interest in nostalgia has led to an upsurge in family and class reunions, most of which are hosted by non-professionals. There is an association for reunion planners—the National Association of Reunion Planners, based in Rockville, Maryland.

This market segment is usually very cost conscious (most attendees pay their own way), and often requires extensive help with planning. If you want to attract the reunions market, you should focus your sales presentations on value and professional expertise.

Military reunions typically draw 100 to 300 people and are much more frequent, meeting annually or biannually, than most class or family reunions.[6] Like class and family reunion attendees, military reunion attendees are very cost conscious. Many reunions in the past were planned by non-professionals, but this is changing. Because of the rising interest in military reunions, publications focusing on them (*Reunion* and *Military Reunion News*) have appeared, and The Reunion Network, an organization offering reunion planning assistance, has been established.

The Reunion Network publishes *TRN News*, a newsletter for military reunion planners (see Exhibit 11). *TRN News* is an excellent vehicle for advertising to this lucrative market segment (the organization provides a list of "reunion friendly" hotels to its members). Other avenues for reaching military reunion planners include direct mail (mailing labels can be obtained from the Service Reunions National Registry) or advertising in military-oriented magazines.

Travel crews include airline personnel, train crews, and bus drivers. Travel crews often have layovers or waiting time between trips. Stays usually range from one to three days. In most cases, airport properties have the advantage in attracting this market segment, but, especially in the case of layover crews or "commuting employees," downtown properties may also be considered due to their proximity to shopping and cultural activities.

Some properties, such as the Congress Hotel in Chicago, have taken extra steps to attract airline travel crews—the property offers a "crew lounge," which includes a washer and dryer and iron and ironing board for crews on a short layover.

The extra business generated by travel crews provides another benefit—travelers who see crews at a property tend to perceive it as a quality hotel. This market can be reached by contacting local or national corporate offices or by offering a discount to travel crew members who recommend the property to their colleagues. Properties may also wish to contract with major travel suppliers to service "distressed passengers" (those whose transportation has been delayed by inclement weather or mechanical problems).

The *trucker* market can be lucrative, especially to budget and mid-scale properties located on well-traveled highways. While most stays are short (many average only eight to ten hours), truckers can help to fill rooms and increase food and beverage revenues (see Exhibit 12).

While there are many independent truckers, most business from this segment is arranged by contracting with major trucking firms. You can begin contract negotiations by contacting corporate headquarters and submitting a written proposal.

Movie crews typically stay on location from six to ten weeks, generating rooms and food and beverage business—and publicity for the property if a movie star is involved in the production. Movie crews usually require 40 to 70 guestrooms and 4 to 6 rooms for office facilities. Rooms for the crew should be similar (usually with one double bed), while special accommodations must be provided for the movie stars and the producer, director, and executive secretary. Room rates are usually discounted somewhat and office space offered free of charge in consideration for the amount of business the crew generates. In addition, such amenities as flowers for the cast and free newspapers are often included.

Exhibit 11 Attracting the Reunions Market

Properties wishing to take advantage of the lucrative military reunions market may join organizations such as The Reunion Network, which publishes TRN News, a free newsletter for military reunion planners. In addition to advertising opportunities, The Reunion Network lists "reunion friendly" properties and conducts seminars to help novice reunion planners stage successful functions.

In order to reach this market, you can contact your state's movie commission or convention and visitors' bureau as well as make personal contact with movie production offices. Familiarization tours are an excellent way to showcase your

Exhibit 12   Advertising to Truckers

Some properties and chains, such as Best Western International, publish directories for truckers. This directory lists Best Western properties throughout the United States. Each listing gives directions for getting to the property, and lists services of interest to truckers, such as a free Continental breakfast, truck washing or repair facilities, and the availability of truck parking and diesel fuel.

property to producers. Producers usually are the decision-makers regarding shooting locations and hotel accommodations.

Military personnel stationed at nearby bases offer the potential for increased weekend room occupancies. You can offer weekend packages at discounted rates to military personnel and their out-of-town guests. You can promote these packages in base newspapers or newsletters, property fliers, and direct mail.

Properties located near courthouses can take advantage of their location and serve *sequestered juries*. The needs of this market will be determined in part by the county sheriff's office or by an appointed court official. In most cases, the jurors, officer of the court, and other court personnel must be housed on one floor for security reasons, and telephones, television sets, and newspapers must be removed from rooms. Sequestered juries must have no contact with hotel employees. All arrangements for meals and transportation are made through the officer of the court.

Conclusion

Most hotels have many markets to which they can sell. Obviously, a hotel cannot precisely fit the needs of every possible market, so hotels focus on satisfying the needs of their principal markets. Frequently, however, demand from these principal markets does not keep hotel occupancies at an acceptable level year-round, and a strong effort must be made to seek out new guests.

International travelers, honeymooners, sports teams and their fans, government travelers, disabled travelers, and other special markets offer an excellent opportunity for increased room occupancies—and profits—to properties with the time and budgets to research and sell to them. As today's hospitality industry becomes increasingly competitive, special markets will become even more important. Properties that take the initiative to target these markets will be in a position to capture their share of the billions of dollars in revenues that special markets generate.

Endnotes

1. "Report of the Travel and Tourism Industry in the United States," by the National Travel and Tourism Awareness Council, 1992.
2. Peter Nelson, "The Challenge of the International Marketplace," *HSMAI Marketing Review,* Spring 1991, p. 8.
3. Some of the facts and figures in this section were taken from two publications by the American Hotel & Motel Association: *The Care and Feeding of Guests from Abroad,* and *The World is Your Market.*
4. "Accommodating the Handicapped Traveler," Information Kit 280, compiled by the American Hotel & Motel Association's Information Center.
5. From "Accommodating the Handicapped Traveler."
6. Bill Masciangelo, "Military Reunions: Today's Hot Market," *HSMAI Marketing Review,* Winter 1992, p. 11.

Key Terms

actual and necessary per diem
adventure honeymoon
Americans with Disabilities
 Act (ADA)
contract per diem
destination wedding

foreign independent travel (FIT)
gateway city
Japanese Assistance Network (JAN)
Language Line Service
straight per diem

Review Questions

1. From what two countries do the majority of international travelers to the United States come?

2. Why is the United States a popular destination for international travelers?

3. What are some typical lodging needs of international travelers? How are lodging properties meeting these needs?

4. What are some ways to find potential international travelers?

5. What percentage of honeymooners use the services of a travel agent?

6. What are some ways to find honeymoon business?

7. What are several key needs of professional football teams?

8. What is a straight per diem?

9. What are three main divisions of disabled travelers?

10. How are properties attempting to meet the needs of disabled travelers?

Appendix

Sample Sales Presentation

The following is a simplified example of a sales presentation. Evaluate the salesperson's presentation and answer the questions at the end of the presentation.

Sales Situation

The Regency Hotel is attempting to book the annual meeting of the Business and Professional Women's Association. A member of the association is planning the meeting and investigating possible meeting sites; a committee will make the final selection decision. The annual meeting will be over a three-day period: a Friday through Sunday in May of next year.

Profile of the Hotel

The Regency Hotel is a high-rise, mid-priced full-service hotel. Guest accommodations are divided into 300 standard guestrooms and 40 suites, all opening onto a central atrium. The hotel is situated on land which borders the largest river in the state. The location is halfway between the airport and the downtown business district, conveniently near a freeway exit.

Food and beverage facilities include a gourmet steak and seafood restaurant, a coffee shop, an atrium lounge, banquet service for up to 500 people, and 24-hour room service. Security features include electronic door locks for guestrooms and an attached parking garage with continuous video monitoring on each level.

All guestrooms have desks, areas suitable for dining, and separate sitting areas. There are phones on the desks as well as next to the beds. Bathrooms feature hair dryers, vanities, makeup mirrors, large towels, and a package of name-brand personal amenities (soap, shampoo, and so on). Every room has skirt hangers, a mini-bar, and a coffee machine. A free local newspaper is left at the door every morning. Suites have the same features as the guestrooms in addition to kitchenettes and separate bedrooms.

The hotel's primary market on weekdays is the business traveler, with families the primary market on weekends. Average occupancy runs 75% on weekdays and 52% on weekends. Average guestroom rate is $78.

Profile of the Prospect

The meeting planner is Ms. Penny Planner. She has been with the association for three years and has handled this meeting for the last two. Initial knowledge of the group came from Ms. Carol Law, the hotel's consulting lawyer and a member of the subject association. During a break in a recent hotel staff meeting, Ms. Law mentioned the upcoming annual meeting of this association to the hotel's marketing director. The marketing director asked a salesperson on the staff, Mr. Sam Salesperson, to investigate the possibilities.

Mr. Salesperson obtained background information about the association and asked Ms. Law about the location of previous meetings, the key personnel involved, and specific problems encountered in previous meetings. His prospect research revealed the following.

Locations of the last two annual meetings:

1. Last year—upstate mountain resort. Time of year—April. Major problems: (1) poor weather limited use of outside recreational facilities—few alternative activities available due to remote location; (2) difficult to understand speakers due to noise and poor acoustics; and (3) slow management response to problems.

2. Two years ago—downtown hotel in the same city as the Regency. Time of year—May. Major problems: (1) mediocre service by employees; and (2) noisy guestrooms (airport nearby) and meeting/banquet rooms (noise from kitchen).

Size of meetings—approximately 200 attendees.

Pre-Presentation Planning

Mr. Salesperson sent a letter and a hotel brochure to Ms. Planner, requesting a meeting to discuss the possibility of using the Regency for the association's annual meeting. He followed up the letter with a phone call to set the date and time for Ms. Planner to visit the property.

He did the following before Ms. Planner's tour of the property:

1. Had his secretary call Ms. Planner's secretary to ask about Ms. Planner's travel schedule and what other properties she might be considering.

2. Sent a memo to all department heads explaining that Ms. Planner would be doing a walk-through on Thursday afternoon and requesting that the word be passed on.

3. Prepared a worksheet which listed the property's features and how they could benefit the prospect.

4. Studied the rooms forecast and budget for May and discussed negotiation limits on price concessions with the marketing director.

5. Contacted the convention service manager, Ms. Sally Service, and asked her to:

   a. Be available for the tour and presentation.

   b. Schedule the sales interview in her office and have refreshments on hand

   c. Set up a typical schoolroom configuration for 50 people in one of the meeting rooms.

    d. Set up audiovisual equipment in the banquet room with a videotape showing various table arrangements and decorations used in the banquet room by past groups

6. Familiarized himself with what was currently in-house in terms of functions so he would know what rooms were available to show.
7. Had the front desk hold keys to specific guestrooms and suites.
8. Set up a signboard in the lobby to welcome Ms. Planner.
9. Had the hotel limousine pick up Ms. Planner at the airport.

Sales Call Objective

    To obtain a commitment from Ms. Planner to recommend the Regency Hotel to the association's selection committee.

Sales Presentation

SALESPERSON: [Meets Planner in the lobby, extends hand and smiles.] Good afternoon, Ms. Planner. I'm Sam Salesperson, the sales manager for the Regency Hotel.

PLANNER: [Accepts handshake with a solemn look on her face.] Hello. Nice to meet you.

SALESPERSON: If you'll come with me, I'd like to show you our Convention Service office. [Escorts Planner to the service manager's office.] Ms. Planner, I'd like you to meet Sally Service. She's the convention service manager who would coordinate the activities for your meeting. Sally, this is Ms. Penny Planner. [Planner and Service shake hands and smile.]

PLANNER: How do you do?

SERVICE: Pleased to meet you. May I offer you something to drink? [Indicates the refreshment table.]

PLANNER: No, thank you.

SERVICE: Then please have a seat. [Gestures to the appropriate chair. Planner and Service are seated in easy chairs next to each other, with Salesperson seated facing them. In the middle is a small, low table to provide a platform for drinks and the presentation handbook.]

SALESPERSON: Ms. Planner, I'd like to begin by briefly explaining the concept of a service manager as we use it at the Regency Hotel. When we book an important meeting such as yours, we always assign one of our service managers to be the primary contact for the meeting planner and key meeting members. Sally will be available to you for coordination and problem-solving from the time we sign the contract until the meeting is satisfactorily concluded. We've been quite responsive to groups such as yours in the past with this system, and I'm sure you'd be pleased with us. [Confident smile.] If I may, I'd like to ask you a few questions about your meeting to be sure we understand your requirements.

PLANNER: Okay.

SALESPERSON: First, what are the exact dates of your meeting?

PLANNER: May 2nd through the 4th, next year. [Service begins taking notes.]

SALESPERSON: And what are the primary services you'll require?

PLANNER: We'll need a banquet hall capable of handling 200 persons comfortably for a sit-down dinner. And we'll need a podium and excellent audio capability for our guest speaker. We'll need at last four smaller rooms big enough for 30 to 75 people, with audiovisual capabilities in each room. In addition to the sit-down dinner, we'd like to have a buffet arrangement two or three times during our stay.

SALESPERSON: [Thinks, "So far, so good."] We can meet those requirements easily. In addition to our excellent guestrooms, we have many suites available. How many of those would you want us to block?

PLANNER: We'll need anywhere from 5 to 20 suites, depending on the response from our more prominent members. Can you handle that many?

SALESPERSON: [Smiles.] Definitely. We have 40 suites.

PLANNER: [Smiles—finally.] I don't think we'll need that many.

SALESPERSON: Would you mind telling us if your group has had any problems with meetings in the past?

PLANNER: Not at all. We had a few problems come up last year, and I found it difficult to get the hotel's management to respond quickly to them. I was also quite disappointed with the acoustics in the meeting rooms. Another problem in recent years has been the weather. Our attendees like to relax, swim, and sun during their free time, but it seems to always rain on the dates of our meetings. Obviously that's not the hotel's fault; but you asked about our past problems.

SALESPERSON: I'm sure you'll find that none of those problems will arise this year in our hotel. If I may, I'd like to give you a tour and show you some of our guestrooms and meeting facilities. Shall we? [Rises from his chair and starts towards the door, with a gesture for Planner and Service to follow.]

PLANNER: [Rises to join Salesperson.] I'd like that. [Tour begins with a walk through the atrium area, past the restaurant entrances.]

SALESPERSON: We're very proud of our atrium. It brings an outdoors feeling into the hotel, even on days when the weather doesn't allow full use of our beautiful grounds. The atrium lounge always provides a bright and friendly atmosphere. We have two excellent restaurants to choose from. This is the Gourmet Room, which can accommodate over 100 people. And here is our coffee shop, which can handle up to 185 guests. [Opens the banquet room door for Planner to enter.] This is our banquet room. We can comfortably serve as many as 500 people for a dinner such as you will have. For smaller groups, we have movable walls to make the room fit the size of the group more comfortably. Does this room meet the needs of your group?

PLANNER: I think so, but it's hard to picture how it would look all set up.

SALESPERSON: If you'll follow me, I think I can give you a better idea of the different arrangements we've used in the past. We have a demonstration videotape for just that purpose. [Walks over to audiovisual equipment and plays videotape.] Did that help you picture your group in this room?

PLANNER: Yes, it helped considerably.

SALESPERSON: [Walks to the podium.] Let me demonstrate the room's sound characteristics. [Gestures for Planner to join him.] We have controls on the podium for all the lighting and audiovisual functions in the room. And, as you can see, they are clearly marked for identification. Sally will gladly provide instruction for their use to everyone who'll use the podium. [Gestures toward the center of the room.] If you'll move to the center of the room, I'll turn on the audio system. [Turns on the system and speaks into the microphone.] The sound quality is excellent. Don't you agree?

PLANNER: Yes, it's fine.

SALESPERSON: [Turns off the sound system.] Our kitchen is behind those barriers. [Points.] The barriers eliminate the noise from that area. And these walls are all designed to keep out noise from outside the room. Our most recent meeting was by Clingaman Corporation last week. The CEO commended us on the acoustical quality of the room. [Walks toward the exit.] Do you think it will satisfy your group?

PLANNER: [Writes on her notepad.] It seems to be adequate. [The tour continues to a meeting room.]

SALESPERSON: [Enters.] This is one of four meeting rooms which can be adjusted with portable walls to accommodate up to 100 persons. We are the only hotel in the city with this capability. This room is set up for a group of 50, which we estimated you would require. We have a rear-projection room behind each meeting room that's capable of handling all types of projection equipment. [Gestures.] Would you like a demonstration?

PLANNER: That won't be necessary.

SALESPERSON: This meets your requirements also?

PLANNER: Yes.

SALESPERSON: [Exits the room.] Then let's take a look at our guestrooms and suites. [They make their way to a standard guestroom. Salesperson unlocks the door with an electronic key card.] As you can see, we utilize electronic locks which are encoded at the front desk when guests check in. Are you familiar with this security feature? [Planner nods her head.] All our rooms have desks, dining areas, and separate sitting areas for after-meeting work sessions or discussions. [Gestures into the bathroom.] Our bathrooms are luxurious and well-lit, with lots of mirrors for ease in making up. Did you notice that we list free personal amenities in the brochure I sent you?

PLANNER: Yes.

SALESPERSON: We feel this helps our guests plan their packing so they can leave the items they won't need at home and travel lighter. I'm sure your members would value that, aren't you?

PLANNER: Yes. [They exit the room.]

SALESPERSON: [Enters a suite.] Our suites have the same features as the guestrooms, but they also have kitchenettes and separate bedrooms. [Gestures.] All our sleeping rooms are quiet because of good insulation and the fact that we're out of the airport traffic pattern, in spite of our proximity to the airport itself. Do you think this suite would be satisfactory for your VIP members?

PLANNER: I think so.

SALESPERSON: [Exits the suite.] Great! Then let's go back to Sally's office and talk over any questions or concerns you might have. [Salesperson thinks, "This is a piece of cake!"]

SERVICE: [Salesperson, Planner, and Service enter the office.] What do you think of our hotel?

PLANNER: [Noncommittally:] It's very nice.

SERVICE: Are you ready for something to drink yet?

PLANNER: Yes, please. I'd like a caffeine-free Diet Coke if you have one. [Salesperson thinks, "I hope we have that!"]

SERVICE: Of course. Please sit down.

SALESPERSON: [Reviews the notes Service passed to him and allows time for Planner to sip her drink.] Let's review what we have agreed on so far. Our banquet room, meeting rooms, and guestroom accommodations all meet with your approval. So let me briefly tell you about other features of the Regency which I think will also please you. Since most of your members will probably arrive by car, they'll appreciate our location next to the freeway—and our parking garage. The garage is well-lit and is continuously monitored by video cameras on each level. [Short pause.] You mentioned earlier that poor service has been a problem for this group in the past, didn't you?

PLANNER: Yes.

SALESPERSON: I hope I can reassure you on that matter as well. We have an extensive employee training program and continually stress the importance of caring for the needs of our guests. I know that sounds like a standard sales pitch, but we really believe in service at the Regency. If I may again refer to our last group meeting, Mr. Clingaman himself praised our service as the best in the state.

PLANNER: [Writes on her pad.]

SALESPERSON: We have 24-hour room service. We offer savings with our free telephone and message service. In addition, we're prepared to offer your group free shuttle service between the airport and the hotel, for those who need it. And we'll provide free transportation for your members who want to visit the many attractions in town. Sally informs me that the local symphony will be performing during your stay with us, and our baseball team will be hosting the Tigers that weekend. [Pauses to let Planner take notes, then begins flipping through the pages in the presentation notebook, showing Planner 5- by 8-inch color pictures of the hotel's facilities.] We have excellent fitness facilities, including a heated pool, an exercise room, and tennis courts,

PLANNER: and there's a jogging trail in the park next to us. Would you like to see some of our banquet rooms?

PLANNER: [Shows signs of being overwhelmed—or is it fatigue?] No, I'm familiar with your food service.

SALESPERSON: Can I assume then that you've dined with us and have been pleased?

PLANNER: [Smiles—thank heaven!] Yes.

SALESPERSON: Excellent! It sounds like we meet all your requirements. Shall we discuss price then?

PLANNER: Yes, please.

SALESPERSON: Good. [Displays a rate schedule in the presentation notebook.] The rate for our standard rooms is $70 per night. Our sites are $150. To cover overhead costs, we charge $200 per session for the banquet room and $50 for each of the meeting rooms. And, as you are aware, our food prices are quite reasonable. I might add that the Regency is the only hotel in the city that actually charges less than dining room menu prices for the same dinners provided at banquets. Is there any additional information you'd like?

PLANNER: I'm convinced your facilities would meet the association's needs. And your reputation for service is quite good. Frankly, that's the main reason I considered your hotel. But your guestroom prices are considerably higher than hotels I've contacted elsewhere in the state, and they don't charge for their function space. I don't think I can sell the total cost involved to the selection committee.

SALESPERSON: [Knowing the answer:] Do you feel our competitors offer the kind of quality in service and function rooms that we do?

PLANNER: No, you have a clear advantage there. And I'm sure my job would be less stressful if we meet here. But cost is an important factor to the association because of its limited budget.

SALESPERSON: I'm afraid our room rates are firm; I just can't adjust that area. If we forfeited the charge for the function space, would you commit to us?

PLANNER: That would help. But isn't there something else you could do as a show of good faith to help me sell the Regency to the committee? [Pause.] How about providing a free cocktail hour on the opening day? I think that would convince them.

SALESPERSON: Fine, if you will commit to us that the Regency will be your only recommendation to the committee.

PLANNER: Agreed. [Smiles and extends her hand to consummate the deal.]

SALESPERSON: [Accepts the handshake and smiles in return.] Great! I'll send you a letter tomorrow summarizing what we've agreed to today.

Review Questions

1. What did the salesperson do correctly? Was anything done incorrectly?

2. Do you think it was a good idea to have the convention service manager sit in on the presentation?

3. Can you point out in the presentation examples of the following?

    a. Open- and close-ended questions

    b. Fact- and feeling-finding questions

    c. Test closes

    d. Objections

    e. Third-party endorsements

    f. Major close

4. Would you make any changes in the presentation? If so, what changes would you make?

Glossary

A

ACCOUNT FILE

A standard-size file folder holding information needed for serving a client's basic business needs.

ACTUAL AND NECESSARY PER DIEM

The maximum amount a government employee can spend regardless of location; usually equal to or greater than the straight per diem rate.

ADVANCE DEPOSIT

A deposit the guest furnishes for a room reservation that the hotel is holding.

ADVERTISING AGENCY

A company that furnishes advertising and marketing services to clients. Ad agencies may be paid by a commission from the media or a predetermined fee from the client.

ADVERTISING RESPONSE TRACKING (ART)

A service offered by some telephone companies that channels calls to a business's regular number when a "dummy" number published in an ad is dialed. The calls placed with the dummy number are counted, providing the business with an accurate picture of how well the ad generated responses.

ADVERTORIAL

A combination of an advertisement and an editorial statement, written by the advertiser, that looks more like a news story than an advertisement.

AFFILIATED HOTEL

One of a chain, franchise, or referral system, membership in which provides special advantages, particularly a national reservation system.

AFFORDABLE-FUNDS BUDGET

A budget that allocates funds based not on need but on whatever is left over after bills have been paid and the owner's profit requirements and other obligations have been met.

AGENCY COMMISSION

A commission media pay to an advertising agency. It is expressed as a percentage (usually 15%) of the gross advertising rate.

AGENCY FEE

A dollar amount agreed upon, in advance, by the agency and client that compensates the agency for all services in lieu of commission.

AIDA

An acronym for *attention, interest, desire,* and *action,* which is a formula used by marketers to catch customers' attention, get them interested, create a desire to buy, and generate action.

AIRLINE TOUR

A tour whose primary mode of transportation is by airplane.

AIRPORT HOTEL

A hotel located near a public airport. Airport hotels vary widely in size and service level.

À LA CARTE

A term that describes meal items priced separately on the menu.

À LA CARTE AD AGENCY

A full-service advertising agency that offers selected services on a negotiated fee basis. Also known as a "modular service."

ALL-EXPENSE TOUR

A tour offering all or most services—transportation, lodging, meals, sight-seeing, and so on—for a pre-established price. The terms "all-expense" and "all-inclusive" are much misused. Virtually no tour rate covers everything. The terms and conditions of a tour contract should specify exactly what is covered.

ALL-SUITE HOTEL

A hotel that features rooms larger than typical guestrooms, with a living or working space separate from the bedroom(s). Suites may also include kitchenettes.

ALTERNATIVE-MEDIA ADVERTISING

Advertising outlets such as movie theaters, ballparks, hot air balloons, inserts in billings, and so on.

AMERICAN HOTEL & MOTEL ASSOCIATION (AH&MA)

A federation of state and regional hotel associations that offers benefits and services to hospitality properties and suppliers. AH&MA reviews proposed legislation affecting hotels, sponsors seminars and group study programs, conducts research, and publishes *Lodging Magazine.* The Educational Institute of AH&MA is the world's largest developer of hospitality industry training materials, including textbooks, videotapes, courses, and software.

AMERICAN PLAN

A room rate that includes three meals.

AMERICAN SOCIETY OF TRAVEL AGENTS (ASTA)

A trade association of travel agents, tour operators, and suppliers to the industry with worldwide membership exceeding 22,000. ASTA's purpose is to promote and advance the interests of the travel agency industry and safeguard the traveling public against unethical practices.

AMERICANS WITH DISABILITIES ACT (ADA)

Legislation passed by the U.S. Congress in 1990, parts of which took effect in January and July, 1992. This act requires commercial operations to remove barriers to the disabled in the workplace and provide facilities for customers with disabilities.

AMTRAK

The name under which the National Railroad Passenger Corporation operates almost all U.S. intercity passenger trains. The intercity trains are usually operated under contract with individual railroads.

AMTRAK TOUR

A rail tour in the United States.

ANIMATED AD

A television ad in which cartoons, puppets, or an animated demonstration is used.

APPOINTMENT CALL (PERSONAL)

Used to introduce a prospective client to the features and services offered by the property, during which the salesperson may or may not attempt to close the sale.

APPOINTMENT CALL (TELEPHONE)

A telephone call made by a salesperson or other representative of a business to briefly introduce a prospect to features and services offered by the business and ask for an appointment to meet face to face.

ATTRACTION

A natural or constructed facility, location, or activity that offers items of specific interest, such as a natural or scenic wonder, a theme park, a cultural or historic exhibition, or a wildlife / ecological park.

AUDIENCE

A group of households or individuals who listen to, view, or read a communications medium.

AUDIENCE PROFILE

A description of the characteristics (sex, age, income, etc.) of individuals or households exposed to a medium. May also refer to the minute-by-minute viewing pattern of a television or radio program.

AUDIMETER

An electronic device attached to TV or radio sets in the sample households of A.C. Nielsen. It records set usage and channel information on a minute-by-minute basis, 24 hours a day.

B

BACKLIGHTING
In billboard advertising, a display board in which the lighting makes the background of the display board "disappear."

BACK OF THE HOUSE
The functional areas of a hotel in which personnel have little or no direct guest contact, such as engineering and accounting.

BANQUET
A formal dinner for a select group.

BANQUET CONTRACT
The form used between hotel and client to confirm banquet arrangements.

BANQUET EVENT ORDER (BEO)
A form that serves as a final contract for the client and serves as a work order for the catering department. Also called a function sheet or banquet prospectus.

BANQUET SETUP
A meal-function setup that generally uses round tables.

BEST-TIME-AVAILABLE PLAN (BTA)
A type of weekly plan for buying radio airtime in which the times the property's ad is aired are chosen by the station. The ad may run at the same time each day, or run as time is available.

BILLBOARD
A large panel designed to carry outdoor advertising.

BINGO CARD
A magazine insert that has numbers that correspond to the numbers assigned to the magazine's advertisements; a reader who wants more information circles the numbers of the ads he or she is interested in.

BLEED AD
An advertisement that runs all the way to the edge of the page(s), leaving no margin.

BOARD-OF-DIRECTORS SETUP
A meeting room setup that calls for a single column of double tables, with seating all the way around.

BODY LANGUAGE
Signals sent from a person's face, arms, hands, legs, and posture that indicate his or her thoughts or mood.

BOOK

To sell hotel space, either to an individual or to a group needing a block of rooms.

BOTTOM-UP METHOD

An upgrading technique used when a guest has already made a reservation or has requested a low-priced guestroom. The front desk or reservations agent simply suggests extra amenities or the merits of a more expensive room, without pressuring the guest.

BREAKOUT MEETING

A meeting that supplements a convention or larger meeting.

BROADCAST ADVERTISING

Advertisements displayed by means of electronics. Includes radio, television, video, and computer-generated graphic ads.

BROCHURE

A printed folder containing descriptive or advertising material.

BUFFET

An assortment of foods offered on a table in self-service fashion.

BUFFET SERVICE

A service style in which hot and cold foods are attractively displayed, and guests help themselves.

BULK OR ANNUAL RATE

A method of buying radio airtime in which a property that runs 250 or more ads a year can purchase airtime for an entire year at a very low rate.

BULLETIN

A type of billboard advertising that is hand-painted directly on the display boards on site, or may be created in the billboard company's studios and then transported to the site and put up on the display board in sections.

BUS

In the travel industry the word "bus" is reserved for a vehicle that provides scheduled service for an individually ticketed passenger. When used to perform any group tour service, the same vehicle is called a motorcoach.

BUSINESS LIST

A type of mailing list that contains the addresses of businesses.

BUTLER-STYLE SERVICE

A service style in which hors d'oeuvres are placed on platters and circulated among guests by servers.

C

CALL REPORT

A document that provides general information about an account (address, contact person, etc.) as well as remarks on the needs of the group and action steps that can be taken to sell the hotel's products and services to the group.

CANCELLATION

A reservation voided at the guest's request.

CASH BAR

A beverage plan for a banquet or other function in which guests pay cash to the bartender who prepares their drinks. Sometimes called a COD bar or an à la carte bar.

CASINO HOTEL

A hotel with gambling facilities.

CENTRAL RESERVATIONS SYSTEM

Part of an affiliate reservation network. A central reservations system typically deals directly with the public, advertises a central (usually toll-free) telephone number, provides participating properties with necessary communications equipment, and bills properties for handling reservations.

CHANNELS OF DISTRIBUTION

The methods by which sellers reach potential buyers. Travel agents, tour operators, and tour wholesalers are part of this system within the tourism industry.

CHARTER

To hire the exclusive use of any aircraft, vessel, or other vehicle.

CIRCULATION

Broadcast advertising: The number of set-owning homes within the station's coverage area. *Outdoor advertising:* The number of people passing an advertisement with an opportunity to view it. *Print advertising:* The number of copies sold or distributed by the publication.

CLOSE-ENDED QUESTION

A question requiring a specific answer that often can be given in just a few words.

COLD CALL

A fact-finding or exploratory call on a prospect with whom there has been little or no previous contact.

COLLATERAL ADVERTISING

Printed material used to advertise products and services, including brochures, folders, posters, fliers, tent cards; and specialty items such as key chains and shoe horns.

COLLATERAL MATERIAL

Printed items (such as fliers, tent cards, and brochures) and specialty items (matchbooks, key chains, etc.) that advertise a business.

COMMERCIAL HOTEL

A property, usually located in a downtown or business district, that caters primarily to business clients. Also called a transient hotel.

COMMERCIAL LIST

A type of mailing list available through commercial mailing list brokers and compilers. Commercial lists are generally rented rather than purchased and are categorized as resident lists, consumer lists, or business lists.

COMMERCIAL RATE

A special room rate, lower than rack rate, agreed upon by a hotel and a company. Also called a corporate rate.

COMMISSIONABLE RATE

The special rate a hotel or other facility quotes, from which travel agents may deduct a commission or upon which the hotel or facility will pay a commission.

COMPETITION ANALYSIS

An evaluation of a business's competition to identify opportunities and unique selling points. Part of a marketing audit.

COMPETITIVE-PARITY BUDGET

A budget based on what the competition is spending; the goal of planners setting up a competitive-parity budget is to approximately match the expenditures of competitors.

COMPLIMENTARY ROOM

A complimentary or "comp" room is a room that is occupied, but the guest is not charged for its use. A hotel may offer comp rooms to a group in ratio to the total number of rooms the group occupies. One comp room may be offered for each fifty rooms occupied, for example.

CONCIERGE

An employee whose task is to serve as the guest's liaison with hotel and non-hotel attractions, facilities, services, and activities.

CONDUCTED TOUR

(1) A pre-arranged travel program, usually for a group, which includes escort service; (2) a sight-seeing program conducted by a guide, such as a city tour. Also called an escorted tour.

CONFERENCE CENTER

A property specifically designed to handle group meetings. Conference centers are often located outside metropolitan areas and may provide extensive leisure facilities. Most offer overnight accommodations.

CONFIRMED RESERVATION

An oral or written statement by a supplier (a carrier, hotel, car rental company, etc.) that he or she has received and will honor a reservation. Oral confirmations have virtually no legal worth. Even written or telegraphed confirmations have specified or implied limitations. For example, a hotel is not obligated to honor a confirmed reservation if the guest arrives after 6 P.M., unless late arrival is specified.

CONSISTENCY

In advertising, refers to the design of advertising messages so that they have a similar look or sound, for easier audience recognition and greater cumulative impact.

CONSUMER LIST

A type of mailing list that is compiled from records of consumer purchases or inquiries for products or services.

CONSUMER MAGAZINE

A publication designed to appeal to the general consumer market, in contrast to a trade magazine.

CONTINENTAL BREAKFAST

A small morning meal that usually includes a beverage, rolls, butter, and jam or marmalade.

CONTINENTAL PLAN

A room rate that includes continental breakfast.

CONTINUITY

An advertising pattern in which ads are distributed evenly over a given time period.

CONTRACT PER DIEM

Incorporates the total cost of accommodations, meals, gratuities, travel expenses, and so on.

COOPERATIVE ADVERTISING

A pooling of marketing dollars by several businesses for promotional purposes in order to increase market impact or reduce marketing costs.

COST PER INQUIRY (CPI)

The cost of advertising based on the number of inquiries the advertising generates.

COST PER THOUSAND (CPM)

The cost of reaching 1,000 households or individuals.

COST-PLUS TRAVELER

An extremely cost-conscious traveler who values no-cost amenities and tends to be sociable.

COVERAGE

The homes that a broadcast station's signal can reach. Also refers to the number of individuals or groups exposed to a specific medium or advertisement within a specific period of time.

COVERS

The actual number of meals served at a food function.

CREATIVE SHOP OR BOUTIQUE

An independent advertising agency that designs and produces ads on a free-lance, per-job basis.

CROSS-SELLING

In internal merchandising, cross-selling is using media in one area of the property to promote a different area. Employees can also cross-sell: employees working at one facility can suggest that guests take advantage of other facilities and services offered at the property.

CRT (CATHODE RAY TUBE)

A computer system's output device, which is usually capable of displaying both text and graphics. Also called a monitor, a display screen, or simply a screen.

CUTOUT

A type of billboard advertising in which part of the illustration extends beyond the display board itself.

D

DEMONSTRATION AD

A type of television ad in which products or services may be shown in use, competing with another product or service, or in before-and-after situations.

DESTINATION

In the travel industry, any city, area, or country that can be marketed as a single entity to tourists.

DESTINATION WEDDING

A wedding held at the honeymoon site.

DIFFERENTIATION

A marketing strategy designed to emphasize the unique selling points of a business and the differences between that business and its competitors.

DIRECT FLIGHT

A journey on which the passenger does not have to change planes. Not necessarily non-stop.

DIRECT MAIL ADVERTISING
Print advertising sent directly to target markets via the mail.

DIRECTOR
An assertive person interested in getting results quickly. One of four personality types of buyers.

DISCOUNTING
Marking down the normal room rates by some percentage or dollar amount. Discounts are usually directed toward particular markets or are instituted during a particular time or season.

DISPLAY ADVERTISING
Advertising on posters displayed (1) inside or outside vehicles such as buses, subway cars, and taxis; (2) at trade shows; and (3) in transportation terminals.

DONUT AD
Prerecorded 30- or 60-second radio ads that leave room for an individual property's message.

DOUBLE CALLING
Making sales calls with two salespeople—usually a new salesperson accompanied by a more experienced salesperson.

DOUBLE OCCUPANCY RATE
A rate used for tours where the per-person charge is based on two to a room.

DOUBLE-PAGE SPREAD
Two facing pages used for a single, unbroken ad—the largest regular portion of ad space sold in a magazine. Also called the center spread if it occurs at the center of the magazine.

DRIVE TIME
The 6:00 to 10:00 A.M. and 3:00 to 7:00 P.M. time periods during which radio listenership is highest and the most money can be charged for airtime.

DUBS
Duplicate tapes of a master audio or video tape.

E

ECOTOURISM
Tourism that promotes enjoyment of nature (without harming the environment), and may include efforts to protect or preserve the visited region.

EMPLOYEE EMPOWERMENT
A program or philosophy that gives employees the authority to make on-the-spot decisions to respond to guest needs—decisions that were previously relegated to those higher in authority.

ENVIRONMENTAL SCANNING

The analysis of trends and factors that will affect a hospitality firm's marketing efforts.

ESCORT

A person, usually employed by a tour operator, who accompanies a tour from departure to return and serves as guide, trouble-shooter, etc.

EUROPEAN PLAN

A room rate that does not include any meals.

EXECUTIVE FLOOR

A hotel floor that features exceptional service to business and other travelers. Also called a business floor or the tower concept.

EXTROVERTED-AFFLUENT TRAVELER

A traveler who is typically young, affluent, and either self-employed, a top-level executive, or a professional. These travelers are not concerned with saving money and favor fashionable properties with lots of amenities.

F

FAIR SHARE

The amount of room nights a property would sell if demand were distributed based on the number of rooms in each property.

FAMILIARIZATION (FAM) TOUR

A complimentary or reduced-rate travel program. A familiarization or "fam" tour is designed to acquaint travel agents, meeting planners, travel writers, and others with a property or destination in order to stimulate sales.

FAMILY RATE

A special room rate for parents and children in the same guestroom.

FEEDER CITY

A city other than the property's city from which guests arrive.

FIXED PLAN

A method of buying billboard advertising space (usually a painted display) in which the ad remains in one location for the entire term of the advertiser's contract.

FIXED POSITION SPOT

A method of buying radio airtime in which a property's message is run in a specific time slot every day over the contract period. This is usually the most expensive way to buy radio airtime.

FLAT RATE

A specific room rate for a group, agreed upon by the hotel and the group in advance. Also called "run-of-the-house rate."

FLIER
A printed advertisement intended for distribution to potential clients or guests, usually by mail.

FLIGHTING
An advertising pattern in which ads are distributed on an as-needed basis over a given time period.

FOLIO
A statement of all transactions affecting the balance of a single account.

FORCED-CHOICE QUESTION
A question that limits an individual to choosing from the alternatives presented by the questioner.

FORECAST
A future projection of estimated business volume.

FOREIGN INDEPENDENT TRAVEL (FIT)
A custom-designed prepaid tour arranged by a travel agent for individual travelers traveling in foreign countries.

FREQUENCY
A measure of how many times the average person in a target market is exposed to an advertising message over a specified time period.

FRONT DESK
The focal point of activity within the hotel, usually prominently located in the hotel lobby. Guests are registered, assigned rooms, and checked out at the front desk.

FRONT DESK AGENT
A hotel employee whose responsibilities center on the registration process, but also typically include preregistration activities, room status coordination, and mail, message, and information requests.

FRONT OF THE HOUSE
The functional areas of the hotel in which employees have extensive guest contact, such as food and beverage facilities and the front office.

FULL POSITION
Newspaper ad space at the top of a page alongside reading matter.

FULL-SERVICE AD AGENCY
An advertising agency that offers clients complete advertising services, including planning, creating, producing, and placing ads as well as sales promotion and research.

FUNCTION BOOK
The master control of all banquet space, broken down on each page by banquet rooms and restaurants, with a page for each day of the year.

G

GATEFOLD

Oversized page or portion of a page added to a regular magazine page.

GATEWAY CITY

A city with an airport that handles direct flights from other countries.

GENERAL LIST

A type of mailing list that is not purchased or rented, but compiled from business and government directories, telephone books, or membership rosters of associations.

GLOBALIZATION

The international consolidation of big business and the growing trend for countries to allow the free transfer of goods and services across national borders.

GOVERNMENT RATE

A special room rate made available at some properties for government employees.

GROSS RATING POINTS (GRP)

A measurement for examining the relationship between reach and frequency. A GRP is the rating (reach) a program achieves, multiplied by the number of times the ad is run (frequency).

GROUND OPERATOR

A company or individual providing such travel services as booking hotel accommodations, arranging sight-seeing tours, arranging transfers, and other related services, exclusive of transportation to and from a given destination. Sometimes called a purveyor.

GROUP RATE

A special room rate for a number of affiliated guests.

GROUP SALES ALLOTMENT

The number of rooms a lodging property sets aside for group and tour business.

GUARANTEE CLAUSE

A clause in a banquet event order or contract in which the client gives the hotel (usually 72 hours in advance of the banquet) a count of the number of persons to be served. Payment is made on the basis of the guaranteed number or the total number actually served, whichever is greater.

GUARANTEED RESERVATION

A reservation that assures the guest that a room will be held until check-out time of the day following the day of arrival. The guest guarantees payment for the room, even if it is not used, unless the reservation is properly canceled. Types of guaranteed reservations include prepayment, credit card, advance deposit, travel agent, and corporate.

GUEST HISTORY CARD

A record of the guest's visits including rooms assigned, rates, special needs, and credit rating.

GUEST MIX

The variety and percentage distribution of hotel guests: individual, group, business, leisure, etc.

GUEST PROFILE

Data portraying significant facts and preferences of previous guests.

GUESTROOM CONTROL BOOK

A book used to monitor the number of guestrooms committed to groups.

GUTTER

The inside portion of a newspaper or magazine where two pages meet.

H

HERRINGBONE SETUP

A meeting room setup in which tables are lined up in rows (one behind the other) on each side of a center aisle; there are usually three or four chairs per table. The tables and chairs face the head table, stage, or speaker's podium at an approximately 45-degree angle.

HOLLOW-SQUARE SETUP

A meeting room setup in which a series of tables forms a square with a hollow middle; chairs are placed around the outside.

HOLOGRAPHY

A visual technique that produces a projected three-dimensional image.

HORIZONTAL CO-OP ADVERTISING

Advertising shared by similar businesses.

HOSPITALITY SALES & MARKETING ASSOCIATION INTERNATIONAL (HSMAI)

A professional society of hotel salespeople, managers, owners, and other sales-minded hotel executives, dedicated to the further education of its members. HSMAI conducts seminars, clinics, workshops, and an annual convention, and publishes a quarterly magazine, *HSMAI Marketing Review,* as well as books and pamphlets on hospitality sales.

HOST BAR

A beverage plan for a banquet or other function in which guests do not pay for drinks; rather, the host is charged, either by the drink or by the bottle. Sometimes called a sponsored bar.

HOTEL REPRESENTATIVE

An individual who offers hotel reservations to wholesalers, travel agents, and the public. A hotel representative or "rep" may be paid by the hotels he or she represents on a fee basis or by commission. Many hotel reps also offer marketing and other services.

HOUSE LIST

A type of mailing list prepared by a hotel that consists of the names and addresses of its previous guests.

HOUSEHOLDS USING TELEVISION (HUT)

A measure of the percent of homes with the television on during a particular hour (viewership of particular programs is not measured).

I

INCENTIVE TRAVEL

Travel financed by a business as an employee incentive.

INCLUSIVE TOUR

A tour in which specific elements—air fare, hotels, transfers, etc.—are included for a flat rate. An inclusive tour rate does not necessarily cover all costs.

INDEPENDENT HOTEL

A hotel with no chain or franchise affiliation, although one proprietor might own several such properties.

INDEPENDENT MOTELS OF AMERICA, INC.

A network of more than 130 independently owned motels and inns, which publishes a directory of its members.

INFLATABLE

A design element made of heavyweight nylon that adds a three-dimensional effect to billboard advertising.

IN-HOUSE PROMOTION

The use of contests, special events, giveaways, and creative activities to stimulate sales and encourage guest satisfaction and repeat or referral business.

INQUIRY PACKET

A hospitality firm's response to a prospect's request for information. An inquiry packet should include a cover letter, printed literature, and a means for the prospect to request additional information.

IN-ROOM REFRESHMENT CENTER

A small refrigerator or cabinet in the guestroom that holds beverages and snack items. Also called a minibar.

INSERT

An advertisement, reply card, or other material inserted between the pages of a magazine. An insert can be bound into the magazine or merely placed between its pages.

INSIDE SALES CALL

A sales presentation made to walk-ins inquiring about the property.

INTERMODAL TOUR

A tour that involves more than one form of transportation (air-motorcoach, for example).

INTERNAL MARKETING

A concept that sees employees as "customers" that must be sold on the property they work for and their importance to its success.

INTERNAL MERCHANDISING

The use of such promotional items as tent cards, posters, and directories to promote a property's facilities and services on-site.

INTERNAL SALES

Specific sales activities engaged in by various employees of a property, in conjunction with a program of internal merchandising, to promote additional sales and guest satisfaction.

INTIMATE SPACE

An area within two feet (arm's length) of an individual.

J–L

JAPANESE ASSISTANCE NETWORK (JAN)

A service that provides Japanese translation via telephone for business and leisure travelers.

KINETIC BOARD

Billboard advertising that uses moving two- or four-sided panels to provide rotating messages.

LANGUAGE LINE SERVICE

A service provided by AT&T that links guests via telephone to interpreters fluent in more than 140 languages.

LETTER OF AGREEMENT

A document listing services, space, and products that becomes binding when signed by both parties.

LETTERSHOP

A business that for a fee will perform mailing chores such as stuffing envelopes, sorting mail, and metering and mailing letters or other mail.

LIFESTYLE AD

An ad that focuses on the consumers of a product or service rather than on the product or service itself.

LIST BROKER

Someone knowledgeable about mailing lists who brings buyers and sellers together.

LOCAL RATE

A rate the media offer to local advertisers that is lower than the national rate.

LOGO

The name of a company or product in a special design used as a trademark.

M

MAILING LIST

A list of the names, addresses, and, in some cases, titles of persons to be reached by direct mail. It can be a commercial, general, or house list.

MAJOR CLOSE

A question or statement at the end of a sales presentation that asks for the sale.

MARKET

A geographic area defined by media coverage or sales patterns. Also refers to a population group that has purchasing power and is a prime prospect for an advertiser's product or service.

MARKET RESEARCH

The use of various techniques to obtain data on past and potential customers or guests. Used by a business to improve its marketing effectiveness.

MARKET SEGMENTATION

Dividing the market into groups of consumers with similar needs, wants, backgrounds, incomes, buying habits, and so on.

MARKET SHARE

The amount of room nights a property sells compared with the total number of room nights within a market area.

MARKETING

A system of interacting activities formulated to plan, price, promote, and make available services or products to potential customers or guests in a particular target market.

MARKETING AUDIT

A systematic and comprehensive evaluation of a business, its competition, and the marketplace.

MARKETING MIX

The combination of the four "Ps" of marketing—product, price, place, and promotion—that is used to achieve marketing objectives for a target market.

MARKETING PLAN

A guide for marketing, sales, advertising, and promotional efforts.

MARKETPLACE ANALYSIS

An evaluation of the environmental trends and forces affecting a business, such as changes in lifestyles and societal values, economic conditions, and technology. Part of a situation analysis.

MASTER ACCOUNT

One folio prepared for a group on which all group charges are accumulated. Also called a master folio.

MASTER CARD

An index card that contains a summary of everything needed for a sales effort, including the organization's name, the decision-maker(s), key contacts, addresses, telephone numbers, and so on.

MASTER TAPE

An audio or video tape on which the music, sound effects, vocals, and so on have been mixed together to create the final finished product.

MEDIA-BUYING SERVICE

A type of advertising agency that specializes in buying radio and television time. A media-buying service does not offer creative services.

MEDIA CLUTTER

The proliferation of advertising in a medium, which tends to reduce the impact of any single ad.

MEDIA OUTLET

An individual newspaper, radio station, television station, magazine, directory, and so on, where advertising can be placed.

MEETING PLANNER

An employee who makes travel and other arrangements for corporate or association meetings.

MODIFIED AMERICAN PLAN

A room rate that includes two meals—typically breakfast and dinner.

MONTHLY PLAN

A method of buying radio airtime in which a property is charged a flat rate for a fixed number of ads, no matter what time slot is selected.

MOTORCOACH

A large highway passenger vehicle used to perform any travel service other than scheduled transportation for individually ticketed passengers. Contains such passenger comfort items as climate control, carpeting, reclining seats, pillow service, etc.

MOTORCOACH CHARTER

A group of people traveling together who select a destination and then contact a motorcoach company to charter or rent a bus to take them to their destination.

MOTORCOACH TOUR

A tour whose primary mode of transportation is by motorcoach or bus.

MULTIPLE-PAGE AD

A magazine ad that appears on three or more pages of the same issue—in direct succession, on alternate pages, or at random.

MUSICAL AD

A broadcast ad that relies heavily on a jingle or musical background to promote a product or service.

N–O

NATIONAL TOUR ASSOCIATION

A trade association of U.S. motorcoach operators federally licensed and bonded by the Interstate Commerce Commission with the purpose of promoting member professionalism and motorcoach tour development.

NEWS RELEASE

A news story about a special event or other interesting item that a business sends to the news media in hopes that it will generate a favorable article, interview, or photograph.

NO-FRILLS TRAVELER

Typically a middle- to upper-management businessperson who only wants a clean, comfortable, and quiet room at a fair price, with little interest in socializing.

NO-SHOW
(1) A passenger or guest who fails either to use or to cancel his or her reservation. (2) A reservation neither canceled nor fulfilled.

OCCUPANCY AND ACTIVITY ANALYSIS
An analysis of a property's past, present, and potential operating statistics. Part of a situation analysis.

OCCUPANT LIST
A type of mailing list that supplies the addresses but not the names of residents.

OPEN-ENDED QUESTION
A question that gives individuals an opportunity to express their feelings and knowledge.

OPTION DATE
The pre-arranged date by which a tentative agreement between a buyer and seller must become a definite agreement or become void.

OUTDOOR ADVERTISING
A business's sign, billboards, and other methods used outdoors to put the business's name and image before the public.

OVERBOOKING
Committing more rooms than are actually available to possible guest occupancy.

OVERSTAY
A guest who stays after his or her stated departure date.

P

PACKAGE
A special offering of products and services created by a hotel to increase sales. There are weekend packages, honeymoon packages, sports packages, and so on. A typical package might include the guestroom, meals, and the use of the property's recreational facilities for a special price.

PACKAGE TOUR
A salable travel product that offers, at an inclusive price, several travel elements that a traveler would otherwise purchase separately. A package tour can include, in varying degrees, any or all of the following elements: lodging; sight-seeing; attractions; meals; entertainment; car rental; and transportation by air, motorcoach, rail, or even private vehicle. A package tour may include more than one destination.

PACKAGER
An individual or organization coordinating and promoting the development of a package tour and establishing operating procedures and guidelines for the tour.

PAINTED DISPLAY

A type of billboard advertising in which the advertising message is painted directly on a wall or display board. A painted display also may be created in the studio and affixed to a display board in sections.

PARTICIPATIONS

A method of buying television airtime in which several advertisers purchase 30- to 60-second spots within a specific program.

PEAK PERIOD

Also known as "in-season," this is the period when demand for a property and its services is highest. Maximum rates may be charged at this time.

PERCENTAGE-OF-SALES BUDGET

A budget based on a percentage of the previous year's sales.

PERSONAL SELLING

A method of securing business through direct personal contact with potential clients or guests.

PERSONAL SPACE

An area two to four feet (.6 to 1.2 meters) from an individual.

PERSONALITY AD

A broadcast ad that relies on the talents or celebrity of the announcer to promote the product.

PLATE SERVICE

A service style in which food is plated in the kitchen, then served to guests.

POINT-OF-PURCHASE MATERIALS

Tent cards, posters, displays, and other materials placed in prominent areas of the hotel to influence buying decisions.

POSITIONING

A marketing term used to describe how consumers perceive the products and services offered by a particular hotel in relation to similar products and services offered by competitors. Positioning strategies attempt to establish in the minds of consumers a particular image of a hotel's products and services.

POSTER

A type of billboard advertising in which sheets are printed with the advertising message and then pasted like wallpaper on display boards.

PREMIUM POSITION BUY

The purchase of a specific position for your newspaper or magazine ad. A premium is paid for this preferred position; otherwise, the ad appears in a run-of-paper position—that is, wherever the publisher decides to place it.

PREREGISTRATION
A process by which sections of a registration card or its equivalent are completed for guests arriving with reservations. Room and rate assignment, creation of a guest folio, and other functions may also be part of preregistration activity.

PRESENTATION CALL
A sales call during which the salesperson presents the features and services offered by the property and attempts to close the sale.

PRE-SET SERVICE
A service style in which the first course is set on the table before guests sit down; in some cases, the dessert may also be pre-set.

PRESS KIT
News releases, fact sheets, photographs, news clippings, and other material, often attractively packaged, designed to give journalists background information about an organization.

PRIME TIME
For television, the period between 7:30 and 11:00 P.M. in which television viewership is highest and the most money can be charged for airtime. For radio, prime time (also called "drive time") includes the 6:00 to 10:00 A.M. and 3:00 to 7:00 P.M. time periods during which radio listenership is highest and the most money can be charged for airtime.

PRINT ADVERTISING
Advertising that appears on the printed page in such media as newspapers, magazines, and directories.

PROBLEM SOLUTION AD
A broadcast ad in which characters discuss a problem and propose the product as the solution. Also called a slice of life ad.

PRODUCT SEGMENTATION
Designing, building, and marketing hospitality products for specific market segments.

PROMOTIONAL CALL
A telephone call made by a salesperson or other representative of a business to introduce special promotions.

PROPERTY ANALYSIS
An evaluation of a business's facilities, services, and programs to determine its strengths and weaknesses. Part of a marketing audit.

PROPERTY INFORMATION SHEET
A summary of what a lodging property has to offer, including the number and types of guestrooms, a description of the atmosphere of the property, number and types of restaurants and meeting rooms, and so on.

PROSPECT CALL

A telephone call made by a salesperson or other representative of a business to gather information and learn the names of decision-makers.

PUBLIC RELATIONS

A systematic effort by a business to communicate favorable information about itself to the public in order to create a positive impression.

PUBLIC RELATIONS CALL (PERSONAL)

A call to maintain the relationship and goodwill enjoyed with a client.

PUBLIC RELATIONS CALL (TELEPHONE)

A telephone call made by a salesperson or other representative of a business to generate goodwill.

PUBLIC SPACE

A non-threatening area over 12 feet (3.7 meters) away from an individual.

PUBLICITY

The gratuitous mention in the media of an organization's people, products, or services.

PUBLISHER'S STATEMENT

Information about a publisher's circulation (broken down by paid subscriptions, number of copies available at newsstands, circulation of regional editions, and so on), subscription rates, advertising rates, mechanical requirements for ads, deadlines for submitting ads, and other information.

PUB-SET AD

An ad designed, written, and typeset by the publishing medium's staff.

PULSING

An advertising pattern in which ads are distributed unevenly over a given time period.

Q–R

QUALIFY

The act of determining if a prospect has a need for or can afford the products and services offered by a property.

QUALIFYING CALL

A telephone call made by a salesperson or other representative of a business to determine if a prospect has a need for or can afford the products and services offered by the business.

RACK RATE

The standard rate established by a property for a particular category of rooms.

RADIO COUPON

A method of radio advertising in which listeners are urged to create their own coupon for redeeming at the advertiser's business.

RATE CARD

A printed statement of advertising rates and general information about a medium.

RATE-CATEGORY-ALTERNATIVES METHOD

An upgrading technique that encourages guests to reserve middle-rate guestrooms. The front desk or reservations agent provides a guest with a choice of three or more rate-category alternatives; in most cases, the guest will seek to avoid extremes and choose a middle-rate room.

RATINGS

A measure of television viewership that represents the percent of individuals or homes tuned to a particular program.

REACH

In print, the number of individuals or households estimated to be in the readership of a given publication or group of publications. In broadcast, the number or percent of an audience exposed to one or more announcements or programs.

READER FILE

A file containing copies of all internal and external memos and correspondence generated by a salesperson, useful for reviewing that salesperson's performance.

RECIPROCAL ADVERTISING

The exchange of an advertiser's products or services to pay for all or part of the medium's time or space. Also called due bill advertising.

REFERRAL PROSPECTING

Asking current clients to identify other individuals or businesses that may be interested in doing business with your property.

REGISTRATION CARD

A printed form the guest completes upon arrival, giving name, address, and other information.

RELATER

A person who tends to view things in terms of how they affect people and relationships. One of four personality types of buyers.

RELATIONSHIP MARKETING

Marketing that views customers as assets and emphasizes retaining customers by nurturing and sustaining a relationship with them.

RELEASE DATE

A date agreed upon by the event organizer and the hotel on which the organizer will either confirm his or her reservation for the space or release the space so the hotel can sell it to someone else. Release dates are usually 60 or 90 days prior to the event.

RESERVATION

An agreement between a hotel and a guest that the hotel will hold a specific type of room for a particular date and length of stay.

RESERVATIONS AGENT

An employee, either in the front office or in a separate department, who is responsible for all aspects of reservations processing.

RESIDENT LIST

A type of mailing list generated from telephone listings, car registrations, and other public records, that contains names and addresses of residents.

RESORT HOTEL

A hotel that provides scenery and activities unavailable at most other properties, and whose guests are typically vacationers.

RETAIL TRAVEL AGENT

An individual qualified to arrange and sell transportation and other travel services and products directly to the public.

REWARDING REMARK

A remark such as "Right," "That's great," or "I agree" that reinforces or confirms what an individual is saying and encourages him or her to continue talking.

RIFLE APPROACH

Concentrating sales or marketing efforts on narrowly defined targets.

ROOM BLOCK

An agreed-upon number of rooms set aside for members of a group planning to stay at a hotel.

ROOM RATE

The price a hotel charges for overnight accommodations.

ROOMING LIST

A list of guests who will occupy reserved accommodations, submitted by the buyer in advance.

ROP COLOR

In newspaper advertising, this is color used in regular sections of the paper and printed on standard newsprint.

ROTATING PLAN

A method of buying billboard advertising space in which the advertiser's message is moved from one billboard location to another at stated intervals to achieve more balanced coverage of a market.

ROUNDS

Round banquet tables.

RUN-OF-STATION PLAN (ROS)

A type of weekly plan for buying radio airtime in which the times the property's ad is aired are chosen by the station and the ad airs in different time slots as time is available. This is one of the least costly ways to buy radio airtime.

RUSSIAN SERVICE

A service style in which food is served from platters or other large dishes, and sufficient food for one table is placed on each platter.

S

SALES

Direct efforts to sell a product or service through personal contact, telephone calls, and mailings.

SALES CALL

A telephone call made by a salesperson or other representative of a business to make a sale.

SALES PROMOTIONS

Promotional activities that are neither personal selling nor media advertising. Sales promotions include offering free samples or discount coupons; staging contests, exhibits, or displays; and attending trade shows.

SALES SUPPORT MATERIALS

Materials used to assist in selling, such as printed brochures, endorsement letters, charts, video brochures, and posters.

SATURATION MEDIUM

A medium that allows an overwhelming concentration of messages to reach a large number of people with considerable frequency.

SCHOOLROOM SETUP

A meeting room setup in which tables are lined up in rows (one behind the other) on each side of an aisle; there are usually three or four chairs per table. The tables and chairs face and are parallel to the head table, stage, or speaker's podium. Also called a classroom setup.

SEGMENTATION
The division of a market into smaller segments.

SELF-MAILER
Direct mail literature that folds up to make its own envelope.

SENATE-STYLE SETUP
A meeting room setup in which chairs are set up in semi-circular rows (with aisles) facing the head table, stage, or speaker's podium.

SERVICE CALL
A telephone call made by a salesperson or other representative of a business to follow up after a sale has been made or merely to keep in touch with a client.

SERVICE CHARGE
A percentage of the bill (usually 10% to 20%) added for distribution to service employees in lieu of direct tipping.

SHELL AD
A pre-designed print ad developed by a hotel or restaurant chain's corporate headquarters that individual properties may use with minor modifications, such as inserting the address and phone number of the property.

SHELL BROCHURE
A printed folder containing descriptive or advertising material that is provided to a chain property by the chain's headquarters. Often space is provided for the property to add its own information.

SHELL MAGAZINE
A magazine with articles of general interest with space for a business to add its own articles or advertising.

SHOTGUN APPROACH
Spreading sales or marketing efforts broadly over the market.

SHOULDER PERIOD
This is a period when the level of business for a property falls somewhere between its peak and valley periods.

SITUATION ANALYSIS
A comprehensive evaluation of a business's current position in the marketplace. Part of a marketing audit.

SLICE OF LIFE AD
A broadcast ad in which characters discuss a problem and propose the product as the solution. Also called a problem solution ad.

SMERF

An acronym for the non-profit-organization market segment, made up of social, military, educational, religious, and fraternal groups.

SOCIAL SPACE

An area four to twelve feet (1.2 to 3.7 meters) from an individual.

SOCIALIZER

A playful and talkative person. One of four personality types of buyers.

SPECIALTY ITEM

Sales tools such as candles, coffee cups, T-shirts, beach towels, and so on that bear the business's name and other advertising information. Also called a premium.

SPECTACULAR

A type of billboard advertising in which special lighting that blinks or changes colors is combined with standard lighting to illuminate the advertising message.

SPLIT TEST

Assigning every other name on a mailing list to one promotion, and the remaining names to another.

SPONSORSHIP

A method of advertising in which an advertiser presents a radio or television program as the sole advertiser or in cooperation with other advertisers.

SPOT ANNOUNCEMENT

A television commercial usually grouped with other spot announcements that air together in clusters or between programs.

SPOT COLOR

The use of a color (other than black) to enhance an advertisement.

STANDARD ADVERTISING UNIT (SAU)

A space one column wide with 14 lines to the inch, used to quote national print advertising in newspapers and magazines.

STANDARD OPERATING PROCEDURES (SOPs)

Written instructions explaining how recurring business activities should be handled in the sales office.

STAYOVER

A room status term indicating that the guest is not checking out and will remain at least one more night.

STORYBOARD

A series of drawings illustrating the characters, action, and dialogue of a proposed television commercial.

STRAIGHT ANNOUNCEMENT AD

A radio or TV ad that simply lists the benefits of the product offered and asks the listener or viewer to act.

STRAIGHT PER DIEM

A dollar figure allocated to government employees traveling on official business that covers lodging, meals, local transportation, and gratuities.

SUGGESTIVE SELLING

The practice of influencing a guest's purchase decision through the use of sales phrases.

SUITE HOTEL

A hotel whose sleeping rooms have separate bedroom and living room or parlor areas, and perhaps a kitchenette.

T

TABLOID

A newspaper smaller than a standard newspaper.

TARGET MARKETS

Market segments that a property identifies as having the greatest potential, and toward which marketing activities are aimed.

TELEMARKETING

The systematic use, often by a specially trained staff of telemarketers with access to computers, of the telephone for marketing or sales purposes.

TELEPHONE SALES BLITZ

The systematic use of the telephone, usually for a short period of time, to gather information, qualify prospects, or in some other way further the marketing and sales success of a business.

TENT CARD

Suggestive-selling print advertising typically placed on restaurant tables or in guestrooms.

TEST CLOSE

A statement or question posed by a salesperson during a sales presentation that seeks to evoke a positive response from the client.

TEST MAILING

Sending out an inexpensive direct mail piece to a targeted audience to measure reader response before sending a more expensive piece to a bigger audience.

TEST MARKETING
(1) The testing of a marketing or media concept in a selected market or markets; (2) an advertising campaign conducted in conjunction with research tools to determine the advisability of extending a marketing program to a broader area of the country.

TESTIMONIAL AD
A type of ad in which a third party praises the product or service of the advertiser.

THEATER SETUP
A meeting room setup in which chairs are set up in straight rows (with aisles) parallel to the head table, stage, or speaker's podium. Also known as a cinema or an auditorium setup.

THINKER
An idea person who is precise, efficient, and well-organized. One of four personality types of buyers.

TICKLER FILE
A file system used to remind salespeople of correspondence, telephone calls, sales calls, or other business activities that must be handled on a particular date. Also called a tracer file, bring-up file, or follow-up file.

TIER MARKETING
The development of multiple "brands" or types of properties by a hospitality firm to appeal to different market segments.

TIMING
In advertising, refers to the scheduling of ads.

TOP-DOWN METHOD
An upgrading technique that encourages guests to reserve middle- or high-rate guestrooms. A front desk or reservations agent recommends the guestroom sold at the highest rate first, and moves down to the next highest price level if this rate is too high. The process continues until the guest is satisfied with the price quoted.

TOTAL AUDIENCE PLAN (TAP)
A type of weekly plan for buying radio airtime in which the broadcast day is divided into four time periods, and the property's ad is aired in each of the periods.

TOUR
Any pre-arranged (but not necessarily prepaid) journey to one or more places and back to the point of origin.

TOUR BROKER
A travel professional licensed by the Federal Interstate Commerce Commission to put together package motorcoach tours in the United States and, in some cases, Canada. Also called a motorcoach broker or tour operator.

TOUR INTERMEDIARY

A travel professional, such as a tour broker, tour wholesaler, or retail travel agent, who arranges group tours.

TOUR VOUCHER

A document issued by tour brokers to be exchanged for accommodations, meals, sight-seeing, and other services. Sometimes called a coupon.

TOUR WHOLESALER

A travel professional who puts tour packages together, usually involving air transportation.

TRACE CARD

A 3- by 5-inch index card used as a reminder to call a client or check a cut-off date, filed by call-back date.

TRADE MAGAZINE

A specialized publication designed to appeal to people in specific industries or professions, in contrast to a consumer magazine.

TRAFFIC COUNT

In outdoor advertising, the tabulation of pedestrians and vehicles passing an outdoor display during a specific time period.

TRANSFER

Local transportation and/or porterage from one carrier terminal to another, from a terminal to a hotel, or from a hotel to a theater. The conditions of a tour contract should specify whether transfers are by private car, taxi, or motorcoach, and whether escort service and/or porterage is provided.

TRANSIT ADVERTISING

Advertising, usually inside cards or outside posters, that appears in or on buses, taxicabs, and—in some cities—the subway.

TRAVEL AGENT COMMISSION

The varying amount a travel agent receives from a supplier for selling transportation, accommodations, or other services.

TRAVEL WRITER

A writer who writes about modes of transportation, hotel accommodations, and business and vacation destinations.

T-SHAPE SETUP

A meeting room setup in which tables are set up in the shape of a block-letter T and chairs are placed around the outside.

U

UNIQUE SELLING POINT

A competitive advantage that a business has over other businesses serving the same target markets.

UNITED STATES TRAVEL AND TOURISM ASSOCIATION (USTTA)

The official U.S. agency for the promotion of travel to and within the United States and its possessions. USTTA is an agency of the U.S. Department of Commerce.

UNITED STATES TRAVEL DATA CENTER

A non-profit organization devoted to the development and standardization of travel research. It publishes statistical compendia and provides indices to measure travel, recreation, and tourism development.

UPGRADING

A sales technique that seeks to move a guest to a better accommodation or class of service.

U-SHAPE SETUP

A meeting room setup in which tables are set up in the shape of a block-letter U; chairs are placed outside the closed end and on both sides of each leg. Also known as a horseshoe setup.

V

VALLEY PERIOD

Also known as "off-season," valleys are times when demand for a property and its services is lowest. Reduced room rates are often offered during valley periods to attract business.

VALUE EQUIVALENCY

A means of measuring the dollar value of the publicity received by a business. Value equivalency is determined by auditing the exact amount of space or airtime given to the business over a period of time, and determining the value of the exposure in terms of what it would have cost to purchase the space or airtime for advertising purposes.

VERTICAL CO-OP ADVERTISING

Advertising shared by dissimilar businesses.

VIDEO BROCHURE

A short video (typically four to six minutes) that presents the products and services of a lodging property, designed to be viewed off-site.

VIDEO MAGAZINE

A video designed primarily for on-site viewing that promotes a lodging property's products and services and may provide information on reservation services, special upcoming promotional packages, and local attractions.

VIDEO NEWS RELEASE

A short video prepared by a business and sent to television stations for possible airing. To be considered a news story rather than a commercial, a video news release must present something that a TV news editor might consider newsworthy.

V-SHAPE SETUP

A meeting room setup in which chairs are set up in straight rows with a center aisle; the rows face the head table, stage, or speaker's podium at an approximately 45-degree angle.

W–Z

WEEKLY PLAN

A method of buying radio airtime in which a property's ad is aired from 10 to 40 times per week. The times the ad is aired depend on whether a total audience plan, a morning-afternoon-night plan, a run-of-station plan, or a best-time-available plan is purchased.

WHOLESALE TRAVEL AGENT

An individual who specializes in putting tour packages together for individual business and leisure travelers. These tours are usually marketed to the public through retail travel agents or the airlines.

YIELD MANAGEMENT

A technique used to maximize room revenues.

ZERO-BASE BUDGET

A budget that starts at zero and forces planners to justify expenditures.

Index

Steven J. Belmonte, CHA
President & COO
Ramada Franchise
  Systems, Inc.
Parsippany, New Jersey

John Q. Hammons
Chairman & CEO
John Q. Hammons
  Hotels, Inc.
Springfield, Missouri

David J. Christianson, Ph.D.
Dean
William F. Harrah College of
  Hotel Administration
University of Nevada,
  Las Vegas
Las Vegas, Nevada

Arnold J. Hewes, CAE
Executive Vice President
Minnesota Hotel & Lodging
  Association
St. Paul, Minnesota

Caroline A. Cooper, CHA
Dean
The Hospitality College
Johnson & Wales University
Providence, Rhode Island

S. Kirk Kinsell
President—Franchise
ITT Sheraton World
  Headquarters
Atlanta, Georgia

Edouard P.O. Dandrieux, CHA
Director
H.I.M., Hotel Institute,
  Montreux
Montreux, Switzerland

Donald J. Landry, CHA
President
Choice Hotels International
Silver Spring, Maryland

Valerie C. Ferguson
General Manager
Ritz-Carlton Atlanta
Atlanta, Georgia

Georges LeMener
President & CEO
Motel 6, L.P.
Dallas, Texas

Douglas G. Geoga
President
Hyatt Hotels Corporation
Chicago, Illinois

Jerry R. Manion, CHA
President
Manion Investments
Paradise Valley, Arizona

Joseph A. McInerney, CHA
President & CEO
Forte Hotels, Inc.
El Cajon, California

William R. Tiefel
President
Marriott Lodging
Washington, D.C.

John L. Sharpe, CHA
President & COO
Four Seasons-Regent Hotels
  and Resorts
Toronto, Ontario, Canada

Jonathan M. Tisch
President & CEO
Loews Hotels
New York, New York

Paul J. Sistare, CHA
President & CEO
Richfield Hospitality Services
Englewood, Colorado

Paul E. Wise, CHA
Professor & Director
Hotel, Restaurant &
  Institutional Management
University of Delaware
Newark, Delaware

Thomas W. Staed, CHA
President
Oceans Eleven Resorts, Inc.
Daytona Beach Shores, Florida

Ted Wright, CHA
Vice President/Managing
  Director
The Cloister Hotel
Sea Island, Georgia

Thomas G. Stauffer, CHA
President & CFO
Americas Region
Renaissance Hotels
  International, Inc.
Cleveland, Ohio